Career Development and Transition Education for Adolescents with Disabilities

Career Development and Transition Education for Adolescents with Disabilities

Second Edition

GARY M. CLARK
University of Kansas

OLIVER P. KOLSTOE
Professor Emeritus
University of Northern Colorado

ALLYN AND BACON
Boston London Toronto Sydney Tokyo Singapore

Series Editor: Ray Short
Editorial Assistant: Christine M. Shaw
Marketing Manager: Ellen Mann
Production Administrator: Annette Joseph
Production Coordinator: Holly Crawford
Editorial-Production Service: Lynda Griffiths/TKM Productions
Composition Buyer: Linda Cox
Cover Administrator: Suzanne Harbison
Cover Designer: Meral Dabcovich
Manufacturing Buyer: Louise Richardson

Copyright © 1995, 1990 by Allyn and Bacon
A Division of Simon & Schuster, Inc.
160 Gould Street
Needham Heights, MA 02194

Library of Congress Cataloging-in-Publication Data

Clark, Gary M.
  Career development and transition education for adolescents with disabilities / Gary M. Clark, Oliver P. Kolstoe. --2nd ed.
      p.   cm.
  Includes bibliographical references and indexes.
  ISBN 0-205-14788-7
  1. Handicapped teenagers--Education (Secondary)--United States.
2. Handicapped teenagers--Vocational education--United States.
3. Vocational guidance for the handicapped--United States.
I. Kolstoe, Oliver P.   II. Title.
LC4031.C59   1994
371.9'0473--dc20   94-347
                                                              CIP

Printed in the United States of America

10 9 8 7 6 5 4 3   99 98 97 96 95

Contents

PART THREE   PROGRAM SUPPORTS

9 Career Guidance and Counseling   292

10 Referrals, Referral Sources, and Interagency Linkages   323

11 Transition of Students from School to Adult Independent Living   345

12 Trends and Issues   376

APPENDICES

Preface

One of the surprises in revising a book is that after several years one can reread certain sentences, sometimes whole passages, with fresh eyes—almost objectively! This experience can be humbling at some points, exhilarating at others. If authors make timely and appropriate changes and bring in new information and new insights, a new edition should be a more substantive, more carefully crafted effort. We hope this second edition of *Career Development and Transition Education for Adolescents with Disabilities* is a new and improved version of our beliefs about secondary special education programming.

One of the things that made this new edition more difficult in some respects than the first edition is the tremendous increase in the last five years in activity related to career development, transition programs and services, and secondary special education. Major laws have been enacted, federal initiatives have increased, local and state education agencies and adult service agencies have moved to new levels of sophistication, the educational reform movement has evolved from general criticism to specific models, and family advocacy and self-determination have become more than ideal proposals. It has been exciting to observe these events, participate in some of them, and try to synthesize the literature that has reflected so much of the change.

In spite of progress since 1989, however, some problems persist and new ones have emerged. Some are educational problems and others are societal. This will always be true, and educators and other advocates for people with disabilities need to review their roles periodically to adapt to the ever-changing configuration of events, people, policies, and resources. Adolescents with disabilities still have unique educational needs that are not being met adequately in the public education system, even though we can say that, on the whole, it is better than it ever has been.

Five years of observation, participation, and reflection have confirmed our initial assumptions and values about secondary special education. The model presented in the first edition is submitted again as both a guide for specific curricula, programs, and services and as a general standard for judging the adequacy of high school programming for youths with disabilities. The model attempts again to broaden the educational choices of *all* high school students to include the academic, personal, social, employability, and daily living skills and knowledge that are needed for a satisfactory and satisfying adult life.

At some points in the book, a strong emphasis is placed on programming that is different from what is typically available in the mainstream of high school programs. It is important to emphasize that when that occurs, we have assumed that the local school has refused to provide such a program for any interested student or that the student and the student's family have chosen the program as the most appropriate and least restrictive alternative. When these programs are made available, they should be outcome oriented and as rigorous as any other course of study in the high school in relation to their unique outcomes. We believe, more strongly than ever, that in ensuring integrity in secondary programming for students with disabilities, educators not only provide them with better education but also affirm the legitimacy of the program as a high school alternative that is both socially and professionally acceptable.

As before, throughout this joint writing effort, we have been aided and encouraged by people who deserve recognition: Stuart E. Schwartz of the University of Florida and Richard Dever of Indiana University for their helpful reviews and proposed changes; Rori Carson of Eastern Illinois University for her comments and suggestions as an instructor using the text; Marianne Notley, for her cartoons; Richard Branham, for his graphic design assistance for the career development and transition education model; Wern-Ing Niew, for her tireless efforts in checking references, assisting in preparation of the revision manuscript, and preparing requests for copyright permissions; Lan-Hsin Pan and Hui-Hsin Pan for their cheerful and gracious volunteering to take scribbled notes and insertions and convert them into neat and readable inserts; and, finally, Raymond G. Short, Christine M. Shaw, and Lynda Griffiths for their encouragement and editorial assistance in getting this second edition into its final form.

G. M. C.
O. P. K.

Career Development and Transition Education for Adolescents with Disabilities

1
Secondary Special Education in Perspective

Progress, for the most part, only substitutes one partial and incomplete truth for another; the new fragment of truth being more wanted, more adapted to the needs of the time, than that which it displaces.—*JOHN STUART MILL*

ACTIVITIES

- Study the life of one of the early workers mentioned in the chapter and report on the experience(s) that shaped his or her influence on the field.
- Trace the influence of the National Advisory Council on Vocational Education beginning in 1963 to determine how the committee has viewed the relationship between vocational education and students who have a disability.
- Examine one of the career education models to determine how it might be modified to more successfully serve students with disabilities.
- Call on representatives of a community organization (such as the chamber of commerce, city commission, business and industrial council, trade union, or trade association) to find out how they provide access to people with disabilities.

INTRODUCTION

To regard people with disabilities as a potentially valuable resource requires a commitment of faith and a recognition that potential must be discovered, nurtured, and developed. It requires a willingness to invest time, effort, patience, and support until a satisfactory level of work and personal living skills can be achieved.

To be certain that each student with a disability has a chance to discover his or her potential, faith must be backed up by educational programs that are realistically crafted to allow students to pursue options to reach their goals.

For the students, their parents, the teachers, and others in the training program, the investments are substantial. Yet, the returns are more than worth it. To convert dependents on tax dollars into tax payers, and to provide anxious parents with emotional strength, employers with able workers, and people who have disabilities with unparalleled feelings of self-worth is a labor of considerable value.

Each local school district has the continuing tasks of charting the educational course for its own locality and of ensuring the availability of education from one generation to the next while balancing pressures from all sectors of the public. Local and state education agencies receive considerable pressure to bring about reforms in public education. Specifically, they are pressured to use a back to basics approach.

Whether schools should provide any kind of career, transition, or even vocational education is far from being an agreed-upon issue. Some circles vigorously resist any departure from teaching the basics. Other circles just as vigorously defend career development and transition education. Those who are of the second view believe that education should prepare young people to assume their rightful places in the adult world—socially, economically, and politically—but that there may be alternative ways of reaching those outcomes.

Recognizing the value of people with some or several disabilities has neither universal acceptance nor wholehearted support. Yet within this large group of people with disabilities, heroes exist: Tom Sullivan, a businessman who, despite his blindness, has become one of the top motivational speakers in the world; Marlee Matlin, the actress who plays a variety of roles, not as a person who is deaf but as a person whose deafness is just one of her personal traits; Stephen W. Hawking, the brilliant physicist who, despite his lack of natural speech and body movement, continues to enlighten us on the origins of the universe; Chris Burke, an actor with Down syndrome who portrayed a teenager with mental disability in the television series, "Life Goes On"; and Mel Tillis, whose singing career is unhampered by a severe stutter. Not only do these people serve as role models for others who have yet to develop their personal skills and abilities to satisfactory levels but they also provide living proof to the world in general of the value of people with pronounced, significant disabilities.

Despite these demonstrations of outstanding contributions to society and the more modest contributions of thousands of other people with disabilities who work, pay taxes, contribute to the nation's gross national product, and otherwise enrich society, there remains a substantial segment of the population that is ignorant of or unable or unwilling to acknowledge the value of people with disabilities. In defense of this segment, it should be pointed out that many of the handicaps imposed by disabilities can only be overcome in the course of training. Thus, the potential value of a person with a disability may not be apparent until considerable effort and time have been invested. For example, without mentors, teachers, parents, and supportive adults and peers, it is unlikely that the talents of these famous persons with disabilities would ever have emerged.

We believe that persons handicapped by some significant disability not only need the opportunity to pursue the development of behaviors, skills, abilities, and attitudes that will allow them equal access to the adult world but they also merit special consideration along the way to circumvent, ameliorate, or eliminate the disability. That is what special education programming and services are all about, and that is what this book is about. Beyond the training and development lies the formidable task of informing society in general and the doubting public in particular of both the potential value and the specific contributions that are the result of that training.

"Things sure haven't changed much over the years, have they?"

This chapter sets the stage for the remainder of the book. First, it discusses major historical attempts to train adolescents and young adults with various disabilities. Next, it examines the guiding principles of secondary education programs. The chapter then highlights the development of special education programs as these efforts have been focused to provide training (within the limits of the U.S. high school) to prepare people with disabilities for the adult world of working and living.

HISTORICAL OVERVIEW

Importance of a Historical Perspective

The value of people to a society and of a society to its people is a complementary arrangement. While people create society with their activities, contributions, products, inventions, and attitudes, societies select from those activities the ones that will be allowed to flourish and become incorporated into the life of the times and places. In turn, these selections give the era the flavor or motif by which the historical periods are characterized.

People who have some characteristic in common can be studied in any society and in any historical period relative to their place in society and the esteem accorded them. People who have some disability, although they may exhibit great individual variability, can be studied as a group because of the common thread of disability that unites them. Their welfare may then become a mirror of the value accorded them by the societies that record their experiences.

A record of persons with disabilities participating as workers in a society is one such instance that reflects their value to that society and contributes to the characterization of that period of history. Chronologically, historical records provide a slide show of changes in values that societies have held toward people who have disabilities. From that kaleidoscopic presentation can emerge patterns on which future directions for action can be built. The best of the past becomes the basis for blueprints for the future, whereas the failures are the warning signs of pitfalls to be avoided.

Classical through the Middle Ages

Historically, work opportunities for persons with disabilities have never been plentiful. A search for evidence of the general value placed by society on people with disabilities as members of the work force does not uncover any systematic efforts to help them secure respected places as working, contributing adults (Kolstoe & Frey, 1965; Sloan, 1963). The records that can be found deal primarily with efforts to train persons with mental retardation and only incidentally people with other kinds of disabilities.

Ancient treatment practices varied, but extermination, asylum, and ridicule were widespread, particularly in western Europe. During the Middle Ages, persons with obvious disabilities were treated differently from persons with problems that were less noticeable. People who were visually impaired or physically disabled, for example, often eked out a livelihood as street beggars and were, if not semiprotected, at least tolerated or benignly neglected. People who were mentally retarded or mentally ill or who had other disabilities that were less apparent were often shunned or otherwise isolated in almshouses, prisons, or institutions. The best they might expect was the opportunity to work at domestic or unskilled tasks closely supervised by more responsible and capable adults in the family or in a monastery. Monks were probably the first people to provide systematic work training to people with disabilities in the chores involved in running the monasteries. The necessary work of cooking, cleaning, gardening, maintenance, and building and repair may have been done by residents who had disabilities. Residents were probably individually trained and supervised for specific jobs—a method closely akin to the technique now called *job coaching*. The pervading view, however, was that these persons, even though sometimes physically and chronologically mature, were perennial children. As such, they were treated as children, disciplined and supervised as children, and often loved as children. Thus, teaching them to perform only simple tasks was consistent with their status.

People with disabilities might not have been considered a major problem to the societies of the Middle Ages and before. The hard labor in agrarian societies guaranteed a certain value would be placed on any necessary service performed by any person. So long as a person did useful work or was not a threat or an irritant to his or her family or other social unit, that person would be accepted. Even beggars who had disabilities were tolerated if they proved to be harmless and contributed to their own welfare or to the welfare of their family. Conversely, if a person behaved in a bizarre or an antisocial manner or if the person was unwilling or unable to work, isolation was a viable way of dealing with the problem. Since human and civil rights were not universally observed, it would scarcely be of great concern if these rights were denied to people with disabilities, nor would it be unusual for such people to perish from lack of food or care. Life for everyone was hazardous and short, even under the best circumstances. One can well imagine that this kind of balance between tolerance and isolation provided a workable method of coping with people who had disabilities.

The Age of Awakening

Not until the events leading to the signing of the Magna Carta by King John of England in 1215 A.D. were civil rights of much concern. Subsequently, the revolt of the British colonies in America in 1776 and the French Revolution of 1793 were expressions of a rising awareness of the lack of individual freedoms. Whether this concern was intended to include people with disabilities is highly doubt-ful. Records of this kind of deference to people with disabilities are not plentiful. Perhaps the absence of records can be blamed on widespread illiteracy, or perhaps the recording of human events simply was not a high priority. However, some thought must have been given to people with disabilities because a royal commission was appointed in England in the early 1900s to find a way of differentiating mental retardation from mental illness. One motive for creating the commission may have been the belief that the same treatment of these different groups was unjust and unproductive.

U.S. Education and Program Principles

From the earliest days of the American colonies, education was highly valued, although simple literacy was probably the goal for many of the colonists. It was common practice for the families living in proximity to each other to pool their resources to support a teacher to provide the opportunity for a basic education for the children in the colony. This cooperative effort seems to have been the beginning of what is now called a *free public education program*. It was not until the early 1900s, however, that education in the schools for children without disabilities began to develop according to two principles that seemed to have universal applicability: (1) the principle of opportunity and (2) the principle of proof.

Principles of Opportunity and Proof

The principle of opportunity simply means that each child should be allowed to enroll in any class open to his or her peers, with no prior restrictions placed on participation.

The principle of proof, however, provides that continuance in the class, experience, or activity is contingent on meeting the standards used to determine satisfactory performance. Unlike the principle of opportunity, the principle of proof imposes a qualitative expectation on the behavior of the student. Thus, each person must prove his or her ability and willingness to meet the standards set for each class. To continue as a bona fide member of the group, a person must constantly prove that he or she has earned the right to be there.

The application of these two principles in governing programs for people with disabilities has a curious history. Earliest records of secondary programs for people with disabilities, as described by Descoeudres (1928) and Duncan (1943) in Europe and Ingram (1960) and Hungerford (1943) in the United States, implied that all persons had to demonstrate progress to stay in their programs. Although no qualitative standards were mentioned, the progression of activities from simple to complex and from concrete to abstract would make it easy to implement a hierarchy of performance objectives. The principle of proof seemed to be operating. However, this practice should not be construed to imply that special education programs were really much different from regular programs. Both have a long history of using tests and other methods of evaluation to assign grades (A, B, C, D, and F) as an index of a person's level of achievement. Those students who get *F*s are presumed to be demonstrating that they have no right to continue in the program. Clearly, the principle of proof has been used for some time with children who have no disabilities for determining who can continue and who cannot, although inter- and intraschool standards vary considerably in their subjective views as to what constitutes failure. It seems possible that the principle of proof played a role in programs for students with disabilities also but probably was tempered considerably in application.

Another manifestation of the principle of proof is the accumulation of units of credit. In 1899, a Subcommittee on History as a College Entrance Requirement made a report to the National Education Association. In that report, the subcommittee used the term *unit* and defined it arithmetically and precisely (Savage, 1953). However, it was not until 1906 that the Carnegie Foundation for the Advancement of Teaching (1909) described how a unit of credit could be established. The foundation described a unit (which became known as the *Carnegie unit*) as the satisfactory completion of a class dealing with some subject that met five days per week for a minimum of 40 minutes each day or a minimum of 120 hours per year. It is clear from several historical accounts (Carnegie Foundation for the Advancement of Teaching, 1909; Encyclopedia of Education, 1971; Savage, 1953) that the Carnegie unit was designed solely to provide a quantitative device for appraising school instruction for college admission. Schools began to recognize 14 Carnegie units of credit as the requirement for graduation as of 1906. The number has increased over the years to the 20 to 22 units required today. It seems reasonable to assume that these units made it easier for college officials to determine eligibility for admission. By embracing the unit concept, colleges and advocates of reform in higher education contributed to the movement to recognize the Carnegie unit as the standard of credit for high school coursework and significantly affected the nature of high school requirements.

Although the agreed-upon measurement of accomplishment in secondary education is a Carnegie unit or some variation of it, the mere accumulation of units is not enough to ensure graduation. Nearly all states have their respective uniform academic requirements. Even though the requirements are minimal, they include classes in English, science, mathematics, and history—the basic blocks of knowledge required to make an industrial society function. Beyond bare literacy, however, most students are afforded the chance to develop to the broadest possible extent by taking classes in a variety of other subjects that also grant units of credit.

Such is not the case for the principle of opportunity. Education has practiced exclusivity from its beginning. Although this point is not within the scope of this book, the interested reader can find documentation in Jordan (1973). Suffice it to say that equal educational opportunity has never been universally practiced in the United States, and the possession of a disability imposes even further limitations on educational opportunities.

Although early on no special educational provisions were made for persons with disabilities, educational opportunities were, ironically, unrestricted. Furthermore, they continued to be unrestricted so long as the standards of expected achievement continued to be met. Obviously, the principles that controlled participation in programs included both the principle of opportunity and the principle of proof.

Development of Programs in the United States

As the United States matured, prevailing social climates had their effects on the treatment of persons with disabilities. The period of the Civil War was a time of great concern for human rights. The mechanism for assuring these rights came from federal laws, probably unevenly administered. Concern for the welfare of slaves was extended to others who were afforded limited human rights, among them people with disabilities. Educators recognized that many persons with mental retardation had been previously denied successful learning because of standards too demanding for them to achieve, and special schools were started to provide them with opportunities for success (Payne & Patton, 1981). The principle of proof was relaxed in these special programs in recognition of the limitations imposed by the disability.

The Victorian era brought marked change to the social climate. Attitudes toward crime and degeneracy became more sharply focused, and new concerns about morality arose. Coincidentally, the emergence of information on the heritability of traits led to the identification of a disability as not only the punishment for presumed behavior transgressions but also as a heritable trait (Goddard, 1912; Dugdale, 1910). A cure for many social problems was sought in eugenics and euthenics. Whether by sterilization or segregation, the prevention of procreation among people with mental disabilities and, by extension, any other person with disabilities whose morals were suspect, quickly put the brakes on any societal movement toward liberal social policies.

With the outbreak of World War I, another swing in the attitude toward people with disabilities occurred. First, the development and widespread use of IQ tests (the Army Alpha and Beta tests) revealed that the number of persons with scores below what was thought to be "normal" was much larger than originally expected (Anastasi, 1976). For the first time, a national picture of subnormality appeared, and it was found to be a large problem. Second, the sudden appearance of many war veterans whose combat wounds left them with permanent disabilities prompted people to recognize the problem as universal. The sudden visibility of people with disabilities acquired in combat may also have had the serendipitous effect of attacking the myth of the heritability of a disability. Certainly, the time was one of compassion, and the result was a scramble to provide services of all kinds.

The Special Class Movement

Often billed as "opportunity" classes or programs, the educational model prevailing after World War II was an exclusive one. Self-contained classes and even schools composed of children sharing the same or similar disabilities proliferated. Equal opportunity was interpreted to mean "modified to compensate for the disability." Blind children, for example, were taught in groups with other blind children. As time went on, two major problems were found to be a consequence of blindness: (1) the inability to travel independently and (2) the cognitive inability to achieve perceptual-spatial closure. Since these issues are largely problems of blind children, the self-contained class model was found to be ideally suited to instruction in these skills. Thus, equal educational opportunity required instruction to be modified to deal with the difficulties imposed by a disability. At the same time, standards of achievement uniquely appropriate to the goals of the instruction were used. Again, the segregated special class and the special school were models well suited to deliver educational services. This service delivery model was dominant until well into the 1970s.

Curiously, within a decade after World War II, both the principle of opportunity and the principle of proof were largely abandoned because the need for them was no longer critical. Opportunity for participation in segregated programs increased almost exponentially beginning in the 1950s (U.S. Department of Education, 1983). Over the next 25 years, nearly any youngster with a mild disability living anywhere in the United States had a class or a program available. It scarcely made sense to advocate for more services because they were nearly universally available to those with mild to moderate disabilities.

The principle of proof, however, was a different matter. From the earliest efforts, it was recognized that educational curricula used with students without disabilities did not provide the kind of content that would help persons with disabilities learn to become independent adults. This led to placement in special classes where the emphasis was on self-development and work skills. Special education teachers rejected the academic criterion and concentrated their efforts on preparing students for work. Looking at some of the data on vocational performance during this period, one can get a picture of rather remarkable success.

Findley (1967) followed up performance of adolescents and young adults in Texas and Colorado and found that

1. IQ was an influencing factor in employment when comparing persons with IQs above 60 with persons with IQs below 60.
2. The above-60 group needed less help and got better jobs, but an equal percentage from both groups got jobs. Most importantly, both groups returned the cost of training in income tax alone in less than 10 years.

In Altoona, Pennsylvania, Dinger (1961) found that

1. Eighty-five percent were employed four years after leaving school.
2. Forty-two percent earned more than a beginning teacher's salary.

Chaffin and associates (Chaffin, Spellman, Regan, & Davison, 1971) found that

1. Sixty-eight percent of a non-work-study group were employed versus 94 percent of work-study groups.

2. Two years later, 75 percent versus 83 percent of persons in these respective groups had jobs.

This was not a significant difference in employment rate, although the work-study group had significantly higher wage rates than the non-work-study group.
In Kent County, Michigan, Warren (1976) found that

1. More than 95 percent of the students from the program were employed.
2. Average starting wage was $2.65 (when minimum wage was $1.65), and the highest wage was $4.85.

These and other landmark studies of work experience and work-training programs during the 1960s and 1970s were basically optimistic, and the lack of sophistication in the research methodology was largely overlooked. One important exception to this neglect was a critique by Butler and Browning (1974) of the studies most often quoted. However, the studies did nothing to raise questions about the work-study model. This was not the case with special education program research, however, particularly research that focused on special classes.

Evolving Program Philosophies

The major accomplishment of the proliferation of special education program research was confusion over what the programs were actually accomplishing for people with disabilities. Although many studies were done to try to assess the effectiveness of special education programs (thus named *efficacy studies*), most of the findings were equivocal. One obvious reason for this is that if there is no agreement on what is supposed to be accomplished, effectiveness cannot be demonstrated. Confining the principle of proof to academic achievement provided the chance for a host of people to criticize the programs (Johnson, 1962; Dunn, 1968; Kolstoe, 1972; MacMillan, 1977). Unfortunately, no amount of depth analysis can help programs that really have no agreed-upon goals or directions in the first place, particularly if the analyses examine only the means and ignore the ends or vice versa.

The 1960s and the Normalization Concept
A goal did emerge as a by-product of the civil rights movement that began in the 1960s. The 1960s were years of idealism in which the major thrust was one of assuring every segment of society the right to participate in the American way of life. Out of this movement came the principle of normalization, the goal of which was to ensure a normal existence for people with disabilities. The principle gained visibility in 1961 when a U.S. delegation from the President's Panel on Mental Retardation (PPMR) visited programs in Europe. The delegates were impressed with the attitudes toward people with disabilities in Scandinavian countries. The head of the Danish services for persons with mental retardation, Neil E. Bank-

Mikkelson (1968, p. 198), originally defined the principle as "letting the mentally retarded obtain an existence as close to normal as possible." Wolf Wolfensberger introduced the principle in the United States in a 1972 publication that described normalization as the "utilization of means which are as culturally normative as possible in order to establish and/or maintain personal behaviors and characteristics which are as culturally normative as possible" (p. 28).

Even a casual comparison of the definitions makes it clear that Bank-Mikkelson (1968, p. 198) spoke of "letting" persons with mental retardation obtain an existence as close to normal as possible, whereas Nirje (1969) spoke of "making [it] available." Wolfensberger (1972), on the other hand, mentioned "utilization of means which are as culturally normative as possible..." (p. 28).

Although much controversy surrounded the meaning of the normalization principle (Roos, 1970; Throne, 1975), there is little doubt as to its effect. The normalization principle established the goal for all people with disabilities to have the right to as normal an existence as possible using the most normal means possible. Essentially, the principle of normalization reestablishes the principle of opportunity and the principle of proof as rights for people with disabilities to achieve as normal an existence as possible using means that are as normative as possible. For many people, however, the traditional academic program is viewed as the most "normalizing" environment available, and academic achievement has become the criterion for success.

CAREER EDUCATION

Historical Development of Work-Training Programs

It was not until 1928 that a specific reference to work training appeared in a book by Alice Descoeudres. The description of an educational program developed by Descoeudres did not specifically include the training methods, materials, or sequences used. What it did describe was the organization of the Society for the Protection of Backward Children. It was the responsibility of the society members to help youths with disabilities find jobs and then to supervise, aid, and advise them in other aspects of living that might be troublesome. Descoeudres' program was located in Belgium. Perhaps because of this, her experiences seemed to have had little influence on U.S. educators. Certainly, no comparable advocacy society was formed in the United States until the National Association for Retarded Citizens was formed in about 1952. Nonetheless, Descoeudres has provided the first record of a systematic effort to include people with disabilities in the labor force.

Attempts to Identify Appropriate Curricula

It fell to John Duncan in England to develop a systematic program of training that would help people with disabilities to become prepared for jobs in society.

Duncan's school at Lankhills, Hampshire, England, was a residential school for youngsters sent by the social services agencies of Hampshire. Although many may have been disabled, many others were children of the streets who had few assets to help them merge into society. In modern parlance, they would probably be categorized as "disadvantaged."

Duncan (1943) discovered that, although the verbal IQs of his young charges averaged about 66, their performance IQ scores were about 30 points higher, averaging 96. He interpreted that discrepancy to mean the youngsters had greater concrete than abstract intelligence, and he designed a program to capitalize on that fact. Duncan analyzed the jobs in the community that demanded concrete intelligence. Jobs such as beekeeping, carpentry, baking, cooking, and other rural domestic jobs were arranged in a hierarchy of steps from using a model to copying schematics, to following written or oral directions, and, finally, designing a new way of performing the task. Duncan kept very careful records of the physical health of the youngsters. For instance, he related the youngsters' rates of growth and general health with the quantity and quality of food they consumed. He was particularly concerned with the relationship of animal protein intake and growth, and his records made him a firm believer in the importance of a well-balanced diet, not only for health but also to facilitate learning and working effectively. He was concerned with both the intellectual and the physical health of his students.

The analysis of community jobs into their component skills and then the incorporation of those skills into the curriculum as practiced by Duncan was also the hallmark of the program developed by Richard Hungerford in New York City in the early 1940s. As the director of the Bureau for Children with Retarded Mental Development, Hungerford (1941, 1943) published a series of tradelike journals called *Occupational Education* between 1941 and 1944. They provided teachers with step-by-step instructions for teaching skills in the needle trades, service occupations, light industry, and various unskilled and semiskilled jobs in which Hungerford had observed youngsters with mental retardation working.

Those methods of determining curriculum content (reports from cooperative community advocates and job analyses) have been expanded and refined since that time and are still far from outmoded. For example, a book by Peterson and Jones published in 1964 contained descriptions of jobs analyzed into their component skills that were successfully performed by persons with mental retardation. Similarly, technical manuals on all subjects from automotive repairs to computer literacy followed that format. However, technical manuals like these are not the only sources for curricular content for work-oriented programs.

In 1958, Oliver Kolstoe and Roger Frey initiated a series of studies that yielded data on successfully and unsuccessfully employed young men with mental retardation. The extensive records kept on the young men made it possible to compare them on personal, academic, social, and occupational skills. The analyses enabled the investigators to go considerably beyond job skills to include the behaviors, knowledge, and attitudes that were displayed by the successfully employed young men. These attributes (Kolstoe, 1961) were incorporated into their work-preparation curriculum and, subsequently, into similar programs across the nation. Thus, in addition to the job performance skills, those academic, personal, and social skills so important to satisfying life-styles were also recognized. These were presented in the book A *High School Work Study Program for Mentally Subnormal Students* (Kolstoe & Frey, 1965). Even though the needs of students with mental retardation were specifically addressed, the curriculum and techniques were presented as being applicable to a much broader range of persons with disabilities. Because many of the young men studied had associated physical and sensory disabilities, those with visual, auditory, motor, perceptual, sensory, and linguistic problems were also included. Thus, the basic work skill development approach became much more widely applicable and acceptable, with the inclusion of the academic, personal, and social skill training that had been found to differentiate between the successful and unsuccessful young men.

Most of the emphasis during the decades before 1970 was on persons with mild mental retardation. Today, many of those persons would be diagnosed and classified as having learning disabilities or behavior disorders. The group classified as moderately to severely mentally retarded was rarely singled out for attention in occupational or job training. It was this group that Marc Gold targeted in the late 1960s to demonstrate that even the lowest functioning among them could perform complex assembly tasks with training (Gold, 1972, 1973). His "Try Another Way" theme caught the imagination of many professionals in secondary special education and rehabilitation and began a trend toward an ideology and technology that culminated in the major movement now associated with the term *supported employment*. This will be discussed fully in a later chapter.

Beginnings of Vocational Education

Another movement to identify curricula appropriate for youth with disabilities had its roots in the 1960s, but it did not become widely accepted until the 1970s. Criticisms of special education services were generally directed at elementary-level programs, partly because there were not many secondary programs of which to be critical. Nonetheless, some criticisms of secondary programs did surface, but they were rather concise regardless of what kind of exceptionality was being discussed. Nearly all the criticisms alleged that the training efforts were restricted to only a few jobs in each area of exceptionality and that the levels of training were so low that they precluded people with disabilities from all but the most menial jobs. People who were visually impaired were often restricted to learning how to tune pianos, cane chairs, or become street musicians. Individuals who were hearing impaired were trained to be linotype operators, dry cleaners, or bakers. Persons with mental retardation were trained for food service or janitorial tasks, and those with physical disabilities were relegated to watch repair or office work (Brolin & Kolstoe, 1978).

Whether the allegations were justifiable or not was largely irrelevant. The charges that training programs limited students with disabilities to few career options and jobs that underutilized their skills were forcefully presented to lawmakers at state and national levels. This caused them to turn their attention to the need for legislation that would free people with disabilities from these restrictive practices.

One other source of major concern was that special education teachers taught not only the academics but also the vocational skills and the skills of independent living. They also did the job placement and follow-up supervision. Although it could be readily acknowledged that the teachers were well trained to teach academic skills, it was more difficult to justify their teaching of work skills and skills of independent living while doing work placement and follow-up. Few, if any, college training programs provided opportunities for would-be teachers to learn those skills, and those programs that did address those skills did so minimally (Clark & Oliverson, 1973). Vocational educators were trained to teach work skills, but they often were reluctant to work with students with disabilities. They feared that if people with disabilities were admitted and successful in vocational education programs, those programs might be thought to have low requirements or standards compared with other, more academic programs. Student safety and their assumed inability to read were further sources of concern.

Despite these concerns, Congress passed the Vocational Education Act of 1963, which specified that persons with disabilities could be included in ongoing vocational education along with their peers without disabilities. The intent of the law was to ensure that students who have disabilities would learn their work skills from people who were experts at teaching work skills (vocational educators) and their academics and daily living skills from experts in those areas (special and other educators).

Unfortunately, no funds were appropriated that would make it financially attractive for vocational educators to serve students with disabilities. As a result, these students were not served in any great number. That began to change, however, when Congress passed the Vocational Education Act Amendments (1968) to the Vocational Education Act. Among the many provisions, two were significant. First, 10 percent of the funds for vocational education were set aside to serve youth with disabilities. Second, each state was required to file a plan with the Bureau of Adult and Vocational Education that described how the funds that were set aside were to be used to serve students with disabilities. The penalty for not providing vocational education programs for this population was the loss of all those funds.

Many states made no more than a token response and did not use all available funds, so it was not until the passage of PL 94-142, the Education for All Handicapped Children Act (1975), that some leverage could be applied to this situation. PL 94-142 stipulated a free and appropriate education for all youth with disabilities. The penalty for noncompliance was more stringent—loss of *all* federal funds to any state that failed to comply. The combination of money to provide services and the threat of the loss of all federal funds for not serving students with disabilities in regular vocational education programs had its desired effect: From 1973 to 1978, enrollment figures increased by 66 percent (U.S. Department of Education, 1983).

The Career Education Movement

As dramatic as these figures are, they tell only a story of quantity. The even more unexpected outcome was the emergence of a concept parallel to vocational special needs education—career education. This was a qualitative flavor added to the rapid increase of services that affected people with or without disabilities.

Definitions

Career education was considered an alternative to the narrow job-preparation approach of vocational education and was also a response to the problems associated with the general education course in the nation's high schools. (General education is basically the course of study leading to minimal graduation requirements and includes anything that is not college preparatory or vocational education.) The career education concept, first presented by Sidney Marland in a speech to school administrators in Houston, Texas, in 1971, was conceived by members of the National Advisory Council on Vocational Education. Marland described the concept in these words:

> I do not speak of career education solely in the sense of job training, as important as it is. I prefer to use career in a much broader connotation—as a stream of continued growth and progress. Career in that sense strongly implies that education can be made to serve *all* the needs of an American—teaching, to begin with, the skills and refinements of the workaday world, for if we cannot at the minimum prepare a man or woman to earn a living, our efforts are without worth. But career education must go beyond occupational skills—the interpersonal and organizational understanding without which one simply cannot exist in a modern nation-state, addressing effectively the matter of living itself, touching on all its pragmatic, theoretical, and moral aspects. That is what I mean in the broadest sense by career education—and that is the way in which I envision the learning process being carried forward in the schools of this Nation, in its homes and businesses, and government offices, and perhaps its streets, since for some, much of what is really educational occurs there. (p. 1)

When Marland introduced the concept of career education, he defined it broadly—that is, not only as preparation to earn a living but also as a way to learn about living itself. Hoyt (1975) defined *career education* as "the totality of experience through which one learns about and prepares to engage in work as part of her or his way of living" (p. 4). He defined *work* (paid or unpaid) as a "conscious effort (other than that involved in activities whose primary purpose are either coping or relaxing) aimed at producing benefits for oneself and/or for oneself and others" (p. 3). In this context, career education was conceptualized as considerably less than all of life or one's reason for living as Marland had visualized it but clearly more than paid employment.

In a later elaboration, Hoyt (1977) defined *career education* as "an effort at refocusing American education and the actions of the broader community in ways that will help individuals acquire and utilize the knowledge, skills, and attitudes necessary for each to make *work* a meaningful, productive, and satisfying part of his or her way of living" (p. 5). He clarified his use of the term *work* by indicating that it "is individualistically decided by the person, not the nature of the task. What is *work* to one person may well be play to another and drudgery to another. The human need to work will, hopefully, be met by others in productive use of leisure-time, in volunteerism, or in duties performed as a full-time homemaker who is not employed for wages" (p. 7). Thus, Hoyt clarified his position on what constitutes productive work—something many conceptualizers have failed to do.

These and various other interpretations have led to confusion about the exact nature of career education. Some people think of it as vocational education and have said that career education is just an old concept dressed in new verbiage. Some have restricted career education to students in the lower track of school programs, while others have included elements for students in all of the educational tracks. Some have felt that career education is not respectable enough to be offered to college-bound students, while others have gone to the other extreme and excluded students with disabilities from their career education offerings.

Many conceptualizers of career education define *career education* as education that focuses on the roles a person is likely to play in his or her lifetime. These include student, paid worker, recreator, family member, citizen, and pensioner. Career education is what people do to learn how to engage in these roles. This is exemplified by the definition approved in December, 1977, by the Board of Governors of The Council for Exceptional Children (Brolin & D'Alonzo, 1979).

Development of Models

So many program variations have been developed that it is impossible to describe all of them. Even when the names of the programs are the same, details differ from school to school and even within the same school from year to year. Rather than this being a cause for concern, it may well be a tribute to the sincerity of the professionals who continuously evaluate their efforts, changing, adding, and discarding elements, materials, and practices as they seek better ways to help young people who have disabilities become better prepared to work and live in a complex and changing society.

Life-Centered Career Education Model
Brolin and Kokaska presented a model (Brolin & Kokaska, 1979; Kokaska & Brolin, 1985) that captured many features of special education work-study programs with their variations and modifications, but broadened them to encompass

the concept of career education for all ages. They defined *career education* in 1983 as a purposeful and sequential planning approach to help students in their career development. They proposed a three-dimensional model of competencies, including (1) stages of career development; (2) school, family, and community experiences; and (3) a set of 22 basic life-centered competencies that collectively contribute to the maturity of youngsters with disabilities.

The 22 major competencies students need to master to become successful as adults were identified from research in the field (Brolin & Thomas, 1971). These have been grouped into three major areas: daily living skills, personal-social skills, and occupational guidance and preparation. The groups are broken down as follows:

Daily Living Skills

1. Managing family finances
2. Selecting, managing, and maintaining a home
3. Caring for personal needs
4. Raising children and living as a family
5. Buying and preparing food
6. Buying and caring for clothes
7. Engaging in civic activities
8. Using recreation and leisure
9. Getting around the community (mobility)

Personal-Social Skills

10. Achieving self-awareness
11. Acquiring self-confidence
12. Achieving socially responsible behavior
13. Maintaining good interpersonal skills
14. Achieving independence
15. Achieving problem-solving skills
16. Communicating adequately with others

Occupational Guidance and Preparation

17. Knowing and exploring occupational possibilities
18. Selecting and planning occupational choices
19. Exhibiting appropriate work habits and behaviors
20. Exhibiting sufficient physical-manual skills
21. Gaining a specific occupational skill
22. Seeking, securing, and maintaining employment

Rather than being presented at that time as a specific curriculum, the Life-Centered Career Education (LCCE) curriculum was designed for the concepts embodied in the 22 competencies to be *infused* into the regular curriculum, beginning with the kindergarten level and extending well into adulthood. Experience with the infusion approach for the past decade led Brolin (1988) to a modified view, however; he now proposes that for some students an alternative curriculum, such as the Life-Centered Career Education Curriculum, must be provided instead of purely academic programs, the goals of which are unattainable for them. The LCCE Curriculum (Brolin, 1992a) was developed to be used through infusion or through seperate instruction.

All life experiences, whether at home, at school, or in the community, are geared to allow each person to learn the behaviors appropriate to his or her life roles at each stage of development. Dependent-children roles interact with the roles of student life until individuals become able to secure jobs and assume the roles of the work world. These work roles may then be superimposed on their adult roles of parent and citizen. Finally, there are expected behaviors that define the role of pensioner or retiree. The behavior requirements of each stage of development differ from those of every other stage. Each stage requires the developing person to learn new skills of living, personal-social relations, and occupational knowledge or behaviors for a variety of life roles. Clearly, career education is forever changing. It has been described as "lifetime learning," seemingly an apt description.

The Experience-Based Career Education (EBCE) Model

The EBCE Model for students with special needs (Larson, 1981) was based on the original Appalachia Educational Laboratory Model (Goldhammer & Taylor, 1972) for students in general education. The program emphasized the opportunity for students to explore possible jobs while still enrolled in school. This necessarily makes the business community an extension of the school, and the program can be successful only if effective coordination between them occurs.

To assure coordination, a learning coordinator manages all aspects of the program. The student's interests and experiences are considered, and a plan is developed that will place the student at a community-based job site for six to nine weeks while a related study plan is implemented. The study plan must embrace both the academic classes needed by the student to fulfill the graduation requirements as well as the opportunity to learn the skills and information required to be successful on the job site. Students do not receive any pay for their experience, nor do the resource persons in the community receive any kind of compensation.

During a student's secondary program, four different job sites can generally be explored. Since the students work for no pay, their evaluation of what kind of work they prefer is unbiased by the money they earn. This allows them to make a more objective choice of full-time employment at the completion of the program. Students complete math, English, or other academic assignments at the work site to show how a worker uses such academic knowledge or skills to complete tasks.

One major criticism of the experience-based program is that the students learn only what they experience. While they may do that well, their experiences are specific to the particular jobs they are in. Even similar jobs in other businesses may not require the same skills or provide the same work climate. Another criticism is that volunteer work is not a strong enough motivator for those students who are poor, who do not have intrinsic motivation, or who do not have the maturity to delay gratification for effort. A third criticism is that experienced-based learning on the job may violate the Fair Labor Standards Act if not handled correctly. The success of EBCE in Iowa, however, is a positive response to such criticisms and demonstrates that there are settings and populations of students with disabilities that can benefit from this model (Larson, 1981).

The School-Based Comprehensive Career Education Model

The most ambitious of the original career education models, the Comprehensive Career Education Model (CCEM), was sponsored by the U.S. Office of Education with the Center for Vocational and Technical Education at Ohio State University, the prime contractor (Goldhammer & Taylor, 1972). Working with six widely dispersed and characteristically different local school districts (Mesa, Arizona; Pontiac, Michigan; Hackensack, New Jersey; Jefferson County, Colorado; Los Angeles, California; and Atlanta, Georgia), its advertised goal was to reform the curricula of these schools and, eventually, the established public school system.

By providing career education information, guidance, counseling, training, curricular guides, and an extensive consultation and evaluation system, modifications and innovations were immediately available to the designated schools. Thus, the programs were able to benefit from their own experiences and from the practices of the other schools to guide their efforts.

While this program was not specifically developed to help students with disabilities, the elements allowed for the inclusion of people with disabilities, with ample opportunities to accommodate their unique needs. However, with the reduction of federal funds for program support from the U.S. government in the 1980s, the model became largely a token attempt at reform rather than a continuing force for reform.

Career Education for Exceptional Children and Youth

Gillet (1981) presented a developmental model specifically for exceptional youngsters that builds around a core program modified to fit the type and degree of disability. It suggests a continuum of services beginning at the elementary level. Learning the meaning of the world of work and developing social competencies form the bases upon which students learn about the requirements of many jobs from which occupational choices are made. Personal adequacy, work habits, skill development, decision-making ability, and the opportunity to participate in a job with constructive supervision are systematically developed.

The program requires the cooperation of pupils, teachers, service staff, parents, administrators, and community leaders to successfully relate special education to career development. The development proceeds through the following stages of career conceptual understanding:

1. Self-understanding in terms of daily activities.
2. Awareness of individual characteristics.
3. Developing proper social relations.
4. Conserving and caring for materials.
5. School as a job.
6. Responsibilities of various family members.
7. Responsibility for one's own actions.
8. Relating of things done in the present to future jobs/roles.
9. Relating work in school and jobs in the future.
10. Work as a productive way of life.
11. Importance of performing a job to the best of one's ability.
12. Both men and women can work in any occupation.
13. The existence of different work values.
14. Likes and dislikes in selected tasks.
15. Each person is a unique individual.
16. What is "interest"?
17. Jobs are dependent upon each other.
18. Study of specific jobs.
19. Meaning of leisure time and examples of leisure activities.
20. Concept of a career cluster.
21. Familiarity with career clusters.
22. Different levels of jobs are found within each cluster.
23. A wide range of jobs exist in each cluster.
24. Identification as a "worker."
25. All people do not have the same abilities and interests.
26. All work and all jobs are important.
27. It takes many jobs to make a functioning business.
28. Reasons for working.
29. Each job has different responsibilities.
30. Locations and times of work.
31. Work can be part time or seasonal.
32. Awareness of nature of individual role and group roles in a work setting.
33. People work for different reasons.
34. Role of work in meeting needs.
35. Concept of volunteerism.
36. Concept of self-employment.
37. Meaning of division of labor, goods, and services.
38. Structure and interrelatedness of the economic system.
39. Determination of likes/dislikes.
40. Relationship between interests, jobs, and leisure-time activities.
41. Exploring specific jobs.
42. Some jobs depend on geographic location and seasons of the year.
43. Decision-making process.
44. Jobs require different kinds and levels of training.

45. The world of work is always changing.
46. Awareness of specific strengths and limitations in relation to work.
47. Some jobs I can do; others I can't.
48. Reasons why people change jobs.
49. Using community resources for leisure activities/jobs.
50. Career advancement.
51. Formulating a general career preference.

The scope and sequence of the program certainly make it a very attractive proposal, but it clearly focuses on work and occupational roles, ignoring personal and social skills and independence in daily living tasks outside of employment.

School-Based Career Development and Transition Education Model

The model chosen for elaboration in this book is a variation of the Marland School-Based Career Development and Transition Education Model (Goldhammer & Taylor, 1972). It was developed by Gary Clark (1979, 1980) at the University of Kansas in the mid-1970s and has gone through refinements and adjustments to bring it to its present state. Chapter 2 provides a detailed description of the model.

Development of Programs

National acceptance of the concept of career education was facilitated by the appointment of Kenneth Hoyt in 1972 to coordinate program efforts in the U.S. Office of Education. However, without the aid of persons such as Melville Appell in the Bureau of Education for the Handicapped (BEH) and the endorsement of the American Vocational Association and The Council for Exceptional Children, career education might not have made quite the impact it has made on students with disabilities. Fortunately, its acceptance has not been confined to the national level. Instead, it has permeated practices at the local level in every corner of the nation. The effect has been to significantly increase opportunities in secondary programs for people with disabilities.

However, career education programs never were implemented nationally. In 1979, at the crest of the career education movement, Reichard studied programs in a five-state area; each state reported having a career education curriculum for students with disabilities. He found that nearly 70 percent of the programs stated they did not schedule field trips to business and industrial settings, even though 60 percent reported they had cooperative work programs through local businesses. Also, 55 percent said they did not provide any job placement help for their students. Most disappointing was that only 25 percent of the students with disabilities at the junior high school level participated in a career education program; at the high school level, only 42 percent of the students with disabilities were involved.

Reichard's (1979) findings were essentially the following:

1. Career education is too frequently viewed synonymously with vocational education or rehabilitation.
2. Of those existing efforts, there appear to be no agreed-upon competencies, philosophies, guidelines, or functional intraagency communications.
3. Knowledge of—or the provision and/or development of—career education materials is nearly nonexistent.
4. Definitions of career education appear to vary significantly among vocational programs.
5. Philosophical differences between administrators and teachers of regular and special classes are evident.
6. Noneducational personnel apparently are not being included in the process.
7. For those programs in existence, accountability—that is, competencies and programmatic evaluations and publications or results—is taking a low profile.
8. Agreement with the career education concept appears to be widely accepted, but implementation is varied.

There is no reason to believe that the problems discovered by Reichard were parochial or that they were characteristic of a specific period of the late 1970s. On the contrary, the need for more programs is greater than ever. Even among existing services, there is plenty of room to improve on the quality and quantity of what is available now or will be in the immediate future.

Attempts to find ways of helping young people with disabilities to learn to work effectively in a complex society have been heavily influenced by what has been successful for youngsters who have no disabilities. The vocational education program that served as a model for the work-study program (cooperative vocational education) was and is successful for students without disabilities. The concept that people should study all aspects of a job while working on the job provides the opportunity to validate theory against practice in an uncompromising world of survival. This concept is at the heart of apprenticeship training programs.

However, the jobs that students with no disabilities were trained for were largely semiskilled, skilled, managerial, or semiprofessional in nature. The training and accompanying study were designed to prepare the person for a specific job. The level of skill required for most of the jobs considered suitable for the students with disabilities was considered both minimal and general. (Keep in mind that teachers' estimates of the abilities of students who are disabled could have been [1] biased, [2] in error, [3] based on the consequences of years of neglect in meeting these needs, or [4] all of the above.) Thus, training programs were thought to need emphasis in general work skills and attitudes. Being on time, not interfering with fellow workers, accepting criticism gracefully, following directions, and being pleasant, honest, loyal, and dependable were judged to be more crucial to getting and retaining jobs than were the more difficult, if not impossible-to-learn, skills of the craftsperson that were being emphasized in vocational education programs. Largely for this reason, the first formal alternative to vocational education—work-study programs in special education—changed the emphasis from training for specific skills to training for generally acceptable employee behavior.

As it became apparent that many people with disabilities were capable of learning higher levels of skills than just general work skills, inclusion of students with disabilities in ongoing vocational education programs, made possible through the Vocational Education Act of 1963 and its subsequent amendments, broadened the training options for students with disabilities. One consequence was the reaffirmation that a goal of all public education was to provide the opportunity for everyone in the school programs to learn how to earn a living. Obviously, vocational education, with its narrow focus on teaching the skills necessary for a person to gain entry to skilled and semiskilled jobs, was too restrictive to be suitable for those who would become managers or enter some profession. Likewise, it was too demanding for people whose abilities were too impaired to learn even entry-level skills for the skilled or semiskilled jobs. In either case, however, whether vocational education or special education work study, the primary emphasis is and always has been on occupational roles in paid competitive employment.

Within this context, the climate was right for a new way to ensure that schools would achieve the goal of allowing all students, regardless of ability level, the opportunity to learn not only how to work but also how to meet the demands of home and family living, community living, and leisure time. Career education seemed to answer all of those needs. After its introduction in 1971, various models were proposed that would be suitable for all students in all schools. However, most models within regular education have emphasized occupational choice and exploration.

TRANSITION

Just as the career education movement of the 1970s was an expansion of the work-study movement of the 1960s, in 1984, Madeline Will, Director of the Office of Special Education and Rehabilitation services, championed the transition movement that extended the career education issue into the realm of adult community services.

Like its predecessors, work-study and career education, the transition movement owed much of its acceptance to the fact that it was introduced as a federal initiative. At such, it carried the weight of legislative legitimacy and substantial funding to support innovative and imaginative programs. It emphasized the preparation of people with disabilities for work, and made possible such innovations as supported employment and job coaching. However, it paid little attention to preparation for independent living. Although the transition from school to work movement has been a needy extension of work-study and career education, greater recognition is needed in the contribution of life skills to successful adult participation in society.

Issues for Future Consideration

The validity of career education for people with disabilities has been well established. There is no question that it represents a healthy evolution from the occupational and persisting life needs curriculum guides of the 1940s and 1950s and the special education work-study models of the 1960s. Augmented by the transition movement of the 1980s, there is a strong movement toward capitalizing on the potential contribution of people with disabling conditions both to society and their own life-styles. Yet, some issues and problems cloud the future and cannot be ignored.

1. The reductions in federal funding beginning in the early 1980s precipitated a need to find alternative sources of financial support for the programs. In many places, state and local education agencies have responded in a commendable fashion. However, career education and transition programs are more expensive than some other forms of education, so it has become a convenient target for cost-cutting movements. Unfortunately, some officials have given little thought to the return on the investment in terms of the increased earning power of trained versus untrained workers. The possibilities of short-term savings have obscured the potential from long-term returns, leading to penny-wise and pound-foolish economies.

2. Perhaps one reason that career development and transition education programs for people with disabilities have been easy to target for financial cuts is that many educators from all disciplines, including special education, are not convinced that the career transition education approach is any better than what existed before its appearance in 1971. The notion that all education should contribute to the preparation of a person for a job is the antithesis of the belief that a major purpose of education is for intrinsic self-improvement. A more moderate position can accommodate both purposes as legitimate goals of education: Education is a major force for improving the human condition both in self-improvement and in vocational competence. This is the thesis of life career development and transition education.

3. Because life career development and transition education is relatively new, it is still at the conceptual and experimental stage of development. The movement is in desperate need of more specific and proven delivery systems, better career development and transition-assessment procedures, and a compre-

hensive scope and sequence curriculum base. With such a promising beginning, however, this scarcely seems to be the time to terminate the movement.

4. Life career development and transition education as a general concept, and particularly the model especially designed for students with disabilities, is in danger of being eclipsed by the current emphasis on back to basics and the call for minimum competency standards. The need or desirability of academic skills is not arguable. What is at issue is the failure to recognize the limitations imposed by various disabilities on a person's ability to master those skills. The injustice of mandating the same levels of achievement for all persons ignores the whole concept of individual differences upon which special education rests. If all persons were equally capable, there would be no need for special education.

5. Life career development and transition education support staff tend to approach their tasks from a discipline perspective. For example, counselors think in terms of counseling objectives and applications, vocational educators think of their vocational training mission, and special educators are ever mindful of needs of those who are disabled. Even those persons who work on different aspects of the services often present their goals differently than do their colleagues. It is a small wonder that local and state boards of education may be confused about what career development and transition education for people with disabilities is trying to accomplish. They hear the loudest, the most persuasive, or the most politically powerful voices. There is little doubt that this situation could be improved if coalitions were formed that would present a united front to these boards and to the public.

6. One consequence of the absence of the coalitions is that the broad goals of life career development and transition education for students with disabilities are difficult to maintain when primary emphasis goes to one component or another, without a sustained, systematic, and balanced approach. A skewed or biased emphasis results in training gaps that are difficult to detect and even harder to fill.

7. A major problem is that special educators are not as accustomed to working with community organizations such as the chamber of commerce, city commissions, business and industrial councils, trade unions, and trade associations as they are with human services agencies. This can have serious consequences, because making an impact within a community requires dealing with and securing the backing of the community's power structure. Again, forming coalitions of persons concerned with people with disabilities would appear to be one way of attacking this problem.

8. Educational policies and practices are difficult to change, and they may be especially vulnerable to short-lived effects if special educators work solely

within their own structures and ignore the needs of the rest of the educational system. This calls for a broader role in education than special educators have played in the past.

CONCLUSION

There is little historical evidence that people with disabilities have ever been considered a valuable labor resource. However, beginning with the 1930s, efforts increased toward training people with disabilities to become employable adults. Early attempts to teach generalized work skills proliferated, spawning variations too numerous to describe. With the passage of the 1963 Vocational Education Act and its subsequent amendments, and later the 1975 Education of All Handicapped Children Act and its amendments, regular vocational education programs became accessible to people with disabilities, and teaching entry-level vocational skills became a more frequent training goal.

The narrowness of this goal led to its inclusion under a broader training umbrella called *career education*. Aided by the career education *Zeitgeist* and federal financing, different models of career education were developed and implemented, and each generated its share of refinements. This book will present what we believe is another refinement.

Work-study and career education models were strengthened considerably by the transition model that extended training into adult and community services. This book borrows from all three movements to present what we believe is another refinement to the existing field.

Even though the book emphasizes secondary-level education programs, it should be remembered that the achievement of full potential is the goal of life career development and transition education and includes elementary-level as well as postsecondary experiences.

2
A Proposed Secondary Special Education Model

The discovery of what is true and the practice of that which is good are the two most important objects of philosophy.— VOLTAIRE

ACTIVITIES

- Examine evidence that supports teaching personal-social skills through *direct* versus *indirect* instructional methods.
- Interview students with differing disabilities to find out what their aspirations for personal, social, and vocational goals are.
- Interview students with differing disabilities to find out what their long-range plans for social, personal, and vocational achievements are.
- Examine the arguments that support a career development curriculum versus a totally academic curriculum.

INTRODUCTION

Wiederholt and McEntire (1980) presented a thoughtful perspective of how the field of special education has approached the provision of educational options for adolescents with disabilities. Before we present a proposal for a secondary special education model that will serve as the philosophical and operational basis for this text, their unique point of view should be reviewed.

In essence, the 1980 article by Wiederholt and McEntire presented the notion that it is not appropriate to consider the value of current educational options simply by using the traditional administrative options for adolescents with educational handicaps—self-contained programs, resource programs, or vocational education. They believe, and with justification, that the programs carrying any one of these labels may differ greatly in effectiveness and have little or nothing to do with the administrative environment. They propose that the examination of a program's basic organizational *rationale* may lead to more useful distinctions between programs. They suggest that such an examination leads to three dominant philosophies or rationales for programs: (1) fit the system, (2) change the system, and (3) ignore the system. These rationales are compared in Table 2.1.

The primary message of Wiederholt and McEntire's 1980 article comes through in their discussion of each of these program rationales. The message is

TABLE 2.1   Rationales for Educating Adolescents with Disabilities

Fit the System Rationale	Change the System Rationale	Ignore the System Rationale
Current models are appropriate.	Current models need improvement.	Current models are inappropriate.
Regular education programs are appropriate for many of the handicapped.	Regular education programs are inappropriate but can be made appropriate for many of the handicapped.	Regular education programs are inappropriate.
Curriculum is predetermined.	Curriculum is predetermined but modified.	Curriculum is not predetermined.
The student is changed to better fit the environment.	The student and existing learning environments are both changed.	New learning environments are developed to fit the needs of the student.

Source: From "Educational Options for Handicapped Adolescents," by J. L. Wiederholt and B. McEntire, 1980, *Exceptional Education Quarterly, 1*, p. 2. Copyright 1980 by PRO-ED, Inc. Reprinted by permission.

one that cannot be overlooked and should be addressed by administrators and teachers in secondary special education. In essence, it suggests the following:

1. For the most part, the needs of exceptional adolescents have been ignored by traditional special education practices.
2. The current emphasis on education of all children and youths has led to a growing awareness that education cannot be geared to one or two common denominators. Alternatives are needed.

When you consider what alternatives are needed and how they might differ from those that currently exist, remember that alternatives can include the existing ones as well as new ones. For example, a high school program exists for almost every adolescent with disabilities in this country. One alternative is to develop an individual education program or provide the necessary support services for any student with educational handicaps to meet his or her needs within that setting. This option may not be sufficient for other students whose individualized education programs may demand changes in the existing high school curriculum or curricular alternatives. Still other students may need something much more specialized than can be provided either within the system or by changes in the system. The issue at point is this: Any one option is not going to meet the needs of *all* secondary special education students.

Ewing and Smith (1981) referred to two basic groups of students with educational handicaps. They are those who require a modification of the learning environment and those who require a modified or different curriculum and set of instructional goals. A model for programming for the needs of all secondary special education students must be one with multiple options. To that end, the model proposed in this chapter is based on a commitment to individualized program *content* (academics, functional academics, life-centered competencies, or vocational), across *learning environment options* (regular classroom, resource room, special class, or special school), and in *instructional approaches* (remedial-tutorial, learning strategies, and community-referenced or didactic instruction) within each content option. The underlying assumption here is that individualization of environment, content, and instructional approaches will lead to the best approximation of what constitutes appropriate education.

PHILOSOPHICAL FOUNDATIONS

The tendency for most special educators is to "fit the system." Too often this is done with the moral and legal mandate of "least restrictive environment" clearly established as the priority in the decision process. Decisions are focused on individual education programs that are expected to be achieved *within* the existing administrative and instructional system. This is another way of saying "fit the system." Parents and administrators may be unaware, however, of the philosophical inconsistencies in today's administrative arrangements for instruction (Clark, 1975a, 1980). The prime example of this is the current problem of delivering specialized, relevant content in administrative and instructional models that do not permit much, if any, attention to content other than what is required for graduation (e.g., regular class with consultation, regular class with resource room support).

Sound programming for secondary special education students without a consistent, clearly stated philosophy is a problem, but it is not the only one. There is the basic dilemma of curriculum options. High school curriculum alternatives typically provide students with choices limited to the following:

1. Preparation for college
2. General education
3. Some type of vocational education
4. Various alternative programs

None of these alternatives currently provides an educational philosophy that is based on a commitment to comprehensive life-career preparation outcomes for students with mild to moderate disabilities and their transition to adult life. Thus, the primary philosophical position presented here addresses the need for secondary special education students to have access to a comprehensive educational program. This should be designed to prepare them for their lifelong career demands. Further, this program should not be viewed as a segregated track with a different diploma or exit document, but rather as a legitimate, approved curriculum option. This option should be open to *any* student in *any* high school and it should be available to students with handicapping conditions if they and their families choose it. Would this approach fit the system, change the system, or ignore the system? It probably would involve a bit of each.

Lifelong career demands are those tasks of living that exist in all areas of careers. We accept the first relevant definition of the word *career* in the *Oxford English Dictionary* (Clarendon Press, 1961, p. 10): "a person's course or progress through life." Career preparation, then, is that formal and informal effort to make one ready for the course of one's life. This course involves various roles (e.g., family member, neighbor, citizen, and worker), various environments (e.g., home, neighborhood, school, and community), and countless events (e.g., home living, mobility, consumer activities, interpersonal relations, leisure activities, and work activities). It also involves many transition periods throughout life, with age-appropriate independent living skills expected in each period. This approach to preparation for life careers—career development and transition education—for individuals with disabilities has been advocated by many authors. They include Brolin (1974, 1983, 1989), Brolin and Kokaska (1979), Clark (1974, 1979, 1981), Clark and Knowlton (1988), Edgar (1987), Goldhammer (1972), Gordon (1973), Gysbers and Moore (1974), Halpern (1985), Hoyt (1979), Wehman, Moon, and McCarthy (1986), and many others.

A logical question at this point is, Why broaden the scope or meaning of *career* beyond what is already for many people a commonly used synonym for *vocation* and *occupation*? Another question is, Rehabilitation with adults focuses on independent living—how does that relate to career development? An equally appropriate question is, Why continue to speak of career development and independent living when *transition* is the currently popular word? Obviously changing terminology does pose some problems in communication. It is important, though, to show the link between career development, independent living, and transition, because they have many common elements. The remainder of this chapter will address some of those commonalities and how they contribute to a secondary special education program model.

EDUCATING ADOLESCENTS WITH DISABILITIES

Assumptions for a Comprehensive Career Development and Transition Education Approach

A proposal for a secondary special education program model that is philosophically centered on the goal of preparation for life-career demands is not new. Brolin (1976, 1982), DeProspo and Hungerford (1946), Hungerford (1941), Kirk and Johnson (1951), Kolstoe (1970), and Martens (1937), among others, have taken similar positions over the past 50 years. They have focused their positions, for the most part, with the student classified as mentally retarded. More recently, Halpern (1985), Kokaska and Brolin (1985), and Clark and Knowlton (1988) have called for a comprehensive career development and transition approach for *all* students with disabilities. We agree with the appropriateness of this philosophy and submit the following assumptions, which provide a foundation for the model that follows later in the chapter:

1. Career development is needed for *all* persons—young and old, with and without disabilities, male and female, poor and affluent, and all races and ethnic groups.

2. One's career is one's progress, or transition, through life as a family member, citizen, and worker. A career is a developmental process and is subject to planning, programming, choices, and changes.

3. Programming in life-career development and transition is concerned with age-appropriate independent living. As such, it promotes protecting each developing person's freedom to make choices and decisions, while assisting him or her to learn what alternatives there are and how to make decisions about them.

4. Significant neglect or adversity in any aspect of human growth can affect one's career development. Significant neglect or adversity during any of life's basic transition periods or during a person's unique transition periods can affect one's adjustment in independent living.

5. Society imposes limits on the life-career development and transitions of persons with disabilities. These factors restrict their independent living.

6. Any person choosing to participate as a producer or consumer in today's complex and changing world must possess a variety of life skills in adaptability.

7. Life-career development and transitions for persons with physical or mental disabilities differ significantly enough in nature or degree from those of persons without disabilities that some special attention to training and services is required.

8. Just as there is a need for different programming between people who are disabled and nondisabled, there is also a need for differentiated programming among the various disability groups and levels of functioning within each population.

9. Life-career development and transition planning and training for any person should begin during infancy and continue throughout adulthood. Early training is especially critical for individuals with disabilities.

10. A democratic philosophy of education and a realistic philosophy of normalization dictate that all students have the same educational opportunities. These philosophies do not dictate, however, that all students have the same specific educational experiences, be in the same instructional programs, or achieve the same educational outcomes.

When an instructional program focused on life-career development and transition demands begins with the question of what educators want students to know, do, or be when they leave high school, the issue of appropriate education inevitably begins with placement. Unfortunately, whether or not students should be placed in a special class, a resource room, or some other administrative arrangement has become the focus of "appropriateness." The decision process frequently becomes distorted when normalization philosophy and advocacy for social equity override individual needs. One might wonder whether the decision makers have truly considered the question, Appropriate for what?

Arguing that outcomes are more important than the nature and location of instructional environments is considered by some as purely subjective and a product of debatable philosophical bias. We submit that there is a body of research that supports the focus on life-centered outcomes. The next section presents data from the literature.

RESEARCH RATIONALE

Two major types of research that support an appropriate educational experience for students with disabilities are adult-adjustment and follow-up studies. Adult-adjustment studies locate people representing certain populations and report how they are adjusting to the tasks of adult living. Follow-up studies follow individuals representing a particular group over time and evaluate them relative to their status on certain variables. Each type of research is represented here.

Adult-adjustment and follow-up studies of identified persons with disabilities are helpful sources of information about the needs of this diverse population and about the implications for educational programming. Studies of this type are typically focused on single-disability categories because of the specific interests of professionals or parents in the long-term effects of various types of programs. The questions asked in these surveys cut across the domains of daily living skills, personal-social skills, and occupational development. Thus, the questions are described briefly for three selected categorical areas: mental retardation, learning disabilities, and deafness.

Mental Retardation

The studies by Butler and Browning (1974), Cobb (1972), and Goldstein (1964) are classic reviews of follow-up studies of persons with mental retardation. More recent follow-up studies have been done by Bruininks, Lewis, and Thurlow (1989), Neubert, Tilson, and Ianacone (1989), Affleck, Edgar, Levine, and Kortering (1990), Haring and Lovett (1990), and Sitlington, Frank, and Carson (1991). The major conclusions from these studies were that although persons with mental retardation appear to adjust satisfactorily in comparison with persons of the same social class who are not retarded, they do have adjustment problems. In addition, their quality of life is less than desirable. Some of the conclusions were as follows:

1. Employment is marginal, with only 30 to 35 percent employed full time, and earnings are at low levels.
2. The majority live with parents.
3. Marriages are unstable.
4. Participation in community activities and leisure-time opportunities are restricted.
5. Money management and social networking are difficult.
6. Health and childcare problems are more frequent.
7. Most persons with mental retardation require one or more nondisabled advocates to provide support in their lives.

Halpern, Close, and Nelson (1986) cited the following rank-order list of independent living difficulties reported by their population of adults with mental retardation:

1. Money management
2. Social networking
3. Home maintenance
4. Food management
5. Conflict over being told what to do versus asking for help
6. Employment
7. Transportation
8. Avoiding/handling problems

Learning Disabilities

Ever since the study by White, Schumaker, Warner, Alley, and Deshler (1980), there has been a continued interest in the postschool outcomes of individuals who have been identified as having a learning disability. This study reported that the individuals classified in school as having learning disabilities had difficulty making friends and relating to parents and relatives, and that employment rates were comparable to adults without learning disabilities, but they were in jobs with significantly lower social status. The investigators also reported that the former students expressed significantly lower aspirations for further education or training. Since that time, there has been an increasing number of postschool outcomes studies. Although there is some discrepancy in some of the findings, probably due in large part to the differences in data-collection procedures and samples, there are some recurring themes in the findings.

Employment outcomes in studies done in the late 1980s and early 1990s (Bruininks et al., 1989; Scuccimarra & Speece, 1990; Sitlington & Frank, 1990; Wagner, 1989) indicate that former students classified as having learning disabilities did not fare as well as the general population, with the average employment rate at about 60 percent one year out of school. Of those who do find work, most are earning no more than minimum wage and many are working only part time. Affleck and colleagues (1990) found in their postschool status study that three years after leaving school, former students are not doing any better over time.

Students served in special resource room programs for individuals with learning disabilities apparently are continuing to have some difficulty in areas of their lives other than employment (Bruininks et al., 1989; Scuccimarra & Speece, 1990; Valdes, Williamson, & Wagner, 1990). Participation in social and recreational activities is directly related to income, so it is not completely clear whether they do not participate because of funds or whether they do not have the knowledge and skills to find ways to involve themselves in the community in activities that do not cost money (volunteer work, church attendance, etc.). Lewis and Taymans (1992) reported similar findings in their study of independent functioning in the community. Kortering and Elrod (1991) concluded from their review of follow-up studies that whatever the statistics show, it is evident that far too many former students find themselves unable to access the community and adjust satisfactorily to adult life.

The Association for Children and Youth with Learning Disabilities (ACLD), now the Association for Children and Adults with learning Disabilities, sponsored an adult adjustment study (Chesler, 1982). This study included a report of the areas of life in which individuals with learning disabilities expressed their greatest need for assistance. The rank-order list included the following:

1. Social relationships, social skills
2. Career counseling
3. Developing self-esteem, confidence (tied)
4. Overcoming dependence, survival (tied)
5. Vocational training
6. Getting and holding a job
7. Reading
8. Spelling
9. Managing of personal finances
10. Organizational skills

This study is important because of the self-reports showing that social and occupational skills were of equal, if not greater, concern than academic skills to students in this group.

Deafness

Although a majority of adults with deafness lead productive, independent lives, follow-up research indicates that being deaf from an early age can significantly affect the personal-social needs of students. Research conducted at the National Technical Institute for the Deaf at the Rochester Institute of Technology revealed that the greatest problems confronting students there were lack of responsibility and poor decision-making skills (Covill-Servo & Garrison, 1978). This finding supported an earlier study that described adolescents and young adults who are deaf as exhibiting immature behavior. That is, they showed egocentricity, easy irritability, impulsiveness, dependency, and suggestibility (Altshuler, 1974).

Historically, individuals with hearing impairments have been more under-employed than unemployed (Moores, 1969; Schein & Delk, 1974; Wagner, 1988). This underemployment seems to occur partly because many lack the personal, social, communication, and technical competencies required for job advancement or upgrading. In part, it may be because these persons are unaware of occupational options available to them and, hence, do not make rational, planned occupational choices (Nash & Castle, 1980; Naidoo, 1989).

Adult adjustment and follow-up studies have not been as focused on other disability groups, but various research efforts and reviews of best practices have led to summaries providing information on their unique needs as well. Those that are mentioned in the next paragraphs were commissioned by the Center for Quality Special Education of Disability Research Systems, Inc., directed by Dr. William Frey.

Behavior Disorders

Wood and Lazarus (1988) described 12 critical educational needs that are especially relevant, if not unique, to the population of students classified as having behavior disorders or emotional impairments. They see these needs falling into two general areas—affective development and academic development. Under affective development, the following educational outcomes should be the concern of school programs:

1. Appropriate emotional development
2. Elimination of inappropriate behavior
3. Assuming responsibility for developing ability in problem solving and decision making
4. Appropriate social skills development
5. Constructive use of school time
6. Parenting and family life education
7. Life-style precautions education

Academic development outcomes will vary, depending on age, severity of the behavioral or emotional problem, personal goals (including interests and preferences), and potential for learning. By definition, these students have psychological problems that interfere with their current functioning, specifically in their academic development and performance. As a result, many of them are not working at expected grade levels for their chronological age and ability levels.

Some are, however, and the needs of this group for continuing their education in postsecondary programs are especially critical in the area of academic development. Some specific academic development needs reported by Wood and Lazarus (1988) that apply to both types of students are:

1. Basic skill development and remediation
2. Functional curriculum instruction (functional reading and communication skills, consumer skills, functional math skills, and independent living skills)
3. Academic survival skills development
4. Acquisition of learning strategies
5. Prevocational, vocational, and career education

Low Vision and Blindness

Alonso (1988) addressed the unique types of needs of students with visual impairments. For example, she stated that students with visual impairments need to have clarification of ongoing needs, along with education system needs, learning adaption needs, and needs related to curriculum additions, curriculum adaptations, component media needs. In the context of career development and transition education, the clarification of ongoing needs and curriculum additions and adaptations are the most critical. They include such outcomes as the following:

1. Skill in conceptualizing and developing short- and long-term goals
2. Developing self-awareness of abilities, interests, preferences, and needs
3. Developing self-confidence for achieving independence
4. Development and use of residual vision
5. Personal management skills
6. Study and organization skills
7. Social and interpersonal skills
8. Physical fitness and health
9. Independent travel skills
10. Reading skills (Braille, print, electronic reading devices, aural reading)
11. Writing skills (Braille, handwriting, typewriting)
12. Occupational information and vocational skills

Speech and Language Impairments

Pistono (1988) took a functional approach to the desirable outcomes for students who are identified as having speech or language disorders. Communication competence in home, school, and community settings is the ultimate outcome. Communication includes talking, listening, gesturing and other nonverbal signaling, reading, writing, interpreting, and interacting. The importance of these as life skills is obvious when applied to the expectations of successful performance in school, satisfying family and friend relationships, understanding expectations and performing successfully at work, and communication in the community.

INDEPENDENT LIVING FOR PERSONS WITH DISABILITIES

Assumptions for a Comprehensive Rehabilitation Approach

Special educators once thought that the state vocational rehabilitation agency was the natural and appropriate bridge to employment and "happily-ever-after" community living for their graduates. This expectation developed during the 1960s when schools saw state vocational rehabilitation agencies taking a new look at special education populations, particularly those classified as mildly mentally retarded. The number of cases closed by vocational rehabilitation increased dramatically from 1960 to 1975. This served only to heighten special educators' expectations that there was someone to assume responsibility for students after they left or completed school. School personnel welcomed the commitment that divisions of vocational rehabilitation were making to the rehabilitation closures (defined as "closed in employment status") of special education graduates and assumed that it was a permanent policy commitment.

At the heart of this optimism was the rather spectacular success of many state departments of education and state vocational rehabilitation agencies in working together through local school districts in programming and funding. Interestingly, even the term *transition* was used in the late 1960s to describe an orderly passage from school or institutional programming to adult services and full community participation (Chaffin, 1968; Younie, 1966). Unfortunately, the momentum waned in the late 1970s as state education agencies and schools became immersed in implementing PL 94-142. During that time, state vocational rehabilitation agencies began quietly withdrawing from school cooperative programs and turning their attention to the demands for services for more severely disabled persons.

Two separate yet parallel movements set the stage for the field to return to the concept of transition. These movements rekindled hopes for an organized, effective process for students and their families. Both occurred in the context of ending school programming and beginning adult living. The first of these was the career education movement as described in Chapter 1 and in the previous section. The second was the independent living movement. While the career education movement was reaching its zenith in the U.S. public education system, the independent living movement was unfolding in the field of rehabilitation with adults. Both have contributed to a return to the goal of interagency cooperation but through a new and improved delivery system—transition programming.

Like the word *transition*, the term *independent living* has both a generic meaning and a symbolic meaning. The generic connotation of independent living may be thought of as the opportunity and ability to participate actively in the community through home and family life, work, and civic and recreational involvement (Pfueger, 1977). Symbolically, however, independent living implies much more than this. One of the early and definitive statements of the meaning of independent living was provided by the Independent Living Research Utilization Project–Texas Institute for Rehabilitation Research (1978). *Independent living* was defined as

> control over one's life based on the choice of acceptable options that minimize reliance on others in making decisions and in performing everyday activities. This includes managing one's own affairs; participating in day-to-day life in the community; fulfilling a range of social roles; and making decisions that lead to self-determination and the minimization of psychological or physical dependence upon others. Independence is a relative concept, which may be defined personally by each individual. (p. 1)

Independent living rehabilitation (ILR) started as a disability-rights movement in the early 1970s by persons with severe physical disabilities in reaction to years of legislation and rehabilitation policies that stopped short of *vocational* rehabilitation. From the beginning, vocational rehabilitation services have been restricted by federal policy to the provision of services only to those for whom there was a "reasonable expectation" that the services would result in remunerative employment. It was the view of many vocational rehabilitation professionals, that independent living services were developed for those for whom a vocational goal was thought to be impossible or unfeasible (DeJong, 1980), rather than a means of making vocational goals feasible.

During the period from 1959 to 1972, Congress made several attempts to pass legislation for special comprehensive rehabilitation services to improve the independent living of persons with disabilities without regard to their ultimate employability. Consumers of rehabilitation services, especially those considered the most severely disabled physically, challenged this concept with the notion that gainful employment is one of several ways an individual can become truly independent. They argued that both comprehensive independent living rehabilitation services *and* vocational rehabilitation services not only were needed but were a basic right. The Rehabilitation Act of 1973 was the first legislation to pass that clearly made a commitment to the provision of vocational rehabilitation services to persons with disabilities who needed more than assistance in gaining employment. Although it did not mandate independent living rehabilitation or vocational rehabilitation services, it did provide a legal base for prohibiting denial of services and discrimination through Sections 501, 502, 503, and 504. It also directed the secretary of the Department of Health, Education, and Welfare to conduct a comprehensive needs study, including research and demonstration projects of various methods of providing rehabilitation and related services to the most severely handicapped individuals (Arkansas Rehabilitation Research and Training Center, 1978).

Because it was a logical extension of the civil rights movement of the 1960s, the independent living movement was receptive to and influenced by other social movements of the 1970s. Among these were consumerism, or self-advocacy, demedicalization and self-care, deinstitutionalization and normalization, and mainstreaming (Dejong, 1983). At the heart of all of these movements was the theme of rejection by the prevailing social system. Using Weiderholt and McEntire's (1980) perspective, all these movements would fall into a rejection of the "fit the system" approach. Their impact on both educators and rehabilitation personnel alike set the stage for a readiness for the concept of *transition.*

TRANSITION FROM SCHOOL TO ADULT LIVING

Edgar (1988), Bruininks and colleagues (1989), Sitlington and Frank (1990), and Valdes and colleagues (1990) have provided a significant body of research findings in their studies of mildly mentally handicapped students who had been in high school special education programs or received special education services while in school. These findings have direct bearing on the issues of transition from school to adult living. Edgar (1988) summarized his analysis of follow-up study data with the conclusion that

1. Few students with handicapping conditions move from school to independent living in their communities.
2. Secondary special education programs appear to have little influence on the adjustment of students to community life.
3. More than 30 percent of the students enrolled in secondary special education programs drop out.
4. Neither graduates nor dropouts of programs involving special education programs or services find adequate employment.

Some view transition primarily as a service-delivery system. Halpern (1985, p. 480) set the tone and substance of transition as a service-delivery concept with the statement, "Living successfully in one's community should be the primary target of transitional services." He went on to specify the thrust of the services to be efforts along three foundation dimensions: the quality of a person's residential environment, the adequacy of a person's social and interpersonal network, and the adequacy of a person's employment. The three-dimensional perspective was highly intentional in an effort to influence a trend toward a unidimensional interpretation of transition—adequacy of employment.

The unidimensional view of transition from school to working life is attributed to Madeline Will by many people as a result of her initiatives and influence on federal priorities as head of the Office of Special Education and Rehabilitative Services of the Department of Education (Will, 1984). Actually, this single-focus view goes back to the influence of Gold (1980) and others who staked an early claim in vocational training of persons with severe disabilities and the supported employment concept (Bellamy, Peterson, & Close, 1975, Rusch, 1986a; Wehman, 1981). In any case, it is clear that Will's priority for federal support in transition efforts is targeted on employment and influences the general perceptions many people have about transition. Politically, there are any number of reasons for focusing transition as a concept on employment outcomes, but it has caused some debate over the interpretation of the concept of transition (Rusch & Menchetti, 1988; Clark & Knowlton, 1988).

We affirm the position of Halpern (1985) and numerous others (Brown, Halpern, Hasazi, & Wehman, 1987; Elliott, 1987; Kokaska, Gruenhagen, Razeghi, & Fair, 1985; Kortering & Elrod, 1991; McDonnel, Sheehan, & Wilcox, 1983, 1985; Wehman, Moon, & McCarthy, 1986) that transition from school to adult living is a broad, life-career focus that parents, school personnel, and adult service agencies should have in developing transition programs. We also support the broader notion of transition described by Edgar (1987), who views it as a *process* with three components: (1) sending agencies, (2) receiving agencies, and (3) the event/process of the handoff between the sending agencies and the receiving agencies.

The *Maryland State Department of Education Transition Guidelines Handbook* (Maryland State Department of Education, 1986) summarizes the issue of focus and interpretation of the transition concept in this way:

> While successful entry into employment is and should be a major goal of vocational preparation during the school years, in keeping with the Maryland State Department's Mission of Schooling, we believe it is equally important to assist students to deal successfully with the nonvocational aspects of community living as well.
>
> Transition should be considered an outcome-oriented process in which the handicapped student has been provided support services throughout the school years and for whom a plan of comprehensive services has been developed to assure, if feasible, an independent community placement, including employment and adequate resources to maintain an appropriate level of independence.
>
> This process of transitioning from dependence as a student to independence as an adult must be accompanied by adequate planning to assure the availability of appropriate support systems. The transition is easier if there has been sound preparation in the secondary school, appropriate planning for postsecondary services, and adequate services for adjustments in the community. (p. 4)

Individuals with Disabilities Education Act

The Individuals with Disabilities Education Act of 1990 (IDEA, PL 101-476) made some significant additions and changes to PL 94-142, Education of the Handicapped Act. Autism and traumatic brain injury were added as separate disability categories in the definition of children with disabilities. Social work services in schools as related services were expanded to any social work services rather than just those in school. Other changes in IDEA related to the addition of rehabilitation counseling as a related service, the definition of *assistive technology device* and *assistive technology service*, and new regulations concerned with the comprehensive system of personnel development, Part B programs affecting infants and toddlers, and some new revisions to the process of planning and documenting the individualized educational program (IEP).

In the context of this book, the most significant provision of IDEA was the mandate for transition planning for students age 16 and older. It placed the initial responsibility for transition planning on state and local education agencies. IDEA used the term *transition services* in the language of the law and the regulations for the first time. Under the law, *transition services* are defined as

> a coordinated set of activities for a student, designed within an outcome-oriented process, which promotes movement from school to post-school activities, including post-secondary education, vocational training, integrated employment (including supported employment), continuing and adult education, adult services, independent living, or community participation... and shall include instruction, community experiences, the development of employment and other post-school

adult living objectives, and, when appropriate, acquisition of daily living skills and functional evaluation. (20 U.S.C. 1401[a][19])

Although 16 years of age is too late to begin planning for many at-risk students, IDEA is a vital new step in educational programming for all identified adolescents with disabilities. That is, transition services must be considered for any student who has an IEP and is 16 years old (or younger when appropriate). Transition services may be provided through *instruction* or *related services*. Instruction can be provided in regular or general education (including vocational education and practical or industrial arts) and special eduction (if it is a specially designed instruction or curriculum).

IDEA legislation makes it clear that programs and services needed by a student should be highly individualized, based on individual needs, preferences, and interests. Programs or instructional arrangements are not to be based on currently available programs and services. The individualized educational program required under PL 94-142 is expanded under IDEA to ensure better individual planning for transition outcomes. The regulations specify that all goals, objectives, instruction, and related services must be planned and delivered within an outcome-oriented process. This process begins with a set of expectations or long-range goals and moves backward to the developing of appropriate current goals to progress toward or reach the desired outcomes.

Program Sequencing

When students are in the elementary grades, the expectations or long-range goals for a child are probably going to be the development of basic academic and socialization skills. The expected level of reading, writing, and arithmetic skills will vary considerably from student to student, but both parents and teachers would ordinarily aspire for the student to reach as high a level of numeracy and literacy as possible. Socialization goals would be for chronological age-appropriate behavior and social functioning. Although IDEA does not require transition planning for elementary age students, it is important that parents and teachers begin early on to work purposefully on values, attitudes, and habits, as well as occupational information and basic prevocational and daily living skills.

Any student who reaches the high school level without the expected academic and socialization outcomes achieved is faced with the choice (the responsibility for which is borne or shared by parents) of pursuing an academic program or some specially designed course of study. If the academic program is chosen, the student will retain basic skills goals and objectives on the IEP and receive a remedial program to work on academic deficiencies or a program that will help the student develop alternative response strategies to the demands of academic work. IDEA requires that transition services be discussed and considered, even when the student or his or her family demands an academic curriculum. The decision to reject the inclusion of any transition goals or objectives must be documented by the school to show that the school complied with the intent of the law. If the student and his or her family choose to work directly on goals and objectives that will enhance the student's postschool adjustment, the school must provide such a program. It is hoped that in both of these case examples, state and local education agencies will provide an appropriate program that will assure that each student will meet the state and local requirements for graduation and a high school diploma.

The progress of each student toward effective adult living should guide all participants in the IEP planning process toward the appropriate decision to fit the system, change the system, or ignore the system. The intent of all federal legislation on behalf of students with disabilities is to assure that each student has the optimum chance to learn to become an effective adult. Therefore, the system should be properly viewed as a facilitating vehicle for the delivery of appropriate content, a choice of learning environment options, and appropriate instructional approaches. It is within this framework that the life career development and transition education model is presented.

PROPOSED MODEL OF CAREER DEVELOPMENT AND TRANSITION EDUCATION

Independent Living for Persons with Disabilities

Reflection on the research literature in career education, independent living, and transition programming leads the thoughtful reader to consider the effects of Wiederholt and McEntire's (1980) three basic options: fit the system, change the system, or ignore the system. What should a school's response be to these options? Do U.S. high schools still value their early goals of civic responsibility, occupational adequacy, worthy home membership, and wise use of leisure time (Resnick & Resnick, 1985)? If so, to choose one of Wiederholt and McEntire's options, one must ask the following questions:

1. Are the educational goals of the past relevant for today?
2. If the goals are still relevant, are the research data presented earlier in this chapter pertinent to the success of today's high schools in meeting those goals?
3. If the research evidence is relevant to the goals, is it strong enough to challenge the appropriateness of current high school programs?
4. If the research evidence is sufficient to challenge the appropriateness of high schools today, is the issue of appropriateness primarily one of inappropriate curriculum or of inappropriate and, thus, ineffective, instruction? Or is the issue a combination of the two?

5. Can the determination of "appropriate education" (Clark, 1980) by means of an individualized education program for any exceptional youth be made without considering the issues raised in the preceding questions?

These questions must not be simply rhetorical. They actually can lead to decisions about program options.

Weiderholt and McEntire's (1980) options provide an action response for student decision making as well as for programs. If the content of a regular high school curriculum is determined to be appropriate for a given student, the student should be permitted to fit into the system. If the curriculum is not appropriate, a change in the system might be needed—either in content or in instructional approach. Kortering and Elrod (1991) referred to this as restructuring schools to prepare students for utilitarian, social, and personal roles. If the curriculum is so inappropriate that changes in the system are not possible, the final option is to ignore the system and develop a new one for the student. IDEA legislation makes it clear that goals and objectives must not be based on existing programs.

Decisions as to how to change a high school program are difficult to make and even more difficult to put into action; the educational reform movement is making it especially difficult to fit or even change the system. Students with handicapping conditions are vulnerable as this change is occurring. At this point, individual curriculum content needs and individual learning styles become the essence of what appropriate education is, and not simply legal mandates and educational philosophies.

It is extremely difficult, but not impossible, to provide every high school student with disabilities with an individualized curriculum for life-career development and transitions without special curricula in place. This means that wherever a student is placed in regular high school curriculum courses for all or a majority of his or her school day, there should be appropriate life-career development and transition skills content within that curriculum. If a student is spending part of the school day in regular classes and part of the day in a resource room, there should be appropriate career development curricula infused or provided separately in both settings. If a student is placed in a self-contained class for all or a majority of his or her school day, there should be appropriate career development and transition skills content, taught from a community-referenced approach.

Viewed from this perspective, *appropriate education* is clearly synonymous with life-career development and transition education. Although this is not a consensus opinion in the field of special education, it is a strongly held view of some leaders of the transition movement, notably Halpern (1985), Wehman, Moon, and McCarthy (1986), Edgar (1987), Brown, Halpern, Hasazi, and Wehman (1987), and Kortering and Elrod (1991). It is also fully affirmed by The Council for Exceptional Children (1978) and the Division on Career Development of The Council for Exceptional Children (Kokaska et al., 1985). The weight of the evidence for a need to do something different bends one to consider the options of changing the current program models before one ignores the system and develops completely new alternatives. The availability of a career development and transition education high school curriculum or course of study that can be the curriculum of choice of any student with disabilities is essential. Making such a choice available to all high school students would, in fact, be changing the system, since many students do not have such an option now. The remainder of this chapter will present some guidelines for what such a curriculum would provide.

Figure 2.1 presents the elements of a career development and transition education model. The focus on the function of life-career development education is clearly based on the four content area components designed for instruction and learning experiences, beginning at the preschool level and continuing through adulthood.

This model includes a focus on work but gives equal importance to other competencies that are critical for life-career roles and transition demands. The curricula of the elementary school, middle school, and junior high school are based on the mutually important elements of (1) values, attitudes, and habits; (2) human relationships; (3) occupational information; and (4) acquisition of job and daily living skills. The level and nature of specific competencies and subcompetencies subsumed under the four elements of the model are not static. As students progress through the grade hierarchy of elementary, middle, or junior high school and move into high school and postsecondary or adult and continuing education, the four basic elements of career development and transition education change as instructional objectives are met and individual needs change.

In Figure 2.1, the four content elements of the model are superimposed over vertical lines that extend upward, undergirding the high school, postsecondary, and adult options for education and training. As a school-based career development and transition education model for adolescents with disabilities, the natural focus is, of course, on what happens during the high school years. This model reflects the basic curricular emphasis options that are available in one form or another in most states. A given school district may have all or only one or two of these options available to students. These options have their unique foci, but the model proposes that every option address systematically the inclusion of *values, attitudes, and habits; human relationships; occupational information;* and *acquisition of job and daily living skills* for students who have disabilities.

Thus, the career development and transition education model advocates the provision of instruction in career development and transition knowledge and skills, regardless of the students' choice of course of study in high school. Again, the intent of IDEA provisions for transition services goals and objectives in each student's IEP is clear—goals can and should supersede existing program options to meet a student's needs. The same concept holds for postsecondary and adult education options. Individuals with handicapping conditions must have access to career development and transition education from preschool through adult working and retirement years.

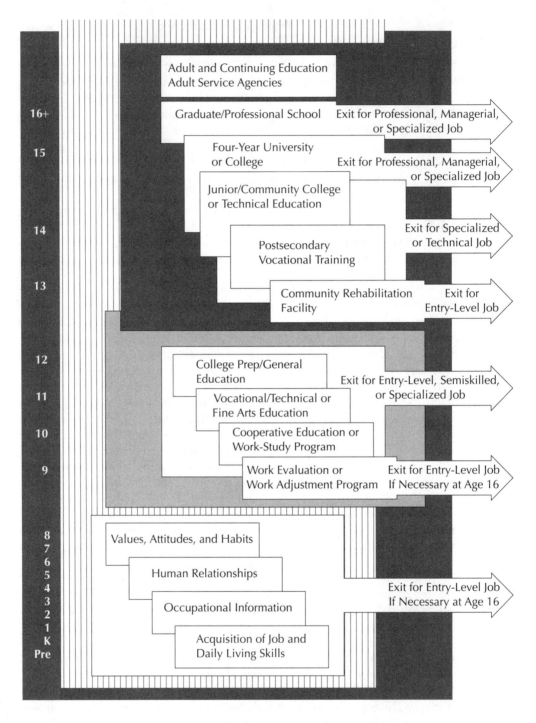

FIGURE 2.1 A School-Based Career Development and Transition Education Model for Adolescents with Disabilities

Although a more detailed elaboration of the original version of the model appears in Clark and White (1980) and Clark (1979, 1981), the following sections provide a description of the basic concepts of each of the current four model components: values, attitudes, and habits; human relationships; occupational information; and acquisition of actual job and daily living skills.

Values, Attitudes, and Habits

A major problem in the school becoming involved in the process of developing and fostering values, attitudes, and habits is the problem in determining *which* values, attitudes, and habits should be taught. Values can be associated with any number of things—money, religious beliefs, race, education, sex, responsibility, integrity, loyalty to country, work, leisure, and so on. Some of these issues are controversial or sensitive.

Some people claim that the school should respond to the need for all of its pupils to establish and maintain value systems that are positive both for themselves and for the social groups to which they belong. Others raise questions as to what constitutes a positive value system and, even if those components can be identified, what the school should do when there is a conflict between that value system and a different one held by someone else within that particular social group. The courts have continually had to provide legal answers to values questions, especially in recent years. But whether the issues have dealt with teaching a theory of evolution, corporal punishment, prayer in the schools, or length, style, or color of a person's hair, they have remained largely unresolved for thousands of individuals despite court decisions.

Raths, Merrill, and Sidney (1966) offered a workable compromise, though not a solution, to the "teach values–do not teach values" dilemma when they suggested that educators should not be concerned with the *content* of people's values but rather with the *process* of valuing. Consideration of this view changes the focus from thinking about whether to teach students certain concepts that are value-laden to how to teach students to select, defend, and act in those concept areas so that they know why they think or believe as they do, *how* their actions are related to those beliefs, and *what* are the probable consequences of their actions.

A compromise in values is not completely acceptable to many who believe the school should maintain and preserve certain moral and social values. To them, a compromise that completely avoids value content begs the question. The position taken here is that the valuing process is of great importance in career development and transition education for students with disabilities, and it should be central to programming in this area. However, the valuing process should not be taught to the exclusion of or apart from certain specific values that are known to be beneficial for individual and group success in life.

People's values are the basis for what they find worthy in other people and in themselves. Values undergird codes of conduct, preferences, beliefs, ideas, and means of decision making. Some values change as people change and as society changes. However, schools and parents should not hesitate to reach a consensus on some specific values and plan instructional efforts toward the goal of teaching those values. Some specific values that have particular relevance for any individual are those suggested by O'Neill and O'Neill (1974, p. 169):

courage	conservation	efficiency
freedom	health	initiative
honesty	perseverance	reliability
cooperation	courtesy	friendliness
respect	tolerance	understanding

Thus far, the rationale for the need to have curricular provisions for developing values and the development of valuing has not dealt specifically with attitudes or habits. The reason for this is that values, attitudes, and habits are so interdependent that a rationale for one is a rationale for the other two. Values, or those beliefs that are cherished, lead persons to assume attitudes or positions that are relatively consistent, which then result in relatively predictable behaviors or habits.

Further rationale for the importance of programming for values, attitudes, and habits goes beyond general educational philosophy. Butler and Browning (1974), Cobb (1972), Goldstein (1964), Henrich and Kriegel (1961), and Mithaug, Martin, Agran, and Rusch (1988) have all concluded from the research literature on adult adjustment of persons with disabilities and personal reports of persons with disabilities that these human variables are of critical importance. In many cases, they seem to be more important for this population than actual job skills in maintaining employment and successfully fulfilling roles in the home and community. Furthermore, the research of Stephens (1972) has strongly suggested that moral judgment (based on values) and moral conduct (attitudes and habits) in children and youths of both normal and below-normal intelligence are developmental traits. As such, they are amenable to change through education and training.

Human Relationships

Historically, the U.S. public school has concentrated its efforts in educating youths in academic skills. Classroom discipline, behavior management, and meeting students' emotional needs have been integral parts of the instructional process. However, these have been taught almost exclusively through rules of behavior and incidental methods rather than through clear-cut, purposeful objectives and procedures. In the past, critics of public education decried this approach and advocated a humanistic philosophy that places personal and social development alongside scholastic achievement as important aims for education (Holt, 1976; Illich, 1971; Ojemann, 1967). More recently, similar proposals have called for the same kinds of curriculum emphases (Cartledge & Milburn, 1986; Kortering & Elrod, 1991; Morse, 1982; Wood, 1982). The challenge from critics is that educators must recognize the school's *formal* role in personal-social development.

The notion of specific, purposeful instruction in the area of personal-social behavior has been rejected by some people, who see it as the responsibility of the family, religious teachers, or, even broader, "everyone's" responsibility. Others have an attitude that "these things work out—just let kids grow up and they'll learn."

Although the family is rightfully viewed as the primary unit responsible for children's basic personal-social development, social learning activities in the company of peers, particularly at school, are important. This is especially true for exceptional adolescents who not only encounter most of the typical painful adolescent experiences that involve human relationships but also those that stem directly from their exceptionality. Their "differentness" elicits overt and covert reactions from others that result in countless painful experiences. Obvious disabilities such as mental retardation with physical stigmata, orthopedic impairments, blindness, or speech impairments pose initial, and sometimes persisting, barriers for satisfactory social relationships. The less obvious disabling conditions—deafness, mild mental retardation, learning disabilities, or emotional disturbance—may manifest themselves in behavioral problems that interfere with social relationships (Kelly, Wildman, Urey, & Thurman, 1979).

According to Campbell (1964), a person's success in human relationships hinges on acceptance or rejection. The criteria for acceptance or rejection are generally classified as pertaining either to personality and social characteristics or to skills and abilities. Research evidence abounds suggesting that friendliness and sociability are correlated with acceptance. On the other hand, social indifference, withdrawal, rebelliousness, and hostility are correlated with rejection. In the area of skills and abilities, research findings indicate that the more intelligent and creative children are more accepted by their peers, while the slow learners and those labeled as mentally retarded are less well accepted, if not rejected. Body size, muscular strength, maturational development, and athletic ability also appear as criteria for acceptance.

From these data, it is clear that students with disabilities, who may differ in both personal-social characteristics and skill performance, need *specific* instruction to deal with those aspects of human relationships that affect their acceptance or rejection. Such instruction should come from every feasible source. It is the position here that some of it should come from the school.

In the past, elementary and secondary special education curriculum guides have included some objectives, activities, and materials focusing on human relationships to some extent. But, to a large degree, they have depended on incidental learning to accomplish the desired ends. In a study of high school special education programs in a Detroit suburban-residential area, Brozovich and Kotting (1984) reported that only 36 percent of the teachers agreed that their curriculum included a specific plan designed to promote students' personal growth, social-emotional development, or mental health. This is not unusual. Rarely, if ever, has any accountability been imposed on programs, teachers, or students to demonstrate specific attainment of goals in this area.

There is certainly a substantial amount of evidence that adults with mild to moderate disabilities have deficits in human relations (Andrasik & Matson, 1985; Bruininks et al., 1989; Nash & Castle, 1980; Scuccimarra & Speece, 1990; Valdes et al., 1990). These studies reflect a growing awareness that schools are either ignoring the issues of personal-social skills through direct instruction or that the incidental learning approach via classroom rules, discussion, counseling and guidance, and related curriculum materials is inadequate.

Career development and transition education must include a deliberate effort to develop skills in creating and maintaining positive human relationships. Any such effort specifically designed for exceptional children and youths must deal with those special and unique problems that involve communication with, and understanding of, others. Examples of these problems include communicating with nonexceptional persons about their ignorance, naivete, or attitudes; working through feelings of anger and hostility that are related to one's exceptionality; communicating feelings about excessive or unwanted assistance and denial of independence; and avoiding tendencies to withdraw.

Career development and transition education programming in human relationships is not typically cited in the literature as a discrete, identifiable component. There are references, however, to social skills training or socialization.

Two studies explored the perceived importance of social skills training from the perspectives of parents, teachers, and other professionals and professionals respectively. Results from both investigations indicated that teachers and related professionals believe that the teaching of social skills is important (Baumgart, Filler, & Askvig, 1991; Sacks, Tierney-Russell, Hirsch, & Braden, 1992). Baumgart and colleagues found also that although a majority of the teachers viewed social skills training as important, there were obstacles preventing them from teaching them. These included teachers' inadequacies in writing appropriate social goals and objectives for IEPs, as well as knowing how to implement specific social skills instuctional strategies or methods. Sacks and colleagues validated the results of the Baumgart study and expanded the notion that teachers and other professionals require further training in teaching social skills.

There is the tacit assumption that human relationships in career development and transition education are important, but rarely are they emphasized as distinct areas of instruction on a parallel with attitudes and values, occupational information, and acquisition of a job or daily living skills. The basic assumptions presented here provide sufficient rationale for emphasizing human relationships as an equally important element of programming for adolescents with disabilities.

A case could probably be made for a similar emphasis on this type of programming for *all* teenagers, based on the literature that reports why people leave jobs or are fired from jobs, dissolve marriages, commit crimes, avoid personal and social interactions in leisure time, and seek anonymity in large urban environments. Nonexceptional students, however, are not the target population for this book. If special educators accept this area as a legitimate component of life-career and transition skills programming, and if it proves to be successful, educators of students without disabilities may move to incorporate it into their programming.

Occupational Information

There is no doubt that from a national perspective, career education programming has emphasized occupational awareness as its primary theme. In fact, *occupational awareness* (or *career awareness*, as it is frequently called) has become a synonym for *career education* for the average teacher. This is unfortunate in three ways. First, as just indicated, the term *career awareness*, when interpreted to be the same as *occupational awareness*, ignores the intent of Kenneth Hoyt (1979), former commissioner of career education, and other career education advocates who would like the word *career* to mean more than one's job or vocation. Second, it has somehow restricted the perspective of what should be taught in the area of occupational awareness to information related primarily to occupational choice alternatives. Third, it has somehow led many to believe that secondary students do not have a need for awareness, but rather should be involved only in exploration and preparation activities.

This narrow perspective of what schools should be providing in the area of awareness and knowledge of career development and transition to the world of work not only shortchanges our children and youth but also decelerates the career education movement. Certainly, it negates the concept of career development and transition education presented here.

Focusing primarily on occupational awareness in the schools has political advantages because federal and state legislators tend to deal with publicly visible problems such as unemployment, job dissatisfaction, and worker alienation. Educationally, however, such a narrow view of what career education encompasses does not make sense when one looks at the needs of adults for occupational information that go far beyond their choices of vocations. Since this is particularly true for adults with disabilities, it is critically important for teenage (better still, preteenage) youths with disabilities to be exposed to a broad perspective of occupational information during a period in their lives when they are forming attitudes and perspectives.

Occupational information, as conceptualized here, involves knowledge of all those aspects of the world of work that are critical for individuals to know about. Those of major importance are discussed briefly in this chapter and include *occupational roles, occupational vocabulary, occupational alternatives,* and *basic information related to some realities of the world of work.*

Occupational Roles

An occupational information program should provide learning experiences that result in a new or expanded awareness of possible roles for exceptional students. In producer/worker roles, there needs to be a stress on the possibility of productive work being inclusive of efforts that are unpaid as well as paid. This includes the work of the student as a learner, work as a volunteer, and the work activities or productivity at home in which one might be involved as a part of daily living or leisure. In consumer roles, there needs to be a stress on an appreciation for those whose work and productivity have made possible the services, conveniences, or environments that people use. Furthermore, exceptional students need to begin learning how to use such services themselves both efficiently and effectively as consumers.

Occupational Vocabulary

Students who are learning about their present and future occupational roles must develop or expand their vocabularies to acquire information basic to such learning. This is somewhat analogous to the student entering law or medical school. The first few months concentrate on the vocabulary, or "language," of the profession. It is said that students in both these professions must acquire up to 20,000 new words during their preparation for work. Exceptional students do not face such a monumental task, but they do have to establish hearing vocabulary skills that are essential for any given occupational information concept or fact. Occupational vocabulary development is necessary for understanding concepts about work roles, what occupations exist, and something about the characteristics of work and work settings.

Occupational Alternatives

Educators of exceptional students should have some general perspective on the theory of occupational choice as it relates to normal growth and development before getting too deeply involved in any type of special programming for children and youth. There are a number of theories, but only one is discussed briefly here to serve as a general base. Ginzberg and associates (Ginzberg, Ginsburg, Axelrad, & Herma, 1951) studied the process of occupational choice and concluded that it is a developmental process. They suggested three stages, or periods—fantasy, tentative choice, and realistic choice. They further stated that occupational choice is a series of decisions made over a period of years, and that each step is meaningfully related to what has been decided before. They have maintained that each decision is a compromise among many factors. Some people have to compromise little, others a great deal. Logic and observation suggest that for individuals with disabilities, a great number of compromises must be made.

Career development and transition education must include a component of information that relates to choice and awareness of occupational alternatives in a way that provides keen sensitivity to the self-esteem needs of students who are disabled. There is time later for personalizing the realities and compromises they must face with regard to who and what they will be. The crux of this position for the elementary and middle school professional is to make children as aware as possible about occupational alternatives. At the same time, professionals must continually accept their students' verbalized choices (regardless of how bizarre or inappropriate from an adult perspective) and affirm the students as persons. Secondary educators have to continue the effort to make students aware of alternatives. However, they must also provide exploration or experience activities that prepare students to set goals as they become ready to make their own choices.

Basic Information on Realities of the World of Work

There is a problematic point in providing occupational information to exceptional youths or information about realities of the world of work. On the one hand, the goal of educators is to encourage students to want to work and be workers; on the other hand, educators have to be honest in pointing out some of the negative realities of work. Chapter 7 deals with some of the realities that are especially important for students with handicaps to learn about. At the high school level, adolescents with disabilities must begin to come to grips with the realities of the world of work so that coping with those realities will be easier later. These realities must be introduced gradually, and the students must receive encouragement with cautious, but realistic, optimism.

Acquisition of Job and Daily Living Skills

A person can have "good" values, attitudes, and habits but still be considered incompetent in personal or work behaviors. A person can be adept in human relationships but still be judged as unskilled in occupational or daily living tasks. A person can have knowledge about the world of work but be unable to maintain a place in it because of lack of skills in job or daily living requirements.

Traditional career education literature focuses on occupational awareness, exploration, and preparation. Values, attitudes, and habits that are emphasized are usually directly related to the goals of developing positive values, attitudes, and habits toward paid work. Similarly, whatever mention is made of human relationships usually relates to social interactions on the job. What is mentioned less frequently is the importance of competence in daily living in one's life-career development and transition to adult living and how daily living competencies critically relate to success in the world of work. These competencies in daily living should receive equal emphasis in training along with acquisition of job skills or competencies.

Job skills and daily living skills overlap in so many ways that there is little reason for debating the necessity of including certain daily living skills in a curriculum model. The basic skills required for reading a recipe for cooking a meal at home are the same skills needed for reading a recipe for cooking in a restaurant on a job. The skills required for driving a car or truck for personal reasons are the same skills required for driving a car or truck in a work setting. The skills needed for selecting and purchasing items for personal use are the same skills required for selecting and buying goods in the work world.

There are scores of daily living demands that require skills or competencies not associated directly with occupational skills. These skills are still justifiable within a career development and transition education context because they are the critical competencies that undergird all life experiences. Failure to acquire competencies in daily living cannot be isolated from a person's success or failure in the world of work. If a person cannot maintain a healthy body, how can he or she work? If a person cannot abide by the laws of a community or state, how can he or she be expected to abide by the laws or rules of the work world? If a person does not know how to use leisure time at home, how can he or she be expected to use a work break effectively? If a person has marital or family relationship problems, how can he or she be expected to perform at work at full potential? Numerous competencies or skills are needed to perform activities not required in one's occupation.

A discussion of the developmental needs of teenagers with disabilities for acquiring job and daily living skills is in order at this point. Any task performance, whether occupational or daily living, requires one or more basic skills. These skills are typically categorized under the domains of cognitive, affective, and psychomotor skills. The basic point of this section is that adolescents with mental handicaps, physical handicaps, or both should have specific programming in basic cognitive and psychomotor skills that have usefulness in preparing them for:

1. Current and emerging work roles during early adolescence
2. Assuming more complex work roles during later adolescence
3. Coping with current and emerging daily living demands
4. Coping with the more complex demands to be made on them in daily living during adolescence

(Affective skills for both occupational and daily living demands were addressed in previous sections.)

Finally, job and daily living skills are not just important for their personal usefulness; they are also important because of society's expectations for everyone to be able to demonstrate these kinds of competencies. There are certain social "penalties" exceptional individuals have to pay if they cannot perform these competencies. Stares, comments by children, embarrassing interactions, and questions from well-meaning but ignorant persons are typical. Competence in as

"Now that's what I call a reliable source."

many skills as possible helps individuals with disabilities to present themselves as either more unobtrusive or more like the "normal" person. Certainly, the more competent they are, the more unobtrusive their deviance becomes, or the more others will tolerate their deviance.

CONCLUSION

A high school special education program model is one that must provide students with life-career development and transition content. The model proposed here is a content model for life-career development and transition. It is proposed as an appropriate framework for all exceptionalities at the high school level, irrespective of the administrative placement of students. However, it is becoming increasingly clear that the current reforms of the public high school make this kind of program content difficult to deliver. At the very minimum, there should be a clear-cut choice for students among curricula or courses of study that includes outcome goals that range from academic achievement to life-career competency development.

Life-career development involves values, attitudes, habits, human relationships, occupational information, and acquisition of job and daily living skills. These are logical areas of instruction when retrospective research data and follow-up study findings are considered. Failure to make such a curriculum one of the legitimate, state-approved diploma options in every high school denies what is appropriate for many students with disabilities who would choose it if given the opportunity.

The importance of establishing life-career development and transition education curricula in various program options in high schools is not currently accepted by many regular educators. Regular education also appears to be moving toward an even more restrictive focus on academics in the future. Advocates for special education students in high schools must know the current trends in educational reform, the implications for students with disabilities, and possible solutions or compromises that can be made within the context of reform.

Career development programming, transition education, career education, life-centered career competencies for adolescents with sensory, physical, or mental disabilities—what term should be used for this approach? As a thematic goal around which content and instructional approaches are woven, a functional, life-career competencies approach speaks to the ultimate issue of *usefulness*. The theme, as we have presented it here, is such that it may completely alienate educators or critics of education who are concerned only about academic excellence and minimum competency standards. For those individuals, we would defer to Marland (1974, p. 13), who quotes Alfred North Whitehead as saying: "Pedants sneer at an education that is useful, but if it is not useful, what is it?" Without apology, that view is supported in presenting this career development and transition education model.

3
Participants in High School Programs for Special Students

There is no one who cannot find a place for himself in our kind of world. Each of us has some unique capacity waiting for realization. Every person is valuable in his own existence—for himself alone.—GEORGE H. BENDER

ACTIVITIES

- Interview students with different kinds of disabilities to determine what characteristics they have in common.
- Interview parents or guardians of students with disabilities to find out what they think are the major problems of their children.
- Study and report on the effects of a specific disability in an urban versus a rural setting.
- Compare the effects of a specific disability on students from Hispanic, Asian, African-American, and Caucasian backgrounds. Describe the effects of poverty on existing specific disabilities as they affect child-rearing patterns.
- Select one of the case studies presented in the chapter and develop a list of questions you think should be included in an assessment focused on values, attitudes, and habits in career development and transition education program planning.

INTRODUCTION

Although the participants in secondary programming for students with handicaps include student populations and instructors, both groups are comprised of a number of subgroups. No two high school programs are alike, even in the same district, because of the diversity of these subgroups. This chapter describes, defines, and explains some of the diversity that makes planning for educational programs for adolescents who have disabilities so enjoyable, challenging, interesting, and, at times, difficult. This will be done by first presenting a perspective on adolescence, next describing the various adolescent subgroups with disabilities, and then describing the professional participants engaged in educational programs and services with them.

ADOLESCENCE

Adolescence may be broadly defined as the transition period from dependent childhood to self-sufficient adulthood. It is a time of conflict, redefinition, and striving for independence. Adolescence may be difficult even for the most intelligent, advantaged, and popular students. For those with disabilities, adolescence may become a Herculean task for which these young people are neither prepared nor capable of dealing. Thus, educators working with a special-needs adolescent population must be reminded of the characteristics and struggles associated with adolescence in general and the effects of this transition period on an adolescent's behavior and personality.

The beginning of adolescence is marked by the genetically and biologically produced onset of puberty. *Puberty* is the time span of physiological development during which the reproductive functions mature. These physiological changes take place over a period of approximately two years. The rate of physical change during this period is greater than at any other time during a person's maturation. The adolescent must deal with a new body and new roles in a very short period of time. New relationships with people of the opposite sex and of the same sex emerge out of both necessity and desire. Masculinity and femininity are established as well as a new body and self-image. Thus, the adolescent is, in essence, involved in the struggle to develop a new sexual identity. This is apparent in the "dating game," in conformity to dress and hairstyles of peers, new relationships with peers and adults, uncommon modesty, and experiments in flirtation and sexual relations, all of which are often perceived by adults as being immature, antisocial, or rebellious behaviors.

The biological change is not the only cause of adolescent conflict, however. The adolescent also is being programmed to fit the expectations of his or her culture. Cultural anthropologists have found that in primitive cultures the period of adolescence is very short (Aries, 1962). Upon reaching puberty, the individual is considered an adult and may be initiated into the adult society through rites and rituals. In Western society, adolescence is an extended period of time during which young persons are expected to pattern themselves after adult standards.

One adult standard of Western culture is for adolescents to begin to emulate the work ethic—and the sooner, the better. Because of the change in the family structure, with one or both parents working outside the home, and the formalization of the workplace, the burden is placed on the school to keep students in school and prepare them for adult roles. Keeping students in school and preparatory status extends the adolescent period through secondary and, often, postsecondary years (Starr, 1986). This extension may lead to conflicts concerning independence and self-sufficiency between parents and their adolescent child. Although the adolescent desires to become self-sufficient, he or she may not have the means to accomplish this goal. Parents, still providing financial support, may impose too many restrictions on the adolescent striving for independence.

Theories of adolescence were developed with the normal young person as the standard of reference. Havighurst (1953) identified some developmental tasks that adolescents must complete in order to become successful adults. Using some of his tasks and adapting others to more current cultural mores, the following tasks are presented:

1. Achieving new and more mature relations with age mates of both sexes
2. Achieving a sexual identity
3. Accepting one's physique and using the body effectively
4. Achieving emotional independence from parents and other adults
5. Achieving economic independence
6. Selecting and preparing for an occupation
7. Preparing for marriage, family life, and intimate relationships
8. Developing intellectual skills and concepts necessary for civic competence
9. Desiring and achieving socially responsible behavior
10. Acquiring a set of values and an ethical system as a guide to behavior

Given a set of challenging development tasks such as those listed, adolescence is more than a matter of hormones and physical maturation. It is also a period of psychological and social change (McDowell, 1981). This change involves a great deal of stress for adolescents with disabilities because the pressures of childhood to conform or achieve intellectual and academic standards expand to include physical, social, and emotional expectations and standards as well. What makes these demands especially stressful for adolescents with disabilities is that there is an increasing discrepancy between the physical development that is so obvious, and the social and emotional development levels that are not so obvious. Parents, teachers, neighbors, employers, and other significant adults all tend to respond primarily to the physical maturation and assume or expect an equal amount of maturational development in the affective areas.

ADOLESCENTS WITH DISABILITIES

Some readers of this text will be generally familiar with the nature and character-istics of each of the major disability groups. Others may be familiar with only one disability group. There even may be some who are new to the field and need an introduction to the general definitions, characteristics, behaviors, and special needs of the variety of students who might be found in any high school program. Regardless of which group a reader might fit into, the information on students in high school special education programming described here is important to bring into focus the young people who need special services at a critical time in their lives.

The definitions provided in every state plan under PL 94-142 for each handicapping condition provide a starting point for those persons who may be placed in some type of special programming in a high school. The major condi-tions that are the focus of this text are the following:

1. Visual impairments
2. Auditory impairments
3. Orthopedic or health impairments
4. Speech or language impairments
5. Learning disabilities
6. Behavior disorders
7. Mental retardation (mild and moderate)

In the early days of special education, segregated programs for each of these groups were the rule rather than the exception. Today, there is less segregation and more heterogeneous groupings in most high school programs.

Visual Impairments

Students with visual problems may be placed in a local high school without regard for the severity of the visual impairment. That is, a student who has a visual acuity of 20/400 with only light perception could be as likely to be in a regular high school program as a student who is partially sighted with a visual acuity of only 20/70 with correction. The major considerations are family goals, independence, mobility skills, available resources, and academic potential rather than degree of loss or severity of impairment.

Visual impairment is legally defined as 20/200 or less in the better eye with correction or with a range of vision that subtends an angle of 20 degrees or less (National Society for the Prevention of Blindness, 1966). Legal definitions are of little or no use for educators, though, because they provide no clue as to the instructional requirements of a student. Knowing that a student can see at 20 feet what a person with normal vision can see at 200 feet does not provide much usable information for the teacher in determining an instructional program. As a consequence, Bateman's (1967) more functional definitions related to primary reading mode are used more frequently. These definitions differentiate between *partially sighted* and *blind* individuals. Partially sighted persons are those who can use their residual vision for reading print materials with the assistance of eyeglasses, special magnifying equipment, large print, or some combination of these aids. Blind persons must rely on Braille as a primary reading medium and other sensory modalities for acquiring information and learning skills.

Individual student characteristics vary greatly, but instructors should be aware that adolescents with visual impairments *may* have one or more of the following characteristics or special needs:

1. Subaverage reading speed and level
2. Limited mobility and orientation skills
3. Restricted range of life experiences
4. Limited spatial orientation
5. Underdeveloped abstract reasoning
6. Peer acceptance and social adjustment problems

The population of students who are visually impaired in public schools is difficult to estimate because of the low incidence of visual impairment generally (7/1,000 school-age children), but the dispersal of students across residential and local community programs and all grade levels makes the probability of working with students who are even partially sighted at the high school level rather low. Even so, a possibility for high schools to have students with visual handicaps exists, and secondary special educators should be prepared to accommodate their students' needs and assist them to move through regular or special programs successfully.

High school teachers may or may not have the support of a consulting teacher for students who are visually impaired. If not, the student can provide much of the information that is needed to make accommodations in seating, lighting, assignments, alternative modalities for learning and test administration, and social inclusion.

Auditory Impairments

Students with auditory impairments range from those who have no hearing ability to those who have difficulty hearing speech, from those who have no speech to those who have near-normal speech, and from those who use manual communication to those who read lips and use speech. There are those who are born deaf and those who become hearing impaired in childhood or adolescence. There are those who choose to identify primarily, or solely, with the deaf community and there are those who want to be accepted as a part of the hearing community. With such diversity, it is difficult to define or characterize students in this population.

As with visual impairment, there is a legal definition of hearing impairment. *Deafness* is defined as when the auditory impairment is 70 decibels (db) or greater in the better ear. Educationally, it is more functional to classify the population into those whose hearing deficits are so severe as to preclude learning through audition (deaf) and those whose hearing deficits are such that, with the aid of amplification, they can learn through audition (hard of hearing).

The degree to which the hearing loss results in personal, social, intellectual, and occupational adjustment problems is related partially to the severity of the hearing loss and the age at onset. The key factors in life adjustment for students who are hearing impaired, however, are communication skills and social acceptance variables. Both of these are influenced by the following characteristics, which occur with greater frequency in groups of people with hearing deficits:

1. Language development may be affected markedly in terms of oral and written expression. Vocabulary, verbal comprehension, grammar, syntax, and spelling may be significantly different than in non-hearing-impaired individuals.
2. Reading level is lower than expected for age and grade level.
3. Intelligence scores on verbal tests are lower. This does not suggest a direct cause-and-effect relationship between hearing loss and intellectual ability, but rather the significant effect verbal reasoning, comprehension, and vocabulary skills have on performance with verbal tests of intelligence.
4. Emotional and behavioral problems interfere with school, peer, and family relationships.

Hearing impairment is a low-incidence disability, but it can vary with geographic location or epidemiology. For example, there are larger numbers of people with hearing impairments in Rochester (New York), Austin (Texas), and Olathe (Kansas), than there are in cities of comparable size in their respective states, simply because deaf communities develop in and around schools for the deaf. Incidence variation based on epidemiological factors were dramatic after the rubella epidemic in the early and mid-1960s. A growing number of students with hearing impairments choose to attend local public schools. Most who do so either have had the benefit of oral instruction or they have enough residual hearing and speech to be able to cope in the regular school environment with support services. A growing number are being placed in local schools with educational interpreters, thus allowing them to keep manual communication as their primary communication system.

Teachers can ease the educational struggles of youngsters with hearing problems by observing a few important practices. Simply being aware that a student has difficulty hearing may alert the teacher to make special efforts to assure the understanding of instructions, assignments, comments, and class discussions. Such consideration may be about all that is required to compensate for the hearing difficulty of many students, but some additional precautions may be taken. The most obvious is to assign the students seats as close as possible to the source of sound. The corollary to that is for a lecturing teacher to stand close to the student with the hearing problems when critical information is presented. Students who are engaged in discussion can be encouraged to face in the direction of the student with the hearing impairment so the sound will be directly toward the student, and the verbal communication will be augmented by the visual cues from the speaker's face and body. The visual cues will be easier to see if the primary light source in the room is behind the student with the impairment rather than behind the speaker. For example, if the classroom has a row of windows along one side, the student should have a desk near the windows and toward the front of the room. In addition, during the course of normal instruction, the use of visual aids, notes, sketches, and key words written on the blackboard or concrete objects to examine will also minimize the possibility of misunderstanding. To accompany instruction, frequent questioning of the student on crucial concepts can reveal problems before they become compounded by additional misinformation.

Orthopedic or Health Impairments

This population represents such a range of physical disabilities that no single quantitative, legal, or medical definition can describe it. In general, this classification encompasses all those who have neuromuscular disorders, musculoskeletal disorders, congenital malformations, or disabilities resulting from disease, accidents, or child abuse. The nature of the disabling condition or health impairment is not as significant to educators as are its effects on cognitive, emotional, and social development. The effects are related to age at onset, the severity of the condition in terms of restricting activity and interaction with others, the extent of visible signs of a disability, and the extent of services and support. In fact, the *Disabilities Statistics Abstract* (1991) has provided statistical data on people with activity limitation, rather than a general classification of orthopedic or health impairments. According to this source, this group comprises 9.8 percent of persons under the age of 18, when mental, sensory, or behaivioral causes for activity limitations are excluded.

Only those high school students who have been referred and determined to need an individualized educational plan because of their physical disabilities or health problems will come to the direct attention of high school instructors. Unless a physical disability or health condition interferes with functioning in a regular classroom, there is no reason to identify or attempt to serve this group. This group of persons with disabilities insists on the distinction between the terms *disability* and *handicap*, although the distinction applies to all disability groups. *Disability* refers to a disorder, defect, or impairment that is visibly or medically verifiable. It is generally regarded as permanent or chronically problematic. In contrast, the term *handicap* refers to a problem or set of environmental problems that can be mitigated or eliminated through accessibility accommodations, prosthetic devices, therapy, adapted equipment, education, or other types of intervention. The concept of handicap is based on the acknowledgment that a disability may interfere with some activities but not all. That is, a person who incurs a spinal cord injury may acknowledge that he or she is handicapped in mobility but not in cognitive activity.

The distinction between the terms *disability* and *handicap* has been behind the development of the World Health Organization's classification system. This system focuses on the functional areas that are affected and on the degree of severity. Such a classification system provides teachers and rehabilitation personnel with much more relevant and functional information than a simple diagnosis of cerebral palsy, muscular dystrophy, or diabetes, for example. The classification system is as follows:

Physical Independence

0   fully independent
1   dependent on aids and appliances
2   dependent on modified environment
3   difficulty with certain activities
4   dependent on others for certain activities
5   difficulty with critical functions (such as feeding, excretion)
6   dependent on others for critical functions
7   dependent on special care
8   dependent on continual care

Mobility

0   fully mobile
1   variable or intermittent restriction
2   difficult mobility; travel may take longer
3   reduced mobility; reduced range
4   limited to neighborhood
5   confined to dwelling
6   confined to room
7   confined to chair
8   confined to bed

Occupation

0   follows customary occupation
1   intermittent inability in customary occupation
2   full time in other than customary occupation
3   less than full-time occupation
4   limited in type and kind of occupation
5   limited in type, kind, and time
6   unable to follow any occupation

Social Integration

0   fully integrated
1   nonspecific disadvantage
2   specific disadvantage reducing quality of life
3   curtailed social relationships
4   behavioral disorders
5   socially isolated
6   unable to relate to others

Economic Self-Sufficiency

0   fully self-sufficient
1   self-sufficient but reduced economic status
2   self-sufficient, with support from others
3   partially self-sufficient
4   not self-sufficient
5   child, not expected to be self-sufficient

There are no unique, personal, social, or intellectual characteristics that can describe adolescents, in spite of the persisting myth that adolescence is a period of "turmoil" (Adelson, 1986). However, Adelson would agree with Carpignano, Sirvis, and Bigge (1982) that adolescence is the most difficult time for any growing youth, disabled or not. All of an adolescent's reactions are intensified, and general stresses related to adolescence, especially in combination with the stresses of having a physical disability or health impairment, present a very difficult problem with which adolescents must deal. Carpignano and colleagues (1982) stated, "Social relationships and peer acceptance are major sources of stress, as are the anxieties and worries about education and employment opportunities.... Adolescents are also subject to the increased concern of parents who now fully realize that their children have limited potential for traditional achievement" (p. 115).

We have no substantial indication that persons with impaired physique or health differ as a group from any other disabled or nondisabled group in their general or overall adjustment. Any blanket generalizations about characteristics would be inappropriate. There is also no clear evidence of an association between types of physical disability and particular personality traits. There is evidence, however, that indicates that physical disability has profound effects on a person's life. These effects come through the process of reaction and adjustment to the disability itself (DeLoach & Greer, 1981; Jourard, 1958; Marinelli & Dell, 1977; Wright, 1960) and through the various sources of stress (parental reactions, hospitalization, limitations in activity, dependence on others, sexual development, and limitations in social relationships) on students who have physical disabilities (Fox, 1980; Goldberg, 1974).

Teachers can make a significant impact on the adjustment problems of students with physical disabilities if they can make a clear distinction between a disability and a handicap in their own interactions with the students. A teacher must remember that, although the disability persists, a handicap can be eliminated by changing the task, the person, or both. Helping students recognize that disabilities do not always produce handicaps may allow them to develop some confidence that they have some control over their roles in life. This may have a critical effect on their personal feelings of worth and sense of destiny. Although there are many sources of information teachers can turn to for suggestions to help them work effectively with students who have orthopedic or health impairments, the writings of Carpignano and colleagues (1982) should be examined.

Speech or Language Impairments

Adolescents with speech or language disorders may or may not be identified with special education programming per se. Generally, they will not require special instructional programs unless their disability is very language oriented, and then they may be classified for specific learning-disabilities programs. It is not uncommon for students with other primary disabilities to have speech or language problems as secondary disorders. There is a tendency to (1) accept the communication problem(s) as a given and pursue no intervention or (2) assign speech therapy intervention a lower priority than the major instructional intervention,

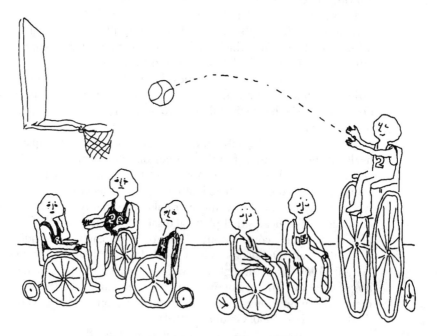

"Boy—I sure wish we had him on our team."

with little or no systematic, long-term efforts. Unfortunately, too often communication disorders are not identified as a specific disability amenable to intervention, but rather as a result or manifestation of the primary disability. This is especially the case with individuals who have mental disabilities.

Speech disorders at the high school level, whether they are a primary or secondary disability, are likely to be well-established patterns and affect students' self-concepts significantly. It is surprising to many that this disability category ranks high in comparison to other disability groups in high school dropout rates. Wagner and Shaver (1989) reported a national dropout rate of 32.5 percent. This category rank fourth behind behavior disorders (54.7 percent), learning disabilities (36.1 percent), and mental retardation (33.6 percent). There is probably no significant difference between rates for students with speech impairments and mental retardation. Wagner and Shaver reported also that secondary students with speech impairments were declassified (deleted from special education classification rosters) at a rate of 18 percent, which is almost three times the rate at which youth in any other category were declassified. The implications for providing more careful attention to this group are clear from these data.

The high school teacher needs to be alert to the existence of communication disorders and must be ready to ensure that the students who have them have the best diagnoses and intervention possible. This begins with an understanding of what constitutes a speech or language problem. Van Riper's (1978) popular definition of *speech defects* suggests that a person has a speech problem when his or her speech differs from the speech of others to the extent that it calls attention to itself, interferes with the intended message, or causes the listener or speaker to be distressed. In short, the speech defect is conspicuous, unintelligible, unpleasant, or embarrassing. The problems are frequently seen in sound production (articulation defects), voice production (phonation defects), stuttering and cluttering (fluency disorders), and physical defects (cleft palate, deafness, or cerebral palsy). Culatta and Culatta (1981) suggested some practical questions to ask in determining whether a person has a speech problem severe enough to warrant referral:

1. Can I understand this person?
2. Does this person sound strange?
3. Does this person have any peculiar physical characteristics when speaking?
4. Is the communication in a style inappropriate to the situation?
5. Do I enjoy listening to this speaker?
6. Is this speaker damaging his or her vocal chords?
7. Does the speaker experience pain or discomfort when attempting to communicate?

Language disorders are much more complex than speech defects, since they involve not only speech but also receptive, integrative, and expressive activities. A student who has difficulty in comprehending questions or directions has a receptive language problem. A student who clearly has greater ability to receive messages than to express them has an expressive language problem. A student who can demonstrate some receptive ability and some expressive ability but has difficulty in coordinating the two is assumed to have some type of integrative deficit in perception, recall, or retrieval of sensory or perceptual input. Language disorders usually affect both oral and written communication, but proper use of facial expressions, gestures, and body language can make oral communication deficits less noticeable.

A high school teacher's primary functions include the following:

1. Be alert to students who have speech or language disorders.
2. Encourage and give information to students and their parents about intervention options.
3. Advocate vigorously for adequate intervention.
4. Assist the speech pathologist by encouraging correct use of speech and language and reinforcing generalization of skills learned in therapy
5. Emphasize tolerance and understanding of students with speech or language dificultties and discourage teasing, disparaging remarks, and other negative behaviors from other students.

Learning Disabilities

Students with specific learning disabilities make up the most heterogeneous of all high school students with disabilities. Abilities range from slow learner to gifted levels, and behavioral characteristics are so diverse as to leave little doubt why this group has practically defied definition. Cruickshank and Paul (1980) reflected this situation in a listing of behavioral and learning deficits found in their review of the literature. Deficits described and reported as more frequent to populations with learning disabilities included problems in the following:

Discrimination	Memory
Sequencing	Impulse control
Affect	Motor behavior
Auditory activity	Visual-motor functioning
Sensory integration	Conceptual and abstract thinking
Language	Spatial orientation
Self-concept	Body image

These deficit areas are generally considered to be the basic processes or elements of cognitive, social, emotional, and motor behavior in school, at home, or in the community.

High school educators usually focus on the academic and behavioral problems of students with learning disabilities. The academic failures of these students in reading, writing, math, language, or spelling are major obstacles in school adjustment, and the personal-social problems that accompany them (or emerge as a consequence of them) are the primary foci of school concerns. These academic and social difficulties make it nearly impossible to differentiate students who have learning disabilities from students who are low achieving. Warner, Schumaker, Alley, and Deshler (1980) reported that behavioral, attitudinal, and test characteristics of students who are low achieving and learning disabled are more similar than they are dissimilar. These findings fueled even further the debate on what constitutes learning disabilities. Researchers agree on the following:

1. There is a difference (discrepancy) between what a student should be able to do and what he or she is actually doing.
2. There are some specific tasks that others can do that students with learning disabilities cannot do.
3. Students' difficulties are centered on one or more basic psychological processes involved in using and understanding language.
4. Students are not learning adequately in spite of the basic integrity of their senses, cognitive ability, emotional state, or lack of opportunity to learn.

The number of students identified as having specific learning disabilities varies considerably according to the definition, assessment procedures, or identification criteria used. Morsink (1981) put this disparity into perspective: "Learning disabilities are extremely varied and complex; they include severe difficulties in learning to read, write, speak, comprehend—even in the broadest sense, to find places on a map, tell time, or ride a bicycle" (p. 356). One can see the difficulty in establishing identification criteria for this population. In fact, this dilemma has reached such proportions that the field has been criticized by legislators who cannot understand the definitions being used and say that they are too loose and ambiguous. Some have complained that learning disabilities is a category for the elite and that primarily middle- and upper-class white students who have reading problems and are hyperactive qualify for placement in special programs for youth with learning disabilities. Ethnic-minority students who cannot read and are restless, acting out, or unresponsive to school rules and routines are more likely identified as mildly retarded or behavior disordered.

Lovitt (1978) issued a logical and responsible challenge to the field by saying that further attempts to define learning disabilities will continue to be useless until those who develop definitions stop using intelligence and achievement tests as the primary means for classifying individuals. He proposed that direct, daily measurement should replace the traditional measures and that such measurement should be complemented by an educational history that relates how a student acquired some of his or her current behaviors, how long it took him or her to learn certain behaviors, the conditions that prevailed while the behaviors were acquired, and the extent to which the student really wants to learn a specific skill.

CRAIG TURNER

Craig is 18 years of age and in his third year of high school. His father is an insurance executive and his mother is socially active in Junior League and a local sorority. Craig is an only child and is very verbal and socially adept. He was in classes for minimal brain dysfunction at a private school for five years prior to returning to the public high school. During his junior high school years at the private school, he was successful in athletics, earning letter awards in football and track.

Reading has always been difficult for Craig, and his current reading achievement level is 1.8. His math performance is 3.6. He does poorly in spelling and writing and is beginning to refuse to do any assignments that require composition and handwriting. In social studies and science, he contributes orally and demonstrates a wealth of information that indicates he acquires information aurally and has good memory skills. His Verbal Scale IQ is 80, and his Performance Scale IQ is 58. His Full Scale IQ is 67.

Craig has been in trouble frequently at school during the past two years. He has not been eligible to participate in athletics because of poor grades and periodic suspensions due to infractions of school rules. He has been truant on numerous occasions and has been caught at school with liquor and various drugs in his locker. He seeks out friends in regular classes from his affluent neighborhood but is not very successful in his attempts. Those who do choose to be with him are those who are having similar problems with grades and school adjustment.

Craig presents two role identities at school. One is the assertive, outgoing, cooperative but "cool" student who has everything under control, including the teachers as they respond to this role positively and cater to his mood and wishes. The other role is the restless, impatient, negative student who communicates nonverbally to everyone, "Stay out of my way—don't hassle me. " His classmates do not trust him, and some are afraid of him. Teachers have tried to establish a relationship with him that is positive, and have succeeded in preventing any classroom conflicts. Most of his misbehavior occurs outside the classroom in other parts of the school.

Craig's parents are well known to school officials because of their response to the school's disciplinary policies. They do not deny the infractions but believe that the school environment is to blame. They have refused to permit Craig to enter into any vocational or prevocational training experiences during his first two years of high school. They believe he has the ability to work in some occupation that has much higher status than what they associate with the school vocational programs. They insist that the school should remediate his reading problem and provide an academic program that will qualify him for high school graduation and possible admission to a community college. Both parents are college graduates and find it difficult to accept any low-status school or employment alternatives.

Craig does not verbalize any occupational interests and has not wanted to be in any high school vocational or prevocational options. His interests appear to focus on cars, movies, professional football, and his stereo equipment. The only part-time job he has ever had was a summer job as a recreation assistant for a children's soccer league. This was obtained for him by his father. His work was satisfactory, but he did not ask to do it again. His parents provide him with a generous allowance each week of $25, so he has spending money all year long.

This approach is not yet an accepted practice, so in the meantime high school programs for students who have learning disabilities are populated by students with a wide range of learning and behavioral characteristics. They differ in abilities, interests, aspirations, and aptitudes, just as all high school students do. Regular and special teachers with students who have learning disabilities have to assess and plan instructional techniques for each individual student.

Zigmond and Miller (1992) made a convincing case in their review of educational program practices for students with learning disabilities. Evidence from data collected since 1975 shows that the traditional models of secondary school services are inadequate. Whether one looks at dropout rates, achievement/ performance levels at school, or postsecondary employment or education, the results are not encouraging at all. The researchers proposed two models that dealt more with substance (outcomes and curriculum focus) than form (administrative placement decisions, such as resource room, consulting model, etc.). In both cases, career development and transition outcomes are integral parts of the models. Perhaps this population is at last getting the attention it needs in those areas that are critical after the school years.

Behavior Disorders

Definitions of behavior disorders typically revolve around two major issues: (1) the inability to establish appropriate, satisfying relationships with others and (2) demonstration of behavior that either fails to meet or exceeds the expectations of those with whom the person comes in contact (McDowell & Brown, 1978). Since these characteristic behaviors are found to a certain degree in normal adolescents, adolescent behavior disorders must be viewed differently than those in children or adults. According to societal standards, the fine line between normal adolescent behavior and disordered behavior is drawn among the degree or magnitude of severity, the rate or frequency of occurrence, the duration of the behavior, and the unique form of the behavior.

The diversity of definitions of behavior disorders prompted a specifically stated definition in PL 94-142 (*Federal Register*, 1977). It was based on Bower's (1969) definition that included characteristics such as the following:

1. An inability to learn that cannot be explained by intellectual, sensory, or health factors
2. An inability to build or maintain satisfactory interpersonal relationships with peers and teachers
3. Inappropriate behavior or feelings under normal circumstances
4. A general pervasive mood of unhappiness or depression
5. A tendency to develop physical symptoms or fears associated with personal or school problems

It also excluded "children who are socially maladjusted, unless it is determined that they are seriously emotionally disturbed" (*Federal Register*, 1977, p. 42478). Some authors have challenged this exclusion (Kaufman, 1981; Nelson, Rutherford, Center, & Walker, 1991) on logical grounds, but even on a practical level most states are making no attempt to deal with the nature of the social maladjustment of the problem students labeled as emotionally disturbed (Grosenick & Huntze, 1980; Epstein, Patton, Palloway, & Foley, 1992).

The kinds of behavior associated with the diagnosis of behavior disorders are so varied that it is difficult to provide a unified list of characteristics or behaviors. Quay and Peterson (1987) described six dimensions of behavior that are useful in showing some distinct clusters or patterns of disorders in behavior in children and youths. These classifications and associated characteristics or traits are shown in Table 3. 1.

Adolescent behavior disorders range from mild to severe, although some would say that, by definition, even mild behaviors are so markedly inappropriate, socially unacceptable, or personally unsatisfying that they are obvious to most observers. In other words, the behaviors must be severe, excessive, and persistent before a teenage student is classified as disturbed or disordered. The relative terms *mild*, *moderate*, and *severe* are appropriate only when used as a continuum of severity within the population already diagnosed as having a severe behavior disorder. McDowell (1981) has given a more specific description of the nature of adolescent behavior disorders from the point of view of relative severity. From this description, we can infer the following:

1. Mild behavior disorders are characteristic of students involved in some type of crisis but who are still able to function within the regular school system with a minimum of support help from a crisis teacher, counselor, or itinerant resource teacher. Disorders that fall within the mild category tend to be transient and may disappear with time-limited interventions or sometimes even without specific intervention.

TABLE 3.1   Quay and Peterson's Dimensions of Behavior

Types of Behavior Disorders	Characteristics
Conduct Disorders	Seeks attention Shows off Is disruptive Annoys others Fights Has temper tantrums
Socialized Aggression	Steals in company with others Is loyal to delinquent friends Is truant from school with others Has "bad" companions Freely admits disrespect for moral values and laws
Attention Problems/ Immaturity	Has short attention span Has poor concentration Is distractible Is easily diverted from task at hand Answers without thinking Is sluggish/lethargic/slow moving
Anxiety/Withdrawal	Is self-conscious Is easily embarrassed Is hypersensitive Feelings are easily hurt Is generally fearful Is anxious Is depressed Is always sad
Psychotic Behavior	Expresses far-fetched ideas Has repetitive speech Shows bizarre behavior
Motor Excess	Is restless Is unable to sit still Is tense Is unable to relax Is over talkative

Source: *Manual for the Revised Behavior Problems Checklist* (Quay & Peterson, 1987).

2. Moderate behavior disorders require some type of intensive intervention (e.g., individual or group therapy, medication, special or resource room placement). These tend to be longer lasting and more debilitating, and they interfere more with functioning at home or school.

3. The severe level is based on a student's inability to function in a high school environment. The adolescent who is severely disordered may have difficulty maintaining contact with reality. The behaviors exhibited are more exaggerated and bizarre. The adolescent with a severe behavior disorder needs a self-contained classroom or possibly placement in a hospital or residential treatment center.

A final note of caution is needed before moving closer to understanding the population with behavior disorders. Critics of the medical or psychiatric view of behavior disorders (Skinner, 1967; Szasz, 1960; Ullmann & Krasner, 1965) have moved a significant proportion of professionals in the field away from a pathological or disease view of the problem. Behavior disorders are now being described as a condition in which significant discrepancy exists between a person's behavior and legal, cultural, moral, or personal expectations (Kauffman, 1981; Nelson & Polsgrove, 1981; Ross, 1980). This description reflects value judgments, which are subjective, change over time, and differ from one environment or culture to another. Given this position, it is possible that the expectations or standards themselves, rather than an individual's behavior, may be inappropriate. The distinction between expected behavior and behavior becomes important when making diagnostic or placement decisions and when attempting some type of intervention to change behavior.

Recent attention to Attention Deficit Disorders (ADD) and Attention Deficit Hyperactivity Disorders (ADHD) by physicians, psychiatrists, mental health professionals, and educators has posed diagnostic and classification problems for schools and even more difficult problems in intervention approaches. The students classified as either ADD or ADHD display many of the classic behaiviors that were originally associated with the children classified as brain injured by Strauss and Lehtinen (1947) and Kephart (1960)—that is, the inability to focus attention long enough to complete tasks, hyperactivity, temper flare-ups with consequent destructive episodes, and impulsiveness.

There is considerable debate about the causes of ADD and ADHD, which leads to a variety of placements in special education programs. Some individuals are placed in programs for students with learning disabilities, some in programs for behavior disorders, and others in programs/services for "other health impaired." At this time, there is not enough research data available to have a great deal of useful information on how to provide these students with appropriate career development and transition programming. Parents and educators have frequently turned to medications for control of inappropriate and exasperating behavior, but there is increasing agreement that this is no cure and that some side

AMY SANDERS

Amy is 16 years old and in the ninth grade in a suburban community. She is the youngest of four children and the only girl. Only one brother lives at home, but he is in and out, depending on his employment. Amy's mother works in a factory and is married to her third husband. Amy's current stepfather works in the same factory but in an supervisory position. He is actively involved in Amy's school and medical problems.

Amy was classified in the mild mental retardation category, but it has been her emotional and behavioral problems that have dominated school responses. She was viewed early as needing a special class, but even there she was seen as different from the other children in the special class. She demonstrated withdrawal, extreme shyness, immaturity, and excessive dependency throughout elementary school. She made no academic progress during the elementary and middle school years, but she made significant progress in her personal and social development during eighth grade. Her current reading and math skills are at a first-grade level.

After one semester in the ninth grade, Amy started to withdraw, showed symptoms of depression, and was unable to function or perform as she previously had at home and at school. She was hospitalized twice for depression, hallucinations, and hearing voices. She is currently taking three medications for her emotional state, but these have been changed frequently in attempts to regulate the dosage. Her behavior at school and home is erratic and she is described by her teachers as "deteriorating" and regressing in all areas and skills where she had once shown much positive growth.

It is known that Amy was a victim of sexual abuse by her natural father, second stepfather, and the brother who is still at home occasionally. Amy's mother reports that she is at the end of her rope. Recently, when Amy wandered from home and asked a stranger for a ride, the family found it necessary to seek respite care for Amy after school.

Amy is now demonstrating manipulative and passive-aggressive behaviors at school. She refuses to respond verbally at times, and frequently cries over trivial incidents and wants to call her "mommy" to come get her when school staff attempt to deal with her inappropriate behaviors. She is lacking in any vocational experience outside the school. She has demonstrated some positive work skills in her school-based work experience when she chooses to work.

effects are more serious than the attention deficits or hyperactivity. In most cases, there will need to be close coordination between career education specialists and medical personnel until such time as research data point to more effective methods of treatment and training. In the meantime, simply recognizing that the behavior or attention disorders are neither willful or controllable by the youngsters can go a long way toward moving teachers and other professionals into meaningful relationships with the youngsters and their families.

Mental Retardation

In only two characteristics are all adolescents classified as mentally retarded alike: (1) they have intelligence quotients of two or more standard deviations below the mean of 100 and (2) there is evidence of two or more types of adaptive behavior deficit, usually including an inability to succeed in school. Otherwise, they vary considerably in most human characteristics. This introductory statement is important for you to put into perspective the most accepted definition used for identifying this population. It is the American Association on Mental Retardation (AAMR) definition (American Association on Mental Retardation, 1992): "Mental retardation refers to substantial limitation in present functioning. It is characterized by significantly subaverage intellectual functioning, existing concurrently with related limitations in two or more of the following applicable adaptive skill areas: communication, self-care, home living, social skills, community use, self-direction, health and safety, functional academics, leisure, and work. Mental retardation manifests before age 18."

This latest revision of the definition for mental retardation places more emphasis than previous definitions on adaptive behavior. The American Association on Mental Retardation recommends the following four assumptions as essential to the application of the definition in diagnosis and classification (American Association on Mental Retardation, 1992):

1. Valid assessment must consider cultural and linguistic differences in both communication and behavioral response factors.
2. The existence of limitations in adaptive behaviors occurs within the context of specific cultural and community environments typical for an individual's age peers.
3. Specific adaptive limitations often coexist with strengths in other adaptive behaviors or skills, or other personal capabilities.
4. With appropriate supports over a sustained period, the functioning level of a person with mental retardation will generally improve.

The similarity, then, among those defined as mentally retarded is an artifact of the definition and is very subjective. For example, assume that two persons have significant deficits in intellectual functioning and adaptive behavior. Knowing that one has an IQ of 65 gives one no single clear notion of what the person's

DARRELL COOMBS

Darrell is 17 years of age and is in his first year of high school. His mother does commercial cleaning with a janitorial service in a city high-rise office building. His father is serving a long-term sentence in prison. Prior to incarceration, he had been absent from the home more frequently than he had been in it and had not held a steady job in 10 years. Both of Darrell's parents are uneducated and unskilled, and have not been able to work steadily at the same time to generate two incomes for the family. Both moved to the city from the rural South as teenagers with their parents.

Darrell is the oldest of five children. He has had difficulty in school from the very beginning. His junior high school years were especially difficult. He was truant frequently and was suspended eight times for various school rule infractions. These included fighting, verbal abuse to teachers, vandalism, and the possession and sale of marijuana. He spent about one year in a juvenile correction center for the possession and sale violation and is back home now under probation. The terms of his probation include satisfactory school attendance.

Academic-achievement test scores for Darrell reveal that he is functioning at about the third-grade level in reading and math (3.1 and 3.2, respectively) but the diagnostician noted that these scores may not reflect his ability, as he did not appear to be showing any sincere effort while taking tests. His intellectual functioning was assessed as Verbal Scale IQ of 66, Performance Scale IQ of 74, and Full Scale IQ of 70. He is described as being verbal and "streetwise" and much smarter than people think. He assumes leadership in his peer group outside of school but is never the primary leader.

Darrell demonstrated some work potential when he began selling newspapers at age 9, and did this for nearly two years. He has worked part time for a neighborhood grocery doing odd jobs. He worked part time for a roller skating rink when he was 15 years old. During that time, he won several cash prizes ($25–$50) in skating contests. His incarceration at the juvenile correction center resulted in the termination of his job. He is interested in getting back into the skating contests and winning a lot more money.

Darrell's family lives in a slum area in extremely substandard housing. Food is nutritious, but there is not much variety or quantity. Darrell rarely eats more than one meal a day at home. The family lives in a two-bedroom house with his grandmother and an aunt. Privacy is impossible, and tensions from crowding and other factors associated with poverty make family interactions difficult and sometimes volatile. This has encouraged much of the life in the street that Darrell participates in and that his younger brothers and sisters are beginning to experience.

capacity to learn, solve problems, acquire knowledge, or think abstractly is as compared to someone with an IQ of 55. Neither does it mean that the person with the higher IQ has a higher level of adapted behavior. Both persons are identified as mentally retarded, but they may be evaluated quite differently—not only on the two factors required for the diagnosis but also in their interests, aptitudes, personalities, physical attributes, and health.

It is fair to generalize, as with the other disability groups discussed, that the severity of mental retardation does lead to differences in performance characteristics. The more severe the mental retardation, the more one can expect to find accompanying physical limitations, problems in language and communication skills, and a wide range of inappropriate social behaviors. The following characteristics are found with greater frequency in populations identified as mildly mentally retarded. They would occur with even greater frequency and severity in persons classified as moderately retarded.

1. Establishing a learning set or frame of reference for novel problems or new learning is difficult.
2. Language deficits are common.
3. Abstract reasoning is limited.
4. Reading skills are at a low level.
5. Reaction time to stimuli is slow.
6. Incidental learning is limited.
7. Short-term memory is inefficient.
8. Transfer of learning and generalization is difficult.
9. Social skills vary widely but are frequently not commensurate with chronological age.
10. Motor development and motor skills are variable but are diminished when retardation is not based on psychosocial factors.
11. Physical impairments or health-related problems are more frequent.

Labels such as *mild, moderate* or *educable*, and *trainable* are used frequently by professionals and others to communicate general expectations without specifying behavior deficits. That is, adolescents labeled mild or educable are meant to be seen as retarded primarily in school. There is also an expectation that they can and will become independent or semi-independent adults. It is assumed that some of them can be educated in regular classrooms with extra help but that others will need special classrooms. Adolescents labeled moderate or trainable, on the other hand, are seen as semidependent and capable of living in the community as participating members with support. In school, they are educated usually in self-contained classrooms with emphasis on community-referenced communication, self-help and daily living skills, social skills, and vocational skills, along with functional academics. Use of these labels, however, poses problems of group stereotyping that can affect individuals and may lead to self-fulfilling prophecies. For that reason, it is best to deal with adolescents labeled mentally retarded as persons first and to help them become who they want to be and can be.

VARIATIONS IN POPULATION CHARACTERISTICS

High school students requiring special education programming vary, then, by definitional factors, physical or mental factors, and educational terminology. The preceding section dealt with these factors, but it is apparent that behavioral characteristics still overlap from one category of exceptionality to another, as well as by degree of severity within categorical areas. Even if each group were homogeneous in disability characteristics, however, there are other ways that populations can vary that affect programming decisions: geographic variables, cultural or ethnic variables, and socioeconomic variables. Each of these will be discussed briefly to highlight the population differences that must be considered in high school programming.

Geographic Variables

People living in the United States have long been aware of geographical factors related to population characteristics. Interests, values, and life-styles are historical phenomena that persist today in spite of the increased mobility of the nation's populace. Yankee ingenuity, Southern hospitality, Midwest work ethnic, East Coast liberalism, Southwest rugged individualism, and Northwest conservationism are examples of regional stereotypes that are based to some degree on both historical tradition and observed differences. Although these regional values and life-styles may be identifiable, they may or may not be reflected in students' attitudes and behavior during their high school years. These influences tend to be adult culture factors that may be resisted by teenagers, then assumed later as adults. When youths with mental or physical handicaps are more attuned to values and life-styles of their parents than of their peers, then some of these regional influences may be observed during the high school years.

Urban-rural factors probably have more direct and lasting effects than do regional factors. For example, the incidence of handicapping conditions is higher in urban areas than in rural areas. The reason for this may be an artifact of proportionately more diagnostic referrals as well as availability of programs for serving people with handicaps. Within each of these geopolitical variables, urban or rural, there are various subcategories. Urban areas, for example, comprise a wide range of urban systems: inner cities of large metropolitan areas, small- to medium-size cities (30,000–150,000), low- to middle-income municipalities adjoining inner cities, and middle- to high-income suburban areas or municipalities (frequently called "bedroom communities").

Urban Issues
Urban schools are usually large enough to be able to offer a range of high school special education programs and services. However, some issues or problem areas for urban districts include the following:

1. *Multicultural populations*. Metropolitan areas particularly have been magnets for multicultural populations, especially migrants and immigrants. Hodgkinson (1985) projected that by the year 2000, one of three persons in the United States will be a member of a racial or ethnic minority. Migrants are of two types—those who move from one part of the country to another to live and those who move around frequently, following crops, construction jobs, or the rainbow. Unlike the immigrants of the past, many today are much like the migrants who are highly mobile and transient. The parents of both groups are frequently ill prepared to cope with the complexities of urban life in a new environment and to provide adequate support for students in special education programs.

2. *Language barriers*. The street language learned by immigrants to the U.S. is quite different from school language. The technical vocabulary and precision of school vocational programs may be overwhelming. Students with learning disabilities or mental retardation, who also may have English language deficits, find high school programs in urban areas extremely demanding and beyond their abilities.

3. *Cultural and value differences*. Youths who are disabled and who live in urban settings present a wide range of values toward school in general and vocational programs in particular. Affluent urban or suburban families, who may not see skilled or semiskilled occupations as being appropriate for their sons or daughters, sometimes insist on an academic emphasis. Families in poverty or lower middle-class working groups may want their children to rise above skilled or semiskilled levels of occupations offered in special education programming and hold higher academic or occupational aspirations. Or, some students feel no family pressures to achieve in school or work and may have learned a negative attitude about work of any kind and do not enroll in any available vocational programs even when they stay in school. Blackorby, Edgar, and Kortering (1991) reported that in their study of students with mild disabilities (learning disabilities, behavior disorders, and mild mental retardation), the ratio of dropouts to graduates was 2:1 among African Americans, Hispanics, and Native Americans, in contrast to a proportion of 1:1 or lower among Caucasian and Asian students.

4. *Size and complexity*. Another issue of urban education that affects career and vocational planning is the size and complexity of the urban environment, especially in large metropolitan areas. Whether inner city or suburban, the diverse needs of urban students result in highly complex and sometimes almost overwhelming administrative and instructional problems. These include the following:
   a. Identification and appropriate placement of students who are educationally disabled
   b. Appropriate curriculum offerings that deal with language barriers, cultural pluralism, and retention of dropout-prone youths
   c. Transportation resources that permit mobility out of inner city or distant suburban neighborhoods

d. Selection and retention of teachers to work with urban students who are educationally handicapped
e. Dropout rates that remain the highest in the nation (Kortering, Haring, Klockars, 1992; Lichtenstein, 1987)

5. *Survival behavior*. The struggle to survive in heavily populated urban areas reaches deep into families of all racial, ethnic, or cultural groups. Economic survival is basic to physical survival, and many students with disabilities are experiencing early the pressures of being an adult in the real world. Having enough money to have a place to live and food to eat is a daily challenge for too many families, and compromises are made in order to have the basics of shelter and food. Just as important, though, is the struggle to survive the social and psychological stresses of poverty, noise, pollution, lack of privacy, and fear. Gangs, child abuse, and both random and directed violence loom as such major problems and concerns that a school may be seen only as a temporary escape, and even then not always as a safe one. Some secondary special education students in a midwest urban city were interviewed informally by their teachers in February of 1992 about their futures. When asked, "What is your greatest fear?" the majority answered that it was a fear of "getting shot" or "being forced to do something bad that they should not do."

Rural Issues

The factors influencing the nature and characteristics of high school students in rural areas are numerous and varied. Rural communities are characterized as conservative and tend to adhere to traditional values (Mertens, Chafetz, & Nunez, 1980). These attitudes tend to provide a positive environment in terms of basic morality, ethics, and personal values that rural youths understand and learn very early. Many of these values, attitudes, and personal and social behaviors are taught in the home, in the local churches, and in community youth organizations such as scouting, 4-H clubs, Future Farmers, and Future Homemakers. Since rural schools are so attuned to the values of the community, they can, at times, reflect what some have chosen to call conservatism and resistance to change that affects the development of resources and programs (Whitson, Korfhage, & Axelrod, 1977). One such example relates to the role of women today. Many rural communities still influence their schools not to encourage and train girls for nontraditional paid occupations except agriculture. Clarenbach (cited in Mertens et al., 1980) suggested that some might argue that resistance is more a function of the insistence on local autonomy than conservatism per se. However, the value messages the young women receive regarding their work role options may still be the same.

Some isolated rural communities exhibit certain characteristics similar to those of developing countries. Rural areas, just as metropolitan areas, have poverty, alcoholism, inadequate housing, unemployment, and underemployment—but without any resources to remedy or improve the situation. The National Rural

Small Schools Task Force ("Rural, Small Schools," 1988) reported that the biggest problem facing small rural schools is that of educating children of low-income families. As many as 2.2 million children in 2,750 rural school districts across the nation suffer from chronic severe "poorness" across multiple areas: family poverty, low per-pupil expenditures, low student outcomes, and limited curriculum offerings. These circumstances influence what all school-age students are like, of course, but in adolescence these effects become more obvious in attitudes and behaviors. If ever there was a group to be labeled "at risk," adolescents are such a group.

Many rural communities that are economically tied to agriculture have migrant workers. Some of these communities are the rural home bases of the migrant families and some are the seasonal homes. Families may leave south Texas, for example, in March or April, boarding up their doors and windows and removing their children from school. They follow the crops, moving north until the end of the fall harvests of the Northwest and Upper Midwest states, then return to their homes in late September or October and return their children to school. Depending on their ages, the children and youths spend decreasing amounts of time in school (even temporary enrollments) and increasing amounts of time in the fields. Schooling back at the home base may last no longer than four or five months a year. Obviously, this pattern is difficult for all the children, but especially for those who have special learning needs. Consequently, many rural schools find themselves facing the need to offer an increasing number of support services—social work, special education, bilingual education, and guidance. Most of them face these needs without adequate financial resources.

Cultural and Ethnic Variables

Cultural, social, and ethnic influences on self-concept and personality development are well established (Easterlin, 1980; Gruber, 1979; Kelley, 1962; La Benne & Green, 1969; Starr, 1986). These influences are at work irrespective of the geographic location or size of a community. That is, cultural, social, or ethnic forces are operating in regional locales and in both urban and rural settings across regions. Urban areas will have many cultural or ethnic groups. Rural areas may have one or two cultural or ethnic groups in relatively small numbers or perhaps a single, predominantly ethnic community. In fact, the United States is the most ethnically diverse nation in the world.

Some urban and rural factors are probably more influential in personality development than are cultural or ethnic variables, so one cannot generalize for any racial, cultural, or ethnic sample without knowing the regional location and size or nature of their community. This is seen in the differences especially between urban and rural African Americans, Native Americans, and Hispanics. The interaction between geographical and cultural or ethnic influences is illustrated in the following brief descriptions.

Urban Ethnic

Within the inner city of many major cities lives an ethnic group that some call "the slum dwellers." At least two-thirds of these people are African American, Puerto Rican, Cuban, Mexican American, or members of some of the new minority groups to the United States, such as Southeast Asian refugees and Mexican and Central American aliens. Many are first-generation newcomers to the United States; some are refugees from rural backgrounds and poverty; and some are fleeing political and economic chaos. Many of the children from these families have experienced family disruption, family losses, and despair from failure, stress, and violence. All had hopes of a better way of life when they arrived, but the slums they find as the only affordable neighborhoods quickly diminish their hopes.

The slum family is usually managed by a woman. This is frequently done by default when the father is absent or has abandoned the family. In more cases than not, the mother is the sole means of support. Male or female, however, the most universal problem shared by those who assume responsibility for individual slum families is an inadequate wage. Inadequate or nonexistent wages result in chronic dependence for many of these families. Others cope through extended families or by working at more than one job. All of these factors affect the children and youths in these families. Many become streetwise and highly enculturated for their neighborhoods and the inner city, but most find school and their environments sources of frustration, failure, and despair.

In contrast to the inner-city ethnic group, there is another urban ethnic group. This group lives between the inner city and the suburbs.

These individuals have postage-stamp row houses in or near industrial or commercial areas. Binzen (1970) described them as "Whitetowners" who are born and raised in these city neighborhoods and rarely think of moving out. He described this group as the working Americans—blue collar and white—who live in the "gray area" fringe of central cities and constitute the majority of the nation's semiskilled and skilled work force.

This population is drawn mainly from ethnic groups that differ from the white Anglo-Saxon Protestant population. Most of these people are second- or third-generation immigrants and descendants of Eastern and Southern European peasants; many others are Irish. Binzen (1970) painted a verbal caricature of this population that is in the process of changing, but the description is still enough on target to capture the flavor of the backgrounds out of which some special education students come: "The Whitetowner male is a steady worker and a family man. He quit school in tenth grade to get a job. His wife, also a native of the area, dropped out of school to marry him two months before her graduation. She was a better student than he was. She manages the family finances. Their house and car are paid for" (p. 3). Binzen pictured the father as a union man who, while uneducated, has strong opinions about law and order, capital punishment, patriotism, Bible reading and prayer in the public schools, busing, "bleeding heart liberals," and physical punishment of children at home and in school.

The values that permeate the Whitetowner urban ethnic population reflect both security and a restrictive, outdated life view for today's adolescents. Those with physical or mental handicaps feel a sense of loyalty and support for their family, but are aware of the handicapism, like racism, that their families and neighborhoods practice. They may be caught between the ambivalence of parents who acknowledge their son's or daughter's disabilities and their responsibility to do their duty on one hand. On the other hand is their hostility toward the efforts of the school district or assistance programs. The children have heard criticisms of those who cannot or do not pull their own weight, who live off government programs, and who ought to be in institutions or special places rather than remaining in the community, causing problems, taking "our" jobs, and making demands on society. The problems in self-concept that result from such mixed messages at home are difficult to address at school—especially if the adolescent is rebelling and acting out at home and school in reaction to family values and traditions.

Rural Ethnic

The major ethnic groups that live in rural areas are Hispanic (primarily of Mexican origin), Native Americans, and African Americans. These three minority groups are associated with specific areas of the country—Hispanics in the Southwest (California, Texas, New Mexico, Colorado, and Arizona), Native Americans in the Southwest, West, and Northwest (Oklahoma, Arizona, California, Utah, New Mexico, Washington, and Alaska), and African Americans in the South (Alabama, Georgia, Mississippi, Louisiana, Arkansas, and parts of Texas, Florida, South Carolina, North Carolina, and Tennessee).

Native Americans are the only major minority or ethnic group that is predominatly rural. They are tending to become more urban, but this group continues to remain the largest group in rural and isolated locales. They are among the most economically depressed groups in the country. Most rural Native Americans (except in Alaska) live on reservations and are extremely poor. The reservation system tends to hinder social and geographical mobility. It is the ancestral home, the place of tribal activity, a family residence, a buffer against the white man's world, and a channel for government assistance.

Culturally, Native Americans have maintained many tribal values about family, tradition, and nature. These valves provide youths with some sense of security as they mature and face changes in themselves and in the larger culture. Although mostly positive, there are times when such values prevent families from agreeing to certain "unnatural" interventions with their sons or daughters with disabilities at school. Hearing aids, for example, would not be acceptable in some tribes for their adolescents. Thus, it is important for special educators to realize that, in this case, the disability of hearing impairment may not be so much something that exists inside a person, but rather a phenomenon that is defined within an ecological context—a social value judgment (Haywood, 1970).

African American and Hispanic populations are more concentrated in urban areas than in rural areas, but they still constitute a significant number of rural

ANNIE SHERWOOD

Annie is 16 years old and new to the community. Her father is a turret-lathe operator at a custom machine tool and die plant. Annie is quiet, somewhat withdrawn, and makes little eye contact with most adults and a number of her peers. She has been in special classes or resource rooms since the fifth grade.

Annie reads at about the fourth-grade level and has a math achievement level of 6.1, with computation higher than numerical reasoning or work problem solving. She has little interest in school except for a stated interest in wanting to get a job as a waitress or cashier at a nice restaurant. She asks frequently about the work-experience program and when she can work. Her intelligence test (WISC-R) scores from two years ago yielded a Verbal Scale IQ of 68, a Performance Scale IQ of 73, and a Full Scale IQ of 70.

Annie is not unattractive physically, but she makes little attempt to dress or groom herself attractively. Her skin is pale and dry. Her long blonde hair is straight and clean but obviously receives little attention. Annie has no close friends at school but talks about a friend at her church. She has never dated but says she wants to get married as soon as she gets out of high school.

School records indicate that Annie's attendance has always been good and that she is a cooperative student. Teachers' comments from previous schools include such statements as:

"Annie S. is a quiet, shy girl who never volunteers for anything but will follow others and do her part. She seems immature about social interactions and somewhat afraid of teachers and adults around the school until she knows them."

"Annie never says a word but is my best and most dependable helper. Junior high school is quite an adjustment for her, and she needs a lot of support and encouragement."

"Annie Sherwood has made noticeable progress in her school skills in her three years at the junior high. Her parents are active in the local church and report that she has been accepted there in the Catholic Youth Organization. She needs to work on her reading and math, or high school will be a real problem."

Annie's family is clearly dominated by the father, who has very strict rules for Annie and her 15-year-old brother. Her mother works part time at a department store. Neither of Annie's parents finished high school, but they want both of their children to finish. Mr. Sherwood was drafted into the Vietnam War and served 18 months in combat. He was partially disabled but was provided vocational training in machine tooling and has been employed steadily ever since. He is active in the Knights of Columbus and in his union. Mrs. Sherwood has worked full time at times in the past. She does all the housework in addition to her part-time job, with help only from Annie. The Sherwoods' house, car, and camper are paid for.

residents. To be African American and rural, or Hispanic and rural means that the person is likely to be poor. The poverty of many rural African Americans is an example of how the social structure feeds the roots of poverty. Education, health services, and economic opportunity have been systematically denied or curtailed over the years, so that domestic service, farm labor, and low-skill, low-paying, nonfarm jobs are the primary occupational opportunities. Rural Hispanic families are found in the same occupational situation, and on every index of socioeconomic status (income, occupation, and education) they are among the lowest. This is especially true of the large proportion who can speak little or no English.

The major effort of rural ethnic minorities to break their poverty cycle and change their social structure is through migrant labor. This is seldom successful, however, as these workers cannot get adequate education; their work is often physically stressful, unhealthful, or hazardous; their housing is often bad; and they are always rootless—strangers in a succession of new environments. Still, not all states regulate labor camps, conditions of travel, working hours of children, and work conditions. Federal law requires registration of crew leaders in at least a minimal gesture toward regulation, but the health and welfare of migratory workers continue to be a problem.

Special education professionals must be responsive to different cultural and ethnic values, styles, and traditions. It is a well-known fact that minority ethnic groups are typically overrepresented in special education programs. Unfortunately, there is very little research on the meaning of disability or its impact on various ethnic groups. The lack of information in this area puts special educators in the position of taking responsibility for finding out the cultural and ethnic perspectives of the parents of their students and how these perspectives affect parent-teacher and student-teacher communication as well as alternatives in educational interventions.

Walker (1991) provided a helpful perspective for addressing some important cultural issues that emerge in school and rehabilitation programs preparing individuals for independence and work. The cultural asumptions that educators and adult service agencies bring to their work (e.g., assessment, planning instruction, placement in jobs, etc.) may be quite different from those of their students or clients from other cultural backrounds. Some of those assumptions and the implications of those assumptions for work include those on page 88.

HENRY BISTIE

Henry is a 17-year-old student in the tenth grade. He lives with his parents as the only child at home, although he has an older brother. The Native-American family is comfortable both within and outside the Native-American community that is a part of the city.

Records indicate that the parents suspected problems from birth with Henry. He never played as a baby, there were allergies to milk and food, and he did not talk until the age of 3. He had frequent temper tantrums, would not let anyone touch him, and he was particularly affected by bright lights.

Henry's school history is marked by numerous changes in placement. School personnel seemed baffled by his behavior and moved him from regular classes to a language development class, then a behavior disorder class, then a learning disability resource room, and even a three-year placement in a self-contained class in a segregated school setting. During junior high school, Henry was placed back in a regular junior high building but in a special class. He attended one year of high school in a special class, but was returned to the segregated, self-contained program at the special school after inappropriately touching female students.

Henry's medical history shows that when he was 7 years old, he was diagnosed as having a complex partial seizure disorder. A secondary diagnosis indicated mild retardation with a Verbal Scale IQ of 70, a Performance Scale IQ of 85, and a Full Scale IQ of 76. He has been on seizure medication since he was age 7. At the age of 10, he was diagnosed as having Tourette's Syndrome.

Despite the fact that he is friendly and eager to please at school, Henry has been hospitalized two times due to out-of-control behavior. There have been several suicide threats and bizarre acting-out incidents. He once cut the telephone line, destroyed a bicycle, and took the family truck. There have been numerous inappropriate sexual behaviors and cruelty to animals.

Henry's only vocational preparation has been within the school setting where he has held several jobs. He is a good worker and eager to please his supervisors, but he becomes extremely anxious when observed.

Cultural Assumptions	Implications for Working
Family boundaries	Life crises and events affect attendance since family is a priority
Quality of life	Independence may be rejected in favor of interdependence
Importance of social status	Different responses to supervisors
Importance of religion	Generosity and community support may be more important than "profit" or advancement
Meaning of work	May view the purpose and nature of work differently
Decision-making style	May value group decision making or may prefer authoritarian style to avoid individual decision making
Belief in change	May not desire individual control and may see situations as fatalistic
Work routines/expectations	May desire main meal at mid-day with rest period or have preferences for type of clothing that is congruent with their health and safety

Walker (1991) stated that the world view of a member of a minority or multinational group is very important for educational and rehabilitation planning. The more professionals know about the culture of an individual with disabilities and his or her living environment and value systems, the more effective the intervention and training efforts can be.

Socioeconomic Variables

It is difficult to categorize or describe the middle-class populations in urban and suburban environments. Popenoe (1985) reviewed some rather familiar descriptors of the middle-class American that set the stage for a brief overview of this group:

1. The middle-class American is not a great reader of books.
2. Television viewing is the most frequent form of entertainment, averaging about 22 hours per week.
3. Most middle-class adults and adolescents do not walk for pleasure or bicycle frequently. Jogging, aerobics, and fitness activities are glamorized and are increasing in frequency but are still engaged in by a minority.
4. Middle-class Americans tend to "neighbor" more than people in other countries. Neighboring may involve giving help, sharing equipment, cooperating in work efforts, and socializing informally.
5. Nearly half of urban and suburban middle-class Americans are actively engaged in church attendance and activities.

6. "Moonlighting" or a second job is common among middle-class families, as are two wage-earners in the family.
7. Mobility is a life-style characteristic of middle-class families with a change of residence at a rate about twice that of Europeans. Most of the moves occur within the same county.
8. Compared with life in Japan and western Europe, the U.S. middle-class life is marked by a high degree of economic security. *Author's note*: This characteristic is probably still acurate for the majority of families, but has seen some slipping during the early 1990s.

The nature of suburban middle-class families has changed considerably from the "Dick and Jane" image of the 1940s and 1950s. The white-collar exodus from the cities to the suburbs led to a stereotyping of suburbia that was characterized by income and life-style. By the 1970s, a broad middle class emerged, making up more than half of the metropolitan population. By 1980, 45 percent of the nation's population was living in metropolitan suburban areas. Although 90 percent of the country's 100 million suburbanites were white, large numbers of ethnic and racial minorities were represented: 50 percent of all Asians, 42 percent of all Hispanics, and 29 percent of all African Americans live in the suburbs (U.S. Census of Population, 1980). The primary change of this class expansion was the upward mobility of blue-collar workers. Their incomes increased significantly enough to enable them to match incomes and status symbols with white-collar workers—suburban homes, numerous household appliances, recreational vans and campers, snowmobiles, boats, and designer clothes.

The milieu of middle-class families in urban and suburban communities has produced a generation of adolescents with a range of values, aspirations, and life-style dreams. Adolescents with disabilities today are confused by the mixed messages of home, school, and society about what is desirable and what is possible. Societal changes have placed stresses on middle-class families. The force of these changes has greatly weakened parents' authority and diminished their enthusuasm for parenting. As parents have yielded their authority and responsibility—sometimes literally, sometimes symbolically—adolescents with disabilities have been seen by many educators as the school's responsibility by default. The adolescents, on the other hand, are increasingly influenced by their peers' values, attitudes, and behavior. Many are more interested in the themes played up by the mass media—sex, affluence, and entertainment (escape) as solutions to problems—than the themes of the high school, which include academic achievement, responsibility, and occupational goals, interspersed with athletic events, proms, and school-related extracurricular activities.

KATHY KOONS

Kathy is a 19-year-old young woman with spina bifida. She has an electric wheelchair that she can control in a very limited way. An instructional assistant works with Kathy to ensure that she is able to get around the school and to assist her with classroom activities. She requires assistance in writing and getting her supplies ready for class, getting her lunch and feeding herself, and controlling her wheelchair.

Kathy is the middle child; she has an older, married sister and a brother who is age 14. Her father is an electrician and her mother does not work outside of the home. The family lives in a very nice house, which has had some modifications made for the wheelchair.

Her school attendance has been very poor. Mrs. Koons has kept Kathy at home for extended periods of time throughout the years, stating that Kathy was not well enough to attend school. The family was told that Kathy would not live to be 5 years old and they have taken care of her every need. The mother does many things that Kathy could do on her own, but it would take her a long time to get it done. When Kathy is at home, she spends the majority of the time in her wheelchair in front of the TV or stretched out on a blanket on the floor. There is nothing that Kathy does at home for herself or the family.

Kathy is in four resource classes (math, language arts, social studies, and vocational exploration), two regular education classes (computers and home economics), and spends one hour a day with the instructional assistant working on daily living and functional living skills. Kathy is working on grooming skills, kitchen skills, making change, telling time, and mobility. She has good verbal skills, but very limited written language skills because of her limited mobility. She is learning to use a computer to enable her to increase her written expressive skills. Kathy has indicated an interest in doing a job that would utilize telephone skills, which is something she feels she could learn to do. Kathy has several friends at school. She says that she would like to have a boyfriend and talks about relationships quite often. She is very concerned about not having someone to marry, being able to leave home, and living on her own.

Kathy's Verbal Scale IQ is 74, Performance Scale IQ is 64, and Full Scale IQ is 69. Kathy is aware of her academic limitations, but she wants to do something with her life. She indicates that she wants to learn to live more independently and to develop job skills. She is older than most of the students in the high school and plans are being made for her to go to a residential center for young adults with physical disabilities where she can have the opportunity to learn many of the things that will allow her to live in a group home and have a job. Kathy is very excited about these plans, but her parents are somewhat hesitant.

INSTRUCTIONAL PERSONNEL AS PARTICIPANTS

The range of instructional programs for high school youths with handicapping conditions results in a variety of instructional personnel. These instructional personnel assume a number of roles—some unique and some arbitrarily assumed or assigned. Role differentiation among instructors is typically influenced by the following:

1. Program size
2. Nature of the population (characteristics, severity)
3. Program complexity
4. Program content
5. Administrative arrangements for delivery of instruction and support services

For now, a brief listing and a description of the major instructional or participant roles is presented. Parents and students are included later in the chapter, because they are, of course, continually engaged in instruction and are important members of the team. Principals and other related administrators also can and do participate in the instructional program by their support and occasional direct contact. However, they are not included here because of the intent to focus only on the first-line instructional personnel. These include the following:

1. Self-contained classroom teacher
2. Resource room teacher
3. Consulting teacher
4. Itinerant teacher
5. Regular education teacher
6. Vocational education teacher or vocational instructor
7. Vocational evaluator
8. Vocational or guidance counselor
9. Work experience coordinator
10. Transition coordinator/counselor
11. Paraprofessional
12. Employer
13. Vocational rehabilitation counselor

Self-Contained Classroom Teacher

The self-contained classroom teacher has the primary responsibility of implementing and sometimes developing the curriculum and course of study deemed appropriate for a given population. In fulfilling this critical role, the teacher provides leadership in IEP development; plans and selects all materials, instructional activities, and equipment; teaches the prescribed content in group or individual sessions; and assesses and evaluates student progress. The self-contained classroom teacher must also be aware of school and community resources that can be used to refer students and expand the school's instructional program beyond the self-contained classroom environment. Typically, the teacher in a self-contained classroom does a great deal of personal, social, and vocational counseling and guidance. Liaisons between the students and their parents, other school faculty, and especially a work-experience coordinator are important in this role to keep the learning process moving and focused on goals. The populations typically served by this type of teacher are low-functioning students with mild to moderate retardation and moderate to severe behavior disorders. When there are enough students to require two or more teachers, the roles of the teachers are usually modified to fit an expanded self-contained program with departmentalization and assumption of specific roles based on interest, training, and experience.

Resource Room Teacher

Wiederholt, Hammill, and Brown (1978) described the primary role of a resource teacher as providing individualized instruction to students who spend one or more periods of the school day in the resource room. The resource room philosophy and instructional approach dictate the specific role activities of the teacher, but they can take the form of a basic skills remedial model, a tutorial model, a learning-strategies model, a functional curriculum model, or a work-study model (Deshler, Lowrey, & Alley, 1979). A resource room may have two or more of these approaches working at one time.

A secondary resource room teacher does most of the instructional tasks that a self-contained classroom teacher does, but may do even more. There is not the same responsibility for curriculum planning, but some unique tasks are required of a resource room teacher. Because of the resource room mission, some of these tasks are offered only infrequently, and others are required more often. Among these tasks are scheduling, collaborative planning, consultation, team teaching with other teachers, making referrals for special individual needs, and coordinating support-service delivery. Serving more students per day, participating in more individualized education program conferences, and providing more written reports of progress are also differentiating factors between self-contained and resource room teachers. Another substantive difference between resource room teachers and self-contained teachers is the resource room teacher's involvement with the academic subject content of the regular education curriculum.

Consulting Teacher

The primary role of the consulting teacher in secondary special education programming is to facilitate the maintenance of identified students with special needs in regular classes with their peers. The concept of a teacher in a consulting role was proposed in the early to mid-1970s by Adelman (1972) and Bauer (1975). Idol, Paolucci-Whitcomb, and Nevin (1986) and Robinson (1988) have developed yet another extension of the concept, with *collaborative consultation*. Collaborative consultation, according to Idol and others, is an interactive process that assumes that regular and special teachers have a wide range of expertise. They must be able to generate creative solutions to mutually defined problems in instruction and classroom management. When a collaborative consulting teacher is available in a school building, he or she will engage in problem solving, cooperative instruction, material modification, monitoring of academic and social behavior, and various other supportive activities while all or most students are mainstreamed during the school day (Robinson, 1988).

Some authorities in secondary learning disabilities (Deshler & Schumaker, 1987) are concerned that high school resource room teachers, unlike elementary and middle school resource teachers, have had to assume far too much responsibility for teaching academic content in subject areas outside their teaching credentials. The preferred alternative for serving those students who spend most of their school day in regular classes is now the consulting teacher or collaborative consulting teacher. Without the heavy work load of a resource room (scheduling, multiple group and individual instruction, supervision, etc.), the collaborative consulting teacher can concentrate on assisting classroom teachers to develop their own educational assessment, prescriptive, and instructional procedures. Direct services to students would be limited to short-term instruction with individual students in regular classrooms to demonstrate special techniques to the classroom teacher or to assist the student in using his or her own learning strategies. The collaborative consulting teacher can also provide teachers or students assistance in transitional planning (Sileo, Rude, & Luckner, 1988). It is important that consulting teachers be informed of the transition goals and objectives set for students who spend all or most of their time in regular classes.

Itinerant Teacher

An itinerant teacher provides more direct services to students enrolled in the regular classroom than does the consulting teacher and, naturally, is not restricted to one building. The itinerant teacher model is used by some smaller school districts that participate in special education cooperatives with other schools. The major role is to provide specialized individual and small-group instruction, although some time is devoted to consulting with regular teachers, parents, and other school staff.

Specialized itinerant instruction includes speech reading, speech, language, or signing for students who are deaf. Itinerant instruction includes Braille writing, Braille reading, or orientation and mobility for students with visual impairments. Specific remedial or tutorial instruction may be needed for any student having a special instructional need not available in the regular curriculum.

Regular Education Teacher

A regular education teacher is a non-special education teacher who assumes responsibility for subject matter instruction for many special-needs students. Teachers of industrial and practical arts, music, graphic arts, physical education, consumer education, English, math, science, or social studies are examples of those who comprise this group. Their roles in relation to youths with handicapping conditions focus on accommodating their instructional styles (course organization, course-requirement options, delivery of content, and testing) and assisting students to adapt to the requirements that all students are expected to complete. In this process, they need to be able to use support-service staff for their own or their students' assistance, be more sensitive to individualized educational planning, and see the unique needs of individuals who have been judged to be capable of successfully achieving the objective of their courses. In the 1988–89 school year, 64.3 percent of all students with disabilities between the ages of 12 and 17 were educated at least part of the day in regular classes (U.S. Department of Education, 1991). This underscores the participant role of regular teachers.

Vocational Education Teacher or Vocational Instructor

Vocational education teachers are those certified teachers who teach vocational skills related to a specific occupational area. Traditional vocational education areas are vocational agriculture, distributive education, office occupations, health occupations, and vocational home economics. Vocational instructors are those experienced tradespersons who teach in vocational and technical schools or programs in specific occupational areas. Examples of areas taught by vocational instructors are the building trades, welding, cosmetology, automotive mechanics, heating and refrigeration, electronics, commercial art, and printing. The roles of these teachers and instructors are the same as those described previously for regular teachers who work with special-needs students.

Vocational Evaluator

The school-based vocational evaluation specialist is a relatively new role. In the past, school vocational assessment was limited to what school psychologists or guidance counselors could provide. Vocational evaluations were sometimes obtained for students through the purchase of evaluation services by state divisions of vocational rehabilitation at community rehabilitation or evaluation centers. These resources still may be used in some instances. However, vocational assessment is increasingly obtained through special and vocational education-assessment programs, mobile vocational-assessment units, or observations of students in simulated or real work situations. The primary roles of the vocational evaluator are as follows:

1. Assess intellectual capacities, aptitudes, interests, and personal-social adjustment.
2. Assess work history, work skills, work attitudes, and work habits.
3. Assess independent living skills (mobility, communication, hygiene, consumer skills, personal and social skills, and home living skills).
4. Assess physical capacity.
5. Assess job-seeking skills.
6. Write useful reports for individualized educational planning.
7. Interpret and communicate vocational evaluation results to students, parents, and school personnel.

Vocational or Guidance Counselor

The roles of vocational counselors in vocational programs and guidance counselors in a comprehensive high school depend on their specific assignments. The school guidance counselor's role will be detailed in Chapter 9. However, in the context of vocational guidance, both the guidance counselor and the vocational counselor have a responsibility to provide occupational information and counseling and guidance. They provide these services in the process of occupational choice, selection of postsecondary training programs, and the application process for training or employment. If vocational assessment is secured outside the vocational school or high school, counselors may get involved in referral; provision of school records; student orientation to vocational evaluation; routing the evaluation report; interpretation of evaluation results; parent conferences; and follow-up activities in planning, placement, or student counseling.

Work Experience Coordinator

The role of the person responsible for obtaining and supervising on-the-job work training carries various titles in schools across the country. These titles include work experience coordinator, vocational adjustment coordinator, vocational counselor, work placement counselor, job coach, designated vocational instructor, work adjustment specialist and various others. Whether full time or part time, the tasks remain essentially the same. The person in this role has many responsibilities, including the following:

1. Coordinate all vocational-assessment data.
2. Conduct job analyses and maintain a file of job and training placement possibilities.
3. Secure job training and employment placements.
4. Supervise training.
5. Evaluate students in job follow-up.
6. Counsel pupils, parents, teachers, and employers on work experience problems.

7. Maintain all legal records related to state and federal requirements.
8. Assist in the development of transition goals and objectives.
9. Develop the curricula and correlate school and work experiences.
10. Coordinate the work experience program with school and community support services.
11. Maintain public relations with school personnel, employers, and parents.

Individuals performing work experience coordination are usually certified teachers with a special education endorsement of some type. Few states have separate endorsements calling for specific training experience or competencies for someone approved for such a position.

Transition Coordinator/Counselor/Specialist

The passage of IDEA with its mandate for transition services planning and coordination has spurred the redefining of secondary special education personnel roles. The need to have one or more persons assigned to implement the transition services requirements for IEP planning and programming for a school district or special education cooperative is obvious when the scope of responsibility is considered. It appears that some schools have redefined the role of the work experience coordinator to include the new transition services responsibilities. Some schools have not reduced any of the traditional responsibilities of the work experience coordinator; others have assigned some of the duties to a paraprofessional job coach. The size of the school and service area have an impact on such decisions.

For those schools that have designated a full-time transition coordinator, the specific responsibilities include the following:

1. Develop formal contacts and working relationships between school and community agencies.
2. Develop a transition services plan and related policies and procedures for the school .
3. Assist in the planning and implementation of a comprehensive functional curriculum focusing on transition outcomes.
4. Coordinate the assessment required for appropriate transition services planning and programming.
5. Provide students and parents with transition information and the critical decision-making and planning areas.
6. Coordinate and participate in the IEP planning for all identified special education students who are 16 years of age and older.
7. Develop a school database of information on students while in school and follow-along data after leaving school.

8. Provide in-service education to teachers, related service personnel, families, and community agency staff.
9. Provide leadership in the development and activities of a local transition council.

Paraprofessional

The role of paraprofessionals in a high school program depends on the nature of the instructional program and the type of delivery system. Primary tasks may include the following:

1. Provide instructional assistance to teachers with individual or small-group activities.
2. Assist with curriculum-based assessment.
3. Assist with classroom management and control.
4. Assist with community-based instruction activities.
5. Supervise students while traveling into community sites.

Any teacher who has had highly competent paraprofessionals, however, acknowledges that professionals' task assignments extend deeply into the teacher's role. Some teachers, in fact, consider their paraprofessionals as their team-teaching colleagues.

An increasingly common special paraprofessional role is that of a job coach. A paraprofessional job coach's role and scope of responsibility depends on the staffing and organization of the school's employment training program. In many ways, there is a direct parallel between the in-school paraprofessional's relationship to the classroom teacher and the paraprofessional job coach's relationship to the work experience coordinator. Examples of duties include the following:

1. Participate in IEP planning and staffings.
2. Implement student vocational training plans.
3. Work with small groups or individual students at community-based work sites in intensive job training and supervision.
4. Work with small groups or individual students in teacher-planned instructional activities related to job choice, job selection, preparation for job interviews, and job-related skills.
5. Conduct informal career development and transition assessment in school and work performance assessment on the job.
6. Transport students to job interviews or community-based instructional activities.
7. Assist in maintaining student records and files.
8. Serve as liaison between employers and the work experience coordinator.

Employer

The role of employers as instructors is very informal, but this informality does not lessen their importance as participants. Some employers are too removed from the training and supervision of student workers to have any direct role. In these cases, designated experienced workers or supervisors who work directly with students do so in place of employers.

Work experience specialists depend on conscientious, committed employers. They see the employers' roles as trainers and evaluators from the best point of view—the potential employer following training. As trainers, they provide the reality that simulated or school-based training cannot begin to provide. As evaluators, they approach the evaluation from the ultimate employment criteria—successful performance in a specific position under real conditions of employment.

Vocational Rehabilitation Counselor

Since the passage of PL 94-142, The Education for All Handicapped Act, the role of the vocational rehabilitation counselor as a participant in high school special education transitional programs has changed. Prior to PL 94-142, the role was prescribed relatively clearly in states that had cooperative work-study agreements. The vocational rehabilitation counselor was authorized to provide extensive rehabilitation services to every special education student accepted as a client. Now, after almost two decades of limited and inconsistent practices within and across states, the inclusion of rehabilitation counseling as an approved related service under IDEA (PL 101-476) is causing many states and local education agencies to redefine the counselor's role with special education students. The following tasks are authorized under federal vocational rehabilitation regulations:

1. Determine eligibility of special education students for vocational rehabilitation services.
2. Determine feasibility of special education students for benefiting from vocational rehabilitation services and make a decision to accept or deny.
3. Provide services to student-clients that are needed but not required of schools under PL 94-142 and for which no duplication of services will occur.
4. Participate in IEP meetings relative to transition services for student-clients.
5. Assist in counseling student-clients, parents, teachers, and employers.

Rehabilitation counseling services as a related service within the school's responsibility is new territory. The delay in giving schools guidance through the federal regulations for this new service led many schools to postpone any action until they knew more how to interface these services with the traditional services of state vocational rehabilitation services. The limited guidance of the proposed regulations defined *rehabilitation counseling* as services provided by a qualified rehabilitation counseling professional, in individual or group sessions, that focus specifically on career development, employment preparation, achieving independence, and integration in the workplace for a student with a disability. The term also included vocational rehabilitation services provided to students with diabilities by vocational rehabilitation programs funded under the Rehabilitation Act of 1973, as amended.

What the Congress intended is not completely clear, but IDEA has opened up a new dialogue between state and local special education agencies with their respective vocational rehabilitation agencies. It is possible that the field will come full circle to the formalized cooperative working arrangements between special education and vocational rehabilitation in the 1960s and early 1970s for schools using the cooperative work-study model developed in Texas (Eskridge & Partridge, 1963).

PARENTS AS PARTICIPANTS

Even if the parents' rights and responsibilities for participation in the planning for their sons or daughters with disabilities were not clearly established in PL 94-142, the emphasis on transition services in IDEA make it patently clear that a partnership is absolutely critical. It is much easier during the elementary years for parents to yield to the schools considerable authority for educational decisions, particularly on the content of the curriculum. For some teachers and parents, school is more or less an end in itself, rather than a means to an end, and the content and substance of what is taught in school is of secondary importance to being there. When a student with disabilities nears the age of entry into high school, the decisions parents and students make are much more critical in that they are no longer focused on the short-term goal of moving through the educational system reasonably successfully, academically and socially. From age 14 on, the educational meter is ticking and choices that are made regarding courses of study (and even specific courses) should be made with outcomes in mind for postsecondary life.

The provisions of IDEA state that those decisions should be made based on the students' needs, preferences, and interests. However, parents must be active participants in the determination of what those needs, preferences, and interests are and be involved in the guidance and teaching process that the schools cannot do alone. Parent/family roles and responsibilities as participants in a career-development and transition-oriented secondary school program include the following:

1. Encourage student self-determination and independence at home.
2. Encourage and facilitate setting goals.

3. Teach, and assist in teaching, daily living and personal-social skills.
4. Encourage the student to work at home and at a neighborhood or community job.
5. Reinforce work-related behaviors at home (work habits, hygiene, grooming, etc.).
6. Explore and promote community resources for transition.
7. Assist in the student assessment process.
8. Assist the student in developing personal and social values, self-confidence, and self-esteem.
9. Work with legal and financial experts, as appropriate, to plan financial, legal, and residential altenatives.

STUDENTS AS PARTICIPANTS

The regulations for IDEA (PL 101-476) state that when the purpose of an IEP meeting is to consider transition services for a student, the school shall invite the student to participate in her or his IEP meeting. For any student who is 16 years of age or older, the annual IEP meeting will always have as one of its purposes to consider transition service needs. It is our position that students of age should be not only invited but encouraged to attend. Beyond that, the school should provide systematic instruction or guidance for students in how they can participate fully. Without that, the invitation and attendance are only token compliance efforts. For a student younger than age 16, if transition services are initially discussed at an IEP meeting that does not include the student, the school is responsible for ensuring that, before a decision about transition services for the student is made a subsequent IEP meeting shall be conducted for that purpose, and the student will be invited to the meeting.

The specific wording of the statute mandating transition services states that the coordinated set of activities described in the definition of transition services "must be based on the individual student's needs, taking into account the student's preferences and interests" [20 U.S.C. 1401(a)(19)]. The students participation in the determination of needs, preferences, and interests should take place during the assessment process used in establishing present level of functioning for IEP planning as well as during the IEP meeting itself.

CONCLUSION

The participants in secondary special education programming are an extremely heterogeneous population. The variations of size, location, population characteristics, and local and state laws and policies make for extremely different educational situations. These variations have implications for differences that one can expect as one is introduced to a given program as a newly employed professional or a prospective employee. If educators understand the differences and use that understanding in providing the best programming possible for identified youths with disabilities, then educators can move closer to being professionals rather than technicians.

4

Assessment in Secondary Special Education

Latent abilities are like clay. It can be mud on shoes, brick in a building or a statue that will inspire all who see it. The clay is the same. The result is dependent on how it is used.—JAMES A. LINCOLN

ACTIVITIES

- Describe the use of the information from academic achievement tests in suggesting career goals for students with disabilities of different kinds.
- Develop a work-sample assessment procedure for the job of grocery clerk.
- Find a situation in the school cafeteria that could be used in an assessment program.
- Develop a system that is nonpunitive to the students for assessing reactions to failure.
- Design a case file folder that will accommodate all the assessment information contained in Chapter 4.
- Develop an assessment battery of both formal and informal procedures that will address the major outcomes for transition planning under PL 101-476.
- Develop an interview questionnaire for students that relates to their current and immediate future interests and preferences for their lives.

INTRODUCTION

The requirements of the Education for All Handicapped Children Act (PL 94-142), its amendment (PL 98-199), and the Carl D. Perkins Vocational Education Act (PL 98-528) all placed an increased emphasis on the purposes for and process of student assessment in special education programming. It was the Individuals with Disabilities Education Act of 1990 (PL 101-476), though, that may be remembered as the major contributor to a shift to a new level of usefulness in assessment. Although assessment was once considered a diagnostic function primarily for identification and classification, it is now intended to be the basis for individual education and transition planning. Whereas assessment was once focused primarily on academic achievement and intellectual assessment, it must now include personal-social skills, daily living skills, career development, and prevocational and vocational skills.

In essence, this view of assessment is what Granger (1982) and Crewe and Athelstan (1984) have called *functional assessment*. That is, assessment that is functional focuses on the measurement of dynamic characteristics of a person in the context of his or her daily living activities, skills, behavioral performances, environmental conditions, and needs. For high school students, that means assessment of their functioning at home, at school, and in the community.

Halpern and Fuhrer (1984) have written a book on functional assessment that makes it clear that the role of functional assessment in the field of rehabilitation is a topic of increasing interest and concern. It has emerged as a major component of state and federal initiatives relative to accountability, nondiscriminatory testing, individualized program planning, and redirection of resources for the benefit of those who are so severely disabled that they are not eligible for rehabilitation services.

In education, there is a similar trend with such terms as *curriculum-based* or *curriculum-referenced assessment* (Albright & Cobb, 1988; Cobb, 1983; Stodden & Ianacone, 1981), *program-related assessment* (Halpern, Lehmann, Irvin, & Heiry, 1982; Irvin, 1988), and *community-referenced assessment* (Rudrud, Ziarnik, Bernstein, & Ferrara, 1984). Assessment from this perspective is the collection and use of information within the context of a person's going through a curriculum or intervention program. The assessment feeds directly into curricular or program decision making, thus making it highly functional.

From a legal point of view, the purposes for assessment in schools relate to the individual education program (IEP) and, in some states, the individual transition plan (ITP). From a practical point of view, the purposes of assessment stem from the types of decisions to be made. Chapter 2 presented a case for a career development and transition approach with adolescents labeled handicapped in high schools. Chapter 3 presented a description of what that population of adolescents might be like and what kinds of information can be obtained through assessment. The task of persons doing assessment, then, is one of asking appropriate questions. Questions are asked to obtain functional information for decision making with students and their parents for educational and transitional goals.

Most of the initial career assessment literature about high school populations with special needs emphasized prevocational and vocational assessment (Cobb & Larkin, 1985; Hursh & Kerns, 1988; Ianacone et al., 1982; McCray, 1982; Phelps & McCarty, 1984; Pruitt, 1977; Roberts, Doty, Santleben, & Tang, 1983; Schneck, 1981; Sitlington & Wimmer, 1978; Stodden, 1980). This is not to say that this has been the most frequent type of assessment conducted with high school students. On the contrary, because academic programming has been the focus of high school programming since the changes in instructional models resulting from PL 94-142, most assessment has been directed at academic achievement and intellectual functioning. Epstein and Cullinan (1992), for example, conducted a survey of assessment practices in programs for adolescents with behavior disorders and found that virtually no tests were listed for vocational and career interest, social skills, critical life events, or other areas central to adolescent students. Why, then, is there more literature on prevocational and vocational assessment?

Probably the basic reason the literature reflects a vocational focus for high school special education programs is that the first of these programs grew out of ties to vocational rehabilitation. Vocational rehabilitation, with its roots in rehabilitation medicine, requires medical, psychological, and vocational evaluations before a person is accepted as a client. The early models of cooperative school work-study programs between schools and state rehabilitation agencies in the 1960s adopted this same approach. This is understandable, since special-needs vocational education and workstudy program placements require prevocational and vocational assessment data. The rapid advancement of vocational evaluation as a discipline in the late 1960s and early 1970s not only strengthened this practice in high schools but also led to a growing body of literature (Fry, 1986).

This chapter proposes a movement away from an assessment emphasis that centers either on academic and cognitive performance or on work or vocational outcomes exclusively. A more useful assessment approach views both of these areas as important but includes daily living skills and personal-social skills as equally important outcomes. It shifts the emphasis to a broad, life-career or transition competencies approach for assessment. This was described as early as 1978 by Brolin (Brolin, 1978, 1983) and since then by others (Elrod & Sorgenfrei, 1988; Epstein & Cullinan, 1992; Leconte, 1992; Peterson, 1983; Sitlington, 1980; Stodden & Ianacone, 1981).

The general goals of assessment, however, are the same whether the emphasis is on vocational assessment or career assessment. The determination of the status of a person's life-style or performance level before, during, and after program interventions, the information needed for present and future decision making, the determination of group status for program planning, and ongoing needs for information for instruction and guidance all comprise the general goals of assessment. The differences lie in what behavior domains are included and the instruments or procedures used. Teachers, counselors, program coordinators, parents, administrators, and the students themselves can benefit from assessment that is done appropriately and competently. *Appropriate* assessment relates primarily to asking the "right" questions (validity), and *competent* assessment pertains primarily to the issues of how well the questions are asked (reliability).

Whether or not a special educator is asking the right questions is a value judgment. The advocates of a vocational rehabilitation or vocational education approach would say that the "right" questions for them emerge out of the domains of occupational interest and aptitude, employability skills, and physical status (Hartley, Otazo, & Cline, 1979; Menz, 1978; Nadolsky, 1981; Phelps & McCarty, 1984). The proponents of maximum academic achievement in the mainstream of education might view the "right" questions as those that focus on academic achievement, diagnosis of deficit areas, or metacognitive skill assessment (Salvia & Ysseldyke, 1985). The advocates of a life-centered career education and transition approach would say that the "right" questions must stem from the domains of daily living skills, personal-social skills, and occupational guidance and preparation skills (Clark, 1980; Leconte, 1992; Halpern, 1985; Kokaska & Brolin, 1985). We and other advocates of the model presented in Chapter 2 support the latter view and believe that the "right" questions come out of the domains of values, attitudes, and habits, human relationships, occupational information, and job and daily living skills. These domains include a concern for academic achievement and vocational behavior but add other critical concern areas as well. In short, these areas give direction as to *what* questions to ask. This leaves the second step to be addressed—How do you get reliable answers to the questions you ask?

Human behavior assessment has been approached from a variety of ways by educators, allied health fields (including vocational rehabilitation), counselors, military personnel, and government, business, and industry. The basic approaches that offer the most promise include the following:

1. Psychometric or standardized testing
2. Work sample
3. Situational
4. Medical appraisal

Each of these approaches will be discussed in terms of its instruments and procedures and its advantages and disadvantages in high school programs for assessment of values, attitudes, and habits, human relationships, occupational information, and job and daily living skills.

THE PSYCHOMETRIC APPROACH

The psychometric approach is the approach most familiar to secondary special educators. Training and experience have led many educators to have opinions about psychometric testing that range from complete acceptance and enthusiasm to complete rejection and hostility. Most educators probably believe something in between these extremes: They know that they have to assess students, but that this assessment process has its problems. Specific concerns include such criticisms as the following:

1. Tests label people and lead to stigma.
2. Tests are imperfect.
3. Test givers are imperfect.
4. Tests can be biased and discriminatory.
5. Tests invade privacy.
6. Test results foster mechanistic decision making.
7. Tests may obscure strengths as they reveal weaknesses.

When the choice of tests and appropriateness for certain groups or individuals is not carefully made, the issues become even more critical. On the other hand, schools must have documented assessment data for individualized placement and educational planning. To achieve this, they look to psychometrics because of their normative information, their speed of administration, their economy, their efficiency, and the ability to focus on specific behaviors of interest.

The types of information typically sought by schools have led school psychometrists to use a variety of tests, among which are intellectual and academic tests, aptitude tests, interest inventories, and personality tests. With the exception of aptitude, interest, and some personality scales, psychometric tests used in schools were not designed for directly assessing life-career development or transition skills. Even in these areas, the test developers had very specific age and ability groups in mind for the normative population. As a result, educators must often choose among a number of reasonably reliable instruments that are not specifically designed to assess career development and transition. This is also true of a few instruments available that are specifically designed for assessing career development but that have questionable levels of validity and reliability. The following sections are meant to shed some light on this dilemma and to offer some alternatives.

Intellectual and Academic Assessment

Although educators, rehabilitation personnel, and others interested in life adjustment for people who have disabilities generally recognize that the tests that yield intelligence quotients (IQs) and academic achievement were not designed to predict adult adjustment, they are still used in school programs for other purposes. Thus, the question to ask is not, Should intelligence tests be used in a high school assessment program? A better question is, Is anything of value for career and transition assessment purposes being collected from these areas?

Intelligence Tests
The chief value of the results from intelligence tests, after their use in classification and placement decisions for special educational programs, is the information that can be gleaned from them regarding specific aspects of intelligence

that relate to life-career roles. This is saying, in effect, that a global IQ is of little value. The tests of intelligence that provide useful information are those that specify various aspects of intellectual functioning through subtests or those that are restricted to the measurement of only one factor. For example, some major factors have been isolated in factor analysis studies (Peck, Stephens, & Veldman, 1964; Tobias, 1964) that appear to be important correlates of vocational adjustment in some specific training and employment domains. Among these are verbal ability, numerical ability, nonverbal conceptual ability, memory, and perception.

Intellectual efficiency and *level of conceptual ability* (abstract verbal reasoning and comprehension) are two factors that relate to two different aspects of occupational adjustment. Intellectual efficiency is considered to be a better predictor of basic employability, level of conceptual ability points more toward probable levels of employment. For example, basic employability predictions would be based on such questions as, Can she obtain and hold a job? and level of employment predictions on such questions as, Would she be able to perform most successfully as a clean-up person, stocker, supervisor, manager, or owner of a grocery store? Intellectual efficiency and level of conceptual ability also are the same two factors operating in prediction of performance in daily living skills and social skills.

Tests of intellectual efficiency and conceptualization specifically designed for predicting basic employability and level of employment are not readily available to all interested users. Such availability may exist in the future, but until that time some general cues as to an estimate of these factors might be obtained from the table below.

A listing of intelligence measures or subtests from intelligence measures such as those listed is frequently interpreted inappropriately. Many people who desperately want more information about the individuals with disabilities with whom they work tend to grasp at any measure and use it. However, the theoretical

Intellectual Efficiency	*Conceptual Ability*
Wechsler scales subtests	
1. Vocabulary	Wechsler scales subtests
2. General Information	1. Similarities
3. Digit Span	2. Comprehension
4. Coding	3. Arithmetic
5. Object Assembly	Stanford-Binet items
6. Picture Completion	1. Verbal Analogies
7. Picture Arrangement	2. Opposites
Porteus Maze Test	3. Absurdities
Raven's Progressive Matrices	4. Abstract Reasoning
Detroit Test of Learning Aptitude	
Devereux Cognitive Process Study	

potential of any instrument can be invalidated by any number of problems associated with validity and reliability of psychological tests. These problems tend to occur with greater frequency in special populations, particularly among persons with mild mental disabilities whose performances are difficult to interpret when there are suspected problems. These problems may include emotional disturbance, motivation to take such tests, English as the second language, and histories of failure experiences that may or may not relate to general intellectual functioning. Consequently, the position taken here in regard to use of intelligence tests or portions of such tests is one of great caution. If the user of such tests is qualified to administer and interpret the tests and is sensitive to the specific applications of information from these tests to decision making for training or employment, then some clues for appropriate decisions are possible. Even then, the information should be used only in conjunction with other information, such as that which is covered in the remainder of this chapter.

Academic Achievement Tests
Achievement tests have been developed to examine people's attainment in academic subjects. This is usually represented by responses indicative of facts and principles known, operations and computational skills acquired, and level of functional comprehension. At the high school level, some special-needs youths have already reached a stage that calls for a shift in emphasis from an academic approach in preparing for life's demands to a functional, life-career development and transition approach. One might question, then, the usefulness of achievement tests in academic subjects for students in career-development programs. If they are basically predictors of future academic success, why should they be used? If primary concerns revolve around such questions as, Can he or she read directions? Can he or she measure flour? Can he or she make change and handle his or her income? are achievement tests going to provide us that information?

Illiteracy is not an insuperable handicap to daily living or employment. Tobias (1964), three decades ago, stated that a very sizable percentage of males labeled as mentally retarded successfully employed after training were unable to read at third-grade levels. This kind of outcome is found also with individuals who have severe to profound hearing loss. On the other hand, the ability to read beyond the fourth-grade level has certainly never prejudiced employers against any applicant. Jobs requiring a high school diploma certainly assume literacy. The specific minimum level of literacy needed for employment success has been debated for more than a decade. Voelker (1963) concluded that academic competency may be more important in determining vocational success than has traditionally been thought. Guralnick (1956) has been among those who have for some time viewed reading deficiencies as serious barriers to many types of employment, if not an insurmountable handicap to getting a job. In spite of the debate over the issue of effects on employability, few would argue that reading problems affect success in consumer activities, community and citizenship roles, and level of employment.

The ability to read, at least at the literacy level, is a desirable objective for many students and parents. As long as a person is enrolled in a school program, teachers will feel some concern (or pressure) for improvement of reading comprehension and vocabulary. The same is true for arithmetic. Young (1956) asserted almost four decades ago that 84 percent of all arithmetic computation for the average adult involved buying and selling. Young also concluded that arithmetic instruction should not concern itself with much beyond this level for youths who are mentally handicapped. This conclusion might be debated on several counts by many today. However, most educators involved with high school youths having special needs agree that a functional approach toward optimal attainment of arithmetic skills is not only desirable but important.

The Basic Occupational literacy Test (BOLT) was developed by the U.S. Department of Labor (1974) in 1972 to address the need for a basic literacy test that would not rely on tests developed for children. It is a test of basic reading and arithmetic skills for use with educationally deficient adults. Reading skills are assessed by a Reading Vocabulary subtest and a Reading Comprehension subtest. Arithmetic skills are assessed by an Arithmetic Computation subtest and an Arithmetic Reasoning subtest. There subtests are available in various levels of difficulty. The content of BOLT items are adult oriented, and, in general, the reading content is similar to that found in newspapers, popular magazines, and nontechnical instruction manuals.

The assessment question at this point becomes more specific: What values are to be gained by using current, standardized achievement test batteries with youths in high school special education programs? As long as any part of the educational program involves the teaching (developmental or remedial) of reading and arithmetic, some assessment and evaluation needs to take place. The effective teacher needs to know the following:

1. At what level each student is functioning for establishing individualized objectives
2. At what level materials should be selected and prepared
3. The specific strengths and weaknesses of individuals and the group
4. The amount of progress (or lack of it) in acquiring reading skills and understanding

With these potential values in mind, can one now answer the question concerning the usefulness of academic achievement assessment affirmatively, and cite such values in using popular standardized achievement batteries currently used in schools? The answer is equivocal, because the skill of the test user is the key to understanding the value of the test results. Unfortunately, not enough secondary special education teachers are thoroughly grounded in psychometrics to be able to use tests in a very sophisticated manner. What alternatives, then, are available for secondary teachers?

One alternative might be an individual diagnostic achievement test such as the Woodcock-Johnson Psycho-Educational Battery (Teaching Resources Corporation, 1977). Burns (1984) indicated that this battery has values, including the following:

1. A generalized profile of a student's strengths and weaknesses in academic skills
2. A "relative performance index" or an overall picture of how a student compares with age peers who are performing in the "average" range or above
3. The opportunity to do an error analysis to determine a student's modality and styles of learning, generalization skills, and reasoning

Daily living and occupational skill demands can be related directly to errors specifically noted in an item analysis. In daily living, for example, 3 of Brolin and Kokaska's (1979) 22 competencies (numbers 1, 5, and 6) and at least 16 of the subcompetencies related to these 3 competencies correspond to the math computational test of the Woodcock-Johnson battery. Thus, assessment data from this battery can yield information for both academic and life skills domains if a teacher will go beyond overall grade-level equivalents and percentile norms.

Another type of achievement test that can be useful is the domain-referenced test. This test is based on the criterion-referenced assessment approach but samples a domain of knowledge or behavioral skills. Best known among this type are the Social and Prevocational Information Battery (Halpern, Raffeld, Irvin, & Link, 1975), Tests of Everyday Living (Halpern, Irvin, & Landman, 1979), PAYES (Program for Assessing Youth Employment Skills) by Educational Testing Service (1979) and Brigance Inventory of Essential Skills (Brigance, 1981). The Brigance Essential Skills are keyed by Sherrie Chrysler of Central Washington University to the career education competencies in the Kokaska and Brolin (1985) book advocating career education for handicapped individuals.

A third alternative is a behavioral or individual criterion-referenced approach. The particular word choice for this approach is attributable to Glaser (1963), but the concept may be known in other disciplines by terms such as behavior analysis, adaptive behavior, and behavior competency. It is a nominal level of measurement that attempts to answer questions that might be posed in behavioral "can–cannot" or "does–does not" terms, It is an individualized approach that provides discrete bits of information that can lead to some predictions. This approach does not emphasize continuous variables, nor does it try to determine the full extent to which an individual can perform, although a refinement in predictions might result from the same individualized perspective. For example, you may want to help John consider his qualifications and abilities as they relate to a delivery person's position for a pharmacy. Crucial criteria to be considered for him in this job would include the following:

1. Does John have a valid driver's license?
2. Can John read address labels?
3. Can John follow directions on a city map?

4. Can John tell time?
5. Can John make change?

The procedure for assessing abilities involved in each of these questions involves breaking down the operations involved in each task into decreasingly complex units that will indicate more precisely where any breakdown in task performance occurs. The following example provides a simplified sequence to illustrate this approach:

Question: Can John make change?

Step 1: Can John demonstrate satisfactorily in five change-making   Yes   No
problem situations that he can make change for (a) $20 bill, (b) $10 bill, (c) $5 bill, (d) $1 bill, and (e) 50¢? If John demonstrates these competencies, the evaluation ceases. If one or more tasks are performed incorrectly, further testing is needed to determine at which level errors are occurring.

Step 2: Can John subtract four-digit numbers using decimals?   Yes   No
($20.00 – $18.78 or $10.00 – $5.98)?
Can John subtract three-digit numbers using decimals?   Yes   No
($5.00 – $2.49)?
Can John subtract two-digit numbers using decimals?   Yes   No
($.50 – $.29)?
If John can perform these operations, his previous errors in making change may have been because of counting errors.

Step 3: Can John count rationally by 10s to 100?   Yes   No
Can John count rationally by 5s to 100?   Yes   No
Can John count rationally by 1s to 100?   Yes   No
If the answer to any of these processes is no, rote counting would then be checked. If counting did not appear to be the problem area, currency recognition might be.

Step 4: Can John recognize the following currency items?
$20 bill   Yes   No
$10 bill   Yes   No
$ 5 bill   Yes   No
$ 1 bill   Yes   No
Half-dollar   Yes   No
Quarter   Yes   No
Dime   Yes   No
Nickel   Yes   No
Penny   Yes   No

This approach has the distinct advantage of providing the important elements of behavior that yield information that can lead to specific training or remediation needs. If the answer to the question, Can John make change? is no, one could make an accurate prediction that John would not be able to function as a delivery person as long as making change remained a crucial task—neither would he be competent in most consumer transactions of everyday life. However, if this task were desirable enough to John for him to learn to make change, an individual criterion-referenced approach could be used effectively to pursue his level of knowledge and understanding of number concepts involved in the process of making change.

The individual criterion-referenced approach has not been developed commercially to any extent because of its inappropriateness for mass utilization and complex standardization problems. Practitioners have not used it extensively because of the demands it places on them to analyze and determine the basic elements of a given operation or task and its time-consuming aspects. These practical considerations must be acknowledged. However, this does not justify complete rejection of it as a viable source of individualized, concrete data that can yield tremendous benefits with people who are mentally and educationally handicapped. Power (1984) provided a good example of a general criterion-referenced test developed by John O. Willis in Appendix B of his book *A Guide to Vocational Assessment*, and Rudrud and others (1984) provided a similar procedure with their "community-referenced" assessment.

A final alternative to academic assessment is to use achievement test batteries that have been developed in past years for adult education populations, such as the *Tests of Adult Basic Education*, Forms 5 and 6, and Survey Form (California Test Bureau/McGraw-Hill, 1987). This particular test has three levels: Level D (difficult), Level M (medium), and Level E (easy). The essential feature of these adaptations is in social-interest level. Concepts oriented toward schoolchildren have been replaced by adult-oriented concepts. Level E omits language testing and tests only reading and arithmetic. It is intended for individuals with severe educational limitations and is geared for reading levels of grade 2 through beginning grade 4. This description is not intended as an endorsement, but serves only to point up an alternative that may provide some refinements in measurement efforts. This battery and others similar to it, such as the *Adult Basic Learning Examination* (Psychological Corporation, 1987), might provide some information pertaining to level of functioning and selection of materials. However, these tests provide very limited information about academic strengths, weaknesses, and progress. Another alternative is needed to answer these questions.

Error analysis and observation of response behaviors during academic-achievement assessment are clinical skills that should be used carefully. Inferences drawn from isolated errors or test behaviors would be highly inappropriate and unprofessional. However, it does not take a skilled clinician or psychometrist to infer that a student has test anxiety if he or she vomits every time he or she has to take a test or be evaluated. Cues from the student's methods of approaching assessment tasks, perseverance, unwillingness to ask for help, or excessive requests for help, lack of confidence by verbalizing expectations for failure or inadequacy and attention to a task are sometimes so apparent that teachers may legitimately make some inferences regarding the student's behavioral strengths and weaknesses under stress.

Evaluators can also make judgments as to ecological stimuli that may have a noticeable effect on individual learner preferences in a training or on-the-job setting. Dunn and Dunn (1978) identified four of these stimuli to which students may respond. These stimuli are *environmental* (sound, heat, light, humidity, and fumes); *emotional* (focus of control, motivation, anxiety, and enthusiasm); *sociological* (responses to supervisors, co-workers, customers, and group work versus individual); and *physical* (coordination, perceptual skills, and mobility). McCray (1982) suggested that students' individual learning styles or preferences come from students' response repertoires within and across these four categories of stimuli.

Patterns of behavior in intellectual or academic assessment, as well as in classroom observations, that indicate risk taking or nonrisk taking, bravado or shyness, and positive or negative outlook toward assigned tasks also provide important data about some of the values, attitudes, and habits of students that relate directly to functioning in life-career roles as student, family member, citizen, and worker.

Aptitude Tests

Test users who recognize the limitations of intelligence and achievement tests often turn to aptitude tests for predicting vocational success or occupational readiness. Neff (1966), some time ago, gave a lucid argument against wholesale acceptance and use of aptitude tests. In spite of the apparent "triumph of empirical logic" in the typical process of developing an aptitude test, he suggested pitfalls:

1. The method of test construction itself does not allow for changes in the characteristics of the labor force upon whose performance the criteria for aptitude tests are based.
2. The requirement that the standardization sample display wide variance in known work capacity is undermined at the outset because the supposedly objective criteria of work performance (for example, supervisor's ratings and measures of productivity) are notoriously unreliable.
3. There are crucial differences between the nature and demands of both the tests and the work situation.

Patterson (1964) also cited several other problem areas, especially those specific to performance aptitude tests: (1) the apparatus or materials used have never been adequately standardized for precision, durability, and interchangeability; (2) the tests have been standardized on adults (although manuals often state without evidence that the tests are appropriate for adolescents); and (3) many of the tests have little but face or "faith" validity because empirical validation is lacking or inadequate.

Aptitude tests are not routinely used in secondary special education programs, but those tests most commonly given in prevocational or vocational training programs are tests of manual skill and dexterity. This primary focus of interest with persons with disabilities may stem from the old belief that they are good with their hands. This is a stereotypical view and does not leave all options open. It is generally agreed, however, that the greatest occupational opportunities for youths with intellectual deficits are in the areas in which physical activity is more prevalent than mental activity. For this reason, the performance aptitude tests that are commonly used to assess manual and finger dexterity, speed, ability to follow directions, persistence, and so on have some direct applicability.

The following manual- and finger-dexterity tests are available and may be used with special-needs adolescents who have full use of their hands and arms:

1. Bennett Hand-Tool Dexterity Test (Bennett, 1965)
2. Crawford Small Parts Dexterity Test (Crawford & Crawford, 1956)
3. MacQuarrie Test for Mechanical Ability (MacQuarrie, 1943)
4. Minnesota Rate of Manipulation Test (Minnesota Employment Stabilization Research Institute, 1969)
5. Minnesota Spatial Relations Test (Paterson, Elliott, Anderson, Toops, & Heidbreder, 1979)
6. O'Connor Finger Dexterity Test (O'Connor, 1926)
7. O'Connor Tweezer Dexterity Test (O'Connor, 1928)
8. Pennsylvania BiManual Dexterity Test (Roberts, 1945)
9. Purdue Pegboard (Purdue Research Foundation, 1968)
10. Stromberg Dexterity Test (Stromberg, 1951)

Paper-and-pencil aptitude tests have the same limitations for use with youths who are mentally and educationally handicapped as do group intelligence and academic achievement tests. Reading becomes a confounding factor that distorts results relating to a person's potential to perform on these tests. Neff (1966) voiced the opinion and concern of many when he stated almost three decades ago that psychometric aptitude tests become entirely inappropriate when the issue is to appraise the work potential of an individual with certain problems. These problems can include chronic behavior disorders and a history of long-term hospitalization, a person with mental retardation with no work history, or a socially and culturally disadvantaged school dropout.

Psychometric aptitude testing does have value for adolescents with disabilities who have reading levels high enough to be able to take the tests. The predictive validity of aptitude tests is questionable, but there is a positive exploration and guidance function that may have as much benefit as the scores, and perhaps more. The most commonly used aptitude test in ninth and tenth grades is the Differential Aptitude Test (Bennett, Seashore, & Wesman, 1982). This test assesses verbal reasoning, numerical ability, abstract reasoning, space relations, mechanical reasoning, clerical speed and accuracy, spelling, and language usage.

"I think we'd better start with the physical skills inventory on this one."

If it is routinely administered in a school district, high school special education staff should ensure that all students are given the greatest accommodation possible in test directions and in responding to the test. Careful orientation of the students before the testing and individual interpretation and exploration of the results afterward are essential for positive outcomes.

The General Aptitude Test Battery (GATB) is a battery of performance and paper-and-pencil tests developed by the United States Employment Service (1982a) for job counseling and placement. Since many high school special education programs refer some or all of their students during some phase of the program to the state employment service, a discussion of this battery is considered appropriate. The GATB consists of 12 subtests yielding nine aptitude scores. The overall validity, however, is questionable due to reading demands (about eighth grade); the speed factor; lack of assessment in mechanical comprehension and reasoning; and the consistent reliance on multiple cutoff scores. Educationally disadvantaged youths from poverty and ghetto environments are likely to fare better than their peers from advantaged homes, but who are considered mentally handicapped. However, they will still suffer from some of the same problems discussed previously in other psychological tests. Schools may find that the GATB given on an individual basis is useful for individual planning. This is especially true for those who can read at least at the eighth-grade level, but automatic administration of it through group referrals to the state employment service is of questionable value for predicting success in vocational education programs or job placement.

The U.S. Employment Service published an alternative to the GATB in 1969 called the Nonreading Aptitude Test Battery (United States Employment Service, 1982b). It was originally developed for use with disadvantaged, hard-core unemployed persons who needed vocational assistance. It was also developed for those who could not take the GATB because of reading deficits or problems in following directions. The 1982 revision of the Nonreading Aptitude Test Battery (NATB) is a substantial improvement over the 1969 edition, according to the U.S. Employment Service. However, Power (1984) reported that it has been disappointing compared to the GATB. Many schools and other organizations, both public and private, have been authorized to use the NATB for counseling and research, but the test is not widely used in such settings or by the Employment Service itself. Information regarding release of the NATB for these purposes may be obtained from state employment services.

One of the few vocational aptitude tests developed specifically for high school students in special education is the Talent Assessment Program (TAP) (Talent Assessment, Inc., n.d.). This battery of aptitude tasks requires no reading and, unlike many aptitude tests, separates learning of the task from performance of the task by giving a practice period before timing. TAP stresses measurement of visual perception, manual dexterity, tactile discrimination, and visual retention of details within the general context of general and mechanical aptitude.

It was only a matter of time before computerized vocational aptitude tests would be available for use with special education students. Several are on the market now, and more are being developed. The Vocational Research Institute (1984)—developers of the JEVS, VITAS, and VIEWS commercial work-sample systems (see section on work samples later in this chapter)—has developed a computerized desktop console that tests cognitive, manipulative, and perceptual aptitudes. It is called APTICOM. APTICOM has 11 separate tests, 7 of which are presented on test panels. These include form perception, general learning ability, numerical reasoning, clerical perception, spatial perception, and verbal ability. The other 4 tests assess manual dexterity, finger dexterity, motor coordination, and eye-hand-foot coordination. It has the same assessment problems of all other vocational aptitude tests, however, and the computerization does not add any significant advantage in overcoming those problems. It does have the potential of sound adaptation for students who are print-handicapped and, may provide an easier response format for some students with physical disabilities. A more portable version of APTICOM developed by the Vocational Research Institute is the newer Vocational Transit.

Another computerized battery is the Microcomputer Evaluation and Screening Assessment (MESA) (Valpar International, n.d.). The MESA is a computerized vocational screening program that combines some of the features of aptitude test batteries, achievement tests, interest inventories, and commercial work samples. It contains 23 subtests, including assessment of academic skills, visual-motor perception and performance, reasoning, visual memory, visual acuity, vocational awareness and interests, physical capacity and mobility, following instructions, and problem solving. It requires no reading on the computer terminal, and there is a high level of student and evaluator interaction.

The Conover Company Limited (n.d.) produced a comprehensive vocational assessment system in its Microcomputer Evaluation of Career Areas (MECA). MECA is a series of work-sample simulations, using full-color graphics illustrating each step of every task of each work sample and using real tools for performing the tasks. The microcomputer software program administers the work-sample assessment through programmed instructions and graphics. A cassette control device can be used for low-reading and nonreading users. The system is organized by career area kits, with each kit consisting of three work samples and a learning-activity packet. These activity packets contain a variety of activities for the user to engage in that are related to the career area. MECA kits are available in several career areas, including automotive, building maintenance, graphic design, cosmetology, custodial housekeeping, electronics, small engines, food service, business and office, manufacturing, distribution, health care, construction, horticulture, and computers.

Interest Inventories

Because interests are basic to motivation for involvement in daily living, citizenship, occupational, and avocational activities, there is some value in trying to ascertain the scope and strength of high school special education students' interests. However, interest inventories are not necessarily the best or only ways to assess interests. Reviewers in Mitchell's *Ninth Mental Measurements Yearbook* (1985) are positive toward only two of the current interest inventories on the market: The Strong-Campbell Interest Inventory (Campbell & Hansen, 1981) and The Self-Directed Search (Form E) (Holland, 1985). Both of these instruments are designed for use with people of high school age and older and for those who have no reading deficits. The Self-Directed Search: A Guide to Educational and Vocational Planning is, unfortunately, a part of the Vocational Insight and Exploration Kit (Holland, 1979), which is not significantly more helpful in expanding users' vocational awareness than is the Self-Directed Search alone (Daniels, 1985). Elrod, Sorgenfrei, and Gibson (1991) found the Self-Directed Search to be helpful in promoting discussion and raising self-awareness levels with students with learning disabilities and behavior disorders. Although they have improved over the years to some degree, interest inventories are still viewed very critically, and even the best ones are recommended with caution.

If the giants of interest assessment are viewed so critically, how much confidence can be placed in the ones frequently recommended for the largest group among the disabled population— those with learning or behavioral handicaps? The commonly recommended interest measures for this group include the

AAMD-Becker Reading-Free Vocational Interest Inventory (Becker, 1975) and the Wide Range Interest and Opinion Test (Jastak & Jastak, 1974). Of these two, only the first one is viewed by test reviewers as having nearly enough assets to warrant its use. One of the reviewers of this single usable one (the AAMD-Becker) even stated, "Perhaps, just perhaps, vocational counseling clients, even if EMR [educable mentally retarded], should be *asked* what their vocational preferences are" (Domino, 1978, p. 1537). Another reviewer, in commenting on the pictorial approach, stated, "All of this in exchange for a relaxation of the necessity to read. Why not simply read to the inventory-taker the items of, say, Holland's (1973) The Self-Directed Search to gain this same benefit and have at hand all the advantages of its clarity, well-developed theoretical framework, associated research establishing its appropriate applications, and concurrent, discriminant, and predictive validity" (Zytowski, 1978, p. 1643).

The concerns that expert reviewers have about interest inventories revolve around the problem of massive usage without ever following the manual explicitly in interpreting the results. Most reviewers concede that the *process* a person goes through inventorying his or her interests is useful. The ultimate concern is that the *product* (test results) gets the emphasis, and the person is somehow subjected to the power of numbers and percentile ranks. This is not unlike the practice with other types of psychometric instruments, particularly intellectual and academic achievement tests. The latter generally have met the American Psychological Association guidelines for test development, however.

A relatively new alternative for interest assessment for low-reading or non-reading students is the Pictorial Inventory of Careers (PIC) (Talent Assessment, Inc., n.d.). The PIC is a unique interest assessment approach in that it uses 35-mm filmstrips rather than verbal statements or printed illustrations. The format consists of 119 scenes of actual work settings, and students are asked to respond to how they feel about the different work situations they view. PIC also presents 11 categories of environmental preferences from which the student may choose. The test results yield information on strong areas of interest, areas students dislike, and areas of little or no real work knowledge.

A more experiential approach to determining interests is the use of hands-on materials such as those in the Project Discovery Training System (Experience Education, n. d.) and the more recent Practical Arts Evaluation System (PAES) (Swisher & Clark, 1991). Both of these were developed as a series of vocational exploration modules. The systems have been modified to encourage their use in systematic vocational assessment. They are designed to give a quick, but valid, exposure to the typical duties, responsibilities, and work tasks of job or occupational areas. Students sometimes discover an interest in an area that they would never have indicated as an interest on an interest inventory or in an interview. If students have never heard of a job or have too little information about a job to be able to consider it as an interest, an assessment program can provide some exposure to broaden the students' base of experience. Field trips, job shadowing, job samples, films, and guest speakers are less formal than something like Project Discovery or PAES, but these can also serve this purpose.

In summary, the alternatives seem to be the following:

1. Use interest inventories selectively and with the assumption that they are useful only as gross screening devices and for structuring a process for self-study and guidance activities.
2. Use exploration activities (formal or informal) to give students an opportunity to experience work activities and environments about which they might know nothing.
3. Use direct interviews that provide another process approach to the goal of better decision making and goal setting through self-awareness.

Self-awareness will not come automatically for many adolescents with disabilities. The interviewer (teacher, counselor, or school psychometrist) plays a critical role in asking the appropriate questions and summarizing and interpreting the responses. The interviewer may use a standard interest checklist or an inventory such as the Gordon Occupational Checklist (Gordon, 1967), the U.S. Employment Service Interest Inventory (U.S. Dept. of Labor, 1982a), or the U.S. Employment Service Interest Check List (U.S. Department of Labor 1982c). A new, computerized interest survey, Career Assessment Survey Exploration (CASE) (American Assessment Corporation, n.d.) is a high-tech example of one of these; the Group Interest Sort (Harvest Educational Labs, n.d.) is another. A skilled interviewer with good rapport, however, can use an informal, conversational approach and elicit just as much information. Hill's (1983) process of indentifying occupational interests using paired comparisons is a good example of this approach. Again, the *process* is the critical idea to keep before the student, with constant reminders that the process of considering alternatives continues as long as one has a desire to do anything.

Personality Tests

It is not surprising that personality evaluations often have been given a low priority in professional work with special-needs populations. Intelligence level and academic achievement have been emphasized in schools in spite of the fact that personality factors often bring persons to the attention of teachers, psychologists, law enforcement officials, and the community. The low priority in the evaluation of personality characteristics and behavior is coupled with a similar approach in training. This skewed emphasis exists in spite of the evidence of more than three decades that documents the greater influence of personal, social, and emotional variables over intellectual and academic achievement in adult adjustment and vocational success (Kolstoe, 1961; Meadow & Trybus, 1979; Peck, Stephens, & Veldman, 1964; Rizzo & Zabel, 1988; Sacks, Tierney-Russell, Hirsch, & Bradon, 1992; Zigmond & Thornton, 1985).

Making a case for personality assessment is difficult because the same dilemmas are encountered as in previous evaluation areas. The challenge lies in trying to convince workers in the field to do the assessment and then reminding them how difficult it is to do. This very difficulty is one reason so little effort has been expended. Psychologists view the job as unrewarding because of the disappointing lack of instruments for personality evaluation, especially for youths with mental and educational handicaps. Reading level is an ever-present problem, poor oral communication skills affect attempts with measures not requiring reading, and the reliability of self-report is often not found.

Tests of personality generally include tests of attitudes, interests, opinions, and adjustment. As these tests are trying to determine how a person feels and acts, they are called *tests of typical performance*. The focus is turned from what a person can do or be to what he or she *is, does,* or *feels* typically. High school students may change in these areas frequently, so what is typical in regard to feelings or behavior becomes difficult to assess except in terms of any current stable patterns.

In personality assessment, the qualitative aspects of behavior are more important than the quantitative. In tests of ability or achievement, a high score is desirable, but in tests of typical performance or "personality," no particular response can be singled out as "good." For example, there is nothing inherently good about an interest in wanting to be associated with important people. There is nothing inherently bad about a male scoring high on sensitivity traits that are typically associated with females. Accurate descriptors of behavior, concerns, or feelings are what are important.

What educators are interested in is assessing characteristic behavior as the best clue to personal values, attitudes, habits, and human relationships. Most people would object to the assumption that a person's stated values and attitudes or observable habits are the total personality; new situations continually arise and a description of "typical" behavior does not indicate what an individual will do in a new situation.

Generally, though, reactions of persons in various situations are viewed as reflections of a more basic and consistent personality structure. The only means one has of inferring that there is such a structure is through behavior. Observing, assessing, and interpreting typical behavior is difficult, and success at doing these things has been varied. The typical approaches used to observe behavior can be categorized as *behavior observations, interviews, self-report devices, rating devices,* and *projectives.* It is not likely that clinical behavior observations or projective techniques will be needed in planning or providing training for most secondary special education students. Self-report devices, interviews, and rating instruments are more commonly used or available, so only they will be discussed here.

Self-Report Devices

Several points on self-report devices have been questioned and criticized since their initial use. Consider the following:

1. Faking is not only possible but probable.
2. Forced choice items such as "never," "seldom," "frequently," and "always" are particularly subject to individual response biases.

3. Items are frequently ambiguous or highly relative to certain situations (for example, "Do you make friends easily?").
4. Responses can be affected by temporary situations (mood, health, and so on).
5. Criteria for establishing validity are inadequate.

Concerns for the accuracy of self-report devices focus primarily on the use of these devices in diagnosing and classifying people. In these days of human and civil rights, one resists this type of invasion of privacy and pressure for a person to reveal himself or herself to others when the consequences of the responses may be negative, such as a restrictive type of placement or limited opportunity. However, if from a curriculum-based assessment perspective one sees social learning, insight, and emotional maturation as possible outcomes from assessment activities, then the devices take on a new perspective. For example, if a student's IEP calls for individual or small group counseling, teachers or counselors may use certain self-report devices to generate topic areas for discussion. Some of these devices are the Handicap Problems Inventory (Wright & Remmers, 1960), the Personal Problems Checklist for Adolescents (Psychological Assessment Resources, 1992), the Tennessee Self-Concept Scale (Fitts, 1965), the Coopersmith Self-Esteem Inventory (Coopersmith, 1981), and the Sixteen Personality Factors Questionnaire (16 PF), Form E (Institute for Personality and Ability Testing, n.d.). If such assessment activities are used in an instructional way and certain patterns of information emerge, then these assessment data are useful in planning future instruction and in making decisions about occupational training or placement and community involvement.

Interviews
Simpson (1981) described the interview as a major source of information in the assessment of adolescents with behavior problems. It is logical to assume that it should also be a prime technique with adolescents who have other handicapping conditions. The interview approach is a straightforward attempt to generate information that is helpful for both the interviewer and interviewee in making decisions. It is critical that the student being interviewed be a full participant in the process. That is, he or she should be told very candidly why the interview is taking place, how the information that comes out will be used, and what roles each participant in the process will play.

In an interview, a student may be asked to

1. Describe himself or herself.
2. Identify personal strengths and weaknesses.
3. Share goals, dreams, or fears.
4. Describe any specific or acute problem or concern.
5. Describe his or her feelings about the problem.
6. Describe how his or her family or the school relate to the problem.

The student should be encouraged to talk about his or her developmental, personality, and school history. He or she should be encouraged to talk about his or her likes and dislikes, interests, and goals for the future, as well as perceptions of his or her parents' goals for him or her. Power (1984) provided an excellent interview guide for difficult clients in Appendix A of his book A *Guide to Vocational Assessment.*

Information from an interview, like a self-report device, may be biased, inaccurate, or limited in value as a result of misinformation or insufficient information. The teacher, counselor, or school psychologist who does the interviewing needs to validate the information through follow-up interviews, parent interviews, or rating scales, with special attention given to any discrepancies in the data from the various sources.

Rating Devices

Rating devices attempt to assess an individual by way of a report from a second person who reacts to the individual personally. Does A consider B pleasant? Dependable? Honest? Stable? As with self-report devices, these second-person rating devices have a number of disadvantages. Among them are the following:

1. Unwillingness or hesitance of persons to make unfavorable judgments
2. Wide differences among raters in leniency or severity of rating
3. Tendency of raters to respond to person rated as a whole (halo effect)
4. Ambiguity of items in terms of the meaning of the attributes to be rated
5. Problems in scaling human behavior

Ratings can be made in narrative form through personality profiles, student descriptions, or letters of recommendation. Sociometrics is a form of a personality rating device, but it is not commonly used with adolescents. Finally, standardized rating scales are another option in rating devices. An example of one of the more frequently used in this area for this population is the Devereux Adolescent Behavior Rating Scale (Spivak & Haimes, 1967).

Interpretation of information obtained from the personality assessments just mentioned can stem from one or more of the following alternative assumptions:

1. The responses obtained are frank, candid reports of a student's typical behavior.
2. The responses obtained indicate the student's public self-concept (that is, they indicate the reputation the student would like to have) but have no concurrent validity from other assessments.
3. The responses obtained are not significant as facts but are accepted as a basis for dynamic interpretation. The interpreter assumes that every act of behavior is meaningful, even when it is inaccurate or inconsistent with other behavior or others' views of the behavior. When a student is

observed to be courteous and considerate of others, dependable, honest, and happy, but responds to the contrary on a self-report device, then the reason for viewing one's self negatively is more important than the item responses. In high school settings, the second and third of these interpretive assumptions are probably most useful.

In summary, personal and social assessment are important in evaluating a student's instructional needs in life-career development and transition— especially in the areas of values, attitudes, habits, and human relationships. Persons involved in making the evaluations must be aware that any self-report device or interview is limited when the student has (1) limited ability to read or hear the questions or items with understanding, (2) limited ability to express ideas verbally through speech or writing, (3) difficulty in reaching self-understanding, and (4) unwillingness to reveal himself or herself honestly. In rating procedures, the limitations of human errors in judgment are the evaluator's major source of frustration. But in spite of the feeling that one's hands are tied, secondary personnel should not surrender and wait for someone to provide a complete battery of personality devices that are valid and reliable. For almost any student about whom important questions have been raised, there is some device, procedure, or approach that can be used. Many of these assessment devices can be used for self-exploration and instructional purposes without obtaining or using scores and percentile ranks.

Adaptive Behavior Scales

Halpern, Lehmann, Irvin, and Heiry (1982) compiled an excellent review of adaptive behavior scales. Because such scales are used frequently with developmentally disabled populations, professionals in that field will be familiar with most of the commonly used ones. However, advocates for students with hearing impairments, visually impairments, learning disabilities, and behavior disorders should become aware of these scales and their potential for use with their respective populations. Among the 20 scales described and evaluated in their publication, the authors included the following for mildly to moderately handicapped persons:

1. Adaptive Behavior Scale for Children and Adults (Nihira, Foster, Shellhaas, & Leland, 1974)
2. Behavioral Characteristics Progression (VORT Corporation, n.d.)
3. Independent Living Behavior Checklist (Walls, Zane, & Thvedt, 1979)
4. Mid-Nebraska Mental Retardation Services Three Track System (Schalock, n.d.)
5. Progress Assessment Chart 2 (Pac Form 2) (Gunzburg, 1963–77)
6. Street Survival Skills Questionnaire (McCarron-Dial Systems, n.d.)

Others to consider are the Functional Assessment Inventory (Crewe & Athelstan, 1984), the Comprehensive Test of Adaptive Behavior (Adams, 1984), the Scales of Independent Behavior (Bruininks, Woodcock, Weatherman, & Hill, 1984), the Vineland Adaptive Behavior Scale (rev. ed.) (Sparrow, Balla, & Cicchetti, 1984), the Checklist of Adaptive Living Skills (Morreau & Bruininks, 1992), and the Transition Competence Battery for Deaf Adolescents and Young Adults (Bullis & Reiman, 1992).

These adaptive behavior scales assess a variety of career-development skills, including the following:

1. Basic developmental skills (sensory development, motor development, and cognitive development)
2. Survival mathematics
3. Survival reading
4. Communication
5. Knowledge of self
6. Emotional and personal adjustment
7. Social and interpersonal skills
8. Self-help and independent living skills
9. Consumer skills
10. Domestic skills
11. Health care
12. Knowledge of community
13. Job readiness
14. Vocational behavior
15. Social behavior on the job

Such a comprehensive array of competency areas so relevant to what life-career development and transition are all about is difficult to find in even 20 instruments, much less the 12 mentioned here as examples. It reminds professionals, though, of the many important life-career skills that might not be assessed in intelligence, academic achievement, aptitude, interest, or personality instruments. McGrew, Bruininks, and Thurlow (1992) demonstrated empirically a significant relationship between measures of adaptive functioning and several community adjustment dimensions. No one instrument will measure all skills, but selected scales, or even subscales, can be used to assess those skill areas related to decisions or questions for any individual student.

The most specific and comprehensive assessment procedure related to life skills and tied directly to a curriculum program is the Life Centered Career Education (LCCE) Knowledge and Performance Batteries (Brolin, 1992b). The LCCE batteries are curriculum-based assessment instruments designed to assess the career education knowledge and skills of special education students, especially those with mild intellectual and severe learning disabilities in grades 7 through 12. The LCCE Knowledge Battery is a standardized criterion-referenced instrument consisting of 200 multiple-choice questions for each of the domains of the LCCE model (Brolin, 1978, 1983, 1989) and the newly developed Life Centered Career Education Curriculum Program (Brolin, 1992a). There are 10 questions for each of the first 20 LCCE competencies. The LCCE Performance Battery is a nonstandardized, criterion-referenced instrument to assess critical life skills. It uses a combination of open-ended questions on worksheets and actual performance activities. The Performance Battery was developed because knowledge itself is not always a valid predictor of a student's ability to perform needed skills.

THE WORK-SAMPLE APPROACH

The work-sample technique grew out of a dissatisfaction with vocational aptitude testing and the traditional job analysis approach. Such dissatisfaction is understandable because people with disabilities are rarely, if ever, evaluated adequately through techniques that have been developed for the majority of the general population.

The basic premise of work sampling has been that if one is interested in determining whether a person can do something, the most practical way is to put the person to work doing the task under conditions as realistic as possible, but that still permit accurate and reliable observation. The refinement of the technique has drawn on the strongest assets of both job analysis and psychometric testing to bring about a situation that has the standardization and statistical strengths of psychometric testing and the personal observation of a person doing prescribed tasks of a job analysis. The logic of this premise seems unquestionable, and there still are many today who advocate it as the most useful approach.

There is no doubt that there are advantages to this approach. Sinick (1962), Neff (1966, 1977), and Overs (1968) very early on and Power (1984) and Hartlage (1987) more recently have suggested the following advantages of work sampling:

1. Work samples are concrete situations that are similar to or that reproduce the tasks or task elements required on a real job.
2. Persons respond more naturally to a meaningful task than to abstract, unfamiliar contents of tests.
3. Observation can be more extensive and lead to direct information rather than inferential judgments.
4. Work samples may eliminate cultural, educational, or language barriers that prohibit the use of any other approach.
5. Many prospective employers are more receptive to satisfactory work-sample performance than to test scores, profiles, or predictions from other sources.

High school special education and special-needs vocational education programs are using work samples increasingly across the nation in school classrooms, school prevocational centers, or through referral to available evaluation and rehabilitation centers. Users of this technique need to keep in mind some of the disadvantages of this approach, because there is still no research evidence to support it as the most decision-effective or cost-effective means of vocational evaluation for school-age populations.

Patterson (1964) has been one of its most severe critics, but others (Neff, 1977; Peterson, 1983; Thomas, Spangler, & Izutu, 1961; Zimmerman & Woo-Sam, 1987) have also pointed up some of its inadequacies. The following summary gives some of the weaknesses to consider:

1. Work samples are not the criteria for determining job success. They are still predictive devices and, as such, they need to be validated, as do any predictive measures. Validity and reliability evidence are still needed.
2. The choice of what work samples to use is subject to question, depending on the characteristics of the community, changes in the nature of jobs, and changes in the nature of task requirements.
3. Work samples can be expensive and time consuming and require constant revision and reconstruction.
4. Equipment may be cumbersome and restricted to an assessment center.
5. Evaluation from observation must be done by trained personnel who are aware of the importance of objectivity and standardization.
6. The primary objective of work sampling evaluation is quantity and quality of production. This negates the evidence that suggests personality factors are more important in job success than productivity for many people with disabilities.
7. Evaluation through work samples is typically a "one-shot" assessment and, as such, assumes aptitude or competency (or lack of the same) without controlling for the variables of motivation, learning, and experience.

Work samples are available through many commercial systems. These systems have been described in a number of publications (Bitter, 1979; Sitlington, 1979; Wright, 1980; Botterbusch, 1982; Brolin, 1982), so they will not be described here. The following sample listing indicates how many are now on the market. Costs for complete systems range from about $1,000 to more than $20,000.

1. Career Evaluation System (Hester, 1982)
2. Carrels for Hands-On Individualized Career Exploration—CHOICE (Career Research Corporation, n.d.)
3. Comprehensive Occupational Assessment and Training System—COATS (Prep, Inc., n.d.)
4. McCarron-Dial Work Evaluation System (McCarron & Dial, 1976)
5. Micro-Tower (Backman, n.d.)
6. Occupational Assessment/Evaluation System (Individualized Rehabilitation Programs, n.d.)

7. Philadelphia Jewish Employment and Vocational Service Work Sample System—JEVS (Jewish Employment and Vocational Service, n.d.)
8. Pre-Vocational Readiness Battery—Valpar 17 (Valpar International, n.d.)
9. Testing, Orientation, and Work Evaluation in Rehabilitation—TOWER (International Center for the Disabled, n.d.)
10. Valpar Component Work Sample Series (Valpar International, n.d.)
11. Vocational Evaluation System (Singer Educational Division, n.d.)
12. Vocational Information and Evaluation Work Samples—VIEWS (Vocational Research Institute, n.d.)
13. Vocational Interest Temperament and Aptitude System (Vocational Research Institute, n.d.)
14. Vocational Skills Assessment and Development Program (Brodhead-Garrett Company, n.d.)
15. Wide Range Employability Sample Test (Jastak & Jastak, 1973)

The relative success of work sampling over the past 20 years has led to its being viewed by many as synonymous with vocational evaluation. This is reinforced frequently in the literature on vocational evaluation, as work-sampling techniques are the focus of the entire process. Schneck (1981), McCray (1982), and Peterson (1983) have put work sampling into perspective for school settings and clearly identify the other important elements to vocational assessment beyond work sampling.

It might be helpful to discuss a terminology problem associated with work sampling. Some people use the terms *work samples* and *work sampling* to refer to evaluation procedures used in real work situations. These can be arranged in either competitive employment situations or subcontract work in sheltered employment situations. Schools sometimes rotate students through four to six work environments during the school year, systematically exposing them to real work settings. The students are evaluated primarily on their interest and aptitude in the various occupational areas, but equally important outcomes are occupational exposure and exploration. This is different from the work-sample concept embodied in the terminology and literature described in the first part of this section. The primary difference relates to the following characteristics of a work sample:

1. Careful selection based on generalized worker traits and skills
2. Structured from job analysis information
3. Provision of standardized instructions for moving through the sample
4. Maintenance of control over conditions
5. Opportunity for close observation and recording of performance

Sitlington and Wimmer (1978) proposed that *job sample* may be a more appropriate term for the informal sampling used in real work settings.

The most important distinction for school programs to make in the work-sample approach is the distinction between work samples designed to predict *trainability* and those designed to predict *employability*. Trainability samples are appropriate when entry-level performance of a job requires skill prerequisites that realistically cannot be taught in a brief orientation or through brief practice on the job. The work samples in this case would be comprised of factors that constitute the basic skills needed for the successful completion of *training*. The employability samples would be those developed for persons who need or are ready for immediate job placement opportunities. This typically includes entry-level jobs that require no special skills other than speed, concentration, eye-hand coordination, and finger or manual dexterity.

One reason the distinction between trainability and employability is important in school settings is because assessment occurs over time. Schools should begin a formal assessment process no later than age 14, or the eighth grade. The goals of planning and decision making differ, depending on whether the assessment is curriculum based (trainability) or focused on decisions regarding employment placement (employability). Using work-sampling procedures for determining trainability can be used to relate to what the school offers in the way of coursework or training. An example of this was described by Swisher and Clark (1991) with a middle school program called the Practical Arts Evaluation System (PAES). PAES was designed to provide assessment information to eighth-grade students, their parents, and school staff for the initial program placement phase of the curriculum-based vocational assessment process for the school district. The PAES model uses an exploration/assessment process that identifies student strengths and instructional needs in practical arts areas of business, home economics, and industrial arts. Generalizable but specific skills were identified in the course offerings of these three practical arts areas and 150 work-sample activities were developed to use in a classroom-based simulated work environment. Students are bused to the program from their home schools and spend up to 90 hours in a semester completing the sequence of work samples. The trainability questions derived for planning included the following:

1. What generalizable and specific skills can the student actually perform?
2. How much assistance is required by the student and what type of instructional intervention(s) will the student most likely need in his or her next prevocational or vocational experience?
3. What is the quality of the student's work at this time?
4. Is the student's work rate at a competitive level at this time?
5. What are the primary areas of student interest at this time?
6. What work behaviors need to be developed?

A similar kind of approach to trainability could be used with selected twelfth-grade students who are interested in postsecondary education or training after graduation rather than employment. Some commercial work samples provide a similar exploration/assessment option that can assist students and their families to make better decisions about choices for adult education, vocational and technical schools, specialized vocational programs, community colleges, or colleges and universities. If educators are ever to make an impact on the *level* of employment of persons with disabilities, we must start early in providing assessment and instructional programs that focus on prerequisite skills for training success in postsecondary education programs. Assuming that most students with disabilities at the middle or junior high school level or at the high school level will "discover" on their own information about their strengths and weaknesses, interests, or a higher level range of options open to them while still in school is naive.

Work samples may be purchased in complete systems or as separate components, or they may be developed locally. A combination of components and locally developed work samples may provide the best compromise, considering economic factors, personnel available, the nature of the population, and local job opportunities. When purchasing commercial work samples, McCray's (1980) *Suggested Guidelines for Evaluating Work Samples* should be consulted. If a school decides to develop its own work samples, the following steps suggested by Sitlington (1979) should be followed:

1. *Decide on samples to develop.* This involves conducting an informal survey of the community to determine which jobs are feasible for the specific handicapped population being served, then ascertaining whether work samples for some of these jobs have already been developed by someone else. Finally, it entails determining which job(s) can be most feasibly and realistically represented in a work-sample format.

2. *Conduct a job analysis.* Once a job has been selected, a detailed, accurate analysis must be conducted to include job tasks, work requirements, physical demands, and environmental conditions. The content validity of the work sample depends almost solely on this step.

3. *Design and construct the work sample.* The job tasks selected for inclusion in the sample must be based on their importance to the job and the feasibility of replicating them in the work sample. These tasks must then be sequenced, with necessary practice sessions and instructions included. Performance on the sample should be measured by number of correct products, number of errors, quality of work, or time required for completion, whichever element is most appropriate for the particular task.

4. *Write a work-sample manual.* For the work sample to be systematically administered and used by other professionals, a manual must be available. It should include two forms of specific instruction—(a) to be given to the individual and (b) to be followed by the evaluator. The Materials Development Center at the University of Wisconsin-Stout has designed a standard format for such a manual that allows agencies and individuals to use work samples developed by others.

5. *Establish norms.* Establishing and updating norms is an ongoing process. The groups with whom the person is going to be compared should be carefully selected and should reflect the population with whom the person who is disabled

will be competing for a job. Percentile scores or standard scores are most often used in establishing norm tables. More information on these methods can be found in any standard measurement text.

6. *Establish estimates of reliability and validity.* This step is one most often overlooked in self-developed work samples, but it is probably one of the most important. Elaborate statistical calculations do not have to be carried out, but it is necessary to see whether the scores obtained are consistent and if the sample measures what it purports to measure. Test-retest reliability is probably the most useful statistic in determining consistency. In terms of validity, it is most useful to determine whether the essential tasks or activities of the job itself are realistically included in the work sample and if individuals who do well on the sample perform well on the real job the sample represents (p. 6).

THE SITUATIONAL ASSESSMENT APPROACH

Situational assessment is probably the most common type of prevocational assessment used in high school occupational or prevocational programs. It has been viewed as an easier and, by some, a better assessment approach than standardized testing or work sampling. Whether or not any approach is easier, better, or more economical than another approach depends on the questions being asked and the importance of the answers. For that reason, it is important to know the nature and limitations of each approach so that appropriate assessment questions and realistic outcomes can be developed.

Situational assessment, because it has been associated with on-the-job training, is typically viewed as an approach that is limited to work situations. If the broader view of life-career education and transition is considered, however, there is no reason that the technique cannot be applied to types of career development and transition other than acquisition of occupational or work-related skills. For example, would not some assessment questions that are frequently posed in employment situations be just as appropriate in home, school, or community situations as on a job? Table 4.1 suggests that this is possible. Some types of academic assessment use a situational approach also when one considers how teachers require students to demonstrate specific skills or knowledge in the context of a written assignment, problem, or experiment.

What this suggests is that situational assessment is a technique for answering questions. It is not a technique limited to one performance site or one performance domain. The fact that most situational assessment for work-experience programs focuses only on work probably reflects no more than an assumption that work is the ultimate criterion for evaluating what high school special education is all about. We believe it is more than work and propose that any assessment area—personal-social, daily living, or job skills—should take advantage of the benefits of situational assessment.

TABLE 4.1 Situational Assessment Questions Applied in Multiple Situations

Situational Assessment Questions	Home		School		Community		Work	
	Yes	No	Yes	No	Yes	No	Yes	No
Can the person be a contributing member of the group?								
Can the person assume responsibility?								
Can the person conform to expected roles?								
Can the person relate to authority?								
Can the person get along with others?								
Can the person take supervision?								
Can the person perform his or her role independently?								
Does the person have self-confidence?								

Situational assessment, as a technique for any performance area, has the following benefits:

1. It provides the opportunity to observe and evaluate individuals in a natural setting or natural task where typical performance is more likely to be manifested than in a testing situation.
2. It provides a realism that cannot be duplicated in other assessment techniques in relation to environmental or situational factors.
3. It minimizes the anxiety produced by formal testing.
4. It allows the individual to be evaluated under different conditions, whether natural or manipulated.
5. It is much more likely to produce assessment results that are more curriculum referenced, leading to better instructional planning.
6. It provides a more realistic view of performance (*does* he or she? rather than *can* he or she?).
7. It provides the unique opportunity of training an individual at the time assessment occurs and within a real-life context.

The disadvantages of the technique are important to consider, also. Some disadvantages are the following:

1. Any one situation is not generalizable to all other situations.
2. Effectiveness is highly dependent on the accurate identification of relevant questions and appropriate data collection.
3. The technique is subject to error and bias because of the human factors involved in the observation, recording, and interpretation of behavior.
4. If a person exhibits inaccurate, inappropriate, or negatively valued behaviors in a situational assessment, it may be very difficult to sort out the critical variables involved.

Situational assessment can employ two main types of data collection: rating scales and functional behavior analysis. Each of these needs to be discussed because data-collection procedures are at the heart of validity and reliability issues in situational assessment.

Rating Scales

The situational approach is frequently based on evaluation by observation and rating of performance on a number of variables. It does not attempt to provide a simple division between those who can make it and those who cannot. Most persons in any role, regardless of ability or educational level, are in the majority on the continuum between those who can make it but have some problem areas and those who have many problems but manage to retain their role. The use of rating devices in the situational approach serves as a basis for describing where a given individual will fall on the continuum and provides information for training needs and placement decisions. Some examples of published rating scales for vocational behaviors are the following:

1. Vocational Behavior Checklist (Walls, Zane, & Werner, 1978)
2. Functional Assessment Inventory (Crewe & Athelstan, 1984)
3. San Francisco Vocational Competency Scale (Levine & Elzey, 1968)
4. Florida International Diagnostic-Prescriptive Vocational Competency Profile (Rosenberg & Tesolowski, 1979)
5. Prevocational Assessment and Curriculum Guide (Mithaug, 1981)

The Sioux Vocational School Social-Interpersonal Behavior Checklist (Bernstein, Van Soest, & Hansum, 1982) is an example of a published rating instrument for social and interpersonal behaviors. Most rating scales used in schools, however, are locally developed or unpublished scales obtained from other professionals.

The quality and value of a rating scale depend entirely on the quality and value of the variables being observed and the skill of the person doing the rating. Rating scales have long been criticized for their reliability problems, but they have been used frequently in spite of their inadequacies. Levine and Elzey (1966) provided the following suggestions for criteria in developing items for a rating scale:

1. The content of each item must be unidimensional. The various levels within an item must reflect different levels of competency for the same behavior.
2. Each item must permit scaling on at least four levels to permit fine discriminations of career competence among individuals.
3. There must be high agreement in the rank ordering of the levels within each item on the continuum of career competence.
4. The items must contain objective behavioral statements that are devoid of value judgments and do not reflect cultural orientations.
5. The items must contain behaviors that are directly observable by the supervisors in their contact with the ratees.
6. The items must contain behaviors that are appropriate to both sexes.
7. The items should be sensitive to detecting increments during the course of training.

Thorndike and Hagen (1969) agree in principle with these guidelines in their suggested steps to improve observational procedures. These include the following:

1. Select the skill or aspect of behavior to be observed.
2. Define the behaviors and levels of skill that are observed and evaluated.
3. Train those who will make the observations.
4. Make the observation of behaviors or performance quantifiable.

Behavior Analysis

The technology developed by professionals in the field of applied behavioral analysis has obvious implications for evaluation of skills and competencies in life-career roles. This technology lends itself particularly for assessment in training when continuous measurement of specific behaviors is needed. Whereas the evaluation approaches highlighted previously are used primarily as one-time or occasional assessments, the behavior-analysis approach includes frequent or even continuous assessments. Furthermore, whereas the basic approaches described previously are usually multidimensional, the behavioral approach usually focuses on only one or two behaviors at a time.

Agran (1986a, 1986b), Alberto and Troutman (1982), Bellamy, Peterson, and Close (1975), Brolin (1982), Dunn and Kruel (1976), Nickelsburg (1973), Sitlington (1979), and many others report the potential or demonstrated success of behavior-analysis procedures in assessment of people who have disabilities. The rationale and technology for this approach have been available for more than two decades (Pennypacker, Koenig, & Lindsley, 1972). The main obstacles to the use of such procedures have been a lack of technological expertise of educators in this approach and a professional commitment to this type of assessment. Frequently, the people who have the expertise use it for intervention. This does not take away the potential of the procedure for assessment information even though an intervention is being conducted (Sitlington, 1979). In fact, the demonstrated success of behavior-analysis procedures involving continuous assessment and continuous intervention procedures contributed to the current attention to curriculum-based assessment in vocational training (Cobb, 1983; Galagan, 1985; Peterson, 1985a; Phelps & McCarty, 1984; Stodden & Ianacone, 1981).

Situational assessment, then, can occur through observations and ratings or observations (continuous or time sampling) and counting frequencies of occurrence of specific behaviors. It can occur at home in daily living tasks or human relationship interactions, at school in academic or on-campus work tasks, or in the community in volunteer or on-the-job placements. It offers a unique means of observing and evaluating a student's performance in actual or near-actual life situations. The limitations of rating scales and raters are ever present, but situational assessment is the most effective means of evaluating certain individuals who are resistive to other types of measurement. However situational assessments are arranged, the type of situation employed for a given individual should be as carefully selected and planned as any other evaluation approach that has been discussed. The situational approach places a student so near the ultimate performance criteria to be predicted that failure can be much more threatening to the student, and potentially more misleading to the staff, than any of the other approaches.

MEDICAL APPRAISAL AND EVALUATION

For many years, educators have been attracted to and have experimented with the medical model (diagnosis, treatment, and prevention or cure). The lack of a sound knowledge base that permits education to follow what should be a simple process in applying the model to learning problems contributes largely to any widespread acceptance of it. The field of vocational rehabilitation has had similar problems in applying the model, but its close ties to medical centers and cases requiring medical treatment have resulted in a modified medical model approach to rehabilitation. Education can benefit from a closer tie to the medical model as well in the use of assessment.

The cooperative work-experience programs established by approximately 45 states in the 1960s and early 1970s were influenced by the rehabilitation model that places an emphasis on early medical appraisal. During the 1960s, schools required little or no medical information unless a student was known to have special health problems or a physical or sensory impairment. The medical examination reports required by state divisions of vocational rehabilitation frequently had significant information in them that teachers or other school personnel did not know. Vision problems, hearing loss, heart murmurs, low-grade infections, nutritional deficiencies, poor muscle tone, and unhealthy gums and teeth were common diagnoses. Some of these physical conditions had implications for occupational training and employment decisions, others for general health maintenance and appearance. Based on the contributions of this kind of assessment information, we support the use of a thorough general medical examination as a valuable supplement to other school assessments. A general medical examination should include an assessment of each of the areas discussed next. It will be obvious in most of the examination areas what the possible values and implications are, but some specific examples will also be given.

Vital Signs

The examining physician should carefully check the vital signs, including blood pressure (for hypertension), pulse (for murmurs, abnormal rhythms, and aneurysms), respiration (for rate and rhythm of breathing, clarity of lungs, and breath capacity), temperature (for low-grade infections and circulation), height, and weight. The height and weight factors are not critical ordinarily, but variations in expected weight for height and extremes in height and weight for age may be symptomatic of health problems. Anorexia, obesity, malnutrition, and abnormal growth caused by glandular malfunctions are examples of adolescent problems that may affect decisions in a school training program.

Medical History

A medical history can be extremely helpful to an examining physician if accurate data are available or can be provided by the student or an accompanying adult. Many youths who are mentally handicapped are not prepared to give accurate medical histories, and some students who are physically disabled may have such long and complex histories that they may have trouble remembering all the details accurately. Whenever possible, the general physical examination should be performed by the student's family physician so that histories are already on record. If there is no family physician, the school should assist the student and his or her parents in preparing to respond to questions about childhood illnesses, previous accidents or surgery, chronic health problems, physical complaints, and family health. In-school activities and home assignments may be helpful in preparing students for the examination and in assisting the examining physician.

Eyes
Vision screening might be administered periodically to elementary-level students in special education, but the chances are that screening has not occurred for three or more years for high school students. A recent vision test is important in making decisions about vocational training or placement and should be done at least once every three years. If a student wears eyeglasses, it is important to keep the prescription up to date. Tests of color vision are also desirable because of the necessity for color discrimination in some occupational settings.

Hearing

Routine examinations of the outer ear, ear canal, and tympanic membrane are important to detect any discharge, foreign objects, or obstructions in the ear. Group hearing tests may be administered periodically in some school districts, but tests should be done every year for high school special education students. Pure tone audiometry tests may not be available in a general physical examination, but physicians should perform some type of hearing test to determine whether more formal testing is needed.

Nose and Throat

The nose and throat are examined visually to detect clinical discoloration, deformities, inflammations, ulceration, suspicious masses, or irregularities. Frequently, this examination reveals dental problems in students who do not get periodic dental and physical examinations.

Cardiovascular System

A cardiac examination beyond the vital signs check is extremely useful in helping students make decisions about occupational alternatives that involve vigorous or prolonged activity. This is necessarily a screening effort only, but it is important. Heart rate and blood pressure should be measured before and after exercise. Palpation (examining by touch) and auscultation (examining by listening with a stethoscope) are basic procedures that should also be conducted.

Chest

Chest examinations may reveal problematic skeletal changes such as scoliosis (especially in adolescent girls), respiratory patterns, lung clarity, and chest disorders or disease. Tuberculin skin tests or chest X rays should be administered, but these should never be substituted for a physician's physical examination and correlation with medical history (Longenecker & Gillen, 1978). Some occupational areas, such as child care and food services, require a negative tuberculin test or X ray prior to placement. Obtaining results from these tests before placement can prevent embarrassment and inconvenience for everyone concerned, not to mention the important health information that positive results on such testing provide.

Neurologic System

Some neurologic data are gathered through a comprehensive examination, but there should be some specific tests of cranial nerves, the motor system, the sensory system, reflexes, and nerve tissue irritation. Neurologic functions are the critical bases for sensorimotor movements, perceptual-motor functions, and reflexes needed in coordinated activity for deliberate task activity, as well as spontaneous reactions to emergencies or hazardous stimuli. These functions are basic to all daily living and work tasks.

Musculoskeletal System

A musculoskeletal examination should focus on an inspection of all extremities, moving joints, the neck, the thorax, the spine, and the pelvis. Attention should be given to gait, anatomic configuration (posture and symmetry), and anatomic defects. Any restrictions in full range of movement or strength should be noted.

Laboratory Diagnosis

The general physical examination should provide the basic laboratory procedures of urinalysis and blood chemistry determinations. The primary purpose of these is general screening for disease detection, disease prevention, substance abuse, and, if the examination is performed by the student's family physician, continuing health care.

General

The physician may want to conduct additional examination procedures. For example, if the physician was aware that the examination was being done to determine the student's work activity potential, he or she would want to check male students' genitalia for hernia symptoms. Other specific procedures might include abdominal examination; examination of the head and neck; examination of skin for acne, eczema, and abnormal growths; or rectal examinations.

Summary

One of the strongest influences state divisions of vocational rehabilitation have had on public school programs upon entering into cooperative agreements has been the improvement of evaluation of physical status. Improved evaluation in this area has provided new avenues for evaluating not only job readiness and potential but also physical behaviors that might be interfering with school performance and expectations. Typically, the general medical examinations required and paid for by vocational rehabilitation agencies go beyond the medical statements required for special class placement in schools. More importantly, there is a strong emphasis on follow-up examinations by specialists when there is any indication that more information is desirable.

Many educators might question the importance of a medical examination and health assessment as part of a prevocational evaluation because of the time and expense involved. If they use the research data that point to personality factors rather than physical factors, as the crucial elements in adult adjustment as support for this position, then their argument falls apart. Evidence shows overwhelmingly the inextricable relationship of physical status to social and emotional behavior. For this reason, an effort should be made to include as much data as possible on physical status and capacity of each student being evaluated. Furthermore, an inappropriate placement that leads to the development or aggravation of some physical or health problem leaves the school and work training placement coordinator extremely vulnerable to liability suits if this type of evaluation has not been done.

The need for career and transition assessment has always been emphasized by those who have experienced the value of having good assessment data for decision making. These advocates are supported now by the explicit mandates in IDEA and the Carl D. Perkins Act, as well as an implied mandate in implementing the Americans with Disabilities Act. IDEA requires that transition services planning in the IEP be based on the *needs, preferences, and interests* of students and that, when appropriate, shall include a *functional evaluation* (IDEA, 20 U.S.C. 1401 (a)(19)). The Carl D. Perkins Vocational and Applied Technology Act of 1990 (PL 101-392) requires *career assessment*, guidance counseling, and career development activities for students with disabilities (Schwarz & Taymans, 1991). These activities are designed to help students in special education in selecting appropriate vocational programs, in determining what modifications might be needed for success, and in facilitating transition planning. The Americans with Disabilities Act prohibits discrimination in employment practices in terms of the denial of a person with a disability, demonstrating that there is a job match based on an assessment of the major job activities versus the individual's functional skills, an analysis of the essential functions of the job, and a determination of reasonable accommodation. *Functional assessment* of individuals and a *functional analysis* of the job are the procedures to use for job matching and exploring feasible accommodation options (Thomas, 1992).

The challenge of getting appropriate assessment information that is then used in developing annual goals and objectives on a student's IEP is one of the critical challenges for school psychologists, school diagnosticians, and special educators. Tables 4.2 and 4.3 present a variety of assessment information needed across an array of assessment procedure alternatives. Chapter 6 will present a way of using selected assessment information from such sources in developing transition services goals and objectives for an IEP.

A sound life-career and transition assessment program should be as carefully planned and developed as any other aspect of a high school special education program. Such a program should be based on some ideas, opinions, or principles that indicate what the high school staff expects of student assessment and what the limitations and sources of error in evaluation are. The program should be based on key questions that give direction to the entire process in terms of what one wants to find out and how to acquire such information.

No single approach to assessment and decision making is adequate. Because of serious deficiencies in most normative samples on standardized psychological and academic measures, the criterion-referenced and functional analysis of behavior approaches seem particularly appropriate for trial in a life-career and transition curriculum. The vocational assessment approaches in current use—such as psychological testing, work samples, and situational assessment—have unique features and should still be used systematically and purposefully with students when it is done by highly skilled and experienced examiners and when their uniqueness can be capitalized on at different stages. Botterbusch and Michael (1985) and Bolton (1987) provide excellent guides for anyone engaged in

TABLE 4.2 Multiple Approaches to Key Questions in Prevocational Evaluation

Key Questions	Personal Interview (Claimed)	Parent Interview (Reported)	Mental and/or Motor Testing	Job Analysis	Work Sample	Situational Assessment	Medical Evaluation
Interest	Yes	Yes	Yes	Yes	Yes	Yes	No
Aptitudes	Yes	Yes	Yes	Yes	Yes	Yes	No
Academic Achievement	No	No	Yes	Yes	No	No	No
Work Ability	Yes	Yes	Yes	Yes	Yes	Yes	No
Personal and Social Adjustment	Yes	Yes	Yes	Yes	Yes	Yes	No
Self-Confidence in Work Ability	Yes	Yes	Yes	Yes	Yes	Yes	No
Ability to Tolerate Pressures and Demands	Yes	Yes	Yes	Yes	Yes	Yes	Yes
Motivational and Incentive Values	Yes	Yes	Yes	No	Yes	Yes	No
Physical Capacity	No	No	Yes	Yes	Yes	Yes	Yes
Physical Condition	Yes	Yes	No	No	No	No	Yes
Physical Appearance	Yes	No	No	No	No	Yes	No
Personal History	Yes	Yes	Yes	No	No	No	Yes

TABLE 4.3 Transition Assessment Checklist

Transition Planning Areas	Have Info.	Need Info.	Comments
Career planning options			
Postsecondary options			
Employment/job training options			
Personal management needs			
Community participation options			
Self-advocacy needs			
Advocacy/legal services needs			
Socialization/friends			
Leisure/recreation needs			
Living arrangement options			
Transportation options			
Medical needs			
Insurance			
Financial or income assistance/support			
Independent living			
Other			

Plans:

Source: Developed by Mary Jo Becker Staab, McPherson County Special Education Cooperative, McPherson, KS. Used by permission.

the assessment of persons with various disabilities, including specific suggestions for test modifications that would be appropriate for persons with visual impairment, hearing impairment, and mental retardation. Medical appraisal should be a routine aspect of the total evaluation process.

CONCLUSION

The process of assessment and evaluation seems overwhelming when presented as an essential program goal. It must be remembered, however, that it is a gradual process that calls for varying types and degrees of information at different times in the high school program and that it need not be the total responsibility of any one person. It definitely is not a procedure that is done at a single point in time by one school staff member; it should involve all school staff at various times. At some points, it may even be an interagency effort (Squires, 1981). High school special education teachers, transition coordinators, or work experience coodinators will probably have the responsibility for coordinating the process and maintaining the records. But information can and should come from others who are oriented to the objectives of the program's assessment and evaluation process. These objectives should include the following:

1. Enhancing self-awareness in students
2. Enhancing awareness in parents of students' interests, abilities, and goals
3. Facilitating growth in students
4. Reducing anxieties in students and parents
5. Solving problems related to students' needs
6. Making decisions related to students' school programs and future options

Anyone interested in developing a comprehensive vocational assessment model for a life-career and transitional education curriculum should refer to the detailed descriptions of Bolton (1987), Halpern and co-workers (1982), Hursh and Kerns (1988), McCray (1982), Peterson (1985b, 1986), Power (1984), Roberts, Doty, Santleben, and Tang (1983), and Stodden, Meehan, Hodell, and Simpson-Ussery (1987a, 1987b).

5
Program Guidelines

The things taught in schools and colleges are not an education, but the means of education.—RALPH WALDO EMERSON

ACTIVITIES

- Analyze the provisions of PL 101-392 (the Carl D. Perkins Vocational and Applied Technology Education Act) for its application to vocational education for students with disabilities.
- Compare the advantages and disadvantages of the general education curriculum for students with different kinds of disabilities.
- Design a course providing an alternative unit of credit that would be better for students with disabilities in terms of life skills to replace an academic Carnegie unit.
- Design an alternative graduation program to the traditional academic program for students who need and choose a functional curriculum.
- Write a position paper taking a stand on inclusion in the regular academic program of a high school for students who cannot successfully achieve in that program with support.

INTRODUCTION

In an effort to provide the best educational experience possible in career and transition education for students with handicaps, educators have turned to many sources for information. Legal influences have played a dominant role, both in the form of lawsuits filed in behalf of students to ensure their legal rights and in the form of federal laws that specify the manner in which certain services will be provided to students. Research findings, educational theories, and practices suggested by experienced practitioners have been other sources of information.

Advances in learning theory have also had a considerable influence on educators, particularly as discoveries about brain functions have been reported. Such new discoveries have provided the impetus for the development of new materials, techniques, and procedures. Teaching techniques have changed rather substantially. However, the goals of education have remained constant ever since the educational reforms of the 1930s.

All these influences have had to mesh with the various policies or courses required for graduation that have dominated—and still dominate—high schools of today. Most curricular patterns still use the Carnegie unit of credit or some variation of it as the standard for determining eligibility for graduation. The method for earning those credits has been as integral to each course offering as has been the content. These social, political, and educational influences have together determined what kind of educational climate one will find in a high school curriculum today. The following sections will elaborate on the major influences on the high school system within which special education services and programs operate.

LEGAL INFLUENCES

Despite the best efforts many professionals made during the early years of special education, criticisms of special education programs were severe. Criticisms included not only concerns for program effectiveness but also concerns for diagnosis and classification, provision of related services, and denial of appropriate services to some populations. Ironically, in these criticisms, special educators have been accused of both sins of omission and sins of commission.

The transgressions in the early days were the failure to include children with severe handicaps in programs in the public schools. These students were excluded because their scores on various tests of intelligence were too low, the students were nonambulatory, or they could not toilet themselves. Schools in those days negated their responsibilities for serving such children. The schools claimed that the youngsters were too limited to learn much, particularly things of an academic nature. Criticisms of this neglect were translated into litigation.

Litigation

In 1973, the Pennsylvania Association for Retarded Citizens (PARC) sued the Commonwealth of Pennsylvania for excluding students with severe handicaps from public schools. In the settlement, the judge ruled that every handicapped child had a right to an appropriate education in the least restrictive environment. He also ruled that a school board could not claim it did not have enough money to provide services. In addition, he stated that every child was entitled to his or her fair share of any available funds. In short, the principle of opportunity was extended to include youths with severe handicaps. Some of these students have even been reclassified as having only moderate disabilities under more contemporary criteria.

Later, failures of omission became the focus of litigation on schools' failures to provide individualized programs and related services (*Rowley v. Board of Education of the Hendrick Hudson Central School District*, 1982). For example, high school students over the years have been denied access to occupational and vocational programs. In the 1980s, a common omission was the denial of appropriate education and of regular high school diplomas through the age of 21 (Kortering, Julnes, & Edgar, 1988).

Charges of "commission" sins alleged that a large number of youngsters were being misassigned to segregated classes for special students based exclusively on their IQ test scores. The tests were presumed to be discriminatory against youths from poor socioeconomic backgrounds. Thus, misassignment to special education programs was alleged to be a consequence (Lilly, 1970; MacMillan, 1977). To add validity to the charge, research in California by Mercer (1973) found that three times more African Americans and five times more Chicanos than their expected numbers as represented in the regular population were in special education classes. Lawsuits such as *Hobson v. Hansen* (1967), *Larry P. v. Riles* (1972), and *Diana v. State Board of Education of California* (1970) established the case for assignment to special education based on more criteria than an IQ score from a single test. The right of "due process of law" to be instituted whenever educational opportunity may be curtailed was firmly established.

Many other lawsuits pertaining to the rights of people with handicaps were heard and settled during the 1970s and 1980s. Nearly all of these cases dealt with some sin of omission or commission. All the cases upheld the spirit of the principles of opportunity and normalization, with the exception of the cases involving regular graduation diplomas (Kottering, Julnes, & Edgar, 1988).

Legislation

Follow-up studies beginning as early as the 1940s of young adult people with handicaps found a surprising number of them working at jobs for which they had received no prior training (Baller, Charles, & Miller, 1967; Brolin & Kolstoe, 1978;

Kennedy, 1962). Experience seemed more of a determiner of the kind of work the people were doing than any training program. Whether that claim is true or not, many individuals came to believe that people with disabilities were being trained for jobs requiring very low levels of skill and that the principle of opportunity was being violated. This indignation led to efforts toward corrective legislation that would ensure people with disabilities would have opportunities open to individuals without handicaps.

In 1963, Congress passed the Vocational Education Act (PL 88-210), which allowed individuals with handicaps to be served in vocational education classes. Not many students were served, however, until subsequent legislation affecting not only vocational education but also special education, federal labor programs, and vocational rehabilitation provided funds to support the programs and, in some cases, enforcement contingencies for schools that did not comply. Each of these laws deserves some discussion.

Vocational Education Amendments of 1968 (PL 90-576)

The amendments used basically the same definitions of *handicapped* as were presented in the 1963 legislation. However, because money was appropriated to implement the provisions, this act had a revolutionary impact on the world of vocational education. For example, each state was required to have an advisory committee (later called a state advisory board). This board was made up of representatives of parents, business, labor, special educators, teachers, and higher education and vocational education leaders appointed by the governor to monitor the plans and practices for compliance with the provisions of the act. The state plan had to describe how persons with handicaps would be served and how the funds allocated to the programs would be spent to help them. It had to show how local plans would be coordinated. A national advisory committee with a membership composition that paralleled the state committees was appointed by the president of the United States. This committee was meant to monitor the state plans and advise the president on the effectiveness of programs and the need for further legislation. If the state plans were not approved by the commissioner of Adult and Vocational Education, the states would receive no funds until they submitted satisfactory plans. This represented approximately 25 percent of the funds to which they would be entitled, so it was important to develop good plans. As a result, the advance planning that went into the development of the state plans was generally quite effective.

Congressional appropriations for funding the amendments were unusually high. The appropriations included 10 percent of all the state grant vocational education funds set aside to support programs for youths with disabilities and 15 percent to support programs for disadvantaged youths. To provide appropriate materials for the programs, a National Center for Vocational Education was established in close proximity to Ohio State University to support research and development of curricular materials for students who are handicapped and disadvantaged. The center was later authorized to support and evaluate programs in career education and to establish a center for advanced study.

The 1968 amendments had an immediate and profound effect in some states on improving opportunities for students with disabilities to participate in ongoing vocational education programs; this was milestone legislation for these students. Although it took some states as many as five years to develop programs within their states that cost as much money as the federal government was willing and able to provide, others used their full set-aside allotments immediately.

The Vocational Education Act Amendments of 1976 (PL 94-482)

In 1976, PL 94-482 funding patterns required the 10 percent set-aside funds to be matched with state and local funds. This was an obvious effort to keep school officials from substituting federal funds for local support of programs. The net effect of the act was an increase in funds available to support programs for students with disabilities, since most states wanted to maximize their federal grant potential and garnered state legislative support for matching appropriations.

Vocational instruction was defined in the regulations applicable to the legislation (*Federal Register*, October 12, 1977) as

(a) For the purpose of these regulations, vocational instruction means instruction which is designed upon its completion to prepare individuals for employment in a specific occupation or a cluster of closely related occupations in an occupational field, which is especially and particularly suited to the needs of those engaged in or preparing to engage in such occupation or occupations.

(b) Vocational instruction may include
  (1) Classroom instruction
  (2) Shop, laboratory, and classroom related field work
  (3) Programs providing occupational work experience and instructional aspects of apprenticeship programs subject to the provisions of Regulation 104.515
  (4) Remedial programs which are designed to enable individuals, including persons of limited English-speaking ability, to profit from instruction related to the occupation or occupations for which they are being trained by correcting whatever educational deficiencies or handicaps prevent them from benefitting from such instruction
  (5) Activities of vocational student organizations which are an integral part of the vocational instruction, subject to the provisions in Regulation 104.513

(c) Vocational instruction may be provided to either
  (1) Those preparing to enter an occupation upon the completion of the instruction; or
  (2) Those who have already entered an occupation but desire to upgrade or update their occupational skills and knowledge in order to achieve stability or advancement in employment.

The purpose of the act was to help improve vocational education, to overcome sex discrimination and sex stereotyping, and to provide part-time employment to enable youths and others who may need it to continue full-time training or retraining. The act even had a special provision that applied to the training of Native Americans. Of particular interest for special educators was the reference to participation in vocational student organizations (for example, Future Farmers of America, Distributive Education Clubs of America, and Vocational and Industrial Clubs of America) as vocational instruction. Even with advances in vocational education opportunities for students with disabilities with the 1963 and 1968 legislation, vocational club access had been limited.

To ensure that national priorities would be served, 10 percent of the allotment to the states had to be used to pay 50 percent of the cost of vocational programs for students with handicaps. Also, 20 percent of the allotment had to be used to pay 50 percent of the cost of programs for disadvantaged students, persons with limited English-speaking ability, and stipends for students with acute economic needs. It took 15 percent to pay 50 percent of the cost of postsecondary programs.

In summary, the 1976 amendments were passed with a clear intent to improve the planning, implementation, and evaluation of vocational education programs and to improve services to special populations.

The Carl D. Perkins Vocational Education Act of 1984 (PL 98-524)

The Carl D. Perkins Vocational Education Act of 1984 was the next major legislation affecting vocational programming for youths with handicaps. A study by David and Hendrickson (1981) of the implementation of the 1976 amendments in states across the nation revealed that states were making greater efforts to serve students with special needs. However, the interpretation of policies affecting the determination of excess costs and matching requirements were sometimes proving to be barriers to local education agencies in spending federal funds for special populations. The regulations of the 1976 amendments, then, appeared to be creating a financial disincentive for placing students with disabilities in regular vocational programs. This and other concerns led to the following major new provisions of the Carl D. Perkins Act:

1. Some 57 percent of the funds allocated to states for vocational education must be spent on special programs and services for special groups. These special groups include handicapped (10 percent), disadvantaged (22 percent), adults needing training or retraining (12 percent), single parents and displaced homemakers (8.5 percent), students in training for nontraditional occupations based on their sex (3.5 percent), and persons in correctional institutions (1 percent).

2. Annual federal appropriations to states for students who are handicapped and disadvantaged must be matched equally by state and local funding. These appropriations must be used exclusively to support the costs of special supplemental services or modified special programs for such students.

3. Local schools must provide their high school students who are handicapped and disadvantaged with certain services. These services include vocational assessment, special instructional services (adaptation of curricula, instruction,

equipment, and facilities), guidance, career-development activities, and counseling services to facilitate the students' transition from school to postschool opportunities.

4. Parents and guardians of students classified as handicapped or disadvantaged must be informed of the options available in vocational education programs at the high school level prior to the students' entering the ninth grade.

5. Local schools must coordinate programs and services for students with handicaps with their individual education programs and in the spirit of the least restrictive environment provisions of PL 94-142.

Carl D. Perkins Vocational Education and Applied Technology Act of 1990 (PL 101-392)

The 1990 Carl D. Perkins Act eliminated set-aside funding for students with disabilities as well as other special populations. Appropriations were directed to those programs that had the highest concentration of special populations. There was a clear mandate, however, that vocational education for students with disabilities be assured. These assurances, which are discussed in Chapter 7, included services that would offer the following:

1. Assistance to students in vocational programs in school to work transition
2. Assessment of student needs for making a successful completion of vocational programs in integrated settings
3. Supplementary services, including curriculum modification, classroom modification, supportive personnel, and instructional aids and devices
4. Guidance and counseling as well as career development activities
5. Counseling and instructional services designed to facilitate transition from school to postschool employment (American Vocational Association, 1990).

Under the provisions of the Carl D. Perkins Act of 1990, every local secondary school receiving Perkins funding must evaluate the effectiveness of all of its vocational-technical programs annually. During the evaluation, local programs must review and evaluate their progress as determined by statewide measures and standards of performance. Program reviews are to be conducted with the full participation of representatives of individuals who are members of special populations. The reviews will identify and adopt strategies to overcome barriers of access to vocational education programs or barriers to success in those programs. The reviews will also include the evaluation of progress of individuals who are members of special populations in vocational education programs (Coyle-Williams & Maddy-Bernstein, 1991).

The federal role in vocational education, particularly for students with disabilities, has increased dramatically since 1976. This increase is placing state and local education agencies in a position to provide many services that have not been available or provided previously. Whether or not state and local education agencies respond fully or not is still up to parents and advocates of students who have disabilities.

Work-Force Training

In December 1973, PL 93-203, the Comprehensive Employment and Training Act of 1973 (CETA), was passed to aid economically disadvantaged people with job training and employment opportunities. People with handicaps were included in the provisions with the passage of PL 95-524, the 1978 amendments. The amendments required that the master plan and the annual reports describe how people with disabilities were being served and how employers allowed part-time work, flex-time hours, and other arrangements for people with disabilities as well as other people who are unable to work full time.

CETA programs were required to be actively involved with agencies providing training and employment opportunities. As a result, many special education teachers used the CETA programs to further the training of their students by placing them in the programs after their special education resources were exhausted. The students most often placed in this manner were those who did not have either the skills or the maturity to go from school work-study programs directly into competitive employment.

As more comprehensive career education practices emerged, training opportunities gradually improved. This improvement was partly recognized by Congress in 1982 when the CETA program was replaced by PL 97-300, the Job Training Partnership Act. This act was specifically designed to serve disadvantaged people but it allowed up to 10 percent of the people served to be persons with disabilities, along with others who had encountered obstacles to employment. Established by local government or by adjacent government entities having populations of more than 200,000 people and being run by a private industry council made up of owners or chief executives of businesses and representatives of educational agencies, the councils could use the funds for the following:

1. Job search
2. Counseling, remedial education, and basic skills education
3. Institutional skill training
4. On-the-job training
5. Advanced career training
6. Programs to develop work habits
7. Literacy training
8. Work experiences
9. Vocational exploration
10. Follow-up services

A variety of other services were designed to meet the criteria of increased employment rates, increased earnings, and reduced welfare dependency. Wages for trainees could be supplemented by up to 50 percent by Job Training Partnership Act (1982) funds. The programs were not designed to attend to problems of persons with disabilities specifically. However, the law is a rich source of support and a welcome addition to the available resources for the training of students with disabilities at the secondary and postsecondary levels.

The Vocational Rehabilitation Act of 1973

In addition to legislation related to vocational education and training of the labor force, some exemplary laws have been passed that further support the principle of opportunity. For example, in 1973, Congress passed the Vocational Rehabilitation Act (PL 94-112). Although the law had many parts, the most important were Sections 503 and 504. Section 503 established not only federal policy but also federal leadership in the practices of hiring, training, advancement, and retention of qualified workers with disabilities. The provisions of Section 503 covered all governmental employment as well as any employer under contract to the federal government for more than $2,500. Under Section 503, qualified applicants with disabilities could not be discriminated against in hiring, selection for training, promotion, or retention. Every business or agency, under the law, must have an affirmative action plan for all employment openings. Also, any government contractor holding a contract for $50,000 or greater, or who has at least 50 employees, must develop and maintain an affirmative action program.

Section 504 affects vocational education or training opportunities for persons with disabilities and states, "No otherwise qualified handicapped individual in the United States, as defined in Section 7(6) shall, solely by reason of his handicap, be excluded from the participation in, be denied the benefits of, or be subjected to discrimination under any program or activity receiving Federal financial assistance." This excerpt clearly shows that the intent of the law is to provide nondiscriminatory access to programs, services, and employment. However, Section 504 goes even further in detailing state agencies' obligations directing them to take an aggressive role in developing state plans to promote both rehabilitation services and expand employment opportunities. This was a landmark piece of legislation in assuring the principle of opportunity to persons with disabilities both in and out of school.

Rehabilitation Act Amendments of 1986 (PL 99-506)

The 1986 Rehabilitation Act made few major amendments to previous legislation. It provided the continuing funding base for all federal-state vocational rehabilitation programs, basing the state allocations on populations and per capita income and the state-matching appropriations. Currently, states must fund at least one-fourth of all vocational rehabilitation programs in order to get a 75 percent federal match.

From a program service perspective, the 1986 amendments of the Rehabilitation Act introduced two new provisions that relate, though not directly, to secondary special education students. The first was the requirement that every individual receiving services of any kind must have an Individualized Written

Rehabilitation Program (IWRP). This was modeled to some extent after the IEP concept and was designed to provide a more carefully planned rehabilitation process. The second provision of note in PL 99-506 was the inclusion of support services, including supported employment programs and services, and an expanded array of support services that will further enable clients who are engaged in other services. These may include interpreter, note taking, and reader services; rehabilitation teaching; rehabilitation engineering; and orientation and mobility training.

Education for All Handicapped Children Act of 1975

The consummate legislation was the Education for All Handicapped Children Act (PL 94-142). Signed into law in November 1975, the law provided that for *all* children with disabilities to receive funds, a school system must make provisions for *all* children with disabilities to have a free and appropriate public education in the least restrictive environment. These provisions should be consistent with the child's educational needs and, insofar as possible, with the needs of children who have no handicaps. This has become the definitive word on the principle of opportunity and the recognition of the principle of normalization.

The principle of proof is not explicitly addressed, but the intent of the law is clear as it relates to individualized education programs. This is the provision that a written IEP must be prepared for each child who has a disability. The program must state the present levels of functioning, long- and short-term goals, services to be provided, and plans for initiating and evaluating the services. The evaluation of each child must be nondiscriminatory and made by a multidisciplinary team. Such a provision does not specify exactly what goals must be written, but it does specify that at least annually they must be evaluated to see what progress is being made in achieving the goals. Although the decision is still left to each school district to decide what individualized education program goals will be, that is certainly better than providing some services but having no idea what goals the services are supposed to serve. Furthermore, it is then possible to use a principle of proof, not necessarily to exclude students who are unable to meet the achievement standards of the IEP, but, more appropriately, to reexamine the goals to ensure that they are realistic for each person in the first place. An acceptable program is one that respects the assurance of equal opportunity for each person to work toward normalization, using the principle of proof for evaluation of progress. The program should readjust the goals or methods if either seems inappropriate to the welfare and development of the student. Phelps and Frasier (1988) pointed out that the least restrictive environment provision clearly suggests that for students of high school age, the least restrictive and most responsive environment includes vocationally related goals and objectives. We agree and add life-career development and transition goals and objectives as well.

The federal rules and regulations for PL 94-142 specifically state that both state and local education agencies must take steps to ensure that students with disabilities have available to them the variety of programs and services available to students who have no disabilities. These programs include industrial arts, home economics, and vocational education (*Federal Register*, August 23, 1977). The

Education for the Handicapped Act Amendments of 1983 (PL 98-199) extended the principle of opportunity for high school special education students even more. This was accomplished through the initiation of programs providing grants to develop model programs for secondary special education and transitional services.

Individuals with Disabilities Education Act of 1990 (PL 101-476)

The Individuals with Disabilities Education Act (IDEA) was the 1990 amendments for the initial Education of the Handicapped Act (PL 94-142). The major provisions of this act affecting secondary special education students have been or will be discussed in various appropriate other sections of this book. It is important to point out in this chapter on program guidelines that this is the first major amendment since the 1975 act that changed the IEP process and established a framework for closer collaboration with other agencies. It introduced and defined transition services in the context of school programs and services for students with disabilities who are 16 years of age and older, and, when appropriate, those 14 or 15 years of age. This act will be discussed in more detail in subsequent chapters.

Americans with Disabilities Act of 1990 (PL 101-336)

The Americans with Disabilities Act (ADA) gives civil rights protection to persons with disabilities in private sector employment, all public services, public accommodations, transportation, and telecommunications. Special educators need to be familiar with ADA since they work with students who will be seeking access to employment and independence in the community. Secondary special educators, particularly, need to be able to apprise students with disabilities and their families about their rights under the act. This responsibility has implications for curriculum content, guidance and counseling services, and parent information services.

The civil rights protection under ADA expands the scope of the provisions of Section 503 and Section 504 of the Rehabilitation Act of 1973. It has its limits in the private sector (it affects only employers with 15 or more employees), but it will have a major impact on public accommodations and telecommunications. Public accommodations include all those businesses and community services that are used every day by most people—restaurants, hotels, grocery stores, laundromats, parks, movie theaters, schools, public community agencies, and the like. Companies offering telephone service to the general public now have to offer continuous telephone relay services at regular telephone rates to anyone using telecommunication devices for people who are deaf.

Consequences of Litigation and Legislation

As administrators and school boards faced the legal consequences of excluding youngsters from services and programs because they had disabilities, efforts to correct the practice took on the extremes of excluding nobody, with little concern over whether the inclusions were benefiting the youngsters educationally. A "zero reject" model proposed to enforce the principle of opportunity for everyone and to suspend any judgments of suitability. However, it enforced no performance standards such as those associated with earning the right to continue in the education class, program, or experience. In short, the model required no principle of proof.

We know of one instance where a teenage youngster, who had mental retardation at such a level of severity that he had no language skills and could barely engage in imitative physical behavior, was transported from his institutional home to a nearby high school daily. There he sat in a resource room where the teacher's aide could get him to respond only to the most rudimentary form of a "pat-a-cake" game.

The program director explained that this youngster was being "mainstreamed" so he could benefit from contact with peers who had no disabilities away from the institution in which he lived. Pressed for further justification, the school personnel explained that they were avoiding a threatened lawsuit if the youngster was not served. Furthermore, in the opinion of the director, the peers with no disabilities were learning a lesson in compassion as they attempted to initiate contact either verbally or physically with the young man. Such procedures have been abetted by the publicity given by the Federal Office of Special Education and Rehabilitative Services to increase annually the number of youngsters with disabilities being served and to increase steadily the amounts of time spent in classes with their peers who are nondisabled.

Obviously, both state and federal laws intended to lead to increases in services and opportunities to participate in activities with peers who have no disabilities. However, the failure to include outcome data in the compliance reports makes it impossible to tell what effect the experiences have had on either the youngsters with disabilities or their peers who are nondisabled. So long as school personnel are not accountable for whether their students are making progress toward well-stated and reasonable educational goals, it is unlikely that outcome data will be generated, gathered, reported, and used to guide program improvements.

As school personnel administer the principle of opportunity to avoid real or possible lawsuits, while serving an ever-widening population of young people, a casualty of the legislative triumphs that brought about these opportunities may very well be the quality of the experiences given formerly excluded youngsters when the principle of proof is ignored. Although this dilemma is not resolved easily, a first step toward solving it is to recognize its existence while examining other avenues for clues to meaningful educational experiences. Eventually, however, outcome data will need to be gathered.

LEARNING THEORY INFLUENCES

Teaching principles that are fairly well established have emerged from the long association between psychologists and educators. Research on learning, validated by trial and error and trial and success, has led to the following understandings:

1. Learning proceeds more effectively when the teacher and the student work as partners, sharing the responsibility for the success of the activity.
2 If there is an immediate need to know or be able to do something, there is a greater interest in learning it.
3. When the student understands clearly what he or she is supossed to learn, and what he or she is supposed to do to learn it, misunderstandings are greatly reduced.
4. It is helpful to the student to be given instructions and materials that are uncomplicated by irrelevant information. Furthermore, if new materials are either associated with already learned information or provided in a format that allows grouping or organizing, the student can assign meaning to them easily.
5. The opportunity to use the information in a variety of ways makes it easier to remember. If the student can put the new information to use, it becomes much more meaningful than if it does not have immediate utility.
6. If there is frequent opportunity to use the newly acquired knowledge or skill, it is more likely to be retained.

There is nothing mysterious about these conditions of learning; they have emerged over a long period of time and seem to have universal applicability. It is helpful, however, to remember their importance if we, as educators, wish to enhance our students' chances for success. Effective teachers make use of these principles in their materials and methods on a daily basis almost as a matter of habit.

To become better teachers, however, educators are frequently forced back into a relationship with past, current, and emerging learning theory to try to better understand the complex relationships of instructional transactions between teachers and students. Innovation, guided by learning theory, moves educators beyond a quasi-technician level of operation in the classroom and closer to a professional level. Therefore, it seems prudent to search for some perspective in learning theory.

LEARNING THEORY PERSPECTIVES

Through the use of theories, psychologists have attempted to provide ways of explaining how people learn. These theories are principles that relate the variables involved in the phenomena of learning and, over the years, they have had an influence on teaching in schools. For example, behaviorism, as a school of psychological thought, became popular around 1915. This occurred when John B. Watson decided that only behaviors that could be observed, and therefore verified by other observers, were legitimate subjects of study. From his early efforts grew the techniques of classical conditioning and operant conditioning. Classical conditioning used a basic paradigm of a stimulus evoking a response (S-R).

The McGuffie Readers, popular in the late 1800s in teaching reading, used the technique of showing the word *cat* and prompting the response of the pupil saying the word correctly. Learning the multiplication tables is another example of the technique in operation. Learning was deemed to occur when the relationship between the stimulus and the response became stable and dependable. Operant conditioning also used the S-R paradigm, but according to that theory, learning occurred when a pleasurable or reinforcing consequence resulted from the response. The effect of the response, not just the repetition of the response, established the stable behavior. For over half a century, educators have depended on the basic S-R model and its variations to guide educational programs.

Classical behaviorists explained a learning handicap as a deficit in the development of S-R relationships. Whether the deficit occurred because of the handicap itself or because of restricted access to environmental stimuli was presumed to vary from person to person. In any event, failure to establish S-R relationships was the major consequence of limited experiences with stimuli.

Those theorists who explain behavior in terms of operant conditioning also point to a deficit. However, their explanation is in the person's response repertoire. In this case, inadequate behavior stems from not receiving the proper reinforcement to a response (Bijou, 1966). Whether the reinforcements are too few, inadequate, or inappropriate, the result is the same: failure to develop proper behavior patterns. The mechanism for controlling behavior is presumed to be the reflex arc. In this explanation, behavior occurs when the individual responds to some environmental event and the response is a satisfactory one.

Perhaps the most fundamental change in thinking is the belief that the reflex arc as a controlling mechanism of behavior cannot explain such behavior phenomena as mental illness, hypnosis, "freezing" under stress, or self-initiated behavior (Miller, Galanter, & Pribram, 1960). Rather than a direct link between a stimulus (S) and a response (R), it appears that an evaluation process occurs between the S and R. Incoming stimuli are monitored and selected for response based on some judgment the individual makes as to the usefulness of the response. Some writers (Bronson, 1983; Kolstoe, 1975b) have suggested that a feedback loop or servosystem is a more adequate mechanism for explaining behavior than is the reflex arc. They base this belief not only on communications information coming from the high-technology industries but also on brain research that has shed new light on how the brain works.

In the behaviorist framework, the brain was depicted as a passive organ responding to incoming stimuli detected and transmitted by sense organs. In the 1980s, Hart (1983) suggested that the opposite may be a more accurate description of its function: He believes the brain is an aggressive organ that actively scans the environment seeking stimuli to evaluate. It is believed to operate as a future-oriented, forward-feed mechanism, continually advancing in thinking with a built-in directive to jump to conclusions whether they are right or wrong. Information picked up by the brain is recycled by rehearsal and endless self-discussion to form new knowledge or relationships, which are immediately incorporated into the ongoing activity of the individual person.

Hart (1983) also stated that the brain has only one organizational form: a series of patterns or structures that control activities much like computers are programmed for different functions. That is, stimuli activate different areas of the brain through circuit gates that operate on a "go" or "no-go" basis, admitting or blocking sensory impulses that activate the programs. These program structures have been called *prosters* (an acronym developed by Hart from the words *program* and *structure*) and are believed to vary in complexity and flexibility. Basic behaviors such as breathing are simple and inflexible. More complex behaviors such as reading are forever changing in form and richness.

The right and left hemispheres of the brain are organized into the same prosters but are specialized for different kinds of thought. Typically, the left hemisphere is employed in symbol selection and manipulation, whereas the right brain more often deals with perception, analysis, choice, and creativity (Ornstein, 1972). Regardless of which mode of thought is used, the brain functions involve pattern analysis and the selection of behaviors by impulsive groupings rather than by disciplined, careful precision. Precision apparently is achieved as a result of feedback information from an ongoing activity relative to the effectiveness of the modes of behavior being used. Precision is achieved and employed in a nonimpulsive manner only after much experience. Practice does make perfect.

When the feedback loop is seen as a monitoring mechanism for controlling behavior, the individual is put in the position of being much more responsible for his or her behavior than if the reflex arc explanation is used. Miller, Galanter, and Pribram (1960) suggested that each person sets standards or expectations of activities in the form of plans of action. The plans may be as simple and transitory as getting up when an alarm clock rings, to as long term as scheduling activities for a day, a year, or a lifetime. The plan sets the course of activities for the person and establishes the expectations of what will constitute satisfactory, acceptable progress. Since the behavior is continuously monitored, a comparison between expected and actual outcomes determines whether the plan should be retained, modified, or replaced with some new, more appropriate plan. It employs formative or ongoing evaluations in a continuous fashion.

The monitoring mechanism described by Miller, Galanter, and Pribram (1960) is TOTE (test, operate, test, exit). The mechanism becomes activated when there is an incongruity between the standards or expectations implicit in a plan and information brought to the brain by thousands of sense impulses from the environment. Perceptual matches assure evaluation of information from all the sense modalities. Any incongruity (test) is an alerting signal that calls for some action (operate) to reduce the incongruity. The effect of the action is evaluated for its effectiveness even before the action is completed (test). If the incongruity is reduced or eliminated, the action is terminated (exit), and the individual continues to follow the new plan or the altered old plan.

The TOTE mechanism is a dynamic explanation of behavior, but homeostasis is sought as a condition, not from an absence of action, but of harmonious action between the ongoing activity of the person. He or she engages in behaviors consistent with the plans and feedback information on whether the behavior works (accomplishes the goal of the plan). It depicts the individual not as a relatively helpless victim of environmental influences, but as an active, self-directed being, evaluating his or her ongoing behavior. It also depicts the person as being able to do something substantive to affect the outcome of his or her activity. More important, the theory accounts for self-initiated behavior (*will*, if one prefers the philosophical term) and personal variability in behavior by recognizing that each person monitors his or her own behavior, a function not included in classical or operant conditioning explanations.

Insistence on including the organism in the learning paradigm has been basic to humanistic psychology for some time (Combs, 1962). However, there has been a dearth of information designed to formulate a new theoretical framework to explain learning. What has been contributed has been another element to the paradigm, so it is composed of three parts: the stimulus, organism, and response (S-O-R). Sometimes the reward or reinforcement may also be included, but the theory is basically behavioristic.

Sternberg (1985) attempted an analysis of the function of the organism in the S-O-R paradigm with his componential theory of intelligence. He confronted his research subjects with problems they had never seen before, then he analyzed the process they used to obtain solutions to the problems. Sternberg wondered about what people do when they do not know what to do. He ascribed the invention of a strategy to solve unfamiliar problems to "intelligence." He described "encoding" as the steps or components his experimental subjects went through to try to solve the problems. This was the action of trying to understand all of the elements of the problem and the nature of the problem. Mapping, the second step, was an attempt to arrange the elements in some kind of orderly fashion. Application, the third step, was the process of seeking a solution to the problem by using all the elements in some meaningful manner. The final step, evaluation, involved making a judgment as to whether the solution was correct.

Through a series of statistical eliminations, Sternberg determined the percentage of total time the subjects gave to encoding, mapping, application, and evaluation. His major finding was that the better problem solvers spent a proportionately greater amount of time on the encoding process. That is, they spent more time trying to understand the nature and elements of the problem than on the other processes of mapping, application, and evaluation.

Smith (1982) applied Sternberg's functional analysis techniques of an organism to subjects who were classified as mildly mentally retarded. While deficient in all the processes, the subjects were particularly incompetent in encoding and evaluation. They not only did not seem to understand the problems but they were unaware that they did not understand very well.

Wansart and DeRuiter (1982) used a variation of this procedure in their book on the psychology of learning disabilities. These investigators explained their findings in a theoretical formulation they described as *constructivism*. Their theory is that the ability to organize chaotic information meaningfully depends on the processes available to the subject to understand (encode) the problem when it is encountered. This theory, which is developmental in nature, is heavily influenced by the work of Jean Piaget. The basic requirement is the recognition of contradictory information in the problem. This reliance on the detection of incongruities before an action is taken and the subsequent evaluation of the consequences of the action provide a link with the subjective behaviorism of Miller, Galanter, and Pribram (1960). This research on process learning could have major implications for new teaching techniques.

Teaching Strategies Drawn from Learning Theory

The acceptance of the feedback-loop theory as central to learning encourages teachers and students to work as partners in the educational enterprise. The teacher is responsible primarily for providing the opportunity for the student to learn those things he or she will need to become an independent, self-managing adult. The student is responsible primarily for interacting with the learning environment to make the knowledge, skills, and behaviors a part of his or her prosters. Clearly, the teacher must be willing to help the student, but the student must likewise be willing to help himself or herself. For the program to be successful, a spirit of mutual responsibility must pervade the learning environment.

Teachers have the additional burden of making sure that learning tasks are fully understood before a student is asked to learn the information or task. Obviously, this calls for considerable ingenuity on the part of the teacher to select materials and present tasks that are understandable to the students. Teachers also have the responsibility of monitoring student progress so each student will be aware of his or her status in the learning process. This ongoing evaluation is mandatory if the student is going to alter his or her behavior in any meaningful way. Finally, of course, the teacher must be able to reinforce correct responses, encouraging the student to invest effort and time in the learning tasks.

CURRICULAR PATTERNS

In 1938, the Educational Policies Commission of the National Education Association presented a report that identified the goals of education as the following:

1. Self-realization
2. Human relationships
3. Economic efficiency
4. Civic responsibility

These goals, however, do not lend themselves to direct outcomes or indicators of program quality. The reforms in education related to outcomes education demand more specific goals.

The most clearly established and validated set of indicators of program quality for secondary special education are those developed and described by Dr. Andrew S. Halpern at the University of Oregon (Halpern, 1988, 1990). The standards of indicators of quality program outcomes were generated from two sources of information: (1) findings from the literature in the field and (2) a recent highly systematic statewide evaluation of secondary special education programs in Oregon. The literature in the field of secondary special education and transition programs over the years has identified four basic domains as the desired pillars of instruction: *academic, vocational, independent living*, and *social/ interpersonal knowledge and skills*. These student outcome indicators and related program characteristics indicators were validated in the Oregon study (Halpern & Benz, 1987) and in an independent external study by Darrow (1990). Halpern and associates have refined the set of indicators to address six major categories of standards: *curriculum and instruction, coordination and mainstreaming, transition, program documentation, administrative support*, and *adult services*. Adult services are beyond the scope and responsibility of school districts, so the indicators for that category are not applicable for schools.

Several states (Oregon, Washington, Nevada, Arizona, and Kansas) have already endorsed the Halpern indicators and standards for the development of a system for follow-along transition programs in their states' secondary special education programs and transition programs. The set of indicators and standards is accompanied by a system of assessment and data collection that makes the approach highly useful for program planning, program implementation, program evaluation, and, ultimately, program accreditation (particularly outcomes-based accreditation).

The procedures of the system are based on current trends in outcomes accreditation in several ways. First, the approach is based on self-evaluation rather than a third-party evaluation. Second, the focus of the assessment is structured around the concept of a set of program standards. Some of these standards are student outcome indicators, some are program-level characteristics or outcome indicators, and some are district-level characteristics or outcome indicators. Most importantly, the set of program standards is based on empirical data and not merely federal or state mandates or current fads in philosophical perspectives. Third, the process of program selection of critical outcome indicators or standards and assessment of them is locally referenced, or even building referenced. That is, needs vary from community to community and even from program to program in the same community. Finally, the assessment and evaluation process provides a foundation for program planning and program change. There is no reason for the results of the assessment to end up as merely a document that signifies some level of compliance or conformity to evaluation requirements. The data focus on needed actions.

The recommended specific indicators for secondary special education program approval in the areas of curriculum and instruction, coordination and mainstreaming, and transition are based on those currently in use in the Oregon

Community Transition Team Model Needs Assessment (Halpern & Nelson, 1990). The indicators that are relevant to and the responsibility of schools are as follows:

Curriculum and Instruction

1. Students with disabilities receive appropriate remedial academic instruction, which prepares them for functioning in their community, including the possibility of postsecondary education.
2. Students with disabilities receive appropriate vocational instruction, which prepares them for jobs in their community.
3. Students with disabilities receive appropriate instruction in independent living, which prepares them for functioning independently in their community.
4. Students with disabilities receive appropriate instruction in social/interpersonal skills, which prepares them for interacting effectively with people in their community.
5. Students with disabilities receive appropriate instruction in leisure and recreation skills, which prepares them for leisure opportunities within their community.
6. Community-based instruction is available as one option within the special education program offerings.
7. Instructional procedures for students with disabilities are designed to ensure that students can perform skills they have learned in new settings (generalization) and that they remember how to use their skills over time (maintenance).
8. Appropriate curriculum materials are available for providing instruction to students with disabilities.
9. Procedures exist for placing students into an instructional program that is tailored to their individual needs.

Coordination and Mainstreaming

10. Specific programs exist for facilitating the social integration of all students with disabilities.
11. Students with disabilities have opportunities to learn prerequisite skills that are needed to participate in the regular academic programs.
12. Students with disabilities have opportunities to learn prerequisite skills that are needed to participate in the regular vocational programs.
13. Teachers of regular academic courses are provided with assistance in adapting their instruction in order to meet the needs of students with disabilities.
14. Teachers of regular vocational courses are provided with assistance in adapting their instruction in order to meet the needs of students with disabilities.

15. A process exists for enhancing program planning and administrative collaboration between special education and the regular academic program.
16. A process exists for enhancing program planning and administrative collaboration between special education and the regular vocational education programs.

Transition

17. Information exists on community services currently available for school leavers with disabilities.
18. Transition goals are addressed as part of the planning process for students with disabilities.
19. A process exists for enhancing collaboration between special education and relevant adult agencies in order to facilitate successful transition of students.
20. Procedures exist for securing parents' involvement in the transition process for their child with a disability.

Curricula and instructional programs and policies have reflected many of these goals for years, but they differ in the content of the curricula to achieve the goals, the administrative and instructional environments used, and the degree of emphasis placed on various goals. Most schools still use an academic curriculum to achieve the 1938 National Education Association goals through such formal credit courses as English, mathematics, science, and social studies. Those schools would claim that self-realization and human relationship goals are achieved also in these courses. These goals are achieved through selected content (literature, social studies, and so on), human interactions in discussions and common experiences, development of confidence and self-esteem through success experiences, and the like. They would likely claim also that the tremendous amount of time and effort spent by students and faculty in extra-curricular activities are valid means of achieving those goals of self-realization and human relationships. Although there are some distinct curricular options or courses of study available in most comprehensive high schools, very few offer only a single-purpose program. Most offer combinations of options. However, the ones that are different enough to warrant being considered as unique are the following:

1. College preparatory or general education
2. Vocational-technical or fine arts
3. Cooperative education or work study

Even though the degree of overlap among these curricula is considerable because of common graduation requirements, there are differences of purpose, requirements, and assumptions that distinguish them from each other and pose special problems to some students with disabilities. The curricula are introduced here as primary curricula options.

College Preparatory or General Education

The oldest and most traditional of the curricular options, the college preparatory program offers a general education in the classical tradition. It evolved historically from the study of academic subjects presumed to be basic to the preparation of philosophers and theologians. Eventually, it evolved to include the present courses presumed to be germane to success in higher education and living in the modern world.

Consisting of classes in English, mathematics, science, social studies, and foreign languages, this option is often perceived as preparation for college, whether it is called that or not, because it provides a broad foundation of courses basic to similar academic areas available in college. Some state colleges and universities, for example, admit any high school graduate on the assumption that completion of this type of curriculum is adequate preparation. In fact, in small high schools where there is only one section taught of each basic academic course, everyone takes the same courses and is exposed to the same content. Only in larger high schools is there a real difference between college preparatory courses and general education courses. In the latter case, there is some justification for differentiating the two and considering them as two separate courses of study.

Whether presented as one or two tracks, a college preparatory or general education curriculum emphasizes the opportunities for self-realization and assumes that students have a certain degree of skill in self-instruction and independent thinking. Various elective courses may include the fine arts and special-interest areas, but seldom would students in this curriculum pursue work-study or life-skills classes as electives. Vocational education electives also would be infrequent, except in rural areas where electives are limited or in the case of those who aspire to become vocational teachers.

In high schools where college preparatory and general education are separate curricula, students with disabilities may opt for either one. Although they are similar in course titles and general subject matter, they differ in some substantive ways. For example, the college preparatory programs typically impose more rigorous standards in both content difficulty and level of performance expectations. In addition, advanced classes in the subject-matter areas often require a greater degree of individual student project work, including original research investigations and reports. In some college preparatory programs, it is even possible for students to take some classes for college credit. However, because both program options are often offered as only one array of course options, and since they both are designed to correspond directly to state guidelines for a high school diploma, they are described here as representing only one curriculum.

Because of the high cognitive demands of the classes, students with learning problems often have great difficulty in this curriculum. Academic rigor or pace of learning becomes an important consideration for students and their families in choosing a course of study. However, there is no question that some students receiving special education services can succeed in the academic or nonvocational curriculum. Although some compensation can be made for some sensory and motor deficits, unless communication can be well established, many students who have disabilities will need a great deal of support to succeed in this type of program. Chapter 6 offers some suggestions that can help students with disabilities compensate for their deficiencies.

An equally important consideration in choosing the regular high school curriculum that is either college preparatory or general education in nature is the content of the course of study available. Level of content difficulty and level of performance expectations are important considerations. But if the content is not relevant for meeting life-skill demands, this curriculum option is questionable from another viewpoint.

Moral, ethical, and legal issues are involved in imposing any curriculum option on a person. The school should not make the decision for any students; the students themselves and their families have that right and responsibility. What the school is obligated to do, however, is make clear what the outcomes of a college preparatory or general education course of study are and what kinds of expectations for performance go with the respective curricular choice. Furthermore, the school should provide the necessary diagnostic services to ensure reasonable predictive success in communicating with students and their families. They should determine whether or not the students have the prerequisites for handling a regular curriculum and how much and what kind of support is likely to be needed.

Vocational, Technical, and Fine Arts Education

Some of the same required general education courses mentioned previously are usually required in vocational, technical, and fine arts programs, but these courses may be modified to fit more nearly the objectives of the curricula. For example, report writing, business English, and personal correspondence may make up the English requirements. Math often is of the practical or business, machine shop, or consumer economics variety rather than basic algebra, geometry, trigonometry, or calculus. The general education classes (sometimes called vocationally related subjects) support the rest of the vocational education curriculum; they are specifically designed to help in the business, industrial, or consumer worlds the students will enter when they finish schooling.

Fine arts programs and vocational and technical programs will be offered as distinctly different programs in larger schools and are vastly different in many dimensions. However, the emphasis on the development of skills and the opportunities for advanced training or early occupational entry by the students are characteristic of both programs, and so they are presented here as one curricular pattern.

The classes in this curricular approach are more practical and applicable to life or occupational skills than are some other classes in the high school. However, students who are handicapped by cognitive, sensory, or motor deficits will need considerable help in finding ways to circumvent the obstacles to learning imposed by their handicaps. In addition, a student requires a rather high level of sensorimotor skill to become a highly skilled machinist, carpenter, typist, musician, or portrait painter, to name just a few. To what degree native talent plays a part in the development of these skills is uncertain. Yet, exceptional craftspersons, artists, and musicians are extremely rare. Many people fail to achieve outstanding performance, despite splendid opportunities and a great personal desire to succeed. When a disability is also present, some exceptional efforts may be required by the individual and others to overcome the obstacles. Fortunately, there are visible public examples around to remind students with disabilities, their parents, and educators of the success of such efforts by some individuals with disabilities.

Arguing the merits of career education

Cooperative Education or Work Study

Like the other options presented thus far, cooperative education and work study may be separate courses of study administered by vocational education or special education personnel, respectively. However, here they will be treated as one type. This curriculum combines study at school with practical experience working in the community as an intern or trainee in a job directly related to the school-based study. An example is a student who works as a salesperson after completing classes in sales techniques and marketing. Teacher training programs in college use a similar procedure when they require prospective teachers to spend several months in student-teaching placement in a classroom under the guidance of an experienced teacher prior to becoming certified to teach. The obvious strength of the curriculum is the combination of studying about a job and the opportunity to experience an actual job situation under the encouraging guidance of a mentor or supervisor.

In this curriculum, occupational adequacy is emphasized, but certainly not to the exclusion of the other goals of education. For students with disabilities, this curriculum has the advantage of allowing them to prove their capabilities in an environment cushioned by a supervisor who can be supportive of their efforts. Often, it allows the job experience to become the direct bridge to employment—a factor not usually present in the general education, college preparatory, vocational and technical, or fine arts curricula. In addition, it can provide the chance for failure to occur in a setting that will not jeopardize the entire career of the student. That is, the student is protected from the harshness of uncompromising job performance in a competitive job situation by the supportive efforts of the supervisor and, if necessary, by the chance to return to school for additional training for the job or some other job before graduating.

INSTRUCTIONAL SETTINGS

Amid the educational controversy of the 1960s and early 1970s, there emerged a variety of suggestions for ways of delivering services to students with disabilities. Dunn (1973) and Chaffin (1967) suggested systems that were similar. Although they differed in detail and nomenclature, they had in common a range of services characterized by the degree of opportunity for students with disabilities to have contact with peers who do not have disabilities and the number and kind of specialized services offered to them. The most normalized contact opportunities and the least amount of specialized services is typical of a regular classroom setting. Between these extremes of "most to least" contact and "least to most" specialized services are resource rooms, partly integrated (cooperative) special classes, segregated programs, and a variety of special schools or programs. At the high school level, the usual service delivery systems employed are those of self-contained classes, partly integrated special classes, resource rooms, and regular class placements with or without itinerant or consulting teacher support.

Within the framework of the integrated programs, academic credits, work-preparatory experiences, and learning skills for independent living provide the content areas that in varying degrees make up the individual education program for each special student. The various contributions to graduation requirements for each component of an integrated program approach often depend on local school district requirements. However, the major objective of the program should be to help the students become employable, self-managing adults.

Class Credit Requirements

Graduation from high school carries a common expectation that any person who has qualified for graduation in any program will have had certain experiences similar to those of any other person who is a high school graduate. It is assumed that the requirements for graduation are similar enough from school to school to assure a certain educational quality among and between graduates. Actually, the similarity of the requirements does not really go much beyond all schools requiring students to earn course credits. What educational experiences made it possible to earn those credits is very much a local matter.

Academics

The minimum number of Carnegie units needed to be earned for graduation in most states is 4.5 to 5 for each year of high school. This amount is increasing. Since 1975, 36 states have raised their academic unit requirements, with 23 of them currently being phased in. Within the 18–20+ required units are usually 4 of English, 2 or 3 of math, 2 of science, and 2 of history or government (Bodner, Clark, & Mellard, 1987). These 10 or 11 units, or "requireds," do not vary much in name from school to school. The variation in content, however, is enormous.

ENGLISH   English classes at the most academically rigorous level might include the study of classical literature, poetry, and composition. The students typically read and discuss the plot, meaning, and style of Chaucer, Shakespeare, the Brontes, Salinger, Twain, Hemingway, Steinbeck, Baldwin, and many contemporary American writers. The poetry of Poe, Burns, Dickinson, Frost, and Angelon might be analyzed and often memorized. Famous speeches such as Patrick Henry's speech on liberty, Washington's farewell to his troops, Lincoln's Gettysburg Address, Monroe's doctrine on the solidarity of the Americas, Kennedy's inaugural address, King's "I Have a Dream" on civil rights, and other examples of stylish prose might be treated in a manner similar to that accorded the poetic form.

In complementary fashion, each student is often required to write poetry, prose, descriptions, essays, and mood pieces that are analyzed, criticized, dissected, and revised within the framework of standard grammatical form and expressive artistry. Students study examples of the best writing to be found and then are challenged and encouraged to try to equal those examples. In secondary schools that advertise their academic rigor, this is the practice; and the rigor may even increase in the future.

However, most states still permit local school districts to exercise some discretion over the content of their curricular offerings. It has been common practice in high school special education and "basic" programs to allow English credit to be earned for classes such as business English, practical English, communications, and functional reading. These classes have as their focus the improvement of students' reading and writing skills at a level as basic as simple literacy for reading job manuals and writing simple reports and summaries. The intent is to prepare students to function as effectively as possible in the communicative life of an industrialized, business-oriented society.

MATHEMATICS   In mathematics at the most demanding academic levels, students are given the chance to learn algebra, geometry, trigonometry, and calculus. The requirements of the "pure," or basic, mathematic functions are usually minimum essentials for the application of those principles to work in scientific inquiry, economic problems, and technical and engineering models. At less rigorous levels in special or basic classes, applied or practical math may never touch on algebra, trigonometry, or calculus because other math functions are applied to solve problems dealing with time, measurement, and money. These math courses are designed to enhance the life-styles of the students or to prepare them for the world of business, industry, or agriculture. Practical math, consumer arithmetic, accounting and bookkeeping, economic and social sciences statistics, and basic computer programming provide alternative ways of earning math credits to satisfy basic requirements in some high schools.

SCIENCE   The sciences may offer students chances to study plants, animals, and human beings and the basic laws that govern their structure and functions. Botany, zoology, biology, chemistry, and physics are basic to working in all the sciences, including the applied sciences of medicine, dentistry, agriculture, and various forms of engineering and manufacturing. At more practical levels, classes in health, sex education, drug and alcohol abuse, and basic technology provide some alternatives for special education or basic science requirement content.

HISTORY AND GOVERNMENT   Historical studies in traditional curricula may include ancient history of any period such as pre-Christian, Medieval, Renaissance, and Exploration (New World and Colonial). Periods characterized by major events such as the Revolutionary War, Civil War, Industrial Revolution, World Wars I and II, the Westward Movement, civil liberties, the space age, and the computer age might also qualify for examination. In addition, social science, geography, political science, and civics are often included in history courses. The social science requirements may be divided into one credit for history and one credit for government. Whether these are separate, interdependent, or simply related is seldom germane to what may be included in the units of credit needed to fulfill the general requirement. That is typically a matter of local custom, and usually the acceptable alternatives are rather broad, as any of several classes are considered acceptable. This choice allows a great deal of flexibility for special education programming in selecting or offering functional content.

In some schools, the functional classes may be taken in lieu of the regular requirements in each area. Passing the courses allows students to earn the credits to meet graduation requirements in the academic areas. This policy may change nationally because of the trend among states to use minimum competency standards exams for determining successful completion of a high school program rather than simply the completion of course units (Bodner, Clark, & Mellard, 1987).

ELECTIVES   From the 8 or 9 elective Carnegie units needed for graduation left after the 10 to 11+ required units have been met, great variability between school districts exists. Generally, at least 4 electives may be earned in vocational classes. Among these classes, some are devoted to learning about jobs, whereas some are dedicated to teaching the skills or performance aspects of an occupation. Depending on the subject studied, the degree of rigor may vary from little to significant. For example, the study of electricity may range from simple wiring to designing electronic components for computers or video equipment. Abilities needed to be successful could range from just being able to connect wires and control units to understanding advanced mathematics and microchip circuitry.

Classes in vocational education are designed to teach the knowledge and skills needed to secure a job at a beginning level in some occupational group. (See Chapter 7 for a more detailed description of vocational education.) Referred to as entry-level skills, the actual requirements are fairly standard from one job to another, since they are determined by what kind of performance employers expect of employees, rather than by teachers or administrators in schools.

As stated earlier, vocational education courses are now supported by funds from the Carl D. Perkins Vocational and Applied Technology Education Act of 1990. Special materials, support services, curriculum and classroom modifications, and even entry requirements designed to allow students to learn those entry-level skills are made possible by the provisions of the law. Although this may not guarantee that the classes will be appropriate to the needs and abilities of the students, the laws and funding make such accommodations possible. To that extent, even though the actual requirements or standards of achievement may not be different for students with and without disabilities, the help available to students who are disabled can be rather substantial.

Usually half a unit of credit can be earned each year in classes that allow students to learn about jobs, with another half-unit from classes that teach the job skills. At the beginning level, classes in occupational information may introduce the job families within which a hierarchy of employment exists. These jobs frequently are in the U.S. Office of Education career clusters, such as the following:

1. Business and office
2. Agribusiness and natural resources
3. Public service
4. Environment

5. Communication and media
6. Hospitality and recreation
7. Manufacturing
8. Health-related occupations
9. Marketing and distribution
10. Marine science
11. Personal services
12. Construction
13. Transportation
14. Consumer and homemaking education
15. Fine arts and humanities

Occupational Analysis and Job Finding may appear as titles of classes or may simply be included as the content of a course with a different title. Quite often, information from vocational assessment determines which of the many occupational clusters or job families will be studied. However, the course content usually is fairly standard, with individualization on assignments.

Successful work behaviors are dependent on the work demands, the expectations of the supervisors, and the setting in which the work is performed. Despite the care exercised in preparing students for work, there is no substitute for the experience of actually working on one or several different jobs. Usually, one or two units of credit can be earned in actual work experience. Typically earned at from a quarter- to a half-unit per semester, the actual amount of credit may be similar from one school system to another but may vary considerably in content and standards of performance expected. Some high schools have a well-defined set of expectations that allow the students to progress through stages of experiences from highly structured to almost unsupervised. Others, unfortunately, have little or no structure and rarely set specific objectives for students.

Units of credit for elective classes students may take, other than the required and the vocational ones in the regular high school curriculum, are usually the same for all students. Whether the student has disabilities or not is seldom a consideration. For the most part, classes in art, music, home economics, health, physical education, social studies, the humanities, child care, or driver education have standard requirements. If any adjustments are made for students with disabilities, they may be in the form of aids or flexible time allowances. The quality of the work performed should be no less for students with disabilities than for students without disabilities.

Special class programs, and sometimes resource room programs, offer elective courses in independent living skills and social skills. These can include minicourses as well as semester-long or year-long courses in consumer skills, family living, community living, leisure-time skills, personal improvement, or human sexuality. In these classes, the requirements are carefully geared to recognize and adjust to the specific needs, abilities, and disabilities of the students, so standards vary considerably from school to school. What is unfortunate is that special education students who need a more functional curriculum are forced to take what they can get—usually in segregated classes or programs.

CONCLUSION

Since it was first proposed, the Carnegie unit of credit has been a common standard used to determine a student's requirements for a high school diploma. All students must meet the minimum requirements of units earned in academic, occupational, vocational, or other classes in whatever amount or pattern is prescribed by state or local school authorities and official accrediting agencies to be eligible for graduation.

Students with disabilities should be afforded the same opportunities for an education as youths who do not have disabilities, subject to the principle of proof as a standard of performance. The principles of opportunity and proof have shaped the directions of programs for students with disabilities. These principles have developed from professional practice, litigation, legislation, and theories of learning and instruction.

Modern educators now recognize the major role of the adolescent learner in the teacher-learner partnership. Good teachers probably have always geared their teaching strategies to the needs and characteristics of their students. It is a promising trend that learning theorists, such as the constructivists, are joining teachers in their quest for effective instructional procedures in which the learner is part of the learning paradigm.

All of these requirements are related to academic principles and instructional settings. They are related as they pertain to graduation requirements in academics, occupational information, vocational education, and other elective classes available in most high school programs.

Curricular options, instructional settings, and class credit requirements may have special appeal or meaning to students with disabilities and their families because of the requirements, standards, or relevancy of the content. Any curricular option, however, should be available to any student to take, subject to the satisfactory fulfilling of the class requirements. Obviously, some curricula are better handled by some students than others. Yet, everyone should have the same opportunity to take the classes and try to meet the performance standards needed to earn course credit. We look forward to the time when the general education curriculum and graduation requirements will acknowledge the importance of direct instruction in life skills and offer more functional content in all course options.

6
Methods and Materials

*The best teacher is not necessarily the one who possesses the most knowledge
but the one who most effectively enables his students to believe in their ability
to learn.*—NORMAN COUSINS

ACTIVITIES

- Write an individual education plan (IEP) objective to teach a value,
attitude, or habit. Use Figure 6.1 as a guide, showing entering, en route,
and terminal behavioral objective statements.
- Develop a list of short stories that feature persons with disabilities as
role models; the stories should be suitable to read in an English class.
- Select a science concept and prepare a lesson plan using a functional
approach to teach the concept.
- Develop a roleplaying incident to solve a problem involving two students who have gotten into a disagreement. One student has a disability
and the other does not.
- Examine different software programs to determine what modifications
need to be made to allow students with various disabilities to use them.

INTRODUCTION

Although Carnegie unit requirements provide the guidelines within which a high school instructional program exists, the guiding element for students with disabilities should be the individual educational program (IEP). It was first stipulated at a national level with the enactment of PL 94-142, the Education for All Handicapped Children Act of 1975, but it has been basic to the individualization of instruction in special education since the earliest recorded history of education (Itard, 1932; Fisher, 1913) and is the most important part of the program.

Every student should have a thorough assessment of his or her abilities, attitudes, interests, and achievements, and from this information the IEP should be constructed and methods and materials selected. Chapter 4 includes a reference to curriculum-based assessment and describes a variety of assessment procedures that could be used in developing instructional objectives for students' IEPs and goals for the program's curriculum focus.

INSTRUCTIONAL OBJECTIVES AND THE IEP

The requirement in PL 94-142 for an IEP for all children and youths with disabilities changed the shape of educational policy and practice in the mid-1970s. The spirit of congressional intent, however, has not been met adequately in relation to appropriate education (Smith & Simpson, 1989; Smith, 1990). Annual goals and objectives have been based more often on the nature of existing programs than on individual needs and preferences. The amendments in the Individuals with Disabilities Education Act (IDEA) were an attempt to provide for adolescents with disabilities—at least a tightening of the statutes and regulations to ensure that individualization is addressed more specifically.

The latest change in the nature of the IEP comes in new language and a new component of the IEP. One new component in IDEA is that the IEP must include "a statement of the needed transition services for students beginning no later than age 16 and annually thereafter (and when determined appropriate for the individual, beginning at age 14 or younger), including, when appropriate, a statement of the interagency responsibilities or linkages (or both) before the student leaves the school setting" [20 U.S.C. 1401 (e)(1)(D)]. The regulations specified that all transition goals and objectives should be entered on a student's IEP. These goals should address the needed match between graduation requirements and postschool outcomes such as postsecondary education, vocational training, integrated employment, and community living, and should include socialization skills for each of these outcome environments. The regulations also required that annual transition goals should be supported by transition services language that would include instruction, community experiences, development of employment, and appropriate interagency linkages. In a departure from previous legislative and regulatory language, the IDEA regulations gave examples of transition goal areas, including work-related behaviors, independent living skills, transportation skills, grooming, and other skills that target a person's employability and success in the community as an adult.

An annual IEP goal is usually supported by two or more short-term objectives that are stated in measurable terms. Whether one accepts the precepts of the operant behaviorist or not, those theorists have been largely responsible for the contribution of formulating objectives that are stated in terms of behaviors that can be observed. This practice has set the standard for the IEP. This is not to deny that objectives that are not readily observable may not be important; it is just that the evaluation of subjective feelings, values, and attitudes is not only difficult to do but the evaluation is derived largely from inferences. Since IEPs require objectives that can be evaluated at least annually, it is only prudent to develop objectives that require a performance that can be observed and therefore are amenable to objective rather than subjective evaluation.

An annual educational goal can be developed from any aspect of the student's needs. Educational goals consist of two or more educational objectives that have a clear relationship to each other. Learning the names or sounds of letters of the alphabet is an example of an educational goal. Learning the sounds of the letters and learning letter combinations are but two objectives to be realized before a person achieves the goal of learning to read.

A behavioral objective is any objective that can be stated in terms of some action that can be observed and evaluated. A behavioral objective has three components: content, conditions, and criteria. For instance, a behavioral objective related to learning the name of the letter R could be stated: "When shown the letter R (the content) and asked to give the name of the letter (the condition), the student will respond with the correct name every time (criteria) it is presented."

The process of arriving at a short-term objective for an IEP is one that considers the *entering behavior* of a student, the *en route behaviors* that must take place to reach intermediate behaviors, and the *terminal objective* you want the student to achieve. An instructional program is developed by laying out a hierarchy of behavioral objectives that start with the highest level at which a learner succeeds (entering behavior) and proceeds in ascending order of difficulty (en route behavior) until the instructional program is achieved (terminal objective) (Gronlund, 1970; Mager, 1968).

An IEP should be finalized in an IEP meeting. This meeting should include the student, one or both parents (guardians or advocates), a local education agency representative, one or more teachers to be involved with the student, and any related services staff. The intent of Congress and the final regulations for implementing IDEA were very clear on the importance of student participation. Students must be invited to participate in the IEP process by providing direct input in the IEP assessment and planning stages with the staff as well as participating in the IEP meeting. Schools must document that they have invited the student and considered the student's needs, preferences, and interests in the goals that are established.

In the past, schools have frequently dealt with the logistical demands of IEP preparation by having one person—typically the teacher most familiar with the student—assume responsibility for preparing the proposed IEP goals and objectives prior to the IEP meeting. Experience since 1978 has shown that high school students and their parents seldom had input into those proposals (Mithaug, Martin, Agran, & Rusch, 1988). Smith (1990) referred to this unfortunate practice as an evolution of the intended IEP process of participation to a process of acquiescence.

Knowing that some compromises must be made because of logistical problems and the difficulty of meeting both the letter and spirit of the law regarding parent participation in IEP conferences, we recommend that every high school student should work with the teacher responsible for preparing the IEP. That process should make it easier for students to participate in their own IEP conferences when parents and school representatives get together. This serves as a secondary benefit to increasing the students' awareness of their needs and developing skills in self-advocacy, problem solving, and decision making.

The IEP must be a written plan that includes the following:

1. The present level of functioning for each performance area addressed

"The first major competencies we shall cover in this unit are..."

2. Annual goals and short-term instructional objectives, including a statement of needed transition services
3. Specific educational and related services to be provided
4. The extent to which the student will be able to participate in regular educational programs
5. The date for initiation of the services and the anticipated duration of services
6. The objective criteria and evaluation procedures
7. Schedules for determining annually whether the instructional objectives are being achieved
8. When appropriate, a statement of the interagency linkages needed, including name of contact person(s) and responsibilities

The statement of transition needs should come out of information from the transition assessment process. The statement should include both a long-term transition goal and a needs statement that relates to the goal. The long-term transition goal is individualized and futuristic to establish a postschool vision for the student. As such, it should focus on desired postschool outcomes related to future living, working, social, and educational environments. The long-term goal and needs statement may be built into the IEP form that a district uses or it can be a brief narrative statement attached to the IEP.

An example of a long-term goal and needs statement for Annie Sherwood (see case study in Chapter 3, pp. 85–86) might look like this:

> The long-term goal for Annie is that she will be employed without ongoing support in competitive employment. She hopes to get married and live in an apartment near her work so she can walk or use public transportation. She hopes to be able to have children and be a good mother. Annie needs to continue her work in reading and math since her motivation is still strong. She may need to switch from remedial to compensatory interventions if there is no progress this year. She needs to have practical applications for consumer reading and math and life skills instruction in personal hygiene, grooming, and sexuality. She also needs specific social skills training on social communication skills (verbal and nonverbal) and some type of instructional activity or strategy that will help her to improve her self-esteem and self-confidence.

Multiple needs like these for Annie might need to be stated in terms of knowledge and skills required for reaching the long-term goals, specific planning or action steps, or both. Not all transition services needs translate into IEP annual goals and objectives. Planning or actions that need to be taken by the student, the family, the school, or an agency outside the school should not be stated as IEP goals or objectives, but rather as staffing notes or action statements that can be written on or attached to the IEP form.

Because every high school student receiving special education should be given every possible opportunity to meet the qualifications for graduation, the state or local high school graduation standards will guide the development of the

IEP to a degree. The career development and transition education model proposed in this book poses problems for some regular and special education professionals when various interpretations of graduation requirements put the model and the graduation requirements in real or apparent conflict. We concur with Edgar (1987, 1988) that it is difficult to be convinced that the current educational system for high schools is producing the outcomes that it should. Too often, either a rigid insistence on completing traditional academic requirements or an amorphous compromise to provide "functional academics" is the option selected. The former is questionable as relevant, and the latter ends up with instructional content lacking in academic or functional integrity. Both of these approaches ignore the educational principle of starting an instructional program with assessed entry behaviors and needs and then developing the program approach best designed to achieve the goals of the program.

The assessment instruments and procedures discussed in Chapter 4 can provide the entry-level behaviors in each area. Entry-level behaviors are the highest level of successful performance in a hierarchy of skills in any area. The IEP should use the success behavior as the entering behavior rather than the next level of behavior—the point at which the person fails in the hierarchy. The success behavior is the first of the en route behaviors that will lead to mastery or the terminal objective of the skill.

The content of the program should be provided by the curriculum of the school and the syllabus of each class. However, many authors have developed lists of competencies needed by people to become successfully employed, self-managing adults. These lists can be used as a guide in the absence of a curriculum focus or when there is concern about the appropriateness of courses required for graduation.

Kokaska and Brolin (1985) described three curricular areas: daily living skills, personal-social skills, and occupational guidance and preparation, which encompass 22 competencies and 97 subcompetencies. Each competency is achieved through the mastery of 3 to 7 subcompetencies that are arranged in a hierarchy from simplest to most complex, and these can be used to develop an IEP. An IEP comprised of 1 or more competencies requires finding the level of skill in each subcompetency group. Then a plan would be developed to teach each subcompetency until all the competencies are achieved. For example, the curriculum area of occupational guidance and preparation, competency number 19 (actually the third of 6 competencies in the area), requires "Exhibiting appropriate work habits and behaviors." The simplest subcompetency is "Follows directions" (number 87). At the next higher level is "Works with others" (88), followed by "Works at a satisfactory rate" (89), "Accepts supervision" (90), "Recognizes the importance of attendance and punctuality" (91), "Meets demands for quality work" (92), and "Demonstrates occupational safety" (93). In this example, the terminal objective could be written: "In a work situation (condition), the person demonstrates the skills required to perform the work required and the work behaviors appropriate to the job (content) consistently *over the duration of the one semester (criteria)."*

The entering behavior could be described: "Given uncomplicated directions to follow, the person will carry out the instructions with no further cues from anyone." En route behavior would follow the same form (content, conditions, and criteria) for each of the subcompetencies in the hierarchy: works with others, works at a satisfactory rate, accepts supervision, recognizes the importance of attendance and punctuality, meets demands for quality work, and demonstrates occupational safety, until the person demonstrates mastery of the terminal objective. Figure 6.1 presents an example of the IEP just described.

Since the instructional objectives need to be specified in each class or experience area, each teacher should participate in writing the IEPs for each student. A master file made up of all the individual IEPs should be kept by the special education teacher, or transition coordinator, who assumes the overall responsibility for the student's needs assessment, program plan, and evaluation of progress. Although this is a heavy responsibility, it ensures that records will be centrally located and that one person will be knowledgeable about all aspects of the student's progress. It is one sure way to guarantee program integrity.

In the model chosen for this book, the four curriculum areas for career-development and transition education are the following:

1. Values, attitudes, and habits
2. Human relations
3. Occupational information
4. Acquisition of job and daily living skills

However, to graduate, most students must accumulate the requisite number of Carnegie units to meet local requirements. Generally, this means that the

---

FIGURE 6.1   Sample IEP Objective Statements

Terminal Objective: In a work situation, the person consistently demonstrates the skills required to perform the work required and the work behaviors appropriate to the job.

Entering Behavior: Given uncomplicated directions to follow, the student will carry out the instructions with no further cues from anyone.

En Route Behaviors:
1. The student works with others in a harmonious relationship.
2. The rate of production of the student is satisfactory for the kind of work performed.
3. The student responds appropriately to the supervision of his or her superiors.
4. The student observes the rules of punctuality and attendance expected of others who work in the same setting.
5. The student performs work that meets the quality standards of the job.
6. In the work setting, the student practices the rules of safety consistent with the job.

---

substance of career development and transition education will need to be infused into the classes from which units of credit can be earned or gain approval for separate credit courses. Thus, instructional offerings must ensure that subject content is able to accommodate the needs of students with disabilities *and* to fulfill the obligation of teaching values, attitudes, habits, human relations, occupational information, job skills, and daily living skills as the student meets the school's requirements for graduation.

TEACHING ACADEMICS

To prepare an appropriate IEP, the present level of knowledge and skill of each student in each academic area must be determined. This may be done by either formal or informal assessment, but it should be done for each class or experience in which the student is to be enrolled. The IEP should then be prepared using the course objectives as a hierarchy of skills or knowledge to be achieved in the class. The matter of presentation should take into account the student's abilities, interests, and motivation, as well as the student's disabilities, so that a reasonable expectation of success can be ensured. It is particularly helpful to include students so that they can feel some sense of partnership in the educational venture and not be confused about what is going to be expected from the class. Including students in the formulating of the goals and objectives for each academic area not only helps to develop realistic objectives but also allows the students to feel a sense of ownership in their educational lives and to be reassured that they can exercise some personal control over the forces in their education. These feelings can have a positive effect on the relationships between teachers and students and can go a long way toward easing whatever anxiety the students may have concerning their ability to be successful in the class.

In the classroom, regardless of whether it is a regular or alternative setting, the major challenge is to help each student progress from one level of behavioral objective to the next. After deciding on the IEP, the teacher has the obligation to analyze the steps required for the student to be able to master the next level of behavior in the march toward reaching the goal of the IEP.

Starting from the initial assessment of the student, the en route objectives should be taught in a sequential manner, from simplest to the most demanding. A systematic way of doing this is to analyze each behavioral objective with regard to the tasks that must be learned to meet the requirements of the objective. This requires the teacher to consider the physical, intellectual, perceptual, and motor skills needed for successful performance. Next, a decision needs to be made concerning which component should be taught first and which should then follow.

This procedure is often referred to as *task analysis*, although it may have other descriptors. Obviously, the procedure may be as detailed as necessary to ensure its success. That is, the teacher may start with a well-conceived plan, only to discover that a vital step has not been mastered by the student. This may require extending the analysis of that troublesome task and breaking down the lessons into even smaller, more manageable ones. For instance, in the example presented previously, if the student has already demonstrated the ability to follow directions (number 87), the next level (number 88) is "works with others."

An analysis of "works with others" reveals that each member of a working team must be able to associate physically with the other team members, understand the task, perceive his or her role in the team effort, and perform the motor acts required by the tasks. Failure to work with others successfully could be a direct result of deficient behavior in one, several, or all of the areas mentioned. The cause of the deficient behavior will need to be corrected before the student will be able to "work with others" satisfactorily. In like manner, each objective will need to be mastered en route to being able to perform the terminal objective satisfactorily.

This progression from entering behavior, to en route objectives, to mastery of the terminal objective can be applied to learning tasks from the very simple to complex objectives, but fundamental to the procedure is the accurate assessment of the learner's status in any hierarchy of behaviors. Once an accurate picture of the requirement of the learning tasks relative to the skills and abilities of the student has been determined, the teaching can proceed in an orderly and meaningful fashion.

It is important to remember that although the selection and presentation of materials used in the teaching is the responsibility of the teacher, the mediation of methods and materials is clearly in the domain of the learner. No one can bring meaning to the lesson except the student. His or her understanding, perception, and acceptance of the learning requirements will determine whether progress can or will be made. That is, the learner is exclusively in charge of whether he or she will accept the stimulus materials as suitable, important, and worthy of time and energy investment. The teacher can arrange the reinforcement and reward contingencies in order to enhance learning, but it is the student who has the power to accept, reject, or modify the rewards offered. If the teacher and the student mutually set the standards to be reached and the rewards for making progress toward or reaching the standards, possible misunderstandings can be reduced to a minimum and a work-oriented classroom climate can be achieved. It is an effort well worth making.

Teaching English

The content of secondary-level English classes usually allows students to study some examples of the best literature written. Whether the samples are modern or ancient, American or foreign, fanciful or expository, the purpose is to expose the students to the finest literary models. Discussion can then lead to the discovery of the skill of the writers in developing plot, mood, expression, description, word choice, and phraseology. Students then may be assigned the task of writing pieces similar to what the famous authors have produced. These efforts are then critiqued by the teacher and peers to point out how the student works can be improved.

Obviously, the academic skills basic to success in English are reading and writing. Any student who lacks the ability to understand the printed word will be unable to benefit fully from a study of the works of famous authors. Furthermore, most students who are unable to read often are unable to write any acceptable prose or poetry themselves. Thus, it is vital to start with an assessment of the reading and writing skills of each student.

Although there are many formal tests that might be used, and should be used if the tests or results are readily available, informal assessment can provide the requisite information just as well. A fairly uncomplicated method is to provide a graded series of reading books and ask the student to read from each. An informal guide to evaluation is no more than 10 errors per 100 words read. This can be used as a guide to determine the approximate grade level at which the student can successfully function. Once a level is determined, age-appropriate materials that deal with daily living adjustments, interpersonal relations, occupations, and/or leisure reading preferences can be used.

A similar assessment technique may be used to determine the level of writing skills. Formal test results certainly provide the most accurate assessment procedures, but informal methods can be used also. Determining writing skill level through informal assessment is somewhat more difficult than determining reading skill level, but it can be done fairly accurately. Readability formulas have been developed by several people (Flesch, 1951; Fry, 1977). They use the number of words in a typical sentence and the complexity of the words written to calculate an approximate grade level to represent the skill of the reader or writer. Some computer software programs can do this. To use one, all a student does is enter into the computer a 100-word sample of writing, and then the student or teacher can call up an analysis of it in grade-level units.

Myklebust (1965) has developed scoring standards for his Picture Story Language Test that provide both quantitative and qualitative language standards for different age levels. The scoring criteria provide a means of arriving at age and sex norms on total words, total sentences, words per sentence, syntax, and a qualitative judgment of sophistication on an abstract-to-concrete dimension. The Myklebust criteria can be used to provide a hierarchy of goals to increase the number of words per sentence, sentences per paragraph, and paragraphs per assignment. In all cases, the entering behavior for the IEP is the actual quantitative score of the student on the Picture Story Language Test.

Since the test itself requires the student to look at a picture and write a story about it, any similar assignment that is age appropriate could be used to provide an informal test of the same type. Then Myklebust's scoring system can be used to determine the level of quantitative and qualitative writing skill shown by the student so an IEP can be developed that is realistic for that person. As the student achieves the quantitative and qualitative IEP goals, the next higher level becomes the next terminal objective. Daily lessons would encompass activities that would lead the student to achieve each goal in the hierarchy.

This system is appropriate for any student who has language difficulties, not just for students with disabilities. The type of disability may be important in order to determine whether specific aids are required to circumvent a specific disability, such as substituting Braille for print so the student can participate in the program. Other than that type of accommodation, the procedure is equally appropriate for any students.

Oral communication skills are appropriate for attention in English classes, and educators are getting support for direct instruction in this area from a specific group within speech pathology—pragmatics specialists. *Pragmatics* is the ability to use verbal and nonverbal language and to participate in conversation that is appropriate to the situation and to the conversational partner (Pippes, Ryan, & Underwood, 1989). Pragmatics specialists believe that communication competencies are necessary for successful educational experiences as well as for a successful transition from school to work and adult living.

Special education teachers who have responsibility for teaching English courses should seek assistance from the school's speech pathology staff in designing and teaching functional communication skills to those students who show characteristics such as the following:

1. Poor comprehension and expression of questions involving who, what, when, where, and why
2. Problems in or an inability to understand indirect question forms, such as "Would you... ?", "Could you... ?", "Will you...?", "Can you... ?"
3. Inability to initiate conversations with strangers, adults, members of the opposite gender, or any other identifiable group
4. Problems in understanding another person's point of view
5. Failure to stay on a topic of conversation or change a topic appropriately
6. Failure to act appropriately upon available information or facts
7. Use of immature speech or language forms
8. Minimal or no use of ritualistic social expressions

Instructional content for pragmatics is fairly obvious from these characteristics, but anyone who has spent much time around adolescents with communication characteristics such as these will see how students could benefit from instruction in communication skills. Topics might include listener and speaker responsibilities; giving and requesting information; giving and taking messages; predicting; advising; disagreeing, criticizing and responding to criticism; apologizing; handling emergencies; expressing feelings; social communication at funerals, weddings, religious ceremonies, and the like; and responding to humor. Resources for more information on age-appropriate pragmatics objectives include McConnell and Blagden (1986) and the Missouri Department of Elementary and Secondary Education (1984).

For resource room teachers who serve as support teachers or learning specialists, teaching high school students how to learn what they need to learn from written materials and how to improve their written and oral communication skills at this late stage is difficult. The Strategies Intervention Model (SIM) (Deshler & Schumaker, 1987; Kline, Deshler, & Schumaker, 1992) provides a variety of learning strategies for students in literature and composition sections of English. Some of these strategies include the following:

1. Word Identification Strategy (ways to decode multisyllabic words quickly)
2. Reading Comprehension Strategy (ways to use visual imagery to form a mental picture of events described, form questions about information that has not been provided by the author, and paraphrase the main idea and important details of each paragraph read)
3. Interpreting Visual Aids Strategy (ways to gain information from pictures, graphs, charts, diagrams, tables, and maps)
4. Multipass Strategy (ways to attack textbook reading assignments)
5. Sentence Writing Strategy (steps for using a variety of formulas when writing sentences)
6. Paragraph Writing Strategy (steps for organizing and writing several types of paragraphs)
7. Error Monitoring Strategy (ways to detect and correct errors in written products)
8. Theme Writing Strategy (steps to organize and write a five-paragraph theme)

Teaching Mathematics

The extent to which information is communicated in terms of numeration or quantity is not only considerable but it is expanding. The language of numbers is so commonly taken for granted that people who are numerically illiterate are simply bewildered by the world around them. In fact, the word *numeracy* has emerged as a term comparable to *literacy* because of increasing attention to this communication mode.

The use of numbers to count, order, group, name, combine, compare, evaluate, describe, and separate things is so basic to nearly all aspects of living that people who cannot participate in the language are isolated from whatever activity is being represented by the number concepts. It is simply expected that all adults will develop basic number literacy as they progress through school.

Fortunately, even though communication through numeric representation is generalizable, the use of numbers is equally appropriate in very specific instances. That is, although numeric skills have wide applicability, it is possible for people to learn to use numbers in specific situations with no need to be aware of the possibility of any generalizable applications. Thus, it may not be necessary to learn the basic functions of numbers to be able to use them effectively in a given task. To be able to put two quarters in a candy machine to get a candy bar does not require the knowledge that a half-dollar, two quarters, five dimes, or various other coin combinations could be given to a clerk to purchase a 50-cent article.

The specificity of numbers makes it possible for people who have limited understanding of numbers to learn to function quite effectively in specific situations. This makes assessment of students' skills somewhat different from the assessment of more general skills, such as reading or writing. In math, knowing a general level of skill by grade-level achievement may not be of much help in the development of IEPs. What is of more use is to identify the math requirements in working and independent living situations and determine whether the student can perform the functions required. Math classes are then structured to teach whatever specific skills are the most important to the student at any given time and place. Importance, in this instance, is an issue of content, which raises the question, How can relevant, age-appropriate content be determined for high school students who have learning difficulties?

Three principle sources of information furnish ideas for math class content: (1) *Dictionary of Occupational Titles* (U.S. Department of Labor, 1977a) descriptions of occupational requirements; (2) outcomes lists from curriculum guides; and (3) specific task analyses. Of the three sources, the *Dictionary of Occupational Titles (DOT)* and its supplement, *The Selected Characteristics of Occupations Defined in the Dictionary of Occupational Titles* (U.S. Department of Labor, 1982), are the most complete and authoritative. To define math requirements, the job the student works on or is preparing for should be determined and the description studied for information about the math requirements. Although some 20,000 jobs are described in the *DOT*, the information in the *DOT* represents the typical job; not every job of that description will be identical. Nevertheless, the *DOT* and its supplements are comprehensive tools and are very useful as general guides to math and other requirements.

Student outcome lists from curricular guides are developed by authors from task analyses of jobs performed by students in programs in their local communities as well as from follow-up studies from other communities or states. For example, independent living skills can yield information about what arithmetic skills people need to maintain themselves in a house or apartment. Both curriculum guides and follow-up studies are related to the lives of students who are, or have been, in the program, so they are relevant to real people and real problems. However, these lists often tend to reflect tasks that are germane to a common handicapping condition and may not be appropriate for people who have some other kinds of disabilities.

One such list comes from the work of teachers in Colorado and Michigan and is presented in a book by Kolstoe (1975b). It incorporates the following skills needed by a person for basic functioning in working and living independently:

1. Can prepare an uncomplicated budget
2. Can calculate pay
3. Can prepare a simple tax form
4. Can compute the cost of a meal from a menu
5. Can compute the cost of maintaining a home or apartment
6. Can identify best buys from newspaper ads
7. Can compute costs of transportation to work
8. Can compute the relative cost of repair versus replacement of appliances
9. Can compute the cost of simple interest when buying on time
10. Understands time cards
11. Can identify the elements in gross and net pay
12. Can measure height, length, width, and weight
13. Knows own clothing sizes
14. Can follow an uncomplicated recipe
15. Can write bank checks
16. Can reconcile a bank account statement
17. Can use a simple calculator
18. Can tell time
19. Can estimate time required to do familiar tasks
20. Can construct a time schedule

The list requires computation, measurement, and time—all basic number skills. Even though the list is far from exhaustive, it covers many of the math skills people need on a day-to-day basis. Furthermore, each item on the list can be isolated to see if the student can perform the skills adequately. If not, specific lessons to teach the skills can then be designed that relate the specific function to the particular life experience the student is demonstrating. Relevance can thus be assured and a general skill can become personally meaningful.

The third source of information for class content—task analysis—is the most time consuming but it is also the most realistic. Actually following the students into their homes, on their jobs, and through their leisure activities requires a huge investment of time. Therefore, it is often more practical to use basic outcomes lists or *DOT* descriptions for most of the course content and then to use task analysis as a supplementary source of information or for specific students with some unique problem.

The process of task analysis has been well described (Gold & Pomerantz, 1978; McCoy & Watson, 1983; Rose, Epstein, Cullinan, & Lloyd, 1981; Sowers, Jenkins, & Powers, 1988). All the descriptions have in common a procedure for dividing a task into specific small steps that can be performed individually. The student is taught each step in the process and then is trained to perform the steps in the proper sequence. The task analysis can be as specific as is appropriate for the student's ability to learn. This simply allows a great deal of flexibility in deciding how much detail to include in each part of the instruction. Thus, task analysis can be adapted to the learning skills of the individual student more realistically than can the other methods of determining content. It is a time-consuming procedure, but it is very realistic and adaptable to many different situations and learner needs. Furthermore, it can be used to supplement the other methods for determining course content.

To whatever extent possible, students should enroll in the regular math classes offered by the schools to fulfill not only the math requirements but their own personal life-career goals. Some students need and can handle math classes such as algebra, geometry, trigonometry, and precalculus. Many students with learning handicaps will need basic classes that have practical applications. Often, these classes are called practical math, basic math, business math, vocational math, or some other title that conveys the idea of the application of numbers to problems of living and working. Commercial instructional materials, such as *Real Life Math* (Schwartz, n. d.), the math series published by Janus Books, or *Math on the Job* (National Center for Research in Vocational Education, n. d.), are examples of math materials that are used in classes like these. Although the course content may deal with practical problem solving, it assumes that the basic knowledge of numbers and symbols and the basic processes of addition, subtraction, division, and multiplication have already been mastered and can then be applied.

To determine whether a student has the basic skills for an advanced or applied math class, a test such as the *KeyMath Diagnostic Arithmetic Test* (Connolly, Pritchett, & Nachman, 1971) is a basic, practical assessment instrument. It consists of three parts and 14 subtests covering nearly all aspects of basic arithmetic skills. *KeyMath* is designed to assess math skills from preschool to ninth-grade levels. One of the unique features of the test is that it contains an equal number of easy, moderately difficult, and hard questions in each subtest. This makes it possible to determine what areas and what levels of math skill the individual needs to address. An IEP can then make use of the behavioral objectives for each subtest provided by the test developers and listed in the appendix of the test manual. Starting with the last successfully answered question in each subtest, the entering behavior is the behavioral outcome for that item listed in the appendix of the test manual. Succeeding outcomes for the other problems in the subtest are arranged in a hierarchy so that en route and terminal objectives are thus provided and can make up the rest of the IEP. The convenience and completeness of this test with the accompanying behavioral outcomes has made it a very attractive educational assessment tool.

In the absence of formal test performance information, the math program for any student can be derived from the regular class curriculum, from outcomes provided in already published curriculum guides and materials, or from task analysis as described in the preceding section on English. As has been stressed repeatedly, it is crucial for realistic instruction to build the IEP on accurate assessment of the student's skills and knowledge leading to the goals of the program, and to then evaluate progress systematically and regularly.

The Strategies Intervention Model (Deshler & Schumaker, 1987) has a learning strategy curriculum strand on math concepts and skills that teachers will find useful. Teachers should also refer to the May/June 1992 special issue articles on teaching math in *Remedial and Special Education* (Vol. 13, No. 3).

Teaching Science

Although the opportunity to participate in any science course offered in the student's high school must be available, the principle of proof should govern a decision on what classes provide a meaningful experience for the student. Figure 6.2 is a checklist that can be used to determine whether the climate, the instructional approach, and the material used in a class are appropriate for the student with a disability who is being considered for a regular science class. In addition, there are implications for the kind of cooperation between the regular and special teacher that will enhance the chances of mainstreaming being a successful experience for the student with disabilities.

The development of an IEP specific to science requires an assessment of the science knowledge and skills of the student. Formal, commercially prepared science achievement tests are so geared to the requirements for college-bound students that they may be inappropriate for students who have other significant learning problems. However, they are generally carefully prepared and standardized and they do cover the subject matter thoroughly. The student's performance can provide an inventory of skills and knowledge but often will provide scant information about the student's ability to apply the knowledge in a practical or applied setting. The real test of science knowledge is whether the student can use it. Two good examples of applied science sexuality education (Brantlinger, 1992) and safety education (Collins, Wolery, & Gast, 1991). Assessing this ability is meaningful for tasks that are specific to the person's living environment, so no formal tests are available to cover this aspect of living. Task analysis (Howell, Kaplan, & O'Connell, 1979; McCoy & Watson, 1983) and criterion-referenced testing (Fimian & Goldstein, 1983; Gronlund, 1973) are the most appropriate ways to determine what the science knowledge and needs of any individual are.

Stefanich and Hadzigeorgiou (1993) stated that students with disabilities often have few opportunities to explore and investigate the world around them outside a supervised setting. Physical, sensory, and cognitive impairments are seen by parents and teachers as automatic constraints to the normal explorations and experimentation with natural or human-made objects that most young people experience. The authors voiced a concern that the lack of these opportunities during childhood and adolescence becomes a barrier to later learning of science concepts, particularly when the instruction in those concepts is primarily expository through lectures and print materials. Stefanich and Hadzigeorgiou gave the following example to illustrate how concepts are typically presented and followed up with questions:

The skip was in the hack. The third man was in the chute. He held the hammer. The rock must draw the button to win the game. The third man pushed from the hack and released the rock. The speed was perfect. The sweepers heard sweep, stop, sweep, stop, sweep. The rock nicked the point at the eight foot. The game was lost. The sweepers were angry.

Where was the skip?   _____

Who was in the chute?   _____

What must the third man do?   _____

What did the rock do?   _____

Why were the sweepers angry? (1993, p. 25)   _____

It is apparent to a person experienced in the game of curling that this is an interesting and colorful description. However, to a person who has never had any exposure to the game and its language, it makes no sense, even though the passage is simple to read and most of the questions can be answered correctly. If we are serious about including students with disabilities in high school science classes, careful attention must be given to assessing the basic level of experience and understanding of the content being presented and certain adaptations must be made in the instruction to provide any prerequisite experiences.

The specificity of the task analysis and criterion-referenced approaches limits their applicability to the individual student. Also, these approaches are not easy to use in developing a science curriculum. This leaves the alternative of depending on the work of others who have developed modified curricula.

Many school systems have developed their own science curricula for students with disabilities, but they may or may not be generalizable to other programs. One group that has developed science materials specifically for students who have limited learning skills is Biological Sciences Curriculum Study (BSCS). Made up of experts in science, the group started in the early 1960s in Boulder, Colorado. Dedicated to improving the teaching of science, particularly the biological sciences, BSCS developed a series of textbooks for secondary schools for students with differing backgrounds and needs.

The first set of materials developed for students with disabilities was called *Me Now* (Biological Sciences Curriculum Study, n.d., c). The program is complete with materials, activities, goals, objectives, and tests to evaluate the student's progress. It deals with the circulatory, respiratory, and excretory systems of the body in a manner that involves the student as an active participant in the lessons and requires no reading skills.

Me Now was so successful that BSCS developed a second program called *Me and My Environment* (Biological Sciences Curriculum Study, n.d., a) to explore the relationship between people and their natural environment. Empha-

FIGURE 6.2 Checklist for Mainstreaming in Science

_____ I. Goals of the science course are compatible with the student's educational goals.

_____ II. The classroom teacher demonstrates a positive attitude toward exceptionality.

III. Instructional Approaches

_____ 1. Activities are consistent with the student's attention span.

_____ 2. Instructional formats promote the social integration of the special student (e.g., peer tutoring, small-group activities).

_____ 3. Instruction incorporates self-paced individualized or small-group learning.

_____ 4. Regular teacher makes appropriate modifications for test taking.

_____ 5. Accommodation is made for student's reading difficulties through the use of alternate materials, peer tutors, or audiotaped text passages.

_____ 6. Duplicate instructional materials are provided to the special education room for student's use.

IV. Appropriate Instructional Materials

_____ 1. Curriculum is flexible to accommodate a variety of student abilities.

_____ 2. Curriculum is flexible to accommodate a variety of student interests.

_____ 3. Reading level of text materials is within reach of most students.

_____ 4. Curriculum stresses hands-on activities.

_____ 5. Curriculum centers on personal needs and experiences of the student.

_____ 6. Concepts are presented at levels of abstraction that the student can understand.

V. _____ 1. Classroom teacher is included in IEP conference.

_____ 2. Classroom teacher meets special students before mainstreaming begins.

_____ 3. Regular and special teachers cooperate to team teach appropriate science topics.

_____ 4. Regular and special teachers cooperate in evaluation and grading of the special student.

_____ 5. Regular and special teachers collaborate periodically to discuss and develop instructional alternatives and curriculum resources.

sizing the ecology systems, _Me and My Environment_ allows students with limited to no reading skills to participate actively in exploring relationships between plants, animals, and humans. The focus is on how people can preserve and protect natural resources.

The third program developed by BSCS is _Me and the Future_ (Biological Sciences Curriculum Study, n.d., b). It is a science program made up of modules that allow students to learn about selected science concepts and, at the same time, to learn about jobs in the field of science. It was designed as a part of the career education thrust, with particular attention given to jobs in science that students with learning handicaps could consider. It allows the student to learn about science in a practical, functional way.

Because each program has well-developed lessons, teachers do not need a science background to be able to use them. In addition, the participatory opportunities with students can make these programs joint adventures of high interest and great practical value. Because they are so well developed, many teachers have found them appealing for use with students with limited learning skills from a variety of causes. However, they do not substitute completely for regular courses in the basic biological sciences, particularly for those who plan to continue their education at the college level.

Teaching Social Studies

Requirements for earning credit in the social sciences vary so much from one school system to another that no set content is generalizable to all. Specific requirements such as a class in the history of a state, a class in pluralistic ethnic culture, a class in the capitalistic economic system, or a class in American government may each fulfill the requirement in a school system. Whatever is required to be studied in a particular school is what needs to be offered to learners with disabilities, but in a manner meaningful to them.

If the students can profit from the regular classes available, these classes should be used to the fullest extent possible. Marsh, Gearhart, and Gearheart (1978) have a number of suggestions that can facilitate the accommodation of students with learning problems in regular classrooms. Parenthetically, these suggestions are applicable to many more classes than just those in the social studies area. These authors suggest that the special education teacher do one or more of the following:

1. Secure the course objectives and schedule so the student can be monitored for due dates of assignments and projects well in advance.

2. Solicit feedback from the regular teacher regarding the student's performance early in the semester so any emerging problems can be detected or anticipated before they become insurmountable.

3. Secure lecture outlines for the student to use as a guide to organizing information in a meaningful sequence. Outlines also can be helpful in learning to identify important ideas, events, and people.

4. Develop a glossary of the technical and unfamiliar words that make up the jargon of the subject studied.

5. Secure or develop concrete models of abstract concepts. Often a picture is indeed worth a thousand words.

6. Solicit permission to substitute oral for written reports or tests. These should be private, not public, sessions between the student and the teacher or aide.

7. When necessary, modify homework assignments to avoid undue emphasis of the student's learning disabilities.

8. Help the student arrange a study schedule that includes the environment as well as the study methods of the students. In this connection, the SQ3R (Survey, Questions, Read, Reflect, Reread) system has been found to be quite helpful to students who have limited reading skills. It is, however, time consuming and can be used only with students who are willing to exert the effort and devote the time to make it a useful method. This approach is expanded upon thoroughly in Alley and Deshler (1979).

9. Help the student prepare for tests appropriately. For multiple choice and true-false or matching questions, there is no substitute for memorizing the material. Essay tests require the student to organize the answer (this may be facilitated by teaching the student to jot down a brief outline before actually writing the answer) and then use complete sentences to present the answer. The student will need to learn to write simple sentences and short paragraphs using words that are correctly spelled. Practice with immediate feedback of results seems to be the best way to teach this writing skill. However, even if the student is allowed to substitute oral for written tests, practice in preparing answers to essay questions can improve the oral presentations.

10. The student needs to understand the test directions, In particular, the student must know the meaning of such words as *discuss, define, compare, contrast, attack, defend, describe, list, criticize, interpret, trace, analyze,* and *summarize.*

Hartwell, Wiseman, and Van Reusen (1983) and Smith, Rice, and Gantley (1981) have provided excellent suggestions for teaching subjects such as social studies in a more self-contained setting. Hartwell and colleagues, for example, recommended a parallel alternate curriculum (PAC). This approach uses a content-centered instructional method in which teachers of students with disabilities, especially those with reading difficulties, can substitute or supplement the students' reading and information acquisition with a variety of other communication options. Students can acquire social studies content from recorded materials, lectures, television, films, group discussions, debates, or any other nonprint media.

Assessing where a student is in relation to knowledge of the social sciences (history, geography, government, etc.) is as difficult as in science. A recent textbook on assessing the abilities and instructional needs of students with disabilities had chapters on math and reading, but none on science and social studies.

Like science, social studies knowledge can be best assessed from a criterion-referenced testing approach in which learning outcomes can be identified. In fact, Hartwell and associates (1983) suggested a sequence for developing any alternative curriculum with the identification of learning outcomes. In some states, such as Texas or California, there are very specific curriculum content areas or "essential elements" that must be covered for every student. There is undoubtedly more flexibility for a school in identifying social studies outcomes when there are no state mandates to meet; the task is more time consuming and difficult in identifying the critical outcomes that should be the goals of social studies. The terminal behaviors should be stated in instructional objectives that answer the question, What does a student need to know or be able to do when he or she leaves school and becomes a citizen, worker, consumer, and adult family member? When these terminal behaviors have been identified, there are some specific materials a teacher can use that are especially designed for adolescents with low reading levels (materials published by Janus Books, Globe Book Company, and others).

TEACHING VALUES, ATTITUDES, AND HABITS

The importance of affect in the lives of students was probably recognized but not often acknowledged as a legitimate element in an academic curriculum until fairly recently. Arthur Combs (1962) was among the first educators in the movement with his work on self-identity in the 1950s. However, Leo Buscaglia popularized the idea of affective education with his book *Love in the Classroom* (Buscaglia, 1972). In fact, humanism became an educational force in the 1970s through the efforts of Buscaglia, Caplin (1969), and Simon (1971).

Starting with an emphasis on discovering the existentialist version of the self, various activities aimed at values clarification became popular and widespread. Most of these used short stories or descriptive events to present a dilemma—a conflict between competing choices of action with no solutions. The more cleverly done materials presented incidents about morality, values, or ethics generalizable to a wide spectrum of social activities. As the dilemma emerged, students had to choose a course of action, identify the consequences of the actions, and defend their choice to the other members of the class. Over time, it became possible to determine the values of the students and to classify their characteristic behavior (liberal vs. conservative, personal vs. social, democratic vs. autocratic, impulsive vs. cautious, etc.). The purpose of the exercises and activities was to allow students to understand their own behavior rather than to provide neat categorical niches into which they could or should fit.

More recent approaches to the understanding of the self have taken the form of student participation in civic projects with accompanying discussions of the goals, procedures, and effectiveness of the activity and a subsequent evaluation of the consequences of the projects. How the students feel about their involvement, effort, commitment, and associations with the people they work with allows for a more realistic appraisal of their values as well as a chance to examine their own approach in terms of social psychological behavior patterns.

Although the study of the development of self-understanding is a rapidly changing field, the idea that school is an appropriate setting in which to evaluate values, feelings, attitudes, emotions, and morals openly as they affect self-understanding seems firmly established. Whether implicitly or explicitly stated, developing self-understanding has emerged as an educational objective that has a direct bearing on a person's quality of life. Duchardt (1992) developed a unique learning strategy through the Strategy Intervention Model (Deshler & Schumaker, 1987) framework on belief systems. Students learn how to analyze a personal failure to achieve some task or goal in terms of what they believe about success and failure (e.g., luck vs. ability, easy vs. hard material, etc.). In this context, belief systems are related to value and attitude systems.

In the career development and transition education model presented in this book, the area of values and attitudes is acknowledged as one of the developmental themes that is fundamental to a person's chances of living and working successfully in society. Furthermore, the personal-social environments of community settings provide many opportunities for practical lessons on human relations, employer-employee conflict resolution, ethical problems, and the importance of honesty, integrity, loyalty, self-control, and responsibility. If there were no other benefits from a career education program, the opportunities for affective education in the psychosocial realism of a work setting might well be enough justification to endorse the program.

Although many exercises for values clarification have been developed for students with learning problems, a more usual approach to the subject has come from conflict events in the students' lives. This approach has been successfully used by the Vocational Evaluation and Training Center (VOTEC) staff in Tucson. This program—jointly sponsored by the University of Arizona Department of Vocational Rehabilitation, the Arizona State Department of Education, and the Public Schools of Tucson—enrolled 10 students with handicaps from each of the five high schools in Tucson in a Vocational Evaluation Center. The students could participate in their choice of six different training programs during one semester of their junior year in high school. Although a values-clarification unit was done as part of the formal instructional program, the most unique part of the program involved crisis intervention counselors. Whenever a conflict occurred between a student and other students or staff, the crisis counselor would sit down with the affected parties to discuss the incident. Using techniques borrowed from Glasser's (1969) *Schools Without Failure*, the incident would be thoroughly explored from the point of view of each person involved. The "reality" of the incident was that even if one person hits another, the fight does not start until the second person hits back. Actions and feelings were then discussed so the students could learn that alternative behaviors may have better consequences than the ones they used. Furthermore, responsibility for conflict was clearly related to the actions of both persons. Subsequent formal classroom sessions very often used the conflict incident as an object lesson to reinforce the notions of shared blame and alternative behaviors that might have had different or better consequences. Because teachers do not need formal counselor training to use Glasser's techniques, the crisis intervention strategy seems to be a useful technique to employ. Interested teachers can learn more about it by reading Glasser's complete perspective.

Sacks, Tierney-Russell, Hirsch, and Braden (1992) conducted a study on social skills training and concluded that a growing number of professional educators and human service personnel view the teaching of social skills as an important effort. Still, the implementation of social skills training strategies appears to be an inconsistent curricular component in schools. Two-thirds of the respondents in the authors' survey reported teaching social skills, but many reported that it was "infused" training into traditional educational curricula. They also reported that the focus of most social skills training was to assist students in maintaining their placements in regular classes, and that little attention was given to other critical social skill outcomes for home, community, and work environments.

Schumaker and Hazel (1984a, 1984b) discussed the most advanced social skills training for adolescents with learning disabilities and concluded that some promising procedures are now available for increasing the use of appropriate social behaviors, decreasing the use of inappropriate behaviors, and learning new social skills. There is still much to learn about how specific social skills are related to general social competence or social standing with peers. In the meantime, however, the procedures that are available and some of the commercially available curriculum materials published by American Guidance Service, Ebsco Curriculum Materials, Human Relations Media, Research Press, the Council for Exceptional Cholldren, and others should be reviewed and evaluated for possible use in social skills instruction. Three social skills curriculum development projects for youth who are mildly handicapped were funded by the U.S. Department of Education in 1981. All three programs were reviewed and evaluated by Schumaker, Pederson, Hazel, and Meyen (1983). Information regarding the distribution of those three social skills curricula is available from the following organizations:

> *Marathon,* Stanfield Film Associates, PO. Box 1983, Santa Monica, California 90406
> *Social Skills Curriculum,* Institute for Research in Learning Disabilities, 3001 Dole Center, University of Kansas, Lawrence, Kansas 66045
> *Social Solutions,* Professional Associated Resources, 2917 Adeline Dr., Burlingame, California 94010

TEACHING DAILY LIVING SKILLS

Assessment of student functioning levels in daily living or independent living skills is improving with the availability of a variety of adaptive behavior scales and specific tests on daily living. These instruments include Tests for Everyday Living, Social and Prevocational Information Battery, Street Survival Skills Questionnaire, and the LCCE Knowledge and Performance Batteries. (Refer to Chapter 4 for more detail.) The domain-referenced approach in developing these tests puts them in a category akin to criterion-referenced tests, but there are some normative data that can be derived from them. Most helpful, however, are specific areas of daily living that are identified as strengths and weaknesses; terminal objectives can be developed from such assessment.

SPECIAL TECHNIQUES FOR INDIVIDUALIZING INSTRUCTION

The individualizing of instruction is aided by a variety of arrangements that have emerged on the educational scene during the past 10 years. These include learning packets, learning centers, computer-assisted instruction, tutorial instruction, group instruction, use of volunteers, peer tutoring, and paraprofessional aides. All have in common the enhancement of learning, and all emphasize individualizing instruction, but they differ from each other in ways significant enough to generate partisan followers.

Learning Packets

Sometimes called learning modules, learning packets are developed to allow students to reach a particular learning objective individually or in small groups. Charles (1980) suggested that a strength of modules is that they organize materials and activities so that students

1. Know what *specific objectives* they are supposed to reach
2. Have *optional activities* from which they choose, all enabling them to teach the objectives
3. Can *direct themselves* through learning activities with minimum assistance from the teacher
4. Can *pace themselves* (work at a rate of speed that suits each person)
5. Have *checkout procedures* that tell them when they have reached the objectives. (p. 116)

Modules can be organized in different ways but generally lend themselves to about 10 parts, according to Charles (1980). These include the following:

Prerequisites	Information or skills the students need to succeed in the module
Time Estimate	A guide for students to know how long the module should take, and a structuring technique for keeping students on task
Goals	One or more clearly stated objectives as to what the students can expect to learn

Prospective	A brief introduction to the module to motivate the students and clarify the activities and goals
Preassessment	A pretest or some other type of assessment to establish entry skill or knowledge or to guide the student as to where to begin in the module
Instructional Objectives	A list of behavioral objectives for the module
Instructional Alternatives	A module plan and list of resources or enabling activities to aid the students in moving through the module
Module Checklist	A blank checklist for students to use to track their progress through the activities and assignments
Postassessment	A posttest or some other assessment activity that serves as an evaluation device for progress
Remediation	A list of activities or resources that students can use to remediate their performance or fill in gaps in their knowledge or skill base

Learning Centers

A learning center is a place where an organized collection of activities and materials allows students to learn about a thing or to achieve specific learning objectives. The design of the learning center may vary by subject and objective, but each center is complete in itself.

Typically, the center is designed for use by only one student or a small group of students at a time. The center is usually a cubicle or a clearly designated area that has a specific purpose stated in behavioral terms and the directions for achieving the purpose. The materials, resources, a workspace, and scheduling and record-keeping sheets are also included.

Learning centers can be used for any subject area, such as math, science, reading, or social studies. Career education learning centers have been developed to provide experience and assessment for students in a number of different jobs. In Carl Hayden High School in Phoenix, Arizona, some 30 different learning centers were developed for students with learning disabilities. They were made of 4' × 8' plywood boards arranged so that each center was shielded from neighboring centers by sidewalls. A stool was provided to allow a student either to stand or sit facing into the cubicle and to work comfortably on the work shelf that was approximately four feet above the floor and between the sides of the cubicle. Each of the three sides above the work shelf contained pictures and instructions of the task to be accomplished. On changing a washer in a faucet, for example, the sides contained various pictures of plumbing fixtures and some questions, such as, How long do you think it will take to change a washer? Make a guess and see how close you come.

A manual with step-by-step instructions encased in clear plastic was on the work shelf. All the tools and materials needed were conveniently placed in labeled boxes within easy reach of the student. The instructions were not only written but they were also presented in a series of pictures and in a series of schematic drawings. An evaluation scheme was also included so students would know whether they had done the job properly. There was also a record sheet for the student to date and sign when the task was completed. The jobs included in the learning cubicles were decided on by the staff after they had surveyed the community to see what kinds of jobs might be available to the students. In addition, some tasks that had to do with routine home maintenance or repair were also included.

The Singer/Graflex System, a commercial system similar to the Phoenix program, was developed by the Singer Company. It consists of the same types of tasks as those just described, but the instruction is an audiovisual presentation that is controlled by the student. All the materials and tools needed are included in the program, so each learning center is complete. The student gets audio instruc-

"At what point do you feel that a teacher should intervene in self-instruction?"

tions from the teaching machine while synchronized pictures of each step of the procedures are presented. At intervals, the student is instructed to turn off the machine, perform specific tasks, and then have the instructor check his or her work to see whether it meets the criteria for mastery. At the end of each learning task, a self-test is available to aid in the evaluation of the student's skill. Although the tasks are commercially prepared and marketed, they are realistic and can be used over and over again. The cost of $1,000 to $1,500 per task, when spread out over a large number of students, makes the investment of $20,000 or more somewhat more palatable. Modules can be used easily in learning centers and often are. The specificity of the tasks, the completeness of the directions, the lack of time limitations, the control of the task by the student, and the end result of a finished product make both modules and learning center instruction quite attractive.

Computer-Assisted Instruction

The use of machines as teaching aids has a venerable place in special education. Beginning with the work of Maria Montessori (Fisher, 1913), who developed self-teaching devices for the children in her school in Rome who had learning problems, special educators have been among the first of the educators to try to adapt educational technology to their fields. Typewriters adapted to print Braille characters for people who are blind have been used. Phonograph records and audiotape recorders have been used in the "talking books" program—the program in which volunteer readers dictate popular and technical books on records and tapes for people who are blind and physically disabled.

In 1965, at Stanford University, a machine called the Optacon was developed. This machine converts printed material such as books and newspapers to tactile sensations transmitted to a person's index finger (Tobin & James, 1974). It transmits the outline of the letters with "pinlike" sensations for "reading." A breakthrough from tactile imagery "reading" was the Kurzweil Teaching Machine in 1976, which scans printed material and converts it into auditory output for electronic or computer speech. More recently, computers have been developed to allow Braille writing machines to feed into the computer, which then projects the words into a loudspeaker that "speaks" the words that are then recorded on tape. This is the high-tech version of the talking books program. Although the first Kurzweil machines sounded monotone and synthetic, machines developed in the 1980s have voice inflection.

People who are deaf have used a variety of machines to amplify sounds, transduce sounds into light or touch media, and filter irrelevant from relevant sounds. Computers play a vital role in visual communication with people who cannot hear.

Many of the innovations used to make machines usable by persons with sensory impairments have been incorporated into the educational programs for students with other learning problems. Talking calculators, voice-activated switches to turn machines on and off, and equipment for an electronically controlled environment (radios, TV, lights, etc.) are used by people with severe orthopedic limitations. Since the 1970s, touch-activated language master and interactive computers have been commonplace in programs that serve people with handicaps.

Beginning in the 1950s, programmed instruction was derived from the operant conditioning work of B. F. Skinner and his students. The technique of dividing learning tasks into their essential steps and designing instruction to assure mastery of each step was quickly incorporated into teaching machines. During the 1960s and 1970s, teaching machines that were used to teach reading and arithmetic were evident in special education classrooms nationwide, and their use triggered a surge of research efforts to test their effectiveness. At first, the programs were linear. But it was not long before branching programs that were activated by wrong answers were developed to provide remedial instruction for students.

Machine programs gave way to television instruction as the lessons became more sophisticated. Graphics, pictures, color, and music could be introduced to make the instructional programs more interesting, varied, and meaningful to the students. By the 1980s, teaching machines that provided programmed learning had practically disappeared from special education programs.

Computer Instructions

Both teaching machines and educational TV lack the response flexibility available in computers. It is small wonder, then, that computers have become standard fixtures in many special education programs. However, computers did not become very useful until after the development of microchips and keyboard programming. To operate the computer, a person needs only to select a disk that has the desired program on it and then press the command keys of the keyboard or other control(s) that the program instructs the operator to do. Appell and Hurley (1984) have described the roles that computers can play in computer-assisted instruction (CAI) as follows:

1. *Patient teacher.* In basic skill work, the computer is tireless, patient, nonjudgmental, and supportive. It can provide students with stress-free *drill and practice*, freeing the teacher for other tasks. It tends to stimulate curiosity, a major component in motivation to learn.

2. *Accessible laboratory.* Many different kinds of scientific experiments can be modeled on the microcomputer. It can *simulate* conditions that would be too dangerous, too costly, or otherwise impractical. The educational opportunities for discovery learning are excellent.

3. *Responsive instructor.* The interactive capabilities of the microcomputer are important in providing tutorial learning experiences for special students. These concept-building activities are enhanced by personal presentation and by stimulation and reinforcement. Students are often less inhibited in their responses, more willing to stick to the task, and less fearful of making mistakes.

4. *Facilitator for problem solving.* Problem-solving skills have become critical to functioning well in the world today. Learning to think logically and creatively about complex events and relationships can be the key to vocational success.

5. *Demonstration device.* Some concepts can be demonstrated with special clarity with the graphic features of the microcomputer. For maps, charts, graphs, and geometric figures, for demonstrating special relationships, and for illustrating consequences of some interaction, graphics have enormous instructional potential.

6. *Musical instrument.* The value of the microcomputer's role in teaching composition and musical theory lies not only in its ability to produce a range of sounds and display the music on the screen. Also important are repetition, correction, reinforcement, and the absence of external pressure to perform. The microcomputer does not get a headache when a student hits the wrong note.

7. *Innovative art supplier.* The microcomputer can provide a blank drawing tablet, a taut canvas, and the tools to create. The color and graphics features allow students to generate images, erase them, modify them, and even store them for later embellishment. For some students whose physical disabilities preclude the use of more traditional art supplies, this role of the microcomputer can be wonderous indeed.

8. *Game board and playing field.* Games played on the computer are highly motivating and exciting to youngsters. The value of games as an instructional aid lies in their ability to teach decision-making skills, increase attention span, improve coordination, and add fun and gaiety to the classroom.

9. *Special study topic.* When you consider the ever-increasing use of the computer in business and industry, government, farming, research and entertainment, it should be obvious that understanding the computer and how it works is becoming an essential area of knowledge. Special students, in particular, will need to be aware and informed about these power-packed devices if they are to compete in the marketplace. Unlike some earlier technologies that educators embraced and then discarded, the roots of this technology are firmly implanted in the world of work.

10. *Powerful prosthesis.* With the addition of creative peripherals to the microcomputer, many physically impaired learners can communicate efficiently for the first time in their lives. Special keyboards, switches, light pens, touch-sensitive screens, voice recognition, speech synthesizers, adapted keyboard commands, and scanners can enable students with serious disabilities to function academically and socially as never before.

11. *Manager.* The microcomputer is a whiz at keeping records, updating files, making lists, and scheduling. It is more efficient than any human at monitoring testing dates, retrieving file data, and cross-checking dates and places. Its word-processing functions are far better than those of any typewriter, and its use for accounting and budget analysis has been widely acknowledged. (pp. 2–4)

The instructions that tell an operator what to do to make the computer perform are contained in the computer software. Software is a program disk written in whatever coded language is compatible with the computer being used. Expert programmers must not only understand the capabilities and limitations of the machines they are writing for but also which language code is compatible with the machine and the program objective. Beginners All-Purpose Symbolic Instruction Code (BASIC) was developed primarily for educational lessons, but other codes such as Programmed Instruction Learning or Teaching (PILOT) may also be used. COBOL, FORTRAN, and LOTUS are more sophisticated machine languages used for more complex educational programs and for business.

Constructing educational programs that can be used by students with unique learning problems makes the preparation of software enormously difficult. Most teachers know what educational objectives they want their students to achieve and they understand the learning disabilities of their students. However, few of them understand the intricacies of any computer language sufficiently to write usable programs for their students. Professional programmers, on the other hand, often do not appreciate the subtleties of learning disabilities on information or skill mastery. Appell and Hurley (1984) pointed to the work of Hofmeister (1982), who criticized software for failing to capitalize on advances made in instructional theory. Budoff and Hutton (1982) discussed the failure of software designers to relate types of handicaps to their software. Chandler (1983) pointed out the tendency of software developers to focus on the technical rather than the educational aspects.

Given the questionable quantity and quality of computer software for career education and the staggering problems associated with developing effective programs, some software writers suggest that educators jump off the computer bandwagon until more research and development has been done. However, this seems to be an unnecessarily cautious approach. The obvious solution to some of these problems is a marriage of the computer programmer's skills and the special educator's knowledge. This promises to happen in the future of computer-assisted instruction, ushering in another bright chapter in the saga of machines improving the lives of people who have disabilities.

Tutorial Instruction

Probably the oldest instructional method—the teaching of a novice by someone more knowledgeable—may be one of the most effective ways to teach. Since there are no constraints on what methods, materials, or evaluations the teacher will use, the technique can be as creative as the tutor and the learner can make it. Furthermore, the subject matter may be as simple or as complex as is appropriate, and the presentation may be as concrete or abstract as is realistic. Additionally, tutoring can be as brief or as protracted as the student's level of mastery dictates. The tutoring may deal with an entire subject and be the only instructional method used, or it may be supplementary to other methods, reserved for extra, intensive help on troublesome parts of a subject.

In the formal academic setting of the schools, tutoring has generally been relegated to a remedial role. Often, special education teachers have tutored their students to help them become better able to participate equally with their peers in regular classes. Sometimes, the tutors help the students with disabilities prepare assignments for the regular class in a resource room. This practice has been so common that it has often been considered to be the traditional resource room role. However, it is just as common to find special education teachers furnishing supplemental materials or experiences over and above what the student may get in the regular classroom.

Who will tutor varies also. So long as the tutor is more knowledgeable than the person being tutored, the technique can be successful. Thus, it is not at all unusual to find some schools that use teaching aides to do one-on-one tutorial instruction. When this occurs, usually the teacher determines what is to be taught and the aide then carries out the instruction. Monitoring the progress of the student as well as the effectiveness of the tutoring procedure may also fall to the teacher. In this way, the teacher is freed to work with larger groups or more comprehensive lessons while the aide does the more routine work. Volunteers have often worked as teachers' aides, particularly in private schools, clinics, and institutions. Although there is no reason volunteers should not function as tutors in public schools, schools often have so many restrictions governing the use of volunteers that the volunteers are more comfortable in private settings. In addition, volunteers often feel they are somewhat more appreciated in the private sector because funding in this sector is difficult and volunteers believe they can make a significant difference in the quality of the programs. If the programs are church or association supported, some tax advantage can be claimed under some circumstances.

One successful form of tutoring is peer tutoring. In public schools, an advanced or more capable student often teaches a younger or less capable student. This is not really a peer situation or instruction by "equals." However, the name has been used to describe the condition of students teaching students whenever it occurs. Whatever it is called, the range of activities and the variety of settings have been almost limitless. We have witnessed in public school settings, elementary-level youngsters teaching children with severe handicaps to feed themselves. We have seen high school students helping students who have disabilities with vocational assessment tasks and later teaching them to dance so they could participate in a school party.

The effectiveness of this kind of tutoring depends on the relationship between the peers and on the skill of the teacher who monitors the relationship. Careful planning, preparation, and interaction can all be negated by an attitude that does not demonstrate mutual cooperation and respect. Any condescension can instantly spoil an otherwise rewarding experience for both the tutor and the tutee. The potential good that can come from peer tutoring is so great, however, that it is well worth considerable effort on the parts of all who are involved to ensure its success.

Tutoring in vocational settings has also been a successful practice in career education. Whether the tutor is a co-worker, a work supervisor, a work coordinator, or someone else, this practice of showing a new worker how to do a job has no equal. It is a practice that underlies the whole apprenticeship program. But it is equally germane to the introduction of a new worker to the most fundamental unskilled job or the periodic application to reach a higher level of efficiency than what is currently demonstrated by the novice. In addition to its venerable past, it appears to have an equally promising future.

Group Instruction

When students have similar educational needs, it is often a good reason to group the students for teaching efficiency. Not only does the grouping make it possible for the teacher to conserve time but often the youngsters in the group improve the learning situation because they help each other learn. Zigmond, Sansone, Miller, Donahoe, and Kohnke (1986) spoke to the issue of efficiency of group instruction versus individual instruction. After their review of several studies, they concluded that there was no evidence that one-to-one instruction is superior to other methods.

Grouping has led to some rather unfortunate practices, however. Certainly the least justifiable practice is grouping by category. Homogeneous grouping by age, for example, has been the common denominator of all schools. Grades made up of children who are within a year or so of each other have been assumed to guarantee that learning requirements and teaching methods will be appropriate for 6- or 7-year-olds, or high school seniors.

In special education, grouping has more often ignored age as a basic requirement, focusing instead on the disability category. Thus, children who have visual disabilities are grouped with others who who have similar disabilities. Special educators have been quick to recognize the artificiality of categorization and have used extensive assessment procedures to determine the nature and extent of the educational needs of the youngsters and the ways in which the disabilities interfere with reaching the educational goals. They have then devised ways of overcoming the handicaps, usually by compensation and sometimes by circumvention of the obstacle to learning represented by the disability. This led to the development of other ways of grouping—namely, teaching groups of youngsters who have a need for a particular kind of compensatory or circumvention treatment. For example, students who are blind may be taught with others who need a Brailler for learning, whereas other students with visual impairments may be grouped in a setting where magnification aids are available. However, even when the device needs are similar, students usually will have highly personal educational needs. Thus, individual instructional programs are common in rooms or classes for students with visual impairments in spite of the fact that all the youngsters may be using Braillers or magnification aids.

At the high school level, grouping has most often been dictated by subject matter. This has generated classes in composition, poetry, American fiction, and a host of other classes all subordinate to the general classification of English. The same practice pervades science, math, social studies, history, music, art, and other subjects. The actual content of the classes is most often related to what curriculum students are in (that is, college preparatory, general education, vocational classes, or fine arts). Thus, a class on the modern American novel could well be suitable for a college-bound student, whereas a student in the general education program might choose a class in business communications, either of which would fulfill a requirement for a Carnegie unit in English. The group or class appropriate for a student with a disability might in this case depend on the student's needs rather than on the nature of the disability or on the kind of learning-support equipment the student might require.

Once the suitability of class content has been determined, the organization of the class should be considered. Simply because a teacher may use large group instruction does not mean that a student with learning problems will not be successful in the class. If the student is able to relate to whatever instructional technique the teacher uses and feels comfortable in the class, those two criteria could be considered the evidence to support the principle of proof. Should either criterion not be met, then immediate intervention of the kinds previously mentioned should occur. Large group instruction need not be automatically condemned. Only when the student demonstrates an inability to achieve or progress toward achieving the goals of the class should the technique be judged inappropriate and other more promising arrangements be made for the student.

Large classes often are divided into smaller groups for various purposes. Within those small groups it is sometimes easier to pursue different assignments than in the larger groups. Under most circumstances, this is a positive arrangement for students with learning handicaps, but only if the groups are thoughtfully formed. For example, group assignments by alphabetical last names, proximate seating, or some other haphazard arrangement is as ineffective as grouping by age. If the student is to benefit from the grouping, then thought should be given to the interests, abilities, attitudes, needs and skills of the group members, such as what is done with cooperative learning groups (Greene, Kokaska, Albright, & Beacham-Green, 1988). Certainly, if one of the group members cannot read well, it may be very important to group that student with another student whose skills compensate for the reading problems of the other group members. The group should be formed in such a way that the learner with the disability will be able to make a contribution to the group project and will benefit from being able to learn from group peers.

INSTRUCTIONAL SUPPORT STRATEGIES

If students are to be successful in the myriad settings available in secondary schools, then every opportunity should be seized to support their educational efforts. There are five sources from which that support may come: administrators, teachers, peers, parents, and the students with the disabilities.

Administrative Support

With the large number of federal and state laws that stipulate the obligation of schools to provide an appropriate education for students with disabilities, administrators have become aware not only of their obligations to these students but also of the penalties administrators may incur should the schools abridge the rights of these students. Since state and federal laws require compliance reports, administrators need to monitor practices in their schools to gather the data they need to complete the reports. However, simple compliance does little to create a climate of support in the schools. The active expression by word and deed that administrators are supportive and appreciative of efforts to help students with disabilites be successful and welcome in the school classes and activities constitutes meaningful support. That message should be communicated by administrators to school boards, teacher organizations, and citizen groups at every opportunity.

Teacher Support

In 1975, the Bureau of Education for the Handicapped initiated a series of Deans grants. These were funds given to departments, schools, and colleges of education to ensure that preservice teacher-education programs would include classes for regular teachers on how to teach students with disabilities in regular classrooms (Grosenick & Reynolds, 1978). Although the results of the grants have not been evaluated effectively, the one consequence is that nearly every teacher has now had some training in how to recognize and teach children with disabilities in regular education settings. In addition, research has pinpointed some of the variables that affect the success of mainstreaming efforts (Miller & Sabatino, 1978). Gottlieb and Leyser in Strain (1982) suggested that one way to facilitate the acceptance of students with disabilities in regular classrooms is to stress the similarities between regular and special education procedures. Strain and Kerr (1981) proposed that to ensure that regular class teachers will be able to teach students who have disabilities effectively, they need to be informed about instructional procedures used in intensive instructional situations. Such procedures are related to (1) targeting behaviors, (2) task analysis, (3) performance assessment, and (4) programming antecedent and consequent events. This is a lot to ask of a high school English teacher who has 175 students to teach each day. Most regular high school teachers do not get this type of teacher education, even with the token required course on exceptional children. Most high school teachers look to the resource room teacher, the consulting teacher, or other support personnel to do the intensive instruction. Greene and others (1988) suggested the teaming of teachers in what they call *collaborative approaches.*

Some regular high school teachers take on the challenge of learning problems and want to make instructional modifications to meet individual student needs. They have demonstrated that changing classroom instruction from predominantly a lecture approach to more active learning, and from a competitive to a cooperative learning style, can work. These techniques protect the self-concepts of the students who have disabilities their peers, and the teachers themselves. Slavin (1980) stated that preservice or in-service instruction for learning those techniques helps to provide a good measure of teacher support for the learners with special needs.

Peer Support

Visualize the following scenes:

Situation 1   The young man hurried down the hall as students around him rushed to their lockers between classes. He would not have been noticed had he not suddenly left the hall by a courtyard exit door. The glass in the door panels permitted an unusual sight. The young man had stopped right outside the doorway, buried his face in his hands, and began sobbing. Shortly, his teacher came by and happened to look out and see him. She moved to investigate and provide some assistance, and by the time they reentered the hall, the bell was ringing for the next period. The teacher later reported that some regular-class students had been calling him "retard" and "dummy."

Situation 2   The couple was well known in the school. She had Down syndrome and he was slow in every behavior and had a severe speech disorder. They were dressed nicely and appropriately for the occasion—the senior prom. They were slow to get started, but once they did, they danced the entire evening. Their dancing was slow and awkward, with constant repetition of the same side-stepping movements, regardless of the rhythm of the music. No one teased them or made any show of rejection. On the other hand, only one person spoke to them the entire evening—a senior girl who worked as a peer tutor daily in their class. They were both delighted about the all-too-brief encounter.

The acceptance of students with disabilities by their classmates who have no disabilities has been the subject of a wide variety of programs and projects. However, the evaluations of the effectiveness of the techniques have not revealed any magic formula for ensuring acceptance. The replacement of a competitive classroom climate by various cooperative techniques has been reported by Slavin (1980) to improve acceptance. Although it may be argued that this is a teacher-controlled procedure, the effect seems to be related to peer attitudes. Certain conditions must be present for the technique to work—namely, an investment of the peer who is nondisabled in the success of the student who is disabled. For example, in team game tournaments (TGT), small groups of teams compete against each other in academic information games. The teams are made up of students of about equal ability. In this system, one high-, one moderate-, and one low-ability person make up each team. Although preparation for the tournament is done by each group working together, in actual performance the students with high ability compete against each other, the students with moderate ability against each other, and the students with low ability against each other. Points earned for correct answers are team points and rewards are team awards. This guarantees each team member a stake in the showing each team member makes.

By pairing youngsters of high status with youngsters of low status, Lilly (1971) was able to improve peer-acceptance scores, but the gains were temporary, disappearing after the pairings were dissolved. Interestingly, improving peer acceptance seemed to have little effect on improving the achievement of the students with disabilities. Teachers looking for high school students with high-status as peer support volunteers need to be aware of some basic high school peer dynamics, and try to obtain the best possible results from the relationship by doing some orientation to both the support student and special education student about some of the possible problems. The Circle of Friends (Perske & Perske, 1988) model may provide structure and guidelines to make a peer support effort maintain effectiveness over time.

In summarizing the effectiveness of various attempts to improve peer acceptance, Strain and Kerr (1981) noted that peer acceptance is influenced more by the acceptability of the behavior of the students with disabilities than by the labels they have been given, that the social standing of the youngsters is important, and that interaction in structured activities influences acceptance.

Parent Support

Since the behavior of students with disabilities is so crucial to their acceptance, some authorities have turned to the parents for help in developing acceptable behaviors. Simpson (1982) advocated involving parents in programs of applied behavior modification. To achieve this, he devised a three-session procedure.

In session 1, the parents are taught to identify and define the most significant problem response. The parents list their concerns about the child's behavior, prioritize the problems, and select one behavior for modification. They then identify the environments and situations in which the behavior occurs most frequently. To do this, they determine which individuals, times, and circumstances are associated with the occurrences.

The parents are then taught to identify the contingencies that support the problem behavior by determining the responses of parents, family, and others that follow the behavior. The parents are then trained to record behavior in a simple, reliable fashion, adjusting the system to fit the skills and abilities of the parents.

In session 2, the parents are first taught to chart the problem behavior in a simple visual display, such as a graph. They are then taught to record the behavior daily and to inspect the baseline data for trends.

Next, the parents are taught to establish intervention and performance goals. The facilitator helps the parents select appropriate consequences for modifying the behavior. To facilitate the procedure, the parents are encouraged to establish appropriate expectations and apply the consequences as they continue to record the behavior.

In session 3, the parents are taught how to analyze and interpret the data and make any necessary changes in recording. Then they are encouraged to apply the model to other behaviors and other children in the family.

The environment of parents in using applied behavior modification suggested by Simpson (1982) was in the home setting, but others have used it in job situations (Payne & Patton, 1981). In addition, the use of contracts between parents, the student, and school personnel has been widely advocated (Management Analysis Center, 1975). The contract involves the preparation of a written agreement that specifies what the parents, the student, and the school personnel agree to do to help the student with disabilities learn the skills necessary for successful entry into a particular kind or class of job. Penalties for not living up to the agreement are confined to school-related sanctions, ranging from extra assignments to expulsion, but they are designed to emphasize the seriousness of the intent of the participants. One obvious problem with these contracts is that penalties are easily found that apply to the students, but it requires some ingenuity to find equally punishing consequences for the parents or for teachers. Thus, the contracts can become unfair. Nevertheless, they are quite popular and are useful for securing parental involvement and support.

Self-Advocacy among Students with Disabilities

The reality therapy movement of Glasser (1969) has had a side effect of forcing students who exhibit undesirable behaviors to learn to take some measure of responsibility for their own misbehavior. The technique has been used effectively in the VOTEC program in Tucson (Management Analysis Center, 1975) and seems well worth employing. The principal consideration is to ensure that the students do not blame their misbehavior on external circumstances, and learn to accept the responsibility for their own behavior. Pride in self-improvement is the ultimate goal of the procedure.

In a reversal of the usual employment of applied behavior management, a Visalia, California, junior high school taught its students to count, chart, and reward positive behavior of their regular classroom teachers, their playground peers, and employers in work situations. In addition to learning to elicit positive contacts from these three diverse groups of people, the serendipitous effect of the project was the improvement in the behavior of the special education students themselves.

Ward (1988, 1992) described self-advocacy in terms of self-determination. He views self-determination as a pattern of personality characteristics, including self-actualization, assertiveness, creativity, and pride. The expected outcome of self-determination behavior among students with disabilities is that they learn to take control of their lives. It is not something that just happens, according to Ward. It is something that is a developmental process that must begin early and have continued encouragement and even specific training.

West and colleagues (1992) provided an excellent discussion of self-advocacy of students with disabilities in *Intergrating Transition Planning. into the IEP Process,* a publication sponsored by the Division on Career Development and Transition of The Council of Exceptional Children. They recommended the following selected suggestions to educators and parents to help prepare children and youths with disabilities develop self-advocacy or self-determination skills:

1. Reinforce the student as a self-advocate.
2. Respond to students who appropriately advocate for themselves.
3. Identify strategies for teaching and practicing self-advocacy and decision making.
4. Identify and include self-advocacy objectives on a student's IEP. Paulson and O'Leary (1991) elaborated on the third suggestion above in their discussion of the IEP planning process. They believe that preparing a student for his or her participation in the IEP meeting is an important instructional task in teaching self-advocacy and they provided specific suggestions on what the student should know about his or her responsibilities in the IEP planning process.

Regardless of the degree of success of the various techniques for improving the chances of students with disabilities to be successful in their career-development programs, there is no better assurance of acceptance than the successful participation of the students themselves. Given realistic goals in an intelligently planned sequence of experiences, the contribution that earned success can make to a realistic self-concept of competence has no parallel. The best way to get acceptance is to earn it.

MATERIALS FOR INSTRUCTION

When President John F. Kennedy initiated a War on Mental Retardation, he appointed a committee of national leaders to help plan the strategy. To gather information, some of the committee members visited various European countries to observe their tactics for dealing with the problem. One provision they encountered was a network of centers of instructional materials for people with disabilities. These repositories of materials—some commercial but most teacher made—were developed to teach specific concepts or skills primarily to children with mental disabilities. They were classroom validated informally. Teachers used them because they worked. And they were available to other teachers who wished to use them. The centers were paid for and maintained through government funds for the benefit of the schoolteachers who had suffered from a severe shortage of suitable materials.

Impressed with the concept, the committee recommended that a similar network be underwritten by the U.S. government. Two centers were started by

1964, and shortly thereafter a network served every region of the country. The purposes of the Instructional Materials Centers (IMC) network included not just gathering and disseminating instructional materials but also developing new materials to fit particular instructional needs of students with disabilities and evaluating commercial materials as they appeared on the market. At the same time, funds were made available to encourage creative people to develop and distribute materials that would meet the needs of students with a wide variety of handicapping conditions. Federal funds to states were used to provide extra funds to local special education programs for the purchase of materials. Thus, developing materials usable by students with many kinds of learning disabilities became a booming business by the 1970s. During the 1980s, the IMC program was so successful at generating materials that government-supported funds for the network were cut back to the point that funding virtually disappeared. Fortunately, the demand has continued and commercially prepared materials continue to appear, generally modified to be geared to videotapes, filmstrips, cassette audiotapes, and computer software. The teacher's dilemma, consequently, is encountering a bewildering and enticing array of excellently packaged materials in which to invest a very limited budget, and very little evaluative information to guide their choice.

It is most unfortunate that, as the success of the IMCs in generating new materials increased, the field has lost the evaluation component that was one of its most valuable provisions. Some school systems have depended on research done by college and university faculties to test the effectiveness of new materials. Not only is this source of information limited in scope but it often takes two to three years to evaluate the materials, yet teachers have immediate needs that cannot be postponed. Therefore, some school systems have formed materials-evaluation committees whose combined judgments are used to decide what materials to purchase. Although this procedure has the advantage of pooling the experience and judgment of the committee members, their selections must fit the general needs of the system and may not provide much help for individual teachers in their own classrooms.

Many textbooks present checklists that teachers can use to help them select materials. These checklists generally caution the teachers to consider reading level; visual and audio supplementary presentations; sequential steps; synthesizing exercises; sex, racial, or disability stereotyping; evaluative provisions; and record-keeping ease. The validity of materials is seldom mentioned because few companies can invest the time and money to find out if the materials do what they are advertised to do. The companies depend on users to report their stories of success or failure, satisfaction or frustration. From this anecdotal information, the company and materials authors can revise subsequent issues of the materials.

Certainly such an approach to validity has some merit, but when a teacher is faced with an immediate need for materials, the decision of what to buy cannot be put off until validity information becomes available. A decision must be made now, and that decision may well take the entire budget for the rest of the school year.

However, there are considerations that can guide the teacher in the selection of materials. First, the material must address a need of the students for whom it is being purchased. One way to determine that need is to list all the objectives from the IEPs of the students. Usually, several students will share objectives.

Second, the theoretical basis that underlies the material should be compatible with the learning theory the teacher uses to teach the objective. If, for instance, Glasser's (1969) reality approach is what will govern classroom activities, then applied behavior analysis or precision teaching materials will not support what the teacher wants to do. Since different objectives will be approached from different theoretical bases, there is no reason materials based on precision teaching techniques cannot coexist with constructivist theory-based materials, but the materials should support each approach the teacher wishes to use.

Third, the materials should lend themselves to self-instruction as well as to group instruction. Flexibility should be built into the design. Sometimes the authors themselves suggest alternative ways in which the materials can be used. More often, a brainstorming session with members of a materials selection committee will turn up some creative uses the authors overlooked.

Fourth, the learning styles of the students should be accommodated. Although it has been popular to think of students' learning styles in sensory terms such as visual, auditory, or kinesthetic and to develop materials for audio, visual, or manipulative presentation, it has become increasingly common to consider logical and analogical styles as related to left- or right-brain functions.

Charles (1980) advocated materials for "adventurers," "ponderers," and "drifters." She has cautioned that every learning style is as good as any other, but each is different. Adventurers, for example, tend to be spontaneous, eager, and active. They approach new tasks with enthusiasm but they often abandon them, with equal enthusiasm, for other tasks. Interesting activities and materials are all that are necessary to get them going. They work well on their own, at least for a time. Ponderers start more slowly but they have more staying power. They like to think and work tasks through to the end. They work well using programmed materials. Drifters have difficulty beginning and following through on activities. They seem to progress when materials and activities are sequenced in small steps. Since they tend to be easily distracted from their work, they require frequent changes of activity and direct support, encouragement, and direction from the teacher. Since there is little agreement on what is meant by *learning styles*, teachers can feel free to make their own categories and then select materials compatible with them.

Fifth, the materials should lend themselves to other support materials. It is most helpful when these support sources are suggested by the materials themselves, but in that absence, teachers can easily decide whether the subjects are treated as isolated or as part of a whole (e.g., a study of railroads versus a study of changing jobs in the transportation industry). Obviously, materials that have some relevance to the life experience of the youngsters may be easier to relate to initially, but schools should constantly try to broaden the horizons of students so materials that lead from a known to an unknown subject can be very acceptable.

Sixth, since some schools have developed curriculum guides, the materials purchased must support the goals and objectives established by the schools themselves. Whether a student qualifies for graduation is determined by the degree to which these objectives are met. Therefore, it may be the wisest course to consider all the other criteria only after correspondence with the curriculum guides has been established.

Some excellent checklists for evaluating materials exist (Phelps & Lutz, 1977; Wimmer, 1980; Kokaska & Brolin, 1985). Supplemented by assessments of relevance, theoretical approach, flexibility, learning style compatibility, and associational relevance information, teachers are in a position to invest their money in commercial materials that will go a long way toward making their work effective and satisfying for themselves and their students. Although one might wish that materials validity research would be done before the materials were marketed, given the economic realities of commercial educational materials publication, teachers must depend on their own application of face validity criteria.

CONCLUSION

The *sine qua non* of special education is to make the subject fit the learners. Educators are better able to do that now because they have a better grasp of instructional design and instructional procedures. Past practices of artificial instructional groupings have been abandoned as more effective individual programs have been developed. Although the limitation on learning imposed by a disability must still be considered, more teachers are becoming skilled at serving students with learning problems in regular classroom settings. Even so, some students still receive most of their instruction from a special teacher in a self-contained setting, and at the high school level that means a teacher must be prepared to teach a variety of subjects.

Since the success of mainstreaming is affected by the climate of the school, it is vital to secure the support of administrators, teachers, peers, parents, and the students themselves for the effort. Although special education has a history of a scarcity of appropriate educational materials, that condition began to be reversed with the development of Instructional Materials Centers, which resulted in a large variety of attractive, commercially prepared materials available at a reasonable cost. That trend has continued with new and established publishing companies increasing the choices for teachers with a variety of textbooks, activity materials, computer software program, audiovisual programs, and teaching aids. Careful selection as to appropriateness, theoretical base, flexibility, compatibility with student learning style, and relevance can ensure a wise investment.

7

Prevocational and Occupational Programming

We cannot cross a bridge until we come to it; but I always like to lay down a pontoon ahead of time.—BERNARD M. BARUCH

ACTIVITIES

- Develop vocabulary lists specific to a particular kind of work (e.g., carpentry or auto detailing).
- Lead a discussion group on the realities of work, emphasizing both the positive and negative aspects of the realities.
- Examine the *Dictionary of Occupational Titles (DOT)* occupation numbering system. Identify the number codes for each function of the *DOT*.
- Study the Carl D. Perkins Act, which governs vocational education relative to providing access for people with disabilities to their programs, and identify the intent of Congress in the specific provisions.

INTRODUCTION

A paradox exists within public education today that affects high school students with handicapping conditions. On one hand, high schools are feeling the pressures of educational reform, with "excellence" and "outcomes" being defined in terms of academic rigor and minimum standards. In response, many high schools are trying to make accommodations for students with disabilities in order for them to achieve success in that increasingly rigorous academic environment. On the other hand, schools are trying to accommodate students with disabilities through individual educational programs that are planned in terms of the students' transition outcomes—that is, adjustment in employment, residential living, and independent living. It is no wonder, then, that teachers, parents, and high school students with disabilities are confused at times as to what school is all about. What kind of message are they getting about what a program should be? Mellard and Clark (1992) reported on a study involving a national sample of school superintendents, directors of special education, and educators of secondary special education teachers. When asked to list exemplary high school special education program attributes, and then to rank the attributes mentioned most frequently by all three groups, the results indicated that administrators and those responsible for the preparation of special education personnel value program organizational attributes much more highly than program outcomes (see Table 7.1). Only 3 of 10 attributes focused on student outcome goals, and they were ranked and weighted low in comparison to the administration- and organization-driven attributes.

How do schools—specifically special educators—deal with the paradox that administrators value program organization more than student outcomes? Typically, they deal with it in different ways with different student populations. That is, if the students have mild learning disabilities, they are likely to respond differently than if the students have moderate mental retardation. The same thing occurs in individual decision making, although other factors enter in here, such as the student's age, the interests and aspirations of the parents, and even such mundane realities as how far away the student lives from school and whether or not transportation is a problem. Student outcomes are the ultimate concern, but the perceived solutions to the problems of the educational delivery system are quite different. It is our opinion that curriculum alternatives related to individual goals and abilities must be of primary concern and that issues such as increased graduation requirements, minimum competency testing, or more (rather than fewer) instructional days obscure the problem with a smoke screen.

The message from the Office of Special Education and Rehabilitative Services of the Department of Education leaves no doubt about where it stands regarding the expected outcomes of students with severe disabilities. Will (1984) clearly established employment as the priority outcome for severely disabled graduates of special education programs. What is intended for mildly handicapped graduates is not so clear, however. This lack of clarity may be because of

TABLE 7.1 Special Education Program Attribute Weights by Group

Program Attribute	DOSE[a] N = 142		SOS[a] N = 67		PTT[a] N = 112	
	Rank	(Mean Wt.)	Rank	(Mean Wt.)	Rank	(Mean Wt.)
Effective staff	1	(16.8)	1	(15.6)	1	(15.5)
Individualized, appropriate instruction	2	(13-3)	2	(13.2)	2	(12.9)
Administrative leadership and support	3	(11.4)	4	(10.5)	3	(12.2)
Regular education support and integration	4	(10.4)	7	(9.7)	6	(8.8)
Program support from staff, parents, business, and community	5	(10.3)	5	(10.2)	5	(9.4)
Successful personal and social adjustment	6	(9.5)	3	(11.3)	4	(10.5)
Successful independent living	7	(8.1)	6	(10. 1)	8	(8.4)
Vocational-career orientation	8	(8.0)	9	(6.4)	7	(8.6)
Employment success	9	(7.3)	8	(7.8)	9	(7.7)
Postsecondary transition curriculum	10	(4.9)	10	(5.6)	10	(6.2)

Source: From *National High School Project, Vol 2: A Quantitative Description of Concepts and Practices for Students With Disabilities* by D. M. Mellard and G. M. Clark, 1992, Lawrence, KS: Department of Special Education, University of Kansas.
[a]DOSE = director of special education; SOS = superintendent of schools; PTT = preservice teacher trainer.

the semantic obfuscation in governmental position papers. For some time, it has been clear that the professional literature on vocational training of those who are "severely" handicapped has included the group of people known in mental retardation classification terms as "moderately mentally retarded." People classified as moderately mentally retarded are considered *severely* handicapped in relation to employment and independent living. In some states, the state vocational rehabilitation agencies include among their "severely" handicapped client populations any persons classified as having mental retardation.

The confusion for educators who are not attuned to such semantic practices is understandable. Although it is apparent that the educational reform movement and the transition movement are on a collision course, the issue of student outcomes and appropriate education is the one that this book addresses.

"Uh—I'm not sure that you're grasping the true concept of mainstreaming."

INSTRUCTIONAL CONTENT FOR PREVOCATIONAL AND OCCUPATIONAL INFORMATION

Numerous curriculum guides, articles, books, and publications outline the instructional content for prevocational and occupational information. Most professionals agree that both knowledge and skills are needed for successful occupational adjustment. This section deals with the knowledge aspect, beginning with prevocational information.

Prevocational Information

Brolin (1976, 1978, 1989), Brolin and Kokaska (1979), and Kokaska and Brolin (1985) approached the delineation of critical prevocational information through the competency approach. They suggested that the competency domain of occupational guidance and preparation of their career education model contains the primary prevocational information needs of an individual. These competencies include identification of the following:

1. The personal values one can meet through work
2. The societal values one can meet through work
3. The remunerative aspects of work
4. Occupational opportunities available locally
5. Sources of occupational information
6. One's own major occupational needs
7. One's own major occupational interests
8. One's own major occupational aptitudes
9. The requirements and demands of appropriate and available jobs

The competencies include understanding of the following:

1. The importance of following directions, working cooperatively with others, accepting supervision, good attendance and punctuality, meeting demands of quality work, and occupational safety
2. The process of searching for a job
3. The process of applying for a job
4. The process of interviewing for a job
5. The behaviors expected in competitive standards on a job
6. The behaviors necessary to maintain postschool occupational adjustment

These kinds of information and knowledge-based competencies represent typical prevocational or occupational information. Part of the problem in specifying exactly what information should be taught, and when, is the overall issue of scope and sequence in schools' curricula. Established scope and sequence for any new instructional content area is rare. The area of occupational information is a good example of this. Chapter 2 alludes to this issue, and Clark (1979), Gillet (1980), and Clark, Carlson, Fisher, Cook, & D'Alonzo (1991) go into some detail about the kinds of information that exceptional children and youth need to learn, beginning in the early childhood years: occupational roles, occupational vocabulary, occupational alternatives, and basic information related to some realities of the world of work. Each of these will be described to show how one can approach the same content suggested by Brolin (1976, 1978, 1989) in a different way.

Occupational Roles

An occupational information program should provide learning experiences that result in new or expanded awareness of possible roles for exceptional students. In producer/worker roles, the possibility of productive work, including paid and unpaid work, must be stressed. This includes awareness of roles such as the work of the student as a learner, the work as a volunteer, the work at home as an unpaid family worker, or the work activities or productivity in which one might be involved as a part of daily living (washing clothes, polishing shoes, repairing a leaky faucet, etc). In consumer roles, there needs to be a stress on the variety of roles one can experience as a consumer—customer, patient, client, renter, borrower, user, and so on.

Occupational Vocabulary

Students who are learning about their present and future occupational roles must develop vocabularies to acquire information basic to such learning (Fisher & Clark, 1992). This is not unlike a student entering law or medical school. The first few months emphasize the language of the profession. It is said that students in both these professions must acquire up to 20,000 new words during their preparation. Exceptional students do not have such a monumental task, but they do have to establish a certain vocabulary base even to begin to understand the world of work. Vocabulary development is not limited to a reading vocabulary, and, in fact, is more likely to be functional in terms of comprehension in hearing vocabulary and speaking vocabulary. From this perspective, it is obvious that occupational information must include purposefully taught occupational vocabulary. This includes general vocabulary necessary for understanding concepts about occupational roles, what occupations exist, and something about the characteristics of work and work settings. Suggested vocabulary words are available through studies by Schilit and Caldwell (1980), Schloss, Schloss, and Misra (1985), and Fisher and Clark (1992).

Occupational Alternatives

Before getting too involved in any type of special career-development programming for youth, educators of exceptional students should have some general perspective on occupational choice theory as it relates to normal growth and development. There are a number of theories, but only one is mentioned in brief here to serve as an example. Ginzberg and associates (Ginzberg, Ginsburg, Axelrad, & Herma, 1951) studied the occupational choice process and concluded that it is a developmental process. They suggested that the occupational decision-making process occurs in three basic stages or periods: fantasy, tentative choice, and realistic choice. They further suggested that the process involves a series of decisions made over a period of years, and that each step is meaningfully related to what has been decided before. The entire process is characterized by a continuous compromise among many factors—abilities, education, social status, age, physical and mental characteristics, geography, and so on. Some people have to compromise little, others a great deal. Individuals with disabilities will experience a greater number of compromises than will individuals without disabilities.

Career education content in the secondary curriculum must include a component of occupational information that relates to occupational choice and awareness of occupational alternatives in a way that provides keen sensitivity to students' needs for self-esteem. In terms of occupational choice development, Ginzberg and associates (Ginzberg et al., 1951) stated that the fantasy period in normal development ends around age 11 or 12. It is not unusual for high school youth with mental, educational, or behavioral disabilities to say that they want to be professional basketball players, movie stars, or rock singers. Given that they are functioning cognitively or maturationally at or below the age of 11, their occupational choices may reflect what others preceive as fantasy choices. Rather than be overly concerned with such verbal behaviors, teachers and counselors need to respond with occupational information that (1) encourages any stated desire to want to work or be productive in a legitimate occupation, (2) teachers and parents should elicit from the students the reasons underlying their stated occupational choices, and (3) begin the process of providing information to the students that affirms or challenges their understanding of what they think they want and what the occupation demands. Sometimes the reasons students give for a fantasy choice are very helpful in suggesting other alternatives.

Basic Information on Realities of the World of Work

There is a point at which providing basic occupational information about the world of work to students with handicaps becomes problematic. On one hand, the goal is to encourage students to want to work; on the other hand, educators have to be forthright in pointing out some of the negative realities of work. This section presents some of the realities—both positive and negative—that are especially important for students with handicaps to know. (*Note:* These appeared originally in a slightly different form in Clark [1979].)

REALITY 1   North American society in general, and the United States in particular, is a work-oriented society. It values work and those who are workers. No one can be directly compelled legally to work in U.S. society, except those few who are ordered by the courts to labor as a punishment for some crime. Even so, there are many formal and informal elements of society operating to "make" people into workers. For many, the system is so effective that unemployment produces high levels of anxiety, personal guilt, or feelings of worthlessness. For persons with disabilities, these feelings may be heightened, even though they may be able to reason that factors beyond their control are responsible for their unemployment.

Some argue that the leisure ethic has replaced the work ethic in U.S. society. Even though the past several years have shown more evidence of worker alienation, an increase in leisure alternatives, and a heavy emphasis on leisure and recreation in the media, the traditional meaning of work is still dictated by the power structure and is still espoused by major societal institutions. Moreover, the fact that most people cannot have any access to leisure or the necessities of life without some means of purchasing them leads people to seek employment. As long as these facts remain, this reality should be communicated to youth in school as part of their occupational information.

REALITY 2   Work, whether paid or unpaid, occurs in a particular locale: the factory, the store, the office, the construction site, the shop, the clinic, or the home. Work can occur in the home for some occupations (cottage industries, artist, writer, telephone answering service, etc.), but by and large a person must go outside the home to work. This fact has two important implications for individuals with handicaps. First, one must be mobile in order to get to work. This requires a set of competencies regarding travel that is critical for getting to the work setting. Choices of work alternatives may be influenced by this reality alone. A second implication is that work is most frequently performed in a public place. A public place has limitations on privacy; it usually has a set of socially expected behaviors, and there are formal or informal standards for dress and social amenities.

Whether these realities are positive or negative to an individual depends on whether the individual is attracted to or uninterested by the nature of work that deals with location. One person might want to work alone at home while another works primarily for the social interaction or the status that might go with a particular locale and its status, behavioral expectations, uniforms, and the like. Choices by one individual may involve no compromises; for another it might involve significant compromise.

Occupational information about these realities is necessary in preparing youths with disabilities for work. Information on mobility requirements, transportation alternatives, and skills needed for use of transportation options are important curriculum content. Occupational information about the expectations of different kinds of work environments in public places for appearance, dress, speech or language, interpersonal relations, and social etiquette provides additional knowledge for students in entering these new and unfamiliar settings.

REALITY 3   Paid work is largely impersonal work. Work for which there is no pay may or may not be impersonal, depending on its nature; the personalized relationships associated with play, recreation, or love are not expected on a job in most situations. In fact, they may be forbidden. This is one reality that youth may have already been exposed to indirectly at home when they detect a different kind or set of expectations by a parent when the parent tells the child to perform a household chore. The child learns that the parent becomes the "boss" and has expectations about *what* is accomplished, *how well* it is accomplished, and, in some instances, *in what way* it is accomplished. The parent temporarily becomes an impersonal work supervisor and acts out a role that is the norm in the work world.

The reality of working for relative strangers who are "all business" may be discouraging to those adolescents who have strong needs for more personal relationships. Although exposing them to this reality runs the risk of seeing them reject the notion of working, it is even more of an injustice to ignore the reality or, worse, distort reality so that they build up unrealistic expectations about the nature of work. Vocational rehabilitation personnel have been critical of special educators who not only do not teach this reality but teach the students that they are special and do not have to measure up in performance. They assert that special education teachers tend to reward their students even when the students do not perform satisfactorily.

If students with disabilities have experienced overprotectiveness from teachers or parents, the impersonality of work may provide them with their first opportunity to produce and be judged honestly on the quality and quantity of their work. Even if the objective opinion of the employer is more negative than feedback from school or home, many young people find the honesty refreshing and motivating. In these cases, the reality of paid work relating to impersonality may prove a positive factor in their work experience. It may be some persons' first experience where the disability is less important than productivity. How many people have you known in your life who might have been voted "least likely to succeed" while they were in school but who blossomed and achieved when given a fair chance to perform in the supposedly cold, cruel world?

REALITY 4   Work has several reward systems. Paid work obviously has the reward of remuneration, but unpaid work may provide the reward of saving money—that is, not having to pay someone else to do the work. There are other rewards of work, however, that should be mentioned. Some people see the value of work as offering them the opportunity to be of service, an opportunity to pursue interests and abilities, a means of meeting people, a way of avoiding boredom, or a chance to gain or maintain self-respect or self-esteem.

Youth need to know that people work for money but that they work for other things also. The question What's in it for me? is not inappropriate as students begin to sort out their values and establish a basis for being able to verbalize, "I want to work because...."

REALITY 5   Work is bound by time. Most workers have starting times and ending times. Certain times are set aside for breaks, for eating, or for cleanup. Many jobs are based on payment for certain hours, with extra payment for overtime. Even when pay is based on piecework, the individual is racing against time to produce or complete as many pieces as possible. There are job benefits that relate to time off and there are penalties or sanctions against being late or slow. To waste time at work is always frowned upon, and if it is chronic behavior, it may be grounds for dismissal from the job.

An inability to discipline oneself to meet time demands or constraints is one of the most serious obstacles to adjustment to work. This is frequently an especially difficult area for some disturbed individuals who have trouble relating to time concepts. It may also be an obstacle to those disturbed youth who have a very rational view of time and believe that those who are slaves to time schedules are the "sick" ones. Nevertheless, while one might appreciate student resistance to the hectic, time-oriented pace of living in the United States, the reality exists, and their understanding of the system and possible alternatives to it must be taught as a part of occupational information.

REALITY 6   Work is seldom performed in complete isolation or independence. Most work involves two or more people who interact in various ways. One of the most important of these interactions is the worker to the supervisor. Another is the interaction with fellow workers or consumers (customers, patients, clients, etc.). Still another is the interaction of the worker with subordinates. Depending on the size and complexity of the work setting, a number of interpersonal reactions are required that may be more critical to staying on that job than is the ability to perform the work tasks.

There may not be a formal communication of expected behaviors in work interactions, but they are communicated nevertheless through modeling, the worker grapevine, and events that occur that illustrate the rewards or penalties meted out to workers. People need to learn these basic expectations so they can develop a response system that shows a balance between dependence and independence in job performance (worker-supervisor interactions) and between the intimate and the casual (employee-fellow worker and employee-consumer interactions).

Although interpersonal and social interactions are a part of most work environments, the reality of having to work for or with other people is not always a demanding factor that sets up a person with disabilities for adjustment problems or failure. This aspect has the potential also for providing the support and positive reward of working that help an employee with disabilities keep a job. The personal rewards of an identity at least at one place outside the home can be significant. Many people without disabilities look for any possible social interactions on the job that compensate for the loneliness of nonwork hours.

REALITY 7   Work settings, like individual workers, rarely exist in isolation. As societies have moved from agrarian work settings to modern, industrial work settings, there has been an increasing dependence and interdependence among workers and work groups. Producers of goods require the services of workers in raw materials, manufactured goods for tools and equipment, transportation services, marketing and distribution services, and business and office services. Periodically, they may need workers in the building trades, communication and media field, custodial and maintenance services, health services, and public services. Likewise, any one of these work groups will have dependent or interdependent relationships with one or more of the others.

Adolescents should become aware of these relationships in order to understand the importance of all types of work groups and to combat some of the occupational stereotyping and status problems that inevitably arise in a study of the world of work and their own fantasies and plans about being a part of it.

REALITY 8   Not everyone who wants to work can obtain work, nor can everyone who obtains work be employed in the work of his or her choice. This final reality particularly affects individuals with mental or physical disabilities. As stated earlier, youths with handicaps should be allowed to have their fantasies about doing various kinds of work, and too much reality too soon can be not only inappropriate but also destructive. Furthermore, withholding some truths from them on this topic is advisable because although people with disabilities as a group are likely to experience unemployment or underemployment, that is not an assured fate for any one individual.

REALITY 9   The choice of an occupational area or a specific job is not a permanent or binding action. Choices, whether made with any compromises or not, can be reconsidered. Most people who make choices about job opportunities at the beginning of their occupational careers do so with the view that most jobs will temporarily meet certain needs and preferences now, but movement up or out of the occupational situation is not only probable, but also desirable. The emphasis that more or less self-actualized professionals in school and rehabilitation settings place on making the "right" occupational choice may send the "wrong" message. That is, young people with disabilities may get the message that because the world of work is so tough and that people with disabilities have to prove themselves even more convincingly than people without disabilities, it is absolutely imperative that they choose the right job the first time.

Adolescents with disabilities should be given the facts about the desirability of exploring one's interests and preferences in several occupations and the assurance that most people in the work force have worked at a number of different kinds of jobs. They also should be given some of the disadvantages of job hopping without any pattern of occupational development or responsibility in leaving jobs inappropriately. Educators and rehabilitation personnel need to remember that what is myth or reality to an adolescent regarding occupational choices and job selection is difficult to know without probing for beliefs and levels of understanding. Nothing can be assumed for any one student.

In summary, the adolescent with disabilities must begin to come to grips as early as possible with the realities of the world of work so that coping with or challenging those realities will be easier later. These realities must be introduced gradually and must include encouragement as well as cautious, but realistic, optimism.

Occupational Information on Prevocational Competencies

There is hardly an end to a description of all the occupational information that one could use in choosing an occupation, seeking training or employment in that occupation, knowing what is required to maintain employment by performing the work routine adequately, and knowing how, as Dever (1985) put it, "to handle 'glitches'" on the job. Most prevocational and occupational information in school curricular content focuses on information related to prevocational competencies; Figures 7.1 and 7.2 are presented as useful guides for teachers and prevocational instructors.

These figures present overlapping but somewhat different views on what should be taught. Each school program must decide for itself what should be taught, to whom, and in what way. School personnel tend to approach these decisions in the easiest possible way. It is not uncommon to hear the expression, "We shouldn't reinvent the wheel." There is some truth to that. But if the result of that approach is to select the wheel that is the most fashionable, the least expensive, the most available, or the easiest to use, without consideration for size, durability, or appropriateness, it is better to choose a wheel that has not yet been invented.

FIGURE 7.1 Basic Work Competencies: What Students Should Know and Be Able to Do as They Enter the Work Force

I. Knowledge and Skills
   A. Academic Skills
      Reading
         Understand basic word meanings
         Demonstrate literal comprehension
         Demonstrate interpretive comprehension
         Demonstrate evaluative comprehension
         Locate information
      Writing
         Demonstrate knowledge of a subject
         Demonstrate clear and consistent purpose and organization
         Demonstrate awareness of intended reader
         Make appropriate word choices
         Use correct capitalization and punctuation
         Spell correctly
         Use complete sentences
         Demonstrate standard grammar use
         Write legibly
      Speaking
         Speak clearly and distinctly
         Use tenses correctly (past, present, future)
         Pronounce words correctly
         Make oneself understood in conversation
      Mathematics
         Understand number and numeration concepts
         Do arithmetic computation
         Do estimation and approximation
         Do measurements
         Understand graphs and tables
         Understand probability concepts
      Reasoning Development
         Use common sense in everyday situations
         Understand problem-solving concepts
         Understand cause-effect relationships
         Do simple cost-benefit analysis
   B. Knowledge of the World of Work
      Demonstrate an Awareness of the Following:
         The concept of work
         Various work environments
         The culture of an organization
         Work-related tools, materials, equipment, vocabulary, basic laws
         Workers' rights and benefits
   C. Career Decision-Making Skills
      Job Possibilities
         Identify personal values met through work

(continued)

FIGURE 7.1 (continued)

Identify societal values met through work
Identify remunerative aspects of work
Understand job classifications
Identify occupational opportunities available locally
Identify sources of occupational information
Explore vocational interests
Job Choices
Identify major occupational interests
Identify requirements of appropriate and available jobs
Make realistic occupational choices
Become familiar with career options
Life Planning and Goal Setting
Develop long-term occupational goals and life plans
Exhibit an understanding of career development as a continuous proces
Expect to change careers over a working lifetime
D. Job Acquisition Skill
Develop job search skills
Develop job application skills
Develop interviewing skills
Adjust to employment standards
E. Independent Living Skills
Care for personal needs
Take action in emergency situations
Buy and care for clothing
Buy and prepare food
Get around in the community (mobility)
Develop basic consumer skills
Develop money skills (managing finances and banking)
Select and maintain a place to live
Manage recreation and leisure time
Participate in civic activities
Maintain relationships with family and friends
II. Behaviors
A. Social Behaviors
Effective Communication Skills
State facts clearly
Express feelings clearly and appropriately
Listen and respond appropriately
Ask for assistance
Self-Presentation
Introduce self
Demonstrate basic hygiene and grooming
Control frustration
Demonstrate patience
Control undue fear and anxiety
Positive Self-Image

FIGURE 7.1   (continued)

Realistic Awareness of One's Own Abilities and Limitations
Decision Making
Interactions with Others
   Demonstrate courtesy
   Demonstrate cooperation
   Demonstrate assertiveness
   Understand the impact of one's behavior on others
   Assess proper behavior for situations
   Seek attention appropriately
   Respect the rights and property of others
   Accept the differences between oneself and others

B. Work Behaviors
Attendance and Punctuality
   Go to work regularly
   Call in when sick or unable to go to work
   Request time off following appropriate procedures
   Know when it is appropriate to take breaks
   Know when it is appropriate to leave work early
Instructions
   Follow verbal instructions
   Follow pictorial instructions
   Follow written instructions
   Follow demonstrated instructions
   Follow multistep instructions
   Remember instructions
Task Orientation
   Attend to task
   Perform repetitive tasks
   Demonstrate work stamina
   Adapt to changes in work task and environment
   Demonstrate organizational skills
   Demonstrate problem-solving skills
   Demonstrate work safety
   Follow shop rules and procedures
   Care for equipment properly
   Work independently (with supervisor present)
   Work alone (with supervisor absent)
   Complete work
Work Pace
   Work at a satisfactory production rate
   Demonstrate efficiency
   Demonstrate productivity
   Respond to time pressure
   Work consistently
Work Quality
   Demonstrate accuracy

(continued)

FIGURE 7.1 (continued)

Recheck work
Discover and correct own errors
Learn from mistakes
Initiative
Attempt new tasks without hesitation
Initiate work tasks
Exhibit self-directed learning
Interaction with Others
Demonstrate an understanding and a respect for the
various roles and work styles found in the workplace
Accept supervision
Respond to correction and criticism
Teamwork
Work cooperatively
Demonstrate a willingness to compromise
III. Work Attitudes
Demonstrate Motivation Through
Interest in work
Enthusiasm for work
Commitment to work
Pride in one's work
Seriousness toward work
Conscientiousness toward work
Demonstrate a Desire to Learn
Demonstrate Ambition
Demonstrate Dependability
Demonstrate Responsibility
Demonstrate Self-Confidence

Source: From *Toward Work: Implementation Handbook* (pp. 46–50) by J. Sowers, 1983, Newton, MA: Education Development Center, Inc. Copyright 1983 by Education Development Center, Inc., Newton, Massachusetts. Reprinted with permission.

There is considerable scope in the content of prevocational and occupational information. It can be simplified and the tasks analyzed with priorities established for which content elements are the most critical for students who are low functioning, students or it can be open ended, reaching for the highest levels of cognitive acquisition for students who are physically, behaviorally, or sensory impaired. Ideally, secondary schools should lay out a scope and sequence curriculum in this area for all students and ensure that all students have access to it. In many schools, hard decisions must be made about how students with special needs can acquire this information.

FIGURE 7.2   Employment Competencies

The student will be proficient in the following areas:
- Referring to want ads and pursuing jobs of interest
- Selecting people to use as personal or job references
- Understanding the differences between private and public employment agencies
- Utilizing the school's job placement services
- Understanding the functions of unions, apprenticeships, professional and trade organizations, civic and fraternal organizations, and the civil service system, and how to use these in getting a job
- Knowing how to write a resume
- Being courteous in using the telephone when searching for a job
- Exhibiting skill in letter writing
- Recognizing the value of walk-in procedures when looking for a job
- Knowing various terminology, words, and abbreviations found on job application forms and being able to fill out an application
- Understanding the importance of personal appearance
- Being familiar with questions routinely asked during interviews and being able to answer them accurately
- Understanding and appreciating the various elements that combine to produce a successful job interview, including evaluation criteria used during the interview, why some applicants are not hired, and how to avoid certain negative impressions by the interviewer
- Showing an awareness of different laws pertaining to employer and employee rights
- Knowing how to give and follow instructions on the job
- Understanding that relationships with co-workers and supervisors are important to job survival
- Recognizing the various factors that produce success on the job and how to self-assess job performance
- Knowing the procedures for terminating employment

If resource rooms are the *modus operandi* for delivery of instruction and support maintenance for regular class instruction, some questions must be asked: Is this content available in one or more elective courses in the regular curriculum? If not, why not? If it is available, is it accessible to *every* student who has been identified as mildly to moderately handicapped? If it is not accessible to *every* student, how can the instruction be delivered?"

If self-contained classrooms or a combination of self-contained classrooms and resource rooms are used, the same questions must be asked, with the addition of these: Is the content currently in the self-contained classroom curriculum? If it is not, why not? How can the instruction be delivered within the context of a self-contained classroom model or in conjunction with another program?

Unfortunately, these questions have not been asked as frequently as the basic question, Is prevocational and occupational information so critical to include that one should sacrifice instructional time from basic academics? Many high school programs buy into the need for both academics and either vocational education or community-based work experience options. The assumption is made that all the content just described will be included in the vocational education classes or will be learned in on-the-job training, thus eliminating the need for prevocational and occupational information being taught purposefully and systematically. We believe that this is a false assumption and that high schools must provide this content as professionally as possible, using all the pedagogy and technology at their disposal.

INSTRUCTIONAL ALTERNATIVES FOR TEACHING OCCUPATIONAL SKILLS

For more than two decades, advocates for students with disabilities have experimented with ways to prepare such students for the world of work. The work of Eskridge and Partridge (1963), Kolstoe and Frey (1965), Younie (1966), Payne and Chaffin (1968), and Freeland (1969) established the community on-the-job training and work experience as a significant model that persists in one form or another. It is clear, though, that this model was designed for youths with mild disabilities, some of whom are still classified as educable mentally handicapped and some of whom are now classified as learning disabled or behavior disordered. A large proportion of these students were from poor families or from culturally different racial or ethnic backgrounds. Programs were designed to motivate students to want to stay in school and find employment through training while in school.

The emergence of secondary programs for all handicapped youth through The Education for All Handicapped Children Act (PL 94-142) and the Carl D. Perkins Vocational Education Act of 1984 (PL 98-524) led to a variety of other models of vocational preparation, including regular vocational education, adapted vocational education, special vocational-occupational programs, work-adjustment programs, and work activities. A description of each of these and a discussion of their merits and limitations follows.

Regular Vocational Education

Clark and Evans (1976), Phelps (1976), Phelps and Greenan (1982), Phelps and Lutz (1977), and Meers (1980) contributed to the literature early in their descriptions of how vocational education as a field can and should respond to its mandate to serve students who have special needs. More recently, Phelps and Frasier (1988) and Hasazi and Cobb (1988) have provided current perspectives of what vocational education is doing to serve students with handicaps. Vocational education is an important means of delivering vocational programming to youth with disabilities.

Vocational education is a term that traditionally had very specific meanings. It has been a major part of the public education system since the Smith-Hughes

Act of 1917. The term has been used loosely in the past few years by many special educators who do not know or appreciate what vocational education has had to do to establish its identity. It is important to establish a clear distinction between vocational education and vocational training (or vocational preparation). Currently, this distinction is not made by many special educators. This muddied situation began when there appeared in the *Federal Register* (1977) this statement: "The term [special education] also includes vocational education if it consists of specially designed instruction, at no cost to the parent, to meet the unique needs of a handicapped student." The same issue of the *Federal Register* defined vocational education as "organized educational programs which are directly related to the preparation of individuals for paid or unpaid employment, or for additional preparation for a career requiring other than a baccalaureate or advanced degree."

Although the latter definition came closer to the traditional definition, the American Vocational Association (n.d.) leaves no doubt as to the specific nature of vocational education in public secondary and postsecondary programs in its publication *Vocational-Technical Terminology*:

> part of a program designed to prepare individuals for gainful employment as semi-skilled or skilled workers, technicians, or subprofessionals in recognized occupations and in new and emerging occupations, or to prepare individuals for enrollment in advanced technical education, but excluding any program to prepare individuals for employment in occupations generally considered professional or which require a baccalaureate or higher degree. (p. 73)

The interpretation made here is that vocational education, as an established discipline, has through tradition, legislative authority, and regulatory policies and procedures, carved out its niche. It does not ordinarily assume responsibility for training in unskilled occupations (day labor and many entry-level service occupations) nor does it train in areas requiring a college degree or professional training. This means, for example, that a youth with very low functioning who is placed in the community with a job coach under a supported employment program is not receiving vocational education from the school; the youth is receiving vocational training or employment training. This means also, for example, that a youth who is placed in a work experience placement in a nursery is not receiving vocational education, but work experience training or occupational training. This even means that a youth who takes a woodworking class or a foods or clothing class may not be receiving vocational education, but rather industrial arts or practical arts training. Unless the program is designated as a state-approved vocational education course of study, it is not vocational education.

A wide variety of alternatives are available to vocational educators in their program development. In reality, however, vocational education is rather limited in what it tries to offer, particularly at the high school level. High school programs typically offer one or more of the "Big Seven," which include the following areas of instruction and some examples of each type:

Vocational agriculture and agribusiness
   Horticulture
   Farm mechanics
   Fertilizers and insecticides
   Animal husbandry
Marketing and distributive occupations
   Wholesale occupations
   Retail occupations
   Warehousing
Health occupations
   Nurse's aide
   Practical nurse
Vocational home economics
   Industrial sewing
   Commercial food preparation
Business and office occupations
   Word processing
   Data processing
   Computer operator
   Bookkeeping
Technical occupations
   Electronics
   Printing
   Graphics
Trades and industrial occupations
   Building trades (carpentry, plumbing, electrical, etc.)
   Heating and refrigeration
   Tool and die
   Manufacturing and processing

Secondary vocational education is offered in several different environments. The comprehensive high school, the area vocational center, the vocational high school, the general high school, and special state schools are the most common places. The largest percentage of all vocational education programs are provided in a comprehensive high school. *Comprehensive high schools* are large high school programs that offer at least five vocational program areas in the same building or on the same campus as the college preparatory and general education programs.

Area vocational centers are popular in communities that are not large enough to have a comprehensive high school or a vocational school. The geographic area usually served by a vocational center usually includes several communities that combine resources to use and support the center. These centers offer only vocational education programs and typically have both secondary and postsecondary training programs. Secondary students who are in their last two years of high school are permitted to leave their home schools and attend the area vocational school for a half of each school day. Transportation and financial support are provided by the sending schools.

Vocational high schools are unique in that while they are separate facilities, they serve only high school students and begin their vocational programming with the students in the ninth grade. Students can get all the academic credit required for high school diplomas at the vocational school. Large school districts are the usual sponsors of such programs, and they may serve adjacent communities that do not have adequate vocational programs or that have students who want a specific type of vocational training that is offered only at the vocational high school.

The *general high school* vocational education program is one that offers fewer than five vocational education programs. Frequently, only two or three vocational training areas are available, along with some industrial and practical arts. In rural areas, vocational agriculture has been a traditional offering, as well as business and office occupations. A third option is often a cooperative education program of some type that depends on the community itself to provide the training environment and much of the instruction.

A final delivery alternative for vocational education is in a *state's residential schools.* For example, most state schools for students with hearing impairments have a vocational education program, much as a comprehensive high school or general high school would. Other vocational education programs for high school students are often found in various state institutions for youths who are behaviorally handicapped or adjudicated. Vocational education teachers or vocational instructors in these programs follow their states' policies for program approval and teacher certification.

It is no secret that students with disabilities have not been welcomed into regular vocational programs in community high school programs. Beginning with initiatives in 1963, and continuing until 1991, every piece of vocational education legislation has attempted to encourage and entice vocational education programs to accept and serve students with disabilities. Weisgerber, Dahl, and Appleby (1980) cited some of the factors involved in this resistance:

- A feeling of personal responsibility that most vocational educators have about the safety of their students when they are working with power equipment or are otherwise exposed to some type of hazard
- An unwillingness of vocational educators to compromise on standards of achievement or alter the course completion requirements to reflect individual differences
- An assumption that it would be harder to place handicapped graduates in jobs, coupled with a recognition that program effectiveness in vocational education depends in large part on the placement rate of course graduates
- A lack of experience by vocational educators in dealing with the handicapped and little knowledge about their capabilities and potential
- A lack of aggressiveness by the handicapped in obtaining assignments to vocational classes. (p. 65)

The 1990 Carl D. Perkins Vocational and Applied Technology Education Act (PL 101-392) appears to reflect the intent of Congress to continue to require access to vocational education programs for students with disabilities, but it dropped the set-aside funds and offered no incentives to state or local education agencies to go beyond the basic requirements of the law. The act now requires that state and local education agencies shall provide the following assurances:

- Vocational education will be provided in the least restrictive environment.
- Students with disabilities will have access to the full range of programs offered.
- Students must be assessed with respect to successful completion of the vocational education program.
- The planning for vocational education will be coordinated among special education, vocational education, and rehabilitation personnel.
- Instruction and counseling services will facilitate the transition of these students from school to postschool environments.
- Supplementary services will be provided that enable students to succeed in their vocational programs.

From the outset, questions from advocates for special populations that had previously been included in specific funding allocations focused on how much schools must spend on services for students with disabilities and still be able to demonstrate these assurances. Department of Education interpretations of the proposed regulations in regard to the question of funding stated that the proposed rules would require school districts to help special populations enroll in vocational education by providing supplementary services if "only to the extent possible from funds under the act" (*Education of the Handicapped*, 1991, p. 1).

Delay in publishing the proposed regulations for PL 101-392 and the extended delay in completing and publishing the final regulations forced states to develop three-year state plans without official guidance on how to meet the new mandate. It remains to be seen what the long-term effects of the changes in the law will be, but there was a clear retreat from previous laws in terms of active advocacy for students with disabilities. It is likely that parents and individuals with disabilities will have recourse only through due process procedures under PL 94-142 and PL 101-476 and the Americans with Disabilities Act (PL 101-336).

Some important gains have been made as a result of compliance reviews by the Office of Civil Rights and the Americans with Americans with Disabilities Act (PL 101-336). But Vocational Education is still not an easily accessible system in many schools. Shapiro and Lentz (1991) reported data for students with learning disabilities that even question the effort. The instructional issue in accessing students with handicapping conditions into regular vocational programs is this: What accommodations must be made for a given student with disabilities so that he or she can participate in the training and complete the requirements of the course? This issue does not speak to changing the requirements of the course in terms of vocational skills or competencies. The curriculum and the outcomes or target competencies remain the same. Accommodations would come in flexibility in the way a student acquires information, prepares and delivers course assignments, and is able to be examined.

Support services to the student could include one or more of the following: audiotapes of readings, notetakers, interpreters, modifications of equipment, architectural accommodations, speech or communication assistance, instructional aids or equipment, peer tutoring, individualized contracts, support personnel, or transportation. Some students might also need additional support outside the classroom or shop in reading or math instruction in order to be successful in the regular program (West et al., 1992).

Instruction in regular vocational training programs is the responsibility of vocational education instructors. Support services to the student or the vocational instructor may be provided by vocational resource teachers, special needs vocational instructors, special needs resource teachers, special education resource room teachers, or special education self-contained classroom teachers. With this arrangement, students have the opportunity to train with peers who have no disabilities and have more vocational training options both in high school and in opportunities for postsecondary vocational training.

Adapted Vocational Education

Adapted vocational education represents program alterations or modifications in a regular vocational education program. Modifications or adaptations are major in that the curriculum or outcomes of the course are changed. For example, if it is not realistic for certain nonreading students to complete an auto mechanics course that moves systematically through engines, electrical systems, hydraulic systems, brake and steering systems, exhaust systems, suspension and chassis systems, and so forth, an adapted program for one or more systems could be developed to permit specialization for students and allow instructors to break down tasks into more carefully developed instructional units to ensure mastery. Thus, a student might complete an adapted vocational education course, taught by a regular vocational instructor, in brake and steering systems or exhaust systems and be placed in a brake and steering or muffler shop.

Students with handicapping conditions who have been determined to be capable of acquiring skills and concepts from a vocational program but who would have difficulty in succeeding in a regular vocational training program (even with accommodations and support services) are the target population for adaptive vocational education. The responsibility for this type of training lies with vocational education personnel, and this type of program should be made to have merit and appeal, even to students without disabilities. The students will still need some accommodations by the instructor and support services in most cases, but it is meant to be as much like a regular vocational education program as possible in terms of course listings and scheduling. Tindall (1980) directed a project leading to an excellent annotated bibliography on modifying curricula for students with disabilities in programs such as these.

A variation of this model is what is sometimes called a special needs vocational class. Classes such as these are provided under the administration and supervision of the vocational education department and are frequently used to serve students who are handicapped and disadvantaged. The content of the curricula in these classes may be prevocational in nature (mostly prevocational and occupational information as described earlier in this chapter), but may also provide some vocational content in a modified form and at a slower pace. Hasazi and Cobb (1988) cite several disadvantages to this type of instructional programming, such as the following:

1. It has increased the degree of segregation experienced by these students and their teachers.

2. Emphasis on generic work skills rather than occupationally specific skills may not be as appropriate for special needs students as for students in general vocational education. Even if it is appropriate, if it serves as a substitute for specific occupational skills training in school and in the community, its value must be questioned.

3. Programs of this type generally assume that specific occupational training will be provided as a follow-up to the generic skills training. Recent follow-up studies of former special education students (Hasazi, Gordon & Roe, 1985; Wehman, Kregel, & Seyfarth, 1985) have indicated that they do not, in fact, receive additional occupationally specific training after leaving high school.

4. The personnel teaching special needs vocational education courses have not been trained adequately to function in a role such as this.

There are some legitimate concerns related to all four of these disadvantages. The segregation issue is a general one that might not be supported in a particular case, because good teaching and positive outcomes are more likely to be associated with a particular instructor than with an administrative arrangement. On the whole, though, one must be concerned with segregation when the motivations are obviously to provide only token compliance with the law or to assume that all students with disabilities are similar and can be taught in the same way in the same type of program.

Some resources for further reading in both regular and adapted vocational education for students with handicaps include these publications:

Employability Skills for the Special Needs Learner (Wircenski, 1982)
Instructional Strategies for Special Education Students in Regular Vocational Classes (Greene et al., 1988)

*Prevocational and Vocational Education for Special Needs Youth: A Blueprint
for the 1980s* (Lynch, Kiernan, & Stark, 1982)
*Puzzled about Educating Special Needs Students? A Handbook on Modifying
Vocational Curricula for Handicapped Students* (Tindall, 1980)
Vocational Education for Persons with Handicaps (Gaylord-Ross, 1988).

Special Vocational-Occupational Training

Special vocational-occupational training programs are those that are designed
specifically for selected vocational or occupational areas that are not available
through an adapted vocational program or that provide training in occupational
areas outside the traditional scope of vocational education. Examples of special
vocational-occupational programs include work-study or work experience programs, general industrial or occupational training through storefront training
centers, special occupational training programs, or on-campus product manufacturing, assembly, packaging, or service delivery subcontracting.

Special vocational-occupational training is usually directed toward a semiskilled or entry-level service occupation for which there is a labor demand or for
which there is an opportunity through job development. Training varies considerably in this general type of employment preparation programming and may not
lend itself to general description or categorization. Frequently, the programs are
innovative and unique because they arose out of necessity. Remember, the students who select this program option, or who have been determined to have
disabilities that suggest great difficulty in successful participation in a regular or
adapted vocational training program, make up the target population for this
general programming approach on the vocational training continuum. This means
that some students are present by choice and others are present by placement.
The specific vocational-occupational training alternatives in a given school may
be limited, or there may be none available at all. The following descriptions
provide examples of these alternatives.

Work-study or *work experience* programs have from the beginning of their
development been justified and supported on the basis of their natural *transition*
goals. Eskridge and Partridge (1963, p. 454) described the Texas Cooperative
Program and results of the two-year pilot project of interdisciplinary cooperation
in a work-study approach: "The soundness of this [pilot project] was substantiat-
ed by the results ... in which approximately 60 percent of the youth were successfully rehabilitated and made the transition from school to the work world."
Younie (1966, p. 32) stated, "The transitional process, although most complex
and little explored, is a vital consideration to include in any work experience
planning." Freeland (1969, p. 13) also used the term *transition* in one of his
stated objectives of a work-study program: "The student's transition from school
to the work world is a guided and smooth one."

The purposes and functions of work-study and work experience programs
vary to some degree from community to community. In fact, work study and work

experience are not even considered the same type of program in some locations. Geographic location, student population characteristics and needs, program philosophy, and community resources are important variables that shape any work-training program into the different programs that can be observed. Even so, there are some common denominators that underlie most all work-study and work experience programs, beginning with the desire and intent to ease the often-difficult transition between school and work by providing training in job skills, attitudes, and work habits. Other more specific common goals include the following:

1. Provide real work experiences in combination with in-school training and general education, enabling students to acquire knowledge, skills, and appropriate attitudes necessary for independent living in the community.
2. Remove the artificial barriers that separate work, independent living, and education.
3. Provide the beginning of connections between school and the community.

The fact that work-study programs in special education were modeled after Cooperative Vocational Education Programs leads one to question the differences between the two. The distinction made in this book is that Cooperative Vocational Education Programs are examples of regular vocational education community-based job training options, and work-study or work experience programs are directed by special educators for students who are not interested in the cooperative programs available in their school or who are unable to succeed in such programs. Cooperative vocational education programs include such programs as cooperative distributive education (DE), cooperative trade and industry (TI), cooperative office education (OE), and occupational home economics (HE) (Kingsbury, 1980). Cooperative vocational education programs are also generally characterized not only by their carefully designed in-school instruction and supervised work experiences but also by their advisory committees and occupationally related student clubs. Distributive Education Clubs of America (DECA) and Vocational and Industrial Clubs of America (VICA) are two well-known examples of student clubs. Special education work-study or work experience programs do not generally follow the cooperative education model in vocational education in the use of advisory committees and student clubs, although there is something to be said for these practices.

Work experience programs that are referred to by that name are also sometimes called work samples, job samples, work exploration, or, in some states, work experience and career exploration programs (WECEP). These programs are usually designed for students who are 14 to 15 years of age and who show a number of indications that they are potential school dropouts. The programs permit students to experience some work exploration and some work success while in a school-related program. Depending on the community, students may or may not earn wages during these exploratory experiences. When students are rotated every six to nine weeks to another work experience, wages are not usually a standard part of the program. Some school programs use on-campus work experience exclusively for their work experience phase, whereas others use only community-based jobs or a combination of the two for work experience options.

Work-study programs are more frequently characterized by more long-term placements and may involve a range of two to four hours per day for beginning students in the program to full-time work placement for students in their last semester, or even during their entire last year. Students may be placed in on-campus paid jobs, but most frequently they are placed in community jobs in competitive employment settings. Students with more deficits in their employment skills might be placed in a supported employment situation in the competitive job market, enclave employment, or mobile work crew. Each of these is discussed in more depth in Chapter 8.

Storefront programs, as a part of special vocational-occupational programming, are not as common as they were in the 1960s and 1970s. Schools are not as inclined to invest in a service station, cafe, nursery, or craft store these days. High costs of rent or purchase and maintenance, insurance, and the negative aspects of segregated training have argued against this particular approach. However, in rural areas and in communities where unemployment is high, there is still room for innovation and dynamic leadership by a teacher or work-study coordinator who has a keen sense of entrepreneurship and can teach some entrepreneuring skills.

Alternative schools and *institutional vocational programs* are not special occupational-vocational programs so much as they are unique training sites where nontraditional regular vocational education, adapted vocational education, and special occupational-vocational programs exist. Alternative schools that blossomed in the late 1960s and early 1970s took several forms, one of which was a "trades" or special occupational training approach. One community in Kansas began such an alternative high school with occupational training programs in health occupations (leading to a licensed vocational nurse certificate), food services, and building trades (students built homes and sold them). The food service program involved not only an in-school training program but also a community work-placement component and a specialized catering service called "Cookie Champs." This particular example reveals a limited range of training options and some interesting alternatives: traditional classroom vocational training, adapted vocational training, community work training, and an entrepreneur model. Many of the students who chose this alternative school had specific learning or behavior disorders.

Institutional programs offering special occupational-vocational training are very similar to alternative schools that offer special training options, with the primary differences being the degree of choice by students for being there and the amount of flexibility for community placements. Training through enclaves and mobile crews are frequently used vocational training options out of institutional programs, but competitive and supported employment training placements are gaining in popularity.

Work-Adjustment Programs

Work adjustment and the work-adjustment process has been described in a clear, straightforward way by Brolin (1976). Although Mithaug (1981) has questioned the value of work adjustment for all disability groups or even all levels of functioning within a specific disability group, there is fairly good agreement on what work-adjustment programming is. Using Brolin's conceptual description, it can be said that work adjustment is an approach to both evaluation and training that has three primary goals: (1) to orient certain persons to the world of work, if they have not had much work experience or have had negative experiences; (2) to develop prevocational skills; and (3) to change specific work deficiencies and maladaptive behaviors that will deter a person from getting and holding a job. The concept grew out of and is still an important part of the field of rehabilitation.

Accomplishing the preceding goals outside the context of a work environment is virtually impossible. Work-adjustment training must be offered through structured work experiences at school or in a rehabilitation facility that provides real work tasks. Using real work tasks, the training focuses on each individual student's needs, whether they are personal-social, attitudinal, related to work readiness, prevocational skills, or actual job skills. Students placed in this component of the vocational continuum should be only those whose deficits are clearly below what would be required for any of the other training options or who are inexperienced because of age or opportunities. Work tasks vary from program to program. Some work-adjustment program options include in-school subcontracting jobs, such as a packaging subcontract for a health-food wholesaler, an enclave work contract in an industrial plant, or mobile work crews. Schools can provide these themselves or they can contract with local rehabilitation facilities, but the issues of responsibility and control are important, and schools should be extremely cautious in passing this type of programming on to another agency.

Scott, Ebbert, and Price (1986) advocated informal work samples as a vehicle for assessing and teaching employability skills and providing work adjustment opportunities. They proposed the use of informal work samples that teachers design in general employability skill areas such as assembling and disassembling, packaging, counting, sorting, matching, sequencing, and using tools, materials, and processes. This approach, in contrast to a school having real work through subcontracts or some type of production or service operation, can be more systematic and more flexible for training of a variety of work skills and behaviors. On the other hand, this approach may be too far removed from the real work world for students to be able to generalize and may become a prevocational version of drill and practice work in academic instruction. It is this latter trap that enough programs have fallen into for the entire notion to attract criticism. Even more detrimental to the prevocational work-sample approach is that some students do not respond well enough in these settings so that their prevocational "readiness" ever reaches the point that would lead to recommendation for placement in competitive employment. Logically, continued prevocational and work-adjustment training is recommended at a community rehabilitation facility. This perpetuates the "readiness" fallacy.

Work Activities

The final component of the vocational training continuum is a program of work activities. This program is designed for students who function at a level such that they would find it difficult to succeed in any type of vocational or occupational training program in the high school. Their needs in basic work skills—such as sorting, assembly, disassembly, product handling, materials handling, or use of tools and equipment—characterize their level of functioning in work environments. These students generally have additional deficits related to success in working that must be addressed. Inappropriate social behaviors, behavior disorders, self-injurious behaviors, and communication deficits are common in this population. The work-activities program focuses on age-appropriate gross and fine motor coordination, on-task behavior, communication skills, mobility skills, personal-social skills, and independent living skills with work tasks as the instructional medium. Since this book is targeted for personnel working with students who are mildly and moderately handicapped in high school programs, this type of program will not be detailed here.

ISSUES IN PREVOCATIONAL AND OCCUPATIONAL PLANNING AND PROGRAMMING

Several important factors can affect what prevocational and vocational programs are offered to students in a given high school. These factors may vary from one community to another, but the following are general issues that persist across most local school districts.

Parental Values

Parents of adolescents with disabilities have a wide range of perspectives on the value of vocational education and vocational training. The traditional view that a high school diploma represents basic academic competence persists, and some parents have a difficult time seeing vocational education or training as a major thrust of a high school course of study. Another variable is the degree to which parents will allow their child to make, or even believe that their child can make, independent occupational choices. Socioeconomic backgrounds, concern for status, and basic views about what a high school education should be about all have an effect on parents' aspirations for their children and the degree to which they can or will accept vocational training in high school, and, if so, what type of training is acceptable.

Postsecondary Vocational Training Opportunities in the Community

Both educators and parents have a tendency to postpone vocational training as long as possible. One way that educators do this is to use the argument that the school need not provide any vocational offerings, or, at best, only a minimum of vocational offerings, because the community has strong postsecondary offerings available. Parents may use these same arguments with their sons and daughters, drawing on their own perceptions of the importance of a regular high school diploma. The lack of postsecondary vocational programs, on the other hand, forces school boards and educators to look at vocational programming as an important alternative to secondary school. The number and kinds of students who might need or want such programs then have an effect on the range of program options in a vocational training continuum.

Labor Market in the Community

All regular vocational education programs must demonstrate a demand for workers in a given area before they can be approved by the state for funding. Community employment levels and the size and nature of the communities enter into the labor market demand. A small town in an isolated area will have few local labor demands, and certain communities—by virtue of their location—will have heavy labor demands in certain kinds of occupational areas and not in others. Program development decisions for youth with disabilities that hinge on the fact that there is a need for general prevocational or general employability skill training for some students may be avoiding the issue of labor demands, but only temporarily. It is a fact that employability skills are vital, but at some point specific occupational skill training for employment must be addressed in program planning and development.

Philosophical Differences in the Field

The philosophical differences between advocates of academic versus vocational programming are not limited to regular and special educators. Some special educators view vocational education and other vocational training alternatives as having lower status for students and, possibly, for themselves. This is found in all categorical groups of teachers but is more common among special education personnel working with populations in which a proportion of the students have intellectual performance levels above the range associated with students with mental retardation. This includes students with learning disabilities, behavior disorders, orthopedic or other health impairments, and visual or hearing impairments. Philosophical differences over academic versus vocational training are probably the most obstructive factors in getting prevocational and occupational training established in high school special education programs.

There is another situation that reflects tension among advocates of occupational and vocational training. This tension has developed recently as advocates for community-based employment and supported employment have challenged more traditional vocational training personnel with their placement success data, their zealous articulation of their philosophical view, and their technology. The message to traditionalists, whether intended or not, is, "You have been ineffective. You have compromised the rights and dignity of persons with handicaps. You, too, can effect appropriate results if you do it our way." This message has been supported by endorsements through federal initiatives for funding of programs using the supported employment-transition model. This creates some dissonance among traditionalists who resent this message and its implications, even though there is some basis to the message.

INDIVIDUALIZED PLANNING FOR PREVOCATIONAL AND OCCUPATIONAL TRAINING

For convenience, this book has dealt with academic goals and prevocational and occupational goals in separate chapters. The establishment of individual goals and short-term objectives forces the participants in the planning process to ask the question, What do we want this student to know or be able to do at the end of this school year? For the student, as a participant in the planning process, the question is, What do I want to know or be able to do at the end of this school year? This question is directly related, of course, to the long-term issue of what the primary objectives are for the high school experience. Each year's IEP should focus clearly on how it will contribute to the final outcome objectives. The new transition services provision in the IDEA (PL 101-476) should increase the response to appropriate prevocational and occupational planning.

An individualized plan that has the individual student's transition from school to adult living as its focus *must* directly address the part that future employment will play. The planners (including the student as well as the student's family) must analyze the school's resources to provide for preparation for employment and make some definite choices about how to achieve the appropriate preparation for employment. Hasazi, Salembier, and Finck (1983) proposed some excellent objectives to provide a framework for planning and evaluating teaching-learning activities from a student-centered and programmatic perspective. They suggested the following student-centered objectives:

1. Develop and implement assessment procedures that identify functional skills and interests related to current and future employment and training opportunities in the community.
2. Provide necessary support services to ensure access to mainstream vocational classes.
3. Provide at least four work experiences, each six to eight weeks in length, in identified areas of interest and skill for students between the ages of 15 and 18.
4. Assist the student in locating and securing employment before graduation.
5. Provide supervision and follow-up services to students in full-time or part-time employment until graduation (or until the student is 22 years of age).
6. Develop individual transition plans with appropriate adult service agencies (i.e., vocational rehabilitation, community colleges, state employment service, or mental health services) for students who need continued service following graduation.

Hasazi and colleagues stated, and correctly so, that in order to plan realistically for these student-centered objectives, certain program-centered objectives must be met. These include the following:

1. Allow for flexible teacher schedules to meet the training and monitoring needs of students placed in community settings.
2. Design and implement a systematic follow-up procedure for contacting students following graduation to determine employment status, utilization of social services, relationship of vocational preparation to present and previous employment, and other relevant information.
3. Develop a "youth find" system for identifying all students with disabilities in need of vocational components in their individual educational plans prior to entering secondary-level programs.

CONCLUSION

The work-study movement of the 1960s, the special-needs vocational education movement of the 1970s, and the transition movement of the 1980s have broadened the options available to schools in providing for students' employment preparation. These movements have also clarified the focus of each so that unique differences among them serve to provide program differentiation for students with different needs, preferences, and interests. There should no longer be groups of professionals arguing for one program type over another. A vocational training continuum makes sense, as does an instructional continuum in academics. This does not suggest that special and vocational educators should now move on to new challenges. All of the program options discussed in this chapter need to be refined and improved until there are workable program implementation guidelines for each type.

The educational reform movement has taken a strong antivocational stance. The implications of these actions are serious. Some states are already reviewing their positions on the role of vocational education in the secondary school and are moving toward a position that places secondary vocational education in the role of providing only exploratory experiences, prevocational (practical and industrial arts) training, and an introduction to technology. Educators must acknowledge the role of politics in the formation of school policies and get involved in the process. Being informed of current prevocational and occupational program planning and development options is critical in making a case in the political arena as well as planning and conducting such programs.

8

Job Placement, Training, and Supervision

Experience is the best of schoolmasters, only the school-fees are heavy.
—*THOMAS CARLYLE*

ACTIVITIES

- Debate the advantages and disadvantages of school-initiated job placement versus student self-initiated job placement.
- Visit a work site and describe the social ecology of the situation. Plan a training program that specifically addresses the social requirements of the job site visited.
- Examine the Fair Labor Standards Act and report on the specific references to training sites for persons with disabilities.
- Conduct a community survey to develop a pool of placement alternatives for students with differing disabilities.
- Develop a training progress evaluation form for a specific job site.

INTRODUCTION

The unique set of competencies required for effective job placement, training, and supervision are not the same as those required for effective classroom instruction. There is some overlap between the two roles in the areas of training and supervision, but the overlap involves more generic competencies, such as basic communication skills, knowledge of how to use resources, and general knowledge of instructional strategies. This chapter is designed to provide specific information on the specialized roles of *job placement, job training,* and *job supervision* since these functions are not commonly taught in special education personnel-preparation programs.

Job placement, training, and supervision responsibilities may be assigned to either a secondary special education teacher (in which case, the title more appropriately used is teacher-coordinator), a work-study coordinator, or a vocational special needs cooperative education teacher. Other titles reflecting similar basic roles are found in school programs, such as prevocational coordinator, vocational adjustment coordinator, vocational adjustment counselor, vocational counselor, job placement specialist, and job coach.

This chapter is meant to prepare one to place students with disabilities in real jobs, assume responsibility for their training on those jobs, and supervise their performance during follow-up. Each of these three basic functions is addressed in separate sections.

JOB PLACEMENT

A philosophical debate has been ongoing in the field for some time as to whether schools should take responsibility for job placement or whether students with disabilities in an employment training program should secure their own jobs. Those who believe that schools are responsible have based their arguments on the belief that the school is responsible for not only the students' learning in this phase of their school program but also for program integrity. They maintain that placement should be based on a job match between a student and a specific job situation, and that schools are more able to arrange that match. They also believe that problems are more likely to occur when a student finds the job and the school endorses it as a job training situation because the proper communications between the school and the employer and the school and the parents fail to occur. Finally, they maintain that while students may find a job in line with their interests, it is more likely that they find jobs just as most everyone else does—by chance. The accommodations that the school has to make under these circumstances result in a loss of control in training and are more likely to result in employer and parent relations problems.

The advocates of students finding their own jobs believe that the students in special education or special needs vocational education programs must learn

the skills of job finding while in school, and the best way to teach those skills is to provide them with training in job finding and then let them demonstrate their aptitude in the skills. They argue that the school or other agencies will not always be available to find jobs for the students and they must learn to function independently. They also view the practical side of the problem in terms of the time it takes to find jobs for students, especially at the beginning of the year, and they rationalize their endorsement of the students' own job finding with the argument that a student is more likely to do better in a job that he or she has found than one that has been found for him or her. They also argue that as students are successful in finding their own jobs, their self-confidence increases. This is viewed as a vital part of their preparation for independence.

Some programs establish a compromise policy and specify that the initial job-training placements that a student has during the tenth or eleventh grade must be secured by the school but the student may find his or her own job for the twelfth grade. Others allow students to find their own jobs but provide them with job leads in previously developed job situations, or, if it is a completely new situation, insist that the job site be analyzed to ensure a job match and that all regular communications concerning the program with employers and parents are made prior to a final approval of the site.

Given the wide range of interests and abilities of students in secondary vocational training programs, it is difficult to say that a school should have a policy on job placement that is either school or student oriented. The basic goal is successful job placement and training that will lead to employment, so flexibility in approach is desirable. On the other hand, not having a policy at all can lead to problems with parents and administrators when difficulties arise in the placement process in the program. If a policy is established, it must be based on realistic knowledge of the work world and anticipation of issues and problems that can occur in a school-community partnership in job training and employment. The following sections address some of these factors.

Knowledge of the Work World

A placement coordinator is going to have a great deal of difficulty in making effective placements without some firsthand or acquired information about the nature of work environments. Chadsey-Rusch and Rusch (1987) have written an excellent description of the ecology of the workplace. They approach the ecology of work environments with the basic assumption that to make a match between a student with disabilities and a job, three basic ecological dimensions of the employment context must be considered.

The first dimension is the physical ecology. *Physical ecology* refers primarily to the architectural and physical designs or layout of environments that may affect behavior, such as enclosed spaces without windows, heights, small work cubicles, presence of loud machines, and so forth. The physical environment can

place demands on a worker that may exceed the demands of the work tasks themselves. An important part of the job match, then, is in matching the student with the physical demands. For example, when considering a work setting, the placement coordinator must analyze the location of the primary work area and any mobility barriers for accessibility; the physical layout of the work area for such variables as furniture dimensions, floor coverings, and climatic conditions; as well as the potential hazards. Beyond these factors, however, the analysis must consider how the physical characteristics of the workplace could affect social and emotional behavior. This involves such factors as the number of people in a given workspace, the degree of isolation imposed by a workspace, and the size of a work space. Chadsey-Rusch (1986), for example, found more frequent social interactions among employees with mental retardation and their co-workers in smaller employment settings.

The second dimension of the ecology of the workplace, according to Chadsey-Rusch and Rusch (1987), is the social ecology. *Social ecology* in a workplace refers to the social interactions and interpersonal relationships that occur between individuals, between individuals and groups, and between groups. This is an area of concern because much of the literature on reasons for loss of employment among persons with special needs has pointed to social deficits as one of the most frequent causes (Greenspan & Shoultz, 1981; Nash & Castle, 1980; White, Schumaker, Warner, Alley, & Deshler, 1980). Given this concern, placement in a work environment should consider carefully not only the possible negative effects that the social ecology might have on a given student but also the possible positive effects to meet certain needs. Any social factors that might result in high levels of stress, social discrimination, or social rejection, or that might contribute to problems in job performance, should be noted in a work environment analysis. On the positive side, there might be some highly supportive social factors inherent in a work setting. Examples of these are the employer's attitude toward persons with disabilities, a nurturing, supportive co-worker or supervisor, or a social support system built into the job through an organization like a union, a bowling league, or informal social networks.

The third ecological dimension of the workplace described by Chadsey-Rusch and Rusch (1987) is organizational ecology. *Organizational ecology* refers to the program or policy factors in a work setting that may influence individual and group behavior. Program or policy factors include such things as management style and structure, size of an organization, employee autonomy, worker rules or regulations, safety procedures, or production quotas. Salaries, employee benefits, and opportunities for advancement are very important organizational factors also. Any number of organizational variables may operate within a work environment and affect the work performance or behavior of a student from a school work experience program in the community. The placement coordinator must be extra sensitive to this dimension, since many of the factors reflecting the organizational ecology are not easily observed by an outsider and are not readily identifiable in a slick company brochure.

Issues in Job Placement

Another area of knowledge of the work world has to do with the many factors involved in job placement itself. This area involves some understanding of labor supply and demand, economic factors in the employment of persons with disabilities, incentives and disincentives for persons with disabilities to work or not work, and legal and moral issues in job placement of persons with special needs. Sometimes this information is more issue based than knowledge based at some points, and should be treated as such.

A general issue in job placement relates directly to the labor supply and demand in a community. Supply and demand for labor depend on such factors as population trends, social trends, changes in occupations, and the economy. Linari and Belmont (1986) provided a thoughtful view of three of these major factors related to employment that should be a part of the information base that placement specialists should have in understanding the work world. They made the following points:

1. *Population trends.* Although there will be a 16 percent increase in overall population growth from 1980 to 2000, it is projected that the population will reflect an aging factor, with fewer in the work force in the 15- to 44-age bracket. This will result in a lower percentage of jobs available for younger people in the work force. Changes in the size and nature of the population will also affect the kinds and amount of goods and services needed (demand) and the size and characteristics (supply) of the work force (Fair, 1980). For example, as a result of population changes, in the 1980s careers in health occupations, domestic services, food and beverage preparation and service, leisure occupations, and construction services are expected to expand (Cetron & Appel, 1984).

2. *Social trends.* Cetron (1983) projected that increased economic demands will require more families to have both spouses working. This will result in both a larger labor supply, hence more competition for jobs, and the creation of an increased demand for domestic and childcare workers, time-saving appliances, transportation needs, and prepared foods.

3. *Occupational trends.* The fields of high technology, agriculture, communications, information processing, environmental conservation, and manufacturing are changing in ways that dramatically affect the work force. Naisbitt (1984) asserted that although the economy of the United States shifted from an agricultural to an industrial base in 100 years, the shift from an industrial base to an information-services base has occurred in only 20 years. Feingold (1984) projected that by the year 2000, 80 percent of the work force will be employed in the field of information services. Manufacturing may provide only 11 percent of the jobs available (down from 28% in 1980) due to foreign competition, robotics, and computer-assisted design in manufacturing. Environmental issues will force attention on conserving natural resources, searches for new energy sources, and

control of pollutants and hazardous waste. The elimination of many traditional jobs in agriculture, manufacturing, and industries such as the oil and gas industry will change the demand for certain kinds of workers at the same time that other new fields are creating new kinds of labor demands. Figures 8.1 and 8.2 show some of these changes.

The effect of the economy on any community's employment picture is obvious, but it is difficult to talk about the specific effects of economic factors for any one community. Most of what appears in the media deals with national economic factors, such as effects of the fiscal policies of the federal government, the monetary policies of the federal reserve board, the balance of trade, or the availability of energy sources and how they affect employment. Some generalizations, however, can be made about how economic variables affect a community's labor supply and demand and how these affect the employment of persons with special needs. O'Brien and Stern (1987) cited two of these generalizations:

1. Placing disabled workers into competitive employment can save taxpayers' money. However, Hill and Wehman (1983, p. 35) cautioned that "most" if not all, of the jobs held by disabled persons would be held by nonhandicapped individuals in their absence." Some displacement of individuals who are nonhandicapped is inevitable when the total number of people looking for paid employment is greater than the number of jobs available. That situation exists, according to Abraham (1983), who estimated that the total number of job seekers exceeds the

FIGURE 8.1 Projections for Industries Providing Services and Industries Providing Goods

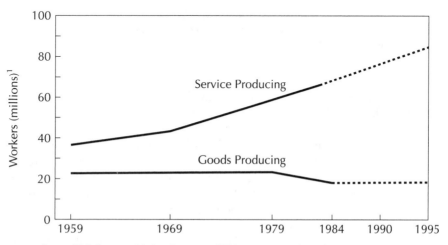

Source: U.S. Bureau of Labor Statistics, 1986.
[1]Includes wage and salary workers, the self-employed, and unpaid family workers.

FIGURE 8.2   Industry Growth through the Mid-1990s

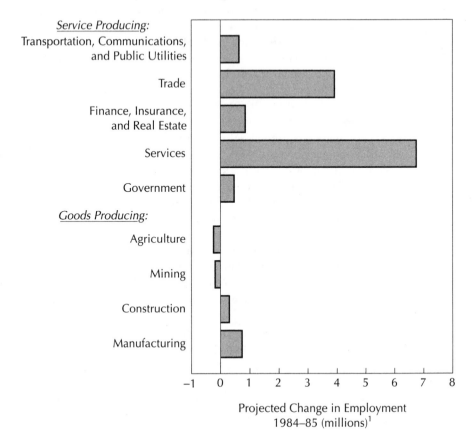

Projected Change in Employment
1984–85 (millions)[1]

Source: U.S. Bureau of Labor Statistics, 1986.
[1]Wage and salary employment except for agriculture, which includes self-employed, and unpaid family workers.

total number of available jobs any time the overall unemployment rate is higher than 3 to 4 percent.

2. The federal government administers several programs intended for the redistribution of income among economic groups in the United States. The major programs affecting persons with disabilities include (a) transfer payments in cash (e.g., Supplemental Security Income) or in kind (e.g., food stamps and Medicaid); (b) education and training programs designed to improve work-force productivity and increase the earning power of special groups (e.g., Job Corps, Job Training Partnership Act, Carl Perkins Vocational Education Act); and (c) direct wage subsidies (Targeted Jobs Tax Credits) or job creation. Unfortunately, these

kinds of income redistribution and "work incentives" may conflict with each other at times and end up being work disincentives.

The job placement specialist needs to be aware of these economic issues and be prepared to discuss them with parents and the community at large, who may see the consequences of job placement in an entirely different light than do schools or employers. One question often raised by parents is, What will happen to the benefits we get once our child begins to earn a salary? The response should include the following facts:

- Under Section 1619(a) of the Social Security Act, a person can continue to receive some Supplemental Security Income (SSI) payments even if earnings are over $500 per month. This is possible because some earnings are excluded from the determination of earned income. Benefits continue until earnings exceed the SSI income limits.
- Parents should notify the local Social Security Office *immediately* regarding employment status and earnings or any change in employment status.
- Should a student exceed the "substantial gainful activity" level of $500 per month, Medicaid coverage may continue even after SSI benefits are reduced or stopped. The amount a student can earn and still receive Medicaid varies from state to state. Contact the local Social Security Office for the amount relative to your state. If the student's earnings are higher than the state's limits, but he or she has special work expenses or medical expenses, the student may still qualify for Medicaid.

Job placement specialists must keep updated on current benefit provisions annually. Benefits change and there are differences between disability classifications.

The federal incentive programs of education and training and wage subsidy will be discussed in a section later in the chapter. At this point, however, another general issue of job placement needs to be discussed, because it involves the federal government. That issue is regarding the legal factors involved in placing students in work situations.

The Fair Labor Standards Act of 1938 and its amendments established the federal guidelines for minimum wage regulations, child labor provisions, and guidelines for obtaining handicapped worker or student-learner certificates for school-work programs. They also provided the legal structure for wages in sheltered workshops. The most critical areas of information for placement personnel in school programs are, of course, the child labor provisions and minimum wage and hour regulations. Figures 8.3 and 8.4 provide summaries of child labor requirements in nonagricultural occupations and in agricultural occupations, respectively. Particular attention must be given to issues of age requirements and hazardous occupations. It is also important to remember that if the age exception regulation for the employment of 14- and 15-year-olds is used for placing students in a Work Experience and Career Exploration Program (WECEP), it must be an approved school-supervised and school-administered WECEP program.

FIGURE 8.3 Employment Standards for 14- and 15-Year-Olds

MINIMUM AGE STANDARD FOR NON-AGRICULTURAL EMPLOYMENT

Oppressive Child Labor Is Defined as Employment of Children Under the Legal Minimum Ages

14   Minimum age for employment in specified occupations outside school hours.

16   BASIC MINIMUM AGE FOR EMPLOYMENT. At 16 years of age youths may be employed in any occupation, other than a nonagricultural occupation declared hazardous by the Secretary of Labor.

18   Minimum age for employment in nonagricultural occupations declared hazardous by the Secretary of Labor.

- No minimum age for employment which is exempt from the child labor provisions of the Act.
- No minimum age for employment with respect to any employee whose services during the workweek are performed in a workplace within a foreign country or within territory as limited by section 13 (f) of the Act.

Note to Employers

Unless otherwise exempt, a covered minor employee must be paid according to statutory minimum wage and overtime provisions of the Act.

EXEMPTIONS FROM THE CHILD LABOR PROVISIONS OF THE ACT

The Child Labor Provisions Do Not Apply To:

- Children under 16 years of age employed by their parents in occupations other than manufacturing or mining, or occupations declared hazardous by the Secretary of Labor.

- Children employed as actors or performers in motion pictures, theatrical, radio, or television productions.
- Homeworkers engaged in the making of wreaths composed principally of natural holly, pine, cedar, or other evergreens (including the harvesting of the evergreens).

OTHER CHILD LABOR LAWS

Other Federal and State laws may have higher standards. When these apply, the more stringent standard must be observed. All states have child labor laws and all but one have compulsory school attendance laws.

HAZARDOUS OCCUPATIONS ORDERS IN NONAGRICULTURAL OCCUPATIONS

(These Orders are published in Subpart E of Part 570 of Title 29 of the Code of Federal Regulations.)

Hazardous Occupations Orders

The Fair Labor Standards Act provides a minimum age of 18 years for any nonagricultural occupations which the Secretary of Labor "shall find and by order declare" to be particularly hazardous for 16- and 17-year-old persons, or detrimental to their health and well-being. This minimum age applies even when the minor is employed by the parent or person standing in place of the parent.

The 17 hazardous occupations orders now in effect apply either on an industry basis, specifying the occupations in the industry that are not covered, or on an occupational basis irrespective of the industry in which found.

The Orders in effect deal with:

1. Manufacturing and storing explosives.

2. Motor-vehicle driving and outside helper.
3. Coal mining.
4. Logging and sawmilling.
5. Power-driven woodworking machines.
6. Exposure to radioactive substances.
7. Power-driven hoisting apparatus.
8. Power-driven metal-forming, punching and shearing machines.
9. Mining, other than coal mining.
10. Slaughtering, or meat packing, processing or rendering.
11. Power-driven bakery machines.
12. Power-driven paper-products machines.
13. Manufacturing brick, tile, and kindred products.
14. Power-driven circular saws, band saws, and guillotine shears.
15. Wrecking, demolition, and shipbreaking operations.
16. Roofing operations.
17. Excavation operations.

Additional information

Inquiries about the Fair Labor Standards Act will be answered by mail, telephone, or personal interview at any office of the Wage and Hour Division of the U.S. Department of Labor. Offices are listed in the telephone directory under U. S. Department of Labor in the U. S. Government listing. (These standards are published in Subpart C of Part 570 of Title 29 of the Code of Federal Regulations, Child Labor Regulation No. 3.) Employment of 14- and 15-year-old minors is limited to certain occupations under conditions which do not interfere with their schooling, health, or well-being.

HOURS-TIME STANDARDS

14 AND 15-YEAR-OLD MINORS MAY NOT BE EMPLOYED:
1. DURING SCHOOL HOURS, except as provided for in Work Experience and Career Exploration Programs.

2. BEFORE 7 A.M. or AFTER 7 P.M. except 9 p.m. from June 1 through Labor Day (time depends on local standards).
3. MORE THAN 3 HOURS A DAY—on school days.
4. MORE THAN 18 HOURS A WEEK—in school weeks.
5. MORE THAN 8 HOURS A DAY—on nonschool days.
6. MORE THAN 40 HOURS A WEEK—in nonschool weeks.

Permitted Occupations for 14-and 15-year-old Minors in Retail, Food Service, and Gasoline Service Establishments

14- AND 15-YEAR-OLD MINORS MAY BE EMPLOYED IN:
1. OFFICE and CLERICAL WORK (including operation of office machines).
2. CASHIERING, SELLING, MODELING, ART WORK, WORK IN ADVERTISING DEPARTMENTS, WINDOW TRIMMING, and COMPARATIVE SHOPPING.
3. PRICE MARKING and TAGGING by hand or by machine, ASSEMBLING ORDERS, PACKING and SHELVING.
4. BAGGING and CARRYING OUT CUSTOMER'S ORDERS.
5. ERRAND and DELIVERY WORK by foot, bicycle, and public transportation.
6. CLEANUP WORK, including the use of vacuum cleaners and floor waxers, and MAINTENANCE of GROUNDS, but not including the use of power driven mowers or cutters.
7. KITCHEN WORK and other work involved in preparing and serving food and beverages, including the operation of machines and devices used in the performance of such work, such as, but not limited to, dishwasher, toasters, dumbwaiters, popcorn poppers, milk shake blenders, and coffee grinders.
8. WORK IN CONNECTION WITH CARS and TRUCKS if confined to the following: dispensing gasoline and oil; courtesy service on premises of gasoline service

(continued)

FIGURE 8.3 (continued)

station; car cleaning, washing, and polishing; other occupations permitted -by this section. BUT NOT INCLUDING WORK involving the use of pits, racks, or lifting apparatus, or involving the inflation of any tire mounted on a rim equipped with a removable retaining ring.

9. CLEANING VEGETABLES and FRUITS, and WRAPPING, SEALING, LABELING, WEIGHING, PRICING and STOCKING GOODS when performed in areas physically separate from areas where meat is prepared for sale and outside freezers or meat coolers.

In Any Other Place of Employment

14- and 15-YEAR-OLD MINORS MAY BE EMPLOYED IN any occupation listed above. 14- and 15-year-old minors may not be employed in:

1. Any MANUFACTURING occupation.
2. Any MINING occupation.
3. PROCESSING occupations such as filleting of fish, dressing poultry, cracking nuts, or laundering as performed by commercial laundries and dry cleaning (except in a retail, food service, or gasoline service establishment in those specific occupations expressly permitted there in accordance with the foregoing list).
4. Occupations requiring the performance of any duties in WORKROOMS or WORKPLACES WHERE GOODS ARE MANUFACTURED, MINED, or OTHERWISE PROCESSED (except to the extent expressly permitted in retail, food service, or gasoline service establishments in accordance with the foregoing list).
5. PUBLIC SERVICE MESSENGER SERVICE.
6. OPERATION OR TENDING OF HOISTING APPARATUS or of ANY POWER-DRIVEN MACHINERY (other than office machines and machines in retail, food service, and gasoline service, establishments which are specified in the forego-

ing list as machines which such minors may operate in such establishment.

7. ANY OCCUPATIONS FOUND AND DECLARED TO BE HAZARDOUS.
8. OCCUPATIONS IN CONNECTION WITH:
   a. TRANSPORTATION of persons or property by rail, highway, air, on water, pipeline or other means.
   b. WAREHOUSING and STORAGE.
   c. COMMUNICATIONS and PUBLIC UTILITIES.
   d. CONSTRUCTION (including repair). Except Office or Sales Work in connection with a, b, c, and d when not performed on transportation media or at the transportation media or at the actual construction site.
9. ANY OF THE FOLLOWING OCCUPATIONS IN A RETAIL, FOOD SERVICE, OR GASOLINE SERVICE ESTABLISHMENT:
   a. WORK performed IN or ABOUT BOILER or ENGINE ROOMS.
   b. Work in connection with MAINTENANCE or REPAIR OF THE ESTABLISHMENT MACHINES or EQUIPMENT.
   c. OUTSIDE WINDOW WASHING that involves working from window sills, and all work requiring the use of LADDERS, SCAFFOLDS, or their substitutes.
   d. COOKING (except at soda fountains, lunch counters, snack bars, or cafeteria service counters) and BAKING.
   e. Occupations which involve OPERATING, SETTING UP, ADJUSTING, CLEANING, OILING, or REPAIRING power-driven FOOD SLICERS and GRINDERS, FOOD CHOPPERS and CUTTERS, and BAKERY-TYPE MIXERS.
   f. Work in FREEZERS and MEAT COOLERS and all work in PREPARATION OF MEATS for sale (except wrapping, sealing, labeling, weighing,

pricing and stocking when performed in other areas).

g. LOADING and UNLOADING GOODS to and from trucks, railroad cars, or conveyors.

h. All occupations in WAREHOUSES except office and clerical work.

Exceptions

WORK EXPERIENCE AND CAREER EXPLORATION PROGRAMS (WECEP) Some of the provisions of Child Labor Regulation No. 3 are varied for 14- and 15-year-olds in ap-

proved school-supervised and school administered Work Experience and Career Exploration Programs (WECEP). Enrollees in WECEP may be employed: during school hours; for as many as 3 hours on a school day; for as many as 23 hours in a school week; in occupations otherwise prohibited for which a variation has been granted by the administrator of the Wage and Hour Division. The State Educational Agency must obtain approval from the administrator of the Wage and Hour Division before operating a WECEP program.

Source: U.S. Department of Labor, Employment Standards Administration, Wage and Hour Division.

FIGURE 8.4   Child Labor Requirements in Agriculture under the Fair Labor Standards Act

---

The Fair Labor Standards Act establishes minimum ages for covered employment in agriculture, unless a specific exemption applies. The Act covers employees whose work involves production of agricultural goods which will leave the state directly or indirectly and become a part of interstate commerce.

Minimum Age Standards for Agricultural Employment

16 years	for employment in any farm job at any time
14–15 years	for employment outside school hours in any farm job that has not been declared hazardous by the Secretary of Labor. No minors under 16 years of age may be employed at any time in hazardous occupations in agriculture, unless exempt.
12–13 years	for employment outside school hours in any nonhazardous farm job, with written parental consent, or on the same farm where their parents are employed.
Under 12 years	for employment outside school hours in any nonhazardous farm job, with written parental consent only on farms where the employees are not subject to the minimum wage provisions of the Act.
10–11 years	local resident children only: for employment outside school hours as hand harvesters of short season crops, for no more than 8 weeks between June 1 and October 15, for employers who receive a waiver from the Secretary of Labor.

(continued)

FIGURE 8.4 (continued)

Any age   for employment in any farm job at any time on a farm owned or operated by the minor's parents or persons standing in place of parents.

The Fair Labor Standards Act extends minimum wage provisions to farm employees, including minors, whose employer used more than 500 man-days of farm labor during any calendar quarter of the previous calendar year. Unless otherwise exempt, employees covered by the minimum wage provisions must be paid at least $4.25 an hour beginning January 1, 1991.

Certain small farms and hand harvest laborers may be exempt from the minimum wage provisions.

Farmworkers are not subject to the overtime provisions of the Act.

Other Child Labor Laws

Most states have laws setting standards for child labor laws in agriculture. When both state and federal child labor laws apply, the law setting the more stringent standard must be observed.

Penalties for Violations

Employers who violate the child labor provisions of the Act may be subject to a civil money penalty up to $1,000 for each violation.

The Secretary of Labor has found and declared that the following occupations in agriculture are particularly hazardous for minors under 16 years of age (No minor under 16 years of age may be employed at any time in these occupations, unless exempt*):

1. Operating a tractor of over 20 PTO horsepower, or connecting or disconnecting an implement or any of its parts to or from such a tractor.

2. Operating or assisting to operate (including starting, stopping, adjusting, feeding or any other activity involving physical contact associated with the operating): corn picker, cotton picker, grain combine, hay mower, forage harvester, hay baler, potato digger, or mobile pea viner; feed grinder, crop dryer, forage blower, auger conveyor, or the unloading mechanism of a nongravity-type self-unloading wagon or trailer; or power post-hole digger, power post driver, or non-walking-type rotary tiller.

3. Operating or assisting to operate (including starting, stopping, adjusting, feeding or any other activity involving physical contact associated with the operation): trencher or earthmoving equipment; fork lift; potato combine; or power-driven circular, band, or chain saw.

4. Working on a farm in a yard, pen, or stall occupied by a: bull, boar, or stud horse maintained for breeding purposes; or sow with suckling pigs, or cow with newborn calf (with umbilical cord present).

5. Felling, bucking, skidding, loading, or unloading timber with butt diameter of more than 6 inches.

6. Working from a ladder or scaffold (painting, repairing, or building structures, pruning trees, picking fruit, etc.) at a height of over 20 feet.

7. Driving a bus, truck, or automobile when transporting passengers, or riding on a tractor as a passenger or helper.

8. Working inside: a fruit, forage, or grain storage designed to retain an oxygen deficient or toxic atmosphere; an upright silo within 2 weeks after silage has been added or when a top unloading device is in operating position; a manure pit; or a horizontal silo while operating a tractor for packing purposes.

9. Handling or applying (including cleaning or decontaminating equipment, disposal or return of empty containers, or serving as a flagman for aircraft applying) agriculture chemicals classified under the Federal Insecticide, Fungicide, and Rodenticide Act as Toxicity Category I, identified by the word "Danger" and/or "Poison" with skull and crossbones; or Toxicity Category II, identified by the word "Warning" on the label.

10. Handling or using a blasting agent, including but not limited to, dynamite, black powder, sensitized ammonium nitrate, blasting caps, and primer cord.

11. Transporting, transferring, or applying anhydrous ammonia.

Additional Information

Contact your local Wage and Hour Division office, listed in most telephone books in the U.S. Government listing, under U.S. Department of Labor, Employment Standards Administration.

Source: Child Labor Bulletin No. 102 (WH Publication 1295).

*Exemptions:

1. Young workers employed on farms owned or operated by their parents.

2. Student-learners enrolled in a bona fide vocational agriculture program are exempt from Items (1) through (6) when certain requirements are met.

3. 4-H Federal Extension Service Training Program and Vocational Agriculture Training Program. Minors 14 and 15 years of age who hold certificates of completion of training under either program in tractor or machinery operation may work outside school hours on equipment in Items (1) and (2) for which they have been trained.

Even the state education agency must obtain approval from the administrator of the regional wage and hour division before it can approve any local education agency work programs.

Most programs allowed for workers with disabilities under the Fair Labor Standards Act, as amended, are straightforward. If there are questions, representatives of the Wage and Hour Division or Child Labor Division are more than willing to assist placement personnel in learning what can be done to facilitate placement of students with disabilities in work settings. The most delicate area of regulatory interpretation of the law has to do with the status of the student as a trainee versus an employee. This is especially important for schools that have their own work-adjustment programs that function much as subcontract rehabilitation facilities. For that reason, the specific wording of the law is presented here as it appears in *Federal Wage and Hour Law: A Guide for Vocational Rehabilitation Facilities* (National Association of Rehabilitation Facilities, 1984):

> Work by handicapped workers which is incidental to a training program is covered by the Fair Labor Standards Act. Only under limited and narrow circumstances can trainees with disabilities or clients be engaged in what would otherwise be covered work and not be compensated. Thus, if a client is put at a work bench or assembly line for evaluation or testing purposes, the client must be paid for time that is spent in producing a product or service. There is a special wage and hour certificate applicable to these situations.... Only if the client is truly *not an employee* can the training/work be considered noncompensable.

The issue of whether or not a student is employed or is in what is called an "employer-employee relationship" goes beyond a placement in a community rehabilitation facility. Simon, Bourexis, and Norman (1993) reported that when students participate in any community-based employment preparation activity, such as a Community-Based Vocational Education (CBVE) program, the placement activities must be in compliance with the federal Fair Labor Standards Act. That is, it is important to establish in writing when a student is not in an employment relationship; otherwise, they are subject to the Fair Labor Standards Act regarding minimum wage, overtime pay, record-keeping requirements, and child labor regulations. Schools and employers should adhere to the following guidelines in order to avoid violation of the provisions of the Fair Labor Standards Act:

• Students with disabilities engaged in vocational exploration, assessment, and training *are not* employees of the businesses in which they might be placed.

• Schools and businesses that engage in activities related to vocational exploration, assessment, and training activities meeting the following criteria *do not* violate the provisions of the Act:

> Participating students must have physical and/or mental disabilities, and competitive employment at or above the minimum wage level is not immediately obtainable.
>
> The students must be at a level of functioning that requires intensive, ongoing support to perform in a work setting.
>
> Student participation will be for vocational exploration, assessment, or training in a community-based placement work site under the general supervision of public school personnel.
>
> Community-based placements will be articulated clearly as a part of the individualized educational program's (IEP) statement of needed transition services in vocational exploration, assessment, or training for each participating student.
>
> Information from the student's IEP will not have to be made available; documentation of the student's enrollment will be required, however, with the local Department of Labor (Wage and Hour Division) and with

the Department of Education. The student and the student's family must be informed fully of the IEP provisions and the community-based placement component. The student and family must indicate voluntary participation in the program and an understanding that the placement does not entitle the student to wages.

The activities of the students in the community-based placement site *do not* result in an immediate advantage to the employer.

Although the existence of an employment relationship is not contingent upon the number of hours spent in the community-based placement, as a general rule, each placement component will not exceed the following limitation during any one school year: vocational exploration, 5 hours per job experienced; vocational assessment, 90 hours per job experienced; and vocational training, 120 hours per job experienced.

Students are not *entitled* to employment at the business at the conclusion of their community-based placement experience under the IEP. However, once a student is employed, the student cannot be considered a trainee (nonemployee) for exploration, assessment, or training at that particular placement site unless the placement involves a clearly distinguishable occupation than the one leading to employment.

Schools and businesses that participate in community-based programs where the students are not employed are responsible for monitoring that all of the preceding criteria are met. If any one of the seven criteria specified in the guidelines are not met, the student will be considered in an employment relationship and can be held responsible for full compliance under the Fair Labor Standards Act. School personnel responsible for administering job-shadowing programs, community job sample programs, community-based vocational assessment, and nonpaid training programs should be familiar with *Meeting the Needs of Youth with Disabilities: Handbook on Implementing Community-based Vocational Programs According to the Fair Labor Standards Act* (Colorado State University, 1994).

Knowledge of Community Resources and Job Placement

There are any number of ways that vocational preparation personnel can and should know about and use the many resources in a community. In the placement process, however, there are some very obvious resources that must be used when they are available and others that may be "invisible" resources. Both of these types are discussed briefly here.

The obvious (or "visible") resources in a community are the agencies or organizations that make it their business to know about the community's employment status. The following are among those in this category of resources: state job service centers, local chamber of commerce, local job training partnership act (JTPA) program, Projects with Industry, state division of vocational rehabilitation, and local advisory committees.

State Job Service Centers

State job service centers or state employment offices offer a variety of services, including information on available jobs in the community, information on trends on new employment possibilities or planned closings of local businesses or industries, assistance in vocational evaluation, and assistance in placement in jobs. Depending on the size of the office, one person may be designated as the placement counselor/advisor for persons with disabilities.

Local Chamber of Commerce

A local chamber of commerce can provide helpful information on the nature of the community, a listing of the types of business and industry in the community, a community map, and other kinds of information related to the growth or expansion of the community and region. This organization is especially helpful to a person who is new to a community. The larger the community, the more printed information is available. The smaller the community, the more personally accessible the officers and members of the chamber are and the more directly they may become involved in placement and community contacts.

Local Job Training Partnership Act Program

The director of the local Job Training Partnership Act (JTPA) and the Private Industry Council (PIC) that serves as the advisory for the JTPA program in a community are very important resources to a placement coordinator. They not only have information about the community that they can share but they also have a direct interest in what the local school(s) can offer them in mutual support of special-needs populations needing employment training. The Job Training Partnership Act of 1982 (PL 97-300) was the Reagan administration's response to pre-1980 election criticism of the Comprehensive Employment Training Act (CETA). It was designed to bring the private sector into a partnership with the federal government in preparing economically disadvantaged and long-term unemployed people to become productive workers. It is a federal, state, and local community partnership, and, for the first time, puts considerable responsibility on local participants for making decisions on how funds will be administered and how programs will be managed.

The JTPA established the local authority role through the election of local administrative officials and Private Industry Councils. The private sector's status as an equal partner in the program is reflected in the PIC's joint policy-making responsibility with the chief locally elected official. The primary features of JTPA that relate to school employment training goals include the following:

1. State and local control is built into the program and local school boards and administrators can use their influence to gain access to JTPA programming.

2. Wages and stipends to trainees are limited but may be a part of a school's proposed JTPA program.

3. All job placements must be in the private sector, in contrast to previous employment training programs that used public service employment predominantly.

4. Youth employment training may be part of adult training programs or be separate programs.

5. There are income eligibility requirements for JTPA program participation, but interpretations of these requirements in some states permit persons with disabilities to be a "family of one," thus making it much easier to qualify under income eligibility. Up to 10 percent of participants in all regular youth and adult programs in Title IIA programs may qualify regardless of income if they have a disability.

6. Of the Title IIA funds, 70 percent must be spent on training. The remaining funds are divided between a maximum of 15 percent for administrative costs and 15 percent for wages, allowances, and support services. At least 40 percent of Title IIA funds must be spent on year-round youth programs. Very importantly, the law mandates no specific *kinds* of programs, so local schools may determine their own needs and develop program proposals creatively. Tindall, Gugerty, and Dougherty (1984) described a number and variety of promising programs that had used JTPA funds in school programs; their text still serves as a good catalog of workable program ideas. Included among these are the Job Corps, which has intensive residential and day employment training for the most economically disadvantaged youths between the ages of 14 and 22, and summer youth programs.

7. There is a 15 percent ceiling on funding for support services to trainees. This makes it critical that schools classify services properly. It will be to the advantage of schools to classify services as training whenever possible. For example, support services that could be classified as training include employer outreach, remedial education, job-related counseling, assessment of employability, job development, job search assistance, books and instructional aids, and training equipment needed for the instructional program (National Association of Rehabilitation Facilities, 1984).

8. Programs are evaluated on the basis of performance standards rather than compliance with regulations or process standards. Performance standards are concerned with demonstrated quality of training and placements, reduction of welfare dependency, wage gains, number of placements, and costs per placement.

Projects with Industry

There are more than 50 Projects with Industry (PWI) programs operating across the nation, but they tend to be in metropolitan areas. PWI programs have been operating for almost two decades. They were designed to establish a positive, cooperative partnership between business and industry, state rehabilitation agencies, and qualified workers with disabilities.

The PWI programs in operation function under one of three major models. The *job-placement model* is designed for people with disabilities who have acquired minimally acceptable work attitudes and behaviors and are considered ready for job entry. The *skills-training model* consists of training in specific, specialized areas for those persons functioning at a higher level and who have appropriate work-related behaviors. The focus of training is on the development of technical and marketable skills. The *work-adjustment model* uses industry and business settings to teach appropriate work attitudes and behaviors. It tries to assist those who are at a lower level of functioning to attain the entry-level skills that are necessary for employment. This model is used most frequently with students from public school programs (Jewish Vocational Service, 1978).

State Division of Vocational Rehabilitation

State agencies designated as responsible for administering federally funded vocational rehabilitation programs and services use various titles, but they all have the same mission—to facilitate persons with disabilities in finding and maintaining employment. To that end, a number of services may be provided to students with disabilities who are eligible for vocational rehabilitation assistance. These services will be discussed more fully in Chapter 10, but one of these services is job placement. If a student is a vocational rehabilitation client as well as a student enrolled in a school program, there is a joint commitment for job placement. Vocational rehabilitation counselors have numerous contacts with employers and other resources that can be valuable in the placement process.

Local Advisory Committees

This type of resource is not used in special education employment training programs nearly as frequently as in vocational education. We consider this an invaluable resource that is available to any placement specialist. It does require effort to recruit, organize, and use a committee, but the payoff can be worth it. Cochran, Phelps, and Cochran (1980) described an advisory committee as a group composed primarily of individuals outside the education profession who are selected from the community to advise educational personnel regarding one or more educational programs or aspects of a program. An excellent handbook on procedures for implementing a community-based work-training program by Parrish and Kok (1985) contains an informative section on activities of advisory committees and some important steps to take in establishing and making the best use of an advisory committee. Advisory committee members can provide a perspective for making placements that is difficult for school personnel to acquire.

To list all of the "invisible" resources available to placement personnel would be impossible. These resources are those that are available daily or those that spring up from nowhere and present themselves as new opportunities. Through one's efforts in community placements, contacts at school through colleagues, and normal, everyday contacts in the community, resource relationships can and do develop. A trip to the dentist may result in a placement for one of your students in the office or a lead to a placement elsewhere. A conversation with the person beside you at a ball game or civic club luncheon may lead to a whole new occupational area that you have never considered before. And, of course, looking through the yellow pages of the telephone directory or city directory or the newspaper classified ads can open up a specific set of alternatives that is just waiting to be explored. Members of civic clubs, community agency workers, ministers, city officials, law enforcement personnel, and recently retired persons from these groups are among those who know their community as well as anyone. Some of these individuals would be willing to work with a school program as a volunteer in job development if asked. The Association for Retarded Citizens (ARC National Research and Demonstration Institute, 1982) developed a training program to prepare volunteers to create new job opportunities (ARC National Research and Demonstration Institute, 1982) that is available to schools that might want to pursue this effort.

State manufacturers' associations often have listings of companies, including products manufactured, services available, size of work force, and names of key company managers. In cities and metropolitan areas where one can be overwhelmed with the sheer number of business and industrial firms, the placement coordinator may find in local libraries some assistance in state industrial directories and other resources, such as the following:

> *Moody's Industrial Manual*
> *Thomas' Register of American Manufacturers*
> *Encyclopedia of Business Information*
> *Dun & Bradstreet's Middle Market Directory*
> *The Wall Street Journal*
> *Business Week*

To know what is going on in the community, what new business is coming to town, or whom to talk to about hiring for some new project, the information is available, starting with one's local newspaper.

Strategies in Job Finding

Some placement personnel rely primarily on their experience in the work world, their ability to develop and use resources in the community, their instincts, their history of being at the right place at the right time, or all of these. Many of these persons are extremely effective and develop excellent reputations among their colleagues for their success in finding jobs. Persons in this league may find the challenge of the job hunt so satisfying that they vicariously experience the pleasure of finding someone else a job as if it were their own. In some cases, the jobs found are not necessarily an ideal job match, but a successful job finder is rarely criticized by administrators for that.

At the other extreme, there are placement personnel who rely primarily on their program visibility via "high-probability" employer contacts, community presentations to organizations to which employers belong, timely and effective media coverage, and, sometimes, the initiative of the students themselves in finding their own jobs. This type of placement person plants the seeds of labor supply and sits back and waits for people to contact the school. Some long-established programs move into this style because the program can begin to proceed on its own momentum in this way after a while. Again, in some cases, the desirability of job match may be sacrificed but is rationalized because of ease of placement or the need to please an employer who has taken the initiative to call.

Both of these placement styles appear to get the job done in terms of number of students placed while in the program. Whether these approaches are more effective in achieving transition outcome goals than a more systematic, technical approach is a researchable question. On the face of it, logic suggests that placement procedures designed to avoid mistakes in placements are more likely to be in the best interests of the individual students, the employers, and the schools. The systematic approach to job placement does not have to deny the effectiveness of personal charisma, persistent contacts and follow-through, "salesmanship," nor the obvious results of good public relations and advertising that attracts employers to the school program. A placement program should incorporate those important features into a systematic approach.

Danley and Anthony (1987) described three basic approaches that have been used by placement personnel with people with disabilities. The three approaches include the following:

1. *Train-Place.*   Train-Place is the traditional model in which the placement specialist places a person with disabilities in a job for which he or she has been trained. The area of training might or might not have been open to choice for the individual, but was presumably determined through some type of assessment. Training may be provided at school (laundry, horticulture, etc.), in a training program separate from school (cosmetology), or in the community.

2. *Place-Train.*   Place-Train is the more recent model that has come out of the supported employment movement. The supported employment model was developed with individuals who have developmental disabilities and began with one of its assumptions that many people with severe handicaps did not transfer their training skills to a job placement. Again, the choice of placement might or might not have been open to choice for the individual. Placement occurs directly in the community and training occurs on the job site where continued employment is expected.

3. *Choose-Get-Keep.*   Choose-Get-Keep is a model originally proposed by Anthony, Howell, and Danley (1984) for persons with psychiatric disabilities who need supported employment services. It begins with the basic assumption that persons with disabilities, and especially those with psychiatric disabilities, need to

choose not only what kind of work they will do but also the type of work and specific location in order to establish the best person-job match. It also provides for the individual to secure the job herself or himself so that there are clear choices for both the individual and the employer. In this approach, negotiations, commitments, and bonding can occur without the involvement of a professional or advocate. The "keeping" stage is that phase that begins with training or placement and follows the supported employment model with time-limited or ongoing support for the person to assure that he or she will be able to keep the job as long as it is desirable.

Another approach that might be appropriate with some adolescents with disabilities is the *Train-Place-Train*. As the first step, a student is given some basic occupational and prevocational training at school in a regular vocational education, adapted vocational education, or special occupational training program, or in the community through a work experience training program. Placement is then arranged in a job site in the community and specific training is provided to ensure that all aspects of the employment situation have been addressed— specific job skills and routines, social and behavioral expectations, transportation arrangements, and self-advocacy strategies. This approach basically takes the Train-Place model and adds the features of the Place-Train model, which is based on supported employment models.

This review of approaches to placement raises two very important questions. First, education and rehabilitation personnel have not allowed enough choice for their students and clients. Mithaug, Martin, Agran, and Rusch (1988) made this point a central one in their book, *Why Special Education Graduates Fail*. These authors say that it is no wonder that graduates lack confidence; fail to understand their own needs, interests, and abilities; and are unable to solve problems independently when their teachers make their decisions.

Second, although the traditional approach of Train-Place seems straightforward and logical, there are now so many vocational assessment methods, intervention strategies, and explanations of work ecology available that placement personnel and individuals with disabilities and their families can become confused as to what approach to take in vocational planning and decision making. The tendency has been to "pick and choose" from among alternative models, resulting in little or no systematic approach to the task. One vocational adjustment coordinator in a newly established work experience program became impatient with the pace of organization and said, "Let's do *something*, even if it is wrong!" Unfortunately, this attitude may reflect what many practitioners feel about trying to be organized and using a systematic approach. "Systematic" sounds too cerebral or too theoretical to teachers and placement specialists in many cases.

A systematic approach to job placement simply refers to the use of well-established procedures used successfully in employment training programs in the past—job development, job analysis, analysis of individual assessment, job worksite modification, and job matching. Each of these will be introduced in the sections that follow.

Job Development

The task of *job development* is one of generating a pool of job placement alternatives so that there are real choices to be made when looking for the best possible placement. This pool of job placement alternatives can be developed in several ways. One of the most commonly suggested activities for a placement coordinator who is new to a community or who is establishing a new work-training program is the community survey. A community survey identifies the local job areas that have vacancies, those that anticipate vacancies frequently because of high turnover rates, and those that hire nonskilled, entry-level employees. These three labor market variables reflect the starting point for placement personnel in knowing whether additional activities in job development are needed.

A community survey can involve both formal and informal information-gathering procedures. Mail or telephone surveys to employers or persons responsible for hiring, use of information from a chamber of commerce and job service center, and regular and systematic analysis of newspaper classified ads will produce the bulk of the information needed. Some very helpful information on high-turnover occupations comes from job service center representatives and personal contacts with employers. It is helpful to organize this information in files or charts by occupational area (e.g., personal services, health occupations, construction/building trades, manufacturing, agriculture/agribusiness).

A community survey may be only a first step in developing a pool of placement alternatives. For example, assume that a community survey reveals that a given community has no available jobs right now and that the high-turnover jobs are stabilizing because of the competition generated by high unemployment. Another procedure in job development in this situation is to identify areas for job *creation* within the community's labor market. This is a task requiring some skill in analyzing jobs and some creativity in using the analysis data for proposing new jobs. This can occur through the creation of a new job by combining elements of existing jobs or by creating entirely new jobs to fulfill unmet needs of the employer. This was done in the early 1960s within the Federal Civil Service system in response to President Kennedy's executive branch initiative to employ workers with disabilities in the federal government. The Civil Service office issued a directive to all federal office personnel directors and supervisors to review all civil service job descriptions with the purpose of identifying tasks that were required that could be performed by someone else with less training or ability. These task elements were to be deleted and combined with other comparable tasks to develop new positions for persons with disabilities. This job development process resulted in the hiring of thousands of people who had mental or physical disabilities.

Job Analysis

Job analysis has already been mentioned as a necessary element of job development, but it is an important part of the job placement process by itself. A job analysis is no more than a systematic way of determining the specific demands of any job. A number of job analysis forms have appeared in the literature or have

FIGURE 8.5 Job Analysis Report

1. Job title _____

2. Description of duties _____

    _____

3. Tools needed _____

4. What kind of job is it?
    __ Clerical
    __ Sales
    __ Agriculture
    __ Service
    __ Self-employment
    __ Factory

5. Job level
    __ Skilled
    __ Semiskilled
    __ Unskilled

6. Experience
    __ Required
    __ None required

7. Employment
    __ Full time
    __ Part time
    __ Seasonal

8. How many people employed?
    __ Male
    __ Female

9. What tests are given?
    __ Employment service tests
    __ Company made test
    __ Other
    __ None

10. What kinds of licenses are required?
    __ Driver's license
    __ Health certificate
    __ Other

11. Must the employee fill out a written report? __ Yes   __ No

12. Must the employee belong to a union?
    __ Yes   __ No

13. How are employees found?
    __ Employment service
    __ Help wanted ads
    __ Labor unions
    __ People come in
    __ Referral by friends
    __ Other

14. Do you have plenty of workers available?
    __ Shortage
    __ Steady supply
    __ More than enough

15. How are employees paid?
    __ Hourly
    __ Weekly
    __ Monthly
    __ Piecework

16. Does the employee
    __ Work alone
    __ Work with others

17. What are the working conditions?
    __ Inside
    __ Wet
    __ Noisy
    __ Dirty
    __ Day work
    __ High places
    __ Outside
    __ Dry
    __ Quiet
    __ Clean
    __ Night work
    __ Low places
    __ Neither

18. Does this job require
    __ Standing

(continued)

FIGURE 8.5 (continued)

__ Sitting
__ Both sitting and standing
__ Lifting
__ Carrying
__ Moving about
__ Driving

19. How much education is required?
__ No formal education
__ Little formal education
__ Elementary school completion
__ Some high school
__ High school diploma

20. How much on the job training is given?
__ None
__ Less than 6 weeks
__ 6 weeks to 6 months
__ Apprenticeship

21. How much adjustment to change is required?
__ None   __ Some
__ Little   __ Frequent

22. Is there much pressure on the job?
__ None   __ Some
__ Little   __ Great

23. How much supervision is the employee given?
__ None   __ Some
__ Little   __ Much

24. Does the employee handle money?
__ Yes   __ No

25. How much memory is required?
__ None
__ Little
__ Memory for oral directions
__ Much

26. Does the employee meet the public?
__ No
__ Seen by public
__ Talks to public
__ Works with public all the time

27. How much reading is required on the job?
__ None
__ Little
__ Addresses

__ Sales orders
__ Patterns
__ Directions
__ Bulletins
__ Letters

28. How much arithmetic is required?
__ None   __ Dividing
__ Little   __ Measurements
__ Counting   __ Sales slips
__ Adding   __ Invoices
__ Subtracting __ Other
__ Multiplying

29. How much writing is required?
__ None
__ Listing
__ Sales orders
__ Production records
__ Information to be read by others

30. What kind of speaking is required?
__ Little
__ Giving messages
__ Asking for materials or tools
__ Giving directions

31. How much strength is required?
Hands: __ None   __ Little
             __ Some   __ Great
Arms: __ None   __ Little
             __ Some   __ Great
Legs: __ None   __ Little
             __ Some   __ Great
Back: __ None   __ Little
             __ Some   __ Great

32. Other pertinent information:

been shared in in-service workshops. Figure 8.5 is an example of one of these. Bragman and Cole (1984) developed a unique approach to job matching that includes a job analysis checklist using five job demand areas: physical demands, environmental conditions, communication skills, intellectual skills, and work situations (Figure 8.6). Each of these areas has specific items of concern that may need to be broken down into even more specific demand information. For example, if manual skills are important for a given job, the form may need to be modified to show the specific manual skills that are required (e.g., reaching, grasping, turning). This particular job analysis checklist is unique in that it is part of a job-match checklist.

Whatever form or procedure is used in a job analysis, the purpose is to assess a specific work environment for a specific job. Job requirements, characteristics of the work setting, and an indication of every anticipated demand give the placement specialist highly useful information for every placement. A job analysis exchange is provided by the Information Service of the Materials Development Center of the University of Wisconsin-Stout, to which a school program can subscribe, but such analyses are general and focus primarily on typical job requirements for someone in a particular occupation. They do not reveal the critical characteristics of a specific location or a specific position. A more specific job analysis form would show a fry cook position at the Kentucky Fried Chicken restaurant on Sixth Street will not necessarily read exactly like one for a fry cook at the Kentucky Fried Chicken restaurant on Twenty-Third Street in the same city. It would show even more differences between a general fry cook and a fry cook at a specific job site.

Analysis of Individual Assessment

The task of *analysis of individual assessment* in the job placement process is to review all assessment and evaluation data on an individual student and determine the student's job interests, strengths and weaknesses, and specific obstacles or limitations that could affect performance on the job that are not directly related to his or her disability or job-related weaknesses. Examples of the latter could include transportation problems, time required to get from school to work, the need to earn a certain amount of money, or temporary constraints because of such factors as probation specifications or having a leg in a cast. Limitations that could be attributed more directly to the disability or disabilities that a student has would vary between persons with the same disability or disabilities and, certainly, across disability areas. Bragman and Cole (1984) provided basic predictors of limitations for various disabling conditions across the generic job demands included in the job-match checklist (Figure 8.6). They referred to these predictors across generic job demands as *handicap profiles*. This approach is a creative way of focusing systematically on job demands by disability areas, but individual differences based on actual assessment data is the only way to follow through with this approach. Bragman and Cole cautioned that the profiles indicate only *possible* areas of consideration and that no individual will have all of these problems and some may have very few, if any.

FIGURE 8.6 Job-Match Checklist

Name of Applicant:

Handicap:

Position:

Job Description:

Generic Job Demands	Critical Job Requirements	Handicap Profile	Items to Question
Physical Demands			
Lifting			
Stooping/Bending/Squatting			
Manual Skills			
Visual-Motor Skills			
Climbing/Balancing			
Prolonged Standing/Sitting			
Visual			
Cosmetic Appearance			
Environmental Conditions			
Extreme Temperatures			
Wet/Humid			
Noise/Vibrations			
Hazards			
Fumes/Dust/Odors			
Communication Skills			
Interpersonal Relations			
Written			
Speech			
Reading			
Hearing			
Receiving Instructions			
Giving Instructions			
Intellectual Skills			
Memory:			
Short-Term			
Long-Term			
Abstract Reasoning			
Planning/Organizing			
Decision-Making			
Numerical Reasoning			

(continued)

FIGURE 8.6   (continued)

Spatial/Form Perception			
Work Situations			
Environmental Stresses:			
Emergency Situations			
Deadlines			
Situational			
Working as Part of a Group			
Working Alone			
Leadership Skills			
Giving Supervision			
Receiving Supervision			
Performing Variety of Duties			
Performing Routine/Concrete			
Duties			
High-Speed Performance			
Driving			
Others:			

Source: From *Job Match: A Process for Interviewing and Hiring Qualified Handicapped Individuals* by R. Bragman and J. C. Cole, 1984, pp. 28-29. Copyright 1984, The American Society for Personnel Administration, Alexandria, Virginia. Reprinted with permission.

Figure 8.7 provides an excerpt of the profiles of six disability groups: visual impairment, wheelchair dependent, learning disability, mental retardation, hearing impairment, and emotional disturbance. Notice that the profile for learning disability shows no primary or secondary limitation considerations for climbing and balancing. Although this generalization might be accurate for most persons with learning disabilities, the likelihood of a given student with learning disabilities having coordination problems that could affect climbing or balance is higher than in the general population. If thorough medical and physical examinations had indicated problems of this nature for a given student, the profile would need to reflect that on the job-match checklist. In other words, the handicap profiles provide generalizations for disability groups as starting points for specific consideration on any individual case. The placement coordinator must analyze each individual's assessment data to personalize the profile.

Job Work-Site Modification

The task of *job work-site modification* can be defined as "work-related changes that enable a disabled person to be employed" (Hester & Stone, 1984, p. 1). Work-site modifications, in one form or another, have been made by or for persons with disabilities for as long as people have worked. These accommodations were often made voluntarily by employers in the past when the person with disabilities was already an employee at the time of the modification or had high

FIGURE 8.7 Disability Profiles

Generic Job Communication	Visual Impairment	Wheelchair Dependent	Learning Disability	Mental Retardation	Hearing Impairment	Emotional Disturbance
Physical Demands						
Lifting		•				
Stooping/ Bending/ Squatting		*				
Manual Skills		•				
Visual-Motor Skills	*		•			
Climbing/ Balancing		*				
Prolonged Standing/ Sitting		*				
Visual	*					
Cosmetic Appearance						
Environmental Conditions						
Extreme Temperatures		•				
Wet/Humid		•				
Noise/ Vibrations					*	
Hazards	*			•		
Fumes/ Dust/ Odors		•				
Communication Skills						
Interpersonal			•	*	•	*

(continued)

FIGURE 8.7   (continued)

Generic Job Communication	Visual Impairment	Wheelchair Dependent	Learning Disability	Mental Retardation	Hearing Impairment	Emotional Disturbance
Relations						
Written	•	•	•	*	•	
Speech			•	•	•	
Reading	•		•	*	•	
Hearing			•		*	
Receiving Instructions			•	*	•	•
Giving Instructions			•	*	•	•
Intellectual Skills						
Memory: Short-Term			•	•		
Long-Term			•	•		
Abstract Reasoning			•	*		
Planning/ Organizing			•	*		
Decision-Making			•	*		•
Numerical Reasoning			•	*		
Spatial/Form Perception	*		•			
Work Situations						
Environmental Stresses: Emergency Situations				*		*

Generic Job Communication	Visual Impairment	Wheelchair Dependent	Learning Disability	Mental Retardation	Hearing Impairment	Emotional Disturbance
Deadlines		•		*		*
Situational						*
Working as Part of a Group					•	•
Working Alone						•
Leadership Skills				*		•
Giving Supervision			·	*	•	•
Receiving Supervision						•
Performing Variety of Duties				•	*	•
Performing Routine/Concrete Duties						
High-Speed Performance		•	•	*		*
Driving	•	•		•		

Source: From *Job Match: A Process for Interviewing and Hiring Qualified Handicapped Individuals* by R. Bragman and J. C. Cole, 1984, pp. 50–53. Copyright 1984, The American Society for Personnel Administration, Alexandria, Virginia. Reprinted with permission.

*Primary considerations

• Secondary considerations

qualifications and potential for productivity. Since the passage of the Rehabilitation Act of 1973, the federal government has required reasonable accommodations in federal employment or any business or industry under contract with the federal government (Section 504). It has also provided some financial incentives for work-site modification. Now, the Americans with Disabilities Act (ADA) requires any employer with 15 or more employees to make "reasonable accommodations" for a person with a disability if that accommodation will allow the person to perform the essential functions of the job. Appendix B provides a checklist of accessibility and usability of buildings and facilities that serves as a guide for needed work-site modification.

Work-site modifications range from the simplest and least costly ones (changing hours, changing work procedures, changing work locations, or changing task assignments) to the most expensive, most complex ones using high technology or rehabilitation engineering for sophisticated equipment or building adaptations. Placement personnel should be alert to discrepancies in the job analysis and the analysis of individual assessment that could be addressed through work-site or job modification.

Early reactions to the section 504 requirements to provide reasonable accommodations in architectural accessibility and work-site modifications were resisted (*Time*, December 5, 1977; *The New York Times*, November 18, 1979; August 3, 1980; *The Washington Post*, June 1, 1980). Employers criticized the concept on the basis of an assumption of high cost and technical complexity. They also interpreted the accessibility requirement too narrowly as *structural* or *architectural* accessibility. Fortunately, the first national survey of work-site modification (Berkeley Planning Associates, 1982) helped to dispel these notions by finding modifications for disabled workers to be largely low cost and simple. About half of the reported accommodations cost *nothing*! About one-third of the modifications cost up to $500, and only 8 percent cost more than $2,000. These findings supported earlier and concurrent studies of specific industries or selected occupational samples (Ellner & Bender, 1980; Pati, Adkins & Morrison, 1981; E. I. du Pont de Nemours & Company, 1982). Still, the response of employers to the concept of work-site modification has been less than enthusiastic, especially from employers in small- and medium-sized firms (Hester & Stone, 1984).

The reaction of employers to Section 504 in regard to reasonable accommodations and workplace modification was not enthusiastic, especially from small- and medium-sized businesses (Hester & Stone, 1984), so the ADA is raising the concerns of a whole new population of employers who must comply with the act. Many are requesting interpretations of the law for their specific situations. The difficulty in interpreting what a reasonable accommodation is is not lessened any by the added regulatory language that provides that accommodation must be made, provided that it does not impose an "undue hardship" on the employer. Placement specialists may decide in some cases that getting the employer to comply with the law in making accommodations may be a legal victory, but the issue of a lack of positive employer attitude and active support may be more of a negative in job matching than a lack of accommodation. Linthicum, Cole, and D'Alonzo (1991) provided an excellent summary of ADA employment provisions that any school employment training program will find invaluable.

School-based job developers and job trainers need to use work-site modifications not only to provide better access to employment under the employment provisions of ADA but also to increase the creative aspects of job alternatives. Meers (1992) reported that technological advances in such areas as laser scanners and electronic switches have revolutionized the traditional time and motion studies that defined so many jobs. For example, automated workstations that can be operated by means of a blink of an eye or a sip-and-puff switch are workable in at least 300 different jobs. In the next decade, technology will expand the range of options for employment even more.

Job Matching

The *job-matching process* is the final task in job placement planning. The task of matching job demands with individual interests, strengths, weaknesses, and expectations brings together all the data available for a logical, intelligent placement. It is designed to take the guesswork and chance out of the process and replace them with reason. In the real world, however, it is never so simple and clear-cut. Decision making in any arena assumes that the decision maker can never know with certainty that he or she has made the *right* decision, but in following decision-making rules, the decisions can be judged as the *best possible* decisions, given the data available. This means that compromises may have to be made at times. The job match is rarely perfect, but more often the *best possible* job match.

Strategies in Job Placement

Job placement specialists eventually develop their own strategies for placing students. These strategies fit individual personalities, community values and responses, and changes in a community's occupational outlook. The literature and experienced placement personnel do have some suggestions for placement coordinators. This section presents some of their ideas.

Payne, Mercer, and Epstein (1974) provided some excellent practical suggestions as strategies in obtaining job placement opportunities. Among these are the following:

1. Use every means possible in making contacts with employers. Use outside organizations—such as Kiwanis, Rotary, Business Women's Clubs of America, Jaycees, and others—to make many employers or personnel managers aware of the program and who you are as the contact person. Use business cards and other printed material about the program to leave behind.

2. Approach every employer with two goals in mind: (a) making the person aware of the school work-training program and how it fits into the entire school vocational continuum and (b) enlisting their willingness to participate in the program. Participation in the program can be as an employer-trainer or as one who will call the program to the attention of his or her friends or others to encourage their participation. Most businesspersons like the idea of working with the public schools, and having the option of promoting the program as one means of participation when they are not able to participate directly gives them a way to do that.

3. An enthusiastic, committed approach, using good sales techniques, works well with employers in initial contacts. The placement specialist should keep the first interview under 10 minutes, unless the employer wishes to discuss the project more fully. Remember that you are asking employers to commit to a program and they have a right to expect something out of it. Be sensitive to what motivates each employer and be prepared to state directly what the program will do for the business and how the school will support their efforts.

The Payne, Mercer, and Epstein (1974) book *Education and Rehabilitation Techniques* contains a section of practical techniques that is impossible to summarize, abstract, or synthesize adequately because of its personal style. For that reason, permission has been obtained to use it intact here:

> Counselors who have approached businessmen on a large scale mention the importance of being physically fit, for the majority of this work requires standing, walking, and, on occasion, some running. Appropriate dress is important for initial business contact success, but caution should be exercised not to overly dress the part. Also, a packet of appropriate forms and program brochures, a booklet of matches for offering lights, a roll of nickels for meters, breath mints, extra pencils, and calling cards represent items which enhance the counselor's effectiveness as well as his efficiency.
>
> The decision to "walk in" on a businessman without an appointment should be considered carefully. The general rule of thumb is that, if the proprietor or manager is readily available, then by all means "walk in." If two or three unexpected "drop in" contacts fail to produce results, use the phone to arrange an appointment. Appointments are appropriate for large businesses and corporations, but smaller, local businesses prefer for the counselor just to drop by during slow hours. In a phone conversation the counselor should state his name, organization, who referred him to the business (if applicable), and that he would like to explain the vocational program. The counselor should tell the employer that it will take less than 10 minutes and ask when it would be convenient to meet. He should *not* ask if the employer is interested or if he *can* meet with him. At *no* time should the counselor ask any question which can be answered "Yes" or "No" because the employer might say "No." The key question to ask is, "When would be a good time for me to meet with you?" This question cannot be answered with a simple "Yes" or "No." If the employer does not want to meet with the counselor, he must at least tell him so in sentence form. Surveys indicate that if the individual under question has to respond in sentence form it is more likely that he will respond positively than negatively....
>
> After getting a foot in the door, the counselor needs something to say. It may help for the counselor to bring a couple of pictures of program activities or clients engaged in work so that the businessman has something to look at while the counselor talks. Another introductory device is the business card, but, if a counselor does not wish to go the expense of printing up business cards, a mimeographed sheet with his name, organization, telephone number, and a description of what he wants to do and why he needs help will suffice....

It is unlikely that the counselor will convince every businessman to participate. However, within a short period of time, he at least should be getting his foot in the door and be having an opportunity to give his presentation to 75 percent of the employers he contacts. If he is falling short of this percentage, he should begin to concentrate on his entry skills because without improving this stage of the business contact he is certain to fail and get discouraged.... (pp. 105–108)

Drake University's National Vocational Rehabilitation Job Development/ Job Placement Institute supports the notion of the importance of placement personnel strategies in employer contacts. The institute suggests that the following errors are common in contacting employers:

1. Marketing to the wrong staff person
2. Bringing up objections before the employer does
3. Overselling the school, client, services, and oneself
4. Talking too much and talking *at* the employer
5. Listening too little and interrupting the employer
6. Using rehabilitation jargon and terminology
7. Not being organized or well prepared
8. Not establishing an identity or purpose of efforts
9. Failing to leave a business card
10. Overemphasizing placement and deemphasizing service
11. Not being genuine or allowing the employer to be genuine
12. Failing to follow up after making contact with the employer
13. Siding with either management or labor
14. Being impulsive or condescending
15. Not knowing when to "back off"
16. Demonstrating a lack of self-confidence

Culver, Spencer, and Gliner (1990) have also suggested some very specific job development and placement strategies that have impact of placement success.

The tone of these two descriptions of *dos* and *don'ts* reflects views of those who have experienced the highly personal interactions that occur in job development and job placement. Academicians may cringe at this approach and resist having to "sell" to potential employers. Excellent classroom or resource room teachers may balk at pressure to assume a style that they think is contrary to the ones that made them effective teachers. The question often comes up when this apparent conflict is discussed: Is there a personality type for job placement personnel? Our response is that there probably is some common trait or cluster of traits among effective placement specialists, but they are not what typically comes to mind when one thinks of the "super salesperson." We have seen individuals with outstanding placement skills who could be described by others who do not know them as "a little old lady in tennis shoes," "a good ole' boy," "hyper," "laid-back," "super organized," "could sell snowshoes at the equator:' or " whatever she's selling I'm buying." Obviously, there is no single stereotype here, yet they all were exceptional communicators with people in the work world and had their own strategies and styles that worked for them.

Most of the emphasis thus far in the job placement process has been on the job placement specialist's approach in finding and making the initial contact with an employer. Once the employer indicates a real interest in the program, whether from a profit, conformity, or humanitarian motive (Payne, Mercer, & Epstein, 1974), the placement specialist moves into an instructional role with the employer. Interest alone does not dispel the myths and notions that are widespread in the business community. Bragman and Cole (1984) reviewed some of these and gave excellent factual responses to each of them that could be used to great advantage at this stage. For example, many employers believe that insurance rates and worker's compensation rates will increase after hiring persons with disabilities. The facts are that of businesses hiring people with disabilities, 90 percent reported that insurance rates did not increase. Brantman (1978) and the U.S. Chamber of Commerce (1974) confirmed these data and assured employers that both insurance and worker's compensation rates are based on the employer's previous record of accidents, and hiring of persons with disabilities will not automatically affect their rates.

However, employers do have certain fears and stereotypes related to persons with disabling conditions, and one of the first steps in developing a relationship with the employer is to explore and respond to employer issues, fears, or concerns (Shrey, Mitchell, & Hursh, 1985). Those interested in more specific information on job development and job placement strategies are encouraged to obtain the following excellent resources:

> *Education and Rehabilitation Techniques* (Payne, Mercer, & Epstein, 1974)
> *Employer Development and Industrial Exploration Manual: A Comprehensive Approach to Initiating School-to-Work Transition Programs for Students with Special Needs* (Shrey, Mitchell, & Hursh, 1985)
> *Employment Incentives Manual: How to Motivate Businesses to Hire Individuals with Disabilities* (Schwartz, 1985)
> *Job Coaching in Supported Work Programs* (Fadely, 1987)
> *Job-Match: A Process for Interviewing and Hiring Qualified Handicapped Individuals* (Bragman & Cole, 1984)
> *Placement in Rehabilitation* (Vandergoot & Worrall, 1979)
> *Procedures Handbook for Special Needs Work-Study Coordinators* (Parrish & Kok, 1985)
> *Supported Employment: A Community Implementation Guide* (Bellamy, Rhodes, Mank, & Albin, 1988)
> *The Supported Work Model of Competitive Employment for Citizens with Severe Handicaps: A Guide for Job Trainers* (Moon, Goodall, Barcus, & Brooke, 1986)

Articles by Nietupski, Hamre-Nietupski, Welch, and Anderson (1983) and Schroka and Schwartz (1982) are also important publications for job placement references. Eigenbrood and Retish (1988) have provided an excellent rating scale for use with employers to evaluate a work experience program and its placement and supervision personnel. Moon, Kiernan, and Halloran (1990) have given an excellent update of legal issues in school-based vocational programs and labor laws.

Job Training and the Focus of Job Placement for Students

The type of job placement that school placement coordinators engage in most often is placement for job training. Only those last-semester students who have been through a work-training program should be ready for employment. Placement personnel and employers must not lose sight of the fact that the purpose of community on-the-job training placements is *training* (Holler & Gugerty, 1984; Parrish & Kok, 1985). Parrish and Kok have used the term *training stations* rather than *jobs* in their discussion of placement, and point out some important differences between the two that involve the employer. These include the following expectations the school program should have of an employer. Employers and trainers must

- Alter their method of giving instructions to meet the demands of each student's learning style.
- Maintain a standard of performance.
- Be willing to spend extra time at first.
- Treat students with respect and courtesy.

These are *minimal expectations*, and no placement specialist should hesitate to communicate these early in the discussion of the employer's participation as a trainer.

Although these are minimal expectations of the employer, there are other factors that might not make a given work situation a good training station. Parrish and Kok (1985) cited a number of reasons given by work-study coordinators for deciding against some available jobs. Among them are inconsistent supervision, nonexistent supervision, frequent changes in supervision, inappropriate environment, bad working hours, inappropriate location, pace of work activity, dangers or hazards, and incompatibility of work situation with a student's interests.

JOB TRAINING

The amount and kind of training that students in special-needs programs need is extremely variable. Certainly, there is a wide range in previous work experience. Work experience, according to Hasazi, Gordon, and Roe (1985), was the primary differentiating factor between employed and unemployed graduates in their follow-up of former special education students. Subjects in a study of characteristics of successfully employed adults with handicaps (Hudson, Schwartz, Sea-lander, Campbell, & Hensel, 1988) gave verbal support to the finding by Hasazi and others claiming that work experience was an important strategy in successful employment. Work experience, then, may be seen as a type of training that proves beneficial in future employment. Obviously, some work experience for youths with disabilities is not ideal in terms of a totally positive experience and varies considerably in the amount of supervision. Still, previous job experience can make a difference in the amount and kind of job training a person needs.

In addition to work experience backgrounds, there are differences in basic physical and intellectual performance levels. An intelligent, highly motivated, student who is visually impaired may require half the job training time that a student who is moderately learning disabled might require for the same job. A student with mild mental retardation should require less training than one with moderate mental retardation, other things being equal. Job trainers must look at speed of learning all job tasks from an individual basis and plan for job training time on the basis of each student's performance. Furthermore, they must analyze performance errors to determine the kind of training the student needs.

The final factor in training variability needs is the nature of the job itself. The job analysis described in an earlier section of this chapter gives the job trainer the same basic information he or she needs to anticipate the kind and amount of training that will be required. A job placement on an assembly line requiring the same psychomotor response repeatedly requires much less training than a job in which multiple responses—sensory, motor, and cognitive—are the norm. Payne (1977) provided a good example of this, with his description of the complex set of task demands of a fast-food kitchen worker. This is an interesting example because of a general criticism in the past of placement coordinators who use food-service jobs more than any other type. The assumption has been made, and erroneously, according to Payne, that food-service placements were all many students with disabilities could handle. In fact, the food services, and especially fast-food services, were used most frequently because they had more job turnover and offered more opportunities for placement. From a job-match point of view, these placements frequently ended in disaster. Many of the students placed in these settings were placed without job analyses, without any systematic training, and were not able to handle the deceptively difficult task demands of the jobs.

One of the points of tension between professionals who have worked with students with mild disabilities in job training over the years and professionals who are currently engaged in supported employment training with students with severe handicapping conditions is an understanding of what constitutes appropriate job training. The amount and kind of support during training comprise the two major points of debate. Perhaps this is an oversimplification. Perhaps it is a matter of systematic planning and delivery of training. The less-than-spectacular success rate of employment of youth with mild disabilities suggests that a more systematic model is needed.

Assuming that it is easier to start with a structured procedure and fade out or omit unnecessary steps than to begin with a loose, unstructured approach and

"Yes , that is an aspect of the traveling salesman that we hadn't considered..."

back up and add new procedures, the job-site training plan of a supported work model (Moon et al., 1986) will be presented here as one recommended procedure. In this approach to job training, a supported employment job trainer or job coach is available to be on a job site for as many hours per day as a student is expected to be in training. This may require full-time availability for some job placements.

It may be helpful to individuals who are new to the ares of job training and supervision to clarify the term *supported employment*. Like many terms that are made up of familar component words (in this case, *supported* and *employment*) the concept behind it carries a number of possible interpretations or ways that it might be demonstrated. In fact, a basic principle in understanding supported employment programs is that they will be delivered in a variety of ways, depending on the resources of the comminity, local economic conditions, available funding, and the type and level of severity of the disabilities of the intended participants in the program.

The following definition of *supported employment* appeared in the *Federal Register:* "the term 'supported employment' contains three elements: (1) Paid, competitive work; (2) an integrated work setting; and (3) the provision of on-going support services" (*Federal Register*, August 14, 1987). The proposed regulations defined "competitive work" to mean "work that is performed on a full-time basis or on a part-time basis, averaging at least 20 hours per week, and for which an individual is compensated in accordance with the Fair Labor Standards Act." "Integrated work setting" was defined as job site settings where (1) most co-workers do not have disabilities, (2) individuals with disabilities are not part of a work group of other individuals with diabilities, or (3) if there are no co-workers or the only co-workers are members of a small work group of not more than eight individuals, all of whom have disabilities, the individuals with disabilities have regular contact with individuals without disabilities other than the personnel providing support services in their immediate work setting. And, finally, "ongoing support services" means continuous or periodic job skill training services.

Supported employment as a federal initiative clearly targeted populations classified as having severe, profound, or multiple disabilities. Until recent years, this population has been considered unable to work and rarely been included in any type of normalized work setting in competitive employment. To ensure that this group was the group served through federal demonstration projects, the Office of Special Education and Rehabilitation Services (OSERS) guidelines specified that supported employment services were not intended for persons with disabilities who might benefit from short-term training that leads to competitive employment (Jackson & Associates, 1985). In spite of this, almost five years after the initiatives were announced and implemented, Kregel and Wehman (1989) found that less than 8 percent of 1,411 individuals involved in supported employment programs in eight states were severely or profoundly disabled.

What has appeared to be a critical factor in both referral and selection of individuals for state-operated supported employment programs is the issue of "ongoing" versus "time-limited" support services. State vocational rehabilitation agencies have a time-limited approach to services, as do most other state agency programs. It is understandable that schools, state vocational rehabilitation agencies, rehabilitation services for the blind, and special programs for targeted groups (mentally ill, traumatic brain injury, autism, etc.) look first to select those individuals who need a supported services approach but have the most potential for success. Gardner, Chapman, Donaldson, and Jacobson (1988, pp. 3–4) stated it this way: "As supported employment enters the mainstream of human services, its definition will no doubt be modified to enable other disability groups to participate in the program."

It is clear that the philosophy and intent of supported employment models are appropriate for school work-training programs for students with mild to moderate disabilities. For more information, the following sources are recommended:

> *Job Coaching in Supported Work Programs* (Fadely, 1987)
> *Supported Employment: Providing Integrated Employment Opportunities for Persons with Disabilities* (Powell et al., 1991)
> *Supported Employment: A Community Implementation Guide* (Bellamy et al., 1988)
> *The Supported Work Model of Competitive Employment for Citizens with Severe Handicaps: A Guide for Job Trainers* (Moon et al., 1986)
> *Toward Supported Employment: A Process Guide for Planned Change* (Gardner et al., 1988)

In the supported employment model, the trainer is responsible for teaching all job skills, for training nonwork skills that are related to the job (social expectations, transportation, grooming, etc.), and for advocacy of the student. The phases of direct instruction in job and job-related skills, according to Moon and associates (1986) are *job orientation* and *assessment, initial training* and *skill acquisition,* and *skill generation* and *maintenance/fading.*

Job Orientation and Assessment

This phase of job training may last two to four weeks. The trainer has to keep in mind that the employer expects the work to be performed up to standards while the training takes place. This means that the trainer must start with learning all the tasks related to the job. The basis for this learning and the training for the student is, of course, a job analysis, but the job analysis must then be extended to task analyses of all job tasks. This leads to a detailed description of each job duty, the equipment or tools needed for each, the amount and kind of communication required, and any special training techniques that would be appropriate. A great deal of modeling is done by the trainer for job and job-related skills. The technique of demonstration, followed by student performance and immediate reinforcement, is critical.

Initial Training and Skill Acquisition

Training youth who are mildly handicapped in job tasks might be accomplished in the orientation and assessment phase without having to follow a systematic training and skill-acquisition procedure. However, job-related skills are equally important and may need this type of training. The research literature conclusions that social and job-related skill deficits are the more common causes of job failure support the contention that work-study coordinators working with students who have mild disabilities need to be much more structured in their training approach in this area. It could be that if a youth with mild disabilities is given the opportunity to train for a challenging job, the initial training and skill-acquisition procedures (Moon et al., 1986) are quite appropriate for even the job-related skills.

The essence of the initial training and skill acquisition phase is good behavioral analysis training. Comprehensive discussions of instructional technologies and behavioral techniques in vocational training may be found in Bellamy, Horner, and Inman (1979); Falvey, Brown, Lyon, Baumgart, and Schroeder (1980); Kim, Siegel, and Gaylord-Ross (1992); Moon and colleagues 1986; Snell, 1978; and Wehman, (1981). The trainer must determine what the primary reinforcers for the trainee are and then develop a reinforcement program that will fade before the trainer's withdrawal from the job site.

During training and skill acquisition, the job trainer must record performance data. The two types of data that are critical are those that (1) indicate how the trainee performs a job duty without any prompting or nonnaturally occurring reinforcement and (2) the number and kinds of prompts (verbal, physical, or modeling) that the trainee needs to perform the job duty. The job coach is concerned during this phase with the trainee acquiring accuracy and independence first. After these have been established, the training emphasis moves to performance rate to bring it up to company standards. Throughout the initial training and acquisition phase, the job trainer monitors on-task behavior and errors. In both cases, problems in these areas might require specific behavioral programs to raise these skills to appropriate levels.

Training for job-related skills such as appropriate dress, riding a city bus, coffee break behavior, using a pay telephone, punching in and out on a time clock, or using a vending machine must occur during this initial training phase but cannot occur during work hours. The job coach and trainee have to arrange time before or after work hours or during lunch or coffee breaks to work on some of these skills. Other persons can assist in or assume responsibility for this training, but it is important that it be done on site. Depending on the learning style and rate of the trainee, the trainer must decide how many of the same behavioral training procedures used in the job training would be appropriate for the job-related skill training. The important thing is the acquisition and maintenance of the skills, and it is probably better to overtrain than to assume the skills will be acquired incidentally or be maintained over time. Chadsey-Rusch (1988) provided a helpful perspective of the social ecology of work settings and the job trainer's or job supervisor's role.

Skill Generalization and Maintenance/Fading

The last phase of job-site training involves the gradual removal or fading out of the job trainer. This process may take from a few days or a week for high-functioning trainees to months for low-functioning trainees. The job trainer must slowly and systematically withdraw from the job and the trainee. The final outcome goal at the outset has been worker independence and productivity that meets the company's standards. Thus, the criteria that the job coach uses in fading from the setting comes from the data that have been collected. On-task behavior, prompting assistance, accuracy or quality of work, and production rate must be reaching independent levels before the trainer can begin to fade out. The fade-out process may begin with any job duty that has been established and maintained for a period of time. It does not have to wait until all job duties have been acquired. The trainer may leave the work area only for a few minutes at first, then extend the time until it appears that he or she can leave the premises.

Moon and colleagues (1986) suggested that the actual schedule of fading is determined not only by the trainee's job performance but also by the needs and personalities of the supervisor and co-workers and the characteristics of the job and the job site. It is possible that some trainees will need some support indefinitely to maintain their independent productivity. This support will have to be provided by a supervisor or co-workers. The job coach or training specialist will have to train these individuals before terminating the job-site training, and be alert to changes in personnel so that reentry into the job site for training of new personnel can occur. Developing natural support systems in a work site is critical and requires some careful planning and implementation (Nisbet & Hagner, 1988; Mangan, 1992).

Advocacy

Advocacy activities are a major part of any work experience or transition coordinator's job description. Advocating for students at school with administrators, guidance counselors, regular teachers, resource or self-contained classroom teachers, parents, employers, and human services agency personnel is a continuous process. The range of activities in advocacy for students in the program is limitless because any activity that promotes better attitudes, accessibility to the community and school, and the success of the student at school and on the job can be thought of as advocacy. Advocacy relating to the thrust of this chapter—job placement, training, and supervision—is more focused but still is limited only by the imagination and energy of the person or persons responsible for these areas of the program. Moon and others (1986, p. 81) provided a helpful set of guidelines for advocacy activities, presented in Figure 8.8.

Neubert and Tilson (1987) proposed a training model especially tailored for special education students who are nearing graduation or those who have recently exited the public school system. The model assumes little or no formal training for employment that occurred during high school. It focuses on that critical stage of transition—the time immediately before and after leaving school. Although it is a postsecondary job training transition model, it could be used or adapted for a student's senior year or last year of public schooling. Referred to as the Job Training and Tryout Model, the model contains four phases, each of which is organized to emphasize certain activities:

Phase I   Use previous assessment data together with new assessment information to develop an individualized employment success plan (IESP).

Phase II   Provide participants eight weeks of employability skills training at an adult education facility.
Provide participants two six-week job try-outs in the community at a real job site, accompanied by a weekly work adjustment seminar.
Assist students in preparing a resume to use in a job search, and provide staff assistance in a supported job search.

Phase III Provide placement services to participants.
Provide support/follow-up needed to participants on the job, particularly for inappropriate work and social behaviors.

FIGURE 8.8   Guidelines for Advocacy Activities

Job Development
- Explain the capabilities of workers with mental retardation to employers and co-workers during job site visits;
- Meet with civic, business, church, and social groups to change social attitudes and educate them on the advantages of hiring workers with handicaps;
- Develop advertising and educational literature pertaining to your job-training program.

Consumer Assessment
- Counsel parents and guardians on benefits of competitive employment for their son or daughter;
- Explain to parents or group home staff the eventual loss of SSI benefits and the trial work period;
- Help parents or residential counselors fill out SSI forms or visit the local SSI representative;
- Work out transportation problems with families or agency staff;
- Outline specific objectives for school or adult program personnel that will improve the employability of prospective employees.

Job Placement
- Make sure the job application is filled out correctly;
- Accompany the consumer to the job interview and speak on his or her behalf if necessary;
- Review appropriate dress and behavior with the interviewee and the family or group home staff;
- Arrange to transport the consumer to the job interview and to the job on the individual's first day;
- Explain the job benefit package to the worker and his or her family or group home staff.

Job Site Training
- Establish rapport with supervisors and co-workers and adhere to the rules of the job site;
- Never allow job training to interfere with the flow of business or the established work schedule;
- Involve supervisors or co-workers in the training if feasible and briefly explain the systematic training and fading procedure;
- Recognize employers, supervisors, and co-workers who promote the employment of citizens with handicaps (e.g., a plaque, awards banquet);
- Establish rapport with co-workers and involve them in the training of the worker;
- Explain to co-workers the disability, background, and behavioral characteristics of the new employee;
- Encourage co-workers to socialize with the new worker and model appropriate ways to do this;
- Have the supervisor complete written evaluations on the worker's performance and discuss results;
- Work out job modifications with the supervisor when needed;
- Keep the family or group home counselors aware of the individual's job progress and problems that may occur;
- Give parents or group home staff the "job rules" such as the procedure for calling in sick;
- Explain pay and benefits to parents and group home staff to prepare them for the eventual loss of SSI and medical benefits;

(continued)

FIGURE 8.8   (continued)

- Do not fade your presence from the job site until you are sure the employee is going to "make it" alone;
- Inform the supervisor and the worker's family or group home staff of the long-term follow-up services you provide for the employee.

Follow-up
- Mail supervisor evaluations on schedule and respond immediately if any problems are indicated;
- Visit the job site and monitor the worker's performance by talking to supervisors and co-workers and by completing task analytic probes, production rate recordings, and on-task observations;
- Keep up with management and supervisor changes at the job site. Personnel changes can seriously affect job performance;
- Find out about any changes in the worker's home situation through the use of parent surveys, phone calls, and home visits;
- Be prepared to go back on the job site at any time for retraining.

Source: From *The Supported Work Model of Competitive Employment for Citizens with Severe Handicaps: A Guide for Job Trainers* (p. 81) by S. Moon, P. Goodall, M. Barcus, and V. Brooke, 1986, Richmond VA: Rehabilitation and Training Center, Virginia Commonwealth University. Reprinted with permission.

	Provide a monthly Job Club program to participants for group problem-solving and support.
Phase IV	Provide job change support.
	Provide job advancement support.
	Provide job coaching or Job Club as needed.

Sowers and Powers (1989) and Siegel, Greener, Prieur, Robert, and Gaylord-Ross (1989) have school-based community work-training models that have excellent success outcomes and should be reviewed by any developing program staff.

JOB SUPERVISION

Many schools that have persons who do job placement and job training also expect them to do job supervision. Thus, even though this chapter has used terms such as *placement specialists* and *job trainers*, and will now refer in this section to *job supervisors*, these roles are generally performed by one person.

The role of job supervisor involves monitoring and evaluating the progress of student workers in a job placement. It also involves the monitoring and evaluation of the job placement itself, which includes observation of every aspect of the job analysis to determine any changes that work against a job match. Within this framework, at least the four following types of supervisory visits are made over the duration of the school's involvement in the work-training program:

1. *Regularly scheduled visits to follow up on the student's performance and the work setting itself.* Regularly scheduled visits are routine and expected by the student, the student's parents, and the employer. *Example*: It has been one week since the job-site trainer faded completely from the work site. Before fading, regular visits were scheduled on Wednesdays to evaluate performance and to find out whether there were any problems from the point of view of the job supervisor or co-workers.

2. *Scheduled visits to address problems or concerns that are beginning to have negative effects on the student's performance or that are expected to have some effect in the near future.* These visits may result from observations made in previous supervisory visits; comments from the employer, job supervisor, or co-workers; reports from teachers or staff at school; or concerns expressed by parents. *Example*: The job supervisor reports on one scheduled visit that the student reported late to work once during the preceding week. During the next week, the employer calls to report that the student had been late two mornings in succession. A visit is scheduled to discuss the problem job-related behavior. Preparation for the visit includes conferences with school staff and the student's family to elicit information about any history of this behavior and possible reasons for the current behavior.

3. *Unscheduled visits to deal with a crisis.* These visits arise out of emergency situations in which a responsible school representative is needed to deal with a crisis. The visits are not anticipated and are primarily for the purpose of diffusing a crisis situation. They do, however, provide another opportunity for student evaluation and monitoring of the work setting. *Example*: The work supervisor at the employment site calls to report that the student has a knife and has cornered one of the employees. The student will not hand over the knife or let anyone near him. The job supervisor must drop everything he or she is doing and proceed immediately to the work site. In this case, again, the primary purpose is to solve a problem, except that this time it is a much more acute problem that needs immediate attention. Important feedback information can and should be gathered, however, once the situation has been handled. It is important for the job supervisor to assess the situation very carefully to determine what caused the incident and to make contingency plans for the future.

4. *Scheduled or unscheduled visits after a student is no longer in formal training and is employed.* This type of follow-up is not only important for a continued show of support for the former student and the employer, but it is also an opportunity to get longitudinal feedback on the program. Follow-up studies are difficult when former students cannot be located; these types of visits increase the likelihood of keeping in touch. *Example*: The job supervisor is in the neighborhood and drops by to see the student (or graduate).

Frequency of job supervision is largely an individual student matter, but a general practice is to visit at least once per week until well after the "honeymoon period" ends for the student, the family, the employer, and the trainer or supervisor. The honeymoon period is that period of time in which it is the perception of the observer or participant that the job situation is ideal and that the job match is a success. It is not likely that these periods for each student will end at the same time, so the supervisor needs to be alert to when they occur and continue monitoring the situation.

Standard evaluation forms are generally used for follow-up visits, and these vary considerably from program to program. More often than not, these forms emphasize social and job-related behaviors more than job skill behaviors. They also tend to be general in nature, leading to some general observation data, but not specific enough to detect problems that could lead to termination or employment difficulties. If the job has been analyzed well, the job duties and social behaviors expected could form the basis for an individualized job evaluation form. A form such as this would prevent the occurrence of what Chaffin, Spellman, Regan, and Davison (1971) experienced. They reported that employers often rated students highly on all the basic job and job-related traits on the form, but would respond "no" to the question at the bottom of the form that asked, Would you hire this person?

Regardless of the kind of job or the nature of the work setting, there are some basic information questions that a job supervisor must ask (and even probe for). Some of these include the following:

- Is the student performing up to company standards? If not, why?
- Is the student improving, performing consistently, or doing less well than during the last visit?
- Are there any job-related skill problems? If so, what are they and what might be contributing to their occurrence?
- Have there been any changes in the work setting? If so, what are they?
- Have there been any changes in the job duties or job-related expectations? If so, what are they?
- Is there anything that the student needs or wants from the school in the way of additional support or assistance?
- Is there anything that the employer needs or wants from the school in the way of additional support or assistance?
- Is the "honeymoon" over for one or more of the participants? For whom? What led to that determination?
- What are the chances for job upgrading or salary increases? If there are possibilities, what does the student need to do to be able to qualify for them?

Neubert and Tilson (1987) found that most of the problems arising on the job in their Job Training and Tryout Project were discovered in the job supervision process and not through employer, parent, or worker information. Careful, systematic supervsion based on the preceding questions will provide critical on going support.

CONCLUSION

The responsibility for placing, training, and supervising students in community-based work-training programs cannot be taken lightly. The relative ease with which some individuals fulfill such responsibility is very deceiving. For most people, it is an awesome responsibility, especially when they realize all that it involves. It borders on the bizarre that the vast majority of states across the nation do not value this professional role enough to recognize it as a legitimate, highly desirable public school position with appropriate certification requirements. It borders on malpractice that state and local education agencies permit individuals to function in such critical outcome areas with no more than some type of academic teaching endorsement, most frequently with only an elementary focus.

Until states and local communities take responsibility for ensuring appropriate training for work experience coordinators, the coordinators will have to be responsible for their own professional development. There is a rapidly growing body of literature that reflects an optimistic philosophy, a demonstrated technology, and a practical agenda for placing, training, and supervising youths with disabilities in community-based employment. Increasing numbers of colleges and universities are offering up-to-date training in vocational training and transition programming for students with disabilities. Individuals in public school roles requiring job placement, job training, and job supervision should seek out these sources of professional development for the sake of the youths they serve, for their own legal protection, and for their own professional pride.

9

Career Guidance and Counseling

The best way in which one human being can properly attempt to influence another is to encourage him to think for himself, instead of endeavoring to instill ready-made opinions into his head.—SIR LESLIE STEPHEN

ACTIVITIES

- Interview a high school guidance counselor about the services offered students with disabilities.
- Examine computer software programs designed to assess interests and preferences to determine how they can assist guidance counselors in their work with students who have disabilities.
- Describe limitations faced by teachers when they attempt to provide all guidance services to students with disabilities.
- Examine and report on some ethical issues faced by school counselors who provide services to students with disabilities.
- Interview a parent of a child with disabilities to determine the parent's feelings about the guidance and counseling services provided to his or her child.

INTRODUCTION

Any consideration of career or transition programming must speak to the role of guidance and counseling. What are the elements of guidance and counseling that function in a high school program? What are the goals of guidance and counseling activities? Who should provide guidance and counseling services to students with special needs? This chapter will try to respond to these questions from the perspective of a high school's program for youths with mild and moderate disabilities. It will focus on the guidance and counseling needs of students and the roles and responsibilities of school personnel in meeting those needs.

ELEMENTS OF GUIDANCE AND COUNSELING

The terms *guidance* and *counseling* are frequently used as two independent concepts, but most school personnel in this field view *guidance* as an umbrella term that includes a number of techniques or approaches, with *counseling* being the heart of the guidance program. Guidance, according to Shertzer and Stone (1981, p. 40), is "the process of helping individuals to understand themselves and their world." They presented counseling in school settings as a technique "to assist students to explore and understand themselves so that they can become self-directing individuals" (p. 172). Since these definitions do not clearly differentiate between the two terms, other than one being viewed as a process and the other as a technique, each will be discussed in greater detail.

GUIDANCE

Educators directly responsible for educating and training high school students with disabilities need to understand the nature and limitations of contemporary guidance programs in order to gain access to their services. Guidance program models have evolved through various forms, including guidance as a vocational choice process (Parsons, 1909), guidance as a process identical with education (Brewer, 1932), guidance as a distribution and adjustment process (Kefauner & Hand, 1941), guidance as a clinical process (Williamson, 1939), guidance as a developmental process (Matthewson, 1962), guidance as a constellation of services (Hoyt, 1962), and guidance as a decision-making process (Katz, 1963; Stefflre & Stewart, 1970).

The most prevalent model for guidance programs in U.S. public schools is the constellation of services model. Hoyt (1982) used his influence strongly in the early 1960s to keep guidance programs broad and focused on education as the organizational system and educators as the primary operators of the system. He believed that guidance services can be successful only if their goals are integrated within the context of the school's educational objectives. He emphasized the opportunities that classroom teachers have for guidance and did not favor them being relegated to minor or passive roles in school guidance programs. He saw schools' guidance counselors as the key figures with major, but not exclusive, responsibility for the complete guidance program (Shertzer & Stone, 1981).

A genuine, working constellation of services focused on guidance services for students with disabilities involves consultation and collaboration. *Consultation* in the guidance program is the process of providing professional or technical assistance among teachers, parents, administrators, school support service personnel (school psychologists, school social workers, school nurses, etc.), community support personnel (community mental health personnel, community health services, physicians, juvenile court personnel, police, etc.), and other counselors. Collaboration usually relates to identifying and solving problems that limit the school's effectiveness with students.

Brolin and Gysbers (1989) addressed the challenge for school counselors in responding to the career development and transition needs of students with disabilities with an optimistic note. They have viewed current trends in guidance in the schools as increasingly being conceptualized and implemented as comprehensive competency-based programs. Gysbers and Henderson (1988) described their proposed model of a comprehensive program as having four program components: (1) guidance curriculum, (2) individual planning, (3) responsive services, and (4) system support. Their program was organized around the need to meet student needs and outcomes. The guidance curriculum component, for example, was made to incorporate Competencies 10 through 15, 17, 18, and 20 of the Life Centered Career Education model (Brolin, 1992a) described in Chapter 6. These competencies, which focus on personal and social skills and occupational guidance, are particularly appropriate for what one would expect in a guidance curriculum and fit in nicely with the current outcomes-based education movement. The individual planning component relates to the counselor's role on the IEP team or as a consultant/collaborator with other school staff in planning for strategies or procedures to help a student. Responsive services would be those assessment, information-giving, referral, or counseling services needed by a student and specified on his or her IEP. The system support component would be the overall support contributions that the counselor makes to the school's operations (testing, scheduling, etc.).

The Gysbers and Henderson (1988) model does not propose that the role of the school guidance counselor be changed dramatically to take on students with disabilities. Rather, it is an attempt to provide a better focus on the various roles of school counselors and to identify percentages of counselor time that should be devoted to carrying out guidance activities in each of the four components in their model.

The positive implications of this model for students with disabilities are that they are much more likely to receive some needed instruction and programming within the mainstream of a school if that school has a guidance curriculum and if counselors are committed to individual planning for all students.

Until comprehensive competency-based guidance program models have replaced the predominant constellation of services model, advocates for students with disabilities must look at any existing guidance and counseling program in terms of the services that are offered and how these services can be accessed. It may be that all of the services that students with disabilities need will never be able to be accessed via the guidance counselor(s) in a school. In those cases, some of the services may have to be provided by others with the support of the guidance counselors. The following sections describe some of the basic guidance services that students with disabilities need, regardless of who provides them.

Assessment

Counselors and teachers using a comprehensive career guidance approach assessment as a basic process for getting information needed in assisting students to make decisions and work toward goals. (Assessment techniques were discussed in detail in Chapter 4.) Assessment, as a functional element of a guidance program, is the responsibility of all personnel who work with students with disabilities, and not just the school psychologist, the vocational evaluator, an educational diagnostician, or the school counselor.

Traditionally, school counselors try to ensure the availability of assessment data to all students, teachers, and parents in the areas of ability (intellectual functioning) and academic achievement. Aptitude, personality, and interest are made available as needed. This means that teachers and parents will probably be limited in IEP planning to ability and achievement data alone, unless other types of testing or assessment are requested. This, again, does not mean that the school counselor as a major guidance staff participant would (or should) be the one to administer and interpret the results of all tests. A counselor should, however, be fully attuned to every student's guidance needs, and should be prepared to facilitate arrangements rather than see students with disabilities as someone else's responsibility.

Information Giving

Information services in a guidance program are designed to provide students with appropriate educational, personal-social, and occupational data needed to understand themselves and their environment. Counselors and teachers can ensure that a significant amount of this type of information is provided systematically when they work together to schedule students in courses that meet each student's individual needs. When available courses are not appropriate for students, information giving may be achieved through course revisions or curriculum development. In a less systematic but a more individualized approach, counselors and teachers should also make available to all students current information on postsecondary education options, occupational information, and information related to adolescent problems and interests.

Information is absolutely critical to the life-career guidance and decision-making process for youth experiencing educational handicaps. Appropriate decisions depend on obtaining comparable, complete, timely, and accurate information about all life-career and transition alternatives under consideration. How to transmit this information is the difficult proplem. Our position is that it must be transmitted through the curriculum, one-to-one counseling with parents, professionals, materials, computer-based information, and guidance systems. Not a single approach is adequate

An interesting psychological subtlety operates in a school in relation to its real commitment to the guidance function of information giving. Information implies a body of knowledge that is of use to someone. Part of that information is in the minds and personal memory systems of counselors, teachers, parents, and other informed sources, but most of it must be in resource documents or systems that can handle large amounts of information—much of which changes rapidly. This suuggests a need for an accessible, central location where this information is easily obtained. A career resource center is one common way of providing that. Such a center serves as an indentifiable source of information to students and increases the likelihood of use. Even then, many high school students may choose not to use it.

Realistically, the percentage of students with disabilities using a central career resource center in a high school may be lower than for students not identified as having special needs. This raises the issue as to why this would be the case. Some special education teachers say that their students do not feel comfortable going to such a center because they do not identify with the rest of the school. The "ours" and "theirs" problem between regular and special education is at the heart of this. One high school counselor in New England in a study of high school programs for youths with disabilities (Clark, Knowlton, & Dorsey, 1989) spoke openly about special education students, IEP students, and "our" students. The interesting distinction was between special students (in this case, students who are mildly mentally retarded) and IEP students (students who are learning disabled and behavior disordered). However, the more telling attitude was the "ours" and "theirs," referring to identified students with disabilities versus students without such an identification.

Discomfort, whether social or ability related, may be an oversimplification of the problem of low usage of a career resource center by students in special programs. Possibly the problem is compounded by other factors, such as general motivation to seek information, receptivity of guidance counselors or guidance staff to students who need more individual attention, the location of the center, a lack of encouragement to students by special class and resource room teachers to use the center, or inadequacy of the center services. The solution to the basic problem—the need for accurate, relevant guidance information—must address the possibility of all of these factors. At a minimum, a high school should address the issue of adequacy of the center's content. Is the center's material limited to college catalogs? Is it focused on occupations requiring only a college education?

Is the material readable and is the information accessible through media other than print? Does the center provide information in career and transition knowledge and skill areas other than education and occupations? Do students identify with any guidance counselor in the career resource center or one specially designed for students who have special needs?

Shertzer and Stone (1981) presented a balanced proposal for the types of information that should be included in a minimally adequate information service. Their three major divisions included *educational information, occupational information,* and *personal-social information.* According to these authors, each type of information service should include these divisions.

Educational Information

Educational data should acquaint students, counselors, teachers, and parents with the following:

1. Full information about the students' own school: policies, regulation, available curricular offerings, extracurricular activities and social activities, high school graduation requirements, and so on
2. Existing local, state, and national postsecondary educational programs: vocational-technical schools, business schools, correspondence schools, proprietary schools, trade schools, apprentice programs, job-training programs, community colleges, and four-year colleges and universities
3. Prerequisites and qualifications for admission to postsecondary educational programs
4. Costs of attending any type of postsecondary educational program
5. Characteristics and descriptions of postsecondary educational institutions
6. Study habits and study skills guides
7. Earnings and other rewards of various occupations
8. Military service (age and qualification requirements, training opportunities, kinds of adjustment problems, etc.)

Occupational Information

Occupational information should include data relevant to the following:

1. Work trends, including labor supply, population shifts, public demand for goods and services, and changes in technology
2. Sources of information for studying occupations
3. Classification of occupations and occupational information
4. Duties of certain occupations and qualifications for employement
5. Preparation needed for occupations
6. Earnings and conditions of employment in occupations
7. Typical places of employment for various occupations

Personal-Social Information

Personal and social information deals with such conditions and factors as the following:

1. Achieving self-insight and understanding
2. Achieving mature relationships with members of the same and opposite sex
3. Understanding one's behavior and one's characteristics
4. Understanding others behaviors and their needs
5. Developing healthy personalities
6. Understanding, adjusting to, and accepting home conditions, family members, and parental expectations
7. Physical and mental health developments
8. Understanding how one differs from others and how one is similar to others
9. Knowledge of dating practices and information related to sexuality and sexual behaviors
10. Personal appearance, manners, and etiquette

Each of these types of information systems needs to be clearly established, accessible, and, at times, taken to the students rather than depending solely on student requests or initiatives.

Computer Information

Computer-based occupational information systems are rapidly becoming part of the common technology of high school guidance programs. The large amounts of information and the rapid changes that occur continuously demand a system more responsive than vertical files in the library or *Occupational Outlook Handbook* editions that are two or more years old.

Over the last 30 years, a number of systems have come and gone. Each new generation of systems, however, has improved in the hardware and software technologies used. The microcomputer boom resulted in significant breakthroughs, not only in sophistication but also in affordable costs for schools. Today, the computer literacy of high school students is well beyond the expectations of even the early enthusiasts. Clearly, there are some definite advantages in using computer-based information systems. Among these are the following:

1. Computers reduce the time counselors and career information personnel must spend in repetitive and routine dissemination tasks.
2. Computers provide almost instantaneous information.
3. Computer technology is still novel enough to be motivational and has moved from information storage to interactive decision-making systems.

4. Information can be updated more easily and more quickly than can print information.
5. Information can be made available in rural and remote areas with portable microcomputers, modems, and other sophisticated equipment.
6. Audio attachments for students with visual impairments or nonreaders open up the systems to new populations.
7. Computers can provide data to teachers and counselors on what information students have obtained and how they have used the system.

Computer-based systems of any kind have their disadvantages, too. Although costs have decreased considerably, some high schools have not believed that computers for guidance purposes are affordable when viewed from a cost benefit in student use. It is critical to keep the information current and to modify the program frequently, and this becomes a problem in some programs. In addition, school personnel's lack of computer background may not permit full use of computer technology. Finally, there is the persistent worry that computer technology will dehumanize the guidance and information process and the fear that counselor and teacher overuse of the computer will substitute for personal attention, one-on-one counseling, and traditional information services (Frederickson, 1982).

Harris-Bowlsbey (1983) made a distinction between computer-based information systems and computer-based guidance systems. Even though they share the common features of storing large data files and sorting and retrieving information about user-defined options on many variables, they are completely different in format. Differences are most evident in the use of assessment instruments. The typical information-emphasis system does not administer assessment instruments, such as interest inventories, ability rating scales, or values inventories at the computer terminal or microcomputer keyboard. In contrast, guidance-emphasis systems such as Apticom or MESA (see Chapter 4 for descriptions) typically make self-assessment instruments or simulations part of the computer input process. Another difference between the two systems is that information systems emphasize local labor market information, whereas guidance systems are more concerned with accurate, timely, national occupational information. A third difference is that information systems generally do not use the computer to teach career-development concepts, such as values clarification, decision-making systems, or job-seeking skills, as do guidance systems. Finally, information systems technically do not store an individual student's records or data, because no long-term interactive process is being monitored. This feature is the heart of the guidance-emphasis system.

Isaacson (1985) has suggested that the opportunity to develop special computer systems for particular groups will be enhanced as the capability of the microprocessor expands and its cost decreases. Rehabilitation agencies and high school special education programs that need much greater detail about physical and mental requirements, working conditions, and job modifications can look forward to access via the microcomputer in the near future. Isaacson placed computer-based systems in optimistic perspective with this statement:

> The degree to which new applications can effectively serve counselors and their clients depends to a large extent on the willingness and ability of counselors to identify needs and transmit those needs to computer specialists in understandable terms. If counselors succeed in communicating, the situation can best be described by that old ungrammatical exclamation "We ain't seen nothing yet!" (1985, p. 377)

Guidance Referrals

The degree to which appropriate guidance services can be obtained for individuals in a high school from outside itself depends largely on the community. Even in the most restricted community, however, there are guidance resources that the school need not duplicate. Certainly, it often requires determined and thoughtful efforts to arrange for the use of these services. But, understanding that, counselors and special education staff can build relationships with community resource persons that lead to referrals and use of an array of guidance assistance services. Because of the broad definition of a comprehensive career guidance program for students with disabilities, the process of referral deserves a full and extensive treatment of its own. Chapter 10 will discuss referral of students for career and transition services that are best obtained from the community.

In the context of guidance and counseling services, there are two important issues that relate to referral decisions:

Issue 1:   Counselors or teachers in the school who decide that a student's problems or needs are beyond their guidance or counseling competencies (but the student or parents will not accept referral) must decide whether to continue services to the student.

Issue 2:   Who should take the initiative for establishing close, direct, cooperative relationships among school and community resources?

In issue 1, the most common argument against continuation of services beyond a perceived level of inadequacy is that such continuation may worsen an already serious situation. We concur with Shertzer and Stone (1981) that the resolution of this issue involves subissues of humanitarianism, practicality, and professional ethics. From a humanitarian perspective, no professional would want to deny services to someone in desperate need, and the question comes down to whether some assistance, however inadequate, is better than none. From a practical perspective, school personnel have to consider their available time, the availability of consultation, and whether there is a reasonable expectation that continuation will make a difference. From a professional ethics perspective, the American Personnel and Guidance Association's (1974) statement of professional ethics for its members is straightforward. Counselors or guidance personnel are expected to terminate any counseling relationships that call for assistance that goes beyond their competencies.

In issue 2, the ideal resolution for initiating cooperative working relationships that make referrals smooth and effective is for schools and community resources to assume mutual responsibility. It is not uncommon for both school and community agency personnel to be critical of the other's failure to initiate, cooperate, and follow through in their relationships with each other. From our perspective, the school is the most stable, established organization in a community, and it is the school's responsibility to take the initiative to make full use of community agency resources because students and the schools are the ones who benefit most from such efforts.

COUNSELING

Counseling in a high school is usually viewed as one part of a guidance program. Any one counselor may approach the counseling relationship from a unique perspective, ranging from an intention to deal primarily with practical information giving for one counselor to working through intense psychological stress with another. Definitions of counseling do not necessarily help in pinning down exactly what counseling is because the definitions tend to be extremely general— "a process of helping people with their troubles (Krumboltz & Thoresen, 1976b, p. 2)—or elusive in their combination of specificity and generality—"Counseling denotes a professional relationship between a trained counselor and a client. This relationship is usually person-to-person, although it may sometimes involve more than two people. It is designed to help clients to understand and clarify their views of their life space, and to learn to reach their self-determined goals through meaningful, well-informed choices and through resolution of problems of an emotional or interpersonal nature" (Burks & Stefflre, 1979, p. 14).

Shertzer and Stone (1981, p. 168) have defined counseling in a straightforward, noninclusive way: "a learning process in which individuals learn about themselves and their interpersonal relationships, and enact behaviors that advance their personal development." Unlike the Burks and Stefflre (1979) definition, this definition does not limit counseling only to a trained counselor. Jageman and Myers (1986) supported this view in their notion that counseling can take place in a relationship between a counselee and a professional, paraprofessional, or nonprofessional counselor. This opens up the counseling role to teachers, teacher aides, parents, employers, school staff, and even peers.

Although the definition of counseling remains difficult (especially when differentiating it from psychotherapy), the nature of the counseling process can be described. For our purposes in discussing the counseling process with high school students with mild to moderate levels of disabilities, the following statements reflect the nature of counseling:

- The counseling process, whether successful or not in terms of outcomes, is characterized by a unique, helping relationship between the person performing the counselor role and the student(s).
- The counseling interaction process includes both verbal and nonverbal communication.
- Counseling may be a service used more by students who are well adjusted and whose mental health is stable than those who exhibit extreme modes of behavior or emotional instability,
- Counseling stresses rational planning, problem solving, and support in the face of situational pressures.
- Counseling approaches, whether selected strategically or naturally and spontaneously, are based more on focusing on everyday reality and conscious observations than unconscious motivations, past events, dreams, or symbolic material.
- Counseling tends to rely on the counselee's positive individual strengths for problem solving or decision making rather than stressing the diagnosis and remediation of personality defects.
- Counseling is ordinarily viewed as a short-term process in which specific problems are identified and outcomes are achieved over a relatively short period of time.

The preceding sections on guidance and counseling suggest that there are some identifiable key elements of a guidance and counseling component. Each of these components reflects a discrete approach, but by way of summary and synthesis, the following statement will try to bring the parts back into a whole as it relates to career development and transition for students in special education programs.

Herr and Cramer (1984) view career guidance as an instrument of human development and mental health. In recognizing the impact of career guidance as such an instrument, they also believe that career guidance and counseling requires a developmental rather than a solely remedial approach. This belief is based on the premise that career guidance and counseling must be conceived as a "systematic program designed to effect certain pre-planned or practitioner-client agreed upon behavioral outcomes" (p. v).

The behavioral outcomes of a comprehensive career and traditional guidance and counseling program are, and should be, the same behavioral outcomes of a career and transition educational program. That is, outcomes related to daily living, personal and social skills, and occupational and vocational adjustment are what practitioners (counselors, teachers, and other professionals) and clients (students and former students) discuss and on which they try to reach some agreement.

The school counselor's role—and the school's role, for that matter—was initially limited to guidance and counseling in vocational choice and vocational planning. Before 1950, vocational guidance was seen as a problem-solving intervention at certain points during a person's life, usually just before graduation

"Funny, I never pictured myself becoming a kabuki dancer before."

from high school, return from military duty, or at occupational change periods in adult years. Williamson (1939) suggested that vocational problems could be boiled down to (1) no choice, (2) uncertain choice, (3) unwise choice, or (4) difficult in choice because of discrepancies between interests and aptitudes.

A movement within the field of vocational guidance during the mid- to late 1940s and continuing into the early 1960s reflected a shift in Williamson's (1939) restricted vocational guidance problem areas to more psychologically oriented problems (Bordin, 1946; Byrne, 1958; Robinson, 1963). The essence of this shift was to focus on both the presenting problems and the symptoms of the problems. These included such things as personal maladjustment, conflict with significant others, lack of information, immaturity, skill deficiencies, and problems in planning, in addition to various vocational choice problems.

Even this shift, however, did not alter the general view that all vocational decision-making problems stem from deficits of one type or another in the behavioral repertoires of the persons presenting their problems. It was also assumed that these problems, when they surface at significant decision points, can be "fixed" or at least ameliorated through vocational guidance interventions.

Even while these changes were occurring among proponents of vocational guidance as a response system to problems at fixed points in time, a subtle but even more significant shift began in 1951 with Donald Super's redefinition of vocational guidance. His redefinition (Super, 1951) and his theoretical position (Super, 1953) began a movement from the occupational choice model to a career decision-making and career-development model. This model, by definition, focuses on a longer time frame for intervention than the "one-shot" approach of the occupational model. It also poses the notion of career guidance as a *stimulus* model as well as an intervention model. In other words, in a stimulus model, guidance and counseling not only respond to existing problems but they also assist students in acquiring knowledge, attitudes, and skills through which they can develop the behaviors necessary to cope with decision points, to acquire an occupational identity, and to develop career maturity (Herr & Cramer, 1984).

Viewing career guidance and counseling as a lifelong developmental process gained a great deal of support in the late 1960s and early 1970s. The introduction of the career education movement in 1970 gave proponents of this view a programmatic vehicle for demonstrating the possibilities of the career guidance model.

Comprehensive career counseling (Crites, 1981) and comprehensive career guidance (Herr, 1982; Herr & Cramer, 1984) are used as descriptors of what the movement begun by Super (1951) has accomplished. The organizing themes of comprehensive career guidance that emerged during the 1970s and the early 1980s, according to these authors, were the following:

1. Efforts to develop decision-making skills
2. Concern for the self-concept
3. Concerns for life-styles, values, and leisure
4. Free choice
5. Individual differences
6. Flexibility and coping with change

If these themes sound familiar, efforts in previous chapters were not in vain. These themes are at the heart of the career/transition model presented in Chapter 2. The career/transition model is, in fact, an extension of the comprehensive career guidance movement. It reflects the intent of its proponents to absorb vocational guidance techniques and strategies and expand them to provide a more appropriate repertoire of interventions to individuals with disabilities in a greater number and variety of settings.

It is interesting to note the parallels between professionals in counseling and guidance and special education in the evolution of the comprehensive career guidance and career/transition models. It appears that there are purists within both fields who advocate a restricted intervention on vocational problems only (Rusch & Menchetti, 1988; Williamson, 1972). These people differ from those who are proponents of a broadened comprehensive view (Herr & Cramer, 1984;

Gysbers & Moore, 1974; Kokaska & Brolin, 1985, Clark & Knowlton, 1988). We reaffirm here the position taken in Chapter 2: To deal only with the vocational needs of students with disabilities and to assume that all of the other consequences of problems related to employment will take care of themselves is not only unrealistic but inappropriate.

GOALS OF GUIDANCE AND COUNSELING ACTIVITIES

As one would expect from the definition given in the introductory section and the descriptions of the elements of a guidance and counseling function, the goals will always be directed toward helping students understand the factors (personal, social, economic, etc.) that have bearing on making educational, vocational, and other personal life decisions, and then the following through on those decisions with action.

Professionals responsible for guidance and counseling with high school youths approach their own goals with a variety of assumptions about career and transition development in the abstract (or ideal) and for career and transition development for youths with disabilities in particular. For example, a regular high school counselor might assume that career-development behavior is developmental for students without disabilities in regular education, but that the career development and behavior of all students with special needs is arrested or retarded significantly. Or, a special education work experience counselor might assume that people in general have multiple potentials regarding occupational or life opportunities, but when pressed about his or her beliefs for persons with disabilities, he or she may acknowledge that occupational and life options for such students are very limited because of their deficits. In both cases, these professionals would likely set their guidance and counseling activity goals or expectations at a different level than someone who had different assumptions about both the nature of youths with special needs and the power of vocational or life-career guidance and counseling.

Another way of putting goals into perspective is to challenge the notion that guidance and counseling, like psychotherapy from a psychodynamic approach, are highly cerebral and can work only with those who have the intelligence and verbal communication skills to deal with problems, information, and decision making at a self-actualization level. Very few people operate at that level in all areas of their lives. Maslow's (1954) need hierarchy has been related to counseling and guidance goals for persons with severe disabilities by both Lassiter (1981) and Jageman and Myers (1986). These authors have delineated possible goal alternatives in guidance and counseling activities with special-needs students with mild or moderate disabilities. Examples are provided for each of Maslow's need levels in Table 9.1.

TABLE 9.1   Examples of Career Guidance and Counseling Goals and Activities Based on Maslow's Hierarchy of Needs

Need	Prevention Goals	Intervention Goals
Physiological Survival Needs	Assist students in learning effects of good eating and drinking habits. Assist students in planning exercise and rest schedules. Assist students in understanding sources of pain and pain-reduction alternatives. Assist students in understanding sexual needs and appropriate responses. Assist students in acquiring knowledge on health and hygiene requirements of a job.	Assist students in dealing with problems of overeating, alcohol or substance abuse, or eating disorders. Provide student support and reinforcement for efforts in accomplishing plans. Assist students with stress-management techniques or making medication schedules work. Provide students assertiveness training. Confront students with inappropriate sexual behavior and modifying behaviors.
Safety/ Security Needs	Assist students in understanding stress in life changes. Assist students in planning for risk events. Assist students in organizing their behavior and environments to establish order and routine.	Counsel students to assist in coping with stress and adjustment to new settings, new people, new demands. Assist students in coping with risk events. Assist students in adjusting to disorganized or chaotic life environments.
Belonging/ Love Needs	Assist students in learning about needing to belong. Assist students in learning appropriate ways of seeking acceptance and love.	Provide accepting support system in a counseling relationship. Provide therapeutic environment and assistance in coping with rejection/ loneliness.
Esteem Needs	Assist students in learning ways of behaving that are seen as successful and confidence building. Assist students in finding places to work, groups to join, or places to live that foster self-esteem. Assist students in understanding conflicts within themselves relative to their disabilities.	Assist students in coping with low self-esteem or mild depression. Assist students in self-evaluation of self-defeating and self-derogatory behavior. Assist students in coping with continuing adjustment demands to their disabilities.
Self-Actualization Needs	Assist students in learning ways of personal growth and self-improvement. Assist students in learning ways of using their strengths to move beyond their present levels of functioning.	Provide students with support and encouragement for efforts in personal growth. Assist students in coping with routine, boredom, and malaise.

KEY PROVIDERS OF SERVICES

Writers in the field of guidance and counseling (Arbuckle, 1962, 1972; Shertzer & Stone, 1981) generally maintain that, although there are a number of important contributors to a guidance and counseling program, the key person is the professionally prepared and personally committed counselor. This position is not a difficult one to defend from a logical and practical point of view, even though some people argue that the teacher is the key person because of day-to-day interactions and knowledge of each student's needs. Lombana (1982) pointed out that the argument that the special education teacher is the best counselor for students with disabilities could logically be extended to conclude that the regular classroom teacher is the best counselor for students who have no disabilities. The main differences between teaching and guidance are inferred from a clear difference between the function of teaching and the various functions of guidance. Since counseling is such an important role in guidance, the differences frequently focus on the dissimilarities between teaching and counseling.

Those who argue in favor of the teacher role being the most important may have an idealized elementary schoolteacher in mind, because it is becoming increasingly clear that high school teachers are being asked to do many more things, few of which are related to guidance and counseling. The typical high school teacher is—by training, by inclination, and by the requirements of a teaching position—a specialist in a subject. It is as a subject specialist that the teacher expects to make a career and meet the expectations of students and their parents. The counselor, on the other hand, is specifically assigned guidance and counseling responsibilities and has some type of training and credentials supporting competency in those responsibilities.

All of this may seem too obvious for discussion. However, the reality of high schools and their hierarchical bureaucracies (Sizer, 1985) breaks through the professional logic and presents a disturbing view of the actual achievement of guidance and counseling goals via this system. To emphasize the persistence of this problem over the years, Arbuckle in 1972 made the following statement:

> Throughout the United States there are tens of thousands of coercive teachers, scores of administrators who are cold and unfeeling, and a school curriculum, a significant proportion of which is dull and deadly, oppressive, and irrelevant. Teachers and administrators should be concerned about these problems, and many of them are very much concerned. But. . . anyone involved in schools surely would have to be blind to be unaware that tens of thousands of young people are being affected in a negative way by their school experience. (p. 789)

All types of students in today's high schools are falling through the cracks of the guidance system. Our view is that this is especially the case for students receiving special services under IEPs. This is not the fault of school guidance counselors, but rather a symptom of some of the issues confronting high school programs today. Some of the more common issues include the following:

- High school guidance counselors are assigned responsibility for providing guidance services to large numbers of students, making significant individual contact difficult and forcing students to be aggressive and persistent if they want to receive assistance.
- High school guidance counselors in small high schools have to be knowledgeable in all areas of guidance; frequently, they have few resources to support their services.
- High school guidance counselors have been assigned administrative support roles over the years (such as scheduling) that have consumed much of their time that could be used for less administrative tasks.
- High school guidance counselors have traditionally spent much of their time helping students to select and apply to colleges. This will continue, if not increase, in response to educational reform policies being implemented and will require more planning for academic course of study decisions.
- High school guidance counselors rarely are required to have any preservice training in even the basic characteristics of exceptional students, much less training in career development or transition guidance for them.
- High school special education teachers are becoming increasingly involved in course selection and scheduling for students on IEPs. This requires more academic planning and guidance in light of new and changing graduation policies.
- Occupational assessment and career/transitional guidance are not available in any systematic form in most high schools. High school guidance counselors claim lack of time or expertise for these services for students in special education services.
- High school special education programs have responded to the guidance and counseling service void for their students by assigning or reassigning teachers to function in similar roles, either on a part- or full-time basis, such as vocational counselors, work experience coordinators, vocational-adjustment coordinators, and so forth. For the most part, these individuals have little or no preservice training for these roles, and only a few states recognize such a role with a certificate or endorsement credential.

Doyle (1971) and Hansen (1971) proposed a solution to the problem of neglect of special education students by school guidance counselors. They both advocated a new professional—a special education counselor who is knowledgeable about disabilities and who is professionally trained for and committed to students with disabilities. This notion met with some enthusiasm at first and was, in fact, made a part of the special services system in Texas and in other states at the elementary school level. It never became a widely accepted alternative due to some counseling field resistance (Baker, 1976; Vandergriff & Hosie, 1979), the difficulties of implementing the idea in higher education counselor-education programs, and the opposition of high schools to the idea.

Some schools are reviewing their guidance and counseling services for students with disabilities in light of the provisions of the Individuals with Disabilities Education Act of 1990 (IDEA), which authorizes the use of "rehabilitation counseling services" [20 U.S.C. 1401(a)(17). Under the final regulations of IDEA, *rehabilitation counseling services* means services provided by qualified personnel in individual or group sessions that focus specifically on career development, employment preparation, achieving independence, and integration in the workplace and community of a student with a disability. The regulations also state that the term *rehabilitation counseling services* includes vocational rehabilitation services provided to students with disabilities by state vocational rehabilitation programs funded under the Rehabilitation Act of 1973, as amended. In essence, this means that students who need the kind of services described under the definition of rehabilitation counseling services should have those related services— as well as who will be designated as responsible for providing them specified on their IEPs. This could mean that, for the first time, a school may now employ someone specifically to provide such services for the school and get reimbursed by the state with special education funds. It could also mean that a student who needs those services and who is eligible for vocational rehabilitation program services may receive such services while still in school and provided by a non-school professional from a state vocational rehabilitation agency. It is also possible that a student might receive rehabilitation counseling services from both a school and nonschool qualified person collaboratively.

In the context of this chapter, is the school guidance counselor among the qualified personnel authorized to provide rehabilitation counseling services? That will depend on the response each state makes to this new provision of the law. Each state will have to develop guidelines specifying who is qualified for employment using special education funds. These guidelines must state what certification, licensing, registration, or other comparable requirements apply to a person who is going to provide the services. This may or may not include public school guidance counselors, just as it may or may not include work experience coordinators, vocational counselors, or others who have been providing services in this area to one extent or another for years.

Hanley-Maxwell and Szymanski (1992) pointed out that rehabilitation counselors' roles in the career-development and transition process depend on a variety of factors. Among these factors are (1) the settings or actual locations of employment of the counselors; (2) the types of disabilities, ages, and needs the students; and (3) the resources available in the setting, from the family, and in the community. Szymanski and King (1989) proposed the following potential rehabilitation counseling functions for transition:

- Career and psychosocial counseling
- Consultation with school personnel regarding the vocational implications of students' disabilities and possible educational accommodations
- Coordination of career planning and preparation efforts

- Job placement, job analysis, job modification and restructuring, and follow-up
- Work-adjustment counseling
- Coordination of job support services
- Coordination of referrals to and coordination with adult service agencies
- Specialized planning and linkage with postsecondary programs
- Development of individual transition plans

In light of the issues reflecting the reality of school organizations, what should be expected of all the individuals typically involved in guidance services? Consider the following as a proposal for what should be exemplary program practice.

School Counselors

In laying out a description of an ideal high school counselor who includes students with disabilities, a caution from Foster, Fitzgerald, and Beal (1980) is appropriate. They have reminded us that no counselor is able to do everything, but any good school counselor can be most helpful in a variety of ways. They provided a long list of ways a good counselor can help students. Included among these ways are some ideas that provide a basis for the following helping role opportunities with students who have special needs.

- Help with social adjustment problems in regular classes or mainstream activities in the school.
- Help with problems that may occur with teachers in regular classes, the resource room, or the special class.
- Provide assistance with questions or decision-making needs about educational goals beyond high school.
- Give help when students find it difficult to establish friendships with members of the opposite sex.
- Provide support when students' interests and goals appear to conflict with those of their parents.
- Help with decision making on appropriate courses in school that are appropriate for students' interests and needs.
- Provide encouragement when students are searching for meaning and values in their lives.
- Give assistance when students need information about their abilities, aptitudes, and interests.
- Help with the development of self-advocacy skills.

The counselor is expected to be ready to help teachers and other school staff also. Hummel and Humes (1984) provided a list of counselor responsibilities that provide a basis for our special focus on the counselor's role with special education teachers and staff. This modified list would indicate that a high school counselor should take on the following responsibilities:

- View special education teachers and staff as members of the guidance team.
- Serve as an interpreter of the school's pupil personnel policies and guidance program and keep students fully informed on the guidance services and activities that are available to the entire school.
- Share appropriate individual student data with both regular and special education teachers with special regard for confidentiality and assist teachers in incorporating those assessment results in curriculum development and instructional planning.
- Assist regular teachers in making referrals to appropriate school personnel, such as the school nurse, school psychologist, school social worker or visiting teacher, or special education staff specialists.
- Assist special education teachers in making referrals to community agency personnel, such as community mental health staff, city or county health staff, and alcohol and drug-abuse information centers.
- Cooperate with the efforts of middle school or junior high school and high school special education teachers in making the student's transition to the high school a smooth and positive one.
- Assist in the planning of special education curriculum development and serve as a resource person for obtaining age-appropriate, relevant guidance materials and information.
- Make current information about job opportunities for students available to special education staff.
- Involve special education teachers and staff in faculty in-service.
- Serve as a liaison between the special education staff and the principal or administrative staff on guidance issues especially related to students in special programs.

Teachers

The role of teachers in the overall guidance concept is well accepted. What has not been laid out in any detail that would permit discussion are the specific guidance functions a teacher has. This is much more of a dilemma at the high school level today, where teachers in regular education are straining at increased expectations and feeling defensive about the criticisms of their efforts, and special education teachers are becoming less and less certain about their roles as special educators.

If high school regular education teachers see any role at all in the Shertzer and Stone (1981, p. 40) definition of guidance—"the process of helping individuals to understand themselves and their world"—it is likely to be in the "understanding their world." The subject emphasis of secondary teachers is so compelling that many resist the imposition of any additional responsibilities. We agree with Foster, Fitzgerald, and Beal (1980), who argued that it is, ultimately, the classroom teacher who spends the largest amount of time with the students. This is especially the case for students with learning disabilities who spend, on the average, 63 percent of their day in regular education classes (Valdez, Williamson, & Wagner, 1990). The classroom teacher sees them about 175 to 180 days per year, and, by attitude and example, is communicating guidance concepts and skills whether he or she intends to or not. The classroom teacher's role in guidance is both direct and indirect, but primarily indirect. Many guidance activities occur indirectly through the following:

- Values supported or rejected before the class
- Incidental references to postsecondary educational and occupational opportunities
- Teachers' modeling of their own attitudes and behaviors involving values (fairness, honesty, acceptance of individual differences, dignity, personhood over ideas, etc.)
- Personal style (job outlook, view of life, organization of his or her environment, time management, decision making)
- Public behavior (citizenship responsibilities, consumer behavior, humanitarian involvement, health, fitness and grooming) and self-sufficiency in independent living activities such as minor housekeeping, automobile maintenance, and financial management

The guidance role, then, of a regular classroom teacher of English, math, home economics, physical education, or any other course should be the following:

- Be open and accepting of students with educational handicaps and those with physical or sensory disabilities.
- Be honest but genuinely caring when communicating discrepancies between expectations for achievement and behavior.
- Make the students' educational experience in the course a meaningful one between the content being taught and life career demands in family living, employment, and community living.
- Assist students in seeking opportunities and making choices in future course selections, extracurricular activities, or occupational exploration related to the teacher's field.
- Provide feedback to special education staff on curriculum needs for special students.
- Be sensitive to the effect of a teacher's personality on students and periodically evaluate one's own personal style of relating to students by asking such questions as:

   Do students see me as a supporter or as an adversary?

   Do students feel that I treat them differently because of their designation as special students?

Do students think that I expect too little of them?

Do students see me as an adult with traits they would like to emulate in their own lives and careers?

Do I see the students as young human beings trying to develop meaningful identities as persons?

Do I make an effort to let students know the behavioral limits within which they can operate in my classroom?

Do I have conferences with my students to let them know that I do know them as individuals and that I care about what they do and how they feel?

Am I listening to what they say and responding to what they feel?

The guidance role of a special education teacher is identical to that of a regular teacher, but it goes beyond it in several respects. Special education teachers frequently have to assume counselor roles by default when the counselor cannot or does not function as outlined previously in the counselor section. However, assumption of the counselor role does not meet all the guidance needs of students with special career development and transition problems. Some of the additional guidance efforts by a special education teacher could include serving as one of the following:

- Interpreter of the school's special education program to parents, employers, and community agencies
- Primary communicator with parents regarding school progress, problems and issues in serving students' needs, and concerns voiced by parents
- Advocate for students in securing support services both during their high school years and after leaving or completing school
- Primary liaison between students and their parents, students or parents and regular teachers, or parents and the school administration
- The students' best and last advocate for ensuring values, attitudes and habits, human relationships, occupational information, and job and daily living skills in the curriculum

Schumaker, Hazel, and Deshler (1985) developed a model for postsecondary transitions of secondary-aged students with learning disabilities. The model, Life-Planning Program, involved instruction in cognitive strategies for learning a process of problem solving, goal setting, and goal implementation. The content areas chosen were career or educational plans, independent living, and social interactions. All of these are associated with guidance functions. Since it is an instructional model, however, the teacher is the most likely professional at the high school level to have the time to implement it.

The Life-Planning Program (Schumaker et al., 1985) presents a learning structure for students called the life-planning process. This process has 10 steps, beginning with defining the problem and ending with rewarding oneself for completing the contract or revising the self-developed contract to recycle through earlier steps of task analyses of subgoals for completing it. The program also includes instruction on how a student can best identify and use personal resources. Because adolescents with learning disabilities have been characterized as having problems in planning, organization, problem solving, and goal setting, direct instruction and practice in such transition-related skills seems ideal for high school students who are mildly handicapped .

The role of a full-time work-study coordinator (also called vocational counselor, vocational adjustment coordinator, and work experience coordinator, among other titles) is basically a specialized guidance and counseling position with a specific focus on occupational, personal-social, and daily living adjustment in the community. Guidance and counseling functions in this professional role overlap considerably with those of the high school counselors and special education teachers. This is why high schools that have a full-time specialist in this role should establish a team approach with clearly specified areas of primary responsibility for the counselor, special education teachers, and the work-study coordinator, as well as support functions for each other.

The specific guidance and counseling role functions of a work-study coordinator include the following:

- Serve as a crisis counselor for students in off-campus activities relating to work, home living, and personal-social problems.
- Serve as an advocate for students in securing and maintaining employment and vocational training.
- Serve as the primary liaison between the school and employers and between parents and employers.
- Secure support services for students who have special needs in their community-based training.
- Ensure a successful transition from school to work and adult life.
- Provide feedback about curriculum offerings in the school program from assessment procedures.
- Provide feedback to students and parents on strengths and weaknesses relative to career and transition planning.

A MODEL FOR GUIDANCE AND COUNSELING ASSISTANCE

If guidance and counseling functions are viewed as desirable and necessary for high school students with disabilities, it is apparent that the provision of the guidance and counseling assistance is far more important than who does it. Guidance and counseling assistance is helping people. In the context of high schools, it is helping students. With that frame of reference, it is easier to separate the words *guidance* and *counseling* from an occupational field or a professional position and give others ownership in what essentially is the process of helping.

Carkhuff (1969, 1972) presented a counseling model that gives some structure to the helping process. We believe that it is useful for persons working with high school students who have special-needs. To synthesize any model that has been described in several publications is to risk oversimplification. That is certainly a possibility here, but Carkhuff has gone to great lengths to present the model in simple terms so that it will be used. *The Art of Helping III* (Carkhuff, Pierce, & Cannon, 1977) is a good example of this.

The basic assumption of the Art of Helping model is that one helps a student with disabilities by *responding* and *initiating*. Responding involves seeing the world through the eyes of the student. Initiating involves seeing the world through one's own eyes and acting on both views of the world by saying or doing something that helps the student. From this basic assumption, there are four underlying helping skills that any professional engaged in *helpful* guidance and counseling must practice: *attending, responding, personalizing,* and *initiating*.

Attending

Generally, attending is being attentive to a student. Being professionally attentive means providing a place for talking that is private and conducive to active listening. Being personally attentive means being physically attentive through active, physical attentiveness to the student with eye contact and body language, by listening with undivided attention, and by using the student's name. Meeting the student's immediate needs for physical comfort, privacy, solitude, or human contact are other ways of being personally attentive.

Beyond the professional and personal attending, the helping person attends by observing while listening. Students give as many cues about how they see the world by their physical behaviors as they do with their verbal behavior. A student's energy level, posture, body language, facial expressions, and grooming should be the focus areas for observation because they give important clues about the student's feelings. If discrepancies are observed between what is being said and the student's posture or energy level, the counselor or teacher is observing an incongruency that is important to see.

Listening begins with undivided attention, but the counselor or teacher should establish as quickly as possible what to listen for. Naturally, one would listen for the reason(s) that the person is seeking help, but the helping professional must also listen for some of the same things that are being observed visually: energy level in the voice, emotional tone, and incongruency in what is being said and the tone and intensity of how it is said.

Listening can be difficult when there are distractions that emerge out of what the student is saying and how it is being said. Some of these distractions can lead to quick judgments and these can get in the way of helping from the very beginning. Active, involved listening keeps the helping person on task and prepared for responding and, at the same time, communicates to the student that here is someone who is open and cares.

Responding

Whereas attending is in itself a type of responding, the responding part of the helping process is more expressive than receptive. The person in the helper role can respond both physically and verbally. Physical responses to a student can be expressed through facial expressions in reaction to what is said, or even through some forms of appropriate physical contact. These nonverbal expressions come out of a natural response to what the student says and feels.

Verbal responses are also responses to the feelings the student expresses and what the student says. Verbal responses are necessary to give the student a chance to see whether the counselor or teacher is getting the message. It is in this type of response that the helper must show empathy. Carkhuff and colleagues (1977) described empathy as experiencing another person's world as if one were the other person. Adolescents—and particularly adolescents who have risked sharing their concerns, questions, or problems with an adult—want desperately to be understood from *their* point of view.

The skill of responding to content (what the student says) and feelings (how the student says it) involves being able to communicate an accurate, perceptive understanding of the unique situation presented by the student. A good response to content to show that kind of understanding rephrases the student's expression in a fresh way. It is *not* echoing the student's own words. The following examples illustrate the difference:

STUDENT SAYS   "Things are not going so good for me. Not at school. Not at home. And not at work. I just can't seem to do anything right for anyone. I've tried everything and nothing works."

ECHO RESPONSE/NO EMPATHY   "Things are not going so good for you at school or home or work and you can't seem to do anything right. When you have tried, nothing works."

EMPATHIC RESPONSE   "You're saying you feel like you have lost it and people at home, school, and work have given up on you."

A good empathic response to the student's feelings demonstrates that the listener has not only understood the message or content but that he or she also understands how the student feels about that message. If the counselor or teacher has been listening and observing the student, it will not be difficult to identify the student's general emotional state (sad, angry, confused, frightened, frustrated, etc.) and the intensity of the feeling or emotion (high, medium, low, controlled, etc.). The helping adult is responding well to the student's feelings when he or she can capture the student's feelings in one or more feeling words. Using the previous example again, the following responses show, in turn, lack of empathy for the student's feelings and then a genuine empathy for the student's feelings:

STUDENT SAYS   "Things are not going so good for me. Not at school. Not at home. And not at work. I just can't seem to do anything right for anyone.

I've tried everything and nothing works." (All this is said with the student sobbing, her head down and her hands over her face.)

INAPPROPRIATE RESPONSE TO FEELING   "Things are not going well for you, huh? Cheer up! Things could be worse. You're not considering suicide are you?"

EMPATHIC RESPONSE TO FELLINGS   "Feeling like you can't satisfy people no matter how hard you try makes you feel like you are stuck at a dead end with nowhere to turn. Maybe even like there is no use trying any more?"

Accurate and empathic responding to content and feelings sets the stage for the counselor or teacher to identify the problem, clarify the real issues related to the problem, and prepare for personalizing the problem for the student.

Personalizing

Personalizing is the key element in the helping process. It is also the most difficult. It requires going beyond what the student has expressed and identifying why his or her experiences are important, what it is about him or her that is causing the situation, how he or she feels about it, and what direction to go. The ability to do this personalizing is what distinguishes the helper from the one being helped. When counselors or teachers facilitate self-exploration, self-understanding, and decision making that leads to action, they are personalizing the student's experience of self.

A more concrete way of explaining personalization is to think of it as a way to respond to the student so that he or she moves from an awareness of the problem and how it feels to have that problem, to (1) an awareness of the effect of the problem situation on him or her, (2) what it is about him or her that causes or contributes to the problem, and (3) what can be done about it. Consider the following examples:

STUDENT SAYS LOUDLY   "I am so mad at them! I hate them! First, they give me a chance to be responsible and then they take it away!"

EMPATHIC RESPONDING   "You feel furious because they backed out on their agreement to let you try."

STUDENT SAYS ANGRILY   "Damn right! They took it all away!"

PERSONALIZING THE MEANING OF THE EXPERIENCE   "You feel angry and cheated because you now are back to being under their control."

STUDENT SAYS QUIETLY WITH TEARS BEGINNING TO FORM   "Yeah...."

PERSONALIZING THE PROBLEM   "You feel put down because in your one chance to be responsible, you blew it?"

STUDENT SAYS   "Right! But I *know* I can be responsible."

PERSONALIZING THE PROBLEM AGAIN   "On the one hand, you say you can be responsible and on the other hand you showed them you were not."

STUDENT SAYS "Yeah, and now I know I'll never get a chance again since I messed up so bad. I just can't seem to figure out what I'm supposed to do when they give me a job. This is the pits!"

PERSONALIZING THE FEELING   "You feel discouraged because you cannot believe they will give you another chance soon and, even if they did, you wouldn't be able to do it?"

STUDENT SAYS "Worse than that! They won't *ever* give me another chance because I just don't have it together and they know it."

PERSONALIZING THE Goal   "You feel down on yourself because you cannot do what your parents ask you to do, and you want to be able to do this."

STUDENT SAYS   "Yeah, I do. But I need some help in figuring out how to do what they ask me to do."

Initiating

The element of initiating in the helping process is focused on assisting the student in formulating and implementing a goal or direction. It is at this point again that any helping person demonstrates what makes a person helpful in solving problems, rather than being just a listener. The counselor or teacher draws on his or her own training and experience in goal setting, establishing instructional objectives, and other, similar experiences to lead the student to a definition of the goal in such a way that both will know when the student has reached the goal.

Carkhuff and others (1977) laid out a sequence of steps for the initiating process. The sequence is presented here, with continuing examples from the student used in the personalizing phase:

Step 1. Define the Goal

DEFINING RESPONSE   "All right, you want to be able to learn how to figure out how to do something when you are given a job. Would you feel that you had learned how to do that if, when you were given a job to do that you had never done before, you would show that you could do it?"

Step 2. Develop the First Step to the Goal

INITIATING RESPONSE   "Your first step is to listen carefully to what someone is telling you to do."

Step 3. Develop Intermediary Steps to the Goal

INITIATING RESPONSE   "What would be some other things you need to learn how to do and practice before you can handle a job alone? Check to see if you have everything you need to do it? Good! Let's write that down. Now, what else? Ask questions if you don't know something? Very important! Let's add that, too. What kinds of questions might you ask? Tell me and I'll write them down. . .Okay, now we have some very specific things for you to do when you are given a job."

Step 4. Initiate a Schedule

INITIATING RESPONSE   "Now that you know what you need to do, when do you want to have your first practice for using all these steps? How many practices do you think you need? All right, if you practice once each week, you will be ready to ask your parents for another chance to do a job alone in one month. You can start tomorrow."

Step 5. Initiate Reinforcements

INITIATING RESPONSE   "What would you like to do to reward yourself for showing me that you can listen and remember what the instructions for a job were in your first practice? What will be the consequences if you don't show up to practice or if you are not able to do the step we are working on for a practice? What will you do to celebrate reaching your goal of handling a job you have never done before all on your own?"

Step 6. Initiate Follow-Through to Ensure All Steps Are Taken

The Carkhuff Helping Model (Carkhuff et al., 1977) incorporates elements of the Carkhuff Institute for Human Technology model of "teaching as treatment" Carkhuff & Berenson, 1976). It is the familiarity of the dominant themes of these two models for educators that make the helping model so appealing, because they parallel the principles of contemporary instructional technology. In comparison to traditional or other counseling models, this approach is most like the behavioral model of counseling (Krumboltz, 1966; Krumboltz & Baker, 1973; Krumboltz & Thoresen, 1976a). The humanistic element of the helping model distinguishes it clearly from the classical behavioral approach, however.

CONCLUSION

The rationale for making guidance and counseling fully available and accessible to students with educational handicaps should be obvious. The concept of a guidance team approach involving high school counselors, regular teachers, and special education personnel simply makes good sense. Unfortunately, logic and common sense are frequently compromised when organizational tradition, funding patterns, infrastructure power struggles, and cost-effectiveness accountability dominate the secondary education component of the public education system. Decision makers do not agree on how to implement many logical and defensible educational concepts, so guidance and counseling for students with special needs is not an isolated problem.

Hummel and Humes (1984) addressed the organizational issues involved in such a decision and took the position that, in spite of arguments for and against the notion, guidance and counseling can be provided best when special education is included under the organizational umbrella of pupil services. From their perspective, a pupil services program unit should be comprised of counseling and guidance services, psychological services, school social work services, school health services, and special education services. Their rationale for this organizational cluster is that special education relies heavily on the other pupil services and that the cause of any individual student can best be served by those who have always been committed to individualization. This is not the case for the instructional unit of high schools. Hummel and Humes revealed the intensity of their position with an indictment that is not unfamiliar to some special educators:

> It is an historical fact that building principals, who represent instruction, have barely tolerated the special education presence. It has also been observed that building principals have been known to divert special education resources to meet the needs of pupils with learning and behavioral problems which do not meet the special education criteria. (p. 54)

The problem we see with this organizational proposal is that it is based on a services approach. Such an approach may do nothing to solve the ever-persisting concerns of specialization, "turf" boundaries, mechanical delivery of services, and lack of a unified program of service delivery. Like the issue of instructional outcome effectiveness (which does not seem to be affected as much by where the activity takes place as by whether the instruction is planned and conducted effectively), guidance and counseling for students with disabilities may occur as well within one organizational plan as another. We would prefer an emphasis on guidance programs rather than on guidance services (Shaw, 1977; Lombana, 1982). An emphasis on services may lead to an activities approach, with activities designed to satisfy selectively the most demanding recipients of those services—students, parents, teachers, or administrators. The services approach clearly opens one up to be *available*, but with no initiative or agenda for meeting guidance needs or accountability for outcomes.

Guidance programming, in contrast to guidance services, is based on an assumption that mutually agreed-upon goals, outcomes, and objectives between guidance providers (counselors, teachers and special education personnel) and special education students and their parents should be the focus of the guidance. Educators make this same argument for instruction; that is, instruction should be based on agreed-upon outcome objectives and not on a predetermined sequence of learning activities. Why not impose the same philosophy on the provision of guidance and counseling? Lombana (1982, pp. 32–33) suggests the following advantages in a program development approach to guidance:

1. A program development approach to guidance allows for the public affirmation of important value and philosophical decisions.
2. Program development has built-in components for feedback so that guidance efforts can be improved.
3. Program development provides counselors with a systematic means of identifying students with unmet needs.
4. Program development offers visibility and public recognition for guidance competence and encourages support of the guidance program.
5. Program planning encourages more positive professional relationships with teachers and administrators.
6. Program planning can lead to increased financial support, the employment of additional staff, and in-service training for counselors.

FIGURE 9.1 Program Evaluation Questions by Phases

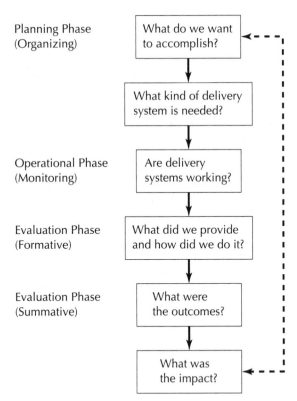

Source: Adapted from *Pupil Personnel Services: A Handbook for Program Development and Evaluation* (p. 97) by F. Wellman and E. Moore, 1975, Washington, DC: U. S. Department of Health, Education, and Welfare.

The necessary, but difficult, part of a program-development approach to guidance is program evaluation. Advantages 2 and 6 in the preceding list would certainly not be obtained without accurate and convincing evaluation data. Figure 9.1 reflects the basic questions that need to be asked and answered in evaluating a program-development approach. Each basic question would probably have numerous subquestions that contribute to each phase. Any school system that has used this evaluation model can attest to its power. But, like any entity with power potential, it must be activated and operated properly or the power is diminished.

Guidance and counseling programs (which can, of course, include services) are vital for making high school experiences for youth with disabilities meaningful in their career development and transition to adult lives in the community. Special educators should insist that guidance and counseling programming be provided for all identified youths for special eduction. If, for some reason, the existing guidance office staff does not assume part or any of this responsibility, efforts should be made to ensure that it happens through some other means.

SUGGESTED READINGS

For anyone interested in pursuing the topic of guidance and counseling for adolescents with disabilities in greater detail, the following books are suggested:

Foster, C. R., Fitzgerald, P. W., & Beal, R. M. (1980). *Modern guidance practices in teaching.* Springfield, IL: Charles C. Thomas.

Foster, J. C., Szoke, C. O., Kapisovsky, P. M., & Kriger, L. S. (1979). *Guidance, counseling, and support services for high school students with physical disabilities.* Cambridge, MA: Technical Education Research Centers.

Harrington, T. F. (1982). *Handbook of career planning for special needs students.* Rockville, MD: Aspen.

Hummel, D. L., & Humes, C. W. (1984). *Pupil services: Development, coordination, and administration.* New York: Macmillan.

Parker, R. M., & Szymanski, E. M. (1992). *Rehabilitation counseling: Basics and beyond* (2nd ed.). Austin, TX: Pro-Ed.

Schiro-Geist, C. (1990). *Vocational counseling for special populations.* Springfield, IL: Charles C. Thomas.

10

Referrals, Referral Sources, and Interagency Linkages

If you don't believe in cooperation, look what happens to a truck when one wheel comes off.—ANONYMOUS

ACTIVITIES

- Examine a remedial program in a high school to determine what services are offered to students with disabilities.
- Interview a school psychologist to determine what services are provided to students with disabilities and their parents.
- Develop an interagency linkage plan for special education, vocational rehabilitation, and mental health.
- Prepare a budget to implement the interagency linkage plan.
- Do the exercise on page 324, and meet with classmates to compare and discuss responses.

Exercise: You have reason to believe that one of your students, Thad, would benefit from a referral to a local child guidance clinic. Thad appears to have emotional problems that make him difficult to work with, and many of the other students seem afraid of him. His most common disruptive behavior in your class is simply to withdraw, sometimes mumbling to himself in a high-pitched whine, which he appears to use to shut out the sound of other voices. You notify the principal of the apparent need for a referral, but he refuses to have any part of it because Thad's mother is a prominent child-behavior clinician at the local university and, in fact, serves as a consultant to the child guidance clinic where you want to refer her son. "If you want to tell the shoemaker that her child has no shoes ," the principal says," go right ahead." Clearly, the best solution is to make Thad's mother realize the need for the referral, and ideally suggest it herself. What kind of information are you going to have to accumulate for your conference with her, and how do you plan to present it? Assuming that Thad's mother goes along with the referral, what sort of information should you try to obtain from her?

INTRODUCTION

The promise of the American Dream—the freedom and opportunity to work and live and lead a satisfying life—is difficult enough to achieve for those who are not disabled, let alone those who are disabled in some significant way. Futurists, whose job it is to chart the trends of the world, point to the pressures faced by children growing up in U.S. society. More than half live or will live in single-parent families. Even in two-parent families, both parents may be working. This leads to the phenomenon of latchkey children—children and youths who carry keys to let themselves into their homes or apartments where they stay unsupervised until a parent comes home from work. These children have a burden of self-management that is, for some, simply too much with which to cope (Rowley, 1987). At school, children have the added problem of facing school reforms that emphasize academic curricula with increasingly demanding standards for success. For many students, this additional pressure to succeed results in failure and stress.

When the problems of disability are coupled with the difficulties seen by the futurists, it is apparent that the obstacles to fulfilling the American promise are substantial. Teenagers who have their other problems compounded by disabilities may need all the help they can get to have any chance at all of achieving even a modest measure of success. To a large degree, their chances for adult adjustment may be determined by the referral resources available. Since the difference between dependency and relative independence could be determined by resources support, this chapter examines referral needs, referral sources, referral strategies, and the interagency cooperation that can make possible the realization of the American Dream.

REFERRAL NEEDS OF HIGH SCHOOL STUDENTS IN SPECIAL PROGRAMS

Although the term *referral* may sound innocuous enough, most high school teachers will have a number of dramatic stories to tell about students who ultimately had to be referred. The reason for the referral may have been a suicide attempt or a student who needed a simple referral initially but somehow slipped through the cracks of the system at every possible juncture until the problem reached crisis proportions. Both types of experiences can prove disheartening and shocking to the teacher who has never encountered such situations.

It is not possible to list and discuss here all the possible needs that students with disabilities might have during their high school years. The examples provided in the following lists will give you an idea of the range and variety of situations that the high school special education teacher or work experience coordinator might encounter. The kinds of services provided by the various referral sources in the next section, Referral Sources and Strategies, provide more information about the types of students who require referral.

Physical Needs

- Poor dental health, resulting in problems of appearance, eating difficulties, bad breath, and absenteeism
- Obesity, resulting in social problems, health problems, and practical problems such as fitting into school furniture and using toilets
- Malnutrition, resulting in frequent illnesses and absenteeism, inability to participate in rigorous activities at school or on job training, and fatigue in classes
- Recurring bruises, scratches, abrasions, or swollen body parts, suggesting physical abuse
- Signs of alcohol or drug abuse, affecting performance at school as well as personal-social relationships

Personal-Social Needs

- Sudden and extreme changes in personal behavior
- Changes in patterns of school attendance
- Signs or direct evidence of illegal conduct
- Complaints from student about being subjected to gang intimidation, "shakedowns," or physical violence, including assault and rape
- Complaints from student about being subjected to sexual harassment at a job site
- Inappropriate sexual behavior
- Evidence of exploitation by real or foster parents, guardians, or welfare agencies

Physical and personal-social needs tend to get the most attention in any discussion of referral needs, but high school teachers and support personnel should remember that referrals can be made for enrichment of students' positive attributes and special interests also. Interest in the positive characteristics that students show at school should receive attention equal to the problem areas, and referrals to appropriate school or community sources can pay dividends in student attitude and performance.

REFERRAL SOURCES AND STRATEGIES

As simplistic as it may seem, to benefit from the resources furnished by individuals and agencies, a person must first be put in touch with the resources. Referrals are mainly for services of two kinds: services related to the training programs in a local education agency and services associated with the community that are related to high school programming and postschool transition planning.

School Program Services Referral

The school reform movement of the mid-1980s increased pressure on students to achieve academically. For some students with disabilities, this often comes as a precondition for being able to get into more appropriate career or vocational education classes. Thus, the pressure increases for students with learning handicaps to do well in academic programs in which they enjoy few of the intrinsic rewards that students without disabilities enjoy. Furthermore, the usefulness of academics to many of the students who have difficulty with reading and abstract reasoning makes the dilemma even worse. Such an unfortunate situation has been difficult to combat and has caused great frustration and misunderstanding, not just for the students in special programs but for their parents and for school personnel as well.

Kokaska and Brolin (1985) developed their career education model around the premise that regular teachers can and should be involved in helping students with learning handicaps acquire various career and transition competencies. They specified how various high school staff can contribute in meeting their 22 basic competencies. Table 10.1 is an adaptation of their listing of possible competency instructional responsibilities for both junior and senior high school personnel.

The most common strategy to assure some success in the basic academic classes has been to seek out mainstream teachers who understand the limitations imposed by various disabilities and who adjust their class requirements accordingly. Referral of selected students to these carefully identified teachers is the best way to guarantee any degree of success in placing students with disabilities in high school academic courses.

TABLE 10.1   Proposed Competency Instructional Responsibilities for High School Instructional and Support Personnel

Competency	Referral/Support Personnel
Daily Living Skills	
1. Managing family finances	Home economics; math
2. Selecting, managing, and maintaining a home	Home economics
3. Caring for personal needs	Home economics
4. Raising children—family living	Home economics
5. Buying and preparing food	Home economics
6. Buying and caring for clothing	Home economics
7. Engaging in civic activities	Social studies; music; art
8. Utilizing recreation and leisure	Physical education; art; music
9. Getting around the community	Driver's education
Personal-Social Skills	
10. Achieving self-awareness	Counselors; art; music; physical education
11. Acquiring self-confidence	Physical education; art; vocational education; music; counselors; social studies
12. Achieving socially responsible behavior	Social studies; counselors; nurse; school social worker; school psychologist; principals
13. Maintaining good interpersonal skills	Counselors; sponsors for extracurricular activities
14. Achieving independence	Counselors; all teachers
15. Achieving problem-solving skills	Counselors; vocational education; science
16. Communicating adequately with others	Language arts; speech; music; art
Occupational Skills	
17. Knowing and exploring occupational possibilities	Counselors; area-specific teachers
18. Selecting and planning occupational choices	Counselors
19. Exhibiting appropriate work habits and behaviors	All teachers
20. Exhibiting sufficient physical-manual skills	Physical education; vocational education
21. Obtaining a specific occupational skill	Vocational education; home economics; typing; driver's education
22. Seeking, securing, and maintaining employment	Counselors

Source: Adapted from *Career Education for Handicapped Individuals* (2nd ed.) (p. 51) by C. J. Kokaska and D. E. Brolin, 1985, Columbus OH: Charles E. Merrill.

Remedial Programs and Services

Remedial academics have been prominent in some programs. These programs have been staffed by remedial specialists, but not uncommonly by volunteers, peers, parents, and resource room teachers also. Basic academic remediation is frequently the primary remedial concern, but other areas can be considered. Other specific remedial specialists may include speech and language therapists, remedial reading specialists, occupational therapists, and physical therapists. These latter sources may prove more helpful in the long run in acquiring and maintaining life-career competencies than academic remediation, but that is a judgment that must be made before outcomes are known.

Counseling Services

Because there are so many adolescents with disabilities who are psychologically damaged by the consequences of their problems, referral for individual personal counseling is common. In some instances, regular counseling sessions are scheduled for groups of adolescents with similar problems. In other instances, in an effort to effect more widespread understanding of the nature and consequences of disability, the counseling sessions may include peers without disabilities. Parents, teachers, and other affected adults (such as employers) might also be a part of such counseling sessions.

The Vocational Technical Education training program (VOTEC) of Tucson, Arizona, has also used crisis intervention counselors to adjudicate altercations or disruptive behavior that occur in that program. The major objective is to bring the antagonists into face-to-face confrontation, with the altercation or behavior as the focus of the discussion. The VOTEC program has made extensive use of Glasser's (1969) behavioral theories, and this has been a contributing factor in their crisis intervention procedure.

School Psychology Services

School psychologists frequently serve primarily in assessment. Assessment for initial identification and placement, periodic reevaluations, and some diagnostic assessment for educational or personal-social adjustment consume much of the school psychologist's time. Training, background, or personal preference may move some school psychologists out of the psychometric role into consultation with teachers on learning or behavior problems, personal adjustment difficulties, interpersonal relationships, and adolescent psychology. Some even seek out opportunities to do some individual or group counseling when their training has included such an emphasis and their school district values that type of service.

High school special educators should cultivate a good working relationship with school psychologists and be very specific with requests for assistance. The growing trend toward comprehensive career and transition assessment is one area where school psychologists could contribute if given specific areas of assessment to conduct. Required reevaluations during the high school years, for example, could be much more useful for individual planning and curriculum development if the assessment could be focused more on occupational interests, aptitudes, job

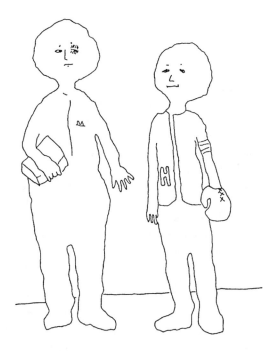

"Perhaps I should clarify exactly what I meant by 'meaningful interaction.'"

and daily living skills, and personal-social development, rather than on intellectual and academic functioning.

School Nurse Services

Students having chronic health impairments often seek out the school nurse for assistance on their own, or referrals are made to the school nurse by attending physicians. High school special education staff, however, should be aware of the needs of these students and be ready to bring the school nurse into emergency or consultation situations.

In other instances, the school nurse can be an important referral source. Students who do not have any chronic health conditions also can benefit from the nurse's services. Students with physical complaints or who become aware of physical symptoms that are not self-diagnosable may need the authoritative opinion of the school nurse in order to respond appropriately. Socially transmitted diseases, problems in sexuality or sex-related behavior, substance-abuse problems, or even less serious physical conditions (such as weight loss, skin care and treatment, or eating problems) all come under the scope of services for the school nurse. High school special education personnel should use the nurse for instructional assistance as well as for referral.

School Social Work Services

When influences outside the school setting interfere with the success of the student, school social services workers can become a resource of significance. Functioning as they do as a bridge between the home and the school, school social workers can evaluate the variables of the home and community setting that could be having an influence on the performance of the young person who has a disability. Although school social workers often can deal directly with a problem, they also broker services, calling on other persons or agencies to supply specific services to the student, the family, or related school personnel.

The actual monitoring of referral sources and services may fall to any of a variety of professionals in the school, such as the guidance counselor, school psychologist, or social worker. Often, however, it becomes one of the chief functions of the special education teacher, simply because that person is the most familiar with the problems and needs of students who are already receiving some special services but who are in need of some additional help. However, regardless of the person who takes on that responsibility, the job can be made easier by use of a technique described by Mathews and Fawcett (1979). These authors have advocated the use of an index card file of services. They list four advantages of such a system: First, it makes it easy to arrange and store information. Second, it permits easy retrieval of information. Third, it helps prevent the loss of needed information. Fourth, it is easily updated. When the file is used for school program services, it contains an index, a set of problem-service cards, and a set of service resources. These authors recommended this technique as being central to efficient community services referral also. Of course, schools with microcomputers can have the same system entered on a database disk and keep it updated even more easily.

Community Services Referral

As described by Mathews and Fawcett (1979), the use of the an index card file for referring people for community services depends on a social service directory that is the heart of the system. This directory lists the problems handled and the services provided by all the agencies in a community. The information is transcribed onto three sets of cards. The first set is an index that lists all of the problems and service categories in the social service directory. The second set consists of problem-service cards. These cards list all the direct services offered, the problems handled, any restrictions to the services, and the agency offering the services. The third set lists the agency's name, address, phone number, office hours, eligibility requirements, appointment policies, and the name of the contact person.

The community services directory should provide information for four kinds of assistance: emergency, financial, health, and program. *Emergency assistance* should identify sources for food, housing, legal, and any other general kinds of help. *Financial assistance* might include bail bonding, supplementary security income, aid to dependent children, food stamps, mortgages, auto loans, banking and credit unions, tax preparation, and financial planning. *Health problems assistance* would include mental health, dental health, visual assistance, and the subspecialties of physical health, preventive as well as corrective. *Program assistance* lists vocational rehabilitation, the state employment service, state and local advocacy groups, rehabilitation facilities, residential programs, and community agencies such as the chamber of commerce, city commissions, business and industrial councils, trade unions, and associations and human services agencies. In addition, some persons might wish to include sources for recreation and other leisure activities. The preceding is only a partial list of referral agency services and will certainly differ from community to community. (See Appendix A for a listing of resource agencies.)

GUIDELINES FOR MAKING REFERRALS

Most school districts have an established policy or procedure for making referrals. This policy frequently includes a standard referral form. Consequently, the following guidelines are general in nature and are basically reminders for common-sense practice:

1. *Involve the administrator responsible for your program in the decision to recommend a referral.* Some administrators want only to be informed on routine cases but insist on involvement for certain kinds of problems or for certain parents.

2. *Involve the parents from the beginning.* Many schools and school personnel have had lawsuits brought against them for providing services without parental permission. By involving the parents in all decisions regarding the referral and obtaining their permission for specific referrals, high school special education staff can not only protect themselves from lawsuits but also may get helpful information and support from the parents. It is a fact, however, that parental involvement might lead to a refusal to cooperate and a denial of permission to refer. Still, parents are the ones with responsibility for their children, and school personnel must involve them.

3. *Provide all important information to the referral resource.* Referral resource personnel need as much relevant information as possible to be able to respond to the needs of the referred student. Write down the important information you want to provide, and organize it so that it can be used more easily. Whenever possible, discuss the information with the resource person to ensure that nothing is misunderstood and that there are no gaps in the information that the person needs.

4. *Inform key people on all stages of the referral.* Key people include the student who is being referred, his or her parents or guardians, other teachers or school personnel who have a need to know, your immediate supervisor, and the referral resource person. Each of these key participants in the referral process have information or a perspective that might be important as the process moves along. Having access to that information or those perspectives requires that these people be kept informed.

5. *Prompt referral resources into action.* Frequently, referral resource persons are overworked and have many other things to do besides respond immediately to a referral form or even to your personal request. Since one cannot ignore a student's needs, it is important to follow up the initial referral after a courteous time period to inquire as to the status of the referral. A referral situation is not always an emergency situation, so there is no rule of thumb as to how long to wait before prompting. There comes a point, however, in any referral that is based on need—either the need disappears or is heightened as time goes on. Prompting, on behalf of a student in need, is a professional expectation and the referral resource person will understand a cheerful but persistent follow-up.

6. *Reinforce referral resources.* The referring professionals should not forget to show appreciation personally and to give recognition to all those people who

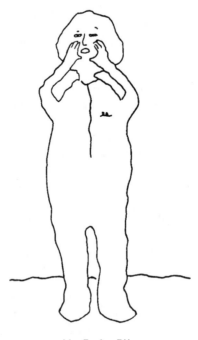

H - E - L - P!!

assist with their services. A short letter or memo of thanks with a copy to the person's supervisor or administrator is one simple way to show both appreciation and give recognition at the same time. Over time, one would need to be creative to keep the reinforcement process genuine and spontaneous.

INTERAGENCY COOPERATION

Reasons for Cooperation

Referral strategies are generally concerned with securing services for students with disabilities to assist them in their training, working, or daily living skills programs. This leaves the impression that each agency or service exists independently of any others, and, like a supply store, elements of the agency are secured one or several at a time to be allocated to a person with a disability. Although this may happen, it is far more likely that agencies are called on to combine their services to provide program support that becomes far stronger than the sum of the parts. Essentially, this calls for interagency cooperation, more commonly known as linkages or coalitions (Steere, Pancsofar, Wood, & Hecimovic, 1990).

In 1978, federal agencies began their collaborative actions first by a joint memorandum and then by position statements followed by a statement of implementation activities. According to Tindall and colleagues (1986), a position statement through an action memorandum was developed in 1978 by the Bureau of Occupational and Adult Education and the Bureau of Education for the Handicapped. The action memorandum (U. S. Office of Education, 1978) proposed a U.S. Office of Education position paper as a basis for joint planning for appropriate comprehensive vocational education for students with handicaps. The position was that an appropriate comprehensive vocational education will be available and accessible to every person who is disabled. One assumption of this position paper was that there would be an appropriate comprehensive vocational relationship between the educational sector and the employment sector to facilitate the transition from school to work.

To implement this position of an appropriate comprehensive vocational education, the U.S. Office of Education identified activities that were to be accomplished at the federal level. The specific interagency activities to be completed were as follows: "Develop the primary interagency and interdepartmental agreements needed in the appropriate comprehensive vocational education effort at the national level and encourage development of similar agreements at state and local levels" (U.S. Office of Education, 1978, p. 2).

These steps were followed by the development of a memorandum addressed to the Chief State School Officers, State Directors of Vocational Rehabilitation, and State Directors of Vocational Education, directing them to follow a similar pattern in their respective states in order to maximize services to people with disabilities. Then, to facilitate the work, a series of research and development activities were funded, including national workshops involving state leaders. These activities apparently resulted in the establishment of some interagency linkage agreements at the state level. The Ninth Annual Report to Congress from the Office of Special Education and Rehabilitation pointed out that Section 613(a) of the Education of the Handicapped Act combined amendments requiring that each State Plan establish interagency agreements between the State Education Agency and other appropriate state and local agencies.

In 1985, a five-year interagency agreement was signed between the Department of Education and the Department of Health and Human Services. The intent of this agreement was to combine the financial and programmatic resources of both agencies to expand employment opportunities for people with disabilities. Specifically, these two federal departments agreed that two key offices in their respective departments would work together to implement a national effort in supported employment. The Office of Special Education and Rehabilitative Services (OSERS) and the Office of Human Development Services (OHDS) Administration on Developmental Disabilities agreed to several important goals. The two most significant ones were the following:

- Strengthen coordination of efforts that lead to meaningful paid employment for persons with severe disabilities.
- Enhance efforts that lead to the expansion of private sector employment opportunities for persons with developmental disabilities (Office of Special Education and Rehabilitative Services, 1985).

Since these actions, most states have initiated or renewed previous interagency agreements to address the issue of transition of youth with disabilities from school to adult living. Some of these agreements are political actions to give the appearance of a proactive stance to prevent pressures from advocacy groups, but most are sincere efforts to respond to needs that have been obvious for a long time. At a local level, interagency agreements have been described by Getzel, Salin, and Wacher (1986) as developing because (1) different agencies may provide the same or similar services, (2) there is a scarcity of funds or resources, (3) there is a chance to offer higher-quality services, and (4) services under such agreements increase in efficiency.

Interagency and Community Linkages

Interagency and community linkages have developed over the years in some states and local communities. School programs characterized by "best practice" or "exemplary programming" have usually included some sort of interagency and community collaboration, usually in the form of an interagency agreement. Rarely, however, has this practice directly affected an individual's IEP. The new definition of "individualized education program" in the IDEA formalizes the concept of interagency and community linkages by making it part of the IEP process [20 U.S.C. Chapter 33, Section 1401(e)(1)(D)]: A statement of the needed transition services for students beginning no later than age 16 and annually thereafter (and, when determined appropriate for the individual, beginning at age 14 or younger), *including, when appropppriate, a statement of the interagency responsibilities or linkages (or both) before the student leaves the school setting.*" The amendments go on to add the following provision: "*In the case where a participating agency, other than the educational agency, fails to provide agreed upon services, the educational agency shall reconvene the IEP team to identify alternative strategies to meet the transition objectives.*"

The IDEA clearly establishes the expectation that the delivery of transition services is not solely a school responsibility (Aune & Johnson, 1992). However, the aforementioned sections charge the school with ensuring that linkages with nonschool agencies occur, rather than waiting for those agencies to initiate something. Although not exclusively responsible for providing all services, the school is clearly responsible for ensuring that needed educational services are provided and that other needed services are addressed in the planning process. Schools have no authority to compel nonschool agencies to participate in the IEP/transition planning process. The only exception would be if the school has a service contract with the agency. In that situation, the state education agency will hold the local school accountable for failing to ensure participation by the nonschool agency under contract. The regulations are clear, however. There is nothing in the provisions of the IDEA that relieves any participating agency, including a state vocational rehabilitation agency, of the responsibility to provide or pay for any transition service that the agency would otherwise provide to students with disabilities who meet the eligibility criteria of that agency.

Elements in Successful Linkages

Whatever the reasons for initiating interagency linkages, Tindall and colleagues (1986) cautioned that, to be successful, great care must be taken in each step of the process, at both the state and local levels of implementation. The following are suggested steps:

1. In selecting the group or committee that will be at the heart of the process, one person must serve as catalyst and be joined by a core group of equally dedicated persons from other agencies. All the members will work together better if they can subordinate any "turf" problems or local agency rivalries to focus on the goal of improving services for people with disabilities. As difficult as that may be, it is worth considerable effort to try to live up to that ideal.

Often, it is expedient to establish the interagency core committee by building on an existing committee. This may be a good procedure, provided the existing committee is not currently involved in some major project, the committee's goals are compatible with those of the linkage committee, and the new leader is already a member of the old committee. It is important to recognize that when a new project is introduced to an established committee, all the assets of the committee are inherited along with all the jealousies, frustrations, inflexibilities, and other liabilities that may have developed during previous work. Obviously, judicious personnel changes can eliminate some of those problems, but sometimes it is prudent to start fresh.

Whatever method is used to establish the linkage committee, it should be limited to as few people as possible yet ensure representation from the public schools, consumer groups, government, and business firms.

The effectiveness of the core group is greatly enhanced if each member has the authority to commit his or her group to whatever course of action the committee decides on. The committee will be even more effective if each member has some significant measure of personal status to contribute. It is a given that each person would be knowledgeable about the needs and services for persons with disabilities available from the sector he or she represents.

2. The linkage committee should be sponsored by some other organization within the community. The committee would then have an overseer or some agency both to protect and monitor it. Although this sponsorship may be from any agency, working as a special task force for United Way, the school board, or a rehabilitation advisory committee guarantees a home base for office and meeting space, plus secretarial services and access to some funds for incidental expenses. Such sponsorship has the added advantage of making it easy to dissolve the committee if it is ineffective. As is always the danger in any such liaison, the core committee will be tainted with the reputation of the sponsoring agency, both good and bad. This may not prove to be much of a problem, but it is a reality and should be recognized and dealt with appropriately.

As the committee begins its work, additional committee members may need to be added. Suggestions for new members can come from any source, but certainly those persons who represent agencies or services called on frequently should receive high priority for inclusion. Again, a careful balance should be maintained between the effectiveness of services increased by adding new members and the efficiency of operating with the fewest possible committee members. Since the goal is to offer optimum services, it is important to add new members only when the effectiveness issue has been carefully considered.

3. As in any cooperative venture, there are barriers that make effective collaborative efforts difficult if not impossible to implement. Tindall and colleagues (1986) pointed out that an issue may become a barrier when (1) the issue generates more concern than the goals, (2) there is reluctance to consider compromises or alternatives, (3) committee members begin to withdraw from the process, and (4) the same issue recurs without being resolved. These barriers generally fall into four categories: those arising from attitudes, those resulting

from policies and regulations, those arising from internal agency operations, and those resulting from environmental barriers (e.g., distance, size of agencies, etc.).

Communication problems are the most usual causes for issues developing into barriers. Each issue will probably generate its own problem and therefore call for a unique solution, but a committee that follows the guidelines for group processes facilitation can generally ward off the stalemates that barriers represent. There are some other considerations that may assist the committee in its work.

Any cooperative effort exposes the members to some elements of risk. The most prevalent aspect is loss of autonomy over jurisdiction, funding, or service. Just recognizing and acknowledging that the risk is present may go a long way toward reducing the anxiety that may fuel the resistance to giving up some autonomy. Quite often, the risk can become less threatening when the possible gains from collaboration are emphasized. Even when that fails, a spirit of cooperation may still be generated from the recognition that resolving an issue will benefit the person with a disability.

When regulations are established by state or federal agencies, they are presented as guidelines to help in the implementation of laws. These guidelines then become the policies that govern services. Barriers develop when there is some confusion over the interpretation or meaning of the policies. This is particularly troublesome when the intent of the law is perceived to conflict with the guidelines. When some inflexible opinion stemming from this confusion becomes an issue, it is helpful to remind the committee that policies and regulations are proposed and passed to enable better things to happen for people with disabilities. Thus, policies and regulations should be interpreted in light of their allowing good things to happen rather than restricting services, At the administrative level, the ultimate criterion may be cost accounting. At the implementation level, it should be service effectiveness. It should be remembered that such an interpretation may put a fellow committee member in real jeopardy with his or her agency administrator and thus may be a threat to the whole collaborative effort. In such a circumstance, it is crucial that committee members marshall whatever forces they can to support their colleagues in behalf of better services to people with disabilities. Such support may make a real impact on someone who is a bit uncertain about confronting his or her superiors with controversial recommendations in behalf of clients. It may well spell the difference between successful and unsuccessful linkages.

Throughout the committee deliberations, a climate of mutual respect should be cultivated. Everyone should be made to feel their presence in their respective agencies is in the best interests of their clients, the committee, the agency, the state, and the nation. If a need for their cooperation did not exist, there would be no need for linkages and no need for the committee. It should be continually stressed that disagreements can serve as a positive mechanism for bringing in all the information pertinent to the problem and clarifying the issues. In the absence of disagreement, not all sides of an issue will be fairly represented, so an issue may not be resolved in the best way possible. However, it is absolutely essential that a solution be searched for and reached. No issue should be allowed to fester.

Areas of Responsibility

As the members of the core committee work to develop some system of collaboration, a clear statement of the services that can be expected from each agency is basic to their deliberations. Any ambiguity concerning who takes responsibility for various tasks inevitably leads to issues that can become barriers to cooperation.

The most common disciplines involved in school career and transition program linkages are special education, vocational education, and vocational rehabilitation. As each discipline or agency contributes its services to a given student, the effectiveness of the services is multiplied. Although special education and vocational education services have been described elsewhere in a different context, they will be reviewed here in summary form. Vocational rehabilitation services will be described in more detail, because they are the primary nonschool, external participants in the interagency linkage.

Special Education
Special education provides the usual educational programs and materials as a part of its ongoing responsibilities to high school youth with educational handicaps. However, it also can be expected to provide for physical education, driver education, career awareness and exploration, and remedial classes when appropriate. Special education also can furnish readers, Braillers, and notetakers for students who are visually handicapped, interpreters for students who are hearing impaired, and aids for those students with physical disabilities while they are in school. Occupational, physical, and speech therapy may also be furnished by special education. Motor development, mobility training, and audiological evaluations are also paid for by special education. In some cases, special psychological, medical, and psychiatric evaluations can be furnished, and special transportation costs can be covered. Finally, special education can provide counseling and provide or arrange for prevocational and vocational evaluations, work-adjustment training, and job placement and follow-up. Comprehensive assessment and evaluation data are especially helpful to vocational education and vocational rehabilitation personnel since they are required to have evaluation data, and duplication of assessment procedures is extremely costly.

Vocational Education
Vocational educators are responsible for assuring access to all regular vocational education programs whenever possible. However, they must go beyond that to provide adapted programs suitable for students with disabilities, if needed. When called for, vocational education specialists must make modifications to ensure access to the program or adapt or modify the curriculum, materials, instructional methods, sequence, duration, content, and type of instructional units. Vocational educators must ensure that appropriate vocational tools and equipment are available and adapt or modify those tools that are inappropriate. Vocational education must also assure a barrier-free environment for the vocational education programs. Any vocational goals on the IEP, must be based on a vocational

assessment, including interests, abilities, and special needs with respect to completing the vocational education program successfully. Special education personnel are to be involved with vocational educators in planning for youth with disabilities or special needs, and their parents must be notified—before the students enter the ninth grade—of the different vocational education programs and services offered.

Federal, state, and local funds may be used for assessment, counseling and guidance personnel, personnel training, supplies, excess costs, advisory committees, surveys, recruitment, and staff development. Perhaps one of the most effective uses of funds is for the modification of equipment to help students with specific disabilities. This can include the following:

1. For students who are visually impaired:
   Instruction in Braille or large print
   Signals keyed to hearing rather than sight
   Special safety devices (for instance, guardrails around moving parts of machines)
2. For students who are hearing impaired:
   Printed rather than verbal instructions
   Signals keyed to sight rather than hearing
   Sound-amplification devices
3. For students who are orthopedically disabled:
   Adaptation of equipment
   Special desks and worktables that accommodate wheelchairs
4. For students who are mentally disabled:
   Simplified equipment and materials
   Visual graphic schematic manuals

Vocational education can also pay for additional staff to coordinate work experiences and arrange summer jobs.

Vocational Rehabilitation Services
Although each state has its own organizational structure for its vocational rehabilitation agency, the substantial federal support to states for the program has resulted in a basic sequence of steps that describe the expectations one could have in any state for seeking and obtaining vocational rehabilitation services. Most states do have separate vocational rehabilitation services for persons disabled by visual impairment and those disabled by all other physical, sensory, or mental impairments. The sequence of service delivery of both, however, is parallel. The steps in vocational rehabilitation generally include the following:

STEP 1. REFERRAL   Students in school programs will ordinarily be referred by the school guidance counselor or by someone in secondary special education. The initial contact, however, can be self-referral; students and their parents may contact the local or area vocational rehabilitation counselor on their own.

Occasionally, referrals are made by physicians, psychologists, ministers, social workers, or caseworkers in social welfare programs. In any case, contact is made and an initial interview is scheduled or conducted at the point of initial contact.

STEP 2. INITIAL INTERVIEW   In the initial interview, the counselor talks with the student and begins developing case management information. The student's own perceptions of his or her disability and how it relates to employment is an important part of this interview. Because most special education students are still minors at the time of referral, it is also important to obtain one or both parents' views on the disability. Initial probes into short- and long-term goals are usually made, but no decisions are made at this point. The counselor will begin arrangements for obtaining any new assessment and evaluation information that is needed. This will usually include a general medical examination, as well as specialist medical examinations, psychological evaluations, and vocational assessment and evaluations, when necessary. If schools have current psychological or assessment data, the counselor may request such data with the student's or parents' permission.

STEP 3. DIAGNOSIS   A vocational rehabilitation counselor must have an authoritative diagnosis of the presence of a physical or mental disability. In addition, there must be some statement or obvious implication relative to the effect of the disability on employability. Thus, examinations and evaluations are scheduled as needed to obtain this type of information and establish official eligibility for services. In this context, it is obvious that vocational rehabilitation insists on current diagnostic data and cannot always use what schools have available. The possibilities are the greatest for sharing of test data for intellectual functioning, adaptive behavior, and personal-social adjustment.

STEP 4. ASSESSMENT   Once eligibility is established through medical, psychiatric, or psychological diagnoses, additional assessment and evaluation are conducted to determine feasibility. Vocational rehabilitation has maintained the concept of feasibility as one criterion for acceptance for services for many years. *Feasibility* is a judgment based on all available diagnostic and evaluation data that the services rendered by vocational rehabilitation are likely to result in successful placement and retention in remunerative employment. In the past, this meant that a counselor could deny services to a person with disabilities, even though the person was clearly eligible. This element of the vocational rehabilitation process was intended to provide some assurance to Congress, legislators, governors, and other persons who must be accountable for expenditure of public funds that rehabilitation services were not provided indiscriminately or capriciously. It put the counselor in a vulnerable position in having to make this determination, but sensitive cases were nearly always determined with the advice and consent of supervisors. It was meant to exclude poor risk referrals so to be able to make better use of limited resources with those who have more positive attitudes and more successful histories in employment and independent living.

The Rehabilitation Act Amendments of 1992 made a major change in the federal regulations in the determination of eligibility and feasibility. The following two amendments are particularly critical:

1. Determinations by other agencies, particularly educational agencies, regarding whether an individual has a disability shall be used to the extent that they are appropriate, available, and consistent with the requirements of the act.
2. It should be presumed that an individual can benefit from vocational rehabilitation services unless the designated state agency can demonstrate, by clear and convincing evidence, that such individual is incapable of benefiting in terms of an employment outcome. When the issue of "ability to benefit" concerns the severity of the disability, the rehabilitation agency needs to conduct an extended evaluation.

School personnel need to know about this aspect of the process of accepting students for services, so that data that speak to feasibility and elegibility are provided during the assessment and evaluation process.

STEP 5. PREPARATION FOR PLACEMENT   Once a student is accepted for services by vocational rehabilitation, an individualized written rehabilitation plan (IWRP) is developed. The plan states what the vocational objective is, what services are required, and how long the services will be needed. Although vocational rehabilitation counselors can provide a variety of services to persons with disabilities, they are required to make use of services offered by other agencies before using their own funds and to stay within the guidelines of the IWRP. When a person is eligible for services, vocational rehabilitation can provide or buy a number of services. This may include medical treatment, surgery, therapy, prosthetic fitting, crutches, wheelchairs, glasses, hearing aids, dental work, and cosmetic enhancement. In the area of training, vocational rehabilitation can pay for tuition, on-the-job-training fees to employers, books, supplies, transportation, readers for clients who are blind, interpreters for clients who are deaf , and aids for clients who are orthopedically handicapped. At the conclusion of training, it can pay for job development, engineering and redesign, and job-seeking skills. Vocational rehabilitation can also pay for licenses, tools, equipment, and supplies, and handle maintenance and transportation during the rehabilitation process.

STEP 6. PLACEMENT   Vocational rehabilitation counselors have a professional stake in the successful culmination of the rehabilitation process, and the placement process is the step in which the counselor may become more active. Large caseloads frequently prevent personal involvement in every placement, however, so placement personnel in public schools, postsecondary training programs, other adult rehabilitation agencies, and the state employment office are used.

STEP 7. FOLLOW-UP   Most state vocational rehabilitation agencies, whether official or unofficial, establish quotas for counselors in achieving successful closures, or "26s," as the counselors call them (referring to the code number for "successfully closed in rehabilitated status" in their quarterly and annual reports). Counselors are encouraged to follow up on their clients for up to a year before closing the case, but a case could be closed within 90 days. Pressure to meet quotas probably has some influence on the length of time a counselor will spend on follow-up. Still, counselors recognize that premature closing of cases is often neither in the best interests of the clients nor themselves, and therefore use that time to deal with those adjustment problems that clients are experiencing while it is much easier to provide services.

Altogether, vocational rehabilitation is an agency that can bring powerful resources to bear on behalf of eligible clients. However, since vocational rehabilitation must use the resources of other agencies first, it will often be unable or unwilling to provide some of its services while the person is a student and therefore the responsibility of the school. (This practice is often referred to as "first dollar.") Since each special education student must have an individual education program, the school can request the attendance of a vocational education representative and a vocational rehabilitation counselor at the IEP meeting. Working together, they can develop the IEP for the school, the individual Transition Play (ITP) required, and the individual written rehabilitation program (IWRP) for vocational rehabilitation. Clearly, such coordinated efforts can do much to focus agency services on common goals. It is no coincidence that this type of joint planning presents such a powerful demonstration of what can be accomplished through linkages.

Cost Considerations

Invariably, the provision of any kind of service carries a price tag of some kind; thus, at some point cost considerations become prominent issues. Gugerty (1986) cautioned that since the use of funds is an expression of an agency's power, prestige, and political influence, it should be treated with great care and respect. Typically, interagency agreements relate to the functions of (1) agreeing on who does what to whom, when, where, how often, under what supervision, and for what purpose; (2) agreeing on definitions, forms, referral methods, entitlements, or the meshing of services; and (3) allocating resources. Both time and money play a governing role in the decision of an agency to commit to an agreement to collaborate. Essentially, the financial structure created must be acceptable to all agencies that are part of the agreement. What Gugerty refers to as "financial bilingualism" simply means that the language and form of the agreement must be consistent with the respective agency, budgetary requirements, constraints, and discretionary authority—that all the agencies speak the same budgetary language so no misunderstandings over finances will interfere with the service goals.

The longevity of the agreements often depend much more on the agencies' knowing what the agreements accomplish than just the cost itself. This kind of information can come from cost analysis, which, in turn, makes possible judgments relative to the effectiveness of the agreements. *Cost analysis* is the systematic analysis of the benefit of the services in relation to the cost and the effectiveness of the services relative to that cost. While it may be asking too much for service personnel to be able to institute the cost-analysis procedures, it could be quite beneficial to insist that performance measures and an accounting system that is capable of allocating costs directly to each part of the services provided should be developed. Although having cost-benefit or cost-effectiveness information is no guarantee that the information will be wisely used, without such information it may be very difficult to justify to each participating agency that its continued cooperation is in the best interests of the client and of the agency and that cooperation is superior to isolated efforts.

Evaluation of Interagency Linkages

Although cost-benefit and cost-effectiveness information is vital to people who must decide whether to continue, alter, or terminate interagency linkages, neither is sufficient unto itself. The deciding factor is whether the clients are better able to pursue the American Dream as a result of the support they receive than without it. As a corollary, the question that needs answering is whether the support is more effective as a result of interagency linkages than when agencies do not cooperate, or when they cooperate only haphazardly. Thus, any evaluation effort must be quite penetrating if it is to be effective. This raises one of the major risks of linkages: incurring the enmity of the people being evaluated simply because they do not want their work in the public spotlight. This fear may have nothing to do with their competence or their integrity. Rather, it may stem from their intrinsic motivation to serve people in a serene atmosphere of relative obscurity in the belief that virtue is its own reward, Although such motivation may be laudable, it does not substitute for data. Yet, that attitude toward service is well worth preserving and once lost is difficult to retrieve. This surely serves to emphasize the importance of a consensual approach to evaluation.

All the members of the linkage committee should be in agreement that data are basic to evaluation. From that should come a full discussion of what the evaluation should cover and who the information will be given to and for what purpose. Given agreement in those areas, a plan for the evaluation can be drawn up.

Although it is customary to designate early on who will be conducting the evaluation, it may be better to wait until the procedures and instruments for data collection have been discussed, since that may dictate who is best equipped to collect a given kind of data. Next, the collection instrument(s) must be designed. These should meet all the standards of test and measurement preparation: objectivity, clarity, brevity, and unambiguousness of interpretation. Obviously, the instruments should be valid. They should measure what they are intended to measure. Since the instruments may be used only occasionally, it is difficult to justify the expense of developing a statistically reliable device. Prudence may dictate a certain level of approximation as being acceptable. Most important, data collection should impose a minimum of interference on the time and energies of respondents. Indeed, if the information can be gleaned from the available records kept by the agencies, that would be ideal.

A decision to evaluate anything always involves comparison with some outside criterion. It is usually a painful experience for those whose results are judged inadequate. If evaluation data are believed to be necessary to ensure the survival of collaborative efforts, then evaluation must be done, but it should be approached with full awareness that the evaluation results can and probably will find their way into the political arena. Therefore, data collection should be as objective as possible. Essentially, if the evaluation is to be done, it should be done with the full cooperation of those being evaluated, by people who have the proper training and experience to do the job well, and with sufficient resources to see the process through to completion.

CONCLUSION

A host of school and community agencies have been developed to provide various kinds of support efforts to persons with disabilities to enable them to live and work successfully. However, these resources are often fragmented and inadequate by themselves. Agency collaborative efforts, often called interagency linkages, have been formed to provide more effective services to people who have disabilities

The linkages may be between school discipline areas, community agencies, or combinations, but they share the common goal of improved support services. The heart of the collaborative effort is a core committee made up of representatives from the various agencies that has full knowledge of all the resources that can be furnished to people with disabilities to help them become successful citizens. Cooperation in furnishing these resources requires a clear understanding of the capabilities and the limitations of each agency, plus a willingness to sacrifice some autonomy, jurisdiction, or ownership for the good of the linkage effort.

The effectiveness of the collaboration should be determined from data generated by accurate cost accounting and objective evaluation procedures. Ideally, these should be integral to the linkage agreement from the start of the effort and should be secured with a minimum of interference to the service providers. However, if persons with disabilities are to benefit from the collaboration, then their welfare must supercede the convenience of the agencies.

11

Transition of Students from School to Adult Independent Living

Be not simply good—be good for something.—HENRY DAVID THOREAU

ACTIVITIES

- Survey the area junior college or equivalent to determine what programs and services are available for persons with disabilities.
- Visit a recreation department of the city or county to find out what obstacles to participation might be faced by people with disabilities.
- Call on the local or state job Training Coordinating Council to determine the scope of its activities.
- Survey the community to find what housing alternatives are available to people with different degrees of independent living skills.
- Visit a sheltered workshop to determine the scope of the services available.
- Interview parents of students with disabilities to determine their postschool goals and concerns.
- Interview students with disabilities during their last year of school to determine their postschool goals and concerns.

INTRODUCTION

In Chapter 2, we affirmed the notion that transition is not only a *process* (Edgar, 1987) but also a multidimensional *service delivery system* based on goals in the domains of adequacy of residential environment, adequacy of social and interpersonal networks, and adequacy of employment (Halpern, 1985). Halpern's transition model, shown in Figure 11.1, illustrates these dimensions and how the high school and community adjustment service agencies should collaborate in providing generic services, time-limited services, and ongoing special services.

One way of explaining transition programming is to describe the major components of the transition process. The components presented in this chapter are those that have appeared in the literature or that have face validity from an organizational or logical point of view.

SYSTEMATIC PLANNING

Systematic planning for movement of youth with handicapping conditions from school to adult community alternatives can and should occur at the state, local, and individual levels. Ideally, a systematic plan should begin with a state plan. This plan may be based on a legislative mandate for transition services (e.g., S.2219, the "Turning 22" Law in Massachusetts), a legislative mandate for transition planning (e.g., HB. 2800 in Kansas), or a voluntary planning policy or memorandum of agreement.

The "Turning 22" Law in Massachusetts was the first and most comprehensive transition legislation to be enacted. It used the basic concepts of PL 94–142 related to free and appropriate education and applied those concepts to free and appropriate services beyond age 22. It mandated an individual transition plan and authorized state funding for services. This legislation became a model for other states. Legislation requiring transition planning is occuring in an increasing number of states, but it has been difficult to enact legislation as far reaching as that in Massachusetts.

A multiagency policy or interagency agreement between senders (schools) and receivers (adult service agencies) can also provide a basis for statewide planning. The agencies ordinarily involved in these agreements are the state department of education (including the divisions of special and vocational education), the state division of vocational rehabilitation, and other specific state agencies responsible for services to persons with disabilities, such as the division of vocational rehabilitation for the blind, state mental health and mental retardation services, developmental disabilities services, social welfare, and, sometimes, state corrections services. These policy-planning documents or planning agreements specify who does what, when, and how. Most states have interagency agreements on transition in place, but there is little evidence to suggest that the

FIGURE 11.1   Halpern's Revised Transition Model

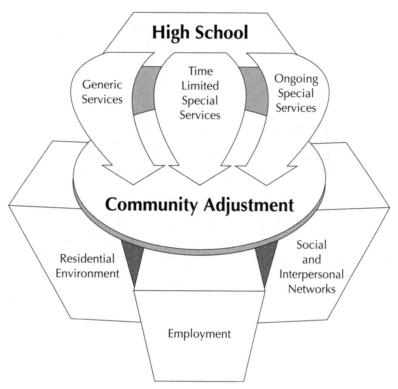

Source: From "Transition: A Look at the Foundations" by A. S. Halpern, *Exceptional Children*, *51*, 1985, p. 481. Copyright 1985 by The Council for Exceptional Children. Reprinted with permission.

agreements are effective or that they carry through into the provision of cooperative services at the local level (Wehman, Kregel, & Seyfarth, 1985a). Overlapping areas from law or regulatory authority have to be addressed, and assurances on "turf" issues have to be included for both the state and local levels before local impact can be felt.

The state of Iowa has tried to address the problem of state-level interagency agreements not carrying over into local community implementation. The Iowa Transition Initiative (Jones, 1988) and the Grant Wood Transition Project (Miller, La Follette, & Green, 1988) provide state and local education agencies with a model for interagency collaboration in transition planning. The Grant Wood Project has special relevance for states using area education agencies, boards of cooperative educational services, or interlocal cooperatives for administering special education programs, since it documents planning, needs assessment, and in-service training at an area level.

Even if there is no state-level planning, senders and receivers at the local level can join together in planning how to make transition work better for its youth and adult population with disabilities. A written plan can be developed but frequently this is much less formalized than planning at the state level. These participants know one another, and planning can come out of daily operations of transition skill training, referral for individual planning, and service delivery. Wehman, Moon, Everson, Wood, and Barcus (1988) proposed a model for local interagency planning that is easy to use or adapt. As at the state level, however, planning by local transition team participants is too frequently focused on the "handoff" (procedures for referral, acceptance for service, and follow-up) rather than sharing information relative to what their respective services and programs will provide or accomplish.

Wehman and Hill (1985) believed that even an excellent secondary program cannot help youth with disabilities unless specific, formalized planning and coordination take place. They warned against focusing exclusively on the transition process while ignoring the quality of transition-skills preparation offered by the schools, and leaving unplanned the development of a range of community adjustment alternatives offered by community agencies. According to Wehman and Hill, a clear plan is vital at the local level and should be based on formal individual transition plans.

It is at the individual level, of course, that planning is imperative. The transition process of an individual student with disabilities leaving school and entering the community can take place without benefit of a state or local transi-

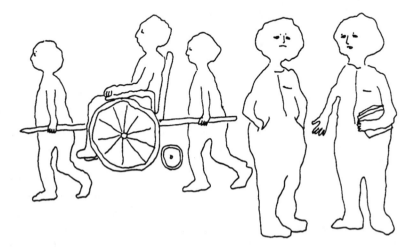

"Sometimes I feel like George takes advantage of our local interagency agreement."

tion plan. The odds against that individual making it these days without an individual transition plan and support team are great, however. There is sufficient evidence from experience with individual educational plans (IEPS) to recognize that having transition goals and objectives on the IEP do not guarantee successful outcomes. On the other hand, not having those goals and objectives is not only noncompliance with the law but is flouting the spirit and logic of purposeful intervention.

Most professionals involved in transition programming welcomed the transition service mandate of IDEA. (PL 101–476). This requires a wirtten plan specifying the transition outcomes to be acquired by the student while still in school and the services to be received prior to and following the termination of schooling by community service delivery agencies. The IEP must include annual goals and short-term objectives related to skills needed for daily living, personal-social interactions, and job performance. It must include the areas of instruction, community experiences, and the development of employment or other postschool adult living objectives. There is also a provision that any one of those areas could be excluded if the IEP team determines that services are not needed in any one or more of those areas. However, a statement that the specific service is not needed and the basis upon which the IEP team is making that determination must be included in the IEP. Transition services should be specified, such as referral plans or procedures to appropriate agencies, networking plans for linking the student to community resource individuals for nonagency assistance, or job placement and follow-up. Specific designations should be made in the IEP for who is to be responsible for every recommended goal, objective, and transition activity. Finally, the IEP should be initiated no later than age 16, but ideally at least three to four years before the anticipated exit for a student so that he or she is more likely to acquire the transition skills that are needed.

COMMUNICATION WITH STUDENTS AND THEIR FAMILIES

In contrast to the independent living philosophy, which focuses on direct input from an adult consumer, school transition programs must include parents or guardians in the planning process and, in effect, consider them, as well as the students, to be "consumers" in transition. The informed cooperation and collaboration of parents or guardians in the transition process is considered a very important component. Informed parents and guardians are those who have been provided or have sought and found information that they needed.

Parent and guardian input on IEPs is a starting point for determining their concerns for the future. Sometimes these concerns are justifiable, and the IEPs should reflect goals that speak to these concerns. At other times, the concerns expressed by parents or guardians are viewed as unrealistic or even inappropriate by professionals. When this occurs, it provides a natural opportunity for dialogue. A common example of this is when a parent or guardian insists that his or her child should be placed in regular academic classes so that graduation requirements can be met and college admission requirements met. If the student is a nonreader and functioning in the mild to moderate levels of adaptive behavior, the parent or guardian is clearly uninformed and needs information based on valid assessment data and college admission criteria.

Students are expressly encouraged to be participants in their own transition planning in the regulations for the IDEA. (PL 101–476). It makes good instructional sense to include adolescents in their school program planning and long-range goal setting. Students may present different preferences than their parents in joint planning, but even that is preferable as a starting point for effective planning than only a one-sided perspective.

It is highly desirable to train parents and guardians, along with their sons and daughters, to be effective advocates and self-advocates for and consumers of services. Some activities toward this end include the following:

1. Orient students and families to local and regional agencies that provide postsecondary services.
2. Familiarize students and families with the specific responsibilities of the public schools (regular, special, and vocational education), vocational rehabilitation, and adult service programs.
3. Prepare students and families to work with various agencies in the transition process.
4. Train students in self-advocacy, beginning with participating actively in their own IEP meeting.

Much of the literature on transition programming for youths and young adults with disabilities stems from research and demonstration programs for those with severe handicapping conditions. Professionals working with families of students who are classified as mildly handicapped may experience a different kind of response than professionals working with more severe disabilities. Proportionately, it is expected that more parents and guardians of students classified as mildly handicapped will be at a lower educational and socioeconomic level. Families that fit this description frequently bring with them a history of negative experiences with schools and community agencies, a limited amount of information about the alternatives for successful adjustment in the community, and diverse views about middle-class values for work and social acceptance.

Expecting low socioeconomic, uneducated students and their families to seek out information or to choose to be active participants in the transition process is unrealistic. On the other hand, failure to try to involve and inform them in a positive way is unprofessional and counterproductive. To assume that students and families do not care or are incapable of positive contributions simply because they do not play by the "rules" is unethical for someone in a helping profession. To assume that it is better to leave the student or family out of the process because of those same reasons is counterproductive because they will passively or actively undermine the efforts of professionals when they sense or actually experience that they are being excluded from the process.

It is not defensible in this multicultural, pluralistic society for teachers or adult service agency providers to impose only one dominant culture's ideas or values on any group. One must take the initiative in collaboration with parents in planning and executing transition planning and programming, expecting in this process to gain insight into the concerns, fears, and limitations perceived by culturally different or impoverished families. Transition planning must reflect a culturally and economically feasible set of life and work alternatives, and professionals rarely can do this independent of families and individuals involved.

The professional's role in encouraging self-advocacy for students and parents might include some of the following:

- Realize that all people have the right to make choices.
- Get to know the students and parents as individuals.
- Ask questions and listen carefully to be sure that you understand not only what the student and family are saying but also what they are feeling.
- Encourage students to set goals for themselves.
- Propose options for decision making rather than giving personal opinions.

COMMUNICATION BETWEEN SCHOOLS AND SERVICE PROVIDERS

The preceding discussion on planning among agencies did not address the critical aspect of implementing those plans. Certainly, there is some question about effective implementation (McDonnell & Hardman, 1985; McDonnell, Wilcox, & Boles, 1983; Edgar, Horton, & Maddox, 1984; Wehman, Kregel, & Seyfarth, 1985b). In fact, Johnson, Bruininks, and Thurlow (1987) maintained that interagency agreements are difficult to implement because of conflicting policy goals, different eligibility criteria, and funding patterns. As difficult as they are to talk about, these topics could be a point of communication at which to begin to break down the barriers of cooperative effort.

It may seem that communication that deals with conflicting policy goals between schools and adult service delivery agencies is not the best place to start. This is probably an accurate assessment of the situation for the local level, but it may not be for the state and federal levels. How can there be any hope for consistent, systematic interagency cooperation at the local level, however, without some consistent, systematic policy at the state and federal levels? Bruininks and Lakin (1985) and Conley (1985) pointed out that over the past 20 years, more than 40 federal laws relating to persons with disabilities have been passed. Many of these work at cross purposes and create serious disincentives to appropriate service delivery, employment, and community integration. It is no wonder that one frequently sees at the local level either nothing happening at all in the way of collaborative effort or a service system that is piecemeal, fragmented, and characterized by gaps in or duplication of services (Johnson, Bruininks, & Thurlow, 1987).

Still, on the basis of demonstrated working relationships at the local level, even without state or federal support for doing so, communication between transition team participants can happen. When it does, it is usually characterized by a focus on the needs of an individual or individuals and a sharing of information about those needs and the service alternatives available or needed. In an interview response for an article in a special issue on transition in *Exceptional Children*, Wehman stated:

> There are two critical aspects of effective coordination. The first is frequent communication, trust, and reciprocal understanding of responsibilities between key agency representatives, parents, and advocacy groups. The second is that coordination and agreements to share resources which are undertaken for the common good of the exiting student are done best at the *local* level. Increasingly, our finding is that no matter how excellent state interagency agreements may be, the real action for change occurs locally. (Brown, Halpern, Hasazi, & Wehman, 1987, p. 547)

Those who work best under informal arrangements find ways to communicate regularly through telephone calls, drop-in visits, sharing information from their respective discipline newsletters or journals, and follow-up contacts to evaluate actions taken. Those who need more of these kinds of activities find regular, planned, goal-oriented staff meetings helpful to keep momentum in the dialogue and collaborative efforts. The more formal, regular schedule approach has the advantages of facilitating more systematic information exchange between transition personnel and being a mechanism for staff development activities, program evaluation, and joint planning for the future.

There is another form of communication between and among service providers at the local level that is much more personal than the local interagency agreement approach and much more systematic than the informal approach. The emergence of the local community transition council as a vehicle for targeting ways and means of improving transition services for a community is an exciting step forward. The forum a local council provides for school personnel, adult service professionals, parents, and all other stakeholders in the transition process is valuable. The notion of pooling financial resources, energy, and commitment to work together toward mutually determined goals is catching on and the rapid development of local councils across the county is a welcome sign of collaboration and improved communication. School personnel interested in initiating a community transition council should refer to publications by Halpern, Lindstrom, Benz, and Nelson (1990), Everson and McNulty (1992), and Johnson, Bruininks, and Thurlow (1987).

TRAINING IN LIFE CAREER AND TRANSITION SKILLS

The theme of the career and transition model presented in Chapter 2 is the goal for systematic, quality training in life career and transition skills. It bears repeating here that it is our basic assumption in writing this book that training for community living for every age period and the transition stages between age periods must occur well before transition from school to adult living. This assumption is supported by Mithaug, Martin, and Agran (1987); they concluded that all transition models contain features that focus on systematic, quality training. Specifically, they found that among other features, the models called for implementation of transition programs that prepare students for postschool life and instruction starting at early ages in community sites.

One of the problems with general program models in education is that they typically stop short of describing the instructional procedures that lead to effective implementation of the programs. This frustrating characteristic of models is not solely the failure of their authors, though. Users of a model must adapt the concepts of the general model to their own situations. If a model is too specific, it does not generalize well to other situations. Hence, the development of specific systematic instructional procedures has to occur at the local level. Guidelines from the model's authors or state guidelines can be extremely helpful, but the local ownership is critical.

A systematic approach to training students with disabilities for life demands and life transitions begins with the development of a locally referenced scope and sequence curriculum. This curriculum should address life-centered career competencies and transition skills in community living, social and interpersonal interactions, and employment. The content of the curriculum should stem from the outcomes for education that teachers and parents have determined jointly. This set of outcomes should serve as a basis for developing IEPs. Even with such a set of outcomes, however, unless there is a systematic approach to the generation of annual goals and short-term objectives, a student could end up with a set of objectives that are skewed toward one area, such as academics, vocational outcomes (Cobb & Phelps, 1983), or arts, crafts, and leisure.

Quality preparation is, of course, like beauty—in the eye of the beholder. Most of the existing school transition models call for quality in terms of age-appropriate, integrated, functional, and community-based instruction. The implication here is that instruction should be increasingly functional rather than increasingly academic, but at the same time should be provided in integrated settings. This common feature of "quality" programs comes out of the literature on vocational transition programming for students with severe handicapping conditions (Wehman & Hill, 1985; Wehman et al., 1988). There is no intent in this book to deny the value of this feature for any student at any level of handicapping condition. However, there is a point at which this is extremely problematic for students classified as having mild mental disabilities (i.e., learning disabilities, mild behavior disorders, or mild mental retardation). The instructional options available to this population in high schools are increasingly academic rather than increasingly functional. The one avenue where some functionality exists within regular education for some students is in vocational education (Hasazi & Cobb, 1988), but this does not happen as frequently as would be desirable (Okolo & Stitlington, 1986). Where the problem most often occurs is in the areas of daily living skills and personal-social skills. Only so much can be taught through incidental learning in integrated academic classes; the rest must be taught systematically and with direct accountability of outcomes to objectives.

The literature for special education is full of proposals for and support of functional curriculum models (Brolin, 1982; Clark, 1980; Edgar, 1987; Kokaska & Brolin, 1985; Mithaug et al., 1988; Polloway, Patton, Epstein, & Smith, 1989). What is functional and what is nonfunctional continues to be in the eye of the beholder, however. The student or parent who insists on an academic high school curriculum may view it as highly functional for achieving the goal of participating with peers who are nondisabled or the goal of going on to higher education. It is because of this personalizing of values, and the goals that emerge from those values, that individual choice in determining what is functional must be maintained. It is important to remember that, just as group norms for tests predict only how well groups will fare academically, group data in follow-up studies of individuals who have been in special education also only predict well for group community adjustment outcomes. The issue of quality in high school programming is an individual matter. The policy implications of this for a high school make it imperative that a high school special education program provide both an option for a regular, integrated course of study with functional content and a functional, life-skills course of study. Each is legitimate for the school to address. Each is worthy of the school's official approval.

Persistent attention to outcomes is another feature of a quality program. The National Center on Educational Outcomes, established in October 1990, works with state departments of education, national policy-making groups, and others to facilitate and enrich the development and use of indicators of educational outcomes for students with disabilities. In their 1993 publication presenting the Center's conceptual model of domains and outcomes, Ysseldyke, Thurlow, and Gilman (1993) presented the following eight major school completion outcomes:

- Presence and participation
- Accommodation and adaptation
- Physical health
- Responsibility and independence
- Contribution and citizenship
- Academic and functional literacy
- Personal and social adjustment
- Satisfaction

The Center views measurement of outcomes to be critical and is working on ways to identify sources of data for each of the school completion outcomes.

Follow-up studies are used effectively by some local school districts as part of their program of services. One might argue that systematic gathering of information from former students and their families should be a part of planning rather than of programming. To the degree that the transition planning process must anticipate numerous possible outcomes and environments for students with disabilities and must accommodate these various possibilities, follow-up studies are indeed a part of planning. It is at the programmatic level, though, that the real value of this process and the resulting information pay off. Because there is a direct relationship between reported outcomes and the career and transition preparation program provided, the issue of quality in programming, as assessed through follow-up studies, needs to be included in a discussion of programming.

POSTSECONDARY VOCATIONAL TRAINING ALTERNATIVES

Formal postsecondary training alternatives include colleges and universities, postsecondary vocational and technical schools, adult education, specialized training in the military, and job training and apprentice programs. Informal training options include both vocational and nonvocational skill training in a variety of community adult service agencies. Each of these will be described briefly.

Colleges and Universities

Common sense and research (Rumberger & Daymont, 1984) indicate that study in two- and four-year college programs have long-lasting impact on success in employment for most people. It is in this context that data on how well students with disabilities do in postsecondary education raise some concerns. Fairweather and Shaver (1991) reported that youths with disabilities who leave high schools are much less likely to enroll in postsecondary educational programs than other high school students without disabilities who leave school (15.1 percent versus 56.0 percent respectively, $p < .0001$). Marder and D'Amico (1992) reported very similar findings (23 percent versus 56 percent respectively, $p < .001$). The breakdown between postsecondary vocational education program enrollment and postsecondary college or university enrollment revealed that the overall difference was due largely to the markedly different participation rates for community colleges and four-year colleges or universities. Youths without disabilities were 3 times more likely to take some community college courses and 10 times more likely to take four-year institution courses than youths with disabilities.

Both the Fairweather and Shaver (1991) and Marder and D'Amico (1992) studies indicated that there were significant differences between specific types of disability groups in their participation rates in postsecondary education. As one might expect, students with visual impairments, speech disorders, deafness, and other physical impairments enroll in postsecondary programs at about the same rates as youths without disabilities. It is the large, predominant group of those students—so frequently referred to as students with mild disabilities (learning disabilities, serious behavioral/emotional disturbance, and mild mental retardation)—that accounts for the highly significant overall differences between youths with and without disabilities in their postsecondary participation. This discrepancy holds, even when demographic variables such as income and socioeconomic status are adjusted in the statistical comparisons.

Many high school students with physical, sensory, or mental disabilities have an interest in and the ability to go to a college or university. The response of colleges and universities to Section 504 of the Rehabilitation Act of 1973 was slow initially, but it is currently better than it has ever been. Student-assistance centers at most community colleges and public and private colleges and universities provide services such as transportation, interpreters, notetakers, tutors, personal and academic counseling, accessibility, and faculty consultation. Increasingly, these centers are offering workshops and credit or noncredit courses in such problem areas as basic skills in time management, listening and notetaking, reading for comprehension and speed, outlining, preparing for exams, taking exams, and writing research papers.

Two college programs especially designed for students with hearing impairments are Gallaudet University in Washington, DC and the National Technical Institute for the Deaf, Rochester Institute of Technology, in Rochester, New York. Both schools have model programs of student assistance and curriculum alternatives. Some colleges and universities have made special efforts to provide special assistance services to college students with physical disabilities. Among these, the University of Illinois has the longest history. Metropolitan State University (Denver, Colorado), the California state community college system, and Johnson County Community College (Overland Park, Kansas) are examples of a growing number of community and state colleges that have unique assistance programs for students with learning disabilities.

Availability of college and university programs is not as significant a problem as accessibility. Some campuses are still partially inaccessible architecturally and some are simply difficult for mobility because of the terrain. Curb cuts, elevators, accessible restrooms and classrooms, lowered drinking fountains, and door-opening mechanisms are important for those with mobility impairments to make a campus more accessible. Accessibility, however, is more than an architectural issue. Program accessibility is also important, and it is at this level that some students with disabilities, especially learning disabilities, have the most difficulty.

Seidenberg (1987) has stated that program accessibility is more the responsibility of high schools in preparation than that of colleges in admission. She has maintained that findings from research on secondary and postsecondary students have identified specific areas of academic need in such areas as reading deficits, study strategies, test taking, and time management. Seidenberg provided a high school curriculum outline (Seidenberg, 1986) to assist high school teachers in preparing students with the prerequisite skills that are needed to meet the demands of college programs. She stated that many postsecondary transition problems can be minimized or eliminated when the high school curriculum is matched to the demands of the college environment and when criterion-based assessment procedures are developed and implemented by high school personnel who are more directly involved in transition planning for students wanting to go to college. This should be coupled with good college selection guidance and assistance in matching a student's readiness and skills with a college or university's demands and expectations.

Postsecondary Vocational and Technical Schools

Postsecondary vocational and technical education programs include vocational and technical schools (public and private) and vocational programs in junior and community colleges. These programs usually last for two years and result in a certificate or an associate's degree, depending on the area. As a result of Section 504 of the 1973 Vocational Rehabilitation Act and the Americans with Disabilities Act of 1990 (PL 101–336), most postsecondary vocational programs have developed support services similar to those found in high schools, colleges, and universities.

Many of the same students who were enrolled in regular or adapted vocational education classes in high school will want to go on for more advanced training. Other students will be those who concentrated on a general high school course of study and who do not have a marketable skill upon graduation. A small number will be those who participated in some type of cooperative vocational education or work study for students with disabilities and who want some specialized vocational training. Hasazi and Cobb (1988) reported that students with special needs historically have had difficulty in enrolling and staying in postsecondary vocational education programs. Brown and Kayser (1985) spoke to the issue of retention when they reported that the primary contributing cause for the disproportionately high dropout rate of students with disabilities was that they were frequently unaware of the special services available to them.

Adult Education

Most adult education programs do not have a strong vocational education component. Some offer courses in auto mechanics, carpentry, or welding, but these and similar courses are designed more for home maintenance and repairs or for hobby and leisure activities. Training in secretarial and office procedures, computer operation, and bookkeeping are the most common and do provide some options, but they are very limited in appeal. Only adult education programs that are highly comprehensive can provide enough alternatives to make adult education a good alternative for postsecondary vocational training.

Specialized Training in the Military

Physical and mental selection criteria exclude many high school youths who see the military as one way of getting some vocational training and as a magic carpet out of their home and community environments. There are a few, though, who are able to pass both physical and mental requirements and enlist in a branch of military service. Once in, they may qualify for or choose training in a variety of occupational areas that support the overall military mission but have employment possibilities when they return to civilian life. The range of options covers more than 300 skill and career fields, including such areas as medical service, food services and hospitality, auto and aircraft maintenance, clerical services, building maintenance and repair, welding, electronics, communications, animal training, military police, fire fighting, transportation, and storage and distribution of supplies.

Military training opportunities go beyond vocational and technical training in skill fields to include college credit for certain career areas. The Air Force, for example, offers four hours of college credit for the physical education provided in basic training and promises prospects that they will earn college credit for most of their training.

Job Training and Apprenticeship Programs

The Job Training Partnership Act (JTPA) of 1982 (PL 97–300) program is the major governmental job training program available at the postsecondary level. Under this program, job training is provided by agencies that have been approved for funding under the JTPA system. This system is a layered system that builds in state and local control of the federal dollars that Congress has allocated for each state. The layers include the state Job Training Coordinating Council (appointed by the governor of each state), service-delivery areas (local governments with a population of 200,000 or more, or a consortium of municipalities with a combined population of 200,000 or more), and a Private Industry Council (PIC) within each one of the service delivery areas. Each part of the system provides input and checks and balances to ensure that this job training program will be used to (1) serve persons who are economically disadvantaged and (2) train individuals for jobs in private business or industry. The vast majority of adults with handicapping conditions who are unemployed will meet the economic criteria for eligibility. In addition to that, 10 percent of all JTPA funds for adult job training may be used for populations that are handicapped or hard to serve populations.

The Job Corps, administered by the U.S. Department of Labor, is another job training program for persons with disabilities after leaving school. It is targeted for youth and young adults from the ages of 14 to 22 and has some attractive features for youths who have dropped out of school before receiving any kind of occupational or transition education. Job Corps training offers those who are the most economically disadvantaged a very intensive job training approach through either a residential or a day program. These programs meet the unique needs of some inner-city youths and young adults, many of whom have been identified with special needs. The training provided through the Job Corps can be offered to an individual for no more than two consecutive years.

Apprenticeship training is a job training alternative that has eluded persons with disabilities (Hasazi & Cobb, 1988). This is in spite of the fact that the Department of Labor requires equal access and opportunity to the program by any participating employer. Labor unions have managed to gain control over most apprenticeship programs because most apprentice training occurs in the construction trades, metalworking, and printing—trades in which the unions have a history of involvement. This seems paradoxical in light of the fact that the only authorized apprenticeship programs available are those administered by states under the authority of the longstanding National Apprenticeship Act of 1937 and come under the funding and administrative responsibility of the Department of Labor.

At this time, the structure for meaningful apprenticeship training exists. The idea of a training relationship built around an agreement between a person who wants to learn a trade and an employer who is part of the competitive labor market is logical and appealing. It is logical in that it starts with a basic assumption that mutual benefit results from such a relationship. It is appealing in its incentives to employers in the wage subsidies and the probability of a direct return to the employer from the investment made in time and effort. Obviously, it is appealing to the apprentice who can learn by experience on the job while getting paid and who will have entered an occupational ladder system that provides opportunities for advancement in skills and earnings. Advocates for persons with disabilities need to learn about this job training alternative and the best ways of gaining access to it.

Informal Job Training Alternatives

Informal job training alternatives are difficult to describe or characterize, They are mentioned here because there is a place for this approach, particularly when the formal options are limited or when an individual needs less structure in a training situation. Informal training can occur through volunteer organizations and activities; short-term one-on-one training by a friend or relative; group work activities as part of family, religious group, hobby, or interest group projects; or even temporary or part-time employment.

In rural areas where there are no JTPA programs, Job Corps, or apprenticeship programs, young adults with disabilities and their advocates have to be creative in finding ways to get training that would provide at least a few entry-level skills. Volunteering to work on a harvesting crew, in a volunteer fire department, in a hospital or nursing home, or in a childcare center, or filling in for vacationing workers in the community provide informal but valuable training experiences. In urban areas, informal training opportunities abound, particularly in volunteer activities, "mom-and-pop" shops, and temporary or part-time work. Wherever one might be, it is important to remember that adults with disabilities without formal training or experience are not that different from any youth who gets work experience and some skill training through part-time jobs, temporary or seasonal job opportunities, and home and community volunteer activities.

POSTSECONDARY PERSONAL-SOCIAL SKILLS AND INDEPENDENT LIVING TRAINING

It is much easier to identify postsecondary training alternatives for vocational training than for personal and social skills and independent living training. These areas, even more so than at the high school level, are left to chance or presumed to be best suited for informal training and incidental learning. The training sources described here are characteristic of the few alternatives that are available.

Colleges and Universities

Most colleges and universities have counseling centers or mental health services to assist all students with personal adjustment problems. Individual and group counseling in these programs are not only available but are accessible to any student at no cost. In addition, residential programs administered by the colleges offer a variety of opportunities for personal-social development through group meetings to solve common problems, special guest speakers on adjustment to college life, and noncredit workshops or seminars on special topics of concern to college-age students, such as problem drinking, recreational drug use, sexuality, suicide, dealing with personal crises, or a special health-related topic such as AIDS. Student-assistance centers may sponsor similar programs to supplement other university programs in these areas. Finally, colleges and universities typically offer courses, seminars, and other instructional options for credit in personal development and human adjustment.

Adult Education

Adult education course offerings are typically subject to the requests of potential students. That is, the tuition must pay for the instructor's salary and other operational costs and there must be sufficient enrollment in adult education courses to justify them. As a result, not many courses are offered on personal and social adjustment. What is more generally available, although not in any systematic way or with any frequency, are courses dealing with certain independent living and leisure-time skills. These may include such courses as cooking, auto mechanics, woodworking, flower arranging, consumer education, or introduction to microcomputers. The adult literacy program component of adult education programming also is definitely related to enhancement of independent living skills. It is one that many adults with learning handicaps should be encouraged to try, since their maturity and motivation may make a noticeable difference in their progress. This type of program is especially appropriate for individuals with disabilities who dropped out before completing a program or acquiring literacy.

Independent Living Centers

The whole purpose of independent living centers is to address personal-social adjustment and independent living problems. Counseling, whether peer counseling or professional, is at the heart of the services of agencies like this and continually focuses on learning to take control over one's life—emotionally, socially, occupationally, and functionally at home and in the community. Even the assistance given in transportation, housing, legal problems, interpreting (for the hearing impaired), attendant care, reading, and training in independent living is designed to increase self-determination and minimize dependence on others (Frieden, 1983).

Mental Health Centers

Two groups that appear to need mental health services more than some other groups classified as having disabilities are those who were classified as students with behavior disorders and students who have mild mental retardation. The latter group is frequently referred to under these circumstances as those with a *dual diagnosis*, because mental health centers generally do not serve persons with mental retardation per se, but rather only those who have some type of severe personal, social, or adjustment difficulty. Community mental health centers or similar agencies offer individual and group counseling to these and other persons in need of assistance in emotional, social, and behavioral problem areas. Some centers use community-based therapeutic activities with the goal of training for functional personal and social skills and independent living at home, at work, and in the community.

RESIDENTIAL AND LEISURE ALTERNATIVES

Residential Alternatives

One of the most discouraging barriers to successful transition for students as they move from school to adult living is the lack of adequate residential alternatives. Persons with physical disabilities find the inadequacy mostly related to architectural accessibility (see Appendix B for an accessibility checklist). Individuals with mild disabling conditions, such as those with learning disabilities, low vision, or who are hard of hearing, may have more alternatives because of their independent functioning levels. Even so, the high cost of housing makes living away from home prohibitive for many, and they often live at home with parents. This is not uncommon even for single young adults who are nondisabled. The practice of living at home or returning home during transition periods among young people decreases some of the negative values attributed by professionals to living at home. Still, the important thing to remember in addressing the issue of residential alternatives is that if there is a need or desire for greater independence in living arrangements, there need to be alternatives.

Schalock and Jensen (1986) indicated that the successful adjustment of people with disabilities is related both to individual behavioral capabilities and the expectations and demands that are specific to a given setting. Residential settings that are most frequently considered as alternatives include the following:

1. Independent living (alone or with a spouse, significant other, or roommates) in a house, mobile home, or apartment
2. Semi-independent living (alone or with someone else) in a house, mobile home, or apartment with periodic supervision
3. Living at home with one or both parents or other relatives with minimal to no supervision
4. Group home living with 6 to 10 other residents under minimal but continuous supervision
5. Family care or foster home living with close and continuous supervision

How do persons with disabilities choose their residential settings? Do they really have much choice? Many do not. The vast majority of adults with disabilities can be classified as low-income persons. This poses an immediate barrier to certain kinds of residential alternatives. Because developers are investing in condominiums and other residential options, rental properties are becoming more scarce and expensive. Rental properties that have been especially designed or adapted for architectural accessibility are still more expensive, and many persons with disabilities have to depend on subsidy assistance from the Department of Housing and Urban Development (HUD). Federal rent subsidies, frequently referred to as Section 8 housing subsidies, are available to low-income people whose incomes do not exceed 80 percent of the area average. A tenant typically pays 25 percent of his or her income toward the rent, and the federal government subsidizes the remainder (Wiggins, 1983). This has been a major development for adults with disabilities in providing some choice in independent residential living.

Halpern, Close, and Nelson (1986) did a comprehensive study on the impact of semi-independent living programs for adults with mental retardation. This program provided placement and supervision as needed in apartments. The initial placement was usually with another person, with the eventual goal of independent living in an apartment alone, or with another person, without supervision. They found that the majority of the clients lived in apartments that were located in relatively clean, integrated apartment complexes that were near grocery stores, laundromats, and restaurants, but one-third lived in neighborhoods of marginal socioeconomic reputation. Although many of the clients were adjusted to and satisfied with their residential situation, a number of problem areas needed to be considered in pretransition skill training as well as direct transition services in the area of residential living. These included such issues as community acceptance, awareness of Section 8 provisions through HUD, choice of apartment mates, access to community resources (particularly transportation), safety and reputation of the neighborhoods, home management skills, and renter rights.

Waiting lists are long at many group home programs, and admission is frequently restricted to those who are participating in a sponsoring rehabilitation facility program. Bruininks, Hill, Lakin, and White (1985) projected that residential services for persons with developmental disabilities are moving in four significant directions: (1) from large to small facilities, (2) from public to private operations, (3) from isolated to integrated community locations, and (4) from self-contained services to community resources and generic services. These trends are still valid today. Although these four directions may be more applicable to the kinds of alternatives available to individuals with mental retardation, other adult agency services will be following these trends with interest and adapting some of the same strategies when appropriate. This is especially true for individuals with emotional or behavioral disorders who do not need institutionalization but are not able to live independently in the community.

In summary, the barriers that exist for providing residential options for adults with disabilities are basically attitudinal, environmental, and socioeconomic. Negative to skeptical attitudes about young persons with disabilities living independently come not only from community neighborhoods, landlords, or apartment managers, but also from parents, professionals, and sometimes the individuals with disabilities themselves. Prime concerns usually focus on fears of exploitation, social discrimination, and health and safety. Environmental barriers result from a lack of accessibility to available residential alternatives, lack of accessible transportation, and dangerous or stressful neighborhoods that pose threats to a person's sense of well-being. Socioeconomic barriers include not only exclusive costs for accessing residential options, but also the prevention of the development of housing facilities in certain neighborhoods under the fear or expectation of property value loss.

Leisure Alternatives

Barriers to leisure alternatives parallel those of residential options in spite of the recent trends in the United States for leisure and recreational pursuits and the popularization of fitness (Maynard & Chadderdon, n.d.). Leisure alternatives, like residential alternatives, are limited primarily by attitudes. Attitudinal barriers to leisure-time participation, for example, are often reflected in a person's feelings of fear and lack of confidence in skills for participation in community activities. Also, both public and commercial recreational facility managers may have some degree of uneasiness about persons with disabling conditions using the same facilities as their clientele who are nondisabled. Sadly, this even includes church memberships, community social groups, and political action groups. Environmentally, there are still numerous barriers preventing participation because of a lack of accessibility to theaters, public buildings, auditoriums, churches, or natural sites such as parks, plazas, and gardens. This is despite the Americans with Disabilities Act of 1990 (PL 101–336). Reasonable accommodation, undue hardship, and exemption of historical sites are provisions of this law that maintain some recreation and leisure participation barriers. Socioeconomic factors limit experiences primarily because of the high cost of participation in so many of the more popular leisure-time alternatives. Again, the low-income status of the vast majority of persons with disabilities restricts their choices considerably.

Planning and providing for leisure-time alternatives should focus on normalized settings and nonspecialized leisure activity options for persons with mild to moderately severe disabilities. To accomplish this, however, the emphasis has to be on preparation of individuals with disabilities to be able to use and enjoy the leisure and recreational alternatives that are available. Cain and Taber (1987) suggested that the educational and rehabilitation systems and disability advocacy groups have contributed to the leisure problems of persons with disabilities. Cain and Taber believe they have done this by attempting to duplicate for students with disabilities some of the after-school and after-work activities that are available to those who are nondisabled. Although these programs obviously provide recreational or leisure experiences, they may not be the best preparation for persons with disabilities for participation in leisure activities in a community of people without disabilities.

Transition services in the area of residential living and leisure alternatives are the responsibility of adult service agencies and the community. Training for residential and leisure skills is the responsibility of parents, public schools, postsecondary education programs, advocacy groups, and adult service agencies. Availability and accessibility to both services and the skills for using them should be planned with the assumption that residential living and leisure activities usually are more an expression of life-style and personality than work, and that one's life-style has consequences for any person's development and well-being.

EMPLOYMENT ALTERNATIVES

Stating that employment alternatives are needed in a transition program is somewhat like stating that engines are needed in automobiles. Determining what those alternatives should be, however, is more like a group of automobile engine experts debating the relative merits of a classic V-8 versus a Slant-6 versus a 350 cc fuel injector, ad infinitum. The current professional debates in the fields of special education and vocational rehabilitation attest to the differences of opinions and philosophies on employment alternatives. The following brief descriptions of the major alternatives should give some basic information for better decision making in this area.

Regular Competitive Employment

There is little argument that students coming out of today's high school programs for youth who are mild and moderately disabled should have the ability to be successful in competitive employment. The statistics (Marder & D'Amico, 1992) do not indicate that they, in fact, are successful in any significant numbers. A more arguable proposition is that students coming out of high school programs for mild and moderately handicapped have the *potential* for being successful in competitive employment with assistance. Chapter 8 presented a perspective on the role of the school in job training, placement, and supervision. In that discussion, the focus was on employment training—one important type of assistance. Placement in a job was to provide training and supervision as a part of the student's high school course of study. In this chapter, the focus is on employment *after* leaving school. The transition from school to employment has a much different context because the school is no longer legally responsible for its former students.

Who is responsible for the employment of persons with disabilities after they leave school? State vocational rehabilitation agencies have been charged with this responsibility, but they have not been given the resources to do the job. Given this reality, individuals have had to look for other service agencies, such as state employment offices, public specialized employment training options (JTPA, Job Corps, etc.), adult developmental programs, and sheltered workshops (e.g., Goodwill Industries, Jewish Vocational Service, National Industries for the Blind, and local rehabilitation facilities). Among these, the probability of placement in competitive employment is favorable, primarily in the state employment offices and the public specialized employment training programs.

Competitive employment is, of course, obtained by large numbers of persons with disabilities on their own initiative. Unfortunately, it is not maintained over time; thus, statistics at any one time reflect a discouraging picture for people with disabilities. Many of those who do obtain their own jobs in competitive employment are underemployed or have resigned themselves to temporary work, part-time work, seasonal work, or migrant labor.

Adult service agencies and placement offices use various forms of incentives with employers to make placements in competitive employment. These include such things as subminimum wage certificates through the Department of Labor, wage subsidies through targeted jobs tax credits, JTPA sponsorship, and the Association for Retarded Citizens–USA on-the-job-training project. The need for incentives varies with the labor market. Placement personnel in one community or region will use incentives, but others have no need and will therefore place adults with disabilities in jobs above the minimum wage scale. This suggests that the labor market factor is a much more difficult barrier to overcome than negative attitudes of employers, even though resistance to hiring persons with disabilities appears to be at work in the private sector.

Supported Employment

Matson and Rusch (1986) made a strong argument that quality of life is directly related to social status and income associated with competitive employment. We would agree with O'Brien and Stern (1988), however, that a significant portion of the population classified as work handicapped are not sufficiently aided by traditional vocational training, public and private sector job programs, vocational rehabilitation efforts, or employer incentives to get and hold even entry-level jobs in competitive employment. More graduates and former students from high school special education programs are among this population than we would like to admit. It is in this context that an alternative such as supported employment has a great deal of appeal.

The supported employment model (Bellamy, Rhodes, Mank, & Albin, 1988; Rusch, 1986a, 1986b; Wehman, 1981; Wehman & Kregel, 1985)—developed for persons considered by professionals and employers for years as very difficult, if not impossible, to place in competitive employment—has been a major breakthrough in employment efforts for persons with disabilities. Wehman and Kregel (1988) identified the problems of the traditional competitive employment placement approach used by vocational rehabilitation counselors and high school work experience coordinators with mild to moderate levels of disability. They pointed out that the critical feature of traditional placement services has been the time-limited feature of the services. Work experience coordinators or job training specialists generally do not have sufficient released time to devote to those who need close and continuous supervision for very long periods, and they provide few or no services after the students leave school. Vocational rehabilitation counselors have active caseloads of clients far beyond what they can handle, and personal follow-up of clients in employment may last for no more than 60 days. Wehman and Kregel stated that, although the time-limited approach may be appropriate for many persons with mild handicaps, other individuals with handicaps seem to require more intensive services to adjust to and maintain employment for extended periods of time.

The supported work model is an extension conceptually of the general notion of community-based job training of the work-study model. It is considerably more sophisticated and, for that reason, is an innovation for the field. Although the early premise of work-study was place in job training, supervise, place in employment, and follow-up, it deteriorated in too many cases to "place and pray." The more sophisticated conceptualization of the supported work approach (or supported employment model) is revealed in Rusch's (1986b) description of its characteristics:

Assessment	Assess work skills and identify job demands of a specific job to achieve an optimal match between the worker and the job being considered for placement.
Placement	From community job survey data, select jobs and work environments most closely matched to an individual's interests and skills. Develop a working relationship with the employer and elicit parental support. Develop mutually agreeable criteria for the evaluation of job performance. Prepare the student for his or her interview and finalize the placement agreement.
Skill training	Train the student for job and job-related skills with one-to-one training procedures, using modeling, shaping, reinforcing, and fading.
Social validation	Evaluate worker effectiveness as perceived by the supervisors, co-workers, and employers through social comparison and subjective evaluation procedures.
Co-workers as change agents	Enlist and train co-workers to assume the role of job coach, evaluators, and advocates for continued support once professionals withdraw.
Maintenance and generalization	Train for maintenance of skills, self-control, and adaptability.

The persisting query by those who are considering using the supported competitive employment model is, Who is going to do it? School personnel are finding it difficult to hire additional personnel, and one-on-one training for extended hours of the day for uncertain lengths of time will surely unnerve school administrators. Vocational rehabilitation counselors have neither the time nor the preparation to serve as support employment specialists; they are looking for service vendors who can provide such a service. The model is so new that not enough people have the combination of skills called for in this approach.

Some professionals with expertise in the area (Wehman & Kregel, 1988) and data from recent research (Harold Russell Associates, 1985) support the position that there are two kinds of personnel needed in job coaching for supported competitive employment. One is a professionally trained person with a bachelor's or master's degree who provides job development, job placement, development of employer relations, and the initial, intensive one-on-one training at the job site. The other is a paraprofessional trained to do maintenance training and to follow along once the student has settled into a routine and the job coach is no longer needed to meet employer expectations for productivity.

The expertise and technology for job coaching that is evolving out of the demonstration models of supported competitive employment programs is providing the fields of special education and rehabilitation with what they have needed to move out of their patterns of programming. The tentative, and sometimes token, efforts made by many work-study coordinators and rehabilitation facility work specialists to achieve employment placement success in the competitive labor market should not be the standards by which one determines feasibility for success. Much more commitment to quality programming is needed than that. More sophistication and effort in job development, work skills assessment, job matching, employer-relations work, parent-relations work, community access work, interagency collaboration work, and, above all, more systematic, behaviorally focused job skills training are needed. There is a growing body of literature on each of these areas that provides the knowledge, guidelines, and technology on how to make these things happen (Bellamy et al., 1988; Gaylord-Ross, 1988; Ludlow, Turnbull, & Luckasson, 1988; Moon, Goodall, Barcus, & Brooke, 1986; Rusch, 1986a; Wehman et al., 1988). There is no longer any excuse for claiming ignorance.

Sheltered Workshops

For years public schools and parents have viewed sheltered workshops as the natural postsecondary placement sites for those with moderate to severe mental retardation and have assumed that most of these youths did indeed find their way there. State and private schools for youths who are visually impaired also have seen special sheltered employment facilities as the primary alternative for those who cannot or do not go on to higher education or some postsecondary training. Educational programs for students with physical disabilities, both in special schools and self-contained day classes in public schools, have expected sheltered employment programs to be a positive alternative for many of their graduates as well. Interestingly, educators of the deaf have never expected this as an alternative for their students, nor has the adult service system ever pushed for the establishment of special facilities of this type for persons with hearing impairments, regardless of the severity of hearing loss.

In general, sheltered workshops have been considered for years to be the basic adult delivery system for adults with severe disabilities—the ultimate back-up program when all else fails. On the other hand, sheltered workshops are not seen as a necessary alternative either by teachers or students with mild mental disabilities (mild mental retardation, learning disabilities, learning disabled, or behavior disorders). Unfortunately, more of the latter group eventually find their way into a sheltered employment program than is realized. (A recent follow-up study of one high school program for midwestern students who are mildly mentally retarded found that almost half of its graduates had been admitted to the local sheltered workshop program.)

The transition movement, and to some extent the independent living movement, brought about a serious questioning of the role of sheltered workshops in the rehabilitation process. Advocates of community-based training and supported competitive employment have challenged the very existence of sheltered workshops and particularly the notion that workshops are the only placement alternative. These challenges began in the 1970s (Greenleigh Associates, Inc., 1975; U.S. Department of Labor, 1977b; Whitehead, 1979) but increased in intensity and open opposition through the 1980s to the present (Buckley & Bellamy, 1985; Wehman et al., 1985; Wehman & Kregel, 1988). The criticisms have focused on major features such as segregation of workers from normal work settings, very low earnings, little or no progress in work skills or behaviors, and the very low rate of movement out of the workshop setting into less restricted and more competitive environments. The challenge to sheltered workshops has had some effect, and some are changing their philosophies regarding their mission from sheltered employment and work activities to training for competitive and supported competitive employment.

Although there is a growing trend to embrace a philosophy of normalization and placement alternatives that reflect the least restrictive environment, the concept of sheltered employment has not only survived but has flourished. The number of these facilities increased dramatically in the past 20 years, and there are waiting lists for nearly all of them. Part of this growth has occurred because these facilities have evolved from essentially terminal employment sites for adults who are severely disabled to multipurpose facilities offering day activity programs, transitional work-adjustment programs, and vocational-evaluation programs for a wide range of severity levels. These services have been needed to fill the void of services not available for increasing numbers of graduates from public school programs, but also for the increasing numbers of residents of state hospitals and schools being moved back into their home communities as a part of deinstitutionalization.

Both public and private facilities providing sheltered employment have had to operate under extreme economic pressures and philosophic inconsistencies. Funding has come from limited local or county mill levies, unpredictable state and federal support, private donations, contracts with the state vocational rehabilitation agency for work evaluation or work adjustment, and subcontracting with business and industry for products and services. Philosophic dilemmas arise when the best interests of the clients are compromised to keep funding sources satisfied. For example, subcontracts are bid at the lowest possible level to get the contract award. Clients are paid at a rate to keep the bids low, and good workers are not encouraged to leave or be placed in competitive employment when it puts a subcontract in jeopardy. Many workshop personnel have no previous training in vocational training for persons with disabilities or in industrial management and are expected to learn on the job. This learning from others like themselves has produced a cycle of low expectations for performance and a restricted view of alternatives. While getting their on-the-job training, sheltered employment personnel have to satisfy Department of Labor regulations, state agencies purchasing their services, business and industrial managers with whom they contract work, boards of directors who may know little about the field, and families of clients being served. It is little wonder that few workshops gain accreditation by meeting the standards of the Council for Accreditation of Rehabilitation Facilities (CARF).

Does this grim picture provide enough evidence that sheltered workshops should be eliminated? The protest and debate over such an effort would be much like the deinstitutionalization movement when the justifiability of large multipurpose institutions was questioned. The issue is also not unlike the criticisms of segregated, self-contained classrooms for all youths with disabilities, when the elimination of special classes is advocated by many critics. We agree with Wehman and Kregel (1988), who stated that the real issue is that of results and outcomes related to individuals' productivity and life-styles and not where the best setting for serving them might be.

The fact that there are more than 5,000 sheltered workshops across the nation with buildings, equipment, personnel, contractual commitments, and thousands of persons with disabilities on their caseloads argues against immediate closings. They can be reorganized, though, to build on their strengths and to refocus their efforts to outcomes that respond to the basic outcomes that we all want for ourselves—decent pay and integrated employment in the community. Some sheltered workshops are already moving in this direction, with programs such as the following:

1. *Mobile work crews.*   Mobile crews go into the community to do a variety of jobs involving specific tasks that are relatively routine—for example, landscaping or lawn care; janitorial work in offices, churches or theaters; highway litter pickup; catering; housepainting; or snow removal. Crews work under the supervision of a staff supervisor, who not only ensures that the work is done efficiently and satisfactorily but also that clients are developing work skills and behaviors that will aid in competitive or supported competitive employment.

2. *Sheltered enclaves.*   Enclaves within a business or industry provide a sheltered approach and integrated setting for employment. From 6 to 10 workers and a staff supervisor move into a work setting and work as a unit to fulfill a role in the operation. Clients are paid directly by the employer in some enclave arrangements (subminimum to above-minimum wage rates), whereas the sheltered workshop pays the clients (nearly always subminimum wage rates) directly out of a contractual fee in other arrangements. The former usually results in

better pay and better worker benefits, but it is not always possible to negotiate that option.

3. *Specialized sheltered employment.* Specialized sheltered employment, or sheltered industry, is an alternative that provides full employment at competitive wage rates for all employed people with disabilties. Facilities such as this may employ only persons with disabilities or may employ the nondisabled when persons with disabilities are unavailable or unable to perform certain jobs. The industry is designed to be competitive in the production of goods and services and may or may not be operating under a nonprofit organization charter. Such a facility is committed to paying at least minimum wage and does not seek any type of workshop status through the Department of Labor. As an alternative to sheltered workshops, the specialized sheltered employment facility does address the major criticism of inadequate wages in traditional workshops. A specialized sheltered facility does not address the issue of segregation, except to the extent that it can employ some workers who are not disabled and provide an integrated setting in that way. This employment alternative raises an interesting philosophical dilemma in determining whether to hire persons without disabilities to achieve an integrated environment, but possibly at the expense of not hiring other unemployed persons with disabilities.

In summary, many alternatives need to be available to adults with disabilities for employment. Dignity, opportunity for personal choice for integration in normalized work settings, and adequate wages are the desired outcomes. Where and how these individuals get the assistance they need to achieve those outcomes is the challenge for society.

GENERIC COMMUNITY SERVICES

The final component of transition programming is that of support services from those basic community resources that most people use and take for granted. Full access to community resources is absolutely necessary for anyone to approach full citizenship. Housing has already been discussed because it is one of the most basic needs. The generic services that persons with disabilities need include transportation, legal services, medical services, financial guidance, and mental health services.

Transportation

Transportation systems have had to accommodate the demand for mobility in the United States. Large cities have developed their public transportation systems with taxis, buses, trains, and subways. Many smaller cities and more rural areas have used privately owned vehicles as the primary transportation source. Available and accessible transportation for adults with disabilities becomes, then, both a practical necessity and a symbol of independence. For many persons with disabilities, it is the key to independent living in the sense that without transportation to educational, vocational, cultural, recreational, and commercial opportunities, one might as well live in an institutionalized environment where everything is provided under one roof. Symbolically, transportation sustains the philosophy of independent living and sense of control in life as it makes persons with disabilities feel that they have access to the same resources at the same price at which they are available to everyone else. The reality, however, is that transportation is not available for many persons with physical disabilities, and the complexity or safety factors may inhibit many who have emotional or intellectual disabilities. In no city in the United States is transportation as available or accessible to persons with disabilities as it is to persons without disabilities (Bowe, 1983).

Advocacy for better transportation systems by consumers who are disabled, families, advocacy groups, adult service agencies, and schools will eventually result in improvements. Until then, individual arrangements have to be made using creative approaches that provide dependable, affordable transportation, such as car pools, volunteers, bicycles, negotiated discounts with taxi companies, and subsidies from the city or county. School and adult service agency personnel need to elicit the collaboration of community leaders and employers in the transportation field to address local, long-term transportation problems that affect the total population of persons who are disabled, elderly, and low-income families, in addition to their assistance in individual arrangements.

Legal Services

Legal problems are difficult to sort out for most people. Adults with disabilities find themselves needing assistance more than ever now that as a group they are more involved in the process of independent living. They experience rental- or lease agreement disputes; civil rights violations; exploitation by high-pressure salespersons, repair and service workers, and personal care attendants; sexual harassment; divorce proceedings; writing wills; filing small-claims suits; and sometimes felonies and misdemeanors. People with disabilities, like everyone else, sometimes need legal assistance. One man in Kansas who had epilepsy was evicted from a low-cost housing apartment complex (HUD Section 8 housing) for doing some computer work in his apartment. This violated Section 8 regulations that specify that living facilities cannot be used for self-employment activities. Legal assistance over an extended period of time finally resulted in an interpretation in his favor. Without it, he was extremely vulnerable and might have joined the homeless.

There is a void in the private sector for legal advocacy in cases involving persons with disabilities. The American Bar Association went as far as to create a Commission on the Mentally Disabled in the 1970s. This grew into several separte efforts, includung publication of what is now called the *Mental and*

Physical Disability Law Reporter, the establishment of a legislative reform section of the American Bar Association to assist in drafting model legislation, and the funding of various demonstration advocacy projects (Vitello & Soskin, 1985). Still, not enough individual case advocacy and assistance is available for people with disabilities.

Medical Services

Health care and medical services are needed by everyone these days, but adults with disabilities have proportionately more need. Chronic health problems, poor nutrition, weight and stress control, physical fitness needs, susceptibility to respiratory infections, dental problems, vision and hearing problems, and preventive medicine needs occur with greater frequency among persons with disabilities. These needs interfere with daily living routines and affect quality of life by adding to existing problems. The availability and accessibility of a variety of kinds of health services to address these needs cannot be taken for granted. Without medical insurance, a Social and Rehabilitation Services card, or Medicaid, access to hospitalization or medical care is routinely denied. Lack of transportation and little or no information or knowledge about health care needs can contribute to inaccessibility.

In short, the transition from the available and accessible services of school nurses, physical therapists, occupational therapists, and physicians' consultations to the maze of adult medical and health care services can be difficult for young adults with disabilities and their families. Training in self-directed care and information on routine medical services, emergency medical services, physical and other therapies, preventive medicine, nutrition, and weight and stress control needs to be available. For those adults with disabilities who are trying to live independently but who find it difficult to cope with the health care system, a client-management system may need to be instituted to assist them in finding and using community health care resources.

Financial Guidance

Somewhat related to legal questions and concerns is information about consumer issues. Not all financial problems or decisions require an attorney, however; the needs that are highlighted here include the following:

- Assistance in financial planning for a limited, and sometimes fixed, income
- Assistance in obtaining financial guidance for planning major purchases, such as homes, lift vans, adapted automobiles, home or apartment adaptations, wheelchairs, electronic devices, and computers

- Guidance in obtaining and retaining entitlements from state and private agencies
- Assistance in money management in general consumer decisions, credit buying, budgeting, and investment of inheritance or trust funds

Mental Health Services

Mental health services should provide an array of options for adults with disabilities to help them in their adjustment to their disabilities, coping with personal and social barriers to daily living and employment, concerns with sexuality, dealing with stress, coping with death or separation from family members, or intensive therapeutic interventions for severe psychological or behavioral disorders. These service options can be provided individually, in groups, or by both means. They can be provided professionally through mental health centers, psychiatric services in hospitals, and individual therapists, or by nonlicensed personnel in postsecondary training programs, independent living centers, religious organizations, vocational rehabilitation services, and various adult service systems.

The availability and accessibility of mental health services to families of persons with disabilities is equally important when their lives are closely involved. Spouses, children, parents, and siblings have many personal and emotional issues to face as they support and advocate for their family member who has disabilities Many parents of young adults have to adjust to some harsh realities of inadequate adult services after having become accustomed to a wide variety of services from schools. Feelings of anger, frustration, disappointment, confusion, and uncertainty are common, and parents need to have some support for dealing with their concerns.

CONCLUSION

The outcomes of the transition process from school to adult living for adults with disabilities depend largely on the availability and accessibility of a community-based system of both specific and generic services. These services can be provided by programs or they can be provided by individuals or informal groups of individuals in a community. It is important to note the distinction between *programs* and *services*. Programs require all the formal elements that characterize a formal operation (funding, personnel, policies, procedures, etc.) and thus demand a certain level of energy and commitment just to get the program planned and implemented. Services, on the other hand, focus on the delivery of a needed response to problems, with the expectation that the outcomes will be satisfying as well as satisfactory. Services can be provided outside the structure of a program as well as within a program. The policy implications of this begin with the recognition that the transition process involves a number of services, but that programs might not be *required* to arrange for those services. Neither programs nor services, however, just happen. Parents, advocates, school officials, and adult service providers have to work together with community support to develop and maintain them.

SUGGESTED READINGS

Some resource materials for those providing guidance and information to students with disabilities wanting to go to college include the following:

Gardner, J. (1987). *Transition from high school to postsecondary education.* Washington, DC: U.S. Department of Education.

Hartman, R. C., & Krulwich, M. T. (1984). *Learning disabled adults in postsecondary education.* Washington, DC: American Council on Education.

HEATH Resource Directory. (1985–86). Washington, DC: HEATH Resource Center.

Mangrum, C. T. II, & Strichart, S. S. (1988). *Peterson's guide to colleges with programs for learning disabled students* (2nd ed.). Princeton, NJ: Peterson's Guides.

National Library Service for the Blind and Physically Handicapped. (1985, October). *From school to working life: Resources and services.* Reference Circular No. 86–1. Washington, DC: Author.

Thomas, C. H., & Thomas, J. L. (Eds.). (1986). *Directory of college facilities and services for the disabled* (2nd ed.). Phoenix, AZ: Oryx Press.

Vogel, S. A., & Sattler, J. L. (1981, December). *The college student with a learning disability: A handbook for college and university admissions officers, faculty, and administration.* Palatine, IL: Illinois Council for Learning Disabilities.

Willingham, W. (1987). *Handicapped applicants to college: An analysis of admissions decisions.* New York: College Enterance Examination Board.

12
Trends and Issues

It is difficult to say what is impossible, for the dream of yesterday is the hope of today and the reality of tomorrow.—ROBERT H. GODDARD

ACTIVITIES

- Discuss the full inclusion movement, stressing what compromises, if any, you would make in high school programming for curriculum.
- Study and critique any of the reports on educational reform as they affect the educational welfare of students with disabilities.
- Discuss the implications of offering different kinds of high school diplomas. Take a position for or against such a policy.
- Devise a program to combat the high dropout rate of students with disabilities.
- Describe your vision of the life-style to which a person with a disability should be able to aspire.

INTRODUCTION

The main job of schools is to prepare young people to take their places as adults in society. How and where preparation may be delivered varies with time, place, and personnel, but there is no shortage of opinion of what U.S. society believes the outcomes should be. Nearly all the descriptors of what constitutes acceptable adult behavior embrace four criteria. An adult is expected to (1) be self-supporting, (2) function in the community independently without care or supervision, (3) behave in ways that are neither threatening nor unacceptable to others, and (4) contribute to the maintenance and improvement of society. Not all grown-ups achieve full status as successful adults using these criteria, and with advancing age, many elderly people lose some aspects of self-care, independence, and even nonthreatening behavior. Still, society can be tolerant in these instances of imperfection largely because the aging process is better understood.

What people do not understand as well is that the handicaps that result from disabilities also affect the attainment of acceptable adult behavior. When persons with disabilities amply demonstrate some or all of the criteria of adult behavior, their disabilities are largely ignored. Those people who are the most competent in their behavior, who come the closest to the expected behaviors of adults, have the best chance of societal acceptance.

This chapter summarizes the elements of the school-based career development and transition education model. We will then discuss some of the major trends as they relate to students with disabilities and will close with a discussion of current educational issues that affect the area.

THE SCHOOL-BASED CAREER DEVELOPMENT AND TRANSITION EDUCATION MODEL

This book is our effort to provide avenues for high school special education personnel that can assist them in helping their students reach the goals of effective adult behavior. Our proposal fully recognizes the effort required of people who have disabilities to learn and exhibit adult behaviors. We know also how much the attitudes of intolerance, ignorance, and bigotry of others can complicate or even prevent the completion of the journey to adulthood. Ideally, society should be willing to accept or even welcome every person in each new generation as he or she enters the adult world. In reality, throughout much of history, this simply has not happened for people with disabilities. Instead, theirs is a story too often filled with instances of cruelty, isolation, and neglect.

Although progress in the recognition of human freedom has been made, it has been far from steady. Still, there are identifiable mileposts. In retrospect, probably the biggest boost came from the American Revolution and the founding of the United States on a constitution of guaranteed freedoms. Coupled later with a public school system that aimed for equal educational opportunity for all, the Constitution provided for people with disabilities as no other movement in history had before. The principle of opportunity was firmly established.

In time, as the violation of that principle became evident, particularly in the experience of people from racial minority groups, the civil rights movements of the 1950s and 1960s resulted in more specific legal guarantees of rights. People with disabilities gradually came to enjoy that same legal protection and the enactment of each piece of civil rights legislation increased the protection of the rights of persons with disabilities. A landmark law, PL 94-142, the Education for All Handicapped Children Act of 1975, followed by the amendments in the Education of the Handicapped Act in 1983 (PL 98-199), the Individuals with Disabilities Education Act of 1990 (PL 101-476), and the Americans with Disabilities Act (PL 101-336), cemented those rights.

The mandating of a "free and appropriate" education for all children with disabilities created the situation in which the interpretation of what is "appropriate" has differed. To some, "appropriate" has meant that the education of the student takes place in a mainstream classroom with few or no special provisions provided. We have taken the position that an appropriate education is one that focuses on outcomes as well as the setting or instructional model. Whether the educational setting is a normalized setting is important, but secondary ultimately to whether the educational program has helped the young person achieve those behaviors of effective adulthood: self-support, independent living, and acceptable, nonthreatening personal behavior.

The proposed model for appropriate education with high school students with mild to moderate disabilities is the school-based career development and transition education model proposed initially by Clark (1979). (See Chapter 2.) It is a lifelong learning concept that starts with the earliest school experience, emphasizing the learning of job and daily living skills, occupational information, human relationships, and values, attitudes, and habits. These knowledges and skills can be learned in any educational setting, but if they are not taught in regular education classes, then provision must be made to ensure they are taught. During the high school years, each student should be allowed to pursue any of the secondary programs offered by the school; college preparatory-general education, vocational technical-fine arts, cooperative education-work study, or work evaluation-work adjustment. Within the option selected by the student, some attention must be given to transition from school to adult life concerns. This is needed for every student with disabilities (16 or older), regardless of the nature or severity of the disability.

In many schools, the special education teacher may function more as a broker, being sure the students with disabilities are receiving instruction that will lead to adult effectiveness. In some schools, the teacher role may be principally instructional. In any case, the major task of the special education teacher is to be sure that the curricular experiences of the student with a disability will lead to effective adult behavior and also to a regular high school diploma or parallel exit document if possible.

The most common expectation of adult behavior is competitive employment. Our transition model acknowledges that some persons will opt to leave the school system to get an entry-level job prior to graduation. Although this is not encouraged, the factors that influence such decisions make it imperative that the school provide as many prevocational skills as possible by the time students reach the age of 16. The relevance of a community-referenced, age-appropriate, adult living outcomes curriculum should have holding power for those who choose not to pursue an academic high school curriculum in preparation for postsecondary education. A range of vocational training options are critical to a population with such a variety of interests and aptitudes. The model oversimplifies the possibilities of the array of vocational training alternatives that could and should be provided in each vocational course of study: regular vocational education, adapted vocational education, and special occupational/vocational training. The field of special needs vocational training has only scratched the surface of creative possibilities in vocational programming. Vocational and special education must work both independently and collaboratively to move beyond the current position.

Work adjustment and work evaluation are a legitimate part of the vocational training continuum if they use short-term, highly specific behavioral objectives and keep a community-referenced and, when possible, community-based focus. The inclusion of these alternatives in a vocational training continuum is not justifiable when they become dumping grounds or holding areas for students who are not wanted elsewhere. At that point where these programs become mini-sheltered workshops and preparatory only for community sheltered employment, they should be eliminated as options.

Since career development and transition education is conceptualized as lifelong learning, postsecondary provisions must include the opportunity to attend whatever educational programs will contribute to reaching the highest level of functioning possible for that person. College—whether junior, community, technical, or university followed by graduate school—may be and often is realistic for some. Nearly all people will, at some time, have a need for adult education programs or continuing education in some form. Probably most will find some combination that will best suit their needs. Certainly, finding appropriate educational resources is aided by the presence of effective interagency linkages and collaborative agreements. The crucial point is that these options for personal development be available and open to persons with disabilities and that adequate guidance and resources to support their efforts exist.

TRENDS IN CAREER DEVELOPMENT AND TRANSITION EDUCATION

Changing Labor Outlook

In February 1988, the William T. Grant Foundation Commission on Work, Family and Citizenship pointed out that between 1979 and 1985, the United States suffered a net loss of 1.7 million jobs in manufacturing. During that same time, millions of new jobs were produced in the retail and service sectors of the economy. Unfortunately, wages for these new jobs average only about half the level of wages for jobs in manufacturing. Even more unfortunately, these new jobs in the retail and service sectors are high-skill jobs. The Hudson Institute reported that low-skill jobs (e.g., helpers and laborers, hand workers, machine setters, transportation workers, and farm laborers) are declining (Johnston & Packer, 1987). This trend continues in the 1990s. Thus, young people with minimal skills often find themselves seeking employment in jobs that offer limited returns on their labor. Furthermore, as more corporations face still more competition in the products they make, there is even greater likelihood that the promise of saving labor costs by the use of foreign employees will become even more attractive in the future. Since opportunities for advancement will often depend on further training in new skills, many people with disabilities face a future that is not bright with promise.

Currently, it appears that the higher-paying jobs are in the high-technology and business areas. These jobs place a premium on training in higher education and the attainment of complex skills. If this trend continues, many people with disabilities may find themselves severely disadvantaged in the competitive labor market. No real solution to the problems created by this trend is immediately apparent, yet it cannot be ignored. Since it is not likely to reverse itself in the foreseeable future, the United States should bring its best efforts to bear on analyzing the tasks and developing training techniques that will prepare students to work in the most promising fields.

Implications of Trends in Changing Occupational Outlook

Developing new training opportunities is only one aspect of the solution to the trend of changing occupational needs. Of equal or greater importance is enabling people with disabilities to participate in the training. A concerted and sustained effort must be launched to convince the general public that many handicaps can be diminished, if not completely eliminated, thus allowing access to the broader range of career training options. Clearly, the myths, stereotypes, and traditional beliefs about the limiting effects of disabilities must be recognized and dispelled. This calls for a public information program so that support for attempting yet untried training options will have public support.

It is not just the public in general that is misinformed or caught up in stereotypes. The history of special education and rehabilitation offers ample documentation of consistently underestimating the potential for achievement possessed by persons with disabilities. If we, as educators, truly believe in the principle of opportunity, we must be sure that our own doubts do not lead to a self-fulfilling prophecy for our students and graduates. We must turn away from the negative aspects of disabilities as we search for and accentuate new, positive avenues for development.

Unfortunately, individuals with disabilities often are their own worst enemies, believing in the limitations of their disabilities, accepting their handicapping condition(s), and failing to develop and capitalize on their abilities. Mithaug, Martin, Agran, and Rusch (1988) indicated that special educators have taught students to do this. As planned and systematic efforts are made to raise the expectations of the general public and professionals in education and adult service agencies, one also needs to address the same kinds of negative attitudes in those persons with disabilities and their families. This means that some changes in one's behavior as well as one's instructional goals must occur.

The Educational Reform Movement

The current debate in this country on what is wrong with the educational system has intensified over the last decade. The reason the debate continues, we believe, is that critics and spokespersons for numerous studies and task force reports continue to confront us with conflicting information, particularly with regard to the outcomes of schooling and the effects of various school alternatives on those outcomes.

The educational reform debate moved from the early reports that focused on what is wrong with the educational system and some possible causes, to proposed solutions for general curriculum or outcomes models. The two reports tht follow give a flavor of the thinking during the early to mid-1980s:

Report: A Nation at Risk
(National Commission on Excellence in Education, 1983)

Theme

1. Educational reform is needed to maintain the ability of the United States to compete in world markets.
2. Better education is needed to achieve economic superiority.
3. The education system should prepare individuals for a technologically advanced society.

Major Recommendations

1. *Content.* High school graduation requirements should be strengthened to include (a) four years of English, (b) four years of mathematics, (c) three years of science, and (d) two years of foreign language (recommended for all college-bound students).
2. *Standards and expectations.* Schools, colleges, and universities should adopt more rigorous and measurable standards, as well as high expectations for student conduct and academic performance; four-year colleges and universities should raise their requirements for admission.
3. *Time.* More school time should be devoted to learning basics. More effective use should be made of the school day; it should be lengthened

or there should be a longer school year. There should be more homework requirements and greater time spent on teaching learning.

Report: High School
(Boyer, 1983)

Theme

1. The world has changed; quality education in the 1980s and beyond means preparing all students for the transformed world.
2. To achieve this goal, a comprehensive school improvement program must urgently be pursued.
3. Without excellence in education, the promise of the United States cannot be fulfilled.

Major Recommendations

Goals

1. Every high school should establish clearly stated goals that are widely shared by teachers, students, administrators, and parents. The goals should focus on the mastery of language, a core of common learning, preparation for work and further education, and community and civic service.

Centrality of Language

2. Elementary schools should build on the child's language skills, and English proficiency of all students should be formally assessed before they go to high school. Remediation programs should be provided if necessary.
3. All high school students should complete a basic English course, with an emphasis on writing. The high school curriculum should include a study of the spoken word.

Core Curriculum

4. The number of required courses in the core curriculum should be expanded from one-half to two-thirds of the total units required for high school graduation.
5. Strengthen courses in literature, history, mathematics, and science and include emphasis on foreign language, the arts, civics, non-Western studies, technology, the meaning of work, and the importance of health.
6. Students should complete a senior independent project.

7. Schools should offer a single track for all students, to include a strong grounding in the basic tools of education and a study of the core curriculum.
8. The last two years of high school should be considered a transition program in which about half the time is devoted to elective clusters.
9. Elective clusters should be carefully designed. Such a program would include advanced study in selected academic subjects, the exploration of a career option, or a combination of both.

Service

10. All high school students should complete a community service requirement.

What is the message from these reports and recommendations? Although they differ in a number of ways, there is a continuing theme of achievement of excellence through increasing the rigor and amount of academic courses in high school programs. Career exploration and preparation for work was mentioned in only one of the proposals reviewed here (Boyer, 1983) and was the only one among the first 11 major reports that did. The term *career education* was not used in either of these reports, although some career education concepts and activities were cited in some of the reform reports.

More recently, *America 2000* (U. S. Department of Education, 1991) took some of the basic concepts of the "effective schools" reform proposals of the early 1980s and the "school restructuring" reform proposals of the late 1980s and laid out a design for system change through the establishment of a national educational agenda. This federal initiative recognized the need for federal involvement in educational reform because of the nation's increasingly culturally diverse population and the increasingly competitive economic global marketplace. The six major goals of *America 2000* include the following:

1. All children in America will start school ready to learn.
2. The high school graduation rate will increase to at least 90 percent.
3. American students leave grades 4, 8, and 12 having demonstrated competency in challenging subject matter, including English, mathematics, science, history, and geography; and every school in America will ensure that all students learn to use their minds well, so they may be prepared for responsible citizenship, further learning, and productive employment in our modern economy.
4. American students will be first in the world in science and mathematics achievement.
5. Every adult American will be literate and will possess the knowledge and skills necessary to compete in a global economy and exercise the rights and responsibilities of citizenship.

6. Every school in America will be free of drugs and violence and will offer a disciplined environment conducive to learning.

Gallagher (1992) gently cautioned educators to applaud public policy statements such as *America 2000*, but at the same time realize that such statements imply that all of the issues targeted are not educational issues so much as societal issues. *America 2000* sends the message that Educational Program = Academic Achievement. Gallagher suggested that it is more like this: "Educational Program + Family + Culture + Physical Environment + Interaction of Factors = Academic Achievement" (p. 50).

While general education was looking to set its house in order, special educators began taking a hard look at its own outcomes and structures. As a result, lively debates emerged around a concept referred to as the *regular education initiative* (Lilly, 1987; Reynolds, Wang, & Walberg, 1987). Skrtic (1991) summarized the issues in the regular education initiative (REI), suggesting that the movement was an evolving concept, grounded in the liberal philosophy of progressive inclusion and was based on several characteristic features, such as the following:

- REI assumes that neither the general education system nor the special education system is adaptable enough today to accommodate the individual needs of students with disabilities.
- REI questions both the ethics and efficacy of current diagnostic and instructional practices associated with special education and argues that there are no instructionally relevant reasons for differentiating between students with and without disabilities, or among the three mild disability classifications (i.e., learning disabilities, mild behavior disorders, and mild mental retardation).
- REI proposes making regular classrooms more diverse instructional settings, and hence reducing the need to use separate educational environments.
- REI argues that the very existence of the special education system is a barrier to developing a capacity within general education for responding to the needs of students with disabilities.

The basic thrust of the REI movement has merged into what some refer to as *inclusive education*. The debate on inclusive education, as with REI, continues to hinge on whether inclusion means full inclusion or partial inclusion, whether neighborhood school or home school district is the only acceptable placement site, whether inclusion for any one disability group might be defined differently than another, and whether there are significant differences in the nature and extent of inclusion between elementary and secondary levels of education. Some propose reforms that are basic to school organization (Skrtic, 1991) and some propose reforms that are based on radically different instructional delivery systems (Thousand & Villa, 1990; Thousand, Villa, Paollucci-Whitcomb, & Nevin, 1992).

Another thrust for reform is coming through outcomes-based education. The concept of outcomes, or "indicators" of performance for an instructional system, may be developed for several levels: exit outcomes, program outcomes, course outcomes, unit outcomes, and lesson outcomes (Spady, 1988). Logically, all outcomes should be derived from exit outcomes—that is, what a student should know, be able to do, or be like when he or she leaves school. The issue of concern here is the difference in values that result when the exit outcomes for a high school graduate are specified in terms of program outcomes.

Should *all* high school graduates be required to demonstrate the following program outcomes, which are commonly proposed as exit outcomes?

Exit Outcome: Demonstrate communication skills
Program Outcome: English—Write using standard written English
    Math—Collect, analyze, and display quantitative information

Educational reform advocates in general education have tended to think only in terms of general education outcomes when outcomes or indicators are specified and appropriate assessment measures are designated for accountability. Special educators would have no difficulty in agreeing that one exit outcome for students identified as having one or more disabilities should be the demonstration of communication skills. A more appropriate program outcome, however, would emerge from an individualized outcome goal related to communication skills (e.g., Write a personal letter; Give oral directions to your residence). It is difficult to be a part of the mainstream of education and have the same exit outcomes when the program outcomes are designed for other students who have different goals and abilities, which are invariably the basis for deriving those students' course outcomes and, ultimately, unit and lesson outcomes.

There is some reason for optimism, however. High schools may begin to consider some program outcomes that are not tied to the traditional outcomes of college preparatory or general education curricula. In June 1991, the Secretary of Labor and the Secretary's Commission on Achieving Necessary Skills (SCANS) submitted an open letter to parents, employers, and educators in the form of a report, *What Work Requires of Schools: A SCANS Report for America 2000* (U.S. Department of Labor, 1991). The Commission based the report on interviews with employers in both private and public sectors, managers of employees, union officials, and U.S. workers. They concluded the following:

- All high school students in the United States must develop a new set of competencies and foundation skills to succeed in today's workplace.
- The qualities of high performance that are characteristic of America's most competitive companies must become the standard for the vast majority of its companies.
- The nation's schools must be transformed into high-performance organizations.

More specifically, the Commission proposed an educational outcome model based on five competencies and a three-part foundation of skills and personal qualities. They proposed that effective workers must be able to use the following:

- Resources—time, money, materials, space, and staff
- Interpersonal skills—working on teams; teaching others; serving customers; and leading, negotiating, and working well with culturally diverse people
- Information—acquires and evaluates information; organizes and maintains information; interprets and communicates information; and uses computers to process information
- Systems—understanding social, organizational, and technological systems; monitoring and correcting performance; and designing or improving systems
- Technology—selecting equipment and tools, applying technology to specific tasks, and maintaining and troubleshooting technologies.

The Commission proposed that workers must have a foundation for competence, requiring the following:

- Basic skills—reading, writing, arithmetic and mathematics, speaking, and listening
- Thinking skills—thinking creatively, making decisions, solving problems, conceptualizing and visualizing possibilities, knowing how to learn, and reasoning
- Personal qualities—individual responsibility, self-esteem, sociability, self-management, and integrity

The SCANS Report (U.S. Department of Education, 1991) gave this particular challenge to educators:

> Educators have to instill in students the perspective on results that the SCANS skills demand. If you do not, you will be failing your students and your community as they try to adjust to the next century. You, more than anyone, are responsible for helping our children develop the skills they need.
>
> Here is how you can help. First, tell your students what the standards are—what is expected of them. Second, give them the benefit of a fair and firm assessment of where they stand and what they need to do. If they pass from grade to grade and receive diplomas without mastering these skills, they cannot make their way in the world of work. Third, inject the competencies and the foundation we have defined into every nook and cranny of the school curriculum. Your most gifted students need this know-how, and so do those experiencing the greatest difficulties in the classroom. We are convinced that if students are taught the know-how in the context of relevant problems, you will find them more attentive, more interested—indeed, more teachable—because they will find the coursework challenging and relevant. (pp. viii-ix)

If this sounds highly familiar, it should. This view of exit outcomes is a contemporary version of earlier views of career education and this book's model of career development and transition.

Implications of Trends in Educational Reform

Secondary special education is caught in the crossfire of the debate between and among all the reform rhetoric and experimentation. It is important to remember that educational reform movements come and go but inevitably have some degree of impact on educational practice. Secondary special educators and advocates for career development and transition should be informed of all views and try to make a difference at whatever level is possible—school district, building, classroom, or individual student.

The emphasis on effective instruction has obscured the need to focus on the outcomes of instruction. There has been a tendency in special education to value programs that conform to practices of meeting the legal requirements of due process assignment, least restrictive alternative placement, zero reject policy, and progressive inclusion, with little concern over whether these practices result in satisfactory adult living outcomes. The effective schools movement seems to have blinded educators to whether the practices produce effective adults, and seems to have made educators feel guilty and concerned over insufficient gains in academic achievement.

Investigators with the National Study of High School Programs for Handicapped Youth in Transition (Mellard & Clark, 1992) reported that directors of special education and superintendents of schools at the local level listed only 3 attributes out of 10 for a quality program that were not compliance related in organization and administration. Even in this area, however, schools do not seem to be doing very well. Judging by the Tenth Annual Report to Congress (U.S. Department of Education, 1988) on the degree of compliance with federal mandates in 24 compliance reviews, none of the states monitor compliance in a satisfactory manner. More specifically, about 24 percent failed to follow the due process provisions adequately and 24 percent did not observe the least restrictive alternative placement procedures.

Although there is no question that compliance with the federal mandates should be a high priority in educational programming, adherence should be tempered by outcomes data. Those who address future reports to Congress need to pay close attention to the life experiences of adults with disabilities, not just to compliance information. The policy and practices of local education agencies are directly related to the priorities of federal and state interpretations of what constitutes compliance. The National Study of High School Special Education Programs for Handicapped Youth (Mellard & Clark, 1992) reflects this in the data showing emphasis on compliance factors associated with least restrictive environment, due process, and individual educational planning procedures, rather than providing an appropriate education (content related to outcomes).

Implications of Trends in the Regular Education Initiative/Inclusive Education

Kauffman, Gerber, and Semmel (1988) agreed with the need for better methods of integrating all youths with disabilities, but argued that eliminating a label may not be beneficial to youngsters because it may deny them services that could help them and it will not eliminate the basic learning problem that prompts the label in the first place. They further pointed out that assigning lack of learner progress to either teacher failure or student failure is naive because it does not recognize either the realities of individual differences or what they call the "staggering complexity of instruction/learning transactions" (p. 8).

We suggest that the proponents of the regular education initiative are concerned primarily with elementary-level efforts today, just as Dunn (1968) and Johnson (1962) were in the 1960s. This leads to undue attention to process (where to place, how to teach, etc.) at the expense of an evaluation of product (whether students find and retain work, have adequate housing, and experience satisfactory and satisfying interpersonal relationships). The considerable time and energy that go into educational reforms such as those described in both the excellence in education and inclusive education reforms detract from the issue of curriculum goals and outcomes for all students across all grade levels. The message of the reform proposals is that academic achievement is the sole criterion of education's effectiveness. This puts such goals on a collision course with career development and transition education programming for many students.

ISSUES

Amid the sweeping changes in administrative structures and educational programming that take place periodically in education, the welfare of students with handicapping conditions can easily be ignored. They are a relatively small group, probably not more than 12 to 15 percent of the total school-age population and, therefore, may be easily overlooked. Furthermore, they are divergent, some being blind or deaf or mentally retarded, and some being physically handicapped or learning disabled or multiply handicapped—and all with differing degrees of severity. Thus, even when they are considered in educational reform proposals, it is difficult to meet the needs of each student because few generalizations of need apply to all of them. There are some considerations that should be kept in mind, however, and these we present as issues.

Issue 1: Elementary versus Secondary Inclusion

Given the continued priority on least restrictive environment and progressive inclusion, are regular high school classes as well suited to assimilating students with disabilities as the elementary school is for its students with disabilities?

Although it can be argued that as students mature they will increase their learning skills and their ability to tolerate increased demands for learning and achievement, there is another side of the discussion. As one goes up the grade-level hierarchy, the discrepancy between students who are handicapped and nonhandicapped in intellectual functioning, academic achievement, learning skills, social experience, and personal maturity becomes greater rather than less. Even though teachers may be well trained to recognize the handicaps imposed by disabilities and to adjust their class requirements accordingly, the fact remains that students who are nondisabled are capable of more rigorous assignments and, consequently, of more sophisticated class participation. The resulting lack of ability to participate in complex problem solving can leave less able students swimming in a sea of confusion. Whether they can profit from peer association in such activities at the high school level is open to question.

Elementary-level programming and high school programming differ in many ways, but the most important difference is in basic goals. Elementary goals focus on teaching the basic tool subjects. High school goals focus on using basic skills to learn new information and skills. Given this primary difference, IEP planners at the high school level must make more difficult decisions about content priorities and placement in integrated settings than at the elementary level. Generally, the principle of proof has been the guide to determine whether a given academic setting is appropriate for a student with disabilities. At such point that the student is overwhelmed by the class atmosphere, the placement is considered unwarranted. Often, with additional tutoring, collaborative instruction, or support, the success of the student can be achieved. But if these or other additional efforts do not clear up the difficulties for the student, it is hard to justify continuing the placement. At that time, it is far better to pursue some other experiences to salvage the self-esteem and learning outcomes of the student than to include the student simply for the sake of inclusion.

Issue 2: Common versus Differentiated Curriculum

Do a democratic philosophy of education and a realistic philosophy of normalization dictate that all people have the same educational experiences?

There is no question that this issue centers on curriculum. The experiences that will allow young people to develop those skills that lead to success as adults have been the concern of special educators for decades. From the early efforts of such people as Descoeudres, Duncan, Ingram, Hungerford, Kolstoe, and Frey, the goal was a curriculum that would allow students with disabilities to learn behaviors appropriate to successful adult living. The holding power of a more relevant functional program has been demonstrated in report after report, not only in reduced dropout rates but also in drawing former students back when they became aware of the new programs. It is not surprising that the special education dropout rate has increased in recent years as the high school curriculum has become more academic.

The curricular focus presented in the school-based career development and transition education model recognizes that vocational education is appropriate in vocational content for many students but is inadequate for adult living instruction and in the development of attitudes, values, and human relations. Often, vocational education may be inappropriate in its level of instruction also; however, this deficiency decreases as vocational educators become attuned to dealing with diverse populations and as better instructional techniques and materials become available. The same can be said for nonvocational courses in the high school. Some of the academic courses and some of the nonacademic courses are appropriate for students with disabilities in both content and level of instruction and some are not. Again, most of these course options do not have a strong emphasis on career development of life skills.

Resnick and Resnick (1985) suggested that the one major question about curriculum that has persisted in U.S. education since 1893, when the first great debate over a common curriculum was held in response to the now-famous report of the Committee of Ten, is the question of a common core for everyone. The most radical recommendation of the committee was its insistence on a core curriculum for high schools. The subjects in this common or core curriculum were to be taught in the same way, with the same demands, for all students. The context for this committee's strong position on a common core was based on a highly cherished egalitarian ideal of access to higher education for everyone, and opposition to the notion of a differentiated curriculum ("tracking"). It made the same basic assumption, however, that has been made by other common curriculum advocates—common outcomes are more important than individual needs, interests, and abilities.

Edgar (1987) stated it about as directly as it can be stated:

> The only solution is a radical (no namby-pamby modification or cosmetic addition to existing programs) shift in focus of secondary curriculum away from academics to functional, vocational, independent living tasks.
>
> With only minimal thinking about this proposal one comes inexorably to the conclusion that such a change in curriculum will result in a *separate education track*. And this track will be populated, primarily, by poor, minority male students. What a dilemma—two equally appalling alternatives; integrated mainstreaming in a nonfunctional curriculum which results in horrendous outcomes (few jobs, high dropout rate) or separate, segregated programs for an already devalued group, a repugnant thought in our democratic society. (p. 560)*

Edgar (1988, 1992), Zigmond (1990), and Kortering and Elrod (1991) responded further to the "appalling alternatives" that Edgar (1987) decried, calling for rethinking the secondary special education programs in content and structure and suggesting possible alternatives for change. All the authors sup-

---

* *Source:* From "Secondary Programs in Special Education: Are Many of Them Justifiable?" by E. Edgar, *Exceptional Children, 53,* 1987, p. 560. Copyright 1987 by The Council for Exceptional Children. Reprinted with permission.

ported content changes that are directly related to current and near-future needs of students with disabilities. All of them also stated or implied that it would be ideal if the instructional content could be provided within the general education curriculum, but if it is not, then it must be provided separately. Edgar (1988) urged consideration of socially valued alternatives for *all* students who do not plan to go directly to college, not just alternative or separate programs for students with disabilities. He used Germany and Australia as examples of educational systems that provide socially valued alternatives for students. Edgar (1992) was more discriminating four years later in his proposals when addressing the needs of students with mild mental retardation. He pointed out that there appears to be no serious move in regular education to provide any new or innovative programs that speak to the needs of nonacademic-oriented students within the context of a regular high school that include students labeled as having mental retardation. As a result of this, Edgar took the position that special educators should be the ones to assume responsibility for appropriate programs for this group.

Issue 3: Special Education Dropouts

What is the effect of current trends and issues in educational reform on retention of special education?

Ever since Hippolitus (1980) cited the Bureau of Education for the Handicapped as the source of documentation for the statistic that special education students had a dropout rate of five to six times the rate of youths without handicaps, there has been an uneasy and growing concern for the problem. Until recently, data sources have been extremely limited in trying to confirm this disproportionate rate of school dropouts. The studies by Edgar (1987), Helge (1991), Jay and Padilla (1987), Kaufman and Frase, (1990), and Valdez, Williamson, and Wagner (1990) are the primary sources of information from retrospective and logitudinal studies available to the field on this issue.

The data collected from the states by the Office of Special Education Programs (OSEP) for the 1985–86 school year was reported in the Tenth Annual Report to Congress and showed that 56,156 students with handicapping conditions over the age of 16 dropped out of high school before completing a program and graduating. This reported number represented about 26 percent of the total number of youth with handicaps who exited school that year and was a 5 percent increase from the previous year (U. S. Department of Education, 1988). It was acknowledged in the Tenth Annual Report to Congress that this figure was an estimate of those who were actually known to have dropped out and did not include youth who had just stopped going to school or whose status was unknown. It was concluded that the 26 percent dropout rate was a conservative estimate. This is in contrast to the dropout data for the general public school school-aged population (including youths who are nonhandicapped and youths with selected mild handicaps) that show rates ranging from a low of 14 percent

(U. S. Department of Education, 1985) to a high of 18 percent (Rumberger, 1987).

In their National Longitudinal Transition Study of Special Education Students, Valdes, Williamson, and Wagner (1990) reported that the percentage of out-of-school youths with disabilities who had dropped out was 32.5 percent across all disability categories. The highest group was behavior disorders/emotional disturbance (49.5 percent) and the lowest were deaf (9.4 percent) and deaf/blind (7.8 perccent). Of the 32.5 percent who dropped out of school prior to completion of a program, the major reasons given by their parents for the dropouts included: "Not doing well in school" (28.1 percent), "Didn't like school/bored" (30.4 percent), and "Had behavior problems" (1 6.6 percent). Of the dropouts, 36.6 percent were from urban areas, 24.6 percent were suburban, and 31.4 percent were rural.

Generally, it is acknowledged that migrant students have higher dropout rates than do nonmigrant students (Kaufman & Frase, 1990; Helge, 1991). Helge has also reported that migrant students have higher rates of disabilities, depression/suicide/low self-esteem, and being victims of child abuse. Many migrant students cross over federal program areas, such as Chapter 1, Title VII bilingual programs, "at risk," and special education. This separation of educational programs and funding sources frequently causes difficulties in programming decisions at the local school level.

The research studies and the OSEP data from states confirm that the dropout rates for youth with handicapping conditions are alarmingly higher than for youth who are nonhandicapped, but not as high as five to six times higher, as previously estimated. The data are extremely difficult to compare across agencies, and cautious interpretations are required. This is especially true when differences across disability groups are studied. What is consistent is that the groups that are most at risk are those with mild mental handicaps: learning disabilities, behavior disorders, and mild mental retardation. Edgar (1987) and Lichtenstein (1988) agreed that those least likely to drop out were those with the most severe handicapping conditions and those who were in self-contained programs.

Lichtenstein and Zantal-Weiner (1988) provided a concise summary of the implications of the dropout data and research findings to date. The following statements are the essence of their research review conclusions:

1. Special educators must develop earlier and more systematic procedures for identifying potential dropouts, and employ better follow-through in providing programs that keep students in school.
2. Special education programs and services must provide earlier and more specialized guidance and counseling services to students with disabilities. These services should be available (a) before entrance into high school, (b) at the point of entry into high school, and (c) continually throughout their high school careers.
3. Secondary educators must be informed of the factors that might lead a student to drop out of school.

With regard to the last conclusion drawn by Lichtenstein and Zantal-Weiner (1988), it is embarrassing to have to admit that secondary educators do not know what critical factors are associated with dropping out of school. Of course, embarrassment for ignorance is easier to defend than guilt for not acting on the knowledge of such factors. Either one of these is sufficiently serious to warrant its inclusion as an issue for the field. The following factors have been presented in various research studies and are presented here as a "starter list" for becoming more informed:

Jay and Padilla (1987)

- Poor academic performance
- Poor social adjustment
- Frequent absenteeism
- Little parental support
- Low participation in extracurricular activities
- Low socioeconomic status
- Alcohol or drug problems

deBettencourt, Zigmond, and Thornton (1987)

- One or more grade repetitions
- Frequent absence and tardiness

Blackorby, Kortering, Edgar, and Emerson (1989)

- Nonattendance
- Verbalization of a dislike for school
- One or more school suspensions or expulsions
- Lack of high school credit accumulation
- One or more dropout attempts after age 16
- One or more transfers between schools or programs in a school district

Valdez, Williamson, and Wagner (1990)

- Not doing well in school
- Didn't like school/bored
- Behavior problems
- Needed/found a job
- Got married/had a child
- Illness or disability

As educators inform themselves of these factors associated with dropout behavior in special education populations, they must remember that these are not presented as causal factors. They are factors that occur with greater frequency than other kinds of factors among responses given by dropouts, parents of dropouts, and school personnel.

Ehren, Lenz, and Swanson (1986) developed a dropout-identification system that is tied directly to a dropout-prevention intervention. In this system, specific causal factors were not inferred from the procedures used. Rather, evaluation data were combined with teacher judgments, a student self-evaluation, and other school records in a decision-making component that concerned itself more with the need for some type of intervention related to learning, home, and social-emotional factors than a predictive identification. *The Florida Dropout Identification System* developed by Ehren and his colleagues and *Preventing School Dropouts* by Lovitt (1991) should be reviewed for possible use in programs for high school youth with disabilities where there is a concern for dropouts.

Issue 4: Common versus Differentiated Exit Documents

Should all students be required to meet minimum-competency standards to qualify for a high school diploma?

What are the issues for secondary special educators in the area of minimum competency standards? At the risk of oversimplification, we believe it comes down to one outcome: Minimum competency standards will inevitably lead to a more restricted definition of the meaning of a high school diploma and, ultimately, a more serious consideration of special or differentiated diplomas.

Florida was the first state to use statewide minimum competency testing for graduation standards. Many students with disabilities (and a large number not identified as disabled) were subsequently denied standard high school diplomas. There is no doubt that if the trend in minimum competency standards moves toward use in graduation determination, students with special needs who are currently eligible for regular high school diplomas will be vulnerable. Bodner, Clark, and Mellard (1987) reported that 17 states had policies requiring either a special or a modified diploma or a certificate of some kind (certificate of completion, certificate of attendance, IEP certificate, etc.) be awarded to special education students who do not meet regular graduation requirements. Of these 17 states that differentiate exit documents, 9 award a special or modified diploma. This represents a significant increase from 1 state identified in 1979 (Galloway, 1979) and 4 states identified in 1981 (Schenck, 1981).

For those who have advocated for nearly three decades for the right of special education students to earn a regular high school diploma, this issue is of great concern. It was easy to argue then, and it is now where minimum standards are not in place, that a high school diploma really has no common meaning. No one has been able to respond to the challenge that the expectations and outcomes for a college preparatory curriculum, general education curriculum, or vocational education curriculum are equivalent in content or rigor. Nor can anyone refute the differences in expectations and outcomes between school districts with variations in size, cultural, economic, or geographic factors. Yet, in most cases, it has been basically a matter of completing a prescribed program of some type in any size or type of community and a diploma is awarded. Although this practice may not be educationally defensible, it has met the American public's demand for equality of opportunity to obtain a high school diploma.

Minimum competency standards are dissolving the general tolerance we have had for these differences in expectations and outcomes. The public's general concern for the low levels of expectations and outcomes is the force behind the minimum competency standards. Now, the first time, in many states, a high school diploma can be operationally defined by *performance level* rather than accumulation of credits or Carnegic units. This is a significant event for special education because the argument for regular diplomas in the past has been based on the completion of a standard number of units using one's own courses of study, curricula, and standards of performance (Safer, 1980).

Unfortunately, special educators are caught in the uncomfortable position of either trying to explain to parents and students the implications of standards that they have had no part in formulating, or defending to school boards and administrators the courses of study and curricula they want to use to satisfy or substitute for graduation requirements. They also frequently find themselves being asked either to remediate deficiencies in students with disabilities who are in an academic curriculum or course of study they have not had any part in determining, or to teach separate courses in those same academic subjects without necessarily having had any training in that subject matter area. This creates considerable conflict for special educators who feel the system is unfair.

In essence, minimum competency standards are in direct conflict with the philosophy of Public Law 94-142, which clearly mandates individual curricula in determining appropriate education, Minimum competency standards for only *one* curriculum take the field of education back to elitism and education for a select population and raise the perennial issue of equity. This conflict demands the use of educational and political strategies by special educators to prevent an erosion of the progress and gains made over the years for the acceptance of the notion of differentiated curricula and standards based on individual differences.

As could be expected, the problems for states have been complex in deciding who will or will not be required to take the minimum competency tests, how modifications can be made in the tests to ensure fairness, and whether to mandate differential diplomas. Court cases have increased in number in challenging the validity and ambiguity of such decisions. The Office of the Assistant Secretary for Civil Rights of the Department of Education provided interpretations of the issue of awarding high school diplomas to students who are educationally handicapped who have completed an individual educational program but who have not met state or local requirements for a regular high school diploma (High, 1983; Daniels, 1988). Both respondents for the office reported that courts that have addressed the issue of diplomas have held that students with handicapping conditions are not automatically qualified to receive a diploma by virtue of attending an educational program if they do not meet the same requirements for receipt of a diploma as those imposed on students who have no handicaps. The federal and state case law on this issue as of 1988 support the official position of the Department of Education. Daniels stated the following:

> It is the position of OCR that Section 504 does not require a school district to award a standard high school diploma to a handicapped student who is unable to satisfy established requirements for the awarding of the diploma. Handicapped students may not be categorically foreclosed from the opportunity to compete for a diploma and to meet graduation requirements...
>
> The Section 504 regulation does, however, require that handicapped students be given adequate notice of the standards that must be met for the awarding of the "regular" high school diploma. In addition, if a high school diploma is conditioned on the passing of a minimum competency test or some other academic achievement test, Section 504 requires that the test results accurately reflect the student's actual achievement, rather than the student's impairment. Thus, appropriate administrative modification to the test format or environment must be made available to handicapped students. (p. 2)

In essence, the OCR holds that if a student with disabilities cannot satisfy the minimum competency testing requirement imposed on potential diploma recipients, and the test accurately reflects the student's impaired skills, the school need not lower its standards or provide the child with a diploma upon successful completion of the goals and objectives outlined in his or her individual education plan. Also, rulings by various courts indicate that appropriate notice to parents is very important. In other words, the child or parent must be advised well in advance as to what standards will be used to determine the successful completion of the requirements for a regular diploma.

Based on this carefully worded, but somewhat flexible, interpretation, the message is that it seems reasonable to proceed on the basis that the awarding of a diploma to a special education student is at the discretion of state or local authority. If a decision is made by local school authorities not to award regular diplomas and, instead, award a "special" diploma or a certificate of completion to special education students, the school must notify the student or parent well in advance of any expected graduation. This interpretation reflects the present unwillingness of the Department of Education to take an advocacy position overriding state and local policies on the issue of awarding regular diplomas to students with disabilities who have been in special programs under IEPs that specified different content or different competencies than those required of other students in the school.

Zeller (1980) posed the underlying questions to these issues very succinctly. He asked three basic questions:

1. What is a diploma?
2. Are different diplomas inherently unequal?
3. Do the criteria established for awarding regular diplomas constitute discrimination if they disproportionally affect special education students? (p. 1)

How do these questions relate to the provision of career development and transition education curriculum options for a wide range of handicapping conditions? According to the national survey of graduation policies of the 50 states and the District of Columbia (Bodner et al., 1987), states and local education agencies are using a variety of plans for awarding exit documents to students. In the absence of any national consensus, professional stance, or federal policy or regulation, this hodgepodge of policies will persist, with litigation shaping policies slowly but surely.

What should secondary special education professionals do if they want to affect policy from a proactive stance, rather than permit litigators or legislators to shape it, using extreme or politically motivated situations? First, it is essential that secondary special education personnel have input into state or local policies on what a diploma means. If they do not, the likelihood of future definitions will be guided by the recommendations of the task forces and commissions that have clearly advocated a more academic curriculum and more rigorous exit standards for high schools. If that happens, special education students stand to lose in two ways: (1) The increased narrowness of performance standards will either eliminate outright many of them who choose to be in regular high school programs but cannot pass the minimum competency tests or (2) the additional liberal arts coursework requirements may eliminate them indirectly because the relevance of the content will become an issue. That is, the students frequently are left with two equally unattractive alternatives: to fail or to enroll in classes in which content is not related to their present or perceived future needs. In either case, the meaning of the regular diploma is defined so that a regular school diploma becomes virtually unattainable or simply undesirable.

If regular diplomas become unattainable by virtue of their academic rigor or are viewed as inappropriate in content or emphasis, will different diplomas or various kinds of certificates be the only options for some students? Are different diplomas so inherently unequal that the courts or the United States Congress would have to take action to prevent such inequities? Given the current pressure to improve the public education system, we suggest that they will not take such action. There are precedents for differentiated exit documents that do not follow the stigmatizing differentiation of regular diploma, special diploma, certificate of completion, or certificate of attendance. In New York, for example, differentiations have been permitted for general education, industrial education, business education, and fine arts. The New York Regents' Examination permits students to show achievement in more than 20 courses, called regents courses. These entitle students to a regents diploma or a special certification on their regular school diplomas (Resnick & Resnick, 1985). This minimizes status or stigma associations with particular programs, because it gives the various special certifications legitimacy within the regular diploma graduation requirements.

Another model of differentiation of exit documents is that which is used in higher education. Universities award diplomas by the various schools (e.g., School of Engineering, School of Arts and Sciences, School of Education). In this model, students choose a school or course of study on the basis of both their interests and occupational aspirations *and* their own self-perceptions of their ability to succeed in the program *or*, more significantly, the school's assessment of their potential to succeed through admission criteria. Selective admission criteria in many colleges have been defended on the basis of limited space available for students and the need to make decisions as to which students should be admitted. In these cases, high achievement or ability measures are rarely questioned, with the exception of challenges of racial discrimination in testing. The primary point is that most students can find a college that will allow them the opportunity to choose a course of study. If performance is unsatisfactory, the student has to decide whether to discontinue schooling or to start over in another course of study. This model clearly differentiates curricula but does not track students; students track themselves.

No one can deny that tracking evokes mostly negative reactions. Not only is there something "un-American" about it, but there are also negative feelings that come out of one's own experiences of being excluded from something in the past. Although most individuals understand competitive selections for scholarships, athletic teams, casts for a dramatic production, or even the cheerleading squad, they perceive a real difference in curriculum tracks. For one reason, there is skepticism that enrollment in the various tracks is truly self-selective. For another, and perhaps most importantly, there are concerns that the instruction received in the various tracks is so inequitable as to make the curricula themselves discriminatory or inadequate. These concerns are validated by critics such as Oakes (1986), who stated:

> Lower track and vocational programs are often detrimental to the students in them. Ample evidence suggests that placement in these programs begins a cycle of restricted opportunities, diminished outcomes, and growing achievement differences between low-track students and their counterparts in higher tracks. These programs do not either appear to overcome student academic deficiencies or to provide them with future access to high-quality learning opportunities. (p. 150)

The dilemma of curriculum differentiation goes back to the first decade or two of this century (Lynd & Lynd, 1929, 1937), so it is not a new problem. So, how does the U.S. education system deal with curriculum and tracking? Obviously, there have been compromises. Public relations language or rhetoric, continued commitment to the comprehensive high school, and provision (in most schools) of an undifferentiated diploma all suggest a stand against tracking. However, in reality, the schools have considerable de facto tracking. Large high schools usually provide several different sets of courses that vary in content or academic rigor that permit and encourage tracking. Students use peers or school guidance counselors to determine the right teachers or courses that will provide the "best" track for them. Rarely are the expectations and standards in these options seen as equivalent by students or faculty. Parents are typically the least aware of the de facto system, and when they are aware, they tend to support it.

The question of inherent inequality in a public high school should not be dismissed lightly, but the primary concerns should be the equality of opportunity to choose a program option and equity among programs. If that can be built into the system, the programs should be able to develop their own courses of study and establish their own performance standards. This system encourages program integrity and more equal opportunity to succeed in a program. We agree with Resnick and Resnick's (1985) conclusion that "there is no sensible way to address the question of curriculum standards in general. Instead, the question of standards must be assessed separately for different programs and different groups of students" (p. 9).

Finally, Zeller's (1980, p. 1) last question should be asked: "Do the criteria established for awarding regular diplomas constitute discrimination if they disproportionately affect special education students?" There appears to be a strong possibility that special education students, minority and ethnic students, and students from non-English-speaking homes have been disproportionately affected (McClung & Pullin, 1978; Pullin, 1980; Smith & Jenkins, 1980). The courts may eventually rule that the problem is in minimum competency testing itself and that the tests systematically discriminate against certain groups. On the other hand, they may rule that the imposition of minimum competency standards based on the value-laden decision to offer only one core or common curriculum option (i.e., the requirements for *a* regular diploma) is discriminatory.

From a practical point of view, what can be gained by special education personnel who advocate a career development and transition focus in working with a single or differentiated diploma system? A single diploma system is an official (but frequently cosmetic) link to the mainstream of education. It suggests that special education students are "like everyone else" and achieve through this system their perceived right to be free of social stigma under a democratic educational system. When special educators and parents buy into this system, they are forced to compromise in a number of ways. Educators compromise when they offer English I or Math 10 for credit to students, knowing that the content and achievement expectations are not equivalent to another section of English I or Math 10. Educators compromise when they use the same grading system as other classes and present students for recognition on the Honor Roll. Educators compromise when they request waivers of the minimum competency examination for some students because they know that some students cannot pass it, yet insist that those students get the same diploma as everyone else. *The acceptability of compromises made for the linkage to mainstream education varies according to the degree that an individual student's needs and personal integrity are sacrificed to a curriculum or a system that is designed for someone else.*

On the other hand, perhaps a differentiated program diploma system is too great a compromise as well. On the positive side, it provides the one element that has never really existed—complete autonomy in determining course of study content based on individual and special population needs. This autonomy frees students with special needs to have a real choice of program options rather than participate in an acknowledged deception that is the only means of achieving a regular high school diploma. However, there is always the possibility that opting out of the mainstream's regular diploma system is a compromise that will lead to the collapse of the concept of mass public education in a comprehensive high school and the emergence of an elitist educational system.

Advocacy for differential programs based on individual differences in these times does not merit serious consideration unless it includes a commitment to two concepts: ligitimacy (official approval) of each program and integrity through adherance to some minimum program performance standards. Legitimacy and offical approval are a commitment to the principle of opportunity. And the principle of proof? One has to look only at the current follow-up studies of graduates and effectiveness studies (Edgar, Levine, & Maddox, 1986; Hasazi et al., 1985; Sitlington & Frank, 1990; Sitlington, Frank, and Carson, 1991) to see the effects of social promotion and ineffective or inappropriate programs. The educational system has allowed students to graduate upon completion of 12 to 14 years of schooling, frequently with nothing more tangible than an attendance record and a collection of Carnegie units or credits as documentation. The United States is the only industrialized nation in the world to grant high school diplomas on the basis of little more than school attendance, acceptable show of effort, and satisfactory conduct. If regular education is questioning its students' final achievement performance in relation to prescribes goals, no less should be done for students with disabilities. In pursuit of excellence, it is neither fair nor appropriate to permit students to graduate without achieving the individual goals set for them. That is the principle of proof.

CONCLUSION

The theme of this book is not a new one to the field. It is not a theme that comes out of strong ideology that demands an ethical or moral professional commitment. It is not a theme that demands that one fit the system, change the system, or ignore the system. It is, however, a theme that has historical roots and a functional view of education that has persisted in U.S. education over the years. It is a theme that is based on a pragmatic approach to educational philosophy, organization, and delivery of instruction. It is a theme that speaks unwaveringly to useful outcomes for youths identified as having handicapping disabilities while they are in school and who will probably encounter additional difficulties in adult living. It is a theme that affirms the rights of students and their families to choose a traditional academic curriculum when they believe it to be an appropriate education. It is a theme that pleads for an equitable alternative for those for whom an academic, college preparatory course of study in high school is neither appealing nor possible to achieve if educational reform continues its current trend.

Resource Agencies

The Accreditation Council of Services
for Persons with Mental Retardation
and Other Developmental
Disabilities
4435 Wisconsin Ave., NW
Washington, DC 20016
(202) 363-2811

Activities Unlimited, Inc.
P.O. Box 324
Helena, MT 59624

Administration on Developmental
Disabilities
Department of Health and Human
Services
200 Independence Avenue, SW
336F Hubert H. Humphrey Building
Washington, DC 20201
(202) 245-2890

Alexander Graham Bell Association for
the Deaf
3417 Volta Pl., NW
Washington, DC 20007
(202) 337-5220

Allergy Foundation of America
118-35 Queens Blvd.
Forest Hills, NY 11375
(718) 261-3663

AMC Cancer Information Center
1600 Pierce St.
Lakewood, CO 80214
(800) 525-3777

American Academy of Cerebral Palsy
and Developmental Medicine
2315 Westwood Ave.
P.O. Box 11083
Richmond, VA 23230
(804) 355-0147

American Alliance for Health, Physical
Education, Recreation and Dance
1900 Association Dr.
Reston, VA 22091
(703) 476-3400

American Association on Mental
Retardation
1719 Kalorama Rd., NW
Washington, DC 20009-2684
(202) 387-1968
(800) 424-3688

American Association of University
Affiliated Programs for the
Developmentally Disabled (35
interdisciplinary facilities working
with the Department of Health,
Education and Welfare)
110 17th Street, NW, Suite 908
Washington, DC 20026

The American Bar Association
Advocacy Center
1800 M St. NW, Suite 200
Washington, DC 20036

American Coalition of Citizens with
Disabilities
1012 14th St., NW, Suite 901
Washington, DC 20005
(202) 628-3470

American Council of the Blind
1211 Connecticut Ave., NW
Suite 506
Washington, DC 20036
(202) 833-1251
(800) 424-8666

American Diabetes Association
600 Fifth Ave.
New York, NY 10020

American Foundation for the Blind
15 West 16th St.
New York, NY 10011

American Kidney Fund
7315 Wisconsin Ave.
Suite 203 East
Bethesda, MD 20814-3266
(800) 638-8299

American Occupation Therapy
Association, Inc.
1383 Piccard Dr.
Rockville, MD 20850
(301) 948-9626

American Orthotic and Prosthetic
Association
1400 N. St., NW
Washington, DC 20005

American Physical Therapy
Association
1111 North Fairfax St.
Alexandria, VA 22314
(703) 684-2782

American Physical Therapy Association
1156 15th St., NW
Washington, DC 20005

American Printing House for The Blind
1839 Frankfurt Ave.
P.O. Box 6085
Louisville, KY 40206
(502) 895-2405

American Self-Help Clearinghouse
St. Clares-Riverside Medical Center
Pocono Rd
Denville, NJ 07834

American Society for the Deaf
814 Thayer Ave.
Silver Springs, MD 20852
(301) 585-5400

American Speech-Language-Hearing
Association
10801 Rockville Pike
Rockville, MD 20852
(301) 897-5700

American Tuberous Sclerosis Association
339 Union St.
P.O. Box 44
Rockland, MA 02370
(617) 878-5528
(800) 446-1211

American Wheelchair Bowling
Association
6718 Pinehurst Dr.
Evansville, IN 47711

Architectural and Transportation
Barriers Compliance Board
330 C Street, SW, Room 1010
Washington, DC 20202
(202) 245-1591

Arthritis Foundation
3400 Peachtree Rd., NE
Suite 1101
Atlanta, GA 30026

Association for Children and Adults
    with Learning Disabilities
4156 Library Rd.
Pittsburg, PA 15234

Association for Education of the Visually
    Handicapped
919 Walnut St., Forth Floor
Philadelphia, PA 19107

Association of Experiential Education
C. U. P.O. Box 249
Boulder, CO 80309

Association on Handicapped Student
    Service Programs in Postsecondary
    Education (AHSSPPE)
P.O. Box 21192
Columbus, OH 43221

Association of Persons in Supported
    Employment (APSE)
P. O. Box 27523
Richmond, VA 23261

The Association for Persons with Severe
    Handicaps
7010 Roosevelt Way, NE
Seattle, WA 98115
(206) 523-8446

Association for Retarded Citizens (ARC)
500 E. Border St., 3rd Floor
Arlington, TX 76010

Beach Center on Families and
    Disabilities
Schiefelbusch Institute for Lifespan
    Studies
3150 Haworth Hall
University of Kansas
Lawrence, KS 66045

Better Hearing Institute Hearing
    Helpline
1430 K St., NW, Suite 700
Washington, DC 20005
(800) 424-8576

Beverly Farm Foundation
3601 Humbert Rd.
Godfrey, IL 62035

Breckenridge Outdoor Education center
P.O. Box 697
Breckenridge, CO 80424

Canadian Association for the Mentally
    Retarded/National Institute on
    Mental Retardation
8605 Rue Berri
Bureau 300
Montreal, Quebec
Canada H2P 2G5
(514) 281-2307

Canadian Cerebral Palsy Association
55 Bloor St., East, Suite 301
Toronto, Ontario
Canada M4W 1A9
(416) 923-2932

Canadian Hearing Society
271 Spadina Rd.
Toronto, Ontario
Canada M5R 2V3
(416) 964-9595
(416) 964-2066

Canadian Hemophilia Society National
    Office
100 King St., West, Suite 210
Hamilton, Ontario
Canada L8P 1A2
(416) 523-6414

Canadian National Institute for the Blind
1929 Bayview Ave.
Toronto, Ontario
Canada M4G 3E8
(416) 486-2500

Canadian Rehabilitation Council for the
    Disabled
1 Young St., Suite 2110
Toronto, Ontario
Canada M5E 1F5
(416) 862-0340

Cancer Information Service National
Line
44 Vinney St.
Boston, MA 02215
(800) 4-CANCER

Center on Postsecondary Education for
Students with Learning Disabilities
The University of Connecticut, U-64
249 Glenbrook Rd.
Storrs, CT 06269-2064

Children's Defense Fund
122 C St., NW, Suite 400
Washington, DC 20001
(800) 424-9602

Closer Look LD Teen Line
1201 16th St., Suite 223
Washington, DC 20036
(202) 822-7900
(800) 522-3458

The Coalition on Sexuality and
Disability, Inc.
853 Broadway, Suite 611
New York, NY 10003
(212) 242-3900
(212) 677-6474

Columbia Lighthouse for the Blind
421 P St., NW
Washington, DC 20005

Committee for the Promotion of
Camping for the Handicapped
2056 South Bluff Road
Travers City, MI 49684

The Compassionate Friends, Inc.
P.O. Box 1347
Oak Brook, IL 60521
(312) 323-5010

Congress of Organizations for the
Physically Handicapped
16630 Beverly Ave.
Tinley Park, IL 60477-1904

Council of Education of the Deaf
c/o Gallaudet University
Seventh St. and Florida Ave.
Washington, DC 20002

Council for Exceptional Children
1920 Association Dr.
Reston, VA 22091

Cystic Fibrosis Foundation
6000 Executive Blvd., #510
Rockville, MD 20852
(301) 881-9130
(800) FIGHT-CF

Dental Guidance Council for Cerebral
Palsy
122 E. 23rd St.
New York, NY 10010

Disabled Living Resource Center
Kinsmen Rehabilitation Foundation
2256 W. 12th Ave.
Vancouver, British Columbia
Canada B6K 2N5

Division of Assistance to States Office of
Special education
400 Maryland Avenue, SW
Donohoe Building
Washington, DC 20202

Down's Syndrome Congress
1640 W. Roosevelt Rd.
Chicago, IL 60608

Dysautonomia Foundation, Inc.
370 Lexington Ave., Room 1504
New York, NY 10017
(212) 889-5222

Dystonia Medical Research Foundation
9615 Brighton Way, Suite 310
Beverly Hills, CA 90210
or
First City Building, Suite 1800
777 Hornby St.
Vancouver, British Columbia
Canada V6Z 1S4

Environmental Travel Companions
Fort Mason Center
Building C
San Francisco, CA 94101

Epilepsy Foundation of America
4351 Garden City Drive, Suite 406
Landover, MD 20785
Epilepsy Information Line
(800) 426-0660
(617) 482-2915

Federation of the Handicapped
211 West 14th St.
New York, NY 10011

Foundation for Children with Learning
    Disabilities
P.O. Box 2929
Grand Central Station
New York, NY 10163
(212) 687-7211

Friedreich's Ataxia Group in America,
    Inc.
P.O. Box 11116
Oakland, CA 94611
(415) 655-0833

Handicapped Children and Youth
P.O. Box 1492
Washington, DC 20013

Help for Incontinent People
P.O. Box 544
Union, SC 29379

Immune Deficiency Foundation (IDF)
P.O. Box 586
Columbia, MD 21045

Independent Living Research Utilization
    Program (ILRU)
3400 Bissonnet, Suite 101
Houston, TX 77005

Information Center for Individuals with
    Disabilities
20 Providence St., Room 329
Boston, MA 02116

Institute on Alcohol, Drugs, and
    Disability (IADD)
2165 Bunker Hill Dr.
San Mateo, CA 94402

Institute on Community Integration
University of Minnesota
109 Pattee Hall
150 Pillsbury Drive SE
Minneapolis, MN 55455

International Association of the Deaf
814 Thayer Ave.
Silver Spring, MD 20910

International Spinal Cord Research
    Foundation
4100 Spring Valley Rd.
Suite 104 LB3
Dallas, TX 75234

Job Accommodation Network (JAN)
West Virginia University
809 Allen Hall
Morgantown, WV 26506

Job Opportunities for the Blind (JOB)
    National Federation of the Blind
1800 Johnson St.
Baltimore, MD 21230

John Tracy Clinic (deafness/hearing
    impairments, deaf/blind)
806 West Adams Blvd.
Los Angeles, CA 90007

Juvenile Diabetes Foundation
    International
60 Madison Ave.
New York, NY 10010-1550
(212) 889-7575
(800) 223-1138

Learning Disabilities Network
25 Accord Park Drive
Rockland, MA 02370

Leukemia Society of America
733 Third Ave., 14th Floor
New York, NY 10017

Life Services for the Handicapped, Inc.
352 Park Ave. South
New York, NY 10010

Little People of America, Inc.
Box 126
Owatonna, MN 55060
(507) 451-3842

Lowe's Syndrome Association
222 Lincoln St.
West Lafayette, IN 47906
(317) 743-3634

Mainstream, Inc.
1030 15th St., NW, Suite 1010
Washington, DC 20005

Muscular Dystrophy Association
810 7th Ave.
New York, NY 10019
(212) 586-0808

National AIDS Information
    Clearinghouse (NAIC)
P.O. Box 6003
Rockville, MD 20850

National Amputation Foundation
12-45 150th St.
Whitestone, NY 11357
(718) 767-0596

National Arthritis Foundation
1314 Spring St., NW
Atlanta, GA 30309
(404) 872-7100

National Association of the Deaf
814 Thayer Ave.
Silver Springs, MD 20910

National Association of the Deaf-Blind
2703 Forest Oak Circle
Norman, OK 73071

National Association of Developmental
    Disabilities Council
1234 Massachusetts Ave., NW
Suite 103
Washington, DC 20005

National Association for Mental Health
10 Columbus Circle
New York, NY 10019

National Association for Retarded
    Citizens
2501 Avenue J
P. O. Box 6109
Arlington, TX 76011

National Association for Visually
    Handicapped
305 East 24th St.
New York, NY 10010
(212)-889-3141

National Association of Mothers of
    Special Children
9079 Arrowhead Ct.
Cincinnati, OH 45231

National Association of the Physically
    Handicapped
76 Elm St.
London, OH 43140

National Association of Private
    Residential Facilities for the Mentally
    Retarded
6269 Leesburg Pike, Suite B5
Falls Church, VA 22044

National Association of Private Schools
    for Exceptional Children
2021 K St., NW
Washington, DC 20006

National Association of Private Schools
for Exceptional Children
P.O. Box 34293
West Bethesda, MD 20817

National Association of Protection &
Advocacy Systems (NAPAS)
900 Second St., NE, Suite 211
Washington, DC 20002

National Association of Vocational
Education Special Needs Personnel
(NAVESNP)
c/o Athens Technical Inst.
U.S. Highway 29 North
Athens, GA 30610

National Ataxia Foundation
600 Twelve Oaks Center
15500 Wayzata Blvd.
Wayzata, MN 55391
(612) 473-7666

National Center for a Barrier-Free
Environment
1140 Connecticut Ave., Suite 1006
Washington, DC 20036

National Center on Disability Services
(NCDS)
201 I.U. Willets Rd.
Albertson, NY 11507

National Center for Education in
Maternal and Child Care
3520 Prospect St., NW
Washington, DC 20057
(202) 625-8400

National Center on Employment of the
Deaf (NCED) National Technical
Institute for the Deaf
Rochester Institute of Technology
One Lomb Memorial Drive
Rochester, NY 14623

National Center for Law and the
Handicapped
University of Notre Dame
P.O. Box 477
Notre Dame, IN 46556

National Center for Stuttering
200 East 33rd St.
New York, NY 10016
(800) 221-2483

National Center for Youth with
Disabilities Adolescent Health
Program
University of Minnesota
Box 721-UMHC
Harvard St. at East River Rd.
Minneapolis, MN 55455

National Cleft Palate Association &
Education Foundation
331 Salk Hall
University of Pittsburgh
Pittsburgh, PA 15261
(412) 681-9620

National Congress of Organizations of
the Physically Handicapped, Inc.
1627 Deborah Ave.,
Rockford, IL 61103

National Committee on Arts for the
Handicapped
1825 Connecticut Ave., NW
Suite 417
Washington, DC 20009
(202) 332-6960

National Council on Disability
800 Independence Ave., SW,
Suite 814
Washington, DC 20591

National Council on Independent Living
(NCIL)
310 S. Peoria St., Suite 201
Chicago, IL 60607

National Crisis Center for the Deaf
Box 484
UVA Medical Center
Charlottesville, VA 22908
(800) 446-9876

National Down Syndrome Congress
1640 West Roosevelt Rd.
Chicago, IL 60608
(312) 226-0416
(800) 446-3835

National Down Syndrome Society
70 West 40th St.
New York, NY 10018
(800) 221-4602

National Easter Seal Society
2023 W. Ogden Ave.
Chicago, IL 60612

National Federation of The Blind
1800 Johnson St.
Baltimore, MD 21230

National Foundation for Asthma, Inc.
P.O. Box 30069
Tucson, AZ 85751-0069
(602) 323-6046

National Foundation of Dentistry for the
    Handicapped
1250 14th St., Suite 610
Denver, CO 80202
(303) 573-0264

The National Foundation for Ileitis
    Colitis
444 Park Ave. South
New York, NY 10017
(212) 685-3440

National Foundation March of Dimes
1275 Manaroneck Ave.
White Plains, NY 10605
(914) 428-7100

The National Foundation for Peroneal
    Muscular Atrophy
c/o Mr. Robert S. Krutsick
University City Science Center
3624 Market St.
Philadelphia, PA 19104
(215) 387-2255

National Foundation of Wheelchair
    Tennis
4000 MacArthur Blvd.
Newport Beach, CA 92660
(714) 851-1707

National Genetics Foundation, Inc.
555 West 57th St.
New York, NY 10019
(212) 586-5800

National Handicapped Sports
4405 East-West Highway #603
Bethesda, MD 20814

National Head Injury Foundation
1140 Connecticut Ave., SW
Suite 812
Washington, DC 20036

National Health Information
Clearinghouse
P.O. Box 1133
Washington, DC 20013-1133
(800) 336-4797

National Hearing Aid Society
20361 Middlebelt
Livonia, MI 48152
(313) 478-2610
(800) 521-5247

National Hemophilia Foundation
110 Green St.
New York, NY 10012
(212) 563-0211

National Icthyosis Foundation
P.O. Box 252
Belmont, CA 94002
(714) 591-1653

National Information Center on
   Deafness
Gallaudet College
Kendal Green
Washington, DC 20002

National Information Center for
   Educational Media
4320 Mesa Grande, SE
Albuquerque, NM 87108

The National Information Center for
   Orphan Drugs and Rare Diseases
P.O. Box 1133
Washington, DC 20013-1133

National Institute of Child Health and
   Human Development
2A03 Building 31, N.I.H.
Bethesda, MD 20205
(301) 496-3454

National Institute for Rehabilitation
   Engineering
97 Decker Rd.
Butler, NJ 07405
(201) 838-2500

National Library Service for the Blind
   and Physically Handicapped
1291 Taylor Street, NW
Library of Congress
Washington, DC 20542
(202) 287-9286
(202) 287-9287

National Mental Health Association
   (NMHA)
1021 Prince St.
Alexandria, VA 22314-7722

National Mental Health Consumer Self-
   Help Clearinghouse
311 S. Juniper St., Suite 902
Philadelphia, PA 19107

National Multiple Sclerosis Society
205 East 42nd St.
New York, NY 10017
(212) 968-3240

The National Neurofibromatosis
   Foundation, Inc.
70 West 40th St. 4th Floor
New York, NY 10018
(212) 869-9034

National Organization on Disability
   NOD)
910 16th St., NW, Suite 600
Washington, DC 20006

National Organization for Rare
   Disorders
1182 Broadway, Suite 402
New York, NY 10001
(212) 686-1057

National Parent Network on Disabilities
   (NPND)
1600 Prince St., Suite #115
Alexandria, VA 22314-2836

National Rehabilitation Association
633 South Washington St.
Alexandria, VA 22314
(703) 836-0850

National Retinitis Pigmentosa
   Foundation
Rolling Park Bldg.
8311 Mindale Circle
Baltimore, MD 21207

National Society for Children and
   Adults with Autism
1234 Massachusetts Ave., NW
Suite 1017
Washington, DC 20005-4599

National Spinal Cord Injury Association
149 California St.
Newton, MA 02158
(617) 964-0521

National Tay-Sachs and Allied Diseases
Association of New York State
94 Washington Ave.
Cedarhurst, NY 11516

National Therapeutic Recreation
Society/National Recreation and Park
Association
3101 Park Center Dr.
Alexandria, VA 22302

National Tuberous Sclerosis
Association, Inc.
P.O. Box 612
Winfield, IL 60190
(312) 668-0787

National Wheelchair Athletic
Association
40-24 62nd St.
Woodside, NY 11377

North American Riding for the
Handicapped Association, Inc.
P.O. Box 100, R.I.B. 218
Ashburn, VA 22011
(703) 471-1261

The Orton Dyslexia Society
724 York Rd.
Baltimore, MD 21204
(301) 296-0232

Office of Deafness and Communicative
Disorders
Department of Education
Room 3416, Switzer Building
400 Maryland Ave.
Washington, DC 20202

Office of Special Education and
Rehabilitative Services (OSERS)
Department of Education
Switzer Building
330 C St., SW
Washington, DC 20202
(202) 245-8492

Outward Bound
690 Market St.
#500
San Francisco, CA 94101

Parent Educational Advocacy Training
Center (PEATC)
228 S. Pitt St.
Alexandria, VA 22314

Parents Helping Parents (PHP)
535 Race St.
San Jose, CA 95126

Parents of John Tracy Clinic
806 West Adams Blvd.
Los Angeles, CA 90007
(213) 748-5481

Prader-Willi Syndrome Association
5515 Malibu Dr.
Edina, MN 55436
(612) 933-0113

President's Committee on Employment
of People with Disabilities
1111 20th St., NW, Suite 636
Washington, DC 20036

Quebec Association for Children with
Learning Disabilities
5003 Victoria Ave.
Montreal, Quebec, Canada H3W 2NZ

Rehabilitation International USA
20 West 40th St.
New York, NY 10018

The Retinitis Pigmentosa Foundation
Fighting Blindness
8331 Mindale Circle
Baltimore, MD 21207
(301) 655-1011

Sex Information and Education Council
of the U. S.
80 Fifth Ave., Suite 801
New York, NY 10017
(212) 929-2300

Shared Outdoor Adventure Recreation
(SOAR)
P.O. Box 14583
Portland, OR 14583

Sibling Information Network
Department of Educational
Psychology
Box U-64 School of Education
University of Connecticut
Storrs, CT 06268
(203) 486-4034

Society for the Rehabilitation of the
Facially Disfigured
550 First Ave.
New York, NY 10016
(212) 340-6656

Special Education and Rehabilitative
Services Clearinghouse for the
Handicapped
Department of Education
400 Maryland Ave., SW
Switzer Building, Room 3106
Washington, DC 20202

Special Education Software Center
(800) 327-5892
(800) 223-2711

Special Olympics, Inc.
1350 New York Ave., NW, Suite 500
Washington, DC 20005
(202) 628-3630

Specialized Training of Military Parents
(STOMP)
12208 Pacific Highway, SE
Tacoma, WA 98499

Spina Bifida Association of America
343 South Dearborn, Suite 317
Chicago, IL 60604
(800) 621-3141

Task Force on Line Safety and the
Handicapped
P.O. Box 19044
Washington, DC 20036

Technical Assistance for Special
Population Program (TASPP)
National Center for Research in
Vocational Education (NCRVE)
University of Illinois Site
345 Education Building
1310 S. 6th St.
Champaign, IL 61820

Tourette Syndrome Association
41-02 Bell Blvd.
Bayside, NY 11361
(718) 224-2999
or
81 Powhattan
Milford Medical Bldg.
Milford, OH 45150

Tripod-Service for Hearing Impaired
955 North Alfred St.
Los Angeles, CA 90069
(800) 352-8888

Tuberous Sclerosis Association of
America
P.O. Box 44
Rockland, MD 02320

United Cerebal Palsy Association
66 East 34th St.
New York, NY 10016

United Leukodystrophy
44105 Yorkshire Dr.
Wayne, MI 48187-2859

United Ostomy Association, Inc.
2001 West Beverly Blvd.
Los Angeles, CA 90057
(213) 413-5510

Very Special Arts USA Education Office
John F. Kennedy Center for the
Performing Arts
Washington, DC 20566
(202) 322-6960

Western Law Center for the
Handicapped
849 South Broadway, Suite M-22
Los Angeles, CA 90014

Wilderness Inquiry
1313 5th St.
S.E. Box 84
Minneapolis, MN 55414

Williams Syndrome Association
P.O. Box 178373
San Diego, CA 92117-0910
(619) 276-2236

Youth Adult Institute
460 West 34th St.
New York, NY 1001

APPENDIX B

Checklist for Accessibility and Usability of Buildings and Facilities

Yes	No	
		Passenger Arriving-Leaving Space
____	____	Is there a safe place designated for passengers to get into and out of cars (may be on the street or off the street)?
____	____	Is that space zoned to prohibit parking?
____	____	If space is at curbside, is the curb ramped up to the sidewalk?
		Walks
____	____	Are public walks at least 48 inches wide (60 inches needed to facilitate passing where wheelchair traffic is heavy)?
____	____	If a walk is sloped, is the grade not greater than 5 percent (1 foot of rise for 20 feet of length)?
____	____	If there are steps in the walks, are there also ramps to bypass the steps?
____	____	If doors open onto walks, is there a level platform at least 5 feet × 5 feet?
		Parking
____	____	Is parking available for persons with mobility impairment either at end of rows or in diagonal or head-in (perpendicular) stalls 12 feet wide?
____	____	Are pedestrian (wheelchair) inclines or sloped walks provided in place of, or in addition to, curbs and steps from parking area?
		Entrances
____	____	Is there at least one ground level or ramped primary entrance usable by persons in wheelchairs?

Doorways

Yes   No

____   ____   Do doorways have a clear, unobstructed opening of at least 32 inches? (Revolving doors are unacceptable unless accompanied by a side leaf door with 32-inch minimum opening.)

____   ____   If there are two leaf doors side by side, does one leaf provide at least 32 inches of clear opening?

____   ____   Do doors in series (vestibule doors) have at least 84 inches between sets?

____   ____   Are thresholds flush with the floor? If not, are they less than 1/2 inch?

Ramps

____   ____   Do ramps rise no more than 1 foot for every 12 feet of length?

____   ____   Does the ramp have handrails 32 inches from the surface on both sides?

____   ____   Do handrails extend 1 foot beyond the top and bottom of the ramp?

____   ____   For rest and safety, do long ramps and sloped walks have level platforms at least every 30 feet?

Elevators

____   ____   Are elevators accessible on the same level as entrance?

____   ____   If this facility is more than one level (including basement, balcony, etc.) are *all* levels served by an elevator?

____   ____   Does the elevator doorway provide at least 32 inches of clear, unobstructed opening?

____   ____   Is the elevator cab at least 4 feet wide by 6 feet deep?

____   ____   Is the space between the building floor and the elevator floor 1/2 inch or less?

____   ____   Are the controls (including emergency switches and light) no more than 48 inches from the floor?

Stairs

____   ____   Do steps have rounded nosings with sloping risers?

____   ____   Are there handrails on both sides of all stairways?

____   ____   Are stairway handrails mounted 32 inches above front edge of stair tread?

____   ____   Do handrails extend 1 foot beyond top and bottom step?

____   ____   Are step risers no greater than 7 inches in height?

Toilet Room

____   ____   Do doors to toilet room (men *and* women) have at least 32 inches of clear opening?

Yes   No

____   ____   Is there at least one toilet stall that is a minimum of 3 feet wide by 5 feet
                   deep?
____   ____   Does that toilet stall have a doorway with 32 inches of clear opening?
____   ____   Does the toilet stall door swing out?
____   ____   Is that toilet stall also equipped with handrails on both sides, 33 inches
                   from the floor?
____   ____   Is the toilet seat 20 inches from the floor?
____   ____   Will the area from the toilet room entrance to the stall allow a wheel-
                   chair to pass (32 inches of unobstructed space)?
____   ____   Is the bottom edge of at least one mirror no higher than 40 inches above
                   the floor?
____   ____   Are lavatories (sinks) mounted so that persons in wheelchairs can use
                   them (29 inches from floor to top of wheelchair armrest)?
____   ____   Are soap, towel, and other dispensers mounted no higher than 40 inches
                   above the floor?

Tub

____   ____   Is a handrail (grab bar) securely mounted at either the foot or head end
                   of the tub that can easily and safely be reached for getting in and out?
____   ____   Is a handrail mounted parallel to the length of the tub to safely facilitate
                   sitting or rising?
____   ____   Does the bottom of the tub have an abrasive, antislip surface?

Shower

____   ____   Does shower stall doorway have at least 32 inches of clear opening?
____   ____   Is shower stall floor level with room floor without an obstructing riser or
                   curb between?
____   ____   Does shower stall have an anti-slip surface?
____   ____   Is there a handrail on at least one side of the shower stall when facing the
                   shower head and also near the stall entrance to facilitate going in and
                   out?
____   ____   Is there a seat in the shower stall?, (*Note:* A folddown, permanent, or
                   portable seat may be used, but it must have a smooth, easy-to-clean
                   surface. A solid mold toilet seat is recommended.)
____   ____   Is the shower equipped with mixing faucet with nonscalding tempera-
                   ture control valve? (*Note:* A hose-type, detachable shower head is
                   preferable.)

Drinking Fountains

____   ____   Are water fountains both hand and foot operated?

Yes   *No*

_____   _____   On wall-mounted fountains, is the spout not higher than 36 inches from the floor?

_____   _____   On floor-mounted models, is there a side fountain 30 inches from the floor?

Phones

_____   _____   Do telephone booth doorways have 32 inches of clear opening?

_____   _____   Are coin drops not higher than 48 inches from the floor?

_____   _____   Are some phones equipped with receiver volume control for the hard of hearing?

_____   _____   Are phones for the hard of hearing readily identifiable?

Controls

_____   _____   Are switches and controls within reach from wheelchair position (not higher than 48 inches from the floor)?

Warnings for Deaf and Blind

_____   _____   Are there raised letters or numbers for identifying rooms?

_____   _____   Are the numbers at the side of the door 5 feet above the floor?

_____   _____   Are potentially dangerous areas identified by knurled door handle or knob?

_____   _____   Are warning signals both audible and visible?

_____   _____   Are signs, lights, and hazardous hanging objects at least 7 feet above the floor?

Glossary of Terms in Transition Programs and Services

Adult services: Adult services include support services and programs provided by both public and private agencies for persons with disabilities. Usually, these services are provided to individuals after they have exited the school system, but there are times when adult services and schools both provide needed services simultaneously. Most public adult service programs have eligibility requirements that vary across agencies.

Advocacy/legal service needs: Advocacy needs could be as simple as a student's need to learn how to advocate for self more effectively. Students may need specific planning for transition that relates to legal advocacy for them or specific legal services they will need. The individualized education program (IEP) team members and families may need to anticipate needs of current students as adults in the areas of guardianship and conservatorship, estate planning (wills and trusts), or parent surrogates. Planning decisions made for a student with disabilities in relation to certain legal issues may affect eligibility for programs and services. Local legal services or the state advocacy and protection agency may be needed to assist the IEP team.

Assistive technology devices and services: Assistive technology devices and services are not specifically listed in the Individuals with Disabilities Act (IDEA) as a related service, but are often provided as "other corrective or support services" necessary to help students with disabilities benefit from their education and school experience. The Office of Special Education Programs (OSEP) has issued a policy ruling that "consideration of a child's need for assistive technology must occur on a case-by-case basis in connection with the development of a child's individualized education program (IEP)." An assistive technology device is any item, piece of equipment, or product system that is used to increase, maintain, or improve functional capabilities of individuals with disabilities. Assistive technology services include any service that directly assists an individual with a disability in the selection, acquisition, or use of an assistive technology device.

Audiology: Audiology services are generally provided by audiologists who screen, assess, and identify students with hearing loss. Audiological services also include referrals for medical or other professional attention for the habilitation of hearing, auditory training, speech reading, speech conservation, determining the need for group or individual amplification, and selecting and fitting a student for an appropriate hearing aid.

Career planning options: Students are provided with options for making tentative and, ultimately, realistic life-career decisions. Systematic provision of career information in coursework at school, occupational exploration opportunities through field trips and job shadowing experiences, community experiences, and summer camps (art, music, computer, etc.) are examples of career planning options.

Community participation options: Students are provided with opportunities to learn and develop age-appropriate life skills in real-life settings. Community-based experiences could include job training, job or work sample tryouts, living skills instruction, community survival skills, job search and application skills, leisure or recreational skills, and so forth. Instruction and experiences are acquired outside of the school environment (also referred to as *community-based instruction* and *community-based education*).

Counseling services: Counseling services are typically provided by counselors who work with students to develop and improve students' understanding of themselves, their awareness of occupational alternatives, and their social and behavioral skills. Guidance and counseling techniques are used with students to assist them and their families in decision making about school and postschool options.

Employment/job training options: Employment and job training options vary widely due to student interests, needs, and abilities, as well as available employment and training placement alternatives

in a community. Planning by the IEP team should consider employment/job training options for an individual after addressing age, interests, aptitudes, motivation, current functioning level of skills, specific requirements and demands of available placements, transportation issues, and support systems necessary. Employment/ job training options include job shadowing, volunteer work, in-school jobs, on-the-job training, supported employment models, and competitive employment.

Financial assistance/support: Eligibility for certain programs are based on the individual characteristics and needs of each student. Some of the procedures for obtaining financial support are cumbersome and involve lengthy application periods. Planning may focus on need for Social Security Income, Social Security Disability Benefits, Survivor's Benefits, food stamps, HUD Section 8 low-income housing eligibility, Medicaid, public health services, and so forth.

Functional curriculum: A functional curriculum is a purposefully designed program of instruction that focuses on teaching specific skills in daily living, personal and social interactions, and employability. Each individual student will have unique preferences and needs, which require individualization of functional curriculum and instruction. Functional curriculum instruction will occur both within and outside of the school setting.

Functional evaluation: A functional evaluation or assessment process is one that is an organized approach to determining the interests, needs, preferences, and abilities that an individual student has in the domains of daily living skills, personal-social skills, and occupational/employability skills. It is a continuous process, using both formal and informal assessment procedures, that provides a basis for planning and instruction.

Independent living: An expanded view of independent living is that it comprises all the demands of living on one's own. This includes residential choices and skills, economic decisions and money management, time management, maintenance of equipment or technological devices, community mobility, involvement in community activities and citizenship responsibilities, and so forth. Some agencies limit their meaning of this term to residential living, but that is not the case in IDEA.

Individualized education program (IEP): The IEP is a written document required of all individuals in school who have been classified as needing special education programs or related services because of some disabling condition. The document should include the student's present level of functioning in each identified needs area, a statement of annual goals for the student, a statement of appropriate short-term objectives with the evaluation approach and evaluation criteria for determining progress toward achievement of annual goals, a statement of any required related services and who will provide them, a statement of needed transition services (beginning at least by age 16), and a statement that relates to the issue of least restrictive environment for the student relative to each of the programs and services to be provided.

Individualized education program planning meeting: The IEP planning meeting is one that occurs at least once annually. The student's present level of functioning is discussed, progress made since the last meeting (for continuing students) is reviewed, and goals and objectives are established for the next year. Every third year, the IEP planning group will conduct an extensive, in-depth review of the student's status based on the comprehensive reevaluation data.

Individualized education program team: The IEP team is a support and planning group made up of the student, his or her parents or guardians, the student's teacher(s), the person responsible for implementing or supervising the implementation of transition services, a school administrator, relevant school support services personnel, and other relevant agency representatives. The team is charged with the responsibility of developing and implementing an individualized education program for the student, based on his or her needs, interests, and preferences.

Insurance needs: Insurance coverage is active during school years while students are engaged in school programs. Community job training, transportation on field trips, and vocational education shops are examples of school-related insurance planning needs. Insurance needs for postschool life planning frequently include health and accident insurance and automobile liability insurance.

Integrated employment: Integrated employment is viewed in most cases as competitive employment, where a person with disabilities has real work opportunities in settings where the interactions are primarily with people who are nondisabled.

Leisure/recreation needs: Leisure and recreation are critical factors in the long-term success of persons with disabilities. Planning ahead for the skills needed to access and engage in leisure and recreation opportunities is a responsibility of the IEP team. There should be ongoing assessment of interests and encouragement of participation in a variety of activities. Accessing leisure and recreational activities through school clubs, parks and recreation programs, sport leagues, church groups, school and public libraries, and community facilities (movie theaters, bowling alleys, skating rinks, parks, etc.)

should be planning and programming goals.

Living arrangement options: Planning for living options after leaving school depends on a variety of factors, beginning with the abilities and preferences of the student. In addition, the living alternatives vary from community to community. Planning should address the need to provide instruction in the basic skills necessary to take full advantage of the living options that are available. This might include the areas of consumer skills, home management skills (cleaning, cooking, laundry, use of appliances, etc.), safety, and dealing with emergencies. Planning for accessing living arrangement options would address the issues of living at home with parents, supervised apartment living, group home life, adult foster care, independent apartment with assistance services, and independent apartment options.

Medical/mental health needs: Planning for the current and future medical or mental health needs of an individual student must involve the student's family. In cases where parents are not well informed regarding the importance of continuing medical or mental health treatment or support, or of the resources in the community for their son or daughter, the IEP team should consider planning for accessing such resources as Arc-USA health insurance, Medicaid, sliding fee scale services (community mental health centers, public health centers, Easter Seal, March of Dimes, and some drug and alcohol centers), and state rehabilitation services.

Medical services: Medical services are considered a related service only under specific conditions. They are provided by a licensed physician and at the present time services are restricted to diagnostic and evaluation purposes. Services do not include direct, ongoing medical treatment. *(See School health services)*

Occupational therapy: Occupational therapy services are provided by therapists who focus on assessing and training students whose disabilities impair their daily life functioning. Emphasis on motor functioning in everyday living demands helps individual students to be more prepared for functioning in the least restrictive environment.

On-the-job training (OJT): Training that occurs on the actual job site while a person is employed and working at the job is referred to as on-the-job training. Training for both job skills and job-related behaviors are taught within a specific job setting by an employer, supervisor, or a job coach employed specifically for that purpose. OJT may be entry-level or advanced skill training.

Parent counseling and training: Parent counseling and training is an increasingly important related service. Counseling and training may be provided when necessary to help the student with a disability benefit from the school's educational program. Specific areas of counseling and training include assisting parents in understanding the special needs of their child, providing parents with information about child/adolescent development, and providing parents with referrals to parent support groups, financial assistance and resources, and professionals outside the school system.

Personal management needs: Personal management needs overlap several other planning areas for IEP teams. Personal management of money, personal belongings, health care needs, personal hygiene needs, dental hygiene needs, and management and use of time are examples of needs in this area. Desirable personal habits—such as self-control of emotions and behaviors, responsibility, and honesty—are also examples of personal management needs to consider in planning for curriculum and instruction.

Physical therapy: Physical therapy services are provided by a therapist following a referral by a physician or other school or health-related professional. Emphasis is placed on increasing muscle strength, mobility, and endurance, and improving gross motor skills, posture, gait, and body awareness. Therapists may also monitor the function, fit, and proper use of mobility aids and devices.

Postsecondary education or training: Any education program beyond high school that has an academic, vocational, professional, or preprofessional focus is considered postsecondary education.

Postsecondary education or training options: Postsecondary education options include adult education, community college, or college or university programs. Any vocational or technical program beyond high school that does not lead to an associate of arts or baccalaureate degree is considered postsecondary training. Postsecondary training may be obtained in public vocational and technical schools, community college vocational or technical programs, private vocational or technical schools, labor union trades/skills training, military vocational or technical skills training, apprenticeship programs, or state/federal employment training programs. Some of these programs require a license or certificate for an individual before being permitted to practice his or her occupational skills.

Psychological services: Psychological services are usually provided by a school psychologist. In addition to psychological testing and interpretation, school psychologists may obtain and interpret information about a student's behavior and con-

ditions for learning or functioning in school environments. Psychologists consult with school staff, assist in planning individual educational programs, and provide counseling for students and parents or lawful custodians.

Recreation therapy: Recreation therapy is included as a related service because all children with disabilities need to learn how to use their leisure time and recreation time constructively and with enjoyment. For those students who need recreation therapy in order to benefit from their educational experience, the therapy usually focuses on improvement of socialization skills, as well as eye-hand coordination and physical, cognitive, or language skills. Recreation therapists assess students' leisure capacities and functions, give therapy to remediate functional difficulties, provide leisure education, and assist students in accessing leisure/recreation options.

Rehabilitation counseling services: Rehabilitation counseling services is a new related service under IDEA. The services are defined in the regulations as "services provided by qualified personnel in individual or group sessions, that focus specifically on career development, employment preparation, achieving independence, and integration in the work-place and community of a student with a disability." The term also includes "vocational rehabilitation services provided to students with disabilities by vocational rehabilitation programs funded under the Rehabilitation Act of 1973, as amended" [IDEA, Sec. 602(A)(1)].

School health services: School health services are typically provided by a qualified school nurse or a specifically trained non-medical person who is supervised by a qualified nurse. These services are available to those students who would be unable to attend school without such supportive health care and monitoring. Services may include clean intermittent catheterization, special feedings, suctioning, administering of medications, and planning for the safety and well-being of a student while at school.

Self-advocacy needs: IEP planning for self-advocacy needs refers to instruction or related services that will help develop an individual student's skills in assuming responsibility for himself or herself at school and in the community. Skill training for self-advocacy in the IEP meeting is a starting goal that is recommended. Skill training should also include awareness of one's own needs and assertiveness training in other settings. (Also referred to as self-determination).

Social work services in schools: Social work services are provided when the whole welfare of the student with a disability must be addressed. Home, school, and community interactions result in complex problems, and educators may not be able to work effectively alone. Social work services in schools are performed by qualified personnel and are focused on mobilizing school and community resources to enable students to learn as effectively as possible in their school programs.

Socialization opportunities. Successful transitions begin while students are still in school. IEP teams should look at each individual student's social skills with peers with disabilities, peers without disabilities, family members, adults at school and the community, and children. Socialization opportunities can be made a part of the instructional program for a student at first as social skills training, but later as a maintenance activity through program and school activities.

Speech-language pathology: Speech and language pathology services are provided by qualified professionals trained to deal

with communication disorders in students. Speech-language pathologists screen, identify, assess, and diagnose communication problems, provide speech and language corrective services, consult on use of augmentative and alternative communication systems, and refer students for medical or other professional attention necessary for the habilitation of speech and language disorders. It is not necessary for students to be manifesting academic problems in addition to speech or language problems for them to be considered eligible for speech-language pathology services under IDEA.

Supported employment: Supported employment may be ongoing or time limited in nature and may occur in competitive or noncompetitive work environments. Ideally, the supported employment opportunity is within the community in a competitive employment setting, and the individual with a disability is provided only the degree of support that is necessary for him or her to perform the job tasks and maintain the expected behaviors and performance level of the job independently. The level and amount of support are decreased over time in an effort to facilitate the person's independence. Supported employment models include competitive employment with support, enclaves within competitive employment, mobile work crews in the community, specialized sheltered employment, and general sheltered employment.

Transition councils: Transition councils or teams are representative groups of persons at the local level who organize to promote, develop, maintain, and improve secondary special education, transition planning, transition services, and adult services for individuals with disabilities who move from school settings to adult living. The councils or teams are comprised of persons with disabilities, their families, school personnel, adult service agency personnel, and members of the community who can contribute to the mission of the council.

Transition services: Transition services refer to a coordinated set of activities for a student, designed within an outcome-oriented process, that promote movement from school to postschool activities, including postsecondary education, vocational training, integrated employment (including supported employment), continuing and adult education, adult services, independent living, and community participation. The coordinated set of activities shall be based on the individual student's needs, taking into account the student's preferences and interests, and shall include, at a minimum, instruction, community experiences, the development of employment and other postschool adult living objectives. When appropriate, activities will also include acquisition of daily living skills and functional vocational evaluation.

Transportation options. Since transportation is key to mobility in a community, transportation options must be considered and planned for in the IEP. Instructional goals and objectives may be appropriate for skill training in accessing available transportation options. Related services goals and objectives may be needed to provide a transportation option that does not exist. Long-term planning should be initiated to try to ensure that appro-

priate transportation options will be available after the student leaves school. Transportation options include the following examples: driving one's own vehicle, taxi service, public transit service, and elderly/handicapped transportation services.

Transportation services: Transportation services may be a related service provided to those students who need special assistance because of their disabilities or the location of the school relative to their homes. Not all identified special education students are eligible to receive special transportation services. For those who are, the school must provide travel to and from school and between schools, provide travel in and around school buildings, and provide specialized equipment, if required, to meet the special transportation needs of students.

Vocational/technical training: Vocational/technical training is training that may be offered at the secondary or postsecondary level to provide students with specific vocational or technical skills. These programs vary from semiskilled to skilled levels, and include such areas as building trades, industrial trades, printing and graphics production, commercial art, health occupations, cosmetology and barbering, food preparation, office machines, computer programming, marketing and distribution occupations, agriculture and agribusiness, automotive mechanics, and automotive body repair.

References

Abraham, K. G. (1983). Structural/frictional vs. deficient demand unemployment: Some new evidence. *American Economic Review, 73,* 708–724.

Adams, G. L. (1984). *Comprehensive test of adaptive behavior.* Columbus, OH: Charles E. Merrill.

Adelman, H. S. (1972). The resource concept—Bigger than a room. *Journal of Special Education, 6,* 361–367.

Adelson, J. (1986). *Inventing adolescence.* New Brunswick, NJ: Transaction Books.

Affleck, J. Q., Edgar, E., Levine, P., & Kortering, L. (1990). Postschool status of students classified as mildly mentally retarded, learning disabled, or nonhandicapped: Does it get better with time? *Education and Training in Mental Retardation. 25,* 315–324.

Agran, M. (1986a). Analysis of work behavior. In F. R. Rusch (Ed.), *Competitive employment: Issues and strategies* (pp. 153–164). Baltimore: Paul H. Brookes.

Agran, M. (1986b). Observational reporting of work behavior. In F. R. Rusch (Ed.), *Competitive employment: Issues and strategies* (pp. 141–152). Baltimore: Paul H. Brookes.

Alberto, P. A., & Troutman, A. C. (1982). *Applied behavior analysis for teachers.* Columbus, OH: Charles E. Merrill.

Albright, L., & Cobb, R. B. (1988). *Establishing a curriculum-based vocational assessment process.* Alexandria, VA: American Vocational Association.

Alley, G., & Deshler, D. (1979). *Teaching the learning disabled adolescent: Strategies and methods.* Denver: Love Publishing.

Alonso, L. (1988). *Unique educational needs of learners with visual impairments.* East Lansing, MI: Center for Quality Special Education.

Altshuler, K. (1974). The social and psychological development of the deaf child: Problems, their treatment and prevention. *American Annals of the Deaf, 119,* 365–376.

American Assessment Corporation. (n.d.). *Career assessment survey exploration.* Homewood, AL: American Assessment Corporation.

American Association on Mental Deficiency. (1975). *Adaptive behavior scale (school version).* Washington, DC: Author.

American Association on Mental Retardation (1992). *Mental retardation: Definition, classification, and systems of support* (9th ed.). Washington, DC: Author.

American Personnel and Guidance Association. (1974). *Ethical standards.* Washington, DC: Author.

American Vocational Association. (1990). *The AVA guide to the Carl D. Perkins Vocational and Applied Technology Education Act of 1990.* Alexandria, VA: Author.

American Vocational Association. (n.d.). *Vocational-technical terminology.* Washington, DC: Author.

Americans with Disabilities Act of 1990. 42 U.S.C., 12101. (PL101-336).

Anastasi, A. (1976). *Psychological testing* (4th ed.). New York: Macmillian.

Andrasik, F., & Matson, J. L. (1985). Social skills training for the mentally retarded. In L. L'Abate and M. A. Milan (Eds.), *Handbook of social skills training and research, (pp. 418–454).* New York: Wiley & Sons.

Anthony, W. A., Howell, J., & Danley, K. (1984). Vocational rehabilitation of the psychiatrically disabled. In M. Mirabi (Ed.), *The chronically mentally ill: Research and services* (pp. 215–237). New York: SP Medical and Scientific Books.

Appell, L. S., & Hurley, K. M. (1984, January). Individualizing instruction with micro-computer software. *Focus on Exceptional Children, 16*(5), 1–11.

Arbuckle, D. S. (1962). *Pupil personnel services in American schools.* Boston: Allyn and Bacon.

Arbuckle, D. S. (1972, June). The counselor: Who? What? *Personnel and Guidance Journal, 50,* 785–790.

ARC National Research and Demonstration Institute. (1982). *Job development workshop.* Arlington, TX: Association for Retarded Citizens.

Aries, P. (1962). *Centuries of childhood: A social history of family life.* (R. Baltic, Trans.). New York: Vintage.

Arkansas Rehabilitation Research and Training Center. (1978, May). *The role of vocational rehabilitation in independent living.* Proceedings of the Fifth Institute on Rehabilitation Issues, Omaha, Nebraska, May 23–25, 1978. Hot Springs, AK: Author.

Aune, E. P., & Johnson, J. M. (1992). Transition takes teamwork!: A collaborative model for college-bound students with LD. *Intervention in School and Clinic. 27,* 222–227.

Backman, M. E. (n.d.). *Micro-tower.* New York: Institute for the Crippled and Disabled Rehabilitation and Research Center.

Baker, L. D. (1976). Preparing school counselors to work with exceptional students. *School Guidance Worker, 32*(1), 5–9.

Baller, W. R., Charles, D. C., & Miller, E. L. (1967). Mid-life attainment of the mentally retarded: A longitudinal study. *Genetic Psychology Monographs, 75,* 235–329.

Bank-Mikkelson, N. E. (1968). Services for mentally retarded children in Denmark. *Children, 15,* 198–200.

Bateman, B. D. (1967). Visually handicapped children. In N.G. Haring & R. L. Schiefelbusch (Eds.), *Methods in special education* (pp. 257–301). New York: McGraw-Hill.

Bates, P. E. Bronkema, J., Ames, T., & Hess, C. (1992). State level interagency planning models. In F. R. Rusch, L. DeStefano, J. Chadsey-Rusch, L. A. Phelps, & E. Szymanski (Eds.), *Transition from school to adult life: Models, linkages, and policy* (pp. 115–129). Sycamore, IL: Sycamore Publishing.

Bauer, H. (1975). The resource teacher—A teacher consultant. *Academic Therapy, 10,* 299–304.

Baumgart, D., Filler, J., & Askvig, B. (1991). Perceived importance of social skills: A survey of teachers, parents, and other professionals. *The Journal of Special Education, 25*(2), 236–251.

Becker, R. L. (1975). *AAMD-Becker reading-free vocational interest inventory.* Washington, DC: American Association of Mental Deficiency.

Bellamy, G. T., Homer, R., & Inman, D. (1979). *Vocational habilitation of severely retarded adults: A direct service technology.* Baltimore: University Park Press.

Bellamy, G. T. Peterson, L., & Close, D. (1975). Habilitation of the severely and profoundly retarded: Illustrations of competence. *Education and Training of the Mentally Retarded, 10,* 174–186.

Bellamy, G. T., Rhodes, L. E., Mank, D. M., & Albin, J. M. (1988). *Supported employment: A community implementation guide.* Baltimore: Paul H. Brookes.

Bennett, G. K. (1965). *Hand-tool dexterity test.* New York: Psychological Corporation.

Bennett, G. K., Seashore, H. G. & Wesman, A. G. (1982). *Differential aptitude test.* New York: Psychological Corporation.

Benz, M. R., & Halpern, A. S. (1987). Transition services for secondary students with mild disabilities: A statewide perspective. *Exceptional Children, 53,* 507–514.

Benz, M. R., Lindstrom, L. E., Halpern, A. S., & Rothstrom, R. (1991). *Community transition team model: Facilitator's manual.* Eugene: University of Oregon.

Berkeley Planning Associates. (1981). *Final report: Analysis of policies of private sector employers toward the disabled.* (Contract HEW 100-79-0180). Washington, DC: Department of Health and Human Services.

Bernstein, G. S., Van Soest, F., Hansum, D. (1982). A social-interpersonal behavior screening instrument for rehabilitation facilities. *Vocational Evaluation and Work Adjustment Bulletin, 15,* 107–111.

Bijou, S. W. (1966). A functional analysis of retarded development. In N. R. Ellis (Ed.), *International review of research in mental retardation* (Vol. 1, pp. 1–19). New York: Academic Press.

Binzen, P. (1970). *Whitetown, U.S.A.* New York: Random House.

Biological Sciences Curriculum Study. (n.d., a). *Me and my environment.* Northbrook, IL: Hubbard.

Biological Sciences Curriculum Study. (n.d., b). *Me and the future.* Northbrook, IL: Hubbard.

Biological Sciences Curriculum Study. (n.d., c). *Me now.* Northbrook, IL: Hubbard.

Bitter, J. A. (1979). *Introduction to rehabilitation.* St. Louis, C. V. Mosby.

Blackorby, J., Edgar, E., & Kortering, L. (1991). A third of our youth: A look at the problem of school dropout. *Journal of Special Education, 25*(1), 102–113.

Blackorby, J., Kortering, L., Edgar, E., & Emerson, J. (1987, August). *Dropouts from special education.* Unpublished paper. Career Vocational Education, University of Washington, Seattle.

Bodner, J., Clark, G. M., & Mellard, D. F. (1987, November). *State graduation policies and program practices related to high school special education programs: A national study.* A report from the National Study of High School Programs for Handicapped Youth in Transition. Lawrence: University of Kansas, Department of Special Education.

Bolton, B. (Ed.). (1987). *Handbook of measurement and evaluation in rehabilitation* (2nd ed.) Baltimore: Paul H. Brookes.

Bordin, E. S. (1946). Diagnosis in counseling and psychotherapy. *Education and Psychological Measurement, 6,* 169–184.

Botterbusch, K. F. (1982). *A comparison of commercial vocational evaluation systems* (2nd ed.). Menomonie, WI: Materials Development Center, Stout Vocational Rehabilitation Institute.

Botterbusch, K. F., & Michael, N. (1985). *Testing and test modification in vocational evaluation.* Menomonie, WI: Materials Development Center, Stout Vocational Rehabilitation Institute.

Bowe, F. (1983). Accessible transportation. In N. M. Crewe, I. K. Zola, & Associates (Eds.), *Independent living for physically disabled people.* (pp. 205–218). San Francisco: Jossey-Bass.

Bowe, F. G., Jacobi, J. E., & Wiseman, L. K. (1978). *Coalition building.* Washington, DC: American Coalition of Citizens with Disabilities.

Bower, E. M. (1969). *Early identification of emotionally handicapped children in school* (2nd ed.). Springfield, IL: Charles C. Thomas.

Boyer, E. L. (1983). *High school: A report on secondary education in America.* New York: Harper and Row.

Bragman, R., & Cole, J. C. (1984). *Jobmatch: A process for interviewing and hiring qualified handicapped individuals.* Alexandria, VA: American Society for Personnel Administration.

Brantlinger, E. (1992). Sexuality education in the secondary special education curriculum: Teachers' perspectives and concerns. *Teacher Education and Special Education, 15*(1), 32–40.

Brantman, M. (1978). What happens to insurance rates when handicapped people come to work? *Disabled Today, 1*(8), 16–17.

Brewer, J. M. (1932). *Education as guidance.* New York: Macmillan.

Brigance, A. H. (1981). *Brigance inventory of basic skills.* North Billerica, MA: Curriculum Associates.

Brodhead-Garrett Company. (n.d.). *Vocational skills assessment and development program.* Cleveland, OH: Author.

Brolin, D. E. (1974). Programming retarded in career education (Project PRICE), Working Paper No. 1. The University of Missouri-Columbia.

Brolin, D. E. (1976). *Vocational preparation of retarded citizens.* Columbus, OH: Charles E. Merrill.

Brolin, D. E. (1978). *Life centered career education: A competency based approach.* Reston, VA: The Council for Exceptional Children.

Brolin, D. E. (1982). *Vocational preparation of persons with handicaps* (2nd ed.). Columbus, OH: Charles E. Merrill.

Brolin, D. E. (1983). *Life centered career education: A competency based approach* (rev. ed.). Reston, VA: The Council for Exceptional Children.

Brolin, D. E. Personal communication, March 1988.

Brolin, D. E. (1988, August). Are we denying special education students a proper education? *The Career Ed-Ucator, 3*(2), 1. (Newsletter of the Career Development Projects, Department of Educational and Counseling Psychology, University of Missouri-Columbia.)

Brolin, D. E. (1989). *Life centered career education: A competency based approach* (3rd ed.). Reston, VA: The Council for Exceptional Children.

Brolin, D. E. (1992a). *Life centered career education (LCCE) curriculum program.* Reston, VA: The Council for Exceptional Children.

Brolin, D. E. (1992b). *Life centered career education (LCCE) knowledge and performance batteries.* Reston, VA. The Council for Exceptional Children.

Brolin, D. E., & D'Alonzo, B. J. (1979). Critical issues in career education for handicapped students. *Exceptional Children, 45,* 246–253.

Brolin, D. E., & Gysbers, N. C. (1989). Career education for students with disabilities. *Journal of Counseling and Development, 68,* 155–159.

Brolin, D. E., & Kokaska, C. J. (1979). *Career education for handicapped children and youth.* Columbus, OH: Charles E. Merrill.

Brolin, D. E., & Kolstoe, O. P (1978). *The career and vocational development of handicapped learners.* The ERIC Clearinghouse on Adult, Career and Vocational Education, Ohio State University.

Brolin, D. E., & Thomas, B. (Eds.). (1971). *Preparing teachers for secondary level educable mentally retarded: A new model*. Final report. University of Wisconsin-Stout, Menomonie.

Bronson, D. B. (1983). Education, writing and the brain. *Education Forum, 46*, 327–335.

Brown, J. M., & Kayser, T. F. (1985). A proposed model for reducing dropout rates among students in postsecondary vocational education programs. *Journal of Industrial Teacher Education, 22*(4), 38–45.

Brown, L., Halpern, A. S., Hasazi, S. B., & Wehman, P. (1987). From school to adult living: A forum on issues and trends. *Exceptional Children, 53*, 546–554.

Brozovich, R., & Kotting, C. (1984). Teacher perceptions of high school special education programs. *Exceptional Children, 50*, 548–550.

Bruininks, R. H., Hill, B. K., Lakin, K. C., & White, C. C. (1985). *Residential services for adults with developmental disabilities.* Logan: Utah State University Developmental Center for Handicapped Persons.

Bruininks, R. H., & Lakin, K. C. (1985). Perspectives and prospects for social and educational integration. In R. H. Bruininks & K. C. Lakin (Eds.), *Living and learning in the least restrictive alternative* (pp. 263–278). Baltimore: Paul H. Brookes.

Bruininks, R. H., Lewis, D. R., & Thurlow, M. L. (1989, January). *Assessing outcomes, costs and benefits of special education programs* (Report Number 88-1). Minneapolis: University of Minnesota, Department of Educational Psychology, University Affiliated Program on Development Disabilities.

Bruininks, R. H., Woodcock, R. W., Weatherman, R. F., & Hill, B. (1984). *Scales of independent behaivior.* Allen, TX: DLM Teaching Resources.

Bryan, D. P., & Herjanic, B. (August, 1980). Depression and suicide among adolescents and young adults with selective handicapping conditions. *Exceptional Education Quaterly, 1*(2), 57–65.

Bryan, T. (1986). Personallity and situational factors in learning disabilities. In G. Pavlidis & D. Fisher (Eds.), *Dyslexia: its neuropsychology and treatment* (pp. 215-230). New York: John Wiley.

Buckley, J., & Bellamy, G. T. (1985). *National survey of day and vocational programs for adults with severe disabilities. A 1984 profile.* Unpublished manuscript. Baltimore, MD: The Johns Hopkins University.

Budoff, M., & Hutton, L. R. (1982). Microcomputers in special education: Promises and pitfalls. *Exceptional Children, 49*, 123–128.

Bullis, M., & Reiman, J. (1992). Development and preliminary psychometric properties of the Transition Competence Battery for Deaf Adolescents and Young Adults. *Exceptional Children, 59*, 12–26.

Bureau of Labor Statistics. (1986). *Occupational outlook handbook, 1986–87 edition.* Bulletin 2250. Washington, DC: U.S. Government Printing Office.

Burks, H. M., Jr., & Stefflre, B. (1979). *Theories of counseling* (3rd ed.). New York: McGraw-Hill.

Burns, M. A. (1984). *Deriving strengths and weaknesses for career/vocational planning from academic achievement assessment.* Unpublished manuscript. Department of Special Education, University of Kansas, Lawrence.

Bursuck, W. D., Rose, E., Cowen, S., & Yahaya, M. A. (1989). Nationwide survey of postsecondary education services for students with learning disabilities. *Exceptional Children, 56*, 236–245.

Buscaglia, L. F. (1972). *Love in the classroom.* Thorofare, NJ: C. B. Slack.

Butler, A. J., & Browning, P. L. (1974). Predictive studies on rehabilitation outcomes with the retarded. In P. L. Browning (Ed.), *Mental retardation: Rehabilitation and counseling* (pp. 198–227). Springfield, IL: Charles C. Thomas.

Byrne, R. H. (1958). Proposed revisions of the Bordin-Pepinsky diagnostic constructs. *Journal of Counseling Psychology, 5,* 184–187.

Cain, E. J., Jr., & Taber, F. M. (1987). *Educating disabled people for the 21st century.* Boston: Little, Brown.

California Test Bureau/McGraw-Hill. (1969). *Tests of adult basic education.* Monterey, CA: Author.

Campbell, D. P., & Hansen, J. C. (1981). *Strong-Campbell interest inventory.* Palo Alto, CA: Consulting Psychologists Press.

Campbell, J. D. (1964). Peer relations in childhood. In M. L. Hoffman & L. W. Hoffman (Eds.), *Review of child development research* (289–322). New York: Russell Sage Foundation.

Caplin, M. (1969). The relationship between self concept and academic achievement. *Journal of Experimental Education, 37,* 13–16.

Career Education Implementation Incentive Act of 1977, Public Law 95–207.

Career Research Corporation. (n.d.). *Carrels for hands-on individualized career exploration.* Salt Lake City, UT: Author.

Carkhuff, R. R. (1969). *Helping and human relations.* (Vols. I and II). New York: Holt, Rinehart and Winston.

Carkhuff, R. R. (1972). *The art of helping.* Amherst, MA: Human Resource Development Press.

Carkhuff, R. R., & Berenson, B. G. (1976). *An introduction to counseling and psychotherapy.* Amherst, MA: Human Resource Development Press.

Carkhuff, R. R., Pierce, R. M., & Cannon, J. R. (1977). *The art of helping III.* Amherst, MA: Human Resource Development Press.

Carl D. Perkins Vocational Education Act of 1984, Public Law 98–524, 98 STAT., 24345–2491.

Carl D. Perkins Vocational and Applied Technology Education Act of 1990, Public Law 101–392, 20 U.S.C., 2301.

Carnegie Council of Policy Studies in Higher Education. (1979). *Giving youth a better chance: Options for education, work, and service.* San Francisco: Jossey-Bass.

Carnegie Foundation for the Advancement of Teaching. (1909, October). *Fourth annual report of the president and of the treasurer.* New York: Author.

Carpignano, J. L., Sirvis, B., & Bigge, J. L. (1982). Psychosocial aspects of physical disability. In J. L. Bigge (Ed.), *Teaching individuals with physical and multiple disabilities* (2nd ed., pp. 110–-137). Columbus, OH: Charles E. Merrill.

Cartledge, G., & Milburn, J. F. (1986). *Teaching social skills to children.* Elmsford, NY: Pergamon Press.

Cetron, M. J. (1983). Getting ready for the jobs of the future. *The Futurist, 17*(3), 15–22.

Cetron, M. J., & Appel, M. (1984). *Jobs of the future—Where they'll be and how to get them.* New York: McGraw-Hill.

Chadsey-Rusch, J. (1986). Identifying and teaching valued social behaviors. In F. R. Rusch (Ed.), *Competitive employment: Issues and strategies* (pp. 273–287). Baltimore: Paul H. Brookes.

Chadsey-Rusch, J. (1988). *Social ecology of the workplace.* The Secondary Transition Intervention Effectiveness Institute, College of Education, University of Illinois at Urbana-Champaign.

Chadsey-Rusch, J., & O'Reilly, M. (1992). Social integration and social skills training—Is there a relationship? In S. Z. Sacks, M. Hirsch, & R. Gaylord-Ross (Eds.), *The status of social skills training in special education and rehabilitation: Present and future trends* (Chapter 5). Monograph supported by the National Institute on Disability Research, Grant No. H133G0096, Special Education Department, Peabody Teachers College of Vanderbilt University.

Chadsey-Rusch, J., & Rusch, F. R. (1987). The ecology of the workplace. In R. Gaylord-Ross (Ed.), *Vocational educa-*

tion for persons with special needs (pp. 234–256). Palo Alto, CA: Mayfield.

Chaffin, J. D. (1967). *Production rate: A variable in the job success or failure of educable mentally retarded adolescents.* Unpublished doctoral dissertation. University of Kansas, Lawrence.

Chaffin, J. D. (1968). *A community transition program for the mentally retarded.* Final Report RII NHO 1731, Parsons State Hospital and Training Center, Parsons, Kansas (supported in part by Social Rehabilitation Services, U.S. Department of Health, Education, and Welfare).

Chaffin, J. D., Spellman, C. R., Regan, C. E., & Davison, R. (1971). Two follow-up studies of former educable mentally retarded students from the Kansas work study project. *Exceptional Children, 37,* 733–738.

Chandler, H. (1983). If we're really on our way, shouldn't we use a roadmap? *Journal of Learning Disorders, 16,* 54–56.

Charles, C. M. (1980). *Individualizing instruction* (2nd ed.). St. Louis, MO: C. V. Mosby.

Chesler, B. (1982, July–August). ACLD committee survey on LD adults. *ACLD Newsbrief, 145,* 1, 5.

Clarendon Press. (1961). *The Oxford English dictionary.* Vol. 11 Oxford, England: Author.

Clark, G. M. (1974). Career education for the mildly handicapped. *Focus on Exceptional Children, 5*(9), 1–10.

Clark, G. M. (1975a). Mainstreaming for the secondary educable mentally retarded: Is it defensible? *Focus on Exceptional Children, 7*(2), 2–5.

Clark, G. M. (1975b). *Prevocational evaluation in secondary special education work/study programs.* Lawrence: University of Kansas Habilitation Personnel Training Project.

Clark, G. M. (1979). *Career education for the handicapped child in the elementary classroom.* Denver: Love Publishing.

Clark, G. M. (1980, August). Career preparation for handicapped adolescents: A matter of appropriate education. *Exceptional Education Quarterly, 1*(2), 11–17.

Clark, G. M. (1981). Career and vocational education. In G. Brown, R. L. McDowell, & J. Smith (Eds.), *Educating adolescents with behavior disorders* (pp. 326–346). Columbus, OH: Charles E. Merrill.

Clark, G. M. (1982). Career and vocational programming. In E. L. Meyen (Ed.), *Exceptional children and youth* (2nd ed.) (pp. 144–167). Denver: Love Publishing.

Clark, G. M., Carlson, B. C., Fisher, S., Cook, I. D., & D'Alonzo, B. J. (1991). Career development for students with disabilities in elementary schools: A position statement of the Division on Career Development. *Career Development for Exceptional Individuals, 14,* 109–120.

Clark, G. M., & Evans, R. N. (1976). Preparing vocational and special education personnel to work with special needs students: A state of the art. In E. K. Abbas & P. L. Sitlington (Eds.), *Issues in the preparation of personnel for the vocational programming of special needs students* (pp. 2–14). University of Illinois, Urbana-Champaign.

Clark, G. M., & Knowlton, H. E. (1988). A closer look at transition for the 1990s: A Response to Rusch and Menchetti. *Exceptional Children, 54,* 365–367.

Clark, G. M., Knowlton, H. E., & Dorsey, D. (1989). Special education for high school students with educational handicaps in a rural setting: A Vermont case study. In H. E. Knowlton & G. M. Clark (Eds.), *National study of high school special education programs for handicapped youth in transition: Volume 1, Qualitative component.*

Lawrence: University of Kansas, Department of Special Education.

Clark, G. M., & Oliverson, B. S. (1973). Education of secondary personnel: Assumptions and preliminary data. *Exceptional Children, 39,* 541–546.

Clark, G. M., & White, W. J. (1980). *Career education for the handicapped: Current perspectives for teachers.* Boothwyn, PA: Education Resources Center.

Cobb, H. V (1972). *The forecast of fulfillment: A review of research on predictive assessment of the adult retarded for social and vocational adjustment.* New York: Columbia University Teachers College Press.

Cobb, R. B. (1983). Curriculum-based vocational assessment. *Teaching Exceptional Children, 15,* 216–219.

Cobb, R. B., & Phelps, L. A. (1983). Analyzing individualized education programs for vocational components: An exploratory study. *Exceptional Children, 50,* 62–63.

Cobb, R. B., & Larkin, D. (1985, March). Assessment and placement of handicapped pupils into secondary vocational education programs. *Focus on Exceptional Children, 17*(7), 1–14.

Cochran, L. H., Phelps, L. A., & Cochran, L. L. (1980). *Advisory committees in action: An educational/occupational/community partnership.* Boston: Allyn and Bacon.

Collins, B. C., Wolery, M., & Gast, D. L., (1991). A survey of safety concerns for students with special needs. *Education and Training in Mental Retardation, 26*(3), 305–318.

Combs, A. (1962). A perceptual view of the adequate personality. In *Perceiving, behaving, becoming.* Washington, DC: Association for Supervision and Curriculum Development Year Book.

Community colleges and students with disabilities. (n.d.). Alexandria, VA: American Association of Community and Junior Colleges.

Comprehensive Employment and Training Act of 1973, Public Law 93–203, U.S. C. 29 874, 918, 919. (1976).

Comprehensive Employment and Training Act Amendments of 1978, Public Law 95–524, U.S.C. 29 893, 899, 906, 942, 991: Supplement V. (1981).

Conley, R. W. (1985). Impact of federal programs on the employability of mentally retarded persons. In K. C. Lakin & R. H. Bruininks (Eds), *Strategies for achieving community integration of developmentally disabled citizens* (pp. 193–216). Baltimore: Paul H. Brookes.

Connolly, A., Pritchett, M., & Nachman, W. (1971). *KeyMath diagnostic arithmetic test.* Circles Pines, MN: American Guidance Service, Inc.

Conover Company, Ltd. (n.d.). *Microcomputer evaluation of career areas.* Omro, WI: Author.

Coopersmith, S. (1981). *Self-esteem inventory.* Palo Alto, CA: Consulting Psychologists Press.

Covill-Servo, J., & Garrison, W. (1978). *Personal-social needs assessment.* Unpublished paper. Rochester, NY: National Technical Institute for the Deaf.

Coyle-Williams, M., & Maddy-Bernstein, C. (1991, December). The 1990 Perkins: Evaluating and improving program effectiveness. *TASPP Brief, 3*(3), 1–6. National Center for Research in Vocational Education, University of California, Berkeley at the University of Illinois at Urbana-Champaign.

Crawford, J. E., & Crawford, D. M. (1956). *Crawford small parts dexterity test.* New York: Psychological Corporation.

Crewe, N. M., & Athelstan, G. T. (1984). *Functional assessment inventory manual.* Menomonie: Materials Development Center, University of Wisconsin-Stout.

Crites, J. O. (1981). *Career counseling: Models, methods, and materials.* New York: McGraw–Hill.

Cruickshank, W M., & Paul, J. L. (1980). *Psychology of exceptional children and youth* (4th ed.). Englewood Cliffs, NJ: Prentice Hall.

Culatta, R., & Culatta, B. K. (1981). Communication disorders. In A. E. Blackhurst & W. H. Berdine (Eds.), *An introduction to special education* (pp. 145–181). Boston: Little, Brown.

Culver, J. B., Spencer, K. C., & Gliner, J. A. (1990). Prediction of supported employment placements by job developers. *Education and Training in Mental Retardation, 25*(3), 237–242.

Daniels, LeG. S. (1988). Personal communication. Office for Civil Rights of the Department of Education, Washington, DC.

Daniels, M. H. (1985). Vocational exploration and insight kit. [Review of *Vocational exploration and insight kit*]. *The ninth mental measurements yearbook* (Vol 2 pp 1675–1676). Lincoln, NE: Buros Institute of Mental Measurement, University of Nebraska-Lincoln.

Danley, K. S., & Anthony, W A. (1987). The choose-get-keep model: Serving severely psychiatrically disabled people. *American Rehabilitation, 13*(4), 6–9, 27–29.

Darrow, M. A. (1990). *A Delphi approach to cross-validation of Halpern's general transition follow-along model for persons with disabilities.* Doctoral dissertation, University of Kansas, Lawrence, KS.

Darrow, M. A., & Clark, G. M. (1992). Cross-state comparisons of former special education students: Evaluation of a follow-along model. *Career development for Exceptional Individuals, 15,* 83-99.

deBettencourt, L., Zigmond, N., & Thorton, H. S. (1989). Follow-up of post-secondary age rural learning disabled graduates and dropouts. *Exceptional Children, 56,* 40–49.

DeJong, G. (1980). The historical and current reality of independent living: Implications for administrative planning. In S. J. Sigman (Ed.), *Policy planning and development in independent living* (pp. 2–6). Proceedings of a Region V Workshop presented by the University Center for International Rehabilitation/ USA, Michigan State University, East Lansing.

DeJong, G. (1983). Defining and implementing the independent living concept. In N. M. Crewe, I. K. Zola, & Associates (Eds.), *Independent living for physically disabled people* (pp. 4–27). San Francisco: Jossey-Bass.

DeLoach, C., & Greer, B. (1981). *Adjustment to severe disability: A metamorphosis.* New York: McGraw-Hill.

Department of Education. (1991). *Thirteenth annual report to Congress on the implementation of the Individuals with Disabilities Education Act.* Washington, D. C.: U.S. Government Printing Office.

DeProspo, C. J., & Hungerford, R. H. (1946). A complete social program for the mentally retarded. *American Journal of Mental Deficiency, 51,* 115–122.

Descoeudres, A. (1928). *The education of mentally defective children* (E. F. Row, Trans.). Boston: D. C. Heath.

Deshler, D. D., Lowrey, N., & Alley, G. R. (1979). Programming alternatives for learning disabled adolescents: A nationwide survey. *Academic Therapy, 14,* 389–397.

Deshler, D. D., & Schumaker, J. B. (1987). An instructional model for teaching strategies on how to learn. In J. L. Graden, J. E. Zins, & M. J. Curtis (Eds.), *Alternative educational delivery systems: Enhancing instructional options for all students* (pp. 391–411). Washington, DC: National Association of School Psychologists.

Dever, R. B. (1985). *Taxonomy of instructional goals and objectives for developmentally disabled learners.* (Field Test

Version). Bloomington: Indiana University Center for Innovation in Teaching the Handicapped.

Dever, R. B. (1989). A taxonomy of community living skills. *Exceptional Children, 55,* 395–404.

Diana v. State Board of Education of California. C-70 37 RFP. District Court of Northern California (1970).

Dinger, J. C. (1961). Post school adjustment of former educable retarded pupils. *Exceptional Children, 27,* 353–360.

Disability Statistics Abstract (1991, December). Disability Statistics Program, School of Nursing, University of California, San Francisco, CA.

Domino, G. (1978). *AAMD-Becker reading-free interest inventory.* [Review of AAMDBecker reading-free interest inventory]. In O. K. Buros (Ed.), *The eighth mental measurements yearbook* (Vol 2, pp 1536–1538). Highland Park, NJ: Gryphon Press.

Doyle, W. C. (1971). *Functions of special education counselors.* ERIC Document Reproduction Service No. ED 065 956.

Duchardt, B. A. (1992). *A strategic intervention for identifying and changing ineffective beliefs for students with learning disabilities.* Unpublished doctoral dissertation, University of Kansas.

Dugdale, R. L. (1910). *The Jukes: A study of crime, pauperism, disease, and heredity.* New York: Putnam.

Duncan, J. (1943). *The education of the ordinary child.* New York: Ronald Press.

Dunn, D. J., & Kruel, D. L. (1976). *A quantitative approach to observation in rehabilitation facilities: Developing a normed behavior observation system.* Menomonie, WI: Stout Vocational Rehabilitation Institute.

Dunn, L. M. (1968). Special education for the mildly retarded: Is much of it justifiable? *Exceptional Children, 35,* 5–22.

Dunn, L. M. (Ed.). (1973). *Exceptional children in the schools: Special educa-tion in transition* (2nd ed.). New York: Holt, Rinehart and Winston.

Dunn, R., & Dunn, K. (1978). *Teaching students through their individual learning styles: A practical approach.* Reston, VA: Reston Publishing Company.

Easterlin, A. (1980). *Birth and fortune.* New York: Basic Books.

Edgar, E. (1987). Secondary programs in special education: Are many of them justifiable? *Exceptional Children, 53,* 555–561.

Edgar, E. (1988, September). Employment as an outcome for mildly handicapped students: Current status and future directions. *Focus on Exceptional Children, 2*(1), 1–8.

Edgar, E. (1992). Secondary options for students with mild intellectual disabilities: Facing the issue of tracking. *Education and Training in Mental Retardation, 27,* 101–111.

Edgar, E., Horton, B., & Maddox, M. (1984). Postschool placements: Planning for public school students with developmental disabilities. *Journal for Vocational Special Needs Education, 6*(2), 15–18, 26.

Edgar, E., Levine, P., & Maddox, M. (1986). *Statewide follow-up studies of secondary special education students in transition.* Working Paper of the Networking and Evaluation Team, CDM-RC, University of Washington, Seattle.

Edgerton, R. B. (Ed.). (1984). *Lives in process: Mildly retarded adults in a large city.* (Monograph No. 6). Washington, DC: American Association on Mental Deficiency.

Education for All Handicapped Children Act of 1975, Public Law 94–142, 20 U.S.C. 1410(i), 1412(2),(A), 1414(a)(i)(C), (1982).

Education for the Handicapped Act Amendments of 1983, Public Law 98–199, 97 STAT., 1357–1377.

Education of the Handicapped, October 23, 1991, *17*(22).

Educational Policies Commission. (1938). *Current school objectives.* Washington, DC: National Education Association.

Educational Testing Service. (1979). *Program for assessing youth employment skills.* Cambridge, MA: The Adult Education Co.

Ehren, B. J., Lenz, B. K., & Swanson, S. (1986, December). *Florida dropout identification system: The research and validation project of the model school adjustment programs. Final report.* Florida Atlantic University, Boca Raton, FL.

E. I. du Pont de Nemours and Company. (1982). *Equal to the task.* Wilmington, DE: Author.

Eigenbrood, R., & Retish, P. (1988). Work experience employers' attitudes regarding the employability of special education students. *Career Development for Exceptional Individuals, 11*(1), 15–25.

Elksnin, L. K., & Elksnin, N. (1990). Using collaborative consultation with parents to promote vocational programming. *Career Development for Exceptional Individuals, 13,* 135–142.

Elliott, B. (1987). *Transition definition for parents.* Resource guide for parents developed through OSERS Grant No. G008530177. Educational Service Unit No. 9, Hastings, NE.

Ellner, J. R., & Bender, H. E. (1980). *Hiring the handicapped.* New York: AMACOM.

Elrod, F. G., & Sorgenfrei, T. B. (1988). Toward an appropriate assessment model for adolescents who are mildly handicapped: Let's not forget transition. *Career Development for Exceptional Individuals, 11* (2), 92–98.

Elrod, F. G., Sorgenfrei, T. B., & Gibson, A. P. (1991). The degree of agreement between the expressed and scale-determined career interests of adolescents with mild handicaps. *Career Development for Exceptional Individuals, 12*(2), 107–116.

Encyclopedia of Education. (1971). Public high school, United States. *Encyclopedia of Education* (Vol. 7). New York: Macmillian

Epstein, M. H., & Cullinan, D. (1992). Assessment practices used in programs for adolescents with behavior disorders. *Preventing School Failure, 36* (3), 20–25.

Eskridge, C. S., & Partridge, D. L. (1963). Vocational rehabilitation for exceptional children through special education. *Exceptional Children, 29,* 452–458.

Everson, J. M., & McNulty, K. (1992). Interagency teams: Building local transition programs through parental and professional partnerships. In F. R. Rusch, L. DeStefano, J. Chadsey-Rusch, L. A. Phelps, & E. Szymanski (Eds.), *Transition from school to adult life: Models, linkages, and policy* (pp. 341–351). Sycamore, IL: Sycamore.

Ewing, N. J., & Smith, J. E., Jr. (1981). Minimum competency testing and the handicapped. *Exceptional Children, 47,* 523–524.

Experience Education. (n.d.). *Project discovery.* Red Oak, IA: Author.

Fadely, D. C. (1987). *Job coaching in supported work programs.* Menomonie, WI: University of Wisconsin-Stout, Materials Development Center, Stout Vocational Rehabilitation Institute.

Fafard, M. B., & Haubrich, P. A. (1981). Vocational and social adjustment of learning disabled young adults: A follow-up study. *Learning Disabilities Quarterly, 4*(2), 122–130.

Fair, G. (1980). Employment opportunities in the 80's for special needs students. *Journal of Vocational Special Needs Education, 3*(1), 18–20.

Fairweather, J. S., & Shaver, D. M. (1991). Making the transition to postsecondary education and training. *Exceptional Children, 57,* 264–270.

Falvey, M., Brown, L., Lyon, S., Baumgart, D., & Schroeder, J. (1980). Strategies for using cues and correction procedures. In W. Sailor, B. Wilcox, & L. Brown (Eds.), *Methods of instruction for severely handicapped students* (pp. 109–133). Baltimore: University Park Press.

Federal Register. (1975). Implementation of Part B of the Education of the Handicapped Act. Washington, DC: Department of Health, Education, and Welfare, Office of Education.

Federal Register (August 23, 1977). Implementation of Part B of the Education of the Handicapped Act, 42(163), p. 42488, 1212.305.

Federal Register (October 12, 1977). 45 CFR Part 104.512.

Federal Register (August 14, 1987). 34 CFR, Part 363, pp. 30546–30552.

Feingold, S. N. (1984). Emerging careers: Occupations for post-industrial society. *The Futurist, 18*(1), 9–16.

Fimian, M. J., & Goldstein, S. A. (1983). Formative evaluation and data management systems for LBP adolescents. In B. J. D'Alonzo (Ed.), *Educating adolescents with learning and behavior problems* (pp. 261–313). Rockville, MD: Aspen.

Findley, W. (1967). *A follow-up of the financial assets and liabilities of mentally retarded youth as related to the cost of vocational training in the public schools.* Unpublished doctoral dissertation, University of Northern Colorado.

Fisher, D. C. (1913). *The Montessori manual.* Chicago: W. E. Richardson Co.

Fitts, W. H. (1965). *Tennessee self-concept scale.* Nashville, TN: Counselor Recordings and Tests.

Flesch, R. (1951). *How to test readability.* New York: Harper and Row.

Foss, G., & Peterson, S. L. (1981). Social-interpersonal skills relevant to job tenure for mentally retarded adults. *Mental Retardation, 19*, 103–106.

Foster, C. R., Fitzgerald, P. W., & Beal, R. M. (1980). *Modern guidance practices in teaching.* Springfield, IL: Charles C. Thomas.

Fox, C. L. (1980). *Communicating to make friends.* Rolling Hill Estates, CA: B. L. Winch & Associates.

Frederickson, R. H. (1982). *Career information.* Englewood Cliffs, NJ: Prentice Hall.

Freeland, K. H. (1969). *High school work-study program for the mentally retarded.* Springfield, IL: Charles C. Thomas.

Frieden, L. (1983). Understanding alternative program models. In N. M. Crewe, I. K. Zola, and Associates (Eds.), *Independent living for physically disabled people* (pp. 62–72). San Francisco: Jossey-Bass.

Fry, E. (1977). Fry's readability graph: clarification, validity, and extension to level 17. *Journal of Reading, 21*, 249.

Fry, R. (1986). *Work evaluation and adjustment: An annotated bibliography.* Menomonie, WI: Materials Development Center, University of Wisconsin-Stout.

Galagan, J. (1985). Psychoeducational testing: Turn out the lights, the party's over. *Exceptional Children, 52*, 288–299.

Gallagher, J. J. (1992). Education as a weak treatment. *Teaching Exceptional Children, 24*(4), 5.

Galloway, J. B. (1979). *Competency testing, special education, and the awarding of diplomas.* Washington, DC: National Association of State Directors of Special Education (ERIC Document Reproduction Service No. ED 185 785).

Gardner, J. (1987). *Transition from high school to postsecondary education.* Washington, DC: U.S. Department of Education.

Gardner, J. F., Chapman, M. S., Donaldson, G., & Jacobson, S. G. (1988). *Toward supported employment: A process guide for planned change.* Baltimore: Paul H. Brookes.

Gaylord-Ross, R. (1988). *Vocational education for persons with handicaps.* Mountain View, CA: Mayfield Publishing.

Gearheart, B. R. (1980). *Special education for the '80's.* St. Louis: C. V. Mosby.

Getzel, E. E., Salin, J. A., & Wacher, G. B. (1986). Developing local agreements. In L. W. Tindall (Ed.), *Handbook on developing effective linking strategies.* Madison: Vocational Studies Center, University of Wisconsin-Madison.

Gillet, P. (1980). Career education in special elementary education programs. *Teaching Exceptional Children, 13*(1), 17–20.

Gillet, P. (1981). Career education for exceptional children and youth. *Of work and worth: Career education for the handicapped.* Salt Lake City: Olympus Publishing.

Ginzberg, E., Ginsburg, S. W., Axelrad, S., & Herma, J. L. (1951). *Occupational choice.* New York: Columbia University Press.

Glaser, R. (1963). Instructional technology and the measurement of learning outcomes: Some questions. *American Psychologist, 18,* 519–521.

Glasser, W. (1969). *Schools without failure,* New York: Harper and Row.

Goddard, H. H. (1912). *The Kallikak family.* New York: Macmillan.

Gold, M. (1972). Stimulus factors in skill training of the retarded on a complex assembly task: Acquisition, transfer, and retention. *American Journal of Mental Deficiency, 76,* 517–526.

Gold, M. (1973). Research on the vocational habilitation of the retarded: The present, the future. In N. R. Ellis (Ed.), *International review of research in mental retardation* (Vol. 6, pp. 97–147). New York: Academic Press.

Gold, M. (1980). *Try another way: Training manual.* Champaign, IL: Research Press.

Gold, M., & Pomerantz, D. (1978). Issues in prevocational training. In M. Snell (Ed.), *Systematic instruction of the moderately and severely handicapped.* Columbus, OH: Charles E. Merrill.

Goldberg, R. T. (1974). Adjustment of children with invisible and visible handicaps. *Journal of Counseling Psychology, 21,* 428–432.

Goldhammer, K. A. (1972). A careers curriculum. In K. A. Goldhammer & R. E. Taylor (Eds.), *Career education: Perspective and promise* (pp. 121–167). Columbus, OH: Charles E. Merriil.

Goldhammer, K. A., & Taylor, R. E. (1972). Career education perspectives. In K. A. Goldhammer & R. E. Taylor (Eds.), *Career education: Perspective and promise* (pp. 1–12). Columbus, OH: Charles E. Merrill.

Goldstein, H. (1964). Social and occupational adjustment. In H. A. Stevens and R. F. Heber (Eds.), *Research in mental retardation.* Chicago: University of Chicago Press.

Goodman, L. (1985). The effective schools movement and special education, *Teaching Exceptional Children, 17,* 102–105.

Gordon, E. W. (1973). Broadening the concept of career education. In L. McClure and C. Buan (Eds.), *Essays on career education.* Portland, OR: Northwest Regional Educational Laboratory.

Gordon, L. V. (1967). *Gordon occupational check list.* New York: Harcourt Brace Jovanovich.

Granger, C. V (1982). Health accounting functional assessment of the long term patient. In F. J. Kottke, G. Stilwell, & J. S. Lehmann (Eds,), *Krusen's handbook of physical medicine and rehabilitation* (pp. 253–274). Philadelphia: W. B. Saunders.

Greene, G., Kokaska, C., Albright, L., & Beacham-Green, C. (1988). *Instructional strategies for special education* students in regular vocational classes: A preserve handbook. Sacramento, CA: Education Transition Center, California State Department of Education.

Greenleigh Associates, Inc. (1975). The role of the sheltered workshop in the rehabilitation of the severely handicapped. Report to the U.S. Department of Health, Education, and Welfare, Rehabilitation Services Administration, New York, NY.

Greenspan, S., & Shoultz, B. (1981). Why mentally retarded adults lose their jobs: Social competence as a factor in work adjustment. Applied Research in Mental Retardation, 2, 23–38.

Gronlund, N. E. (1970). Stating behavioral objectives of classroom instruction. New York: Macmillan.

Gronlund, N. E. (1973). Preparing criterion-referenced tests for classroom instruction. New York: Macmillan.

Grosenick, J. K., & Huntze, S. L. (1980). National needs analysis in behavior disorders: Severe behavior disorders. University of Missouri-Columbia.

Grosenick, J. K., & Reynolds, M. C. (1978). Teacher education: Renegotiating roles for mainstreaming. Reston, VA: The Council for Exceptional Children.

Gruber, J. E. (1979). Self in transition: Change and continuity in self-esteem after high school. Palo Alto, CA: R & E Research Associates.

Gugerty, J. J. (1986). Cost considerations in establishing and maintaining interagency linkages. In L. W. Tindall (Ed.), Handbook on developing effective linking strategies. Madison: Vocational Studies Center, University of Wisconsin-Madison.

Gunzburg, H. C. (1963-77). Progress Assessment Chart 2 (PAC Form 2). Bristol, IN: Aux Chandelles, PAC Department.

Gunzburg, H. C (1975). Psycho-therapy with the feebleminded. In A. A. Clarke & A. D. B. Clarke (Eds.), Mental deficiency: The changing outlook (3rd ed., pp. 708–728). New York: Free Press.

Guralnick, D. (1956). Vocational rehabilitation services in New York City for the mentally retarded. American Journal of Mental Deficiency, 61, 368–377.

Gysbers, N. C., & Henderson, P. (1988). Developing and managing your school guidance program. Alexandria, VA: American Association for Counseling and Development.

Gysbers N. C., & Moore, E. J. (1974). Career guidance, counseling and placement: Elements of an illustrative program guide. Columbia: Career Guidance, Counseling and Placement Project. University of Missouri-Columbia.

Hallahan, D. P., & Kauffman, J. M. (1982). Exceptional children: Introduction to special education (2nd ed.). Englewood Cliffs, NJ: Prentice Hall.

Halpern, A. S. (1985). Transition: A look at the foundations. Exceptional Children, 51, 479–486.

Halpern, A. S. (1988). Characteristics of a quality program. In C. Warger & B. Weiner (Eds.), Secondary special education: A guide to promising public school programs. Reston, VA: The Council on Exceptional Children.

Halpern, A. S. (1990). A methodological review of follow-up and follow-along studies tracking school leavers from special education. Career Development for Exceptional Individuals, 13, 13–28.

Halpern, A. S. (1992). Transition: Old wine in new bottles. Exceptional Children, 58, 202–211.

Halpern, A. S., & Benz, M. (1987). A statewide examination of secondary special education students with mild disabilities: Implications for the high school curriculum. Exceptional Children, 54, 122–129.

Halpern, A. S., & Benz, M. R., & Lindstrom, L. E. (1992). A systems change approach to improving secondary special education and transition programs at the community level. *Career Development for Exceptional Individuals, 15*(1), 109–120.

Halpern, A. S., Close, D. W., & Nelson, D. J. (1986). *On my own: The impact of semi-independent living programs for adults with mental retardation.* Baltimore: Paul H. Brookes.

Halpern, A. S., & Fuhrer, M. J. (1984). *Functional assessment in rehabilitation.* Baltimore: Paul H. Brookes.

Halpern, A., S., Irvin, L., & Landman, J. J. (1979). *Tests for everyday living.* Monterey, CA: CTB/McGraw-Hill.

Halpern, A. S., Lehmann, J. P., Irvin, L. K., & Heiry, T. J. (1982). *Contemporary assessment for mentally retarded adolescents and adults.* Baltimore, MD: University Park Press.

Halpern, A. S., Lindstrom, L. E., Benz, M. R., & Nelson, D. (1990). *Community transition team model: Team leader's manual.* Eugene, OR: University of Oregon

Halpern, A. S., & Nelson, D. J. (1990). *Secondary special education and transition teams: Procedures manual.* Eugene University of Oregon.

Halpern, A. S., Raffeld, P., Irvin, L. K., & Link, R. (1975). *Social and prevocational information battery.* Eugene: University of Oregon, Rehabilitation Research and Training Center.

Hanley-Maxwell, C., & Szymanski, E. M. (1992). Transition and supported employment. In R. M. Parker & E. M. Szymanski (Eds.), *Rehabilitation counseling: Basics and beyond* (2nd ed.). Austin, TX: Pro-Ed..

Hansen, C. E. (1971). The special education counselor: A new role. *Exceptional Children, 38,* 69–70.

Haring, K., & Lovett, D. (1990). A study of the social and vocational adjustment of young adults with mental retardation. *Education and Training in Mental Retardation, 25*(1), 52–61.

Harold Russell Associates. (1985). *Supported and transitional employment personnel preparation study.* Boston: Authors.

Harris-Bowlsbey, J. (1983, December). The impact of computers on career guidance and assessment. In R. C. Rodgers (Ed.), *Measurement trends in career and vocational education: New directions for testing and measurement, No. 20* (pp. 63–76), San Francisco: Jossey-Bass.

Hart, L. A. (1983). *Human brain and human learning.* New York: Longman.

Hartlage, L. C. (1987). Diagnostic assessment in rehabilitation. In B. Bolton (Ed.), *Handbook of measurement and evaluation in rehabilitation* (2nd ed., pp. 141–149). Baltimore: Paul H. Brookes.

Hartley, N., Otazo, K., and Cline, C. (1979). *Assessment of basic vocational related skills.* Greeley: University of Northern Colorado.

Hartwell, L. K., Wiseman, D. E., & Van Reusen, A. (1983). Parallel alternative curriculum for LBP adolescents. In B. J. D'Alonzo (Ed.), *Educating adolescents with learning and behavior problems* (pp. 381–419). Rockville, MD: Aspen.

Harvest Educational Labs. (n.d.). *Group interest sort.* Newport, RI: Author.

Hasazi, S., & Cobb, R. B. (1988). Vocational education of persons with mild handicaps. In R. Gaylord-Ross (Ed.), *Vocational education for persons with handicaps* (pp. 331–354). Mountain View, CA: Mayfield Publishing.

Hasazi, S., Gordon, L., & Roe, C. (1985). Factors associated with the employment status of handicapped youth exiting high school from 1979 to 1983. *Exceptional Children, 51,* 455–469.

Hasazi, S. B., Salembier, G., & Finck, K. (1983). Directions for the 80's: Vocational preparation for secondary mildly handicapped students: *Teaching Exceptional Children, 15,* 206–209.

Havighurst, R. J. (1953). *Human development and education*. New York: Longman's, Green.

Haywood, H. C. (1970a). *Social-cultural aspects of mental retardation*. New York: Appleton-Century-Crofts.

Haywood, H. C. (1970b). Some perspective on socio-cultural aspects of mental retardation. In H. C. Haywood (Ed.), *Social-cultural aspects of mental retardation* (pp. 761–778). Proceedings of the Peabody-NIMH Conference. New York: Appleton-Century-Crofts.

Helge, D. (1991). *Rural, exceptional, at-risk*. Reston, VA: The Council for Exceptional Children.

Henrich, E., & Kriegel, L. (1961). *Experiments in survival*. New York: Foundation for Child Development (formerly the Association for the Aid of Crippled Children).

Herr, E. L. (1982). Comprehensive career guidance: Future impact. *Vocational Guidance Quarterly, 30*, 367–376.

Herr, E. L., & Cramer, S. H. (1984). *Career guidance and counseling through the life span: Systematic approaches* (3rd ed.). Boston: Little, Brown.

Hester, E. J. (1982). *The career evaluation system*. Niles, IL: Career Evaluation Systems.

Hester, E. J., & Stone, E. (1984). *Utilization of worksite modification*. Topeka, KS: The Menninger Foundation.

High, J. L. (1983). Personal communication. The Office for Civil Rights of the Department of Education, Washington, DC.

Hill, D. S. (1983). A process for identifying the occupational interest of handicapped students using the method of pair comparisons. *Career Development of Exceptional Individuals, 6*, 93–99.

Hill, M., & Wehman, P. (1983). Cost benefit analysis of placing moderately and severely handicapped individuals into competitive employment. *TASH Journal, 8*(1), 30–38.

Hippolitus, P. (1980). Mainstreaming: The true story. *Disabled USA, 3*(9), 5–8.

Hobson v. Hansen 269 F. Supp. 401 (D.D.C.) (1967); 393 U.S. 801 (1968).

Hodgkinson, H. L. (1985, June). *All one system: Demographics of education—Kindergarten through graduate school*. Washington, DC: Institute for Educational Leadership, Inc.

Hofmeister, A. M. (1982). Microcomputers in perspective. *Exceptional Children, 49*, 115–121.

Holland, J. L. (1973). *Making vocational choices*. Englewood Cliffs, NJ: Prentice Hall.

Holland, J. L. (1979). *Vocational exploration and insight kit*. Palo Alto, CA: Consulting Psychologists Press.

Holland, J. L. (1985). *Making vocational choices: A theory of vocational personalities and work environments*. Englewood Cliffs, NJ: Prentice Hall.

Holler, B., & Gugerty, J. (1984), Reflections about on-the-job training for high school special education students. *Career Development for Exceptional Individuals, 7*, 87–92.

Holt, J. (1976). *Instead of education*. New York: Dutton.

Horton, B., Maddox, M., & Edgar, E. (1984). *The adult transition model: Planning for postschool services*. Child Development and Mental Retardation Center, University of Washington, Seattle.

Howell, K. W., Kaplan, J. S., & O'Connell, C. Y. (1979). *Evaluating exceptional children: A task analysis approach*. (Vol. 2). Columbus, OH: Charles E. Merrill.

Hoyt, K. B. (1962, April). Guidance: A constellation of services. *Personnel and Guidance Journal, 40*, 690–697.

Hoyt, K. B. (1975). *An introduction to career education*. Policy Paper of the United States Office of Education, DHEW Publications No. (OE) 75–00504. Washington, DC: U.S. Government Printing Office.

Hoyt, K. B. (1977). *A primer for career education.* Washington, DC: U.S. Government Printing Office.

Hoyt, K. B. (1979). Career education for exceptional individuals: Challenges for the future. In C. J. Kokoska (Ed.), *Career futures for exceptional individuals.* Reston, VA: The Council for Exceptional Children.

Hoyt, K. B. (1982). Career education: Beginning of the end? Or a new beginning? *Career Development for Exceptional Individuals, 5*(1), 3–12.

Hudson, P. J., Schwartz, S. E., Sealander, K. A., Campbell, P., & Hensel, J. W. (1988). Successfully employed adults with handicaps. *Career Development for Exceptional Individuals, 11* (1), 7–14.

Hummel, D. L., & Humes, C. W. (1984). *Pupil services: Development coordination, administration.* New York: Macmillan.

Hungerford, R. H. (1941). The Detroit plan for the occupational education of the mentally retarded. *American Journal of Mental Deficiency, 46,* 102–108.

Hungerford, R. H. (1943). *Occupational education.* New York: Association for New York City Teachers of Special Education.

Hursh, N. C., & Kerns, A. F. (1988). *Vocational evaluation in special education.* Boston: College-Hill.

Ianacone, R. N., Hunter, A. E. C., Hiltenbrand, D. M., Razeghi, J. A., Stodden, R. A., Sullivan, W. F., and Rothkopt, L. R. (1982). *Vocational education for the handicapped: Perspectives on vocational assessment.* (Personnel Development Series: Document 7). Champaign, IL: University of Illinois Office of Career Development for Special Populations.

Idol, L., Paolucci-Whitcomb, P., & Nevin, A. (1986). *Collaborative consultation.* Rockville, MD: Aspen.

Illich, I. (1971). *Deschooling society (World perspectives series, Vol. 4).* New York: Harper and Row.

Independent Living Research Utilization Project. (1978, May). *Final draft.* Houston: Texas Institute for Rehabilitation and Research.

Individualized Rehabilitation Programs. (n.d.). *Occupational assessment/evaluation system.* Long Beach, NY: Author.

Individuals with Disabilities Education Act of 1990 (IDEA), PL 101–476, §602a, 20 U.S.C., 1401.

Ingram, C. P. (1960). *Education of the slow-learning child* (3rd ed.). New York: Ronald Press.

Institute for Personality and Ability Testing. (n.d.). *Sixteen personality factors questionnaire, Form E.* Champaign, IL: Author.

International Center for the Disabled. *TOWER system.* New York: ICD Rehabilitation and Research Center, International Center for the Disabled.

Irvin, L. K. (1988). Vocational assessment in school and rehabilitation programs. In R. Gaylord-Ross (Ed.), *Vocational education for persons with handicaps* (pp. 111–141). Mountain View, CA: Mayfield.

Isaacson, L. E. (1985). *Basics of career counseling.* Boston: Allyn and Bacon.

Itard, J. M. (1932). *The wild boy of Aveyron.* New York: Appleton-Century-Crofts.

Jackson & Associates. (1985). *Executive summary: National Leadership Institute on Supported Employment.* Unpublished paper, Olympia, WA.

Jageman, L. W. & Myers, J. E. (1986). *Counseling mentally retarded adults: A procedures and training manual.* Menomonie: University of Wisconsin-Stout Materials Development Center.

Jastak, J., & Jastak, S. (1973). *Wide range employability sample test.* Wilmington, DE: Jastak Associates.

Jastak, J., & Jastak, S. (1974). *Wide range interest and opinion test.* Wilmington, DE: Guidance Associates of Delaware.

Jay, E. D., & Padilla, C. L. (1987). *Special education dropouts: The incidence of and reasons for dropping out of special education in California.* Menlo Park, CA: SRI International.

Jay, E. D., & Padilla, C. L. (1988). *Dropping out of special education: Preliminary findings from the National Transition Study.* Unpublished manuscript, Menlo Park, CA: SRI International.

Jewish Employment and Vocational Service. (n.d.). *Philadelphia Jewish employment and vocational service work sample system.* Philadelphia: Author.

Jewish Vocational Service. (1978). *Program models for Projects with Industry.* Chicago: Research Utilization Laboratory, Jewish Vocational Service.

Job Training Partnership Act of 1982, Public Law 97–300, 29 U.S. C. 1512(a)(b), 1604, 1605, 1632 (1982).

Johnson, D. R., Bruininks, R. H., & Thurlow, M. L. (1987). Meeting the challenge of transition service planning through improved interagency cooperation. *Exceptional Children, 53,* 522–530.

Johnson, G. O. (1962). Special education for the mentally handicapped: A paradox. *Exceptional Children, 29,* 62–69.

Johnston, W. B., & Packer, A. H, (1987). *Workforce 2000: Work and workers for the twenty-first century.* Indianapolis, IN: Hudson Institute.

Jones, D. (1988). *Iowa transition initiative:* Summary. Des Moines, IA: Drake University Mountain Plains Regional Resource Center.

Jordan, T. E. (1973). *America's children: An introduction to education.* Rand McNally.

Jourard, S. M. (1958). *Personal adjustment.* New York: Macmillan.

Katz, M. (1963). *Decisions and values: A rationale for secondary school guidance.* New York: College Entrance Examination Board.

Kauffman, J. M. (1981). *Characteristics of children's behavior disorders* (2nd ed.). Columbus, OH: Charles E. Merrill.

Kauffman, J. M., Gerber, M. M., & Semmel, M. 1. (1988). Arguable assumptions underlying the regular education initiative. *Journal of Learning Disabilities, 21,* 6–11.

Kaufman, P., & Frase, M. (1990). *Dropout rates in the United States: 1989.* Washington, DC: National Center for Education Statistics.

Kefauner, G. N., & Hand, H. C. (1941). *Appraising guidance in secondary schools.* New York: Macmillan.

Kelley, E. C. (1962). The fully functioning self. In A. W. Combs (Ed.), *Perceiving, behaving and becoming: ASCD Yearbook, Vol. 62* (pp. 9–20). Washington, DC: Association for Supervision and Curriculum Development.

Kelly, J. A., Wildman, B. G., Urey, J. R., & Thurman, C. (1979). Group skills training to increase the conversational repertoire of retarded adolescents. *Child Behavior Therapy, 1*(4), 323–336.

Kennedy, R. J. R. (1962). *A Connecticut community revisited: A study of the social adjustment of a group of mentally deficient adults in 1948 and 1960.* U.S. Office of Vocational Rehabilitation, Washington, DC.

Kephart, N. C. (1960). *The slow learner in the classroom.* Columbus, OH: Charles E. Merrill.

Kim, C-H, Siegel, S., & Gaylord-Ross, R. (1992). Simulated and *in situ* vocational social skills training for youths with learning disabilities. *Exceptional Children, 58,* 336–345.

Kingsbury, D. (1980). Work experience and cooperative placement programs. In G. D. Meers (Ed.), *Handbook of special vocational needs education* (pp. 169–204). Rockville, MD: Aspen.

Kirk, S. A., & Johnson, G. O. (1951). *Educating the retarded child.* Cambridge, MA: Riverside Press.

Kline, F. M., Deshler, D. D., & Schumaker, J. B. (1992). Implementing learning strategy instruction in class settings: A research perspective. In M. Pressley, K. R. Harris, & J. T. Guthrie (Eds.), *Promoting academic competence and literacy in school* (pp. 361-406). San Diego, CA: Academic Press.

Knowlton, H. E., & Clark, G. M. (1989). *National study of high school programs for handicapped youth in transition. Vol. 1: Qualitative component.* Grant No. GOO8530217. Lawrence: University of Kansas. Department of Special Education.

Kokaska, C. J. (1964). In-school work experience: A tool for community adjustment. *Mental Retardation, 2,* 365–369.

Kokaska, C. J., & Brolin, D. E. (1985). *Career education for handicapped individuals* (2nd ed.). Columbus, OH: Charles E. Merrill.

Kokaska, C. J., Gruenhagen, K., Razeghi, J., & Fair, G. W. (1985, October). Division on Career Development's position statement on transition. In D. E. Brolin (Ed.), *Proceedings of the International Conference on the Decade of the Disabled: Transition to work and adult life* (p. 28). Las Vegas, NV.

Kolstoe, O. P. (1961). An examination of some characteristics which discriminate between employed and not-employed mentally retarded males. *American Journal of Mental Deficiency, 66,* 472–482.

Kolstoe, O. P. (1970). *Teaching educable mentally retarded children.* New York: Holt, Rinehart and Winston.

Kolstoe, O. P. (1972). Special education for the mildly retarded: A response to critics. *Exceptional Children, 35,* 51–55.

Kolstoe, O. P (1975a). *Mental retardation: An educational viewpoint.* New York: Holt, Rinehart and Winston.

Kolstoe, O. P. (1975b). *Teaching educable mentally retarded children* (2nd ed.). New York: Holt, Rinehart and Winston.

Kolstoe, O. P. & Frey, R. M. (1965). A *high school work study program for mentally subnormal students.* Carbondale, IL: Southern Illinois University Press.

Kortering, L. J., & Elrod, G. F. (1991). Programs for mildly handicapped adolescents: Evaluating where we are and contemplating change. *Career Development for Exceptional Individuals, 14,* 145–157.

Kortering, L., Haring, N., & Klockars, A. (1992). The identification of high-school dropouts identified as learning disabled: Evaluating the utility of a discriminant analysis function. *Exceptional Children, 58,* 422–435.

Kortering, L., Julnes, R., & Edgar, E. (1988). *The proper discharge of our responsibility to educate handicapped students: An instructive review of the case law pertaining to graduation.* Unpublished manuscript, Experimental Education Unit, University of Washington, Seattle.

Kregel, J., & Wehman, P. (1989). Supported employment: Promises deferred for persons with severe disabilities. *Journal of the Association for Persons with Severe Handicaps, 14*(4), 293–303.

Krumboltz, J. D. (1966). Behavioral goals for counseling. *Journal of Counseling Psychology, 13,* 153–159.

Krumboltz, J. D., & Baker, R. D. (1973). Behavioral counseling for vocational decisions. In H. Borow (Ed.), *Career guidance for a new age* (pp. 235–283). Boston: Houghton Mifflin.

Krumboltz, J. D., & Thoresen, C. E. (Eds.). (1976a). A *behavioral counseling: Cases and techniques* (2nd ed.). New York: Holt, Rinehart and Winston.

Krumboltz, J. D., & Thoresen, C. E. (1976b). *Counseling methods.* New York: Holt, Rinehart and Winston.

Kugel, R. B., & Wolfensberger, W. (Eds.). (1969). *Changing patterns in residential services for the mentally retarded* (pp. 179–188). Washington, DC: President's Committee on Mental Retardation.

La Benne, W. D., & Green, B. I. (1969). *Educational implications of self-concept theory.* Pacific Palisades, CA: Goodyear.

Larry P. v. Riles, USLW 2033 (U.S. June 21). (1972).

Larson, C. (1981). *EBCE State of Iowa dissemination model for MD and LD students.* Fort Dodge: Iowa Central Community College.

Lassiter, R. A. (1981, December). *Work evaluation and work adjustment for severely handicapped people: A counseling approach* (pp. 13–18). Paper presented at the International Roundtable for the Advancement of Counseling Consultation on Career Guidance and Higher Education, Cambridge, England.

Leconte, P. (1992). Back to basics. Holistic appraisal: A fundamental principle of vocational assessment and evaluation. *Vocational Evaluation and Assessment Bulletin, 6*(1), 1–4. Washington, DC: The George Washington University.

Lenz, B. K., & Deshler, D. D. (1989). The strategies instructional approach. *International Journal of Disability, Development and Education, 36,* 203–224.

Levine, S., & Elzey, F. F. (1966). *Personal-social and vocational scale for the mentally retarded.* San Francisco: San Francisco State College, Cooperative Research Project No. 1891.

Levine, S., & Elzey, F. F. (1968). *San Francisco vocational competency scale.* New York: Psychological Corporation.

Levine, S., & White, P. E. (1961). Exchange as a conceptual framework for the study of interorganizational relationships. *Administration Science Quarterly, 5,* 583–601.

Lewis, K., & Taymans, J. (1992). An examination of autonomous functioning skills of adolescents with learning disabilities. *Career Development for Exceptional Individuals, 15*(1), 37–46.

Lichtenstein, S. (1987). *A study of the post-school employment patterns of handicapped and nonhandicapped graduates and dropouts.* Unpublished doctoral dissertation, University of Illinois at Urbana-Champaign.

Lichtenstein, S. (1988). *Dropouts. Perspectives on special education.* Concord, NH: Task Force for the Improvement of Secondary Special Education.

Lichtenstein, S., & Zantal-Weiner, K. (1988). Special education dropouts. ERIC Digest 451. ERIC Clearinghouse on Handicapped and Gifted Children, Reston, VA.

Lilly, M. S. (1970). Improving social acceptance of low sociometric status, low achieving students. *Exceptional Children, 37,* 341–347.

Lilly, M. S. (1971). A training based model for special education. *Exceptional Children, 37,* 747–749.

Lilly, M. S. (1979). *Children with exceptional needs: A survey of special education.* New York: Holt, Rinehart and Winston.

Lilly, M. S. (1987). Lack of focus on special education in literature on educational reform. *Exceptional Children, 53,* 325–326.

Linari, R. F., & Belmont, R. M. (1986). 2001: Employment odyssey or opportunity for persons with handicapping conditions? *Career Development for Exceptional Individuals, 9,* 34–41.

Lindstrom, L. E., Ard, W., Benz, M. R., & Halpern, A. S. (1991). *Community transition team model: Management information system manual.* Eugene: University of Oregon.

Linthicum, E., Cole, J. T., & D'Alonzo, B. J. (1991). Employment and the Americans with Disabilities Act of 1990. *Career Development for Exceptional Individuals, 14*(1), 1–13.

Lombana, J. H. (1982). *Guidance for handicapped students.* Springfield, IL: Charles C. Thomas.

Longenecker, D. P., & Gillen, J. C. (1978). Physical diagnosis. In R. B. Taylor (Ed.), *Family medicine: Principles and practice* (pp. 388–402). New York: Springer-Verlag.

Lovitt, T. C. (1978). The learning disabled. In N. G. Haring (Ed.), *Behavior of exceptional children: An introduction to special education* (2nd ed., pp. 155–191). Columbus, OH: Charles E. Merrill.

Lovitt, T. C. (1991). *Preventing school dropouts: Tactics for at-risk, remedial, and mildly handicapped adolescents.* Austin, TX: Pro-Ed.

Ludlow, B. L., Turnbull, A. P., & Luckasson, R. (1988). *Transition to adult life for people with mental retardation—Principles and practices.* Baltimore: Paul H. Brookes.

Lynch, K. P., Kierman, W. E., & Stark, J. A. (1982). *Prevocational and vocational education for special needs youth: A blueprint for the 1980s.* Baltimore: Paul H. Brookes.

Lynd, R. S., & Lynd, H. M. (1929). *Middletown: A study in contemporary American culture.* New York: Harcourt Brace.

Lynd, R. S., & Lynd, H. M. (1937). *Middletown in transition.* New York: Harcourt Brace.

McCarron-Dial Systems. (n.d.). *Street survival skills questionnaire.* Dallas, TX: Author.

McCarron, L., & Dial, J. (1976). *McCarron-Dial work evaluation system: Evaluation of the mentally disabled—a systematic approach.* Dallas: Common Market Press.

McClung, M. S. (1978). Are competency testing programs fair? Legal? *Phi Delta Kappan, 59,* 397–400.

McClung, M. S., & Pullin, D. (1978). *Competency testing and handicapped students.* Cambridge, MA: Center for Law and Education. (ERIC Document Reproduction Service, No. ED 164 64).

McConnell, N. L., & Blagden, C. M. (1986). *Resource of activities for peer pragmatics.* Moline, IL: Lingui Systems, Inc.

McCoy, K. M., & Watson, N. R. (1983). Methods of instruction: A process-task approach for LBP adolescents. In B. J. D'Alonzo (Ed.), *Educating adolescents with learning and behavior problems* (pp. 233–259). Rockville, MD: Aspen.

McCray, P. M. (1980). *Suggested guidelines for evaluating work samples.* Menomonie, WI: Materials Development Center, Stout Vocational Rehabilitation Institute.

McCray, P. M. (1982). *Vocational evaluation and assessment in school settings.* Menomonie, WI: Materials Development Center, Stout Vocational Rehabilitation Institute.

McDonnell, J., & Hardman, M. (1985). Planning the transition of severely handicapped youth from school to adult services: A framework for high school programs. *Education and Training of the Mentally Retarded, 20,* 275-284.

McDonnell, J., Sheehan, M., & Wilcox, B. (1983). *Effective transition from school to work and adult services: A procedural handbook for parents and teachers.* Unpublished manuscript, University of Oregon, A Specialized Training Program, Eugene, OR.

McDonnel, J. J., Sheehan, M., & Wilcox, B. (1985). Transition issues facing youths with severe disabilities: Parents' perspectives. *Journal of the Association for Persons with Severe Handicaps. 10*(1), 61–65.

McDonnell, J., Wilcox, B., & Boles, S. M. (1983). *Issues in the transition from school to adult services: A study of parents of secondary students with severe handicaps.* Eugene: University of Oregon, Center on Human Development. (ERIC Document Reproduction Service No. ED 240 381).

McDowell, R. L. (1981). Adolescence. In G. Brown, R. L. McDowell, & J, Smith (Eds.), *Educating adolescents with be-*

havior disorders (pp. 10–29). Columbus, OH: Charles E. Merrill.

McDowell, R. L., & Brown, G. B. (1978). The emotionally disturbed adolescent: Development of program alternatives in secondary education. *Focus on Exceptional Children, 10*(4), 1–15.

McGrew, K. S., Bruininks, R. H., & Thurlow, M. L. (1992). Relationship between measures of adaptive functioning and community adjustment for adults with mental retardation. *Exceptional Children, 58,* 517–529.

MacMillan, D. L. (1977). *Mental retardation in school and society.* Boston: Little, Brown.

MacQuarrie, T. W. (1943). *MacQuarrie test for mechanical ability.* Monterey, CA: CTB/McGraw-Hill.

Mager, R, F. (1968). *Developing attitudes toward learning.* Palo Alto, CA: Fearon.

Management Analysis Center. (Circa 1975). *Improving occupational programs for the handicapped.* Final report of a project funded by the Bureau of Education for the Handicapped, U. S. Office of Education, Washington, DC: Office of Education, Department of Health, Education, and Welfare.

Mangan, T. (1992, Spring/Summer). Promoting integration on the job: Building natural support in the workplace. *What's Working,* 1, 5. Institute on Community Integration, University of Minnesota.

Marder, C., & D'Amico, R. (1992, March). *How well are youth with disabilities really doing? A comparison of youth with disabilities and youth in general.* A Report from the National Longitudinal Transition Study of Special Education Students. Menlo Park, CA: SRI International.

Marinelli, R., & Dell, A. (1977). *The psychological and social impact of physical disability.* New York: Springer.

Marland, S. P. (1971). *Career education now.* Speech presented January 23, 1971, to the Convention of the National Association of Secondary School Principals in Houston, TX.

Marland, S. P. (1972). Career education now. In K. A. Goldhammer & R. E. Taylor (Eds.), *Career education: Perspective and promise* (pp. 33–41). Columbus, OH: Charles E. Merrill.

Marland, S. P., Jr. (1974). *Career education: A proposal for reform.* New York: McGraw-Hill.

Marsh, G., Gearheart, C. K., & Gearheart, B. R. (1978). *The learning disabled adolescent: Program alternatives in the secondary school.* St. Louis, MO: C. V. Mosby.

Martens, E. H. (1937). Occupational preparation for mentally handicapped children. *Proceedings and Addresses for the Sixty-First Annual Session of the American Association on Mental Deficiency, 42,* 157–165.

Maryland State Department of Education. (1986). *Maryland State Department of Education transition guidelines.* Baltimore: Author.

Maslow, A. H. (1954). *Motivation and personality.* New York: Harper and Row.

Mathews, M. R., & Fawcett, S. B. (1979). A community-based information and referral system. Monograph 17, *Journal of the Community Development Society, 10,* 13–25.

Matson, J., & Rusch, F. (1986). Quality of life: Does competitive employment make a difference? In F. R. Rusch (Ed.), *Competitive employment issues and strategies* (pp. 331–337). Baltimore: Paul H. Brookes.

Matthewson, R. H. (1962). *Guidance policy and practice.* New York: Harper and Row.

Maynard, M., & Chadderdon, L. (n.d.). *Leisure and life-style: A cross national report on issues and models for people with disabilities.* East Lansing, MI: Michigan State University Center for International Rehabilitation.

Meadow, K., & Trybus, R. (1979). Behavioral and emotional problems of deaf children: An overview. In L. Bradford and W. Hardy (Eds.), *Hearing and hearing impairment* (pp. 395–403). New York: Grune & Stratton.

Meers, G. D. (1980). *Handbook of special vocational needs education.* Rockville, MD: Aspen.

Meers, G. D. (1992). getting ready for the next century: Vocational preparation of students with disabilities. *Teaching Exceptional Children, 24*(4), 36–39.

Mellard, D. F., & Clark, G. M. (1992). *National High School Project. Vol. 2: A quantitative description of concepts and practices for students with disabilities.* Final report for Grant No. GOO8530217, Office of Special Education and Rehabilitative Services. Department of Special Education, University of Kansas.

Menz, F. (1978). *Vocational evaluation with adolescents: Description and evaluation of a program with reluctant learners.* Menomonie, WI: University of Wisconsin-Stout, Stout Vocational Rehabilitation Institute, Research and Training Center.

Mercer, J. (1973). The myth of 3% prevalence. In R. K. Eyman, C. E. Meyers, & G. Tarjan (Eds.), *Sociobehavioral studies in mental retardation: Papers in honor of Harvey F. Dingman* (pp. 1–18). Monographs of the American Association on Mental Deficiency. Washington, DC: American Association on Mental Deficiency.

Mertens, D. M., Chafetz, S. E., & Nunez, A. R. (1980). *Policy study for rural vocational and adult education.* Columbus, OH: The National Center for Research in Vocational and Adult Education.

Miller, G., Galanter, E., & Pribram, K. (1960). *Plans and the structure of behavior.* New York: Holt, Rinehart and Winston.

Miller, R. J., La Follette, M., & Green, K. (1988). *Perceptions in implementing transition planning: Transition planning procedural manual and inservice training package.* Cedar Rapids, IA: Grant Wood Area Education Agency.

Miller, S. E. (1990). *Environmental factors related to at-risk adolescents' experiences in high school.* Unpublished doctoral dissertation, University of Pittsburgh.

Miller, T. L., & Sabatino, D. A. (1978). An evaluation of the teacher consultation model as an approach of mainstreaming. *Exceptional Children, 45,* 86–91.

Minnesota Employment Stabilization Research Institute. (1969). *Minnesota rate of manipulation test.* Circle Pines, MN: American Guidance Service.

Missouri Department of Elementary and Secondary Education. (1984). *Resource guide for special education, II-A.* Jefferson City, MO: Missouri State Department of Education.

Mitchell, A. M. (1978). *Career development needs of seventeen year olds: How to improve career development programs.* Monograph of the National Vocational Guidance Association and the Association for Measurement and Evaluation in Guidance (divisions of American Personnel and Guidance Association), Washington, DC.

Mitchell, J. V, Jr. (1985). *The ninth mental measurements yearbook* (Vol. 2). Lincoln, NE: The Buros Institute of Mental Measurements, The University of Nebraska-Lincoln.

Mithaug, D. (1981). *Prevocational training for retarded students.* Springfield, IL: Charles C. Thomas.

Mithaug, D., Horiuchi, C., & Fanning, P. (1985). A report on the Colorado statewide follow-up survey of special education students. *Exceptional Children, 51,* 397–404.

Mithaug, D., Martin, J. E., & Agran, M. (1987). Adaptability instruction: The goal of transitional programming. *Exceptional Children, 53,* 500–505.

Mithaug, D. E., Martin, J. E., Agran, M., & Rusch, F. R. (1988). *Why special education graduates fail: How to teach them to succeed.* Colorado Springs, CO: Ascent Publications.

Moon, S., Goodall, P., Barcus, M., & Brooke, V. (1986). *The supported work model of competitive employment for citizens with severe handicaps. A guide for job trainers* (rev.). Richmond, VA: Rehabilitation Research and Training Center, Virginia Commonwealth University.

Moon, M. S., Kiernan, W., & Halloran, W. (1990). School-based vocational programs and labor laws: A 1990 update. *Journal of the Association for Persons with Severe Handicaps, 15*(3), 177–185.

Moores, D. (1969). The vocational status of young deaf adults in New England. *Journal of Rehabilitation of the Deaf, 2,* 5.

Morgan, D. I. (1979). Prevalence and types of handicapping conditions found in juvenile correctional institutions: A national survey. *Journal of Special Education, 13,* 283–295.

Morreau, L. E., & Bruininks, R. H. (1992). *Checklist of adaptive living skills.* Allen, TX: DLM.

Morrow, D., Thorton, H., & Zigmond, N. (1988). *Graduation and postsecondary adjustment: Follow-up of urban-bound learning disabled students (Final Report).* University of Pittsburgh.

Morse, W. C. (1979). The helping teacher/crisis teacher concept. In E. L. Meyen, G. A. Vergason, & R. J. Whelan (Eds.), *Instructional planning for exceptional children: Essays from Focus on Exceptional Children* (pp. 308–324). Denver: Love Publishing.

Morse, W. C. (1982). The place of affective education in special education. *Teaching Exceptional Children, 14,* 209–211.

Morsink, C. V. (1981). Learning disabilities. In A. E. Blackhurst & W. H. Ber-

dine (Eds.), *An introduction to special education* (pp. 391–425). Boston: Little, Brown.

Myklebust, H. P. (1965). *Development and disorders of written language* (Vol. 1). New York: Grune and Stratton.

Nadolsky, J. (1981). Vocational evaluation in the public school: Implications for future practice. *Journal of Vocational Special Needs Education, 3*(3), 5–9.

Naidoo, R. M. (1989). *An examination of parents' and teachers' expressed attitudes towards occupational expectations for deaf persons.* Unpublished doctoral dissertation, University of Kansas.

Naisbitt, J. (1984). *Megatrends: Ten new directions transforming our lives.* New York: Warner Communications.

Nash, K. R., & Castle, W. E. (1980, August). Special problems of deaf adolescents and young adults. *Exceptional Education Quarterly, 1*(2), 99–106.

National Assessment of Educational Progress. (1978a). It's what you don't know that "hurts." *NAEP Newsletter, 11*(5), 1.

National Assessment of Educational Progress. (1978b). Wrap-up: Social studies/citizenship. *NAEP Newsletter, 11,*(5), 1–2.

National Assessment of Educational Progress. (1979). Are 17 year olds prepared? Doors open to "real" consumer world. *NAEP Newsletter, 12*(3), 1, 3–4.

National Association of Rehabilitation Facilities. (1984). *Job Training Partnership Act (PL 97–300): An analysis and guide.* Washington, DC: Author.

National Center for Research in Vocational Education. (n.d.). *Math on the job.* Omro, WI: Conover Company.

National Commission on Excellence in Education. (1983). *A nation at risk: The imperative for educational reform.* Washington, DC: Author.

National Society for the Prevention of Blindness. (1966). *NSPB fact book: Estimated statistics on blindness and vi-*

sual problems. New York: National Society for the Prevention of Blindness.

Neff, W. S. (1966). Problems of work evaluation. *The Personnel and Guidance Journal, 44,* 682–688.

Neff, W. S. (1977). *Work and human behavior* (2nd ed.). New York: Aldine-Atherton.

Nelson, C. M., & Polsgrove, L. (1981). The etiology of adolescent behavior disorders. In G. Brown, R. L. McDowell, & J. Smith (Eds.), *Educating adolescents with behavior disorders* (pp. 30–59). Columbus, OH: Charles E. Merrill.

Nelson, C. M., Rutherford, R. B., Center, D. B., & Walker, H. M. (1991). Do public schools have an obligation to serve troubled children and youth? *Exceptional Children, 57,* 406–415.

Neubert, D. A., & Tilson, G. P. (1987). Critical stages of transition: A challenge and an opportunity. *Journal for Vocational Special Needs Education, 10*(1), 3, 7.

Neubert D. A., Tilson, G. P., & Ianacone, R. N. (1989). Postsecondary transition needs and employment patterns of individuals with mild disabilities. *Exceptional Children, 55,* 494–500.

Nickelsburg, R. (1973). Time sampling of work behavior. *Mental Retardation, 2*(6), 29–32.

Nietupski, J., Hamre-Nietupski, S., Welch, J., & Anderson, R. J. (1983). Establishing and maintaining vocational training sites for moderately and severely handicapped students: Strategies for community/vocational trainers. *Education and Training of the Mentally Retarded, 18,* 169–175.

Nihira, K., Foster, R., Shellhaas, M., & Leland, H. (1974). *AAMD Adaptive behavior scale for children and adults* (1974 rev.). Washington, DC: American Association on Mental Deficiency.

Nirje, B. (1969). The normalization principle and its human management implications. In R. B. Kugel & W.

Wolfensberger (Eds.), *Changing patterns in residential services for the mentally retarded.* Washington, DC: U.S. Government Printing Office.

Nisbet, J., & Hagner, D. (1988). Natural supports in the workplace: A reexamination of supported employment. *Journal of the Association for Persons with Severe Handicaps, 13,* 260–267.

Oakes, J. (1986). Keeping track, Part 2: Curriculum inequality and school reform. *Phi Delta Kappan, 68,* 148–154.

O'Brien, J., & Stern, D. (1988). Economic issues in employing persons with disabilities. In R. Gaylord-Ross (Ed.), *Vocational education for persons with special needs* (pp. 257–295). Palo Alto, CA: Mayfield.

O'Connor, J. (1926). *O'Connor finger dexterity test.* Chicago: Stoelting.

O'Connor, J. (1928). *O'Connor tweezer dexterity test.* Chicago: Stoelting.

Office of Special Education and Rehabilitative Services. (1985). National news: Interagency agreement signed. *OSERS News in Print, 1*(1), 9.

Ojemann, R. (1967). Incorporating psychological concepts in the school curriculum. *Journal of School Psychology, 5,* 195–204.

Okolo, C. M., & Sitlington, P. L. (1986). The role of special education in adolescents' transition from school to work. *Learning Disability Quarterly, 9,* 141–150.

O'Neill, N., & O'Neill, G. (1974). *Shifting gears.* New York: M. Evans and Co.

Ornstein, J. H. (1972). *The mind and the brain: A multi-aspect interpretation.* The Hague: Nijhoff.

Overs, R. (1968). *The theory of job sample tasks.* Milwaukee: Curative Workshop.

Parrish, L. H., & Kok, M. R. (1985). *Procedures handbook for special needs work-study coordinators.* Rockville, MD: Aspen.

Parsons, F. (1909). *Choosing a vocation.* Boston: Houghton Mifflin.

Paterson, D. G., Elliott, R. M., Anderson, L. D., Toops, H. A., & Heidbreder, E. (1979). *Minnesota spatial relations test* (rev. ed.). Minneapolis, MN: Educational Test Bureau.

Pati, G., Adkins, J., & Morrison, G. (1981). *Managing and employing the handicapped. The untapped potential.* Lake Forest, IL: The Human Resource Press.

Patterson, C. H. (1964). Methods of assessing the vocational adjustment potential of the mentally handicapped. *Training School Bulletin, 61,* 129–152.

Paulson, J., & O'Leary, E. (1991). *Developing and writing transition services within the IEP process.* Unpublished manuscript, Great Plains Instructional Material Center, Des Moines, IA.

Payne, J. S. (1977). Job placement. How to approach employers. In R. L. Carpenter (Ed.), *Colloquium series on career education for handicapped adolescents.* West Lafayette, IN: Special Education Section, Department of Education, Purdue University.

Payne, J. S., & Chaffin, J. D. (1968). Developing employer relations in a work study program for the educable mentally retarded. *Education and Training of the Mentally Retarded, 3,* 127–133.

Payne, J. S., Mercer, C. D., & Epstein, M. H. (1974). *Education and rehabilitation techniques.* New York: Behavioral Publications.

Payne, J. S., & Patton, J. R. (1981). *Mental retardation.* Columbus, OH: Charles E. Merrill.

Pearl, R., Donahue, M., & Bryan, T. (1986). Social relationships of learning disabled children. In J. Torgeson & B. Wong (Eds.), *Psychological and educational perspectives on learning disabilities* (pp. 193–225). New York: Academic Press.

Peck, J. R., Stephens, W. B., & Veldman, D. J. (1964). *Personality and success profiles characteristic of young adult male retardates.* Austin, TX: University of Texas, Cooperative Research Project No. S-116.

Pennsylvania Association for Retarded Children v. Commonwealth of Pennsylvania, 343 F Suppl. 279 (E.D., Pa), 1972.

Pennypacker, H. S., Koenig, C. H., & Lindsley, O. R. (1972). *Handbook of the standard behavior chart.* Kansas City, KS: Precision Media.

Perske, R., & Perske, M. (1988). *Circles of friends: People with disabilities and their friends enrich the lives of one another.* Nashville: Abingdon Press.

Peterson, M. (1983). *Vocational assessment of special needs students: A concept paper.* Unpublished manuscript, Committee on Vocational Assessment, Mississippi State University, P. O. Drawer, GE, Mississippi State, MS.

Peterson, M. (1985a). Models of vocational assessment. *Career Development for Exceptional Individuals, 8*(2), 110–118.

Peterson, M. (1985b). *Vocational assessment of special students: A guide.* Starkville, MS: VOC-AIM.

Peterson, M. (1986). *Vocational assessment of special students: A procedural manual.* Starkville, MS: VOC-AIM.

Peterson, R. C., & Jones, E. M. (1964). *Guide to jobs for the mentally retarded* (rev. ed.). Pittsburgh: American Institute for Research.

Petry, C. (1992). Social skills instruction: A guide for school practitioners. In S. Z. Sacks, M. Hirsh, & R. Gaylord-Ross (Eds.), *The status of social skills training in special education and rehabilitation: Present and future trends* (Chapter 3). Monograph supported by the National Institute on Disability Research, Grant No. H133G0096, Special Education Department, Peabody Teachers College of Vanderbilt University.

Pfueger, S. (1977). *Independent living: Emerging issues in rehabilitation.* Washington, DC: Institute for Research Utilization.

Phelps, L. A. (1976). *Instructional development for special needs learners: An inservice resource guide.* Urbana, IL: University of Illinois at Urbana-Champaign, Department of Vocational and Technical Education.

Phelps, L. A., & Frasier, J. R. (1988). Legislative and policy aspects of vocational special education. In R. Gaylord-Ross (Ed.), *Vocational education for persons with special needs* (pp. 3–29). Palo Alto, CA: Mayfield.

Phelps, L. A., & Greenan, J. P (1982). Delivering vocational education to handicapped learners. *Exceptional Children, 48,* 408–411.

Phelps, L. A., & Lutz, J. (1977). *Career exploration and preparation for the special needs learner.* Boston: Allyn and Bacon.

Phelps, L. A., & McCarty, T. (1984). Student assessment practices. *Career Development for Exceptional Individuals, 7*(6), 30–38.

Pippes, M. K., Ryan, J. A., & Underwood, A. (1989, December/January). Pragmatics: The transition link. *Missouri Lincletter, 11*(3), 1–3. Newsletter published by Missouri LINC, University of Missouri-Columbia.

Pistono, K. S. (1988). *Unique educational needs of learners with speech and language impairments.* East Lansing, MI: Center for Quality Special Education.

Polloway, E. A., Patton, J. R., Epstein, M. H., & Smith, T. E. C. (1989, April). Comprehensive curriculum for students with mild handicaps. *Focus on Exceptional Children, 21*(8), 1–12.

Popenoe, D. (1985). *Private pleasure, public plight: American metropolitan community life in comparative perspective.* New Brunswick, NJ: Transaction Books.

Powell, T. H., Pancsofar, E. L., Steere, D. E., Butterworth, J., Itzkowitz, J. S., &

Rainforth, B. (1991). *Supported employment: Providing integrated employment opportunities for persons with disabilities.* New York: Longman.

Power, P. W. (1984). *A guide to vocational assessment.* Baltimore: University Park Press.

Prep, Inc. (n.d.). *Comprehensive occupational assessment and training system.* Trenton, NJ: Author.

Pruitt, W. A. (1977). *Vocational work evaluation.* Menomonie, WI: Walt Pruitt Associates.

Psychological Assessment Resources, Inc. (1992). *Personal problems checklist for adolescents.* Odessa, FL: Author.

Psychological Corporation. (1987). *Adult basic learning examination.* Newark, NJ: Author.

Pullin, D. (1980, August). Mandated minimum competency testing: Its impact on handicapped adolescents. *Exceptional Education Quarterly, 1*(2), 107–115.

Purdue Research Foundation. (1968). *Purdue pegboard.* Chicago: Science Research Associates.

Quay, H. C., & Peterson, D. P. (1987). *Manual for the revised behavior problems checklist.* Coral Gables, FL: Authors.

Raths, L., Merrill, H., & Sidney, S. (1966). *Values and teaching.* Columbus, OH: Charles E. Merrill.

Rehabilitation Act of 1973, PL 93–112, 29 U.S.C. 723(a), 721(a)(9), 793, 794, 795(a), 795(g) (1982).

Rehabilitation Act Amendments of 1984, PL 98–211.

Rehabilitation Act Amendments of 1986, 29 U.S.C., 701, PL 99–506.

Reichard, C. L. (1979). Project RETOOL Report. Reston, VA: The Council for Exceptional Children, Teacher Education Division.

Research Utilization Laboratory (1977). RUL Number 6: *Guidelines for interagency cooperation and the severely dis-*

abled. Chicago, IL: Jewish Vocational Services.

Resnick, D. P., & Resnick, L. B. (1985, April). Standards, curriculum, and performance: Historical and comparative perspective. *Educational Researcher, 14,* 5–20.

Reynolds, M. C., Wang, M. C., & Walberg, H. J. (1987). The necessary restructuring of special and regular education. *Exceptional Children, 53,* 391–398.

Rizzo, J. V., & Zabel, R. H. (1988). *Educating children and adolescents with behavioral disorders: An integrative approach.* Boston: Allyn and Bacon.

Roberts, J. R. (1945). *Pennsylvania bi-manual work sample.* Circle Pines, MN: American Guidance Service.

Roberts, S., Doty, D., Santleben, S., & Tang, T. (1983). A model for vocational assessment of handicapped students. *Career Development for Exceptional Individuals, 6,* 100–110.

Robinson, F. P. (1963). Modern approaches to counseling diagnosis. *Journal of Counseling Psychology, 10,* 325–333.

Robinson, S. M. (1988). Collaborative consultation as part of special education services: Questions to consider. *Collaborative Consultation Newsletter, 1*(3), 1–2. Department of Special Education, University of Kansas, Lawrence.

Roos, P. (1970). Normalization, de-humanization, and conditioning—Conflict or harmony? *Mental Retardation, 8*(4), 12–14.

Rose, T. L., Epstein, M. H., Cullinan, D., & Lloyd, J. (1981). Academic programming for behaviorally disordered adolescents: An approach to remediation. In G. Brown, R. L. McDowell, & J. Smith (Eds.), *Educating adolescents with behavior disorders* (pp. 213–237). Columbus, OH: Charles E. Merrill.

Rosenberg, H., & Tesolowski, D. G. (1979). *Florida International diagnos-tic-prescriptive vocational competency profile.* Chicago: Stoelting.

Ross, A. O. (1980). *Psychological disorders of children* (2nd ed.). New York: McGraw-Hill.

Rowley, J. (1987). From your president. *Phi Delta Kappa Newsletter, 32,* 1.

Rowley v. Board of Education of the Hendrick Hudson Central School District, 458 U.S. 176 (1982).

Rudrud, E. H., Ziarnik, J. P., Bernstein, G. S., & Ferrara, J. M. (1984). *Proactive vocational habilitation.* Baltimore: Paul H. Brookes.

Rumberger, R. (1987). High school dropouts: A review of issues and evidence. *Review of Educational Research, 57,* 101–121.

Rumberger, R., & Daymont, T. (1984). The economic value of academic and vocational training acquired in high school. In M. Borus (Ed.), *Youth and the labor market: Analysis of the national longitudinal survey* (pp. 157–191). Kalamazoo, MI: Upjohn Institute for Employment Research.

Rural, small schools: Miles to go, promises to keep. (1988, Summer). *SEDLETTER, 1*(2), 1–2. (Newsletter published by Southwest Educational Development Laboratory News, Austin, Texas.)

Rusch, F. R. (Ed.). (1986a). *Competitive employment issues and strategies.* Baltimore: Paul H. Brookes.

Rusch, F. R. (1986b). Supported work: An introduction. *Interchange, 7*(1), 1–5. Secondary Transition Intervention Effectiveness Institute, College of Education, University of Illinois at Urbana-Champaign.

Rusch, F. R., & Menchetti, B. M. (1988). Transition in the 1990s: A reply to Knowlton and Clark. *Exceptional Children, 54,* 363–365.

Sacks, S. Z., Tierney-Russell, D., Hirsch, M., & Braden, J. (1992). Social skills training: What professionals say they do. In S. Z. Sacks, M. Hirsch, & R.

Gaylord-Ross (Eds.), *The status of social skills training in special education and rehabilitation : Present and future trends* (Chapter 1). Monograph supported by the National Institute on Disability Research, Grant No. H133G0096, Special Education Department, Peabody Teachers College of Vanderbilt University.

Safer, N. D. (1980). Implications of minimum competency standards and testing for handicapped students. *Exceptional Children, 46,* 288–290.

Salvia, J., & Ysseldyke, J. E. (1985). *Assessment in special and remedial education* (3rd ed.). Boston: Houghton Mifflin.

Savage, H. J. (1953). *Fruit of an impulse: Forty-five years of the Carnegie Foundation, 1905–1950.* New York: Harcourt, Brace and Company.

Schalock, R. L. (n.d.). *Mid-Nebraska mental retardation services three track system.* Hastings, NE: Author.

Schalock, R. L., & Jensen, C. M. (1986). Assessing the goodness-of-fit between persons and their environments. *The Journal of the Association for Persons with Severe Handicaps, 11,* 103–109.

Schein, J., & Delk, M. (1974). *The deaf population of the United States.* Silver Spring, MD: National Association of the Deaf.

Schenck, S. J. (1981). *Ramifications of the minimum competency movement for special education.* Paper presented at the annual meeting of the American Educational Research Association, Los Angeles, April 13–17. (ERIC Document Reproduction Service No. ED 207 234).

Schilit, J., & Caldwell, M. L. (1980). A word list of essential career/vocational words for mentally retarded students. *Education and Training of the Mentally Retarded, 35,* 113–116.

Schinka, J. A. (1895). *Personal problems checklist for adolescents.* Odessa, FL: Psychological Assessment Resources.

Schloss, P. J., Schloss, C. N., & Misra, A. (1985). Analysis of application forms used by special needs youths applying for entry-level jobs. *Career Development for Exceptional Individuals, 8,* 80–89.

Schmitt, P., & Hall, R. (1986). About the unique vocational adjustment needs of students with a learning disability. *The Directive Teacher, 8*(1), 7–8.

Schneck, G. R. (1981, March). Program improvement in vocational assessment for the handicapped. *Interchange.* Newsletter of the Leadership Training Institute/ Vocational and Special Education Project, University of Illinois at Urbana-Champaign, pp. 1–6.

Schroka, J. S., & Schwartz, S. E. (1982). Job placement of handicapped persons: A positive approach. *Career Development for Exceptional Individuals, 5,* 116–121.

Schumaker, J. B., & Deshler, D. D. (1987). Implementing the regular education initiative in secondary schools. *Journal of Learning Disabilities, 21*(1), 36–42.

Schumaker, J. B., & Hazel, J. S. (1984a). Social skills assessment and training for the learning disabled: Who's on first and what's on second? Part 1. *Journal of Learning Disabilities, 17,* 422–431.

Schumaker, J. B., & Hazel, J. S. (1984b). Social skills assessment and training for the learning disabled: Who's on first and what's on second? Part 2. *Journal of Learning Disabilities, 17,* 492–499.

Schumaker, J. B., Hazel, J. S., & Deshler, D. D. (1985). A model for facilitating postsecondary transitions. *Techniques, 1,* 437–445.

Schumaker, J. B., Pederson, C. S., Hazel, J. S., & Meyen, E. L. (1983). Social skills curricula for mildly handicapped adolescents: A review. *Focus on Exceptional Children, 16*(4), 1–16.

Schwartz, P (1985). *Employment incentives manual: How to motivate businesses to hire individuals with disabilities.* Bellingham, WA: American Council on Rural Special Education, Western Washington University.

Schwartz, S. E. (n.d.). *Real life math.* Northbrook, IL: Hubbard.

Schwarz, S. L., & Taymans, J. M. (1991). Urban vocational/technical program completers with learning disabilities: A follow-up study. *The Journal for Vocational Special Needs Education, 13*(1), 15–20.

Scott, M. L., Ebbert, A., & Price, D. (1986, Summer). Assessing and teaching employability skills with prevocational work samples. *The Directive Teacher, 8*(1), 3–6.

Scuccimarra, D., & Speece, D. (1990). Employment outcomes and social integration of students with mild handicaps: The quality of life two years after high school. *The Journal of Learning Disabilities, 23,* 213–219.

Seidenberg, P. L. (1986). *A framework for a curriculum foundation program for college-bound learning disabled students.* (Position Paper Series: Document No. 3). Greenvale, NY: Long Island University, Demonstration Model Transition Project,

Seidenberg, P. L. (1987, January). Curriculum-based assessment procedures for the college-bound high school student with learning disabilities. *Interchange, 7*(2), 2–5. College of Education, University of Illinois at Urbana-Champaign.

Shapiro, E. S., & Lentz, F. E. (1991). Vocational-technical programs: Follow-up of students with learning disabilities. *Exceptional Children, 58,* 47–59.

Shaw, M. C. (1977). The development of counseling programs: Priorities, progress, and professionalism. *Personnel and Guidance Journal, 55,* 339–345.

Shertzer, B., & Stone, S. C. (1981). *Fundamentals of guidance* (4th ed.). Boston: Houghton Mifflin.

Shrey, D. E., Mitchell, D. K., & Hursh, N. C. (1985). *Employer development and industrial exploration manual: A comprehensive approach to initiating school-to-work transition programs for students with special needs.* Dublin, OH: International Center for Industry, Labor and Rehabilitation.

Siegel, S., Greener, K., Prieur, J., Robert, M., & Gaylord-Ross, R. (1989). The community vocational training program: A transition program for youths with mild handicaps. *Career Development for Exceptional Individuals, 12*(1), 48–64.

Sileo, T. W., Rude, H. A., & Luckner, J. L. (1988). Collaborative consultation: A model for transition planning for handicapped youth. *Education and Training in Mental Retardation, 23,* 333–339.

Simon, S. (1971). Values clarification vs. indoctrination. *Social Education, 35,* 902–905.

Simpson, R. L. (1981). Screening and assessment strategies for behaviorally disordered adolescents. In G. Brown, R. L. McDowell, & J. Smith (Eds.), *Educating adolescents with behavior disorders* (pp. 79–101). Columbus, OH: Charles E. Merrill.

Simpson, R. L. (1982). *Conferencing parents of exceptional children.* Rockville, MD: Aspen.

Singer Educational Division. (n.d.). *Vocational evaluation system.* Rochester, NY: Singer Educational Division, Career Systems.

Sinick, D. (1962). Client evaluation: Work task approach. *Rehabilitation Record, 3*(2), 6–8.

Sitlington, P. L. (1979). Vocational assessment and training of the handicapped. *Focus on Exceptional Children, 12*(4), 1–11.

Sitlington, P. L. (1980). The assessment process as a component of career education. In G. M. Clark & W. J. White (Eds.), *Career education for the handicapped: Current perspectives for teachers* (pp. 79–91). Boothwyn, PA: Educational Resource Center.

Sitlington, P. L., & Frank, A. R. (1990). Are adolescents with learning disabilities successfully crossing the bridge into adult life? *Learning Disabilities Quarterly, 13*, 97–111.

Sitlington, P. L., Frank, A. R., & Carson, R. (1991, October). *Iowa statewide follow-up study: Changes in the adult adjustment of graduates with mental disabilities one vs. three years out of school.* Iowa Department of Education, Des Moines, IA.

Sitlington, P. L., & Wimmer, D. (1978). Vocational assessment techniques for the handicapped adolescent. *Career Development for Exceptional Individuals, 1*, 74–87.

Sizer, T. R. (1985). *Horace's compromise: The dilemma of the American high school.* Boston: Houghton Mifflin.

Skinner, B. F. (1967). What is psychotic behavior? In T. Millon (Ed.), *Theories of psychopathology* (pp. 324–337). Philadelphia: W. B. Saunders.

Skrtic, T. M. (1991). *Behind special education: A critical analysis of professional culture and school organization.* Denver: Love Publishing.

Slavin, R. E. (1980). Cooperative learning. *Review of Educational Research, 50*, 315–342.

Sloan, W. (1963). Fourscore and seven. *American Journal of Mental Deficiency, 68*, 6–14.

Smith, G. J. (1982). Analogical reasoning profiles of mentally retarded and normal adults judged against Sternberg's unified componential theory of human reasoning. *Dissertation Abstracts International, 42*, 3560A.

Smith, S. W. (1990). Individualized education programs (IEPs) in special education—From intent to acquiescence. *Exceptional Children, 57*(1), 6–14.

Smith, J., & Jenkins, D. S. (1980). Minimum competency testing and handicapped students. *Exceptional Children, 46*, 440–443

Smith, J., Rice, S. R., & Gantley, B. I. (1981). Teaching subjects and skills to troubled adolescents. In G. Brown, R. L. McDowell, & J. Smith (Eds.), *Educating adolescents with behavior disorders* (pp. 238–279). Columbus, OH: Charles E. Merrill.

Snell, M. (1978). *Systematic instruction of the moderately and severely handicapped.* Columbus, OH: Charles E. Merrill.

Sowers, J. (1983). *Toward work: Implementation handbook.* Newton, MA: Education Development Center, Inc.

Sowers, J., Jenkins, C., & Powers, L. (1988). *Vocational education of persons with physical handicaps.* In R. Gaylord-Ross (Ed.), Vocational education for persons with handicaps (pp. 387–416). Mountain View, CA: Mayfield.

Sowers, J., & Powers, L. (1989). Preparing students with cerebral palsy and mental retardation for the transition from school to community-based employment. *Career Development for Exceptional Individuals, 12*(1), 25–35.

Spady, W. G. (1988). Organizing for results: The basis of authentic restructuring and reform. *Educational Leadership, 46*,(2), 4–8.

Sparrow, S. S., Bella, D. A., & Cicchetti, D. V. (1984). *Vineland adaptive behavior scales.* Circle Pines, MN: American Guidance Services.

Spivak, J. S., & Haimes, P. E. (1967). *Devereux adolescent behavior rating scale.* Deveon, PA: Devereux Foundation Press.

Squires, S. (1981, July). Interagency cooperation relative to vocational assessment for the handicapped. *Interchange.* Newsletter of the Leadership

Training Institute/Vocational and Special Education Project, University of Illinois at Urbana-Champaign, pp. 1–5

Starr, J. M. (1986). American youth in the 1980's. *Youth and Society*, 17, 323–345.

Steere, D., Pancsofar, E., Wood, R., & Hecimovic, A. (1990). The principles of shared responsibility. *Career Development for Exceptional Individuals*, 13, 143–153.

Stefanich, G., & Hadzigeorgiou, Y. (1993). The role of the teacher in meeting the needs of students with disabilities. *Journal of Science for Persons with Disabilities*, 1(1), 23–30.

Stefflre, B., & Stewart, N. (1970). *Principles of guidance* (6th ed.). New York: McGraw-Hill.

Stephens, W. B. (1972). *The development of reasoning, moral judgment and moral conduct in retardates and normals, Phase 11*. Unpublished paper, Temple University, Philadelphia, PA.

Sternberg, R. J. (1985). *Beyond IQ: A triarchic theory of human intelligence*. New York: Cambridge University Press.

Stodden, R. A. (1980). *Vocational assessment of special needs individuals: Project final report, phase II*. Commonwealth of Massachusetts, Division of Occupational Education.

Stodden, R. A., & Ianacone, R. N. (1981). Career/vocational assessment of the special needs individual: A conceptual model. *Exceptional Children*, 47, 600–609.

Stodden, R. A., Meehan, K. A., Hodell, S., & Simpson-Ussery, S. (1987a). Curriculum-based vocational assessment handbook for the mildly handicapped student: Project intervention *No. 1*. (U.S. Department of Education Contract No. 158–GH–5008). Honolulu: University of Hawaii Department of Special Education.

Stodden, R. A., Meehan, K. A., Hodell, S. & Simpson-Ussery, S. (1987b). *Curriculum-based vocational assessment handbook for the moderately handicapped student: Project intervention No. 2*. (U.S. Department of Education Contract No. 158–GH–5008). Honolulu: University of Hawaii Department of Special Education.

Strain, P. S. (Ed.) (1982). *Social development of exceptional children*. Rockville, MD: Aspen.

Strain, P. S., & Kerr, M. M. (1981). *Mainstreaming of children in schools*. New York: Academic Press.

Strauss, A. A., & Lehtinen, L. E. (1947). *Psychopathology and education of the brain-injured child*. New York: Grune and Stratton.

Stromberg, E. L. (1951). *Stromberg dexterity test*. New York: Psychological Corporation.

Super, D. E. (1951). Vocational adjustment: Implementing a self-concept. *Occupations*, 30, 88–92.

Super, D. E. (1953). A theory of vocational development. *American Psychologist*, 8, 185–190.

Swisher, J., & Clark, G. M. (1991). Curriculum-based vocational assessment of students with special needs at the middle school/junior high school levels: The Practical Arts Evaluation System. *The Journal for Vocational Special Needs Education*, 13(3), 9–14.

Szasz, T. S. (1960). The myth of mental illness. *American Psychologist*, 15, 113–118.

Szymanski, E. M., & King, J. (1989). Rehabilitation counseling in transitional planning and preparation. *Career Development for Exceptional Individuals*, 12, 3–10.

Talent Assessment, Inc. (n.d.). *The pictorial inventory of careers*. Jacksonville, FL: Author.

Teaching Resources Corporation. (1977). *Woodcock-Johnson psycho-educational battery*. Boston: Author.

Thomas, C. W., Spangler, D. P., & Izutu, S. (1961). Some fundamental propositions in the construction of evaluation units in vocational rehabilitation. *The Personnel and Guidance Journal*, 39, 536–589.

Thomas, S. W. (1992). *Transition issues in vocational assessment.* Paper presented to a Kansas Vocational Evaluation and Work Adjustment Association conference, Emporia State University, Emporia, KS. July 27.

Thorndike, R. L., & Hagen, E. (1969). *Measurement and evaluation in psychology and education.* New York: Wiley & Sons.

Thousand, J., & Villa, R. (1990). Sharing expertise and responsibilities through teaching teams. In W. Stainback & S. Stainback (Eds.), *Support networks for inclusive schooling: Integrated interdependent education* (pp. 151–166). Baltimore: Paul H. Brookes.

Thousand, J., Villa, R., Paollucci-Whitcomb, P., & Nevin, A. (1992). A rationale for collaborative consultation. In W. Stainback & S. Stainback (Eds.), *Controversial issues confronting special education: Divergent perspectives* (pp. 223-232). Boston: Allyn and Bacon.

Throne, J. M. (1975). Normalization through the normalization principle. Right ends, wrong means. *Mental Retardation, 13*(5), 23–25.

Tindall, L. W. (1980). *Puzzled about educating special needs students?* Madison, WI: Wisconsin Vocational Studies Center, University of Wisconsin-Madison.

Tindall, L. W., Gugerty, J. J., & Dougherty, B. (1984). *Promising programs which use Job Training Partnership Act funds for the vocational education, training and employment of handicapped youth.* Madison, WI: Vocational Studies Center, School of Education, University of Wisconsin-Madison.

Tindall, L. W., Gugerty, J. J., Getzel, E. E., Salin, J. A., Wacker, G. B., & Crowley, C. B. (1986). In L. W. Tindall (Ed.), *Handbook on developing effective linking strategies.* Madison, WI:

University of Wisconsin-Madison Vocational Studies Center.

Tobias, J. (1964). *Evaluating vocational potential of retarded adults through psychological tests.* Paper presented at American Psychological Association, Los Angeles.

Tobin, M. J., & James, R. K. (1974). Evaluation of the Optacon: General reflections on reading machines for the blind. *Research Bulletin: American Foundation for the Blind, 28,* 145–157.

Turnbull, A. P. (1988). The challenge of providing comprehensive support to families. *Education and Training in Mental Retardation, 23,* 261–272.

Ullmann, L. P., & Krasner, L. (1965). *Case studies in behavior modification.* New York: Holt, Rinehart and Winston.

U.S. Census of Population. (1980). *Volume I, Characteristics of the population: Chapter A, Number of inhabitants* (PC80–1–A1). Washington, DC: U.S. Government Printing Office.

U.S. Chamber of Commerce. (1974). *Study on group insurance costs.* Sacramento, CA: California Governor's Committee for Employment of the Handicapped.

U.S. Department of Education. (1983). *Report of services to adolescent handicapped, 1968–1982.* Washington, DC: U.S. Government Printing Office.

U.S. Department of Education (1985). *Digest of education statistics.* Washington, DC: Center for Education Statistics.

U.S. Department of Education. (1987). *To assure the free appropriate public education of all handicapped children.* Ninth Annual Report to Congress on the Implementation of the Education of the Handicapped Act. Washington, DC: Author.

U.S. Department of Education. (1988). *To assure the free appropriate public education of all handicapped children.* Tenth Annual Report to Congress on the Implementation of the Education of the Handicapped Act. Washington, DC: Author.

U.S. Department of Education. (1991). *America 2000: Sourcebook.* Washington, DC: Author.

U.S. Department of Labor. (1974). *Manual for the basic occupational literacy test. Section 1: Administration, scoring, and interpretation.* Washington, DC: Author.

U.S. Department of Labor. (1977a). *Dictionary of occupational titles* (4th ed.). Washington, DC: U.S. Government Printing Office.

U.S. Department of Labor. (1977b). *Study of handicapped clients in sheltered workshops* (Vol. 2). Washington, DC: Author.

U.S. Department of Labor. (1982a). *Manual for the USES interest inventory.* Minneapolis: Intran Corporation.

U.S. Department of Labor. (1982b). *The selected characteristics of occupations defined in the Dictionary of Occupational Titles.* Washington, DC: U.S. Government Printing Office.

U.S. Department of Labor. (1982c). *U.S. employment service interest check list.* Washington DC: Author.

U.S. Department of Labor. (1991, June). *What work requires of schools: A SCANS report for America 2000.*

U.S. Employment Service. (1982a). *General aptitude test battery (GATB).* Washington, DC: U.S. Government Printing Office.

U.S. Employment Service. (1982b). *Nonreading aptitude test battery (NATB).* Washington, DC: U.S. Government Printing Office.

U.S. Office of Education. (1978). Memorandum on cooperative agreements. In L. A. Phelps (Ed.), *A compendium of interagency agreements: Vocational education, special education, and vocational rehabilitation.* Champaign, IL: Leadership Training Institute/Vocational and Special Education, University of Illinois.

U.S. Senate. (1975). *Our nation's schools.* Ninety-Fourth Congress, First Session, Preliminary Report, Committee to Investigate Juvenile Delinquency. Washington, DC: U.S. Government Printing Office.

Valdes, K. A., Williamson, C. L., & Wagner, M. (1990, July). *Statistical almanac, Vol. 2: Youth categorized as learning disabled.* The National Longitudinal Transition Study of Special Education Students (Contract 300-87-0054), SRI International, Menlo Park, CA.

Valpar International. (n.d.). *Microcomputer evaluation and screening assessment.* Tucson, AZ: Author.

Valpar International. (n.d.). *Valpar component work sample series.* Tucson, AZ: Author.

Valpar International. (n.d.). *Prevocational readiness battery.* Tucson, AZ: Author.

Van Riper, C. (1978). *Speech correction:* Principles and methods (6th ed.). Englewood Cliffs, NJ: Prentice Hall.

Vandergoot, D., & Worrall, J. D. (1979). *Placement in rehabilitation.* Baltimore: University Park Press.

Vandergriff, A. F., & Hosie, T. W. (1979). PL 94–142: A role change for counselors or just an extension of present role? *Journal of Counseling Services, 3* (1), 6–11.

Varela, R. A. (1983). Organizing disabled people for political action. In N. M. Crewe, I. K. Zola, & Associates (Eds.), *Independent living for physically disabled people* (pp. 311–326). San Francisco: Jossey-Bass.

Vitello, S. J., & Soskin, R. M. (1985). *Mental retardation: Its social and legal context.* Englewood Cliffs, NJ: Prentice Hall.

Vocational Education Act of 1963, PL 88-210, 26 U.S.C. 5 (1964).

Vocational Education Act Amendments of 1968, PL 90–576, U.S.C. 1262(c), 1263(b), (F), (1970).

Vocational Education Act Amendments of 1976, PL 94–482, U.S.C. 2310(a), (b) (1982).

Vocational Research Institute. (n.d. a). *Vocational information and evaluation work samples.* Philadelphia: Jewish Employment and Vocational Service.

Vocational Research Institute. (n.d. b). *Vocational interest temperament and aptitude system.* Philadelphia: Jewish Employment and Vocational Service.

Vocational Research Institute. (1984). *Apticom.* Philadelphia: Jewish Employment and Vocational Service.

Voelker, P. H. (1963). The value of certain selected factors in predicting early postschool employment for white educable mentally retarded males. *Dissertation Abstracts, 23,* 3242.

VORT Corporation. (n.d.). *Behavioral characteristics progression.* Palo Alto, CA: Author

Wagner, M. (1988). *Preliminary findings from the transition of hearing impaired students from secondary school to adulthood.* Unpublished paper prepared for 1988 meeting of the American Educational Research Association, New Orleans, LA. Menlo Park, CA: SRI International.

Wagner, M. (1989). *The transition experiences of youths with disabilities: A report from the National Longitudinal Transition Study.* Stanford, CA: SRI International.

Wagner, M., & Shaver, D. M. (1989). *Educational programs and achievements of secondary special education students: Findings from the National Longitudinal Transition Study.* Presentation to the Special Education Interest Group at the meetings of the American Educational Research Association, San Francisco.

Walker, M. L. (1991, Fall). Rehabilitation service delivery to individuals with disabilities: A question of culture competence. *OSERS News in Print, 4*(2), 7–11.

Walls, R. J., Zane, T., & Thvedt, J. E. (1979). *Independent living behavior checklist.* Morgantown, WV: West Virginia Rehabilitation Research and Training Center.

Walls, R. J., Zane, T., & Werner, T. J. (1978). *Vocational behavior checklist.* Dunbar, WV: West Virginia Rehabilitation Research and Training Center.

Wansart, W. & DeRuiter, J. (1982). *Psychology of learning disabilities: Application and educational practice.* Rockville, MD: Aspen.

Ward, M. J. (1988). The many facets of self-determination. *NICHCY Transition Summary, 5.* 2–3. (Available from NICHCY, P. O. Box 1492, Washington, DC 20013.)

Ward, M. J. (1991, September). Self-determination revisited: Going beyond expectations. *NICHCY Transition Summary, 7,* 2–4, 12. (Available from NICHCY, P. O. Box 1492, Washington, DC 20013.)

Ward, M. J. (1992). OSERS initiative on self-determination. *Interchange, 12*(1), 1–7. Champaign, IL: Transition Research Institute, University of Illinois.

Warner, M. M., Schumaker, J. B., Alley, G. R., & Deshler, D. D. (1980, August). Learning disabled adolescents in the public schools: Are they different from low achievers? *Exceptional Education Quarterly, 1*(2), 27–36.

Warren, F. G. (1976). *Report of the Kent County Educational Training Center.* Grand Rapids, MI.

Wehman, P. (1981). *Competitive employment: New horizons for severely disabled individuals.* Baltimore: Paul H. Brookes.

Wehman, P., & Hill, J. W. (Eds.). (1985). *Competitive employment for persons with mental retardation: From research to practice, Vol. 1.* Richmond, VA: Rehabilitation Research and Training Center, Virginia Commonwealth University.

Wehman, P., Hill, M., Hill, J., Brooke, V. Pendleton, P., & Britt, C. (1985). Competitive employment for persons with mental retardation: A follow-up six years later. *Mental Retardation, 23,* 274–281.

Wehman, P., & Kregel, J. (1985). A supported work approach to competitive employment of individuals with moderate and severe handicaps. *Journal of the Association for Persons with Severe Handicaps, 10,* 3–1 1.

Wehman, P., & Kregel, J. (1988). Adult employment programs. In R. Gaylord-Ross (Ed.), *Vocational education for persons with special needs* (pp. 205–233). Palo Alto, CA: Mayfield.

Wehman, P., Kregel, J., & Seyfarth, J. (1985a). Transition from school to work for individuals with severe handicaps: A follow-up study. *Journal of the Association for the Severely Handicapped, 10,* 132–139.

Wehman, P., Kregel, J., & Seyfarth, J. (1985b). What is the employment outlook for young adults with mental retardation after leaving school? *Rehabilitation Counseling Bulletin, 29,* 91–99.

Wehman, P., Moon, M. S., Everson, J. M., Wood, W., & Barcus, J. M. (1988). *Transition from school to work: New challenges for youth with severe disabilities.* Baltimore: Paul H. Brookes.

Wehman, P., Moon, M. S., & McCarthy, P. (1986, January). Transition from school to adulthood for youth with severe handicaps. *Focus on Exceptional Children, 18*(5), 1–12.

Weisgerber, R. A., Dahl, P. R., & Appleby, J. A. (1980). *Training the handicapped for productive employment.* Rockville, MD: Aspen.

Wellman, F., & Moore, E. (1975). *Pupil personnel services: A handbook for program development and evaluation.* Washington, DC: U.S. Department of Health, Education, and Welfare.

West, L., Jones, B. L., Corbey, S., Boyer-Stephens, A., Miller, R. J., & Sarkees-Wircenski, M. (1992). *Integrating transition planning into the IEP process.* Reston, VA: The Council for Exceptional Children.

White, W. J., Alley, G. R., Deshler, D. D., Schumaker, J. B., Warner, M. M., & Clark, F. L. (1982). Are there learning disabilities after high school? *Exceptional Children, 49,* 273–274.

Whitehead, C. W. (1979). Sheltered workshops in the decade ahead: Work, wages, and welfare. In G. T. Bellamy, G. O'Connor, & O. C. Karan (Eds.), *Vocational rehabilitation of severely handicapped persons* (pp. 71–84). Baltimore: University Park Press.

Whitson, K. S., Korfhage, M., & Axelrod, V. (Eds.). (1977). The rural community. In Career Guidance, Counseling Placement, and Follow-Through Program for Rural Schools. *State of the art review: A comprehensive review of the strengths and limitations on the rural home, school, and community for improved career guidance programs.* Research and Development 118A1. Columbus, OH: The Center for Vocational Education.

Wiederholt, J. L., Hammill, D. D., & Brown, V. (1978). *The resource teacher: A guide to effective practice.* Boston: Allyn and Bacon.

Wiederholt, J. L., & McEntire, B. (1980, August). Educational options for handicapped adolescents. *Exceptional Education Quarterly, 1*(2), 1–10.

Wiggins, S. F. (1983). Specialized housing. In N. M. Crewe, I. K. Zola, & Associates (Eds.), *Independent living for physically disabled people* (pp. 219–244). San Francisco: Jossey-Bass.

Will, M. (1984). *OSERS programming for the transition of youth with disabilities: Bridges from school to working life.* Washington, DC: Office of Special Education and Rehabilitative Services.

William T. Grant Foundation Commission on Work, Family and Citizenship. (1988). The forgotten half Non-college bound youth in America. *Phi Delta Kappan, 69,* 409–414.

Williamson, E. G. (1939). *How to counsel students.* New York: McGraw-Hill.

Williamson, E. G. (1972). Trait-and-factor theory and individual differences. In B. Stefflre & W. H. Grant (Eds.), *Theories of counseling* (2d ed. 136–176). New York: McGraw-Hill.

Willingham, W. (1987). *Handicapped applicants to college: An analysis of admissions decisions.* New York: College Entrance Examination Board.

Wimmer, D. (1980). Selected issues in using career education materials with handicapped students. In G. M. Clark & W. J. White (Eds.), *Career education for the handicapped: Current perspectives for teachers* (pp. 93–106). Boothwyn, PA: Educational Resources Center.

Wimmer, D. (1981). Functional learning curricula in the secondary schools. *Exceptional Children, 47,* 610–616.

Wircenski, J. (1982). *Employability skills for the special needs learner* Rockville, MD: Aspen.

Wolfe, B. (September, 1980). How the disabled fare in the labor market. *Monthly Labor Review: Research Summaries,* 48–52.

Wolfensberger, W. (1972). *The principle of normalization in human services.* Toronto: National Institute on Mental Retardation.

Wood, F. H. (1982). Affective education and social skills training: A consumers guide. *Teaching Exceptional Children, 14,* 212–216.

Wood, P., & Lazarus, B. (1988). *Unique educational needs of learning with emotional impairments.* East Lansing, MI: Center for Quality Special Education.

Wright, B. A. (1960). *Physical disability—A psychological approach.* New York: Harper and Row.

Wright, G. N. (1980). *Total rehabilitation.* Boston: Little, Brown.

Wright, G. N., & Remmers, H. H. (1960). *The handicap problems inventory.* Lafayette, IN: University Book Store.

Young, M. (1956). Academic requirements of jobs held by the educable mentally retarded. *American Journal of Mental Deficiency, 62,* 792-802.

Younie, W. J. (1966). *Guidelines for establishing school work-study programs for educable mentally retarded youth.* Vol. 48 (10). Richmond, VA: Special Education Service, State Department of Education.

Ysseldyke, J. E., Thurlow, M. L., & Gilman, C. J. (1993). *Educational outcomes and indicators for students completing school.* National Center on Educational Outcomes in collaboration with the National Association of State Directors of Special Education, University of Minnesota.

Zeller, R. (1980). *Information and resources on graduation requirements and handicapped students.* Unpublished document developed with the Northwest Regional Resource Center, Eugene, OR, pp. 1–7.

Zigmond, N. (1990). Rethinking secondary special education programs for students with learning disabilities. *Focus on Exceptional Children, 23*(1), 1–22.

Zigmond, N., & Miller, S. E. (1992). Improving high school programs for students with learning disabilities: A matter of substance as well as form. In F. Rusch, L. Destefano, J. Chadsey-Rusch, L. A. Phelps, & E. Szymanski (Eds.), *Transition from school to adult life: Models, linkages, and policy* (pp. 17-32). Sycamore, IL: Sycamore Publishing.

Zigmond, N., Sansone, J., Miller, S. E., Donahue, K. A., & Kohnke, R. (1986). *Teaching learning disabled students at the secondary level.* Reston, VA: The Council for Exceptional Children.

Zigmond, N., & Thornton, H. (1985). Follow-up of post secondary age learning disabled graduates and drop outs. *Learning Disabilities Research, 1,* 50–55.

Zimmerman, I. L., & Woo-Sam, J. M. (1987). Assessment of adults with mental retardation. In B. Bolton (Ed.), *Handbook of measurement and evaluation in rehabilitation* (2nd ed., pp. 283–297). Baltimore: Paul H. Brookes.

Zytowski, D. G. (1978). Wide range interest and opinion test. [Review of *Wide range interest and opinion test*]. In O. K. Buros (Ed.), *The eighth mental measurements yearbook* (Vol. 2, pp. 1029–1030). Highland Park, NJ: Gryphon Press.

Author Index

Subject Index

Acknowledgments:
pp. 129–130 from "Vocational Assessment and Training of the Handicapped" by P. L. Sitlington, 1979, *Focus on Exceptional Children*, 12(4), p. 6. Copyright 1979 by Love Publishing Company. Reprinted with permission. **p. 187** from "The Role of the Teacher in Meeting the Needs of Students with Disabilities" by G. Stefanich and Y. Hadzigeorgiou, 1993, *Journal of Science for Persons with Disabilities*, 1(1), p. 25. Copyright 1993 by the Journal of Science for Persons with Disabilities. Reprinted by permission. **pp. 194–195** from *Individualizing Instruction* (2nd ed.) (p. 116) by C. M. Charles, 1980. St. Louis, MO: C. V. Mosby Co. Reprinted with permission of the author. **pp. 198–199** from "Individualizing Instruction with Micro-computer Software" by L. S. Appell and K. M. Hurley, 1984, *Focus on Exceptional Children*, 16, pp. 2–4. Copyright 1984 by Love Publishing Company. Reprinted with permission. **pp. 276–278** from *Education and Rehabilitation Techniques* by J. S. Payne, C. D. Mercer, and M. H. Epstein, 1974. New York: Behavioral Publications. Copyright 1974 by Behavioral Publications. Reprinted with permission. **p. 390** from "Secondary Programs in Special Education: Are Many of Them Justifiable?" by E. Edgar, 1987, *Exceptional Children*, 53, p. 560. Copyright 1987 by The Council for Exceptional Children. Reprinted with permission. **p. 398** from "Keeping Track, Part 2: Curriculum Inequality and School Reform" by J. Oakes, 1986, *Phi Delta Kappan*, 68, p. 150. Copyright 1986 by the Phi Delta Kappan. Reprinted with permission. **p. 399** from "Standards, Curriculum, and Performances: Historical and Comparative Perspective" by D. P. Resnick and L. B. Resnick, 1985, *Educational Researcher, 14*, p. 9. Copyright 1985 by the American Educational Research Association. Reprinted with permission.